Venetian Humanism in an Age
of Patrician Dominance

VENETIAN HUMANISM
IN AN AGE
OF PATRICIAN
DOMINANCE

Margaret L. King

PRINCETON UNIVERSITY PRESS

PRINCETON, NEW JERSEY

Published by Princeton University Press, 41 William Street,
Princeton, New Jersey 08540
In the United Kingdom: Princeton University Press,
Guildford, Surrey

Library of Congress Cataloging in Publication Data will
be found on the last printed page of this book

ISBN 0-691-05465-7 ISBN 1-597-40616-3(pbk)

This book has been composed in Linotron Sabon

Clothbound editions of Princeton University Press books
are printed on acid-free paper, and binding materials are
chosen for strength and durability

Printed in the United States of America by Princeton
University Press, Princeton, New Jersey

Frontispiece: Guarino Veronese Presents the Strabo to the
Venetian humanist and patron Jacopo Antonio Marcello.
Attributed to Andrea Mantegna. Albi, Bibliothèque
Municipale, MS 77, fol. 3ᵛ

FOR MY FAMILY, WITH LOVE:

Reno and Marie King
Robert E. Kessler
David and Jeremy King Kessler

CONTENTS

Part One

CONTENTS

Part Two

CONTENTS

ACKNOWLEDGMENTS

WITHOUT the assistance I have received from individuals and institutions, I could not have written this book. An American Council of Learned Societies Fellowship freed me from one year of teaching duties, and a Brooklyn College sabbatical from a second. A grant-in-aid from the ACLS, four grants jointly funded by the City University and its Professional Staff Congress, and two from the Gladys Krieble Delmas Foundation made seven trips to Venice possible. Brooklyn College monies and a grant from the American Philosophical Society permitted me to buy essential microfilms to read at home when I couldn't read abroad. Columbia University through its University Seminar program has graciously extended library privileges to me as an Associate of the Seminar on the Renaissance. The support of Brooklyn College and the Department of History for my research efforts has been invaluable.

My research called me to archives and libraries in Italy, Spain, France, and England, where I received courteous assistance from librarians sympathetic to my bewilderment, haste, and extraordinary requests. I note especially the assistance I received from the professionals at the Archivio di Stato, Biblioteca Nazionale Marciana, and Biblioteca of the Museo Correr in Venice, and the Biblioteca Universitaria and Biblioteca of the Museo Civico in Padua.

I am grateful to the publishers of the *Renaissance Quarterly* and the *Journal of Medieval and Renaissance Studies* for permitting me to reprint in revised form sections of my articles appearing in those journals: respectively, "Personal, Domestic and Republican Values in the Moral Philosophy of Giovanni Caldiera," 28 (1975), 535-74, and "Caldiera and the Barbaros on Marriage and the Family: Humanist Reflections of Venetian Realities," 6 (1976), 19-50. Upon the first article is based section 2, upon the second, sections 1 and (in part) 10 of Chapter Two.

Over the years many friends have made suggestions, passed on references, and offered criticisms: among them Patricia Labalme, Donald Queller, Albert Rabil, Lewis Spitz (my dissertation advisor). The members of the Columbia University Seminar on the Renaissance and of the Executive Board of the Renaissance Society of America have provided fellowship in this mission, and many gems of advice. And I recall with fondness my colleagues in the Archivio di Stato in Venice—

the *topi di Archivio*—with whom I shared mid-morning coffee breaks (no more than ten minutes), summer heat, and unmitigated winter cold: Stanley Chojnacki, Robert Finlay, Paul Grendler, Deborah Howard, Martin Lowry, Jill Moore, Reinhold Mueller, Richard Rapp, Guido Ruggiero, James Williamson, and others. Gladys Krieble Delmas, from whose exceptional generosity a whole generation of scholars has benefited, has in recent years greeted me when in Venice with encouragement and interest. My Venetian hosts Giovanna and Franco Marzollo have made the city a home to me and my husband.

In these days when publishers prefer short and simple books, I acknowledge with special gratitude my debt to R. Miriam Brokaw of Princeton University Press. She looked seriously at a gargantuan manuscript from an unknown historian, with the result now before you.

One figure overshadows this book. Paul Oskar Kristeller, a great scholar and cherished friend, has taught me my trade. I regret the errors which mar this work, but regret them most of all because they would pain him. Its virtues are very much due to his guidance.

My family deserves much more than a dedication. For years they have labored in my vineyard. My mother screened articles, looked up references, typed, numbered, and filed. My father gave me a word processor (when that miracle was new, but still almost too late) and insisted I use it. He has supervised each disk and printout since. My husband provided endless support, and suffered dinners alone, cold dinners, no dinners, on many late nights. A journalist, he insisted on the deletion of many polysyllables in the manuscript. I have indulged myself with a few. My sons David (born between Chapter Three and the Profiles) and Jeremy (born between the penultimate and final revisions) bravely bore their mother's absence. They know that Mommy makes words and think that might be all right for her; they have other ambitions.

This book is theirs more than mine.

GUIDE TO THE FORMAT
OF CITATIONS IN NOTES, PROFILES,
AND BIBLIOGRAPHY

BECAUSE of the great length of the apparatus in this book, the notes do not give full first references. Full publication information is provided in the bibliography.

The primary sources cited in notes, bibliography and profiles are those to which I have access—not necessarily the best. In some cases where a manuscript source is given, other manuscript versions abound; in some cases, an existing printed version has not been seen. For the core group figures, these circumstances are explained in the profiles. The notes and profiles of core group figures list some works not actually seen if they are essential. There titles are given with the notation "not seen" and are accompanied by data of publication or location to the extent that they are known. Where useful, guidance to further information about the work is provided. The bibliography includes only those works actually seen by me. Thus the profiles are a more comprehensive guide to the work of core group figures than the bibliography. Where a primary work exists in more than one manuscript or printed version, the bibliography gives the version I have used; the profiles may cite alternate versions, or provide guidance to a listing of alternate versions, or merely indicate that the work is widely diffused in manuscript or available in several printed editions. The many manuscript catalogues and standard reference works that were consulted but are not explicitly required for citation in the notes are also excluded from the bibliography.

In the notes and profiles, archival sources are cited in short form, using the abbreviations given in the table of abbreviations that follows and in parentheses in the bibliography after the title of each documentary series. The Arabic numeral immediately following refers to the register (volume) of that documentary series; c. and cc. signify *charta* and *chartae*. Both for archival documents and manuscript sources, the r for *recto* is normally omitted, whereas v is always shown to indicate *verso*. I have throughout used the old or original enumeration of archival documents. All dates are given according to our calendar, not as they appear in the documents *more veneto* (whereby the year begins on 1 March). All citations of documents in the profiles are from the Archivio di Stato in Venice unless specific note is made; elsewhere, a documentary citation is preceded by ASV (for the Venetian archive) or other indication of location.

In the notes and bibliography, manuscript locations are indicated with city (Anglicized), library, and shelfmark. Manuscripts from the Biblioteca Nazionale Marciana (Venice) and Biblioteca Apostolica Vaticana (the most frequently cited), however, are given only in abbreviated form: Marc. Lat., Marc. Ital., Vat. Lat., Vat. Ottob. Lat., Vat. Chis., etc., without preliminary "cod.," and followed by shelfmark. Information about the manuscript (age, fabric, etc.) has not been included. References to catalogues in which such information appears or from which the manuscript was located have also been omitted unless, in isolated cases, an explicit reference is required. For manuscripts, fol. and fols. are used for folio and folios.

Some works consist of one or a few letters or similar material and are not formally titled as they appear in manuscripts or printed editions. I have supplied a title in brackets: [*Epistolae*], three [*epistolae*], etc.

Works in manuscript and older printed editions often have elaborate titles that are not standard in all versions. Titles have been shortened, therefore, to essential information, although I have not standardized the titles in violation of the word order given in the version I cite. Honorific appellations or titles preceding names (*illustrissimus, reverendissimus, dominus*, etc.) and editorial information extending the titles especially of older printed works are often omitted. Older editions are cited with information about place, date, and printer in Anglicized, modernized, and condensed form.

Punctuation of manuscript and old (fifteenth- and sixteenth-century) editions is altered to conform with modern usage. Emendations have been suggested sparingly and where necessary for sense.

Names of authors normally (always for core group figures) are given in a standardized Italian form. When the name reappears in the title in a Latin form, I have usually omitted it from the notes and bibliography. In the notes, profiles, and bibliography, V and G signify *vecchio* (elder) and *giovane* (younger). These terms are used when two related figures with the same name are discussed in this work.

ABBREVIATIONS

Offices and Titles

Amb.	Ambassador
Avog.	Avogador di comun
CX	Member of the Consiglio dei Dieci (Council of Ten)
Capt.	Captain
Card.	Cardinal
Cons.	Consigliere
Duc. el.	Ducal elector
Pat.	Patriarch
Pod.	Podestà
Prov.	Provveditore
Sav. gr.	Savio grande
Sav. tf.	Savio di terraferma
Sind.	Sindaco

Archival Sources

ASV	Archivo di Stato di Venezia
AN	Archivio Notarile
AC	Avogaria di Comun
BO	Balla d'oro
CLN	Collegio—Notatorio
CX	Consiglio dei Dieci
MC	Maggior Consiglio
SGV	Segretario alle Voci
SMS, SM, ST	Senato-Miste, Mar, Terra, respectively

Books (full citation in bibliography)

CTC	*Catalogus translationum et commentariorum*
CVQ	*La civiltà veneziana del Quattrocento*
CVR	*La civiltà veneziana del Rinascimento*
CVT	*La civiltà veneziana del Trecento*
Comm., ed. Predelli	*I libri commemoriali della republica di Venezia*, edited by R. Predelli
DBI	*Dizionario biografico degli italiani*
DBIRP	Domenico Morosini, *De bene instituta re publica*
DFE	Pietro Barozzi, *De factionibus extinguendis*
DN	Lauro Quirini, *De nobilitate*
DR	Lauro Quirini, *De republica*
DRF	Paolo Morosini, *De rebus ac forma reipublicae venetae*
DRU	Francesco Barbaro, *De re uxoria*

ABBREVIATIONS

DVEP	Paolo Morosini, *Defensio venetorum ad Europae principes*
Iter	P. O. Kristeller, *Iter Italicum*
LQU	*Lauro Quirini umanista*
OCP	Ermolao Barbaro the Elder, *Orationes contra poetas*
RERV	*Rinascimento europeo e rinascimento veneziano*
SCV	*Storia della cultura veneta*
UEUV	*Umanesimo europeo ed umanesimo veneziano*

JOURNALS

ASI	*Archivio storico italiano*
Annales: ESC	*Annales: économies, sociétés, civilisations*
Atti del [R]IV di SLA	*Atti del [Regio] Istituto Veneto di scienze, lettere ed arti*
AV, NAV, AVT	*Archivio veneto*, and its sub-series, *Nuovo archivio veneto, Archivio veneto tridentino*
BHR	*Bibliothèque d'humanisme et renaissance*
BIS	*Bollettino dell'Istituto Storico per la storia e cultura veneziana* (continues as *Studi veneziani*)
GSLI	*Giornale storico della letteratura italiana*
IMU	*Italia medioevale e umanistica*
JWCI	*Journal of the Warburg and Courtauld Institutes*
NRS	*Nuova rivista storica*
RQ	*Renaissance Quarterly*
RSI	*Rivista storica italiana*
SV	*Studi veneziani* (continues BIS)

OTHERS

NS	New Series
SLA	Scienze, lettere ed arti
Epist.	*Epistola/ae, Epistole, Epistolario*

A City Without Walls

Nec celsis Urbs est circumdata muris
—Pietro Barozzi

THE TOURIST is no stranger to the miracle of Venice. He arrives, shall we say, by train—for by that means his realization is most poignant. For hours he has been whipped across fields, through mountain tunnels and sleeping towns; now he wakes, startled, in a dusty palace at the city's limit. He descends to a platform choked with carts and peddlers, uniforms and costumes of all descriptions, the clatter of a dozen languages and the litter of half the world. He strides along the platform, through the station, down the steps, to the water's edge, and stops. The world of shrieking rails, sleek steel and massed concrete is confuted at the verge of what in Venice serves as Main Street: the Grand Canal, snaking through the city in a sinuous line no architect designed, though architects, struck by the play of water, mist, and light, have adorned it. Down that waterway now he journeys, cradled and rocked by waves, slowed by fog, cowed by storms, through waters yielding, capricious, and ancient. He has entered that paradoxical city which once ruled, she claimed with cautious bravado, a quarter and an eighth of the Roman world.

A city built on water: it is a phenomenon nearly inconceivable even when the *palazzi*—weightless and lacy, solid and elegant, soigné, rotting—float before one's eyes. For in Venice, nature is reversed, matter yields to vapor, substance walks on water. Her historians have long commented on the scene. She floats, wrote the medieval chronicler Giovanni Diacono, amid the sea and the waves, "wondrous." She arose providentially amid water and marsh, "unprecedented," wrote the chancellor Lorenzo de' Monaci. As though without foundation, wrote the humanist Bernardo Giustiniani, her buildings soar from the waters.[1]

---

[1] Giovanni Diacono in his *Cronaca veneziana*, cited by G. Fasoli, "I fondamenti della storiografia veneziana," p. 17: Venice, "que Adriatici maris collecta sinus, interfluentibus undis, positione mirabili." De' Monaci in his *Oratio ad serenissimum principem et ducem Venetorum in laude et edificatione alme civitatis Venetiarum*, pp. 483-97 in

This floating city was in another sense paradoxical to the contemporary observer, who probably lived, if he lived in a city, surrounded by walls marking sharply the boundary between urban and rural existence. Within the walls, there was refuge; from the ramparts, the city was defended. Venice, a city without walls, was anomalous. "Miraculous" that she was founded only on water, without walls, wrote Antonio Broianico. Planted in the sea, wrote Leonardo Giustiniani, she was circumscribed not by walls but, beyond the waters, distant shores. Alone among cities, remarked his son Bernardo, Venice has "no walls, no gates, no fortifications." Yet she stood invulnerable.[2]

Provoking endless comment and undimmed wonder, the uniqueness of Venice's situation in the Adriatic littoral has permitted her apologists to offer useful explanations for that invulnerability. If not encased in walls, how was she defended? By the favor of God or the saints; by the industry and devotion of her people; by the sober diligence of her rulers; by the excellence of her institutions. Indeed, were these not surer defenses than barren walls? Such "vacua moenia," Paolo Morosini said, the first Venetians renounced when they fled the ravaged mainland to find safety in the sea. Though she has no walls, Pier Paolo Vergerio wrote, the city is well armed. The citizens, wrote Guarnerio d'Artegna, "are the walls of the city on which the republic depends." The city's rulers, added Francesco Barbaro, are "the walls of the city." The city's laws, commented Pietro Contarini, are "the walls and defense of the city." Not her physical posture, said Domenico Morosini, but her institutions—"ordinamenti"—defend the city; and again, "not the walls, but institutions" protect her. Not walls and buildings but the citizens joined in common effort defend the city, wrote Gasparo Contarini. Fortunate city, wrote Paolo Paruta, whose citizens render you "though without walls, powerful and safe." Two centuries earlier, the archhumanist Petrarch had also pointed to the immaterial civic qualities which, more than her material wealth and power, made Ven-

---

M. Poppi, "Un'orazione del cronista Lorenzo de Monacis per il millenario di Venezia (1421)," p. 492: "Surexit igitur favente Deo in aquis et paludibus sine exemplo maxima civitas." B. Giustiniani in his *De origine urbis venetiarum rebusque gestis a venetis libri quindecim*, col. 9: the buildings "ut sine ullo fundamento solidiori in tantam altitudinem exsurgant." The Barozzi quotation in the epigraph is from that author's *Versuum atque hymnorum libri III*, p. 218.

[2] A. Broianico's *De divina origine reipublicae venetorum*, fol. 2: "Urbs liquido firmata solo/ sine moenibus ullis molibus immensis/ pelago subnixa profundo mirandis es fixa modis/ operaque deorum." L. Giustiniani, *Funebris oratio ad Georgium Lauredanum*, p. 12: "cum eo tot opportunas fluminum derivationes adeo commodo adjacentes quaquaversum regiones, tot cingentium littorum quasi moenia vallumque conspicio." B. Giustiniani, *De divi Marci Evangelistae vita, translatione et sepulturae loco*, col. 171: "non menia, non portas, nullasque denique arces extructas."

ice strong: she was "rich in gold but richer in fame, mighty in her resources but mightier in virtue, solidly built on marble but standing more solid on a foundation of civil concord, ringed with salt waters but more secure with the salt of good counsel!"[3]

We are not compelled to believe the "myth of Venice" that lurks behind these words. We would be foolish to do so. But it would be foolish, too, to deny that Venice, fashioned on sterile sand bars that a perilous age had made safer than solid ground, was a uniquely successful city. Her vibrant success had many sources. Among them was the constitution she slowly evolved, which achieved a new clarity at the brink of the age we call the Renaissance—a constitution that was administered effectively, on the whole, by a delimited and hereditary ruling class whose interests lay in nurturing as well as exploiting their city. These noblemen defended Venice with a citizen navy and rented troops. They decided policy in large councils and select committees. They protected food and water supplies and administered strict justice. They fostered civic festivals and rituals that promoted cohesion among the people and devotion to the city.

They pursued their ends by more subtle means, as well. They were conscious of trends in the world of ideas that could threaten or promote civic stability. At the dawn of the fifteenth century, they appropriated the humanist movement, novel and vigorous among the mix of the intellectual traditions of the burgeoning Italian Renaissance.[4] They did

---

[3] For the explanations of the sources of Venice's invulnerability, see the literature on the "myth of Venice" cited in Chapter Two n. 231. P. Morosini, *De rebus ac forma reipublicae venetae* [DRF], III, 233: "abeundum sibi populoque universo . . . relinquendum vacua moenia ac lares hostibus decreverunt, et in proximas sedes diverterunt." P. P. Vergerio, *De republica venetorum*, p. 40: "Hec igitur cum nullis sit muris nulloque vallo cincta, munitissima tamen est omnium, quas noster orbis habet." Guarnerio in L. Foscarini's *Epistolae* [*Epist.*], fol. 40: "cives qui muri appellati sunt civitatis." F. Barbaro, *De re uxoria liber* [DRU], p. 29: "sic natos ad laudem [the nobility] moenia civitatis appellare poterimus." P. Contarini, *In funere Marci Cornelii oratio*, p. 208: "leges solas esse urbis nostrae moenia et propugnacula." D. Morosini in his *De bene instituta re publica* [DBIRP], pp. 19, 241: "sono gli ordinamenti infatti e non la sua posizione lagunare ad aver salvato sempre Venezia da ogni nemico"; "non le mura, ma le istituzioni difendono la città." G. Contarini, *De republica venetorum libri quinque* (Leiden, 1628), as quoted in P. Gothein, *Francesco Barbaro (1390-1454)*, p. 75. P. Paruta, *Orazione funebre in lode dei morti nella vittoriosa battaglia contra i Turchi*, p. 115: "O avventurata città, che nel seno delle tue leggi nudrisci tai cittadini, che . . . ti rendono senza mura fortissima e sicurissima." F. Petrarch, *Letters*, p. 234 (*Epist. seniles*, IV, 3), often quoted in the literature on the Venetian myth. The topos that the citizens are the real walls of the city is ancient. Already traditional, it appears in Thucydides (II.78.3; VII.77.7); note also St. Augustine (*Sermo de urbis excidio*, VI, 6): "Civitas est in civibus non in parietibus."

[4] Here and henceforth, that definition of humanism is adopted which has been posed by P. O. Kristeller in his many works: see especially his essay "The Humanist Movement," at pp. 21-24. For the development of the terms "humanist" and "humanism"

so by hiring and firing professional intellectuals, by providing or denying opportunities for expression, as powerful men are wont in any time or place to do. They did so, most remarkably, by themselves entering the ranks of the humanists and thus defining intellectual culture for the first nine decades of the fifteenth century. And those who did so were not the least members of that aristocracy, not the excluded or politically disaffected, but to a great extent among the most privileged of the city's jealous rulers. Dominated by the patricians in their ranks, the humanists of Venice accommodated themselves to the interests of the city's ruling class. They, too, undertook the defense of Venice, and served as walls that would make her invulnerable.

The role played by the humanists of early Renaissance Venice as protective walls of the city is traced in this book. To do so, it has been necessary to name the humanists—each one; to define their place in Venetian society; to survey their works. The first of these tasks has proved to be immense, requiring extensive research to elucidate the careers of many less-known figures, and the coordination of an unruly secondary literature for others. It has been assigned to Part II of this book. There a core group of ninety-two humanists active from 1400 to 1490 is defined, the definition defended, and each figure introduced with a bio-bibliographical profile designed to give the reader access to existing literature or, in its absence, to provide from new sources critical data otherwise unavailable. The core group definition and profiles are fundamental to the narrative in Part I, which performs the other tasks named and presents an interpretation of Venetian humanism. Its three chapters have, respectively, these aims: to view the society of Venetian humanists in action; to analyze key works closely and to

---

(the latter not used until the nineteenth century), see A. Campana, "The Origin of the Word 'Humanist,' " and P. F. Grendler, "Five Italian Occurrences of Umanista, 1540-1574."

See also the principal studies of the development of Italian humanism providing guidance to further exploration: by H. Baron, *The Crisis of the Early Italian Renaissance*; E. Garin, *Italian Humanism* and *La letteratura degli umanisti*; P. Monnier, *Le Quattrocento*; V. Rossi, *Il Quattrocento*; G. Saitta, *Il pensiero italiano nell'umanesimo e nel rinascimento*; A. Tartaro and F. Tateo, *Il Quattrocento: l'età dell'umanesimo*, I, especially Tateo, *La cultura umanistica e i suoi centri*; G. Toffanin, *History of Humanism*; C. Trinkaus, *In Our Image and Likeness*; G. Voigt, *Il risorgimento dell'antichità classica*. *Renaissance Humanism*, a two-volume collection of essays surveying the state of humanist studies, edited by A. Rabil, Jr., will be published shortly by the University of Pennsylvania Press. For Venetian humanism in particular, see the essays in *Storia della cultura veneta*, III:1 [SCV, III/1], with a rich bibliographical apparatus. The specialized studies in the *Miscellanea di studi in onore di Vittore Branca*, III:1 and 2 [*Misc. Branca*, III/1, III/2] should be consulted for the most recent bibliographical references. For an interpretative overview with which this study fundamentally concurs, see F. Gilbert, "Humanism in Venice."

survey, naming scores of others, the whole of that group's literary production; and to trace the course of Venetian humanism from its origins through three fifteenth-century generations to its new configuration at the brink of the following century.

An overview of Quattrocento humanism in Venice follows, then, that both presents the full range of evidence known to this author and poses a hypothesis about the nature of that phenomenon. Every attempt has been made not to anticipate the ideals often found in humanism—those familiar ideals of the dignity of man, of civic liberty, of the dynamic will and explosive power of the word—where they may not exist, or exist only dimly, intertwined with lesser, perhaps, but more urgent notions. Every attempt has been made to avoid the quest for a philosophy central to humanism, but to search instead intently for the characteristic elements of Venetian intellectual culture in the Quattrocento. These dwell at the intersection of patrician interest and humanist studies. Power and thought met, and men of ideas became walls of the city.

Part One

ONE

The Humanists: *Ordo litteratorum*

1. THE NEW LEARNING

Far from his native Greece, the learned Manuel Chrysoloras died in 1415 during sessions of the Council of Constance that was to resolve the schism of the Latin Church and burn John Hus. More than any other single figure, Chrysoloras had stimulated among the humanists a love of Greek learning. Yet none among his friends and students, struck though they were by their loss, composed his eulogy. It was written and delivered by the young Venetian nobleman, Andrea Giuliani. Urged to the task by his teacher Guarino Veronese, a former pupil of Chrysoloras, on behalf of the learned of Italy, Giuliani lamented the death of their majestic guide and inspiration.[1]

For Venetians had by this time joined the community of those who loved the *studia humanitatis*. Giuliani himself had fallen under their spell. At the advanced age of twenty-three, he had undertaken a program of literary studies. Eight years later, then a young statesman pressed by official tasks, he spoke upon the invitation of a group of his peers about the ideal of eloquence central to humanism.[2] May God

---

[1] For the circumstances surrounding Giuliani's oration, see especially R. Sabbadini, *Vita di Guarino Veronese*, pp. 28ff. Poggio Bracciolini reveals in his letter to Guarino congratulating that scholar on his protégé's performance that Giuliani alone had publicly eulogized Chrysoloras: "Andreas vero Julianus summe est a nobis collaudandus qui cernens ignaviam nostram, qui nullam ne mortuo quidem pro suis in nos singularibus meritis gratiam referremus, sua opera, suo studio, nos ad operam concitavit, et tarditatem nostram sua diligentia sublevavit" (*Epist.*, ed. Tonellis, I, 24). To avoid encumbering an already heavy apparatus, figures mentioned in this narrative will not routinely be identified in the notes. For core-group figures refer to the profiles in Part Two. Some figures—including Venetians and resident and transient foreigners not of the core group—are identified in the notes to sections 6-11 of the preface to Part Two on excluded, marginal, and peripheral figures. Humanists who are well known to a scholarly audience (such as Poggio and Guarino, introduced here) are not discussed except in their relation to the Venetians.

[2] The *Oratio super principio orationum M. Tullii Ciceronis*, in K. Müllner, *Reden und Briefe italienischer Humanisten*, pp. 115-18, with Müllner's introduction outlining the relevant circumstances. Giuliani's age and political activities are known from his own words: "... primarum ... litterarum praecepta post tertium et vigesimum aetatis meae annum ingressus sum ..."; "... [me] publicus magistratus nostrique communis officii cura solicitat ...." (116). The translations provided throughout are deliberately free, eliminating distracting superlatives and circumlocutions. In citing Latin texts from

3

give me the capacity to describe to you, he implored, "the divine eloquence of these orations of Cicero—for I know that my gifts are not equal to the task to which I am moved not by my own will, but assume it gladly so I might accede to yours."[3] Curiosity about the new learning had invaded the hearts of the sober guardians of imperial Venice.

Fired with love of the humanities, Venetians carved time from busy lives to study the "divine eloquence" of ancient masters. Once the hero of Chioggia, where Venice had fought to the death with Genoa and won, Carlo Zeno was later disgraced for an indiscretion in the matter of accepting gifts from enemies of the state. In retirement, he took up the *studia humanitatis* full time—not, as his eulogist Leonardo Giustiniani put it, like a busy man engaged in a variety of tasks, but like a philosopher or orator, a professional. He studied as though life offered no pleasure more intense.[4]

Giustiniani might have been describing himself. In his youth a poet of sensual love whose rhymes were sung by gondoliers, later in life the author of exquisite sacred verse, Giustiniani yearned for quiet days filled with deep thoughts and intense memories. On the island of Murano, in retreat from the plague and tedious obligations, he admired the natural symmetries of nature and artful harmonies of music, and pondered problems of moral philosophy and of history.[5] Eagerly, he

---

printed editions, I have duplicated the editor's text, omitting brackets and editorial signs (unless essential to the meaning) and unnecessary capitalizations. In citing from manuscript versions, I have supplied convenient punctuation and capitalization, but followed orthographical peculiarities, making no attempt at standardization. Obscure words are bracketed. Where I have supplied a word to make a meaning complete (or otherwise emended or commented upon the text), such words, comments, and emendations are similarly bracketed. For the Cicero oration and Giuliani's late start in humanist studies, see also M. Pastore Stocchi, "Scuola e cultura umanistica fra due secoli," at pp. 101, 107.

[3] "Nihil est, patres clarissimi, quod mihi dii immortales optabilius largiri potuissent, quam ut hodie tantam vim ac rationem dicendi mihi dedissent, ut harum orationum Ciceronis nostri divinam eloquentiam atque artem vobis exponere valerem, cum in me non tantum ingenii sit, ut huius rei magnitudini satis opportune satisfieri posse cognoscam; quod tamen onus non tam automate quam ut voluntatibus vestris adductus libenter assumam." Giuliani, *Oratio super principio*, p. 116.

[4] For Zeno, J. Zeno, *Vita Caroli Zeni*, and L. Giustiniani, *Funebris oratio pro Carolo Zeno* are essential. For Zeno's literary activities, see Jacopo Zeno's *Vita*, pp. 135-37, and Guarino's letter to Carlo repeating Francesco Barbaro's description of his studies, in *Epist.*, ed. Sabbadini, I, 136; for his Greek learning in particular, see A. Pertusi., "L'umanesimo greco dalla fine del secolo XIV agli inizi del secolo XVI," pp. 199ff.; also L. Giustiniani's *Funebris oratio pro Carolo Zeno*, p. 143. Guarino dedicated to Zeno his translation of Plutarch's *Themistocles*; Kristeller, *Iter*, I, 418. A volume of Zeno's orations were among the books owned by his grandson Jacopo; cf. E. Govi, "La biblioteca di Jacopo Zeno," p. 58.

[5] This letter is in Guarino, *Epist.* I, 292-97, and previously published also by Sabbadini

reflected upon the nature of the republic, the governance of the family, the fortunes and misfortunes of Venetian ancestors, the happiness of past ages, and the tragedy of this one: "and all that those many minds, each in its age, had thought of any matter, I in an instant can know."[6] Nothing delighted him more than fellowship with those books which provided him that harvest.

Ermolao Barbaro the Younger also rejoiced when duty or accident removed him from the press of duties and allowed him time for studies. The republic will do quite well without me, he wrote Giorgio Merula, "but without letters I shall not survive."[7] In Padua, where he had taken refuge from the rumor of plague, he devoted his leisure to his beloved studies. A few years later, when ambassador to Milan, he crowed to his friend Girolamo Donato about the chief benefit of his assignment: the opportunity for serious study. "The shades of Dioscorides and Aristotle," he wrote, "have won me this legation."[8] And later still, when his embassy to Rome had resulted in ecclesiastical preferment and Venetian disfavor, he welcomed again the opportunity for study. "A great part of my life has always been devoted to study," he wrote to Ugolino Verino; "now it shall be the whole."[9] And to Antonio Calvo: "Born to letters, pledged to letters, without letters I cannot exist. . . . O happy calamity, which has restored letters to me and me to letters, and indeed myself to myself."[10] With his dearly-won time, he completed his emendation of Pliny.[11]

Books were the object of this passion for learning that suffused so many Quattrocento Venetians and engaged them with the other humanist circles of Italy. They discovered, borrowed, copied and collected books with fervor. Francesco Barbaro had congratulated Poggio Bracciolini for his momentous discoveries of ancient manuscripts dur-

---

with a discussion in R. Sabbadini, "Sugli studi volgari di Leonardo Giustiniani," pp. 363ff.

[6] ". . . hic de rei publice statu, hic de rei familiaris gubernatione, hic de antiquis casibus et fortunis civitatis civiumque nostrorum; hic de felicitatibus superioris seculi, de calamitate huius etatis, de gloria, de virtute ceterisque rebus humanis semper aut utiliter aut festive quippiam disputatur et que tot ingenia de unaquaque re omni sua etate collegerunt brevi ego momento cognosco." Guarino, *Epist.*, I, 294-95.

[7] ". . . sine me respublica nihilominus incolumis florensque est, ego sine litteris non supersum." Barbaro, *Epist.*, ed. Branca, I, 54.

[8] "Credo Dioscoridis et Aristotelis manes impetravisse mihi legationem." Ibid., II, 14.

[9] ". . . magna pars vitae meae . . . litteris semper fuit dicata, nunc erit tota." Ibid., II, 66.

[10] "Litteris natus, litteris dicatus, sine litteris esse non possum. . . . O foelix calamitas, quae litteras mihi et me litteris, imo ipsum mihi me restituit." Ibid., II, 70.

[11] The *Castigationes plinianae et in Pomponium Melam* [1493]. For patricians' yearning for studious leisure, see also M. Pastore Stocchi, "Scuola e cultura umanistica," p. 121.

ing the Council of Constance, but was even more delighted when he made a discovery of his own.[12] As Venetian ambassador to the papal curia in 1426, he one day strayed from his path and stumbled upon a treasure in a dismal warehouse attached to the monastery of Santa Maria di Frascati. Amid barrels of wine lay Greek books, beautifully written, worthy of the library of a Varro or a Ptolemy, neglected and unread. Barbaro described his triumph to his friend and mentor Guarino Veronese "that you may know that in this age the good fortune and diligence of one 'barbarian' (Barbaro) unearthed near Rome these treasures of Greek learning which the Roman people allowed to be hidden and buried in squalor and dirt."[13] Gregorio Correr was also proud of his discoveries in a monastic library near Basel: he had rescued Salvianus' *De providentia Dei*, as he put it, "from German dungeons."[14] Books were lost as well as found. Lauro Quirini mourned the devastation suffered when Constantinople fell to the Turks: "More than one hundred twenty thousand volumes," he lamented. What Greek literature had achieved "through such length of time, with so much labor, with such industry" had "perished, alas, perished"—how can we restrain our tears?[15]

Venetians engaged with non-Venetians in the circulation of important texts. Leonardo Bruni asked Pietro Miani to give to Chrysoloras Bruni's copy of *The City of God*, and to request that scholar to bring to the curia any interesting Greek manuscripts.[16] Gasparino Barzizza copied Giovanni Corner's text of Pliny, and emended the Venetian's manuscript of Cicero's *De oratore*.[17] Guarino Veronese received from

[12] Barbaro's letter to Poggio in his *Epistolae* in the *Diatriba praeliminaris in duas partes divisa* [Quirini, *Diatriba* = I; *Epist.*, ed. Quirini = II], II, 1-8. The letter to Guarino described below in Barbaro, *Centotrenta*, ed. Sabbadini, pp. 70-71 and Guarino, *Epist.*, I, 549-50.

[13] ". . . ut intellegeres hac aetate unius Barbari fortunam et diligentiam thesauros quosdam graecae disciplinae prope urbem romanam repperisse, quos populus romanus in squalore ac sordibus sepultos iacere ac latere patiebatur." *Centotrenta*, ed. Sabbadini, p. 71.

[14] Correr, *Epistola ad Caeciliam virginem de fugiendo saeculo*, in G. B. Contarini, *Anec. ven.*, p. 42. The *Epistola* is also translated in M. L. King and A. Rabil, Jr., *Her Immaculate Hand*, pp. 93-105. The patrician Archbishop of Crete Pietro Donato also made a notable discovery in 1436 of a codex of geographical works; see R. Sabbadini, *Le scoperte dei codici latini e greci ne' secoli XIV e XV*, edited by E. Garin, I, 119ff.

[15] "Ultra centum et viginti milia librorum volumina . . . devastata. Ergo et lingua et litteratura Graecorum tanto tempore, tanto labore, tanta industria inventa, aucta, perfecta peribit, heu peribit! Ecquis vel adeo rudis rerum est vel adeo ferrens, ut se a lacrimis possit abstinere?" L. Quirini, *Epistola* to Pope Nicholas V, p. 227, in "Epistole storiche sulla caduta di Costantinopoli e la potenza dei Turchi," edited by A. Pertusi. For Quirini's reactions, see Pertusi, "L'umanesimo greco," p. 248.

[16] L. Bruni, *Epist.*, ed. Mehus, II, 52. Miani was one of the earliest Italians engaged in the study and collection of Greek texts; see Sabbadini, *Scoperte*, I, 63.

[17] For the Pliny manuscript, see Barzizza's letter to Corner in *Gasparini Barzizzii*

Leonardo Giustiniani a copy of Plutarch's life of Themistocles and had to remind Andrea Giuliani to return Pliny's letters, since the owner required them.[18] Ambrogio Traversari received from Francesco Barbaro a rare Lactantius codex, which he promised to emend and return with Xenophon's *Agesilaus*, and employed Leonardo Giustiniani as agent in acquiring materials he needed for his busy scribes.[19] Pietro Donato's will carefully provided for the return of books he had borrowed over the years from the Florentine exile Palla Strozzi.[20] Ludovico Foscarini wrote to Guarnerio d'Artegna that Thucydides, for several days now his guest, was on the way home, but that he was in urgent need of more books from that bibliophile's store: "Without Greek friends I cannot lead a decent life here—I beg you, send me Appian or Herodotus."[21]

As books circulated, libraries formed. Pietro Barbo's favored histories; Giovanni Marcanova's, medicine; Georgio Valla's, mathematics and science.[22] The large inventoried collections of Pietro Barozzi, Pietro Donato, Jacopo Zeno, and Marcanova were willed to Paduan libraries.[23] The patrician Domenico Morosini prohibited by his will the dispersion of his collection; the commoners Marcantonio Sabellico and Pietro Cirneo bequeathed theirs, respectively, to family and

Bergomatis et Guiniforti filii opera, edited by J. A. Furiettus, pp. 209-10, and C. Colombo, "Gasparino Barzizza a Padova," pp. 4ff. For the correction of the *De oratore*, see Barzizza's letter to Corner in R. Sabbadini, "Codici latini posseduti, scoperti, illustrati da Guarino Veronese," cols. 397-98, and R. Sabbadini, *Storia e critica di testi latini*, p. 81.

[18] For Plutarch's Themistocles, see Giustiniani's words to Guarino in the latter's *Epist.* I, 138; Guarino's reminder to Giuliani at I, 306.

[19] For the loan of Lactantius and the promised Xenophon, see Traversari's letters: *Aliorumque ad ipsum epist.*, ed. Mehus, II, 279-81 and 283-84. For Leonardo Giustiniani's aid, see ibid., pp. 316-17 and 320-21. Barbaro had also sent Traversari a catalogue of his books: R. Sabbadini, *Scoperte*, I, 63. For Traversari's literary relations with both Barbaro and Giustiniani, see C. Stinger, *Humanism and the Church Fathers*, index.

[20] See G. Fiocco, "Palla Strozzi e l'umanesimo veneto," p. 353.

[21] "Tuchidides hospes noster post multos hos dies domum reverti deliberavit; fas non est aliquid sui temporis prorogari. Verum quia eius consuetudine mirum in modum dellectatus sum, nec videor posse iocundam in his regionibus sine graecis comitibus vitam agere, te hortor et horo, ut Appianum vel Herodotum ad nos mittas ...." Foscarini, *Epist.*, fols. 215ᵛ-216.

[22] For Barbo, see R. Weiss, *Un umanista veneziano: Papa Paolo II*; for Marcanova's library, L. Sighinolfi, "La biblioteca di Giovanni Marcanova"; for Valla's, J. L. Heiberg, *Beiträge zur Geschichte Georg Vallas und seiner Bibliothek*, pp. 109-29, and P. L. Rose, "Humanist Culture and Renaissance Mathematics," pp. 65-104, esp. pp. 94ff.

[23] For Barozzi, see esp. E. Govi, "Petri Barocii bibliothecae inventarium"; for Donato, P. Sambin, "Ricerche per la storia della cultura nel secolo XV"; for Zeno, E. Govi, "La biblioteca di Jacopo Zeno"; for Marcanova, L. Sighinolfi, "La biblioteca di Giovanni Marcanova," and M. C. Vitali, "L'umanista padovano Giovanni Marcanova (1410/1418-67) e la sua biblioteca."

teacher.[24] The precious libraries of Marco Barbo (some 500 volumes) and Pietro Tommasi (130) were scattered.[25] During his visit to Venice in 1433, Ambrogio Traversari—finding little of interest in monastic libraries—admired the private collections of Francesco Barbaro, Tommasi, and Giovanni Corner, the latter's particularly remarkable for the elegance of its manuscripts.[26] In Crete, Lauro Quirini became an entrepreneur of books.[27] As duke of that Venetian island, the nobleman Marco Lippomano arranged to copy the pseudo-Aristotelian *Mechanics*; as a tourist in Constantinople, the commoner Jacopo Languschi transcribed with Giovanni Aurispa a valuable text of Cicero.[28]

Pietro del Monte purchased all the books he could find, according to the Florentine bookseller Vespasiano de' Bisticci, and kept a scribe employed in his house.[29] Guglielmo Quirini asked Febo Capella to acquire books for him in Milan, and Pietro Miani arranged to have books shipped from England on a Venetian vessel.[30] Some books journeyed from library to library. A Catullus first copied by Girolamo Donato the Elder formed part of the collection of his kinsman Pietro Donato, then passed successively to Giovannino Corradini, Francesco Barbaro, and Ermolao Barbaro the Younger.[31] Leonardo Sanuto's collection circulated to family and friends, with each transaction carefully noted.[32] The libraries of Marcantonio Morosini and Daniele Renier provided texts used by Aldo Manuzio's press.[33] Pietro Marcello the Elder was the divulgator in Venice of Cicero's letters to Atticus, and Domenico Bollani's manuscript of Petrarch's *Epistolae familiares* provided the text for that work's *editio princeps*.[34] Cardinal Bessarion

[24] Morosini's testament in ASV, AN, Testamenti C. Rizzo, B. 1227.122, c. 2ᵛ, and B. 1229.152, #23. Sabellico's, published by A. Zeno, *Istorici delle cose veneziane*, I, lxviii-lxxi. For Cirneo's, see G. dalla Santa, "Un testamento ed alcune note biografiche di Pietro Cirneo."

[25] For Barbo's, see G. Gualdo in DBI, VI (1964), 249-52, and G. Zippel, "La morte di Marco Barbo cardinale," p. 203 and n. 2; for Tommasi's see S. Connell, "Books and Their Owners in Venice, 1345-1480," pp. 175-82.

[26] A. Traversari, *Hodoeporicon*, pp. 61-64; R. Sabbadini, *Scoperte*, I, 94.

[27] See V. Branca, "Lauro Quirini e il commercio librario a Venezia e Firenze."

[28] For Lippomano, see D. Geanakoplos, *Greek Scholars in Venice*, p. 50, and J. Monfasani, *George of Trebizond*, p. 6; for Languschi, see Connell, "Books," p. 168.

[29] R. Sabbadini, *Scoperte*, I, 115.

[30] For Quirini, see G. dalla Santa, "Di un patrizio mercante veneziano del Quattrocento e di Francesco Filelfo suo debitore," p. 75; for Miani, dalla Santa, "Uomini e fatti dell'ultimo Trecento e del primo Quattrocento," p. 46.

[31] P. Sambin, "Ricerche . . . P. Donato," pp. 57ff.; R. Sabbadini, "Codici latini," pp. 379-80.

[32] The record of his book transactions on fols. 159ᵛ-160 of his cash book and ricordanza: ASV, Giudici di Petizion, B. 955. I am grateful to Reinhold Mueller for this reference.

[33] G. degli Agostini, *Notizie*, I, xl.

[34] For Marcello, see R. Sabbadini, "Antonio da Romagno e Pietro Marcello," p. 218; for Bollani, DBI, XI (1969), 290.

donated his famous library of Greek manuscripts to Venice in 1468, persuaded by Paolo Morosini, thinking that in that cosmopolitan city they would find a wide readership. Ironically, his books arrived with pomp, but languished, inaccessible, for years.[35] Bernardo Bembo's collection, descended to the Vatican, gives evidence of loving accumulation. It includes a copy of Leonardo Bruni's translation of Plato's *Phaedo*, transcribed and annotated by Bembo himself when not yet twenty, and a manuscript of Petrarch's *On the Solitary Life* in the author's hand. The autograph was carefully verified by Bembo, who duly noted on the guard-leaf that the hand was "undoubtedly" Petrarch's, though "hastily written."[36]

For not only ancient authors, but modern works and translations were read and discussed by Venetian humanists among themselves and with non-Venetian friends. Leonardo Giustiniani discussed with Ambrogio Traversari the latter's translation of Diogenes Laertius, and urged the Florentine monk to interest himself in sacred works written in the language of the people.[37] Pietro Dolfin defended to Pietro Barozzi his commissioning for transcription works of the Florentine Leon Battista Alberti: to the Bishop Barozzi's scolding, the Abbot Dolfin replied that the works, though admittedly not religious, were not antireligious.[38] Leonardo Bruni sent one of his works to Jacopo Foscari for comment—"since you are, as I have gathered from your letters, an admirer and lover of my works"—and Marco Dandolo accepted the criticism of his work by Battista Guarini.[39] Ludovico Foscarini asked

[35] For Bessarion's collection and its donation to the doge, see L. Labowsky, *Bessarion's Library and the Biblioteca Marciana*; useful brief accounts are also by G. Fedalto, "Stranieri a Venezia e a Padova," p. 509, and A. Pertusi, "L'umanesimo greco," p. 254. For the abuse of Bessarion's codices, see M. Lowry, "Two Great Venetian Libraries in the Age of Aldus Manutius," pp. 133ff.

[36] For Bembo's collection, far richer in precious manuscripts than can be indicated here, see C. H. Clough, *Pietro Bembo's Library as Represented Particularly in the British Museum*, and P. de Nolhac, *La Bibliothèque de Fulvio Orsini*, pp. 91ff. and passim. See also the studies listed in his profile in Part II. For the Bruni translation, V. Cian, "Per Bernardo Bembo—II," pp. 68ff.; for the Petrarch manuscript, P. Rajna, "Il codice Vaticano 3357 del trattato 'De vita solitaria' di Francesco Petrarca." In addition to those mentioned in the previous notes, the following libraries are recorded: those of Ermolao Barbaro V and G, Zaccaria Barbaro, Antonio Calvo, Fantino Dandolo, Domenico de' Domenichi, Jacopo Foscari, Leonardo Giustiniani, Niccolò Leonardi, Giovanni Lorenzi, Giorgio Merula, Niccolò Sagundino, Niccolò Leonico Tomeo; consult the "Discourse" section and related notes in the pertinent profiles. Of ninety-two core group figures I am aware of, twenty-six actively engaged in the collection of books and antiquities.

[37] Traversari, *Epist.*, ed. Mehus, II, 305-306 and 307-308, 313-14 and 315-16, respectively.

[38] P. Dolfin, *Epist. CCXLII*, ed. Martène & Durand, III, col. 1160; "... et si non religiosa, non tamen religioni contraria expetere opuscula ...."

[39] Bruni, *Epist.*, ed. Mehus, II, 109: "... ut tuis litteris ad me scriptis perspexi, tu

Damiano dal Borgo for his works, and Bernardo Giustiniani requested of Francesco Capodilista copies of the orations of Guarino Veronese and George of Trebizond—his teachers—so that their fame could be spread abroad.[40] Pietro Tommasi praised Poggio Bracciolini's dialogue *On Avarice* to Francesco Barbaro and encouraged Guarino to translate Chrysoloras' works.[41] Niccolò Canal begged Francesco Filelfo for his translation of Xenophon's *Cyropaedeia*, which he required for companionship, along with the poet Paolo Marsi, at the Battle of Negropont; "and who could more typify that century," wondered Marsi's biographer, "than this general who, leaving on a difficult enterprise, wished to have with him a philosophical book and a humanist poet?"[42]

Some works by Venetians received high acclaim from the audience beyond the lagoons. Andrea Giuliani's oration for Chrysoloras circulated widely—a sign of favor—and was praised enthusiastically by Gasparino Barzizza, Poggio Bracciolini, and Guarino Veronese.[43] Francesco Barbaro's *On Marriage* was even more of a success. Extant in a multitude of contemporary manuscripts, it was celebrated by Ambrogio Traversari and Pier Paolo Vergerio.[44]

The humanists enticed each other to the joys of the intellectual life. Niccolò Barbo exhorted Andrea Trapesunzio—his teacher's son—not to abandon literary studies for a soldier's career.[45] Ermolao Barbaro the Younger encouraged his junior contemporary Giovanni Pico della Mirandola in Greek studies, and bestowed advice on Giorgio Merula, charged to write the history of the exploits of his Milanese masters.[46] Jacopo Zeno praised the antiquarian Ciriaco d'Ancona for recovering lost antiquity single-handedly, calling him "the one and only liberator and preserver, patron, and parent of antiquity."[47] The Venetians re-

---

meorum operum comprobator simul, atque amator es." Dandolo's letter to Guarino in A. Medin, "Gli scritti umanistici di Marco Dandolo," pp. 374-75.

[40] Foscarini, *Epist.*, fols. 99-100; B. Giustiniani, *Orat. et epist.*, sig. L.

[41] Tommasi's letter to Barbaro in E. Walser, *Poggius Florentinus, Leben und Werke*, pp. 432-35; for his recommendation to Guarino, see A. Segarizzi, "La corrispondenza famigliare di un medico erudito del Quattrocento (Pietro Tommasi)," p. 241.

[42] A. della Torre, *Paolo Marsi*, 173-74. The contemporary Marino Sanuto's comment is also interesting: he called the learned general "atto più a leger libri che a governar le cose di mar," quoted in S. Romanin, *Stor. doc.*, IV, 347, n. 1.

[43] For Barzizza, his *Opera*, p. 210. For Guarino, his *Epist.*, ed. Sabbadini, I, 81-83. For Poggio's words, see above, n. 1.

[44] Traversari, *Epist.*, ed. Mehus, II, 294; Vergerio in *Epist.*, ed. Smith, pp. 360-62.

[45] N. Barbo, *Epist.*, fols. 50-55ᵛ.

[46] Ermolao Barbaro G, *Epist.*, ed. Branca, I, 85-86, and I, 44, 52, 71ff., and 98, respectively.

[47] ". . . ut solum et unicum antiquitatis liberatorem ac servatorem, patronum atque parentem te benemeritum omnes uno ore, una voce, una sententia cognominandum

ceived in their turn encouragements to study from abroad. Gasparino Barzizza begged of Daniele Vitturi news of his studies, and Leonardo Bruni and Poggio Bracciolini urged the young Jacopo Foscari to further efforts in his; Guarino commended Foscari's vast learning.[48] In Rome, the papal *camerarius* Andrea Fiocchi found his duties prevented study, and urged his former student Paolo Barbo to devote himself while he still could find the time to the *studia humanitatis*: "later you will grieve the loss of so precious a treasure."[49] In Florence, Ficino wrote of the joys of philosophy to several Venetian friends—to Marco Aurelio, Febo Capella, Sebastiano Badoer, Ermolao Barbaro the Younger, Marco Barbo, Girolamo Donato, Pietro Molin, and above all to Bernardo Bembo and Antonio Vinciguerra, his "Castor" and "Pollux."[50]

Venetian humanists were involved, too, in the quarrels of the age. Francesco Barbaro resolved the debate between Poggio Bracciolini and Guarino Veronese on the relative merits of Caesar and Scipio, and healed the tensions between Niccolò Niccoli and Leonardo Bruni, and between Niccoli and Francesco Filelfo. He and Pietro Tommasi were instrumental in reconciling Poggio and Filelfo, and Jacopo Foscari had been involved as the recipient of Poggio's invective against Filelfo.[51] The acrimonious dispute between Poggio and Valla involved several Venetians: Barbaro and Tommasi again, and Lorenzo Zane.[52] Venetians were the objects of such invectives as well: Leonardo Bruni denounced Lauro Quirini, who had questioned his understanding of

---

putarint." Zeno's laudatory *epistola* to Ciriaco in L. Bertalot and A. Campana, "Gli scritti di Iacopo Zeno e il suo elogio di Ciriaco d'Ancona," p. 326.

[48] Barzizza, *Opera*, ed. Furiettus, pp. 176-77; Bruni, *Epist.*, ed. Mehus, II, 96-97; Poggio Bracciolini, *Epist.*, ed. Tonellis, I, 150-53; Guarino, *Epist.*, II, 292-94.

[49] ". . . lugebis postea nequicquam tanti precii thesaurum amisisse." From Fiocchi's letter to Barbo in G. Mercati, *Ultimi contributi alla storia degli umanisti*, I, 128.

[50] Letters to various Venetian figures are among Ficino's *Epist.* in his *Opera omnia*, I:2, 607-994. For letters (and allusions) to the figures named, see the index to the *Opera omnia* by P. O. Kristeller in his *Supplementum Ficinianum*, II, 357ff. Translations of the letters in books I, III, and IV of the twelve books of Ficino's *Epist.* are in the three completed volumes of *The Letters of Marsilio Ficino*; see indices. For Ficino's Venetian correspondents and relations, see also Kristeller, "Marsilio Ficino a Venezia." The reference to Castor and Pollux is in Ficino's greeting to both Venetians (*Epist.*, p. 810): "Salve semper Bernarde mi Castor, salve rursus Antoni mi Pollux."

[51] For Barbaro's involvement in these controversies, see Quirini, *Diatriba*, chap. ii, pp. 37ff. For Tommasi's, see his extensive correspondence with Poggio and Filelfo in Walser, *Poggius Florentinus*, pp. 455ff., and Guarino's with Tommasi in Guarino, *Epist.*, ed. Sabbadini, II, 568-72. For Foscari, see Poggio's three letters to the Venetian in his *Epist.*, ed. Tonellis, I, 150-54 and 177-78.

[52] For this incident, see G. Zippel, "Lorenzo Valla e le origini della storiografia umanistica a Venezia," pp. 104ff. In addition, for Barbaro's role, Quirini's *Diatriba*, pp. 53ff.; for Tommasi, cf. Connell, "Books," p. 176, and Kristeller's introduction to "Tre trattati di Lauro Quirini sulla nobiltà," edited by K. Krautter et al., p. 33; for Zane's, R. Weiss, "Lorenzo Zane arcivescovo di Spalato e governatore di Cesena," p. 165.

Aristotle, as arrogant and ignorant.[53] Poggio Bracciolini accused Jacopo Zeno of "insane greed."[54]

2. Learned Friends

Venetians were involved in the wider world of Italian humanism not only through the written word, but through actual contact in cities beyond their own. Sent abroad by the Signoria as ambassadors, governors, or secretaries, they often looked forward to assignments that offered leisure for study and discourse with learned men. When Paolo Barbo declined the office of podestà of Verona to accept a more arduous magistracy at home, Ludovico Foscarini marveled at his decision—"You are nourished on hard work, like the gods on nectar"—and regretted that Barbo would not be able to enjoy the tranquillity one found in the podestariate, or pleasant conversation.[55] About to embark on the same office Barbo had declined, Foscarini shared with Girolamo Barbarigo his yearning for that opportunity to return to the studies he had pursued since childhood.[56] As he had hoped, he did engage in the literary life of Verona, as is demonstrated by his profound friendship with the woman humanist and recluse Isotta Nogarola.[57] Foscarini's term as governor of Friuli also yielded intellectual pleasures. "Here I find quiet," he wrote Girolamo da Ponte, "here I find new strength, here I am refreshed, here I enjoy letters, here I resume my interrupted studies . . . ; we are always hearing issues proposed by experts, or debating about some learned matter or other, or discussing history."[58] His studies in Udine were particularly fruitful because of the proximity of San Daniele and Guarnerio d'Artegna's library, "than which none in all of Italy or the world is more renowned."[59]

During his two embassies to Florence, Bernardo Bembo engaged to the fullest in that city's brilliant intellectual life.[60] He became close to

---

[53] Bruni, *Epist.*, ed. Mehus, II, 134-47.

[54] ". . . tu . . . qui neque pudori neque honori parcis ob insanam auri et argenti cupiditatem." Poggio's invective to Jacopo Zeno, in *Opera omnia*, IV, 653.

[55] "Sed tu vir studiosissimus qui sicut dii nectare aluntur sic maximis negotiis nutriris . . . ." Foscarini, *Epist.*, fol. 257^v.

[56] Ibid., fol. 80.

[57] See especially P. Gothein, "L'amicizia fra Ludovico Foscarini e l'umanista Isotta Nogarola," and M. L. King, "The Religious Retreat of Isotta Nogarola." See Foscarini's profile for notes to the correspondence with Nogarola and others with whom that nobleman formed ties during service abroad.

[58] "Hic quiesco; hic recreor; hic refitior; hic litteris fruor; hic intermissa studia revoco; . . . semper aut causas a peritissimis audimus aut in aliquo doctrine genere contendimus, aut in ystori[i]s versamur." Foscarini, *Epist.*, fol. 206^v.

[59] ". . . qua nulla . . . in universa Italia nec orbe celebrior est . . . ." Ibid., fol. 242.

[60] For Bembo's stay in Florence and contacts there with the Medici and learned men,

Landino, Poliziano, and above all Ficino, in whose circle he became a star. "You ask what the Academy does?" Ficino wrote him. "It loves Bembo. What else does it do? It reveres Bembo. Every man among us agrees that Bembo above all is worthy of love and reverence, for his breast is the temple of the Graces, and his mind the fount of the Muses."[61] He developed warm relations also with Florence's Medici rulers from the years of his first embassy until at least 1494, when he welcomed Pietro and his sons, now exiles, in Venice.[62] Bembo's relations with Florence's literary elite, so close in turn to the Medici center of power, was far from irrelevant to his diplomatic mission: he formed with Florence, when tensions with Venice were high, "a real and genuine literary alliance."[63] When he was podestà of Ravenna, a few years later, he displayed his gratitude to Florentine friends by erecting for the bones of Dante, that Florentine exile still not permitted to go home, a splendid tomb.[64]

Francesco Diedo also joined a circle of learned men while podestà of Brescia. His *Life of San Rocco* he wrote in part to please that healing saint and win divine favor for the plague-struck city; in part it was written to please the city's learned men—for no recent author, adequately trained in the *studia humanitatis*, Diedo pointed out, had before undertaken the task.[65] And Francesco Barbaro found opportunity during his podestariate in Verona to discuss nature, "the queen of all things," and the relationship of God to man with Francesco da Crema, with whom he wished "not only to delight, but also to live" in studies.[66] When podestà of Padua, Ludovico Foscarini conversed with, among other learned men, the Trevisan Bernardino Bononigena, who dedicated to him a book of verse, including one, notably, about the nature of the poetic impulse.[67] As ambassador to Naples, Barbone Morosini came to know Antonio Panormita and George of Trebizond,

---

see V. Cian, "Per Bernardo Bembo—I," and "Per Bernardo Bembo—II"; F. Pintor, "Le due ambascerie di Bernardo Bembo a Firenze e le sue relazioni coi Medici"; della Torre, "La prima ambasceria di Bernardo Bembo a Firenze." Also for Ficino and Bembo, Kristeller, "Marsilio Ficino e Venezia," pp. 477ff.

[61] Ficino, *Letters*, II, 25.

[62] For Bembo's hospitality, see Cian, "Per Bernardo Bembo—I," p. 359.

[63] Ibid., p. 361.

[64] For Florentine reactions see Pintor, "Due ambascerie," p. 813, and E.-G. Ledos, "Lettre inédite de Cristoforo Landino à Bernardo Bembo," pp. 723-24.

[65] ". . . Non admirari non possumus aliquot aetatis nostrae doctissimos viros hoc scribendi sive interpretandi munus non sumpsisse, tantumque apud barbaros, et in obscuro delituisse passi sunt . . . ." *Vita Sancti Rochi*, fol. 34.

[66] ". . . non modo tecum studiis delectari, sed etiam vivere . . . ." Barbaro in *Centotrenta*, ed. Sabbadini, p. 112.

[67] Bononigena's *Epistolarum atque epigrammatum libellus*, introductory letter, fols. 2-3, and the verse noted, fols. 24-31ᵛ.

CHAPTER ONE

then at that court.[68] Niccolò Sagundino, on his mission to Naples, developed close ties with the humanist circle of that city: Bartolomeo Facio, Theodore Gaza, Giovanni Pontano, Andrea Contrario (a Venetian resident there), and particularly Antonio Panormita, at whose request Sagundino translated Onosander's *De optimo imperatore*.[69] Contrario became during his second stay in Naples a member of the Academy, beloved of Pontano, as he had been in Rome a familiar of Gaza and Lorenzo Valla.[70]

Within Venice also, amid the press of daily business, the learned gathered. The opening words of Lauro Quirini's response to Poggio's *On Nobility* alludes to such a gathering: "A few days ago, as is our daily habit, we went to the Rialto, so that we might discuss a matter concerning literary studies with the learned men who throng to that place."[71] Amid the marketplace babble near that famous bridge, humanists conversed. Matteo Collazio also alludes to that custom. Recently at the Rialto his friend had raised with him an issue that concerned Domenico Morosini: the nature of "civility" in rhetoric.[72] Marcantonio Sabellico's dialogue on the restoration of the Latin language is set under the portico of the Ducal Palace.[73] And in Candiano Bollani's trialogue, a philosophical conversation takes place among three men who find each other on the streets of Venice—easy enough, remarks one interlocutor, in this city of philosophers, to stumble upon a group of scholars.[74] In this setting, it is not surprising to find Lauro

[68] See his letter to Barbaro in the latter's *Epist.*, ed. Quirini, p. 269.
[69] See Sagundino's letters written from Naples or written from Venice to those in Naples among his *Epist. et opusc.*; cf. F. Babinger, *Johannes Darius*, pp. 25ff. He salutes all these figures in a single letter to Iunius Cassius of Florence (cod. 62, fol. 62), and reveals Panormita's encouragement of the Onosander translation. Elsewhere he admires Panormita's work: *Epist. et opusc.*, cod. 62, fol. 94.
[70] See R. Sabbadini, "Andrea Contrario," pp. 386-87 and 381, respectively, and V. Branca, "Ermolao Barbaro 'poeta' e la sua 'presentazione' alla corte degli Aragonesi."
[71] "Superioribus diebus iuxta quotidianam nostram consuetudinem ad Rivumaltum profecti eramus, ut in eo loco . . . aliqua de studiis litterarum cum doctissimis viris, qui in eo frequentes advenerant, communicaremus." Quirini's *Epistola* to Pietro Tommasi, cosigned by Francesco Contarini and Niccolò Barbo, in "Tre trattati di Lauro Quirini sulla nobiltà," ed. K. Krautter et al., p. 67.
[72] "Nam paucis ante diebus mihi in Rivoalto casu factus obvius inquit: Modo Matthaee cum viro gravissimo Dominico Mauroceno sumus in re letteraria versati, post multa, credo quo me pertentaret, ut fit, dixit se quaedam habere dubia, neque hactenus comperisse: qui ea sibi solverit, ea quae ferebat difficilia, haec esse . . . ." Collazio, *De verbo civilitate*, not foliated, sig. a-i.
[73] The *De reparatione latinae linguae libri 2* [*De rep. lat. ling.*], in M. Sabellico, *Opera*, fols. 109-15ᵛ, opening at fol. 109.
[74] "Episcopum non recte intelligerem, nisi et tu Candiane in hac flebili civitate philosophantium non verbis sed factis sudasses; in qua quidem facile est invenire frequentantem gymnasium hoc vel achademiam. . . ." C. Bollani, *Trialogus in rebus futuris annorum XX proximorum*, fol. 2.

Quirini teaching Aristotle's *Ethics* daily on a street corner, or Ermolao Barbaro the Younger doing so in his house.[75]

For the great houses of Venice must often have been, even in this century as they certainly were in the next, the sites of intellectual discourse.[76] Francesco Negri urged such hospitality upon the wealthy men to whom he addressed his *On Aristocracy*—which, since he was himself a shiftless *littérateur* in search of refuge, it was surely in his interest to do. From his prescription, nevertheless, can be inferred an image of literary gatherings in palatial settings not wholly detached from fact. "Let your house be . . . above all . . . ," wrote Negri, "an academy of philosophers, all of whose halls and gateways, galleries and arcades, resound day and night with wisdom, echo with poetic and oratorical utterance, ring with philosophical truths, where Apollo with his nine sisters may for perpetuity establish a home."[77] With less bombast, Filippo Morandi da Rimini described the crowds of learned who met in Francesco Barbaro's house, and with whom Barbaro himself, "transformed into a humble philosopher," conversed.[78] That custom had already begun with Francesco's father Candiano, in whose house Gasparino Barzizza stayed more than once, sought out by a crowd of studious youths.[79] In those early years, too, Carlo Zeno opened his house to the learned, according to Leonardo Giustiniani.[80] Pietro Miani's was also the setting of lively discussions, such as that described by Pietro del Monte.[81] Later in the century, the Corner or Dandolo houses may have set the scene for learned conversations in

[75] For Quirini's self-starting pedagogy, see Barbaro, *Centotrenta*, ed. Sabbadini, p. 49, digesting Barbaro, *Epist.*, ed. Quirini, App. 62; for Ermolao's, see his *Epist.*, ed. Branca, I, 78-80.

[76] For the sixteenth-century *cenacoli*, see O. Logan, *Culture and Society in Venice, 1470-1790*, pp. 71ff., and P. L. Rose, "The Accademia Venetiana."

[77] ". . . ut domus prius vestra sit . . . philosophantium academia, cuius atria cuncta, intercolumina, vestibula, porticus, dieque noctuque, sapientiam resonent, poetica, oratoriaque dictamenta redoleant, gymnica sophismata perstrepent; ubi perpetuam sibi sedem, novem sororibus comitatus, constituat Apollo." *De aristocratia*, fol. 137.

[78] "Quid est igitur quod amplius tuas frequentem aedes Barbare; quid est quod tuos queram recessus revisere, ubi in corona litteratorum hominum mei ordinis te continebas, si quando vacuum suis curis tua te respublica permittebat; et quid festivius nobis omnibus ea significatione amoris in nos tui, ut inter nos sic versareris, ut ex uno principum civitatis qui habereris et eras in humilem philosophum te converteres, confabularaeris adcurate et copiose in omni genere litterarum." *Oratio in funere Francisci Barbari*, fols. 8-12, at fols. 9ᵛ-10.

[79] See Barzizza, *Opera*, ed. Furiettus, pp. xxviiiff., 141ff.; C. Colombo, "Gasparino Barzizza," p. 13.

[80] "Maximus fuit in eo colendi ingenii ardor et vehemens optimarum artium studium. Multos ille eruditissimos ac summos viros hospitalitate donavit." *Funebris pro Carolo Zeno oratio*, p. 143.

[81] Del Monte, *De vitiorum inter se differencia et comparatione*, fols. 3ᵛ-5.

which the foreigner Raffaele Zovenzoni and the still adolescent Ermolao Barbaro the Younger sparkled.[82] Clusters of humanists also gathered around learned visitors. Florentine ambassador to Venice in 1448, Giannozzo Manetti was sought out by Lauro Quirini and Pietro Tommasi; and Filippo Buonaccorsi, ambassador from Poland in 1486, was surrounded by a small university of humanists.[83] The "academy" of Aldo Manuzio that emerged in the last decade of the century had its precursors in an earlier period.[84] Venice was even before his advent a home for learned men.

A common dedication to learning was the basis of many friendships. The remarkably intense sympathy between the two Dalmatian clerics Maffeo Vallaresso and Lorenzo Zane, initiated wholly through formal correspondence, was based on the regard of each for the other's eloquence.[85] "All my letters," wrote Zane in a typical communication, "Are abject, ugly, pale, rude, rough, poorly thought out, without learning," while you command "an elegant abundance of words . . . the greatest knowledge of the good arts, . . . and in sum a certain incredible magnitude of mind."[86]

Francesco Barbaro's words to Ludovico Barozzi reveal how friendly relations were cemented in a joint commitment to learning. "Since you are dedicated to the *studia humanitatis* and to learning, in which I also delight, I am not surprised that you feel drawn to me, as your elegant letter shows, by that mutual and sweet chain."[87] That "sweet chain" was also responsible for Barbaro's close relationships to Zaccaria Trevisan the Elder, his political and literary mentor, and to Lauro Quirini, his protégé.[88] A shared devotion to the *studia humanitatis* also informs the warm friendships of Ermolao Barbaro the Younger with Girolamo Donato and Antonio Calvo; of Leonardo Giustiniani

---

[82] See B. Ziliotto, *Raffaele Zovenzoni*, pp. 37ff. I suspect a leading role was played by Marco Corner, a known patron of the arts and employer of humanist tutors for his children; cf. della Torre, *Paolo Marsi*, pp. 193ff.

[83] For Manetti's and Buonaccorsi's visits, see Part Two, Preface, n. 14.

[84] For Aldo's circle, see Chapter Three, section 6.

[85] See their letters in M. Vallaresso's *Epistolae*, especially at pp. 145ff., 376ff., 378ff., 382ff., 386ff., 388ff., 584ff.

[86] ". . . omnia mea sunt abiecta, horrida, jeiuna, inculta, dura, callide minus excogitata, inerudita . . . ."; "Vero enim vero tu . . . verborum copiam elegantem, . . . summam bonarum litterarum cognitionem, . . . denique incredibilem quandam ingenii magnitudinem habes . . . ." Ibid., pp. 378, 379.

[87] "Et quia studiis humanitatis et doctrinae deditus es, quibus ego quoque delector, non miror, cum hoc communi et suavi vinculo nobis adstrictus sis . . . ." Barbaro's *Epist.*, ed. Quirini, App., p. 115.

[88] For Barbaro's relations with Trevisan, see A. Gnesotto's preface to the DRU, pp. 11ff. and P. Gothein, *Zaccaria Trevisan il Vecchio*, pp. 122ff. For those with Quirini, see Barbaro, *Centotrenta*, ed. Sabbadini, pp. 39, 45, 47, 49, 57.

with Pietro Tommasi; of Ludovico Foscarini with Paolo Barbo, Vitale Lando, and Candiano Bollani.[89] Foscarini's words to Bollani suggest the strength of the bond uniting members of Venice's patrician elite who had shared a common experience: "since no greater, no more profound, no more radiant cause of our mutual affection will ever be found. We shared the same studies, the same schools, the same troubled times, the same opinions. Very greatly have these common experiences of private studies, these responsibilities of public office, this consensus of like wills, always prevailed powerfully between us both."[90] Common schooling is also suspected from Foscarini's assurance of friendship to Niccolò Canal: "I have always loved you for your unique virtues, great merits, daily intercourse, and the much more than old, but rather ancient friendship between us from our earliest years."[91]

Pietro Dolfin's deep and lifelong friendship with Pietro Barozzi, grounded in love for learning, dated from their youth, when both were students of Pietro Perleone, teacher in one of Venice's famed public schools. As they had once studied together, Dolfin wrote Barozzi in Belluno from Venice, so now though their bodies were parted, their spirits were joined.[92] Eusebio Priuli in his funeral oration for Barozzi also describes the love between those two friends and a third co-student, the future doge Leonardo Loredan: "They were mutually affected by such love, joined by chains of such probity, that like a braided rope which is hard to break, they always loved each other to the extent that it is possible in mortal life."[93] Niccolò Barbo's intimacy

---

[89] For Barbaro's friendship with Donato, see the former's *Epist.*, ed. Branca, II, 19ff., 27ff., 43ff.; with Calvo, see I, passim, and especially II, 64. For Giustiniani's friendship with Tommasi, see his letter in B. Giustiniani, *Orat. et epist.*, sig. K2ʳ⁻ᵛ. For Foscarini's with the figures named, see his *Epist.*, fols. 201, 203ff., 204ff., respectively.

[90] ". . . quia nulla maior, nulla gravior, nulla illustrior necessitudinis causa unquam reperietur. Fuimus in eisdem studiis, eisdem collegiis, eisdem periculosissimis temporibus, eisdem sentenciis. Hae conventiones longissime consuetudines privatorum studiorum, sortes publicorum munerum, consensus comunium voluntatum, semper inter nos binos plurimum valuerunt." Foscarini, *Epist.*, fol. 204ᵛ. I have translated *collegiis* as schools because of the context; the word might also signify associations or sodalities. I have not learned what teacher or school experience Foscarini may have shared with Bollani or Canal, below.

[91] ". . . quem ego unum semper propter singulares virtutes, summa merita, diuturnam consuetudinem et ne dum institutam, sed inveteratissimam a primis annis benivolentiam maxime colui." Ibid., fol. 173.

[92] "Accipies vero animum tibi deditissimum, atque ita certe affectum; ac dum olim in litterarum studiis pariter versabimur, corpore absens, spiritu [praesto?] sum." Dolfin, *Epistolae et orationes*, p. 13; this passage not in the version in *Epist. CCXLII*, ed. Martène & Durand, cols. 938-40.

[93] ". . . qui tanto amore invicem afficiebantur, tantae probitatis vinculis connectebantur, ut tamquam funiculus triplex, qui difficile rumpitur, quoad in humanis egere, mutua se benivolentia semper prosecuti fuerint." Priuli, *Oratio funebris*, in Martène & Durand, *Veterum scriptorum collectio*, III, col. 1218.

with Paolo Barbo—to whom he indiscreetly offered advice on discretion—was probably also based on a friendship that began in early studies.[94] The appeal to schooltime ties was explicitly but unsuccessfully made by Jacopo Zeno, referring to early-childhood relations, common studies, country, class, blood, and "conformity of souls" to Pietro Barbo, one-time friend, now rival, enemy, and pope.[95]

3. Schools and Teachers

The schools of Venice in which such friendships were forged are famous.[96] Their fame is noted not only in contemporary report, but is evidenced by the volume of modern scholarship about them. Venice's role as a nursery for professional educators was perhaps the most significant one she played in the evolution of the new culture.[97] Private and local schools already existed when the fifteenth century opened. In the coming years, noblemen entreated educators to come to the city to open schools and tutor their sons.[98] A series of scholars heeded their call, coming to teach for a few months or years, then leaving for adventures elsewhere: Francesco and Giovanni Mario Filelfo, George of Trebizond, Cristoforo de' Scarpis, Giovanni Pietro Vitali d'Avenza (da Lucca), Antonio Baratella, Paolo Marsi among others. Two of the three great educators of the humanist movement—Guarino Veronese and Vittorino da Feltre—taught in Venice early in their careers, and afterwards retained Venetian ties. Two others—Gasparino Barzizza and Pier Paolo Vergerio—worked on the perimeters of Venice and had

[94] See his letter to Barbo in the latter's *Epist.*, fols. 56-59ᵛ; his interesting cautions to give no opportunity for even the slightest criticisms at fols. 57ff. In the cases of Niccolò and Paolo Barbo here, and of Jacopo Zeno and Pietro Barbo, below, I have not learned what school experience or which teacher, if any, was shared.

[95] "Neminem—video cui eque ac mihi gaudendum—sit, cum nos patria, generisque nobilitas communis, coniunctio sanguinis, vitae ab ineunte aetate, puerilibusque ipsis annis societas, studia eadem et animorum conformitas, beneficia summa, innumera, et immortalia in me tua, vita omnis mea semper tibi dedita et dedicata diuturnaque fidelis et accurata servitus mea ita coniunxerunt, tot tantisque devinxerunt vinculis, ut tu mihi solus parens, dux, dominus . . . semper extiteris." Zeno, *Oratio* to Pietro Barbo on his elevation to pope, cited by Zonta in his preface to Zeno's *Vita Caroli Zeni*, i, n. 4.

[96] For the Venetian schools, see J. B. Ross, "Venetian Schools and Teachers, Fourteenth to Early Sixteenth Century," pp. 523ff.; and M. Pastore Stocchi, "Scuola e cultura," both of whom review a larger literature, some of which is cited where needed in the notes of this and subsequent chapters.

[97] The opinion of Monnier, *Le Quattrocento*, I, 174ff.

[98] The notable efforts of Leonardo Giustiniani are described by P. H. Labalme, *Bernardo Giustiniani*, pp. 17ff. Consider also the efforts of Giovanni Corner to find a tutor for his son Federico: Colombo, "Gasparino Barzizza," pp. 1ff. and the letters on pp. 17ff. and 23ff. M. Pastore Stocchi, "Scuola e cultura," p. 102, points out that private instruction, not public, was the norm in Venice.

Venetian friends.[99] The most remarkable phenomenon, however, in the history of education in Venice is the evolution of the public schools. Their story, launched in 1403 by the will of an ardent Aristotelian, progressed through a series of Senate decrees to culminate by the last third of the century in the three schools at San Marco and the Rialto: two devoted to the rhetorical subjects of the *studia humanitatis*, and one to the philosophical studies that never lost favor in Venice.

The Venetian humanists studied with tutors and private teachers and at the public schools in Venice, and with tutors and teachers abroad.[100] Francesco Barbaro and his nephew Ermolao Barbaro the Elder, Leonardo Giustiniani and his son Bernardo, Fantino Vallaresso and his nephew Maffeo, Andrea Giuliani and his citizen friend Pietro del Monte, Marco Aurelio, Tito Livio Frulovisi, studied with Guarino either in Venice or Verona. Francesco Barbaro and Leonardo Giustiniani studied with Gasparino Barzizza in Venice or Padua, as did their friends Andrea Giuliani and (perhaps) Daniele Vitturi. Giovanni Marino and Gregorio Correr studied with Vittorino da Feltre; Bernardo Giustiniani, Pietro Perleone, and Giorgio Merula with Francesco Filelfo; Pietro Barbo, Candiano Bollani, and the friends Niccolò Barbo and Francesco Contarini with George of Trebizond.

At the public school of San Marco (the first, or chancery school), Giovanni Pietro Vitali d'Avenza (da Lucca) taught Ludovico Donato and the future teacher Benedetto Brognoli; Pietro Perleone taught the friends Pietro Barozzi and Pietro Dolfin, and the future secretary Antonio Vinciguerra; and Brognoli taught Daniele Renier and the immigrant Pietro Cirneo. At the second San Marco school, Giorgio Merula taught Marco Dandolo, and Giorgio Valla taught Paolo Pisani. At the famed Rialto school, Niccolò Barbo and Francesco Contarini, together still, and Ludovico Donato, Sebastiano Badoer, and Zaccaria Trevisan the Younger studied with Paolo della Pergola, and in later years, Francesco Negri with Domenico Bragadin.

Here patterns cease, for the educational experiences of our human-

---

[99] For Vergerio, see for example the profile of Niccolò Leonardi. For other figures, see Part Two, Preface, sections 9 and 10.

[100] Lists of the students of teachers are rare. School connections are known from happenstance: comments in letters, orations, dedications. It is easier to reconstruct university careers, which are not, strictly speaking, relevant to the matter of humanist education, but surely played an important role in shaping Venetian humanism, since so many of the city's humanists attended the university, receiving formal degrees in arts and laws. More than half of our core group humanists (fifty-one, including four merely probable cases, most of them patricians) attended Padua. A handful studied instead at the universities of Bologna or Pavia. Both school and university attendance, where known, are indicated under the "Education" rubric of the profiles, which should be consulted for documentation of the statements made below.

ists were disparate. They studied in Venice with private teachers: Jacopo Zeno with Damiano da Pola, Bernardo Giustiniani with Cristoforo de Scarpis, Jacopo Foscari perhaps with Bartolomeo Facio; Domenico de' Domenichi and Antonio Vinciguerra with the prominent Venetian physicians Pietro Tommasi and Giovanni Caldiera. They traveled abroad to study with the Byzantine scholars Manuel Chrysoloras (Pietro Miani), John Argyropoulos (Pietro Perleone), Demetrius Chalcondylas (Giovanni Lorenzi and Niccolò Leonico Tomeo), Constantine Lascaris (Giorgio Valla, later Pietro Bembo), and Theodore Gaza (Giovanni Lorenzi, and the friends Ermolao Barbaro the Younger and Girolamo Donato). Or they sought out Italian teachers of imposing reputation: Lorenzo Valla (Ludovico Donato and Lorenzo Zane) and Pomponio Leto (Ermolao Barbaro the Younger, and Marcantonio Sabellico), or many others of lesser fame.

The school careers of only some of our humanists are known. The literary achievements of others testify that they received an education in the *studia humanitatis*. Others who have left no significant written testimony of their learning may have nevertheless received a humanist education. For humanist learning was diffused in the patriciate beyond the limited group studied here. Many figures known to have had a humanist education did not otherwise stand out in intellectual life. Their existence suggests that there were many others not known or knowable from the available documents. Francesco Filelfo, for instance, had hopes of Domenico Barbarigo (perhaps his student), who was urged to emulate his father's learning.[101] He must also have eyed the promising young Gabriele Moro, who eventually abandoned his studies to enter public life. "Always be reading something, or writing, when it is possible, in your public duties," Filelfo advised weakly.[102] In spite of his teacher's encouragement, Moro seems to have played no further role in Venetian humanism. There were many learned patricians in Venice, according to Filelfo, even if few of them attained the level of a Francesco Barbaro.[103] Yet they excelled so in the liberal arts and eloquence, he wrote the Doge Pasquale Malipiero, "that they

---

[101] F. Filelfo, *Epist. fam.*, fols. 150-51ᵛ.

[102] "Lege semper aliquid aut scribe, cum tibi licet per publica munera." Ibid., fol. 3. See also later letters to Moro, fols. 3ᵛ and 8ᵛ.

[103] The passage in which Filelfo laments Barbaro's death indicates an intellectual culture widespread in the ruling class but mediocre in quality: "Magna est nostro saeculo, permagna eloquentiae iactura iniecta, Venetis vero omnibus plane singularis, qui talem virum amiserunt, qualem habent alterum neminem. De doctis atque disertis loquor. Nam viros graves et sapientes scio esse Venetis poene innumerabiles. Sed qui idem et graece esset, et latine eruditus, quem alterum habeatis illustrem audio neminem." Ibid., fol. 82ᵛ.

all equal antiquity in their speech and judgments."[104] George of Trebizond praised the great men of Venice for having already achieved
the ideal republic Plato had envisioned. The equals of kings in dignity
and authority, "in the experience and knowledge of divine and human
things they even excel kings."[105] And Giovanni Caldiera attributed
humanist competence to the whole of the governing elite. In Venice,
"the noble citizens of the senatorial order who are judged by the
testimony of other nations to be learned in all the virtues and good
arts . . . have by great diligence and effort become eloquent not merely
in their maternal tongue but in Latin and Greek."[106] Behind these
exaggerations is suspected a wholesale commitment of the elite inner
circle of Venice's nobility to humanist education, and the need for a
small army of pedagogues.

Teachers and tutors were chosen carefully by employers, and respected by their pupils. From abroad, Ludovico Foscarini entreated a
certain Filippo to teach his son, who had been restive during his father's
absence and required a steadying hand: "If paternal love does not
blind me, he is not of slothful mind, but if he seems hard and slow,
he should not be deterred, but enlivened and enflamed because those
eager for honor and truly desirous of glory undertake the most difficult
[tasks]. . . . Born of me and taught by you, I believe it is neither right
nor possible that Niccolò remain ignorant and unlettered."[107]

The outcome of Niccolò's training is unknown, but successful students were devoted to their teachers who provided both a literary and
a moral education. The youthful Ermolao Barbaro the Elder, still a
student, wrote admiringly in a preface to Ambrogio Traversari of his
mentor Guarino, from whom he was learning Latin and Greek and
the path to a good life.[108] A respectful alumnus, Giovanni Barbo, wrote

---

[104] "Videmus enim vel aetate nostra, patricios quosdam Venetos tantum in utroque
genere [he speaks of "artes liberales atque eloquentia"] claruisse, ut [cuncti] omni
possent antiquitate et dicendo et iudicando comparari." Ibid., fol. 115ᵛ.

[105] "Nam et regum more vivunt et dignitate atque auctoritate regibus non cedunt;
usu vero peritiaque rerum et divinarum et humanarum etiam reges ipsos excellunt."
From the *Praefatio* to George's translation of Plato's *Laws*, in F. Gaeta, "Giorgio da
Trebisonda, le 'Leggi' di Platone e la costituzione di Venezia," p. 501.

[106] ". . . illius nobilissimi senatori ordinis cives qui omnium virtutum ac bonarum
artium ceterarum nationum testimonio peritissimi iudicantur . . . non solum maternam,
verum Latinam ac Grecam eloquentiam summo studio ac exercitatione adepti sunt."
G. Caldiera, *Orationes*, fols. 46ᵛ-47.

[107] ". . . et si paternus amor non fallit, non est pigerrimi ingenii, et si tardioris
duriorisque esset, non deterreri sed animari accendique debet [*cod.* debes] quod ap-
petentes honoris et vere glorie cupidi ad difficilima se convertunt. . . . Nec ius nec fas
esse credo Nicolaum apud te doctum et ex me natum literarum imperitum ignarumque
esse . . . ." Foscarini, *Epist.*, fols. 95ᵛ-96.

[108] "Quod cum pro virili parte assequi constitueram, Guarino patri et praeceptori

Guarino to inquire about a grammatical matter, proudly inserting his own letter in his collection of classical and humanist texts.[109] Maffeo Vallaresso composed when still young a grammar textbook clearly modeled on Guarinian principles.[110] Long graduated from Vittorino da Feltre's school, Gregorio Correr remained his teacher's close friend.[111] When struck by a long and painful illness, Pietro Perleone was lovingly attended at his bedside by loyal pupils and friends.[112]

Giovanni Quirini's consolatory piece to a fellow student on the death of their teacher Benedetto Brognoli suggests what role the teacher played for young Venetians, and their attitudes of gratitude and respect. Brognoli always treated his students lovingly, wrote the former pupil, "as though he himself had fathered them."[113] So much of his time was spent in speculation, or in wide reading, or in the education of his students, that he could never eat a meal in peace. He taught with public salary for forty years, training so many students "that few men can be found in this city learned in good letters who cannot and should not thank him for their skills."[114] Bartolomeo Zamberto (like Brognoli, a public teacher of humanities in Venice), in his funeral oration for Giorgio Valla, similarly stressed his mentor's diligence and concern. Having taught in Pavia, Genoa, and Milan, he was considered worthy of Venice. Established there, "with such sweetness of soul, with such virtues, with such learning did he bind to himself the students who flocked to him, that all those students listened to George alone,

---

meo me totum tradidi, ut quemadmodum eius industria diligentia et caritate effectum est, ut a teneris ut aiunt unguiculis latinarum litterarum quicquid sunt prudentiam et suavitatem degustarim, sic graecam humanitatem ac disciplinam ab eo cognoscere queam, cognitamque pro viribus percipere, perceptam, ad bene vivendum iucundeque convertere." E. Barbaro, trans. of Aesop's *Fables*, fols. 3ᵛ-4.

[109] The letter on pp. 247-48 in P. O. Kristeller, "An Unknown Letter of Giovanni Barbo to Guarino."

[110] See A. Segarizzi, "Una grammatica latina del secolo XV."

[111] See Correr's account of a meeting with Vittorino about the plight of Cecilia Gonzaga in his *Epistola ad Caeciliam virginem*, p. 33.

[112] "Assidua certe corona et frequenti illustrium civium et doctissimorum adolescentium cetu lectus in quo egrotus iacebam circundatus erat alii consolando alii hortando alii iuvando alii studium operam pecunias res fortunasque suas omnes policendo nullum humanitatis benivolencie atque amicicie officium reliquerunt." Perleone, *epistola* in Vat. Chis. J VI 215, fol. 177ᵛ. The three letters in this codex to Marcantonio Morosini (fols. 176ᵛ-177) and Vitale Lando (fols. 177-78ᵛ, cited above) reveal that Perleone received lavish attention on his sickbed.

[113] "Discipulos vero ita semper benigne erudivit, ac si ex seipso procreati fuissent." *Consolatoria oratio pro obitu eximii ac integerrimi viri Benedicti Brugnoli utriusque preceptoris*, sig. Bii. Giovanni Quirini, like Bartolomeo Zamberto to be discussed below, is a late figure not belonging to the core group; but Brognoli, like Valla, of whom Zamberto speaks, does belong.

[114] ". . . ut perpauci existant hac in urbe nostra, qui bonas litteras docti sint: qui ei non possint ac debeant referre acceptum." Ibid., sig. Biii.

imitated George alone, embraced George alone, and looked upon George alone sharply and clearly expounding."[115] Even allowing a margin for the excesses of panegyric, it seems that these teachers were cherished.

4. A Training in Values

They were cherished, perhaps, for their tender guidance of young minds in the *studia humanitatis*, but also valued because they understood clearly, accepted fully, and articulated lucidly the function that a humanistic education should have for their main audience in Venice, the sons of the patricians who directly and self-consciously ruled the city. With a sharp sense of mission, they defined for young listeners the purpose of their studies. The knowledge of philosophy is essential, Sabellico advised a "dense crowd" at the Rialto school, and should be diligently sought, "so that you may be judged worthy of this city in which you were born and educated . . . [and] worthy of the fortune which the Venetian name promises on sea and on land."[116] On another occasion, he echoed the same theme. Knowledge of philosophy, the culmination of a liberal education, is particularly useful for patrician youths: "So that you can as best as possible benefit the republic in the Senate, and the citizens in the marketplace, both by advising and acting, in order that you not appear to be born for yourselves alone, but for your country . . . and your friends."[117]

Francesco Negri delineated the same pedagogical rationale. Young aristocrats should study the liberal arts, he advised, so that they can eventually replace their fathers as rulers of the republic. Thus educated, they will confer the greatest possible benefit on the city, and bring

---

[115] ". . . tanta animi clementia talibus moribus talique doctrina discipulos undique conuolantes sibi deuinxit ut omnes discipuli unum Georgium audirent, unum Georgium immitarentur [*sic*; I read *immitarentur* in Marc. Lat. XI, 6 (3811), fol. 6ᵛ], unum Georgium suspicerent atque intuerentur, argute atque enucleate disputantem." From *In funere Georgii Vallae Placentini philosophi praestantissimi oratio*, pp. 306-307. For the esteem accorded Valla, see also Heiberg, *Beiträge zur Geschichte Georg Vallas*, pp. 22ff.

[116] ". . . et nobis imprimis Veneti adolescentes, ut et patria clarissima, in qua nati sumus et educati, tandem digni videamur . . . digni hac fortuna, qua Venetum nomen terra marique pollet." Sabellico's oration *De cultu et fructu philosophiae* in his *Opera*, at fol. 78. The oration was recited, the title (fol. 75ᵛ) informs us, "in Rivoaltino gymnasio frequentissimo philosophorum consessu." Sabellico uses "we" but means "you"; he is neither a patrician nor Venetian-born. In this and the following passage, I have substituted the appropriate pronoun.

[117] ". . . ut in senatu rei publicae, in foro civibus, et consulendo et agendo quam maxime prodesse possimus, ut non nobis solum nati videamur, sed patriae, . . . et amicis . . . ." Sabellico's oration *De usu philosophiae* in *Opera*, fol. 79.

their fathers great joy.[118] If it educates its youth well, the patriciate will give birth not to Catilines, Sullas, and Gracchi, but Scipios, Marcelluses, Fabiuses, Publicolas, Camilluses—"For who ever [could be so foolish] as to expect . . . that a republic in the hands of the ignorant could long survive?"[119] "But by what means . . . can your sons attain that kind of wisdom which will then be so greatly needed when you . . . relinquish to them the reins of your republic" if not through literary studies?[120]

Matteo Collazio also saw the *studia humanitatis* as the proper tool of the patriciate. Instruction should be given in ethics so that the republic will have good *patresfamilias*. "But there are also in the city certain disciplines whereby those youths who are its future rulers acquire the faculty of pure speech, the gateway to eloquence [and] good morals, and are trained to govern the republic."[121] These are the grammatical arts—poetry and history certainly, and above all politics or civil science. Patricians must entrust their children to good teachers of the liberal arts, advised Marino Becichemo in a similar statement, and not allow them to have military instruction only: "Thus will the reins of the republic always be in the hands of the best men—for the republic is best governed not by all the citizens, but by a few, who should be respected and revered, just as in a battle the credit for victory goes not to all the soldiers but to a few who should be rewarded for their merits."[122] And Francesco Pisani, a patrician student of a later generation, admonished his fellow students to the diligent study of philosophy "so that our republic, which always abounded with ex-

[118] Negri addresses patrician fathers regarding the benefits of education: "Tantum enim haec civitati pietas proderit, quod et vos non mediocri sane laeticia diffundemini, quum in tam probatos iuvenes filios vestros evasisse videritis, et illi non minori quidem gloria, quum tempus erit, remp[ublicam] de manibus vestris suscipere poterunt." Negri, *De aristocratia*, fol. 98.

[119] "Nam quis est ille . . . qui unquam speret remp[ublicam] ab ignorantibus susceptam diu posse servari?" Ibid., fol. 104. Those destructive and productive Romans in the passage preceding.

[120] "Sed quo pacto . . . ad hanc poterunt filii vestri prudentiam pervenire, qua tunc maxime opus erit quum vos eis reip[ublicae] vestrae retinacula relinquetis?" Ibid., fols. 95v-96. Pedagogy is a major theme of Negri's work; see the discussions at fols. 97ff. and 139vff.

[121] "Sunt quaedam etiam in civitate disciplinae unde acquirant adolescentes futuri politici purum sermonem, ad eloquentiam aditum, bonos mores, et ad gubernanda[m] etiam remp[ublicam] instruantur." *De verbo civilitate*, fol. aiiv.

[122] "Sic semper in manibus optimorum sunt R[ei] P[ublicae] habenae, cuius optima gubernatio non est omnibus civibus, sed paucis attribuenda, qui colendi sunt ac venerandi, quemadmodum in pugna non est ad omnes milites, sed ad paucos victoria referenda, quibus merita premia elargienda sunt." M. Becichemo, *Panegiricus Principi Leonardo Lauretano dictus*, sig. avii.

cellent men who were in peacetime an ornament of their *patria*, and in wartime a great aid, shall never lack for them."[123]

Education in the liberal arts—that is, a humanist education—is described by these commentators not as a goal in itself, but as the tool by which the noblemen of Venice, that city's only enfranchised group, could mold its descendants in their own image. Thus trained, they would be willing to shoulder the responsibilities of their class and able to govern the state. Humanist education, though new in content and method, becomes here the agent of inherited power, the vehicle by which patrician culture can reproduce itself. It was an education not only in the good arts, but in character, responsibility, and destiny. It was the crucible of patrician culture.

5. THE IDEAL OF EXCELLENCE

It was recognized as such by the patricians themselves, who nurtured no doubts about their right to rule and to bestow that prerogative upon their offspring. Francesco Barbaro delineated for his son Zaccaria expectations that he match or exceed that nobleman's paternal example in learning, virtue, and republican service. "Be sure that you adorn your name with the glory of virtue and the good arts rather than dull it through depravity. Cultivate the promise which your mind held forth from your earliest youth, and [cultivate] above all else piety, from which derives not only immortal glory but also the greatest pleasure and utility. If [your teacher] Lorenzo Cesano is there, work hard to cultivate your mind with his knowledge and virtue, lest you allow those seeds of virtue given you by God and nature to perish—while if you permit them to mature, you will recognize yourself as born for the honor of your country and for the glory and amplification of our family."[124] Alluding to his own extraordinary efforts in Brescia, which he defended for Venice against Milan's besieging army, he offered Zaccaria the encouragement that those labors would be repaid with glory. Then he urged equal diligence on his son: "Wherefore if

---

[123] ". . . ut nostrae reipublicae, quae semper clarissimis viris abundavit, qui pacis tempore nostrae patriae ornamento, belli vero non parvo adjumento extiterunt, numquam sint defuturi." Pisani, *Oratio de universae philosophiae ornamentis*, pp. 265-66.

[124] "Cura ut cum laude virtutis et bonarum artium potius illustres nomen tuum, quam obscures pro ignavia. Expectationem, quam nobis dedit indoles tua ab ineunte aetate, et super omnia pietatem cole, quae non solum gloriam immortalem, sed etiam maximam jucunditatem et utilitatem parit. Si Laurentius Cesanus istic est, da operam, ut literis et moribus suis colas ingenium tuum, ne semina illa virtutis, quae tibi a Deo et a natura data sunt, perire patiaris; quae si adolescere permiseris, ad laudem patriae, ad gloriam, et amplitudinem gentis nostrae te natum esse cognosces." Barbaro, *Epist.*, ed. Quirini, p. 74.

you love me as much as you do, see that with sound morals and the studies of the good arts you protect for perpetuity the inheritance of glory bestowed upon you, so that you may be no less an asset to our posterity than [your ancestors] have been to you."[125] Zaccaria had acquired not only the wealth but the obligations specific to his dynasty and social standing. "We were so born and so bred," Francesco wrote, admonishing Zaccaria not to mourn too deeply the death of a relative, "that we must bear all things calmly. . . . Take care to excel so much in the studies of the good arts that in you all may behold the standard we set ourselves; and just as you must be [by nature] the heir to our wealth, so may you be [by will] heir to our honor and glory."[126] Disciplined in mind and character through an education in the *studia humanitatis*, Zaccaria would be able to fulfill the responsibilities of his class and meet the expectations of his father.[127]

Francesco Contarini must also have borne the weight of paternal expectation, of social responsibility, and of state obligations. In striving to fulfill them, he became a model young patrician. Contarini's behavior and attitudes became articulated as an ideal in a famous oration delivered by his friend and fellow-student Niccolò Barbo when Contarini received his doctorate in arts in Padua in 1441.[128] The accomplishments of Contarini's ancestors set for the young nobleman a formidable standard, said Barbo. The family was already long established when Attila stormed Italy, forcing them and other resourceful inhabitants of northern Italy to found the new city of Venice. Since that time, members of the Contarini family had always figured among the greatest citizens, and even the doges of Venice. In recent years, men of the Contarini clan continued to sustain that ancestral glory. Among them were Zaccaria, Luca, and Niccolò, the great-grandfather, grandfather, and father of Francesco. Zaccaria was not only a first-

[125] "Quare si me diligis quantum profecto facis, da operam ut honestissimis moribus et optimarum artium studiis hereditatem gloriae tibi partam in perpetuum tuearis, ut non minori ornamento sis posteris nostris, quam nos tibi." Barbaro in *Centotrenta*, ed. Sabbadini, p. 97.

[126] "Ita enim nati et ita instituti sumus, ut omnia aequo animo ferre debeamus. . . . Da operam ut in studiis bonarum artium tantum proficias, ut in te omnes recognoscant mores nostros; et sicut heres fortunae esse debes, ita laudis et gloriae sis . . . ." Ibid., p. 93.

[127] Where Barbaro sees humanist studies as a part of the development of patrician character, a commoner humanist less touched by Venetian cultural values may think differently. Guarino Veronese exhorted Andrea Giuliani to literary endeavors with quite another plea: Giuliani shared his patrician status with many, but his learning was unique to him; *Epist.*, ed. Sabbadini, I, 83.

[128] N. Barbo's *Oratio in laudem Francisci Contareni.* The following review of Contarini's ancestry summarizes fols. 60-72ᵛ of that oration. The theme of Venetian origins, already well established in the historiographical tradition, here makes an appearance.

rate politician—a veteran, among other things, of sixty-three embassies—but a learned man as well. He was so outstanding "in every field of knowledge," in wisdom and eloquence, that he could be judged the "city's greatest and foremost ornament."[129] He was greater, perhaps, even than Cicero, that orator who had saved Rome from the nefarious Catiline; for "by following so many roads, visiting so many peoples, journeying through so many lands, crossing so many seas, by his eloquence he was able to save his *patria* from infinite perils."[130] Though Zaccaria had established learning as part of the family tradition, his son Luca did not continue it. Instead he engaged in trade, generating wealth beneficial to the city and to posterity.[131] But Zaccaria's grandson Niccolò, Francesco's father, was also learned. Many contemporaries had heard Niccolò speak expertly on civil and canon law, on philosophy, on theology, and beheld him with admiration.[132] His remarkable intelligence won him early entry to the Senate, and election as ambassador to Savoy. On that mission, he tragically died.

Upon Francesco rested the obligation to imitate the learning and patriotism of his father and his ancestors, Barbo continued. From his earliest childhood, "judging that it would be unworthy to fall short of the great glories of his ancestors," he decided not to "consume that patrimony in luxury and pleasures, but instead gave himself with the greatest desire and ardor of soul to letters and to study."[133] Though born wealthy—"nourished on abundant riches and delights"—yet he yearned for knowledge to the degree that "no relaxation could lure

---

[129] "Viro in omni studio atque doctrina praestanti"; "ut putaretur esse civitatis maximum atque praecipuum ornamentum." Ibid., fol. 68. For the sixty-three legations, see fol. 69.

[130] ". . . qui tot itinera conficiendo, tot populos adeundo, tot terras peragrando, tot maria transeundo, facile [*cod.* faciens] eloquentia sua patriam ab infinitis periculis liberare potuerit." Ibid., fol. 69ᵛ.

[131] Spokesmen for the Venetian aristocracy often felt compelled to defend that group's commercial activities; note below, Caldiera's and Domenico Morosini's praise of Venetian wealth, and Paolo Morosini's apology for the nobility's involvement in trade, Chapter Two, Sections 2, 5, and 4, respectively. Barbo here glorifies Luca's commercial role. In turning to trade, Luca could leave a worthy patrimony to his sons as well as benefit the republic, for the well-being of the city depends on money (fols. 69ᵛ-70). Thus every city needs merchants, and Luca's wealth, then, was not for his own glorification but for his patria and posterity (fol. 70ʳ⁻ᵛ).

[132] For Niccolò's learning, ibid., fol. 71. Niccolò is representative of those learned patricians who were found in Venice prior to the patrician absorption of the humanist tradition; see below, Chapter Four, Section 1.

[133] ". . . indignum esse existimans a tantis maiorum suorum laudibus degenerare, non quemadmodum plurimi amplissimum a patre [*cod.* patrae] patrimonium relictum in luxu et voluptatibus consumere statuit, sed tanto animi desiderio atque ardore se ad litteras atque studium contulit." Barbo, *Oratio in laudem Francisci Contareni*, fol. 73ʳ⁻ᵛ. Francesco's studies and achievements described from here to the end.

him from his studies, no pleasure seduce him, nor sleep ever restrain him."[134] Although grown men have not thought it improper to seek relaxation in the time left them from public and private business, Francesco studied without cease—and this when he was "not in his manhood, not in youth, not in adolescence, but in the early years of boyhood." He seemed not to be the subject, but the master of time.[135]

He sped ahead of other children in his work, studying dialectic with Paolo della Pergola and oratory—Latin and some Greek—with George of Trebizond. In his youth, Francesco mastered as much philosophy as others did in a lifetime; and he so excelled in oratory that he seemed "not to be born to it, but appointed to it by God."[136] By such training, Francesco was prepared to serve his city, adorned "with every art that ever flourished amid a free people and that ever prevailed in any well-constituted republic."[137]

By age sixteen, Francesco had progressed so far in his studies that he spoke publicly before the visiting brother of the emperor of Constantinople: "So subtly did he argue about life, on the virtues of men, on the nature of things, that the king himself with great kindness, delight, and courtesy, kissed him, while earlier in the presence of all he had said distinctly that he had never before either seen nor read nor heard of an adolescent to whom our Francesco should defer in such wondrous and excellent mastery of so much knowledge."[138]

In this past year, continued Barbo's oration, Francesco also twice spoke "elegantly" in the Senate (the youngest speaker ever to do so) on the subject of the preservation of wealth.[139] And a few months

[134] ". . . in amplissimis divitiis atque deliciis enutritus, tamen ad disciplinarum studia incenderetur, ut eum neque ocium abstrahere neque aliqua ludi voluptas avocare, neque somnus unquam valuerit retardare." Ibid., fol. 73^v.

[135] ". . . hunc non in virilitate, non in iuventute, non in adolescentia, sed in ipsis puericiae primordiis ita egisse, ut non sibi tempus, sed ut ipse tempori superesset." Ibid., fol. 74^v.

[136] ". . . ut ad eam non natus sed tamquam a deo electus cunctorum existimatione crederetur." Ibid., fol. 76^v.

[137] ". . . ne artem illam inspectam atque incognitam tanquam post terga relinqueret, quae si unquam in omni libero populo floruit, et si unquam in omni bene constituta re pu[blica] valuit . . . ." Ibid.

[138] ". . . de vita, de moribus hominum, de naturis rerum ita subtiliter disputavit, ut eum rex ille magna cum benignitate gaudio, mansuetudine oscularetur, cum antea coram omnibus clara voce dixisset se nullum unquam aut vidisse aut legisse aut audisse adolescentium cui Franciscus noster cederet in tanta tot doctrinarum mirabili atque egraegia disciplina." Ibid.

[139] "Nam in hoc anno transacto frequenti saenatu bis copiose luculente ac eleganter causam suam de conservandis possessionibus dixit, in ea aetate constitutus in qua omnium confirmatione nullus unquam tale quid facere fuerit ausus." Ibid., fols. 76^v-77. The deed was remarkable particularly because of Francesco's age: "Magna haec et praeclara non in adolescente, sed in iuvene quoque apparerent." Ibid., fol. 77.

earlier, "at a great gathering of all the most noble citizens," he had delivered a "subtle" disputation, in which he was not "vanquished by the sublimity" of the matters he dealt with, nor "confounded by their magnitude," nor "routed by their multitude."[140] All admired the great intellect, vast knowledge, elegant mastery of detail. The achievement was remarkable in itself, more remarkable in a young man. Now age twenty-one, Francesco was neither an adolescent nor a youth, but a man, on account of his virtue which is the mark of manhood. Splendid in fortitude, prudence, and justice, he was most remarkable for his temperance: for he "not frequently but always coerced, repressed, and crushed every lust, every irrational impetus of soul with a certain firm and moderate control."[141] Virtuous and learned, he would bestow upon posterity a greater glory than he had received from his awesome Contarini forebears.

Not only were humanist studies the vehicle by which the patrician consciousness was formed, as it was for Contarini, but humanists, as Niccolò Barbo did here, defined the type of a patrician personality. Many other orations in which humanists praised, lamented, or exhorted each other also contributed to the definition of that type. Indeed, that appears to be the primary function of much of the oratorical genre in Venice. School and university orations, funeral orations, orations delivered to honor visiting dignitaries present the interwoven components of the patrician ideal: humanist learning (remarkably precocious, and continuous with philosophical studies as was common in Venice), an austere morality, and a consciousness of duty to dynasty and patria. Virtue was linked to learning, and virtue and learning alike were seen to glorify clan and class and to benefit the republic.

Zaccaria Trevisan the Younger had before him the model, as had Francesco Contarini, of an illustrious and learned father: Zaccaria the Elder. On the occasion of the son's doctorate in law, Marco Donato praised the father to encourage and inspire the son.[142] The father's

---

[140] "Quid vero dicam de illa praestantissima repetitione ac subtilissima disputatione quam his mensibus elapsis egit in magno cunctorum nobilissimorum civium concursu cum tanta ingenii sui laude ac gloria? In qua non sublimitate rerum uinci, non magnitudine confundi, non multitudine obrui potuit. Qua ex re non solum divinum illud ingenium summum quid admirationis omnibus attulit, sed etiam incredibilis eius scientia atque doctrina cunctis concivibus nostris qui eum ad audiendum accesserant ita maximae patuit; ut eius mirabilem ac inauditam eruditionem non mediocri laude in caelum usque transferent." Ibid., fol. 77.

[141] ". . . non saepenumero sed semper omnem libidinem, omnem irrationabilem impetum animi firma et moderata quadam dominatione coercuit, compescuit, atque confregit . . . ." Ibid., fol. 81ᵛ.

[142] The following summarizes M. Donato's *Oratio in laudes Zacharie Trivisani.* Reference will be made to the full manuscript version unless the Gothein edition is indicated. The oration deals with father (fols. 155ᵛ-161ᵛ), then son (fols. 161ᵛ-163ᵛ).

loyalty, prudence, justice, fortitude, generosity and clemency were famous. In patriotism, he equaled or outclassed the two Catos, Scipio, and Julius Caesar. He was knowledgeable in canon and civil law and in philosophy, and expert in poetry and oratory "which breathe life into the other sciences, clothes and adorns them."[143] Now the son is heir to the father's achievement, "who even if he never did anything at all that could be called great, yet by his father's splendor alone would be made illustrious and immortal."[144] But he should not passively accept glory from his father's radiance, but acquire glory and honor by imitating his example. The young Zaccaria had already taken up this challenge, showing early achievements in virtue and learning. Singularly mature, abhorring all temptations at that very age—adolescence—when most are prone to vice, he behaved so modestly that he seemed bound for a sacred rather than worldly career. He assiduously studied all the sciences, and particularly the poets and orators, from whom he learned "to speak elegantly, write correctly, and [enunciate] properly."[145] Proceeding from these elementary studies to philosophy and law, he came to that pinnacle of achievement—a doctorate in law—which this oration celebrates. For by his diligent studies, hard work, and sleepless nights, he had "recovered [his] father's glory," concluded the eulogist, "exceeded your ancestors, and [surpassed] yourself."[146]

The key elements of the ideal outlined by Barbo are here as well: precocious moral and intellectual achievement spurred by paternal and ancestral expectations. They reappear in Pietro Marcello the Younger's depiction of Domenico Grimani. Like Contarini and Trevisan, he was the heir to the formidable achievements of his ancestors.[147] His father Antonio had been a wealthy and eloquent patriot, eventually doge of Venice. Domenico had acquired by birth these "gifts of nature," and augmented them by "assiduous study and constant diligence and other virtues."[148] Though raised amid the "abundance of delights" his family's wealth provided, he had from adolescence (that vice-prone age)

---

[143] ". . . qui ceteras scientias reficiunt, denudatasque vestiunt et exornant . . . ." *Oratio*, ed. Gothein, pp. 57-58.

[144] ". . . qui, etsi nil unquam egisset, quod egregium dici posset, solo patris splendore illustris et immortalis effectus esset. . . ." Ibid., p. 59.

[145] "In quibus expollitissime loqui, rectissime scribere, tutissime pronuntiare didicit." *Oratio*, fol. 162ᵛ.

[146] "In quibus omnibus patris gloriam exhausisti, maiores tuos et te ipsum superasti . . . ." Ibid., fol. 163ᵛ.

[147] Grimani's forebears are praised at length on fols. 110-12 of Marcello's *Oratio in adventu Cardinalis Grimani*.

[148] "Has vero naturae praestantissimas dotes ita tu assiduo studio et continua diligentia ceteris virtutibus illustranda curasti . . . ." Ibid., fol. 112ᵛ.

avoided luxury and sloth and devoted himself to liberal studies, in which he still as an adult excelled, "so that not only in Italy but indeed in all the world wherever literary studies flourish, there is scarcely any who can compare to you."[149] The promise of greatness, the foundations of which had been laid in childhood with the careful formation of morals and style of life, had now been realized: he had acquired a cardinalate, and his Venetian admirers had hopes as well that he would ascend to the highest dignity of pope. He never did, and disappointed in this one regard the expectations held of him. "Know that a great burden has been laid upon you," Leonardo Bruni had written to Jacopo Foscari, alluding to the glorious standard set for that youth of his father's, the Doge Francesco's, achievement.[150] Just such a burden lay on Grimani and his peers who were required by their achievements of learning and virtue to sustain the glory of their family and social order.

6. HUMANISM AND PIETY

The fusion of learning and virtue was an objective named frequently in humanist culture. But virtue was a term richly ambiguous in the fifteenth century. It connoted, on the one hand, the moral ideal of the Christian religion as comprehended in the Middle Ages; on the other, a renewed classical ideal, secular and modern, proud and aggressive, destined for embodiment in Machiavelli's hero. In Venice, concepts of antique virtue were welcomed and adopted into humanist culture. But Venice's humanists—and their culture—remained staunchly pious, and humanist learning at times joined the battle of the medieval Church against passion and instinct.

Francesco Contarini, Zaccaria Trevisan the Younger, and Domenico Grimani were all commended, as has been seen, for having as youths resisted the seductions of lust and amusement and devoted their energies instead to studies. That topos is frequently encountered. Cristoforo Moro also, according to Bernardo Bembo, "passed all the years of his adolescence in the study of theology," and by his Christian virtue had earned not only the highest position in the republic (he had just been elected doge), but a place in heaven.[151] Such youthful asceticism hu-

---

[149] ". . . ut non solum in Italia sed in toto prope orbe terrarum ubi literarum studia florent vix ullus tibi merito comparandus esse videat[ur] . . . ." Ibid.

[150] "Magnum tibi onus impositum esse cogita." Bruni, *Epist.*, ed. Mehus, II, 97.

[151] ". . . adolescentiae annos transgressus divinarum rerum studio . . . ."; "Has igitur princeps noster virtutes per hunc laudatissimum vitae curriculum ita respexit . . . ut non ad amplissimas dignitates modo in hac urbe nostra . . . , non ad hoc tam amplum fastigium quod superioribus diebus luculentissime est consecutus, verum ad caelestia

manist authors also discerned and esteemed in those whose virtue was not linked to the new learning: Marco Corner, according to Pietro Contarini, rescued his youth from sensuality and devoted it to hard work;[152] Giorgio Loredan, according to Leonardo Giustiniani, fled the passions that beset him in adolescence to take refuge in labors by which his body and mind were prepared for civic and military obligations.[153] Yet even when corseted, the passions of youth were suspect. The very young were barred from government in Venice, while the most respected offices were reserved for the old whose experience *in se* bore fruit of wisdom: "There are no wise men who are not old," wrote Domenico Morosini, adding sourly, "and even then, very few."[154]

Did the adolescents of Venice's patriciate in fact avoid as a class the intense passions peculiar to that age? Few would find that claim wholly credible. But the ideal of adolescent self-restraint seems to have been generally respected. And certainly, in their maturity many among the Venetian humanists, however they had weathered the turbulent years of youth, were pious by profession and in practice. Perhaps, since piety is expected of ecclesiastics, the examples of Pietro Barozzi and Marco Barbo are not compelling. Yet these humanist clerics, at a time when the moral corruption of the clergy was widespread and notorious, appeared to have given to the poor abundantly of their own substance. Barozzi, habitually generous, had in a year of particular need supplied the Paduan population with grain and money in quantities sufficient to save many from death.[155] Barbo died in Rome, the "most honored" of the cardinals, clothed in a hair shirt, rich in books, poor in ducats— for he had given all his wealth to the poor.[156] But not all the pious among Venice's humanists were clerics. Laymen as well found in established Christianity solace for the soul and hope for their city.[157]

About to embark on the journey to Crete, to which island-colony he had been elected doge, Candiano Bollani put the final words to his commentary on Genesis and asked his friend, a Carthusian monk of

---

ipsa, quod maxime optat, accessus quidam ei facillimus relinquatur." B. Bembo, *Gratulatio ad Christophorum Maurum*, pp. 282-83.

[152] Contarini, *In funere Marci Cornelii oratio*, p. 206.

[153] Giustiniani, *Funebris oratio ad Georgium Lauredanum*, p. 16.

[154] "Sapientes non nisi senes et illi perpauci." DBIRP, p. 128. Patricians could enter the Great Council at age twenty-five, in exceptional cases earlier. For the tendency to assign important offices to the very old, see R. Finlay, "The Venetian Republic as a Gerontocracy."

[155] C. Marcello, *In reverendissimi episcopi Petri Barocii funus oratio*, p. 106.

[156] Zippel, "La morte di Marco Barbo Cardinale," pp. 197, 202-203.

[157] For the tendency of Venetian patricians in this epoch toward the spiritual life, see S. Tramontin, "La cultura monastica del Quattrocento."

no particular stature, to pray for him.[158] Here is indeed a case of the blending of active and contemplative lives, when a nobleman of impeccably orthodox conviction devotes his leisure to reflection on Scripture, and pauses for the aid of prayer before assuming office! Ludovico Foscarini consulted a battery of spiritual advisers. To Matteo Contarini he spoke bravely of how the bodily pain he suffered aroused him to love of God.[159] To Moro Lapi—a simple monk, prolific of pious works in the vernacular yet with but limping competence in Latin, correspondent of several highly placed patricians—he confessed his fear of demons, and of sin.[160] To the saintly Patriarch Lorenzo Giustiniani, he deplored the immorality of conspicuous display and lamented the brutality of his own—not the enemy's—soldiers.[161] With Francesco Trevisan, who had also the confidence of the doge, he shared his grief at the death of his father, a pious layman who wished to be buried in the habit of a Franciscan friar.[162]

Francesco Barbaro, Venice's arch-humanist, was active in monastic reform and, like Foscarini, an intimate of holy men who could proffer advice and consolation.[163] Poised to set out from Zoppola to Venice, he anxiously wrote two monks—one Carthusian, one Camaldulensian—for their prayers and their advice: should he travel when there was danger of the plague?[164] He wooed the monk Giovanni Capistrano, inviting friendship in a letter accompanied by a generous gift of wine. That wealthy and powerful man who had taken under his protection learned commoners, poor noblemen, whole cities, implored

---

[158] Bollani, *Libri XVIII in tria priora capita Genesis*, dedicatory letter to Andreas Pannonius Cartusiensis, fol. [0ᵛ].

[159] Foscarini, *Epist.*, fol. 188ᵛ. He writes the patriarch of Venice, who was probably at the time of this letter (date uncertain) Matteo Contarini.

[160] Ibid., fol. 207ᵛ. Florentine by birth, Lapi was a Camaldulensian monk at San Matteo di Murano. See Lapi's very interesting works—letters, autobiographical notes, transcriptions from others' works, vernacular translations from Latin—in Marc. cod. Lat. XIV, 295 (4348), a contemporary codex of 312 folios described by Kristeller, *Iter Italicum*, II, 270. These works indicate relations also with Marco Barbo, Pietro Foscari, and Giovanni Marcanova. Lapi deplores his inability to master Latin, fol. 93ᵛ.

[161] Foscarini, *Epist.*, fols. 149ᵛ, 123ᵛ.

[162] Ibid., fols. 37ᵛ-39 for Foscarini's words to Francesco; fol. 46ᵛ for his father's piety. Foscarini's several intimate letters to this monk are addressed to "the Carthusian Francesco." I am identifying him with the Carthusian Trevisan, an intimate of many patricians; see Agostini, *Notizie*, I, 79. Trevisan's intimacy with the doge and the Venetian political process is evident in the first letter cited above, as well as in several others; see especially fols. 57-58ᵛ, 166ᵛ-67ᵛ, 194-96.

[163] For Francesco's reformism, see for example Quirini, *Diatriba*, pp. 261ff., 271ff., 284ff.; *Epist.*, ed. Quirini, pp. 15-16, 54. For his piety see also B. Bughetti, "Alcune lettere di Francesco Barbaro riguardanti l'Ordine Francescano."

[164] See Barbaro's *Epist.*, ed. Quirini, pp. 138-39, 139-40; *Centotrenta*, ed. Sabbadini, p. 50.

Giovanni in the name of God to "receive me in your faith and your protection."[165] No casual Christian, Barbaro was one of many Venetians fascinated by the preaching friar San Bernardino, whose cult of veneration of the holy name of Jesus he joined. Poggio Bracciolini, a humanist of a different stripe, bemoaned Barbaro's custom of heading manuscript pages with the radiant IHS of the holy name: "I rejoice that at last you have become a Christian," he mocked, then grieved that a wise and learned man should engage in such vulgar folly.[166]

Barbaro's veneration of the holy name suggests more than conventional acquiescence to the credos of his age; it suggests profound conviction. His friend Leonardo Giustiniani also underwent a process of spiritual deepening akin, in his case, to conversion. The love poems of his youth for which he was justly famed he renounced, and devoted later years to religious *laudi* of great sensitivity.[167] In his prose works, as well, urged by his brother the Patriarch Lorenzo, he progressed from secular to religious concerns. "For daily you urge me with your incredible piety," Leonardo wrote his brother in the dedicatory letter to the life of Nicholas of Myra he had translated from the Greek, "that I direct my studies and my thoughts above all to attaining the blessed life and [my] soul's immortality, and after sailing so long that I finally seek a harbor."[168] The seriousness of his spiritual concern is evident elsewhere than in communications with the heroically ascetic patriarch. To the preacher Francesco of Rimini whose words had inspired many, Leonardo expressed gratitude for the liberating consolation he had received. Francesco was his "harbor," in which he found peace.[169] Leonardo urged the monk and humanist Ambrogio

[165] *Epist.*, ed. Quirini, pp. 198, 234-35, App. pp. 77-78, 79; *Centotrenta*, ed. Sabbadini, pp. 51-52. "Te igitur hortor in Domino, ut ita me in fidem, ac tutelam tuam recipias . . . ." *Epist.*, App. p. 79.
[166] "Iam tandem gaudeo te factum esse Christianum . . . ." Poggio, *Epist.*, ed. Tonellis, I, 261. San Bernardino greatly impressed the Venetians. See Bernardo Giustiniani's reflections on the friar's great impact on his life, *Orat. et epist.*, sigs. Lᵛ-L2; and descriptions of the encounter of that friar with Cristoforo Moro, later doge, by Bernardo Bembo in his *Gratulatio ad Christophorum Maurum*, p. 285, and P. Barozzi, *Oratio ad Christophorum Maurum Ducem*, p. 153. Also Tramontin, "Cultura monastica," p. 448 and n. 87.
[167] For guidance to the various editions of the *canzoni* and the *laudi*, see the studies cited in Giustiniani's profile. M. Dazzi, an enthusiast of Giustiniani's secular poetry, sees no profound reorientation in the religious (*Leonardo Giustiniani, poeta populare d'amore*, pp. 80ff.). To my mind, the reorientation was notable and serious, apparent in the prose as well as poetic works.
[168] "Me etenim quotidie pro tua incredibili pietate admones ut studia cogitationesque meas ad beatam vitam animique immortalitatem adipiscendam potissimum conferam et post longam navigationem aliquando de Portu cogitem." Preface to Lorenzo of the *Vita Beati Nicolai Myrensis Episcopi* in the patriarch's *Opera omnia*, I, liii.
[169] Giustiniani, *epistola* in G. B. Contarini, *Anec. ven.*, p. 81.

Traversari to have his busy scribes provide vernacular books on sacred subjects so that less-educated readers might have access to them, and reproved his friend for devoting too much time to the study of secular authors.[170]

The tension between secular and sacred studies was also felt by Gregorio Correr, a pupil of the humanist pedagogue Vittorino da Feltre, and in his youth an author of secular verse and an enthusiast of Virgil.[171] For two years he had wavered between his life of civilized studies and a life devoted to God. Swayed finally by the example of his holy uncle, he renounced secular for sacred learning.[172] Years later, though, the writings of the ancient pagans still tempted him. Exhorting a Carthusian novice to read only holy books, Correr admitted his weakness. "Let no literature delight you other than that written in the name of our Lord. This will be easy for you; it was harder for me. I had loved the foolish learning of the world, and the seductions of secular letters—and even now, I have not ceased to love them."[173] Like Correr, Ludovico Foscarini urged the young Jacopo Foscari to love not the pagan authors, but "ours," and to find truth in the gospel of Christ.[174] Like Correr, too, Pietro Dolfin abandoned the secular studies he had loved when he entered the religious life, and mourned his former devotion to them in a long autobiographical letter to his friend, later abbot, Pietro Donato.[175]

Though the religious experience of these Venetian humanists was sometimes intense and personal, they saw religion as a civic as well

---

[170] Traversari, *Epist.*, ed. Mehus, pp. 313ff., 315ff. on *volgare* works, pp. 307ff. on secular authors. These letters are Traversari's to Giustiniani, from which is inferred Giustiniani's message.

[171] *Epistola ad Caeciliam virginem*, pp. 213ff.

[172] This hesitation described in his *Soliloquium ad Deum de vita sua et de vita et obitu beatae memoriae Antonii Episcopi Ostiensis et Cardinalis patrui sui*, in Contarini, *Anec. ven.*, pp. 15ff.

[173] "Nullae te delectent litterae praeter eas, quae in nomine Domini nostri scriptae sunt. [T]ibi hoc facile erit, mihi difficilius esset; inanes saeculi disciplinas et gentilium litterarum illecebras sectatus sum, et adhuc sectari non desino." Correr, *Epistola ad novitium Carthusianum de commodis vitae regularis*, in Contarini, *Anec. ven.*, I, 30.

[174] L. Foscarini, *Gesta martyrum Victoris et Coronae*, fols. 66-67ᵛ. We should turn above all to the saints, "qui gravissimis meritis, non vulgaribus exemplis, non comunibus precibus indefessi adiuvare non desinunt" (67ᵛ).

[175] The letter to Donato in his *Epistolae CCXLII*, ed. Martène & Durand, pp. 915-19. Antonio Vinciguerra on his deathbed ordered all but a few of his works burnt: ". . . sint omnes combuste, arse, brusade et cunsumate in igne, sic quod hab (sic) eis non habeatur vestigium"; see the testament in B. Beffa, *Antonio Vinciguerra Cronico*, p. 178; also the discussion of della Torre, *Di Antonio Vinciguerra e delle sue satire*, pp. 225ff. It is not known whether Vinciguerra repudiated these works because he found them artistically or morally inadequate. Certainly the *satire*, which he did not condemn, are highly moralistic. In Vinciguerra's action may be found another case of the forswearing of secular literary involvements.

35

as a private concern. Pietro Contarini believed that no quality was more highly valued in Venice than piety, of which the witnesses were "the frequent ceremonies, the elaborate ornaments of prelates, the bones of saints brought from all over the world."[176] The whole city could benefit from communal expressions of piety. Domenico Morosini recommended public preaching as a cure for the plague and argued that the devoutness of senators would assure the benevolence of God to the city.[177]

Nothing was so likely, however, to win divine indulgence than the presence of relics, hundreds of which Venice proudly possessed. The respect for these relics invades even the official language of the Senate, as in this passage from an act by which 10,000 ducats were allotted to purchase a garment worn by Christ. "In that our ancestors strove and sweated continually for the honor of God and the increase of the Christian religion and of our city's devotion, not considering the risks, labors and expenses which they might face, and brought to this city from every part of the world . . . the bodies and various relics of the saints . . . our city has been adorned with many holy and devout and venerable bodies and many relics of the saints by whose merits and prayers it must be believed that this city has been often saved and every day is saved and protected from many adversities, by the grace of God."[178] Bernardo Giustiniani appealed for the city's welfare not only to God, to Mary, and the evangelist Mark, but to the relics of seventy saints which Venice housed; for he firmly believed that relics protected the city. By the "vigilance and patronage" of Saint Mark above all, the city's protector and almost her founder, Venice was rendered "unconquerable and impregnable."[179] Ermolao Barbaro (the

---

[176] "Testes sunt frequentissimae cerimoniae, ditissima antistitum ornamenta, sanctorum ossa toto orbe quaesita." *In funere Marci Cornelii oratio*, p. 203. He was speaking of "religio," "qua nihil sanctius in hac urbe habetur, nihil ornatius colitur, nihil diligentius observatur."

[177] For the recommendations of preaching to oppose the plague, see pp. 11ff. of C. Finzi's introduction to the DBIRP; Finzi also prints (Doc. 5, p. 259) the relevant Senate act introduced by Morosini when *provisor super pestem*. For Morosini's recommendation of senatorial piety, see pp. 108, 240.

[178] "Quantum progenitores nostri vigilaverint continue et insudaverint pro honore dei et augmento christiane religionis et devotionis huius nostrae civitatis, non habentes respectum ad pericula labores et expensas quod haberentur, et ad hanc civitatem nostram conducerentur ex omnibus partibus mundi, . . . corpora et diverse reliquie sanctorum . . . ista civitas nostra ornata est multis sanctis et devotissimis corporibus et venerabilibus ac multis reliquiis sanctorum quorum meritis et precibus credendum est civitatem istam liberatam esse quampluries et omni die liberari atque tueri a multis adversitatibus gratia dei mediante." ASV, ST 3, c. 169, 26 August 1455. A more noxious example of public concern for sanctity is the Senate's foundation of the western world's first Jewish ghetto in 1516; see R. Finlay, "The Foundation of the Ghetto."

[179] Giustiniani, *Orat. et epist.*, sig. D2; Labalme, *Bernardo Giustiniani*, p. 305. Dil-

Elder) concurred: adorned with "so many and such saints," the city, become God's particular joy, would never perish.[180]

If the humanists, along with other Venetians, trusted in the relics that protected their city, they feared those outsiders whose denial of Christianity—in their eyes, perverse—threatened the cohesion of the community. The cleric Pietro Bruto devoted two of his works and much of his energy to combatting the Jews of Vicenza where he was vice-regent and lieutenant to the Bishop Giovanni Battista Zeno.[181] Paolo Morosini wrote a famous apology for Christianity against the Jews—the first book published in Padua.[182] Ludovico Foscarini vigorously testified—against others who had doubted them—of atrocities committed by Jews. Concurring with Fantino Dandolo, who had denounced Jewish doctors who both killed the bodies of Christian patients and damned their souls, he praised Ermolao Donato, who had chosen to suffer from his wounds rather than be treated by a Jewish doctor.[183]

7. SERVING THE REPUBLIC

Concerned, even anxious, about the welfare of their souls and of their city, these humanists selected from the writings of antiquity not those values which displaced, but those which complemented a traditional piety. Piety prohibited a vaunting of self. But both piety and ancient example sanctioned a commitment to the republic. To that suprapersonal goal the humanists dedicated themselves ardently. In this consists the "civicism" of the Venetian humanists: not that they, as citizens, saw the fulfillment of the human personality in social action; but that their freedom of self-expression, limited by cultural convention and religious norm, both sets of standards reinforced by humanist teachers,

---

igent and conspicuous veneration of those same seventy saints was seen as a sure indication of the piety of Cristoforo Moro; Pietro Barozzi, *Oratio ad Christophorum Maurum*, p. 150. For the cult of Saint Mark as the "nucleus of civic consciousness," see E. Muir, *Civic Ritual in Renaissance Venice*, pp. 78ff.

[180] "Nec deseret hanc urbem, quae ... est tot ac tantis sanctorum corporibus ornata ac munita, ut nunquam adduci possim illam facile perituram, tamquam Dei peculiarem." E. Barbaro, *Epistola ad D. Celsem Veronensem*, col. 104.

[181] Bruto's *Epistola contra Judaeos* and *Victoria contra Judaeos*.

[182] Morosini's *De aeterna temporalique Christi generatione in judaice improbationem perfidiae*.

[183] *Epist.*, fols. 259ᵛ-262ᵛ for his long letter to Antonio Gradenigo on Jewish atrocities; his reference to Dandolo, fol. 234ᵛ; to Donato, 237ᵛ. Jews were subjected to restrictive legislation in 1443, but were permitted to practice medicine; see Agostini, *Notizie* I, 80. G. Gardenal's "Lodovico Foscarini e la medicina" studies Foscarini's attitude toward Jewish doctors as expressed in several letters, and relates them to the general course of Venetian anti-Semitism.

they permitted themselves with their new power of eloquence the expression of civic devotion.

Son of Leonardo, the famous poet, humanist, and statesman, nephew of the awesomely pious Lorenzo, and of the powerful states-man Marco, whose achievement would not so have paled had his brothers' been less remarkable—Bernardo Giustiniani exemplifies this pattern of subordination of self to republican service.[184] His heritage scarcely permitted deviation (at least conscious or public deviation) from that ideal. He modestly accepted the insignia of knighthood offered him by the king of France. But he had previously refused the honor three times, imitating in self-sacrifice his father Leonardo.[185] He was rewarded with admonishments and a lecture.[186] Even in death, Giustiniani humbled himself. He had by his testament prohibited with characteristic but extreme modesty all pomp at his funeral, and had arranged for an obscure tomb near the body of his saintly uncle Lorenzo.[187] Disappointed that when Giustiniani died no funeral ora-tion was permitted to celebrate his accomplishments, Ermolao Barbaro the Younger wrote a letter of praise to that humanist and statesman's grandson, Marco Dandolo. Is it right, wailed Barbaro, "that the bones of such a man should lie unhonored by marble, unwitnessed by any eulogy?"[188] The virtues that the dead nobleman cultivated in his youth here reached a climax of self-effacement. The glory of his ancestors culminates in the modesty of the son.

Personally self-deprecating, Giustiniani had excelled in humanist studies and devoted his eloquent pen to the will of Venice. Barbaro particularly admired Giustiniani's wedding of literary interests to re-publican service—a marriage in which he himself was to fail singularly. "Those literary studies in which [Giustiniani] had always excelled since childhood he pursued not in retirement or for himself nor closeted in domesticity," but for the welfare of the republic.[189] He had employed

---

[184] In this judgment I follow Labalme, *Bernardo Giustiniani*.

[185] B. Giustiniani's *Oratio pro militia ad regem Franciae Ludovicum*, sigs. E3ᵛ-E4 for his father's renunciation and his own previous three. He had deliberately followed the "exemplum paternum," reminding his listeners of the wise dictum ". . . ne transgrediaris terminos, quos patres tui posuerunt tibi" (sig. E4).

[186] Ludovico Foscarini's letter to Giustiniani (*Epist.*, fols. 238ᵛ-42) congratulates him on his knighthood, then prescribes for him a nobleman's code of moral behavior: wise use of wealth and diligent striving to meet the lofty expectations that all have of him.

[187] Giustiniani's will in P. H. Labalme, "The Last Will of a Venetian Patrician (1489)."

[188] "Nunquid propterea laturi estis ut ossa tanti viri sine marmoris honore, sine ulla eulogii testatione iaceant?" Barbaro, *Epist.*, ed. Branca, II, 49; his letter praising Gius-tiniani, II, 48-49.

[189] "Illa sua et propria quod fere quamdiu vixit principem in urbe sua locum tenuit, qui studia litterarum, in quibus a puero semper eminuit, non ad vitam umbratilem aut sibi nec intra domesticos parietes exercuit, sed reipublicae commentariis ab urbe condita

his eloquence in directions beneficial to Venice: by writing a history of the city since its foundation, by serving as ambassador (an office in which his skills were useful) on important and difficult missions to European rulers, by administering magistracies of several kinds in Venice and her subject cities, in all of which he performed "wisely and virtuously." His eloquence was heard in the government councils, as well. For twenty-five years, wrote Barbaro, "there was no greater authority in the Senate, none presented his opinion with greater weight."[190] When all the Senators were inclined to act one way, he was best able to persuade them to another. When the Senate was exhausted by debate, it still listened with attention to him. His speech was considered, elegant, sparkling, and solid; he was in voice and gesture the perfect orator. "I have learned more from him in the Senate than from six hundred volumes of the rhetoricians in the schools."[191] Giustiniani, a model patrician, put the *studia humanitatis* to work in public service.

Giustiniani was surely remarkable, as Barbaro depicts him; he was a humanist of first rank. But he was not unique. Venice offered the members of her ruling elite many opportunities to employ their humanist learning in the public arena. Debating skills were useful in the government councils, oratorical skills in embassies and magistracies abroad, and managerial skills in offices at home. Barbone Morosini was one such patrician trained in the *studia humanitatis* who placed his knowledge and capabilities in public service: he was "long experienced in various and important republican offices and learned in every branch of literary studies and of law," said Francesco Barozzi.[192] Ludovico Foscarini called him "an elegant humanist, a wise lawyer, a sharp dialectician, a profound philosopher."[193] Though he wrote no major works, Morosini must have spoken on public occasions of which there is no other record than his friend's description: "in eloquence

---

perscriptis, legationibus ad principes Europae maximis et difficillimis quibusque gestis, magistratibus urbanis et peregrinis omnibus sapienter et innocenter administratis, ut nemo iura populis prudentius aut castius aut aequabilius praebuerit." Ibid., II, 48.

[190] "Per quinque porro et viginti annos fere nulli maior auctoritas in curia, nullius maior in sententia dicenda gravitas . . . ." Ibid.

[191] "Fateor me plura in eo genere ab illo in senatu didicisse quam ex sexcentis rhetorum voluminibus in scholis." Ibid., II, 49.

[192] ". . . et in maximis ac diversissimis rei p[ublicae] nostre muneribus diutissime exercitus ac preterea omnis generis litterarum et iuris praecipue peritissimus . . . ." F. Barozzi, *Oratio pro doctoratu Jacobi Molini in gymnasio patavino*, fol. 28.

[193] ". . . humanitate ornatissimus, iuris consultissimus, dyaleticus acutissimus, philosophus gravissimus . . . ." Foscarini, *Epist.*, fol. 202. Foscarini devotes this entire letter (to the Patriarch Matteo Contarini), summarized here to Morosini's praise: fols. 201ᵛ-202ᵛ, 204, 205ʳ⁻ᵛ.

and forceful speech he was exceeded by none; candidly challenging errors of private behavior and public policy, always defending, gracefully and weightily, the cause of truth, he applied the greatest wisdom, the greatest force, the greatest goodness, his blameless soul to the glorification of virtue and damnation of vice."[194] The importance of such a man to the city is inestimable, continued Foscarini. He was not merely a prudent man, but a prophet, a complete and perfect senator. Carlo Zeno, who came to the *studia humanitatis* after a lifetime of hard experience of the political world, also understood their usefulness to civic life, and applied his skills to the daily task of governing. Leonardo Giustiniani did not describe his feats of eloquence in detail, since the members of his audience had witnessed Zeno firsthand: "You when you came to the Senate often heard his rich voice and his profound opinions, always with the greatest admiration."[195]

Venice was surely not, like the ideal republic designed by Plato, a city ruled by philosopher-kings. But the patrician humanists viewed each other as such and were encouraged to do so by admirers outside their ranks. Giustiniani, Morosini, and Zeno defended truth and damned injustice in the Senate. Trained in the *studia humanitatis*, they were thereby better suited, in the eyes of contemporary observers, to perform the offices that were their province by birth. Their humanist teachers—Sabellico, Negri, Becichemo, Collazio, transmitters of the classical tradition—had told them so. And they reinforced each other in that conviction. When Girolamo Barbarigo was elected procurator of Saint Mark, Ludovico Foscarini was pleased but not surprised: this was the office for which he had been born and educated.[196] To Vitale Lando, recently elected governor of Ravenna, Foscarini wrote that he rejoiced for the republic, which always profited when ruled by the wise.[197]

---

[194] ". . . in dicendi vi [et] elloquentia nemini cedebat; libero animo publicos privatosque erores redarguens, causam veritatis semper ornatissime gravissimeque defends, summam sapientiam, summam vim, summam bonitatem, integerimum animum ad virtutum gloriam et vitiorum damnationem afferebat . . . ." Ibid., fol. 202.

[195] ". . . qui saepe, cum in Senatum rogati convenissetis, suavissimam illam vocem gravissimasque sententias maxima semper cum admiratione audivistis." Giustiniani, *Funebris oratio pro Carolo Zeno*, p. 143. Giustiniani had just described thus Zeno's understanding of the utility of letters: "Vidit sane, vir sapiens, quantum ad gloriam atque laudem haec litterarum ornamenta conducant. Quod cum phylosophiam potissimum ac oratorium munus, tum ad bene beateque vivendum, tum ad publicam hominum utilitatem conferre intellexisset . . . ."

[196] "Quia dignitatem ex tua naturali consuetudine, parentis institutione administra[sti] summa virtute qua omnibus semper gratissimus fuisti. Eritque comodissismus gradus ad promissam tuis meritis omnium juditio, mihi vero speratam et optatam dignitatem." Foscarini, *Epist.*, fol. 354ᵛ.

[197] Ibid., fol. 203ᵛ.

Foscarini himself was an exemplar of learning wedded to republican service. Benedetto Bursa observed that his learning in all the arts, philosophy, and law uniquely suited him to the task of government. "For the government of cities and peoples you have been exceedingly well and uncommonly trained."[198] Foscarini's knowledge of law, Bursa cannily pointed out, was particularly useful. "For whatever city or people has been delegated to you by the powerful order of the Venetian Senate, it is never necessary to send with you a team of learned lawyers for you to have as advisers in any case of civil or canon law; whenever there is need of any advice or counsel of this sort in the performance of your office, you yourself are capable of providing that advice from your own knowledge and skill."[199] Though he passed new laws not in the city's constitution, yet the people accepted them and praised their author: "Your orders, though they were not incorporated among the city's written laws, yet so pleased the citizens, so did they take root in their souls, that even without official promulgation they shall endure forever in the mouths of men. For always in the midst of the marketplace, and the favorite gathering places, the citizens themselves ... remember your words and counsels."[200] And he protected public revenues from "rapacious men," and diligently managed the public debt, so enriching the treasury that he "freed this city from its ancient monetary problems ... and raised it up from great poverty and wretchedness."[201]

This depiction of a humanist's practical management of provincial office is perhaps matched by Francesco Negri's account of Paolo Morosini, called the "wise," one of Venice's leading humanists. When Venice's water supply was suffering from contamination, Morosini advised some drastic feats of hydraulic engineering.[202] Just what role

[198] "Ad gubernationem igitur civitatum et populorum cum eximie atque unice doctrina sis ornatus . . . ." Bursa, fol. 7ᵛ of the *Oratio ad Ludovicum Foscarenum*, in his *Orationes tres*.

[199] "Itaque quecunque urbs aut populus decernatur tibi per Senatum Venetum gravissimum ordinem, numquam necessarium est addere tibi comites iuris peritos quos tecum monitores habeas in ratione ista civili aut in causa aliqua pontificii iuris; quocumque enim eiusmodi consilio et admonitione opus esset ad magistratum tuum gerendum, valeas [*cod.* valeres] consulere tibi ipsi solus et eiusmodi admonitionem omnem ex scientia et facultate tua repetere." Ibid., fol. 7ᵛ.

[200] "Quae institutiones tuae etiam si forte in monumenta publica redacte non sint, tamen ita civibus placuerunt, ita in suis animis insederunt ut sine litteris publicis semper elucere et in ore hominum extare perpetuo possint. Semper enim in foro medio et celebribus locis loquentium ipsi cives . . . te repetent et verba et consilia tua commemorabunt." Ibid., fol. 8.

[201] ". . . ut urbem hanc vetere difficultate numaria pressam recrearis et ab inopia et miseria magna erexeris." Ibid.

[202] ". . . aquas omnes fluviales quae a leva ab eo loco in venetas lacunas defluere

was played in Morosini's apparently successful analysis of Venice's perennial water problems by a humanist education is unclear. But Marco Dandolo's training in law, as well as the rhetorical skills cultivated by early humanist nurture, encouraged the Council of Ten to dispatch him to Padua to consult with experts about a momentous issue of the day: Henry VIII's divorce.[203] Morosini and Dandolo, like Foscarini, were surely figures of whom Domenico Morosini would have approved. Knowledge—"*scientiae*" and "*disciplinae*"—was essential in those who ruled the city, he wrote, which more greatly profited from the wisdom of its rulers than their wealth. Wise governors are "like prophets, inspired by the holy spirit."[204]

Francesco Barbaro had tried to convince Santo Venier of the utility of humanist studies for the rulers of the republic.[205] They had once discussed the subject in Dalmatia where, in the city of Zara, Venier was now governor. Greek and Latin writers, Barbaro contended, "with their lofty minds and exquisite learning left many weighty and beautiful writings to posterity concerning the education of the young and the management of the city."[206] Since those works are of use to Venice, "many patricians in our own age I have seen so committed to these *studia humanitatis* that the republic can anticipate from their learning utility and aid no less than those scholars derive pleasure and honor."[207] Even though there have been many worthy men who were uneducated, Barbaro argued, still they would have been still more excellent "if they had joined to their superior natural gifts, in the manner of famous men, the benefits of learning."[208] The ancients have bestowed upon us, through their writings, models of virtue, "which if our citizens hold before themselves in administering the republic,

---

incipiunt, quae incolae Jesulum appellant usque ad dextram, ubi apud Clodiam urbem lacunarum istarum semicirculas clauditur, aggere eminenti ac per quattuor stadia lato claudi censebat." Negri, *De aristocratia*, fol. 92ʳ⁻ᵛ. Morosini's surname, often repeated, is given here: "Paulus Maurocenus quem . . . etiam sapientem appellabant . . . ." Morosini held the office of *savio super aquis* in 1453-1454 and supervised extensive work to protect the fresh water supply from the river Brenta: ASV, ST 3, cc. 76, 99, 103ᵛ.

[203] ASV, CX-Sec. 2, cc. 60ᵛ-61ᵛ, containing a letter of 12 May 1530; also another on the same matter, c. 62, 17 May. The first letter refers to "la prudentia et dexterita del ingenio vostro" (c. 60ᵛ).

[204] ". . . profecto vates sunt existimati quasi afflati spiritu divino." Morosini, *DBIRP*, p. 78. For the necessity of knowledge, p. 81.

[205] This important letter in *Centotrenta*, ed. Sabbadini, pp. 65-66.

[206] ". . . qui pleraque summis ingeniis exquisitaque doctrina de ingenuis moribus et institutis urbanis graviter et ornate scripta posteris reliquerunt . . . ." Ibid., p. 65.

[207] ". . . aetate nostra complures patricio loco natos tanta cura in haec studia humanitatis ferri viderem, ut non minus utilitatis et adiumenti resp. quam ipsi studiosi iucunditatis ac ornamenti sperare possint." Ibid.

[208] ". . . si clarissimorum hominum exemplo ad eximiam naturam adiumenta quoque doctrinae coniunxissent." Ibid.

by that reflection upon illustrious men, they shall become more prudent and capable."[209] To illustrate his point, Barbaro sent Venier with this letter, "so that I might serve myself and you and the city itself," Cicero's letter to his brother Quintus on the administration of public office.[210] Cicero's advice is immediately pertinent to the Venetian situation, Barbaro felt, and could be used to guide her officials: "If they were to read this work daily and reflect upon it, and tend carefully and diligently to the greatness and comfort of our republic, the republic itself would consider at once all the other writers of the best arts and Marcus Tullius Cicero to have deserved well of it, and would offer them great thanks."[211] The texts of the ancients are seen here, and described as such to a man in the center of power by another destined for that position, not merely as tools for the development of the mind, but as handbooks of effective management.

Barbaro would probably have approved the strong words of Agostino Valier, written more than a century later: "Whoever commits himself to literary studies and, so trained, does not apply them to the needs of the republic, can scarcely avoid the reprobation of learned men."[212] Inclined to do so by their teachers' urgings and parental admonitions, if not by fear of the reprobation of the learned, patrician humanists did to a remarkable degree employ their learning in activities useful to Venice. The day-to-day business of government councils, it has already been noted, provided occasion for the exercise of oratorical skills. Embassies to foreign rulers gave opportunity for some of the most famous orations of the epoch: those of Zaccaria Trevisan the Elder, for instance, to the rival popes; of Bernardo Giustiniani to the king of France and the University of Paris; of Ermolao Barbaro to the Emperor Frederick III and imperial heir Maximilian.[213] The

[209] ". . . quas cum sibi proponent in administranda rep. cives nostri, illustrium virorum cogitatione prudentiores ac fortiores erunt." Ibid.

[210] "Ideoque quia tibi et mihi et ipsi civitati morem gererem, mecum statui ut gravissimam eius ad Q. fratrem proconsulem epistulam velut de magistratus institutione commentariolos ad te mitterem . . . ." Ibid.

[211] "Haec enim si quotidie legent et commentari volent, et ipsius reipublicae amplitudini ac commodis accuratius ac diligentius servient et ipsa respubl. tum ceteris optimarum artium scriptoribus, tum M. T. Ciceroni bene de se meritis magnas gratias habebit et dicet." Ibid., p. 66. Ludovico Foscarini assessed the utility to the republic of learning when he attributed the success of the defense of Brescia to the will of God and the knowledge of the classics; see G. B. Picotti, "Le lettere di Ludovico Foscarini," pp. 220-21.

[212] "His artibus quicunque se studiis litterarum tradiderit si instructus non redit in patriam, profecto vix potest doctorum hominum reprehensionem effugere." Valier, *Epistola ad Laurentium Priulum*, p. 300.

[213] Trevisan's orations to Gregory XII and Benedict XIII in Gothein, "Zaccaria Trevisan," pp. 34-42, 43-46 resp.; Giustiniani's orations *Pro militia* and to the University

triumphs or deaths of citizens and friends of Venice spurred other orations as famous: Leonardo Giustiniani's on Carlo Zeno, Andrea Giuliani's on Chrysoloras, Marcantonio Sabellico's on Zaccaria Barbaro.[214] The funeral orations were perceived as particularly important, perhaps because at a time when the restraints were placed in Venice upon the material or conspicuous honoring of individuals, alive or dead, these eulogies were verbal monuments permitted by law. Such orations teach posterity the achievements of great men, George of Trebizond commented, and "render cities themselves immortal," remarked Francesco Negri.[215]

Usefulness to the republic was also considered by patrician humanists when they selected works for translation from the Greek. Francesco Barbaro and Leonardo Giustiniani translated between them five lives from Plutarch, portraits of exemplary leaders or citizens.[216] From the vast corpus of Greek literature, they tended to those works which were useful to an educated elite of rulers. Bernardo Giustiniani, similarly, chose to translate Isocrates' oration to Nicocles, and Lauro Quirini chose Dio Cassius' rendition of an oration by Julius Caesar, both works in which the qualities of ideal rulers are implicitly defined.[217] Patrician taste for translation of this kind moved others to do them as well. When George of Trebizond, then in Naples, translated Plato's *Laws* and described the enterprise to Francesco Barbaro, that nobleman grasped well the significance of the work and its potential benefits to patrician culture.[218] George had explained how Venice's constitu-

of Paris in his *Orat. et epist.*, sigs. E4ᵛ-Fᵛ; Barbaro (G's) *Oratio ad Federicum imperatorem et Maximilianum regem Romanorum* in his *Epist.*, ed. Branca, II, 110-20.

[214] Giustiniani's and Giuliani's orations previously cited. Sabellico's *Oratio in funere Zachariae Barbari* in his *Opera*, fols. 70-71.

[215] "Quamquam omnes antiquitatis mores plurimum laudare soleo . . . , ille tamen ceteris michi videtur prestantior, quo institutum est clarissimorum virorum vitam ac laudes in funere recenseri . . . et ad imitandas virtutes eorum huiusmodi oratione, quicunque audiunt, incitantur atque inflammantur." George's *Oratio funebris in Fantinum Michielem*, p. 445. ". . . civitates . . . ipsas immortales reddent," Negri, *De aristocratia*, fol. 150. Note Marcantonio Sabellico's comment in his *Oratio in funere Zachariae Barbari*, fol. 135ᵛ: ". . . nulla gens in terris, nullus populus, nulla civitas . . . tanta defunctos pietate prosequatur, ac veneratione, quanta vestra haec . . . ."

[216] Barbaro's lives of Aristides and the elder Cato, dedicated to his brother Zaccaria, in Plutarch's *Vitae*, first in the edition of Brescia, 1499; I have seen the Paris 1514 edition where those lives appear on fols. 114-20, 120ᵛ-126, respectively. Giustiniani's of Cimon and Lucullus to Henry Lusignan, King of Cyprus, and of Phocion to his brother Marco in Plutarch's *Vitae*, II, fols. 1-22 and 123-34ᵛ.

[217] Giustiniani's translation of Isocrates in *Orat. et epist.*, sigs. H6ᵛ-I6ᵛ; Quirini's from Dio Cassius in J. M. Muccioli, *Catalogus codicum manuscriptorum Malatestianae Caesenatis Bibliothecae*, II, 233-36.

[218] See Gaeta, "Giorgio da Trebisonda"; Monfasani, *George of Trebizond*, pp. 72, 102ff.; Pertusi, "L'umanesimo greco," pp. 225, 233ff.; for the text of the preface, see above n. 105.

tion resembled the one recommended by Plato, and suggested that the noble founders of the city, learned then as now, had consulted that philosopher's work. It is clear to me, he wrote, "that your ancestors, who laid the foundations of your city, learned surely from this book what makes a republic flourish and endure."[219] Barbaro's response was eager. "How much what you wrote about Plato's *Laws* delighted me is more easily sensed than explained. For when our city was because of historical circumstances founded from the remains of other noble cities, and established by great and illustrious men who could find no safety elsewhere, partly by divine, partly by human counsel, and when in time the city grew so much, our ancestors not without cause turned to Plato and other wise men to understand and learn how to acquire and retain civic liberty, and to increase and amplify public majesty."[220] "But indeed, either the love of country deceives me," he continued delightedly, "or this republic, which has always lived by its own laws, was constituted with such pure morals, such just laws, such honest decrees that, as you say, our rivers appear to have risen from Plato's springs."[221] Barbaro promised his support in a project so full of appeal for learned statesmen: "So I urge you . . . to write a little preface worthy of the author and the greatness of the work and to dedicate to [me] the *Laws* of our Plato, and I shall so disseminate them among our citizens, so that in time you will receive ample fruit for your labors. This will please me so, that you could do nothing to please me more."[222]

Many of the patricians' original works were in the same way written on topics related to political life, and even on matters of urgent public interest. Lauro Quirini's works on nobility and the republic, for instance, are political in focus, as are the "historical letters" of his later

---

[219] ". . . majores vestros, qui Reipublicae vestrae fundamenta jecerunt, ex his certe libris omnia, quibus Respublica diu felix esse possit, collegisse." F. Barbaro, *Epist.*, ed. Quirini, p. 290.

[220] "Quantum etiam me delectarunt, quae scribis de legibus Platonis, facilius intelligi quam explicari potest. Nam cum urbs nosta temporum culpa ex ruinis nobilissimarum civitatum condita et a magnis et clarissimis viris, qui alibi salvi esse non poterant, instituta sit partim divino, partim humano consilio, eodem rerum tenore in tantam magnitudinem venit, ut non sine causa majores nostri a Platone aut a sapientissimis viris aequandae et retinendae communis libertatis et augendae ac amplificandae publicae majestatis rationem habuisse et didicisse videantur." Ibid., p. 293.

[221] "Sed profecto aut me amor Patriae fallit, aut ista Respublica, quae suis semper legibus vixit, ita sanctis moribus, ita aequo jure, ita honestis decretis instituta est, ut ex fontibus Platonis rivuli nostri, sicut dicis, manasse videantur." Ibid.

[222] "Caeterum te hortor ut . . . cum praefatiuncula, quae digna sit auctore et magnitudine rei, inscribas nobis leges istas Platonis nostri, et ego illas ita disseminabo apud cives nostros, ut aliquando non mediocrem fructum sis consecuturus laborum tuorum. Hoc ita mihi gratum erit, ut facere mihi gratius fere nihil possis." Ibid., p. 295.

years provoked by the Turkish advance.[223] Paolo Morosini wrote three major works in defense of Venice, all responding directly to foreign comment or inquiry. The *Letter to Cicco Simonetta*, indeed, was written at the request of the Senate, who wished Venice's case clearly stated by one of its own senators.[224] Girolamo Donato's ardent defense of Venice, similarly, answered the accusations made against the republic by King Charles VIII.[225] Pietro Barozzi wrote *On Extirpating Factions* for Bernardo Bembo, podestà of Bergamo, a city beset by chronic civic strife. "You asked," wrote the bishop to his friend, "once you learned that factions and internecine hatreds were rife in that city, that I show you how best to eliminate them and to reestablish mutual love among the parties."[226] These patricians were prompt to employ their pens in the defense of Venice and her interests.

They did so most energetically in the writing and commissioning of histories. Some wrote to record events of current interest: Francesco Contarini, for instance, described Venice's military ventures in Tuscany, in which he was a key participant; and Jacopo Zeno wrote a brief and straightforward account of a Paduan conspiracy.[227] Others wrote histories of Venice or her doges.[228] Yet, despite the abundance of historical literature produced by patrician humanists, attempts were repeatedly made to interest nonpatricians in writing histories of Venice.[229]

Ludovico Foscarini was particularly active in that search. He approached the Veronese Damiano dal Borgo: "I know with what bril-

---

[223] Quirini's three works on nobility—the *Epistola ad Petrum Thomasium*, the *De nobilitate contra Poggium Florentinum* [DN], and the *De nobilitate responsio quid iuris*; the *De republica* [DR]; the letters to Pope Nicholas V, Ludovico [Scarampo] Trevisan, Pope Pius II, and Paolo Morosini. An analysis of Quirini's major works on nobility and the republic appears in Chapter Two, Section 3.

[224] P. Morosini's *Defensio venetorum ad Europae principes contra obtrectatores* [DVEP]; *Lettera a Cicco Simonetta [Lettera]*; *De rebus ac formis reipublicae venetae* [DRF]. An analysis of all three works appears in Chapter Two, Section 4. For the Senate request, see the *Lettera*, fol. 1ʳᵛ: "domandatime de la Signoria mia quale commandandome gli dovesse dechiarire per qual modo la signoria mia se habia acquistato tanto imperio non havendo pocho tempo inanti habuta parte alcuna in terra ferma."

[225] Donato's *Contra Caroli Regis Francorum in Senatum Venetum calumnias apologia*.

[226] "Rogasti, quando vigere in ea urbe factiones et odia intestina intellexisses, ut qua potissimum ratione extingui atque ad benivolentiam mutuam revocari possent ostenderem." P. Barozzi, *De factionibus extinguendis* [DFE], p. 50. An analysis of Barozzi's work appears in Chapter Two, Section 6.

[227] F. Contarini, *De rebus in Hetruria a Senensibus gestis*; J. Zeno, *Descriptio coniurationis patavine*.

[228] For the histories written by Venetians, see Chapter Two, Section 8.

[229] For accounts of these attempts, see A. Pertusi, "Gli inizi della storiografia umanistica del Quattrocento"; F. Gilbert, "Biondo, Sabellico, and the Beginnings of Venetian Official Historiography"; Zippel, "Lorenzo Valla."

liance, with what elegance our history will sparkle when you have adorned it."[230] And the Neapolitan Porcellio Pandoni: how pleased we would be, he wrote, if we had a "worthy and excellent poet . . . by whose industry the wartime deeds of Venice would be noted for posterity."[231] And the Venetian Jacopo Ragazzoni: "Your pen is suited for the writing of history—exert yourself diligently in this matter, do not neglect what you can do so well."[232] And to Flavio Biondo, who had already begun a history, Foscarini gave some specific advice. He urged writing about three kinds of men: the "great, who died in sanctity, their lives more glorious than the golden temples you admire so much" (referring to Biondo's interest in ancient monuments); the "strong," who include not only famous soldiers, but those who wielded "literary arms" as well in the defense of the republic; and the "wise," whose life and character are more important to the community than any institutions.[233] Biondo had, in fact, written on Venice, as had Pier Paolo Vergerio at the request of Zaccaria Trevisan the Elder; and so had Poggio Bracciolini.[234] But neither Biondo nor any other candidate—Lorenzo Valla, Giovanni Mario Filelfo, George of Trebizond, Pietro Perleone—was hired at this time in Venice to write her history. Eventually, Venice found the historian she wanted: Marcantonio Sabellico, whose history—bland, prolix, and uncritical—perfectly suited a patrician audience.[235]

[230] "Scio equidem quanto nitore, quanta ellegantia res nostre fulgebunt cum tu eas exornaveris . . . ." Foscarini, *Epist.*, fol. 151.

[231] ". . . quod vatem insignem et prestantissimum habeamus, cuius industria res venetorum bello geste posteritati mandabuntur." Ibid., fol. 119. Porcellio did in fact write on Venetian history; see Pertusi, "Inizi," pp. 290ff.

[232] "Hystorie enim accomodatus est stilus tuus—in hoc te studiosius exerceas, nec negligas quod optime facis." Foscarini, *Epist.*, fol. 215ᵛ.

[233] "Optimis enim viris qui per sanctimoniam ex vita nostra demigraverunt, maior gloria debetur quam templis auratis, que tu tanta religione colis. Pro fortissimorum laude arma litteraria non minus capescenda arbitror quam illi militaribus usi sunt strenue in patriae salute defendenda. Sapientum vero vita et mores ornandi sunt, quom omnibus institutionibus anteponuntur." Ibid., 253ᵛ-254. Barbaro also encouraged Biondo to write Venetian history; see especially the letters of 31 March 1440 and 13 November 1440, both capsulized in *Centotrenta*, ed. Sabbadini, pp. 33 and 34, the former published at p. 101.

[234] For Biondo's *De origine et gestis venetorum* and fragmentary *Populi Veneti historiarum liber I*, Vergerio's *De situ et conditione et republica urbis venetiarum*, and Bracciolini's *Oratio in laudem rei publicae venetorum*, see Pertusi, "Inizi," pp. 292, 272 and 289ff., respectively; for Vergerio's work, see also Robey and Law, "Venetian Myth," where the text is printed at pp. 38-50. Coriolano Cippico also composed a history of a Venetian naval campaign—the *Petri Mocenici venetae classis imperatoris contra Ottomannum Turcarum principem rebus gestis libri III ab anno 1470 ad 1474*—at the urging of Marcantonio Morosini.

[235] His *Rerum venetarum ab urbe condita libri XXXIII*. For judgments on Sabellico's work, see Pertusi, "Inizi," pp. 330ff., and G. Cozzi, "Intorno all'edizione dell'opera di

Patrician humanists had as their object in writing history or having others do it the defense and glorification of their city. Even in their private communications, political or military matters were a central concern. Ludovico Foscarini's letter to Paolo Morosini exhorting Venice to action against the Turkish advance is a striking example, and one of that author's most compelling works.[236] Equally moving is Foscarini's lament for the depredations wrought on the Veronese *contado* by unruly troops. Don't send any more soldiers here, he wrote Barbaro; they have brought "chains . . . poverty, nakedness, squalor, deformity, grief, shrieking, everywhere, a giant mirror of death."[237] Foscarini's candor here was matched by Barbaro's, who assessed his enemy, some thought, rather too favorably, and who denounced Senate strategy—had his own been followed, he rasped testily, Italy would be at peace.[238] And Barbaro begged his correspondents incessantly for political information. "I urge you . . . ," he wrote characteristically to Lorenzo Zane, "that you write me about the republic, even if about something which should be communicated to no one else."[239] These humanists never strayed far from the center of power, though they clothed their shrewd and forceful thoughts in sinuous Latin.

In the Senate and in the piazza, in translations from the Greek, in works on Venice and its history, in correspondence, patrician humanists applied their skills in the service of the republic. They took to heart the message of other Venetians who described learning as a social cement, a force that held the city together. Filippo Morandi da Rimini attributed to the magnificent figure of *eloquentia* an array of social functions. "I am that Eloquence," she intoned, "who inhabits free cities. I move the minds of patricians engaged in the discussion of important matters to do what I wish. I proclaim wars, peace, truces,

---

Marcantonio Sabellico," p. 170. Pertusi remarks that Sabellico's history was admired not by humanists, but by politicians who approved especially the "parte di propaganda o di publicistica espressa in un latino abbastanza brillante tale che far breccia nelle corti più umanisticamente impegnate" (p. 331).

[236] Foscarini's *Epist.*, fols. 15-19ᵛ. Picotti's assessment in "Le lettere di Ludovico Foscarini," p. 32: "La lunga lettera a Paolo Morosini è tra le più belle ed eloquenti scritture del nostro, è la parola d'un cuore che ama sinceramente la patria, che ne piange le sventure, che si sente sopraffatto dei tristi presagi."

[237] "Catenae . . . paupertas, nuditas, squalor, deformitas, luctus, clamor ubique et plurima mortis imago . . . ." Barbaro, *Epist.*, ed. Quirini, p. 249. Foscarini consistently deplores war. The correspondence related to his Genoa mission is especially striking; see G. Zippel, "Ludovico Foscarini." Barbaro shares his love for peace, but is tougher than Foscarini: for assessments of his correspondence, see ibid., and N. Carotti, "Un politico umanista del Quattrocento: Francesco Barbaro."

[238] Barbaro, *Epist.*, pp. 227, 155, respectively—both comments to Febo Capella.

[239] "Te . . . hortor ut . . . ad me de republica scribas, etiamsi cum nullo alio communicandum esset." Barbaro in *Centotrenta*, ed. Sabbadini, p. 85.

leagues, decrees; I propose laws. . . . For the protection of the republic and augmentation of the empire I arouse the very armies and camps."[240] And in another place, he listed the advantages that had accrued to the republic by the self-sacrificing labors of the wise men of antiquity. Had they, instead, wallowed in luxury, "medicine could not bring you health if you were ill, nor could a lawyer assist you in court; no one would protect widows, orphans would be neglected; what protection could ruling majesty provide to an ignorant people, who would there be to rule the state wisely?"[241] The liberal arts, commented Sabellico, "protect the dignity and fortunes of the citizen and the whole body of the republic."[242] Without eloquence, the voice of the *studia humanitatis*, "there never would have been instituted human society among men, no concord could have joined mortals together . . . we would have no cities, no villages . . . no laws, no morals, no institutions, no associations, no assemblies, no leagues, no links would join man to man."[243]

8. CLIENTS

If the links between man and man were forged with eloquent phrases, they chained some men more tightly than others. Though most were, not all the humanists of fifteenth-century Venice were noble. A population of nonpatrician humanists, native and foreign, transient or resident in Venice or her territories, looked to patricians for direction and support. Patricians willingly took up the role as patrons to their clients.[244]

Gabriele Concoreggio was a particularly articulate client.[245] A Mil-

[240] "Ego illa sum eloquentia que in liberrimis urbibus habito . . . . Ego patriciorum mentes in consultandis maximis rebus quo velim exagito. Bella indico, pacem, inducias, societates, scita, leges pono. . . . Ego pro tutanda re publica atque imperio proferendo legiones ipsas et castra succendo." *Invectiva in vanissimos homines*, fols. 46ᵛ-47.

[241] ". . . neque hic medicina salutem invalido tibi dare posset, neque te alter litibus expediret; patrocinaretur nemo viduis, pupillum quis tutandum susciperet, praetoria maiestas ignaro populo quid cautum praestare posset, imperia magistratus consultus quis regeret?" Morandi, *Symposium de paupertate*, p. 179.

[242] ". . . qui civium dignitatem et fortunas, qui totum corpus reipublicae tuentur." Sabellico, *Opera*, fol. 78.

[243] "Nulla unquam inter homines humana societas esset inita, nulla inter mortales coaluisset concordia . . . nullas urbes, nulla oppida haberemus . . . non leges, non mores, non instituta, non coetus, non conciliabula, nullo foedere, nullis vinculis homo homini iungeretur . . . ." Ibid., fol. 74.

[244] For these "important people" who were nevertheless dependent on the nobility, see G. Ruggiero, *Violence in Early Renaissance Venice*, pp. 59ff. and 82ff. Ruggiero observes an ominous process as early as the fourteenth century: "this group of important men without noble status was being converted into a client class" (p. 61).

[245] See Quirini, *Diatriba*, pp. 97ff., 198ff.

anese humanist teaching in Brescia, he was encouraged by Zaccaria Barbaro, Francesco's son, to turn to that statesman for assistance. He did so, using the opportunity of Barbaro's promotion to procurator of Saint Mark, which occasioned a letter of congratulation. To his best wishes, he appended a statement of his desperate condition. His house was full of children and nearly bare of food. Competition was severe. "Now what I can hope in such a throng of pedagogues, I simply don't know. There is no one who does not prefer ignorance to learning, no one who would not rather push his children through school, so that they write in Italian, not Latin."[246] Concorregio begged of Barbaro a government position as secretary, assuring that patriot that though born in Milan, he hated tyrants, and would be loyal to Venice. "I come, therefore, to you—my hope, my salvation, begging counsel and aid. Great men do not spurn their clients."[247] Despite Concoreggio's forceful plea, Barbaro appears to have taken no action until the teacher's second letter, a year later.[248] There, Concoreggio described his circumstances in greater detail. The increased salary that Barbaro as captain had procured for him years earlier was reduced by a third three years after the Venetian's departure. Since then, he had struggled constantly for increases no sooner given than taken away. At this point, the city owed him more than six hundred lire and seemed intent on cheating him of it. Meanwhile, impoverished by the presence of children, he needed help. He asked Barbaro to write to the present podestà, the learned Ludovico Foscarini, "and so commend me to him, that I may in no way feel that your usual kindness and mercy toward me have died. If you do this, which I do not doubt you will do, you will preserve your servant in loyal clientage."[249] Clearly, Barbaro was expected to do as he was told, as though he were as much in need of a client as was Concoreggio of a patron.

Pier Paolo Vergerio was not quite so confident of Carlo Zeno's

[246] "Nunc quid in tanta paedagogorum turba sperem, prorsus ignoro. Nemo est, qui non malit indoctum quam doctum adire, nemo est, qui non malit liberos propere expediri, et potius vulgariter quam latine scribere." Barbaro, *Epist.*, ed. Quirini, p. 216.
[247] "Ad te igitur venio, spem, salutem, consilium, auxiliumque expetens. Summi viri minores et clientulos non sunt aspernati." Ibid.
[248] See *Centotrenta*, ed. Sabbadini, pp. 56, 59. Concoreggio's second letter in Barbaro's *Epist.*, ed. Quirini, pp. 330-31.
[249] ". . . et me ita sibi commendare, ut tuam in me solitam benignitatem, et clementiam nulla ex parte sentiam esse sopitam. Hoc si feceris, quod facturum non dubito, servum tuum fideli patrocinio servaveris." Ibid., p. 331. Barbaro obeyed Concoreggio, writing Foscarini that "our Brescians," known to both men as ferocious warriors, should strive to excell as well in the arts of peace, and recommending that a good position be found for Concoreggio; ibid., pp. 331-32. Bernardo Giustiniani also appears to have felt obligated to satisfy a client's demands; when his attempt to aid the man failed, he abjectly apologized; Giustiniani, *Orat. et epist.*, sigs. L3v-L4.

patronage, but was certainly pleased to be absorbed into that hero's circle.[250] Vergerio warmly thanked the friend who had brought him to Zeno's attention. Because of your words, he wrote, that great man "renowned in peace and war and easily the first citizen of his city, wishes me to be his friend. How can I thank you enough for so great a service?"[251] Arguing that it was in no way shameful to serve a man of such magnitude, Vergerio went to greet him. He had barely uttered his first sentence when Zeno spoke: "He called me by name, taking me completely by surprise, and said that he had heard much about me, and loved me even before he met me; now that I was known to him, he wished me as a friend and not the least among them."[252] For several years, Vergerio sustained his contacts with Zeno, writing the kinds of letters that gratify great men: one congratulating the Venetian on his marriage, another praising him for his victory over the formidable Maréchal Boucicault.[253]

Though Vergerio had not been able to greet the returning hero, as was perhaps his duty, and as so many did, he explained to Zeno that his loyalty was undiminished. "If I could see you more clearly with my eyes than I behold your image in my soul when you are away . . . I would not have delayed coming to see you as soon as I heard the announcement of your return; but, since sight, I judge, adds little to the fruit of friendship, and since the glory of your name has been spread at home and abroad even to those by whom you have never been seen, I easily permitted myself to stay home, failing to number among the first to come and greet you."[254] With this elaborate apology, Vergerio acquitted his responsibility as a client perhaps to Zeno's satisfaction by describing in detail the latter's triumphant campaign.[255]

Francesco Filelfo and Guarino Veronese were both major humanist

[250] For Vergerio's 1398 encounter with Zeno in Bologna, see Robey and Law, "Venetian Myth," pp. 25ff.

[251] ". . . ille me tantus vir, bello ac pace preclarus et in urbe sua omnium facile primus, in amicum sibi desideraret. Quam tibi ego dignam gratiam possum pro huiusmodi beneficio reddere?" Vergerio, *Epist.*, ed. Smith, p. 222.

[252] ". . . ille inter prima fere salutationis verba, cum tale nichil sperarem, nominatim me compellavit, et audisse se multa de rebus meis testatus est, et dilexisse antea quam cognosceret, nunc cognitum in amicum velle et inter suos non postremum . . . ." Ibid., p. 223.

[253] Ibid., pp. 251ff., 269ff.

[254] "Si te ego certius coram visurus oculis fuissem quam absens animo video . . . nichil essem moratus quin ad primum reditus tui nuntium visurus te protinus venissem; verum, quoniam oculorum conspectu minimam esse accessionem in amicitie fructu iudico, et te nominis tui gloria domi forisque parta etiam ad eos quibus nunquam es visus, longe lateque presentem refert, facile michi permisi ne loco nunc moverer, neve te venientem inter primos salutaturus adirem . . . ." Ibid., pp. 269-70.

[255] Ibid., pp. 270ff.

figures in their maturity. When young, however, they had both sought
the assistance of patrician patrons in Venice. Filelfo, encouraged by
Venetian friends, went to Constantinople to learn Greek. He stayed
there several years. On his return, with wife, children, and a valuable
library of Greek books, he stopped in Venice. But the plague had
struck the city, and the friends from whom he expected assistance or
employment were not there. He lamented to each in turn: to Leonardo
Giustiniani, Francesco Barbaro, Marco Lippomano, Daniele Vitturi.[256]
"Your former and most beautiful favors to me," he wrote Giustiniani
in characteristic words, "by which I am bound in perpetual observance
to you, I could never forget or think less splendid."[257] Though they
had all been helpful in the past, no help was forthcoming now. Filelfo
sought greener pastures in other cities, though he retained contacts
with some Venetian friends.[258] Nearly forty years later, however, he
still required the aid of a powerful Venetian. He wrote frankly to
Marco Barbo, the bishop of Vicenza, asking to be adopted among the
prelate's clients.[259] And on behalf of his son, Giovanni Mario, he
turned to a powerful patrician: Bernardo Giustiniani, the son of Filelfo's erstwhile patron, Leonardo. Giustiniani had agreed to assist
Giovanni Mario when Filelfo wrote him delightedly: "For when I see
that same friendship which first prevailed between your father and
me, and then has been so great with you that it could not be greater,
has been transfused as though by a kind of hereditary law to our
posterity, it appears that I and all my family have acquired a wonderful
patrimony. So I rejoice, that you have so responded to my wishes, and
I commend you for being so generous, so kind, so like your father."[260]

Like Filelfo, Guarino had enjoyed patrician support for his trip to

[256] Letters to these patricians from October to November 1427 are the first set appearing in Filelfo's *Epist. fam.*, fol. 1ʳ⁻ᵛ.

[257] "Nam pristina vestra illa erga me et pulcherrima beneficia neque oblivisci unquam
possim, nec minus digna censere, quibus sum obstrictus perpetua observantia." Ibid.,
fol. 1.

[258] The contacts were not always friendly, since he quarreled, without breaking ties,
with Francesco Barbaro and Leonardo Giustiniani in a famous tangle over the rights
to books he had brought with him from Greece. For this controversy, see dalla Santa,
"Di un patrizio mercante"; the comments of A. Oberdorfer, "Di Leonardo Giustiniano
umanista," pp. 118ff.; the recent justification of D. Robin, "A Reassessment of the
Character of Francesco Filelfo (1398-1481)," pp. 205ff.

[259] Filelfo, *Epist. fam.*, fol. 187.

[260] "Nam cum video eam amiciciam, quae mihi primum cum patre tuo, sapientissimo
atque summo viro, maxima fuit, deinde tecum tanta est, ut nihil ad cumulum queat
accedere, transfudi est tanquam haereditario quodam iure in posteros nostros, non
mediocre mihi atque meis omnibus patrimonium adeptus videor. Itaque non possum
mihi non laetari plurimum, quod optatis meis ita respondeas, ut tibi gratulandum
existimem, quod ita humanus es, ita benignus, ita patris tui simillimus." Ibid., fol. 115
(a).

Constantinople. Years later, he was still appreciative of Paolo Zane's financial and moral support. Guarino's son Niccolò had encountered in Venice Marco Zane, the son of the humanist's former patron. Guarino wrote him to express, on behalf of both father and son, gratitude to son and father: "Love me, as you have already begun, and include my son Niccolò in the number of your intimates, and continue to number me, whom you kindly accepted long ago, among [the friends of] the Zane family. [In you still] lives and will live on . . . Paolo Zane, my patron and benefactor, by whose guidance and well-wishing I went to Constantinople and there, honorably sustained by his wealth, slaked my thirst for Greek learning. . . . For his sake, therefore, who was the ornament and glory of your family, I beg you also to love my family, now yours."[261] Even when Guarino was well established in Ferrara as tutor to the d'Este household, he was deferential to Venetian friends. When a rumor circulated that Guarino had written an epigram mocking Venice, the humanist hastened to ask his old friends Andrea Giuliani and Leonardo Giustiniani to defend him against that charge.[262] Giustiniani responded comfortingly that no one believed the rumor among "our magnates," who had long experience of Guarino's loyalty. "For our leaders judge you to be not so much Veronese as Venetian, [you] who built the first foundations of your life, character, and learning among us, who always particularly cherished the friendships, sodalities, and hospitalities of the leaders of our city, who have so many times extolled beyond the stars the glories of Venice in your elegant writings and words."[263] Guarino, one of the century's leading humanists, was a trusted servant of Venice.

None of these figures just discussed spoke explicitly, when they

[261] ". . . oro ut me, ut diutius coepisti, amare pergas et filium Nicolaum in tuorum intimorum numerum ascribas meque in Zana familia iam pridem [vestris] meritis acceptum serves. Vivit vivetque . . . Paulus Zane patronus et benefactor meus, cuius ductu et auspicio Constantinopolim petivi et in ea suis opibus honorifice substentatus graecarum litterarum sitim sedavi . . . . In eo etiam, qui familiae vestrae decus et splendor extitit, diligas et meos iam tuos obsecro." Guarino, *Epist.*, ed. Sabbadini, II, 611. (This relationship also discussed by Pertusi, "L'umanesimo greco," pp. 190-91.) As in Filelfo's case, Guarino's connections with powerful patricians assured protection for his sons, as well. Girolamo Guarini won the favor of Bernardo Giustiniani (Giustiniani, *Orat. et epist.*, sig. L^r-v), and Gregorio Guarini's courtship of Caterina Caldiera was assisted, but not successfully, by Francesco Barbaro (the four relevant letters are in Guarino's *Epist.* II, 556-60; the first three are also in Barbaro's *Epist.*, ed. Quirini, pp. 85, 118-19).

[262] Guarino, *Epist.* II, 363-65.

[263] "Te enim non tam Veronensem nostri homines quam Venetum iudicant, qui prima vite morum et eruditionis fundamenta apud nos ieceris, qui amicitias sodalitia hospitalitates principum civitatis nostre inprimis semper colueris, qui laudes Venetorum totiens elegantissimis scriptis ac verbis tuis super astra extuleris." Ibid., II, 372; also in A. Oberdorfer, "Alcune lettere inedite di Leonardo Giustiniani," p. 315.

addressed potential patrons from the Venetian patriciate, in the tones that Giovanni Mario Filelfo assigns the "client" in the model letters he devised for such cases in his book on epistolography.[264] Yet the pattern of the relationship of client to patron that Filelfo presents there may be a clue to the nature of such relationships in the world of northern urban Italy—and suggests that they were commonplace. The letters are intoned at three different levels of intimacy from "gravis" to "familiarissimus." The "formal" writer points out the advantages of clientage to the patron. Servants, even sons, may be factious and rebellious, whereas clients remain loyal. The "familiar" writer outlines for the patron the obligations he owes his clients. The "intimate" writer stresses the emotional link between subordinate and superior: "I am your client," he writes, "you are my patron. There is nothing of mine which does not pertain to you. . . . For just as I consider that I was created by you when you took me into your clientage, so you do not owe me merely counsel, but favor and aid. . . . For to none do I cede in benevolence toward you and in rare and unbroken faith. Others of your clients are perhaps richer, finer in body, more noble in origin, but none loves you more than I."[265] Did the patrons in such relationships respond affectionately and helpfully to such pleas?

9. PATRONS

They did. When Benedetto Bursa wrote lamenting his great poverty, Leonardo Giustiniani dispatched to him three hundred gold florins, outraged that life could be so hard in a rich city like Bologna.[266] But perhaps he extended more valuable aid to Giovanni da Porto, a lawyer in need of a job. He is dear to me, Giustiniani wrote recommending the supplicant to his friend Barbone Morosini, "because of his love for me and his service to the republic"; it is now your duty to aid him. "It behooves you now to remember that you are a citizen and indeed a nobleman of Venice, who should so far as it can be done with propriety and by the fruits of your studies, improve and advance

---

[264] The *Epistolare Marii Philelfi* is an early humanist work of the *ars dictaminis* tradition, incorporating many of its conventions. For that tradition in general, see R. Witt, "Medieval 'Ars Dictaminis' and the Beginnings of Humanism." The following discussion is based on the exemplary letters at Titulus XXVII.

[265] "Ego tuus sum cliens; tu patronus es meus. Nihil meum est quod ad te non pertineat . . . . Ut enim creatus abs te censeo quando me in clientelam admisisti, sic mihi non consilium debes solum, sed favorem ac auxilium. . . . Nulli enim cedo benivolentia in te singulari ac inconcussa fide. Sunt alii fortasse tibi clientes ditiores, meliores corpore, nobiliores genere, at nullus tui amantior." G. M. Filelfo, *Epist. fam.*, "familiarissimus."

[266] M. Morici, *Per gli epistolari di due discepoli e di un amico di Guarino Guarini*, p. 19.

those deserving well of our republic."[267] Patronage was a duty for these patricians, not merely an occupation of leisure hours.

Francesco Barbaro—once again so articulate where others are silent—defined the obligation of patronage to Paolo Correr, then podestà of Padua, to whom he was recommending a Trevisan physician. "Thus the greatest and wisest rulers of cities in the best times judged themselves most grand and worthy if they gathered about themselves in honorable positions those who had committed themselves to the good arts and finest disciplines." Therefore I beg you to take "this excellent and learned man Antonio, a citizen of Treviso and dear to me, first among your clients," satisfying "both his virtue, and my expectation."[268] Barbaro had made a similar request of Marco Lippomano, and later thanked him for assisting the client recommended. "Once I began this prefecture," wrote Barbaro grandly from Brescia, "by the example and custom of my ancestors, I placed all the Brescians"—all of them!—"in my protection and clientage. Wherefore, as I should, I give you thanks for treating the lawyer Ambrose so kindly, so that because of your good deed he offered great thanks to me. What he wished, or what you did, I do not know. But I am pleased that my recommendation could accomplish this much, that your action has joined this man to us in perpetuity."[269] Once again, these noblemen perceive patronage activity as an obligation, the performance of which could bear the desired fruit of a client's eternal loyalty.

[267] ". . . mihi perquam carissimus est . . . erga r.p. merito, tum veteri et privata in me benivolentia et caritate. . . . Tua nunc interesset meminisse te civem et quidem patricium venetiarum esse qui quoad cum dignitate et fructu studiorum tuorum fieri possit, benemeritos de nostra rep. honestare atque extollere debeas." Leonardo in Bernardo Giustiniani, *Orat. et epist.*, sig. K3ᵛ.

[268] "Sic etiam summi ac sapientissimi principes civitatum temporibus optimis amplissimum sibi pulcherrimumque judicabant, si eos, qui bonis artibus et praestantissimis disciplinis studuissent, in honesto loco dignitatis apud se collocarent . . . . Quae cum ita sint, a te etiam atque etiam peto, ut Antonium praestantissimum ac eruditissimum virum, civem Tarvisinum et mihi carissimum, inter tuos primum suscipias, deinde in hac reformatione existimationis ipsius ita rationem habeas, ut et virtuti suae et expectationi meae satisfacias." Barbaro's *epistola* in Quirini, *Diatriba*, pp. 244-45.

[269] "Postquam inii hanc praeturam, ex more et instituto majorum Brixienses omnes in tutelam et clientelam meam suscepi. Quare sicut debeo, tibi gratias habeo, quia Ambrosium jurisconsultum ita benigne tractasti, ut merito tuo ingentes mihi gratias dixerit. Quid sibi velit aut quid a te sit consecutus, nescio. Sed mihi congratulor meam apud te commendationem tantum potuisse, ut officium tuum praestantem virum nobis in perpetuum devinxerit." *Epist.*, ed. Quirini, p. 72. In an oration to the Brescians (*Diatriba*, 321-23), Barbaro formally adopts those he had led—". . . in tutelam ac clientelam meam magnanimam civitatem istam suscipio . . ." (p. 321). Note also his grandiose and patronizing tone in addressing the Veronese: *Centotrenta*, ed. Sabbadini, pp. 109-10. The term *clientela* often connotes a warm and trusting relationship. Ludovico Foscarini thus referred to his own family's reliance on the saints: "O clementissimum patronum [Saint Victor], qui clientuli sui curam exactam gerit." *Gesta*, fol. 86ᵛ.

Ludovico Foscarini exerted himself strenuously for his clients. He had presented the work of Porcellio Pandoni to the pope, who approved of it, as Foscarini assured the Neapolitan poet. In Venice, too, Porcellio was well reputed. Porcellio was grateful for Foscarini's assistance, and urged him to greater efforts: he was interested in a post as papal secretary.[270] When a rumor circulated against the physician Pantaleone Quagliano, Foscarini wrote in his defense. "Pantaleone has never said nor thought anything improper. Since boyhood he has cherished honor, the friendship of good men, study, and knowledge. He has to the utmost sought, pondered, and tried to achieve esteem. On which account, there is no one of his order in deeds more pious, in healing more effective, in performing responsibilities more diligent."[271] Jacopo Ragazzoni was a particular favorite. From Rome, Foscarini wrote that he would approach the pope on Ragazzoni's behalf. "No office of zeal, none of piety shall you lack; if my efforts can bring you any good fortune I shall think it mine."[272] In time, Foscarini did as he had promised. "At last your poems were given to the pope, written on parchment by the industry of an excellent scribe, lest anything be omitted that might enhance them."[273] Foscarini was present while the poems were read. The pope praised them, and the whole gathering of prelates was impressed. Ragazzoni's introduction had been successful. "I delight in your learning, I shall support your studies and encourage your industry. Wherefore from your elevation to glory, I expect the fruit to redound to me, and those close to me and to all good men."[274] Foscarini had brought his beloved client to the attention of the pope, and now hoped to reap a profit of reflected glory.

Next to Francesco Barbaro, perhaps, the most active patron among this group of patrician humanists was Bernardo Bembo. An array of learned men from the many cities the statesman had visited in his official role addressed works to him. A sampling of these, gathered

[270] The presentation of Porcellio's work and report of his reputation, Foscarini, *Epist.*, fols. 33ᵛ, 34ᵛ; Porcellio's expectations at fol. 67ᵛ.

[271] "Nihil a Panthaleone impium dictum excogitatumve reperietur. Honores a pueritia, bonorum amicitias, studia, disciplinas dillexit. Existimationem quam maximam optavit, cogitavit et conatus est adipisci. Ex quo factum est, quod sui ordinis nemo in bene agendo san[c]tior, in medendo salubrior, in retinendis officiis dilligentior videri potuerit." Ibid., fol. 273. The *ordo* is the professional one of physicians.

[272] "Nullum studii, nullum pietatis officium tibi deerit; si qua tibi bona fortuna opera nostra eveniet, meam putabo." Ibid., fol. 25ᵛ.

[273] "Tandem pontifici data sunt carmina tua pergameno singulari librarii conscripta industria nequid deesset quod ad ea illustranda pertineret." Ibid., fol. 61ᵛ. The following is a summary of the whole letter appearing there.

[274] "Tua doctrina delector, tua studia iuvabo, tue industrie favebo. Quia ex tua laude ac dignitate mihi, meis et bonis omnibus fructum reddundare expecto." Ibid.

by Bembo himself, included works by Giovanni Jacopo Cane, Marsilio Ficino, Cristoforo Landino, Paolo Marsi, and Filippo Morandi da Rimini.[275] Not a passive recipient of such literary gifts, the learned Bembo was asked to read and comment on such works before their publication.[276] Bembo also enjoyed the intimate companionship of learned men. At his bidding, the poet Paolo Marsi of Pescina (who memorialized the journey in the verse collection *Bembice*) and the Venetian secretary Antonio Vinciguerra accompanied him on his embassy to Castille.[277] Vinciguerra was Bembo's companion during his first embassy to Florence, and was included with Bembo in conversations with Ficino's circle.[278] Bembo's letters do not survive to tell us of his patronal sentiments. But sympathy colors the words he thoughtfully penned at the end of a manuscript of Filippo da Rimini's poems on Venice, addressed to him: "These are the hand of the author and the mind of an octogenarian. This poor fellow died when nearly ninety, a fine poet, in 1497 . . . in Venice."[279]

The figure of a sympathetic patron tending to the needs of a dependent if assertive nonnoble client was often encountered. But there were, naturally, exceptions to this pattern. Sometimes the patron found the client unworthy. Ludovico Foscarini, for instance, once refused to assist the delinquent brother of Tito Livio Frulovisi, and Francesco Barbaro advised Francesco della Sega of his client's deficiencies.[280] Sometimes the person seeking aid was noble himself, but poor or powerless or temporarily disadvantaged. Pietro Barozzi, already an orphan, pleaded his great need to the pope when the death of his uncle Giovanni, the patriarch of Venice, left him penniless and vulnerable.[281] Maffeo Vallaresso, who had friendly relations with many noblemen whom he addressed as equals, assumed a distinctly humbler tone toward the powerful Cardinal Pietro Barbo, later Pope Paul II. Vallaresso flattered and petitioned the cardinal, studding his verbal expressions of gratitude with gifts from his remote Dalmatian see: paintings and

[275] The famous Ferrara ms: Bibl. Comunale Ariostea, cod. II 162. Descriptions in Kristeller, *Iter Italicum*, I, 58-59, and G. Baruffaldi, "Relazione."

[276] See della Torre, "La prima ambasceria," p. 260.

[277] For a description of the journey as recorded in Marsi's works, see della Torre, *Paolo Marsi*, pp. 149ff.

[278] For Bembo's Florentine journey, see above, Section 2.

[279] "Auctoris hec sunt manus et ingenium senis octogenarii. Moritur miselus hic fere nonagenarius, poeta bonus, anno salutis MCCCCLXXXXVII die [. . .] Venetiis." Ferrara, Bibl. Comunale Ariostea, cod. II 162, fol. 115.

[280] Foscarini, *Epist.*, fols. 191-92, 196ᵛ-197; Barbaro's *epistola* in *Centotrenta*, ed. Sabbadini, p. 123.

[281] See Barozzi's *Oratio in morte Johannis patrui Patriarchae Venetiarum* in *Orazioni, elogi e vite*, I, 103-27.

medals (Barbo's special passion), figs, and barrels of fish.[282] Ludovico Foscarini lectured Zaccaria Trevisan (the Younger) on his responsibility toward poor noblemen: "You have always been accustomed from your singular mercy toward the poor and from your generosity of soul toward noblemen to take willingly into your *clientela* needy patricians."[283] Recommending the disadvantaged Simone Diedo, Foscarini continued: "Absolutely incredible are your virtues with which the whole of Italy resounds, but none is more gratifying to heaven than this, that you, illustrious by the glory of your name do not neglect inferiors, and none is more pleasing to the senators than that you, most noble, protect nobility."[284]

10. PATRICIANS AND COMMONERS

Just as some noblemen were poor or powerless, moreover, and perceived as dependent clients, some ordinary citizens came from prominent backgrounds, and were treated nearly as equals by patrician friends. Candiano Bollani describes a conversation between himself and two citizen friends—the secretary Jacopo Languschi and the future Bishop Domenico de' Domenichi—where a consciousness of unequal social positions does not intrude on a tone of perfect amicability.[285] The citizen Pietro del Monte, similarly, in his dialogue inveighing against an unnamed enemy of oratory portrays easy relations with patrician friends.[286] More striking is the position of Pietro Tommasi, a citizen doctor, who became the friend and frequent correspondent of Francesco Barbaro and Leonardo Giustiniani, and was known to many humanists within and outside of Venice. Giustiniani invited him to be bolder in a friendship that had long existed "by nature itself," not merely by will, or common studies, or exchange of obligations: "You tell me that you will come to me on what day I command—that neither befits your dignity nor my merit. It is just that occasionally the requirements of office should relax for private obligations and intimacies. Therefore you should prescribe to me by your judgment

---

[282] Vallaresso, *Epist.*, especially pp. 84-85, 256-58, 493-97; for offers of gifts, especially pp. 4 bis, 124, 329, 411-12.

[283] "Consuevisti pro tua singulari misericordia in pauperes, pro animi generositate in nobilles, libentissime patricios egentes in clientellam suscipere." Foscarini, *Epist.*, fol. 236.

[284] "Magne incredibillesque sunt virtutes tuae quibus universa resonat Italia, sed nulla superis gratior quam iam quod tu gloria nominis illustris inferiores non negligas; nulla senatoribus iocundior quam quod tu nobillissimus nobillitati faveas." Ibid. For the problem of poor noblemen in Venice in the sixteenth century, see B. Pullan, "Poverty, Charity, and the Reason of State," pp. 27ff. For the financial pressures on noblemen, see D. Queller, "The Civic Irresponsibility of the Venetian Nobility."

[285] C. Bollani, *Trialogus in rebus futurum annorum XX proximorum.*

[286] The *Invectiva adversus ridiculum quendam oratorem.*

the day and hour in which I may meet with you so that we can talk as you wish whether of the republic or of private matters. I shall defer to you unless public business prevents me."[287] Giustiniani is gracious, but Tommasi had been deferential. The patrician's cordiality does not wholly erase the line that was drawn in Venice between noble and commoner.

The physician Tommasi was a member of that group of commoner humanists which most nearly approached the status of noblemen. His consciousness of the honor accorded the class of physicians in Venice pervades the opening statement of the oration he delivered on their behalf to the city's illustrious ally and powerful guest, Count Francesco Sforza.[288] On occasions of the greatest moment, when all other citizen groups came forth to honor foreign or native worthies, the College of Physicians, proud and secure, stood aloof. Our presence here before you is unusual, Tommasi informed the count, "especially since, from the founding of the city up until this present day, we have come to greet no one. There have come to this city prelates of every kind, cardinals and popes, princes, satraps, and kings, [yet] to none was it the habit of the men of this order of medicine to bow. And what is more amazing, when our new and illustrious ruling doges are created, it is the custom that every group of our city, each individual order, each society, steps forth both to make obeisance and to congratulate him with joyous, festive, and incredible applause—yet the college of physicians by the indulgence of this republic for the sake of its particular dignity has been absolved from this duty."[289] Nevertheless they, too, wished to encourage him in his great venture, promise their prayers, and offer to do what is necessary for his good health.[290]

As a physician, Tommasi was able to provide valuable services to

---

[287] "Nostrum . . . amorem non voluntas modo nostra aut studiorum similitudo aut intercessio officiorum, verum etiam natura ipsa . . . vixisse videtur . . . . Quod autem ad me venturum te dicis quo die iusserim id neque tuae dignitati convenit neque meo merito. Quandoquidem in privatis officiis atque congressibus interquiescere magistratuum iura par est. Itaque tu diem et horam qua te conveniam tuo arbitratu prescribes mihi seu de repu[blica] seu de privata tibi mecum ut ais loquendum est. Ego tibi adero nisi me negotium publicum ad se vocabit." In B. Giustiniani, *Orat. et epist.*, sig. K2ʳ⁻ᵛ.

[288] *Oratio pro collegio phisicorum coram illustrissimi comite Francisco Sfortia.* Little is known about this professional body; see J. B. Ross, "Venetian Schools," p. 529 n. 31.

[289] ". . . praesertim cum ab urbe hac condita hunc usque diem neminem adierit. Fuerunt hanc ad urbem prelati omnis generis, cardinales, pontifices summi; fuerunt principes, satrape ac reges; ad nullum simul cedere consuerunt huius ordinis phisici homines. Quodque magis mirabitur, creantur principes novi nostri incliti duces, pro more civitatis omnis cetus, singulus ordo, queque societas cum inclinatum, tum congratulatum gradiuntur ad eum jocundo, festivo incredibilique applausu, collegium phisicorum rei publicae indulgentia dignitate quadam ab hoc munere est absolutum." Tommasi, *Oratio*, fol. 78.

[290] Ibid., fols. 78ᵛ, 84.

patrician friends: he cast horoscopes—since astrology was one of the fields in which physicians were learned—and gave medical advice. On one occasion, he wrote a *consilium*, a small handbook of sensible health recommendations for two noblemen about to undertake in the service of Venice the hazardous journey across the Alps.[291] Francesco Barbaro, who had taken a vacation on Tommasi's advice and found his health restored,[292] was so much convinced of the healing powers of doctors, that he applied the language of healing to political analysis: "What should we do," he wrote Tommasi, "to relieve or liberate the republic from this sickness, which, lest I am deceived, will not yield to the usual remedies? . . . but indeed a stronger medicine is needed capable of healing so great and so pernicious a disease."[293]

Barbaro here and elsewhere takes Tommasi into his confidence and discusses matters of political concern.[294] That confidence is a measure not only of Tommasi's loyalty, it seems, but also of his status—for he was party to knowledge to which only a limited circle of patricians had access. Tommasi was able on one occasion, for instance, to assure Barbaro that his communications from Brescia were well received in the Senate.[295] On another, he advised Barbaro to write the Brescians, whom he had ruled during a historic siege; they were now demoralized, Tommasi had learned, in the face of new attacks.[296] Ludovico Foscarini also trusted Tommasi with frank discussions of political affairs. Heartsick about the fall of Constantinople, Foscarini wrote the doctor that if his advice had been followed, the city would have been spared.[297] In another letter, he lambasted the peace made with the invaders, then realized that discretion was called for: "But after peace was sworn by decision of the Senate, nothing more should be said . . . I shall contain my words."[298] Here Tommasi, though not a noble, is Foscarini's intimate.

[291] *Consilium medicum.*

[292] Cf. *Centotrenta*, ed. Sabbadini, p. 54; *Epist.*, ed. Quirini, App. pp. 100-101.

[293] "Quod nobis quoque faciendum esset ad levandam Remp[ublicam] aut liberandam hac aegritudine, quae, nisi fallor, consuetis remediis tolli non valet, sed majore profecto opus est medicina, quae tantum ac tam perniciosum malum sanare possit." Barbaro, *Epist.*, ed. Quirini, p. 147.

[294] For examples beyond those given here, see *Centotrenta*, pp. 33, 47, 48.

[295] Ibid., pp. 32, 99-100.

[296] Barbaro, *Epist.*, ed. Quirini, App. pp. 36-38; cf. *Centotrenta*, p. 46.

[297] "Quotiens memoria repeto que tu graviter in Campo Catellano nobis . . . loquutus es cum longe ante videris calamitatem urbis Constantinopolitane impendere, totiens maxime doleo piissimis consiliis et cogitationibus tuis ab illis qui plurimum poterant creditum non fuisse, quasi cruentam miseram et crudelissimam huius barbari historiam non audivissemus . . . ." Foscarini, *Epist.*, fol. 71.

[298] "Sed postquam Senatus consulto pax iurata fuit tacendum est . . . . Ego verba continebo," Ibid., fol. 77[r-v].

Another learned physician known to Barbaro—Giovanni Caldiera—was not on such terms of intimacy with them or other patricians.[299] Indeed, his words betray an exaggerated deference toward the nobility. In his substantial work *On the Excellence of the Venetian Polity*, Caldiera praises as a just institution the exclusive right of the nobility to rule, and their right to bestow that privilege on their descendants. In defining the nature of "magnificence" in his work *On the Virtues*, Caldiera takes delight in describing the weightless obligations that go hand in hand with aristocratic privilege: noblemen should celebrate their daughters' weddings lavishly; they must construct splendid homes, fortresses and cities meant to endure "perpetually," and churches in which divine offices are devoutly performed. They are particularly suited to these functions which adorn and benefit society. Having acquired their wealth from their parents and without labor, they are not inhibited—as would be members, presumably, of Caldiera's own class—from easy spending.[300] Caldiera's admiring attitude toward aristocratic privilege is heard again in his funeral oration for Orsato Giustiniani, the admiral of the Venetian fleet who had recently died a hero's death in the Morea. After praising Giustiniani's family, health and stature, Christian and patriotic zeal, the orator remarked upon his wealth: "For in performing his legations and public magistracies, he always wore golden robes, lined moreover with silk, which were so numerous and so precious that they would have clothed all the patricians of Italy."[301] His house was commensurately splendid, ornamented with gold and silver where other houses displayed only "common stone."[302] In his liberality and magnificence, Giustiniani not only equaled kings, but surpassed them, "so that when he went as ambassador to the emperor, whether Sigismund or Frederick III, he was thought to be the emperor himself, rather than the emperor's orator, just as when he went on Venice's behalf to Alfonso, the illustrious king of Aragon, or other great kings, he was said to be the king himself. . . ."[303] Affluent himself, and descended from a proud citizen

---

[299] For Barbaro's acquaintance with Caldiera, see the Guarino-Barbaro correspondence cited above, n. 261.

[300] The *De praestantia venetae politiae [De politia]; De virtutibus moralibus et theologicis libri octo [De virtutibus]*. A discussion of these works and the third work of the trilogy, the *De oeconomia veneta [De oeconomia]*, appears in Chapter Two, Section 2.

[301] "Nam semper in legationibus suis et publicis magistratibus gerendis semper aureas vestes et que infime magis siricias induebat quarum tantus erat numerus, tanta pretiositas, ut omnibus Italie patriciis [*cod.* patricibus] sufecisent." *Oratio in funere Orsati Justiniani Sancti Marci Procuratoris ad senatum populumque*, fol. 94ᵛ.

[302] ". . . omnis domus aparatus maximus, quare non secus et argento et auro utebatur quam cetere domus uti sutilibus [*sic*] soleant." Ibid.

[303] "Ita ut cum vel Sigismundum vel Federicum Secundum [*sic*; Tertium] imperatores

family, Caldiera was nevertheless in awe of this rich and eminent nobleman.

In lamenting the death of another physician, his friend and the friend of the two noblemen Francesco Barbaro and Andrea Giuliani, the physician Niccolò Leonardi betrays a similar attitude toward the patrician class.[304] In describing Andrea's career, Leonardi illuminates not only that physician's attitude toward Venice's rulers, but his own as well, and perhaps that of many of his coprofessionals. Born in Venice and excellently trained, Andrea "was so much linked by love to the noblemen and other citizens of this city of Venice that they preferred him to all others; who, or perhaps because of his good fortune, prospered so well, that it would be difficult to hope for a better or happier [experience]."[305] Since his house was full of children of both sexes, he arranged to have them instructed in the best arts, "so that they would be not only learned but well bred."[306] As in their education, Andrea's children imitated the pattern of patrician culture in other ways, as well. "He adorned them with clothing worthy of his station, so that crowned with good breeding and adornment they could easily enter the circles of patrician youths. And the girls he rendered so brilliant with honesty and good manners that he could even place them as wives to patrician husbands."[307] Recognizing that Venice was a city devoted to commerce, he had his sons trained in mercantile activities. Enriched by the practice of medicine, which brought him in contact with wealthy noblemen, Andrea strove to raise his children so that the men could become as much like patricians as possible, and so that

orator adivisset, Orsatus hic potius imperator quam imperatorius orator credebatur; sicut cum ad Alfonsum inclitum Regem Aragonum [*cod.* aragonium] et ceteros maximos reges pro veneto dominio orator adisset [*cod.* adiset], potius Rex ipse quam regius orator diceretur." Ibid., fol. 96ᵛ.

[304] Leonardi's *Oratio in funere Magistri Andreae phisici venetiarum*, in this form actually a letter to Barbaro and Giuliani; perhaps the work was delivered as an oration, and subsequently directed in written form to the two noblemen. I am inclined to identify the physician Andrea, who clearly was a well-known figure in Venice, with the physician Andrea de' Mussolini, who treated Zaccaria Trevisan V in his final illness; see Gothein, "Zaccaria Trevisan," p. 49. The following summarizes the substance of the whole brief work.

[305] ". . . huius Venetiarum urbis nobiles ac reliquos cives tanto sibi amore coniunxit ut hunc pre ceteris omnes expeterent; qui vel suis auspitiis tam pulcre sucessit ut dificile sit melius an felicius optare." Ibid., fol. 120.

[306] "Nam cum liberis domum refertam haberet, claram atque optimam utriusque sexus indolem optimarum disciplinarum et bone institutionis magistros prius designavit ut non modo eruditi verum etiam recti morigerati essent." Ibid.

[307] "Vestibusque pro sua dignitate ornavit ut patriciorum adolescentulorum moribus et ornatu coronasset cetus facile ingrederentur; puellas vero honestate moribus doctibus ita claras reddit ut et patriciis viris etiam uxores collocaret." Ibid.

the women could actually marry into—and thus associate his family with—the noble class.

How Leonardi managed his own household is not known, but the echo of the physician Andrea's outlook on the world is detected in the terms of the will of Leonardi's son Girolamo.[308] A learned physician like his father and a dutiful son, Girolamo wished to be buried next to Niccolò in the Church of San Lorenzo. A wealthy man, he mentions in his will money he inherited from his father, four houses, and a country villa. After specifying carefully provisions for the return of several books he had borrowed from other doctors and learned men, and noting that he lacked legitimate children, he arranged to provide for his illegitimate son Vittore a good education, suitable clothing, access to needed books, and professional training in medicine. If he had legitimate daughters, however, Girolamo continued, that provision was to change. "I wish, that if there be one or two daughters, that they be married to Venetian noblemen and have 2000 ducats each [as dowry]. But if there are many, let them be married to citizens from the people, with a respectable dowry as my executors see fit."[309] But if *all* his legitimate offspring were female, Girolamo added, "let them all be married to noblemen."[310] Daughters or no, the bulk of Girolamo's wealth was to descend through males—through the illegitimate Vittore, if no legitimate sons were born to him. And if Vittore were to inherit and have in turn no heirs, a boy of poor but honest family should be chosen, designated heir, and given the Leonardi name. Girolamo shows here a concern with dynasty and status befitting an aristocrat. Members of a privileged profession, the physicians of Venice (and among them the physician-humanists) were close enough to the patriciate to be able to imitate their noble friends in culture and in dress, and to aspire, through their daughters and their fortunes, to be joined to the nobility by blood.

Tommasi, Caldiera, and Leonardi, though commoners, were privileged men. They perceived the abyss between their social position and that of patricians, yet they counted those elevated individuals as

[308] Certainly Niccolò's old age was difficult, and he was unable to place at least two of his sons as he had wished; see his letter to Pier Paolo Vergerio in Vergerio's *Epist.*, ed. Smith, pp. 95-98. It appears from Girolamo's will, however, that Niccolò's daughter (Girolamo's sister) Justina had married the nobleman Ludovico Venier. Girolamo's will (15 March 1466) in ASV, AN, Testamenti Tomei, B. 1240.183.

[309] ". . . volo quod si fuerit una aut duo dentur duobus nobilibus Venetis et habeant duo mille ducatorum pro quodlibet. Si vero plures essent maritentur civibus popularibus cum honesta dote quae commissariis videbitur." Girolamo's will. The sum of 2,000 ducats would have been considerable even in an era of inflated dowries.

[310] ". . . maritentur nobilibus omnes." Ibid.

friends. Pietro del Monte, of a substantial citizen family, was also comfortable with patrician friends. He required their aid to launch a Church career that took him out of Venice to contend with a different and cooler hierarchy. In Venice or abroad in papal service, his letters through the years show him seeking the aid of powerful men.

Del Monte is treated with great cordiality by Ludovico Foscarini, who alludes to a common background and training that crossed the boundary between classes: "There has always been warm feeling between us: born in the same city, educated by the same teachers, trained in the same disciplines, and joined together not only by our own loyalty, but by the friendship between our fathers."[311] Intimate relations with at least some members of the Venetian aristocracy did not blunt for del Monte, however, the reality of his own dependence. That consciousness underlines his profession of delight in performing a service Pietro Barbo had committed to him. In view of that prelate's status, his obligation was clear: "For why should I not undertake labors on your behalf, since you were born of noble lineage and are the pope's nephew, and deserve my profound reverence. Not only the devotion and reverence which I owe the pope urges me to love you, serve you, obey you, indeed, bow to your rule. But also duty to my patria moves me, which since it is common to us, demands that service of me, since I owe my efforts, my labors, and my obedience to your nobility."[312] To Andrea Giuliani, he recalled with gratitude the kindnesses that nobleman had proffered to his distressed family: "You restored the decorum and dignity of my house and family, almost entirely destroyed through the evil actions of certain others, by your counsel and prudence. With many sleepless nights and labors you snatched my inheritance from the maws of the impious, nor did you permit it (because of the foreign air to which it had wrongly been exposed) to be plundered, despoiled, or squandered. My dear mother, my one brother, hearing my counsels and cautions, you protected in your sanctum. In all, the whole cause of all our fortunes you received into your protection and tutelage, to the extent that all my household has been restored by you and liberated from pressing danger."[313]

[311] "Optimo semper inter nos animo fuimus; eadem urbe nati, eisdem praeceptoribus edocti, eisdem disciplinis eruditi, et nedum fide nostra, sed parentum nostrorum amicitia coniuncti." Foscarini, *Epist.*, fol. 281^v.

[312] "Cur enim tui causa labores non subeam qui, cum ex generosa prosapia natus sis et pontificis maximi nepos, magna debes a nobis observantia venerari. Urget me siquidem devotio et reverentia quam pontifici debeo, ut te diligam, te observem, tibi morem geram, tuo denique imperio obsequar. Sed et patrie necessitudo me provocat, que cum nobis comunis sit id a me exigit, ut nobilitati tue meos favores, meos labores et obsequia impendam." Del Monte, *epistola* in J. Haller, *Pier da Monte*, p. 30.

[313] "... domus ac familie mee honestatem ac dignitatem quorundam malis artibus

Although well-connected to members of the Venetian nobility, del Monte depended ultimately for his advancement (since he had chosen that course) not on them, but upon the pope. The pope had sent him on an important mission to England, where del Monte defended tirelessly (as he had also at Basle) the principle of papal authority. Though he had served well, he felt he was insufficiently rewarded. In writing Ermolao Barbaro the Elder from London, he appealed to a friendship begun as schoolfellows, and congratulated the nobleman on a recent preferment. When you have the opportunity, he continued, pressing his friend, intercede for me with the pope to provide me with some kind of benefice: "so that when I go there I may be able to live life, even if not abundantly and magnificently, at least in a mediocre way. For I have always struggled to keep my expenses moderate. It was already time, after I had joined the clerical ranks and had borne many hardships and discomforts for the sake of the pope, that I should taste at last the sweetness of ecclesiastical benefices. Yet even though I wrote often on this matter to many of those living there, still I was never able to gain my wish, but rather was I telling stories to deaf ears."[314] The pope remembered him, del Monte continued, whenever there was hard work to be done, but forgot him quickly when it was time to distribute rewards. "The pope himself, whenever any difficult or laborious matter needs to be done pertaining to the peace and quiet of the Church or his own dignity, immediately remembers me, and without any prompting, knows that it is I who am his legate to this kingdom. Then he orders, commands, and imposes on my shoulders some burdens, and knows my labors are fruitful for him and the Church. These I undertake not unwillingly, but gladly and joyfully. For so my loyalty and reverence toward him require. But when it is time for

---

pene radicitus eversam tuo consilio tuaque prudentia erexisti. Tu hereditatem paternam multis partam vigiliis ac sudoribus ab impiorum faucibus extraxisti neque eris alieni occasione, quod iniuria contractum erat, diripi distrahi aut lacerari permisisti. Tu carissimam matrem fratremque illum unicum meis monitis meisque consiliis audientem tuo exilio protexisti. Denique omnem omnium fortunarum nostrarum causam in tutellam tuam ac patrocinium suscepisti, adeo ut per te restituta sit omnis domus mea et ab imminenti periculo liberata . . . ." Ibid., pp. 90-91. On another occasion of grave need—he had been captured and imprisoned while traveling with the Curia through hostile territory—del Monte was rescued in part by the intercession of Francesco Barbaro; see *Centotrenta*, ed. Sabbadini, pp. 74, 75-76.

[314] ". . . quo, cum istic ero, vitam etsi non habunde atque magnifice, at saltem mediocriter ducere valeam. Nam satis semperque meis sumptibus militavi. Tempus iam esset, ut, posteaquam militia clericali adscriptus sum multa quoque damna atque incommoda pro statu pontificis pertuli beneficiorum ecclesiasticorum dulcedinem aliquando degustarem. Qua de re etsi sepius multis istic existentibus scripserim, nunquam tamen voti compos fieri potui, sed potius surdis visus sum narrasse fabulam." Del Monte, *epistola* in Haller, p. 18.

benefices, for honors, for the rewards of labors, he forgets me entirely, speaks not a word of me, I fall from memory. I am never named, no one knows me."[315]

During the same period, del Monte was in frequent correspondence with the Florentine humanist Poggio Bracciolini, then a member of the papal curia.[316] Del Monte spoke repeatedly to Poggio of his desire to return. He wished to return to the Curia, he wrote on one occasion, "where even if living is slim, if fortune in no way smiles, yet in your company and that of other learned men, in which I greatly delight, I shall console my poverty and make it lighter and milder; and daily I shall be made if not wealthier, at least more learned and more virtuous."[317] After the Venetian's return not from England, but a later embassy for the pope to France, Poggio congratulated him for having impressed the monarch of that country, "who at least does not shy away from learning, and from familiarity with learned men."[318] The Florentine, having had some experience with the struggle for recognition as a man of letters, perceived his Venetian friend as having the same need. Neither poor nor helpless, del Monte nevertheless did not find that advancement came easily. Even his promotion to bishop of Brescia, which he owed to the pope, was accomplished over the objections of Venice. The Brescian Council, who hoped for a Brescian bishop, complained to the Serenissima that del Monte had not been approved by them, and moreover "was not of the nobility, but the populace of Venice."[319]

Domenico de' Domenichi, born, like del Monte, of an august citizen family, also made his career in the Church, outside of Venice, while

[315] "Ipse pontifex, cum quid arduum ac laboriosum pro pace et quiete ecclesie ac dignitate sua agendum occurrit, illico memor est mei et nemine monente scit me in hoc regno eius fungi legatione. Tunc precipit imperat et humeris meis quecunque honera imponit meosque labores sibi et ecclesie fructuosos esse cognoscit. Quos ego non invitus, sed lubens gaudensque suscipio. Ita enim mea in sanctitatem suam fides ac reverentia postulat. Verum ubi de beneficiis, de dignitatibus, de laborum retributione agitur, mei prorsus est immemor, nullum de me verbum facit, a memoria decido, nusquam nominor, nullus me cognoscit." Ibid.

[316] Their correspondence tabulated in Poggio's *Opera omnia*, IV, 738-39.

[317] "... ubi etsi victus tenuis ducendus erit, si fortuna nequaquam arriserit, tua tamen et aliorum doctissimorum virorum consuetudine, qua sane plurimum delector, inopiam meam consolabor, leviorem quoque ac mitiorem constituam, atque in dies si non ditior at saltem doctior ac melior efficiar ...." Zanelli, "Pietro del Monte," 7, p. 361 n. 2. Also Walser, *Poggius Florentinus*, pp. 450-52; summary but no text in Haller, *Pier da Monte*, p. 143.

[318] "Itaque magnum aestimandum est esse principem, qui saltem non abhorreat a doctrina, et doctissimorum familiaritate." Poggio, *Epist.*, ed. Tonellis, II, 281.

[319] "... quod non est de numero nobilium licet sit de vulgo Venetiarum." Archivio Comunale di Brescia, Provvis., 1442, 11 May, Reg. 492, c. 91, cited by Zanelli, "Pietro del Monte," 8, p. 50 n. 2.

remaining friendly with patricians at home.[320] And he, too, was a strong advocate of papal authority; as a canon lawyer, he was a resource of great use to the papacy. He was made bishop of Torcello against Venice's wishes, as del Monte had been opposed in Brescia. Later, when he himself held the see of Brescia, he wrote on the pope's behalf a work critical of Venice's ecclesiastical policy.[321] More successful than del Monte in obtaining preferment in the Church, he was equally alienated from Venice as he pursued his career abroad. Yet in the oration he gave in response to the grant of Roman citizenship, he spoke of Venice's kinship to Rome, and reaffirmed his loyalty to the city of his birth.[322] And on a journey through Venice shortly before he died, he arranged to build a family chapel in the Church of San Zaccaria.[323]

Del Monte and de' Domenichi were aided materially and psychologically by Venetian ties and patrician power as they forged successful church careers. The priest Francesco Negri, in contrast, born in Venice of Dalmatian parentage, was unsuccessful at establishing himself in Venice or elsewhere. Indeed, prior to his departure from the city, he had been imprisoned on suspicion of disloyalty.[324] After leaving Venice, he lived nearly thirty years abroad—in northern Italy, in Hungary, to which country he accompanied Cardinal Ippolito I d'Este, in Rome and the south, working as private teacher and courtier. Years later he reflected on his past: "He still has not found rest, this pauper Negri," he wrote of himself, an "old man and nearing his final year, without any benefice or income, he leads his life in the greatest poverty. But if the rewards of virtue are rightly hoped for, what hope should remain for me?—[I], who have taught and written, for about forty-five years, in every field and in both languages. I taught both publicly and pri-

---

[320] He corresponded with Francesco Barbaro (see *Centotrenta*, ed. Sabbadini, pp. 41, 42, 43, 55) and Francesco's son Zaccaria (Sabbadini, "Andrea Contrario," pp. 431-33), his nephew Ermolao V (cf. Agostini, *Notizie*, I, 438), and his grandson Ermolao G (his *Epist.*, ed. Branca, I, 3-4). The last spoke of the unbreakable links between their families: "Taceo privatas res tuas, quibus tibi nos coniunctissimos facis, cum ita de nobis in dies bene merearis alligesque, ut solus qui nos exolvat Hercules sit expectandus. Veniet autem nunquam; annexos itaque habebis semper." Barbaro, *Epist.*, I, 4. Domenichi also corresponded with Maffeo Vallaresso (the latter's *Epist.*, pp. 523-24, 560-61), and had relations with Candiano Bollani, the governor of Brescia, when he was Bishop, to whom he dedicated a philosophical work (see H. Jedin, *Studien über Domenico de' Domenichi*, pp. 27, 108), and Pietro Barbo (ibid., pp. 11, 23ff.).

[321] His election to Torcello: Jedin, *Studien*, pp. 8ff.; for his *Epistola de non exigendis decimis . . . ad Venetos pro papa*, see ibid., p. 29.

[322] Ibid., p. 38; Jedin "Gasparo Contarini e il contributo veneziano alla riforma cattolica," p. 105.

[323] Jedin, *Studien*, p. 40.

[324] See G. Mercati, *Ultimi contributi*, II, 47ff.

vately in many places, and under my rod have trained many learned men."[325]

Negri's most important work, *On Aristocracy*, he devised and wrote as a tool for gaining reentry to Venice.[326] Carefully molded on the skeleton of another's work—the real author unacknowledged—Negri's importunate plagiarism flatters the nobility, glorifies the role of the pedagogue in the mental and moral formation of that class, and sympathizes with the poor (among whom he ranked) who dwelt in a community ruled by the wealthy.[327] Those who rule do so justly, according to Negri, because their superior virtue has elevated them above others. That virtue descends by blood, so that future generations are able and expected to meet the standard set by their ancestors. Ruled by such worthies, Venice justly rules her empire, and her subjects delight in their servitude.[328] The nurture of the young rulers of the city should be delegated to learned and amply rewarded pedagogues who should train them in the liberal arts, which perfect character.[329] The poor should be exempted from wartime taxation lest, oppressed beyond bearing, they desert their patria or succumb to vice; the burden of war should be borne by the wealthy who enjoy the benefits of political supremacy that are its harvest. At home, wealth should be expended for the public utility, not private pleasure.[330] "It is useful, indeed, and to a citizen family fitting to have—I confess it—a splendid and ample house: but it is more useful to provide for the republic in a time of pressing danger."[331] Remember our origins, Negri cautioned, associating himself with Venice's rooted citizenry, and our ancestors who lived in humble cottages: "how ample, how broad then was their

[325] "Non restat tamen quin pauper Niger, homo senex et iam ad scalarium annum accedens, sine aliquo sacerdotio aut proventu in summa paupertate vitam degat. Quod si virtuti premia iure speranda sunt, quid mihi spei reliquum est? qui per annos circiter quadraginta quinque in omni facultate et in utraque lingua et legi et scripsi. Legi tam publice quam privatim in plerisque locis multosque sub mea ferula in doctissimos viros eduxi . . . ." Negri, ibid., II, 97.

[326] *De aristocratia*. The first redaction of the work, begun 1493 and completed by 1495, was dedicated to Doge Agostino Barbarigo. Subsequently, it was rededicated to the Ferrarese Ippolito d'Este, to a second Venetian Doge, Leonardo Loredan, and to Pope Clement VII. The text was modified to suit the non-Venetian dedicatees. See Mercati, *Ultimi contributi*, II, App. pp. 40ff.

[327] Jacopo della Porcia's *De reipublicae Venetae administratione domi et foris liber* is the exploited source. For the exposure and explanation of the plagiarism, see Mercati, *Ultimi contributi*, II, App. pp. 44ff.

[328] *De aristocratia*, fols. 122ᵛ, 12ʳ⁻ᵛ, 11ᵛ-12 for these points.

[329] See above, Section 5.

[330] Negri, *De aristocratia*, fols. 28-31ᵛ, 35-40ᵛ.

[331] "Utile quidem, et familiae civili honestissimum est (fateor) ornatissimas et commodissimas aedes habere, ast utilius imminente periculo reip[ublicae] providere." Ibid., fol. 36.

empire?"[332] It is better to lavish no money on luxuries, but instead to invest in the education of one's children, counselled Negri, the chronically unemployed teacher under whose rod had sprung up learned men.[333]

At the end of the work, the suppliant author posed his plea to the Doge Agostino Barbarigo. Among all the learned men who flock to your throne, he wrote, "I am the least: . . . yet a servant devoted to your Serenity from my earliest years, . . . I come with a small work, yet written in my own hand, to salute you, and all my goods, my family . . . , and above all myself I devote to you. We are all yours, most excellent fathers, willing subjects of your domination. Test us however you wish: you will find us indeed as faithful in deed as in word."[334] Negri listed his credentials as teacher, as rhetor, as author—noted his poverty—then concluded: "[I was], moreover, what is most important, in this city of Venice born, bred, and taught, and wish also for the dignity and welfare of Venice to die, if need be. Therefore, as you do to others, with your usual clemency and kindness, receive your citizen and priest, whose work, faith, and integrity, if you test it, you will perhaps not regret having found numbered among the others of your republic so faithful a servant."[335]

Negri's humble plea is undoubtedly exaggerated. Yet it suggests the lot of the professional humanist who, though born in Venice, could not satisfactorily establish himself there. Andrea Contrario faced a similar experience. Born of a naturalized citizen family, Contrario as a young man belonged to Francesco Barbaro's circle in Venice.[336] By

---

[332] "Meministisne, patres, quo tempore maiores nostri, humili tecto contenti, soli reip[ublicae] vacabant; quam amplum, quam latum erat imperium eorum?" Ibid., fol. 37.

[333] Ibid., fol. 40r-v.

[334] "Ego quoque minimus inter ceteros doctores minister, vestrae tamen Serenitati[s] servus ab ineunte aetate dicatus, tum exiguo munere, propria tamen manu exarato, salutaturus advenio, tum omniaque bona mea, parentes, . . . cognatos, agnatos, meque inprimis ipsum vobis devoveo. Vestri sumus omnes, excellentissimi patres, vestraeque servituti quam libentissime subditi. Facite, quum volueritis, de nobis periculum: invenietis profecto non minus re quam verbo fideles." Mercati, *Ultimi contributi*, II, App. p. 58.

[335] "Sumus praeterea, quod praecipuum est, et in Veneta hac civitate nati, educati, et instituti, et pro Venetum etiam dignitate et salute emori volumus, si opus erit. Vos igitur vestrum civem et sacerdotem solita ut caeteros facitis clementia et benignitate suscipite; cuius si operam, fidem, integritatem experiemini, non pigebit fortasse tam fidelem inter caeteros reip. vestrae servulum ascriptitium invenisse." Ibid., II, App. p. 59.

[336] Filippo Morandi da Rimini, for example, first approached Barbaro at Andrea Contrario's urging, suggesting Contrario's intimacy with the great man; see Barbaro's *Epist.*, ed. Quirini, App. p. 119. Domenico de' Domenichi, writing to Zaccaria Barbaro, referred to Contrario as Francesco's "favorite"—"olim genitoris tui delitias"—Sabbadini, "Andrea Contrario," p. 432.

middle age, however, he had left Venice and had begun a series of residences in Rome, Naples, Bologna, Florence, and Siena, always in search of work. He had set out for Venice armed by the friendship of Barbaro, among others, and had developed links to other powerful men thereafter. During the pontificate of Pope Paul II he flourished, at one point receiving the adequate but not lavish salary of eight ducats per month. During his last years in Naples, he received a stipend from the royal court.[337] But though he managed to survive, his situation was certainly, like Negri's, precarious. Curiously, the only two professionals among the native-born Venetian humanists—men who lived, or tried to live, by their pens—encountered similar difficulties as they attempted to establish themselves abroad, having failed to make a place for themselves at home.

11. Outsiders

In contrast to the native Venetians who never established themselves in Venice are the foreign humanists who took up residence in that city. Most were teachers of the *studia humanitatis*.[338] As foreigners in the direct or indirect employ of Venetian patricians, they were understandably concerned to gain the approval of those great men. Francesco Filelfo congratulated Pietro Perleone on his new position in Venice, understanding well that his friend's future depended on the generosity of patricians: "That you have taken yourself to the Venetians, those clearly eminent men, I not only approve, but also applaud. For I confidently hope in the future that rewards equal to your learning and virtue will accrue, and that very soon. For these Venetians are such that they never allow themselves to be conquered by a favor, but always pile favor upon favor. And they strive earnestly to be deserving. Therefore, I congratulate your good fortune, that you have at last obtained a position where you may shortly acquire worthy emoluments and also great honor."[339]

[337] For Andrea's attempts to find patrons, see especially his letters to Pope Pius II in Sabbadini, "Andrea Contrario," pp. 415-16, 419-23. For his remuneration under Pope Paul II and King Ferdinand, ibid., p. 386. Contrario was, like Negri, a priest; as for Negri, membership in sacred orders did not interfere with humanist activities or offer satisfactory alternative employment.

[338] Some taught in the public schools, others in a private school or as tutors in a private household. Filippo Morandi da Rimini left teaching for a variety of other roles. The exceptions are Niccolò Sagundino, a foreigner, who obtained a post as secretary, and Paolo Ramusio, who obtained a law degree and then clerked for Venetian governments abroad.

[339] "Quod ad Venetos te receperis, viros plane optimatis, non solum probo, sed etiam laetor. Facile enim futurum spero, ut doctrinae virtutique tuae paria praemia referantur. Idque propediem. Ii enim sunt Veneti, ut numquam se beneficio vinci patiantur, sed

Perleone did come to enjoy ample patrician support, as attested by the letters he wrote to well-wishers during an illness, perhaps his last, late in life. To Marcantonio Morosini and Vitale Lando he expressed great appreciation for kind concern—acknowledging to the former a gift of chickens that were a great consolation to him in his poverty. To the latter, he reviewed the assistance accorded him by Lando and other noblemen, concluding that, indeed, he owed them his life: "From which it appears that to you and the other excellent men to whom my health was a concern I owe my life and confess that I am glad to be in their debt."[340]

Acting on this perception of the generosity of Venetian noblemen, Filelfo urged his sons to go to that city. To his son Senofonte he explained that "the Venetians alone, I have found, in Italy, at this time, revere virtue. The other cities or principalities are stations, not gateways. . . . Furthermore I warn and exhort both you and Mario, and command you both by paternal law, do nothing bold, nothing insolent. If you are modest and quietly restrained, there is a most comfortable place ready for you, and perpetual."[341] His son Giovanni Mario did go to Venice, and appeared before doge and Senate to demonstrate his abilities. In their presence, he dictated extemporaneously to a bank of thirty-two secretaries compositions proposed on the spot—improvisation was his forte. The next day, he submitted evidence of his writing ability. His efforts met with success; he won the competition held in 1460 for the position of teacher at the new school of rhetoric. Francesco wrote to thank his friends and his son's new patron, the Doge Pasquale Malipiero.[342] But Giovanni Mario, not heeding his father's advice, behaved neither modestly nor soberly. He quarreled with Perleone and George of Trebizond (then in Venice), two competitors with him for the position of historian that Ludovico Foscarini, among others, wished to establish.[343] The young Filelfo left

---

officium semper officio cumulent, et maximo opere promereri studeant. Gratulor igitur felicitati tuae, qui in eos sis loco tandem collocatus, ubi et emolumenta sis non vulgaria, et laudem item maximam brevi assecuturus." Filelfo, *Epist. fam.*, fol. 99ᵛ.

[340] "Quo fit ut tibi reliquisque optimis viris quibis mea salus cure fuit vitam debeam et debere me velle profitear . . . ." Perleone, *epistola* in cod. Vat. Chis. J VI 215, fol. 177ʳ⁻ᵛ. For the chickens, fol. 176ᵛ.

[341] "Nam soli Veneti mihi visi sunt, hac tempestate, in Italia, qui virtutem colant. Reliquae vel civitates vel principatus stationes sunt, non portus . . . . Praeterea te ac item Marium moneo atque hortor et pro jure paterno vestrum utrique iubeo, nequid agatis temere, nequid insolenter. Si modestia volueritis et gravitate uti, quietissima istic vobis et commodissima sedes parata est, eaque perpetua." Filelfo, *Epist. fam.*, fol. 110. The following account of Giovanni Mario's experience in Venice is from G. Favre, *Vie de Jean-Marius Philelphe*, pp. 88ff.

[342] The letter to the Doge in Filelfo, *Epist. fam.*, fol. 115ʳ⁻ᵛ.

[343] Nasty quarreling among competitors was common. Tito Livio Frulovisi offered

Venice in a huff, sealing his departure with a nasty invective directed against George of Trebizond. Perleone, Francesco's old friend, complained to the father about the son; Francesco, furious with his offspring, mollified Pietro.[344]

The Corsican priest Pietro Cirneo was able to establish himself securely in Venice with the favor of a patrician family, although his rewards fell far short of the "not vulgar emoluments" that Francesco Filelfo anticipated from patrician employers. At first he worked for the printing presses, abandoning that tedious labor whenever funds allowed him to engage in serious studies. These he pursued under the tutelage of another resident foreigner, the more famous Benedetto Brognoli, with whom he studied for twelve years, having begun as an adult at age thirty-three. Meanwhile, he entered the household of Andrea Capello as tutor to that nobleman's two sons. In that household where he labored by day, he studied—as he himself tells us—all night, daunted but not thwarted by a jealous rival (his roommate). His labor for the family was not sufficient to support him. Capello arranged a church position for Cirneo in the nearby Santa Maria Mater Domini, by which he could supplement his income. At his death, Cirneo left to his heirs a substantial library and some few sparse possessions. He appears to have felt great affection for the Capello family, which had protected though not enriched him. Of the twelve ducats they still owed him, he forgivingly ordered six restored.[345]

Though his long years of Venetian residence were filled with success and acclaim, Giorgio Merula did not, like Perleone and Cirneo, commit himself permanently to his adopted city. One of the great philologists of the century, his interests precisely suited Venetian tastes. Born in Alessandria, he came to Venice in 1465. Beloved by Venice's learned patricians, he held for nineteen years the chair of rhetoric the surly Giovanni Mario had abandoned. His relations with learned noblemen are marked by the trail of dedications of his critical works: to Ludovico Foscarini, Marcantonio Morosini, Bernardo Giustiniani, Domenico

as a solution the recommendation that a government school be established in each quarter of the city and staffed by a paid public teacher; see the introduction of C. W. Prévité-Orton to the *Opera hactenus inedita Titi Livii de Frulovisis de Ferrara*, p. x n. 9.

[344] Giovanni Mario's *Invettiva contro Pietro Perleone e Giorgio Trapezunzio*; for Francesco's attempts to soothe Perleone, see Favre, *Vie de Jean-Marius Philelphe*, p. 92.

[345] The testament is summarized (not published) in G. dalla Santa, "Un testamento." For Cirneo's struggle and devotion to study, see the autobiographical passages of his *De rebus corsicis libris quattuor a temporibus romanorum usque ad annum MDVI*, cols. 483-506.

Giorgi, Jacopo Zeno, and Bernardo Bembo, among others.[346] Even
after he left Venice for a more attractive position in Milan, he remained
friendly with Ermolao Barbaro the Younger, the most conspicuous
figure of Venice's late-century humanism. On Barbaro's youthful and
lonely death, Merula sent the nobleman's friend Antonio Calvo a letter
of praise and lament.[347]

Before Barbaro had entered that last phase of his life in Rome, he
had taken a role in finding a successor for Merula at the school of
rhetoric. On Merula's advice, he favored Giorgio Valla of Piacenza,
a humanist of philological and encyclopedic interests. The Senate offered Valla the position. When Valla did not respond, Barbaro anxiously wrote Merula: "For I have promised the [city's] leaders that he
would come, and assumed that the salary was settled. That shall be,
as we wrote, 150 ducats, a nearly unprecedented sum; it remains only
that I honor the pledge, which I gave the fathers concerning him. Daily
and hourly I am summoned; my goose will be cooked, not merely if
he does not come at all, but if he delays."[348] In the end, Valla came
to Venice in 1485, always hoping to be able to return to Milan. After
teaching eleven years, he fell under the suspicion of the Council of
Ten, was imprisoned, released, and died three years later.[349]

Merula had been lured to Milan after nineteen years in Venice. Valla
would have preferred Milan to Venice—and was imprisoned, in fact,
because of his relations with the Milanese—and his Venetian career
was marked by difficulty. Venice seems not to have been hospitable,
in spite of the high opinion of her rulers held by Francesco Filelfo, to
two of the most important humanists who came to her from abroad.
Marcantonio Sabellico, however, knew how to serve his masters well,
and settled comfortably into the Venetian milieu. His history of Venice
won the enthusiastic approval of the Senate.[350] His works on Venice
or on subjects of interest to Venetian rulers he poured out and dedi-

[346] For his relations with these figures, see F. Gabotto and A. Badini Confalonieri,
"Vita di Giorgio Merula," first part, 282ff.; also Merula's profile.

[347] In A. Zeno, *Dissertazioni vossiane [Diss. voss.]*, II, 394-95. For Barbaro's last
years, see Chapter Two, Section 10.

[348] "Pollicitus enim sum principibus venturum eum simulatque constituta merces esset;
ea porro, quemadmodum scripsimus, centum quinquaginta nummorum, quanta fere
nemini decreta; reliquum est ut fidem, quam de ipso patribus dedi, praestem. Singulis
et diebus et horis appellor ut decoquendum mihi sit, non dico si non venerit omnino,
sed si venire distulerit." Barbaro, *Epist.*, ed. Branca, I, 78.

[349] For Valla's 1496 trial, see F. Gabotto, "Giorgio Valla el il suo processo in Venezia
nel 1496," and G. dalla Santa, "Nuovi appunti sul processo di Giorgio Valla."

[350] Not, however, as had been supposed, the official post of public historiographer;
see F. Gilbert, "Biondo, Sabellico."

cated to an array of powerful patricians: *On the Site of the City of Venice*, for instance, to Girolamo Donato; *On Venetian Magistracies* to Doge Agostino Barbarigo; *On the Office of Governor* to Antonio Corner, the governor of Vicenza.[351] His attitude toward these noblemen was servile. From some, he sought favors.[352] Launching his funeral oration for Zaccaria Barbaro, he sketched his position as client of all of Venice's great men, the dead as well as the living: "There is nothing, most Serene Prince, Fathers, and revered gentlemen, which I have either more often nor more conscientiously prayed of God Almighty, than that if I have any talent, any skill in speaking, any beauty or abundance of expression, if, finally, my studies have been or can be of any use, it is proper for me to employ them at every time, in every place, on any occasion, and to celebrate your honor and glory that for the sake of the public and private beneficence of your order toward me, I should be grateful not merely toward you, great Prince Agostino, and toward these patricians who with you today both felicitously and wisely govern Venice, but [I] also should remember gratefully and dutifully those who have departed from this life."[353] As the beneficiary of the public and private generosity of the noble class, Sabellico had a long and successful career in Venice—even receiving in retirement a generous pension of two hundred ducats, "lest failing or in health, he be forced to experience poverty."[354] It is a mark of Sabellico's success that his Venetian-born friend, Francesco Negri, whose experiences were noted earlier, turned to him for aid. He appealed to the closeness between them rooted in their "similar condition," referring to the work he had

[351] The *De situ venetae urbis libri tres, De venetis magistratibus liber unus*, and *De praetoris officio*. See profile for other works.

[352] Note the obsequious tone, for instance, of his letters to Sebastiano Badoer (fols. 9v-10) or Girolamo Donato (fol. 35); he requests favors of Girolamo Giorgi (fol. 26v, 42v-43), Domenico Grimani (fol. 45v), Bernardo Bembo (fol. 49); all references from his *Epist. fam.* in the *Opera*.

[353] "Nihil est, serenissime princeps, patres et viri amplissimi, quod ego aut saepius aut intentius sim solitus a deo optimo maximo precari, quam sive ingenii in me est, sequid dicendi facultas, siquis cultus copiae in sermonis, siquis denique meorum nunc est studiorum usus aut deinceps esse poterit, hunc ipsum ita mihi omni tempore, loco, occasione disponere liceat, vestrisque laudibus et ornamentis accommodare, ut pro publica et privata amplissimi ordinis uestri in me beneficentia non in te tantum, Augustine princeps optime, et in hos viros patritios, qui hodie tecum rem Venetam tam feliciter quam sapienter administrant, grato sim animo existimandus, sed grata etiam piaque in eos memoria, qui ex hac vita decesserunt . . . ." *Oratio in funere Zachariae Barbari*, fol. 70.

[354] ". . . stipendium tamen suum annuum ducatorum ducentorum in senii sui sustentatione consequi et habere consuetis temporibus debeat, ne senex vel valitudinarius pauperiem experiri cogatur . . . ."; from a Senate act of 29 July 1505, Zeno, *Istorici*, I, lviii. The pension was equal to full salary.

designed to reestablish himself in Venice: "Promote my *Periarchon* [the *De aristocratia*]," he pleaded, "among your patricians."[355]

Filippo Morandi da Rimini, an immigrant of prominent family from that city, has left the most substantial statement of the condition of a nonnoble humanist in a city dominated by patricians. He dedicated to Francesco Barbaro his *Conversation on Poverty*, as a poor man offering to a wealthy one a gift of words constituting a plea for assistance.[356] The dialogue presents several forms of poverty, and while lamenting or condemning most, honors two: the traditional poverty of the Christian in search of salvation, and the voluntary poverty of the sage who sacrifices material comfort to the pursuit of learning— a figure with whom Filippo certainly identified. Filippo, hoping to mollify the terrifying figure of poverty by whom he had been bedeviled, wrote in the preface to Barbaro, with a fitting literary tribute. He hoped as well to move Barbaro's heart.

If that was his aim, he achieved it. Barbaro became Filippo's patron. The role the nobleman played for his client in the years before Barbaro's death is noted from the words of the unusually expressive funeral oration Filippo delivered in his honor. "For a while I was permitted to enjoy you, you, Barbaro, whom I called my second father, you, Barbaro, who was my promoter and my never-failing defender, you, Barbaro, the pillar and refuge of my fortunes."[357] Filippo lamented the ill fortune that had betrayed him, "orphaned of an incomparable friend and patron, and a first and present protection of my whole existence."[358] He recalled fondly the congregations at Barbaro's home of learned men. But when he dwelled on those pleasures, he was overcome with grief at the loss of "Francesco . . . my one solace, whom I called my Cicero, my Demosthenes and Hortensius, whose speech I so admired, so venerated, that I always hung from his words and anchored there all my thoughts and all my life's principles."[359] Filippo's

[355] "Periarchon nostrum, ubi et tu quoque decantatus es, apud hos patritios tuos pro tua humanitate foveto . . . ." Sabellico, *Opera*, fol. 48.

[356] For this interpretation, see M. L. King, "A Study in Venetian Humanism at Mid-Quattrocento," especially Part Three; for Filippo's diligent search for a patron, Part One.

[357] "Nam dum te frui mihi licuit, quem parentem alterum adpellabam Barbarum, quem fautorem et defessum numquam propugnatorem meum Barbarum, quem columen et perfugium fortunarum mearum Barbarum." *Oratio in funere Francisci Barbari*, fol. 9ᵛ. The choice of Filippo as a eulogist shows at once the esteem the Riminese native enjoyed in Venice, and public recognition of his relation to Barbaro.

[358] "Sic de me triumphavit [i.e., fortuna sua] orbato amici incomparabilis et patroni praesentia et tutela omnium apud me rerum prima." Ibid., fol. 10.

[359] ". . . Franciscum . . . solacium meum unicum, quem meum Ciceronem adpellabam,

dependence on his patron, it seems, was absolute. With profound meaning, he cried to the patrician Senate: "Barbaro, it is I, it is I, that you by dying have killed. You were worthy of vital life, not death; when you gave up your noble spirit, it is indeed I that you summoned to the grave."[360] With the support of patricians, these teachers gained a reasonable livelihood. Without it, they were vulnerable.[361]

12. THE ORDER OF SCRIBES

Holding a more secure position were the government secretaries, largely drawn from the citizen class. For them, as for the physicians examined earlier, humanist studies were a secondary concern. Their primary occupation was to serve Venice. As key servants of the Venetian republic, they shouldered heavy responsibilities (the consciousness of which encouraged their cohesion), and enjoyed rare privileges.[362] Marcantonio Sabellico outlined the duties of a secretary in his dialogue *On the Duties of Scribes*.[363] Marco Aurelio, a secretary and humanist, is the main speaker. The scribe should come from a substantial background, recommends Aurelio, and possess several virtues. He should know several languages, excel in speaking, and be expert in law—all these—though frankly some ignorant secretaries had ascended to high positions. Tenacious loyalty is as essential as learning. The scribe should be discreet—for he was entrusted with sensitive business—and urbane, able to deal smoothly with people. He should be industrious and prudent. The accomplishments of the army of Venetian secretaries lent them a fine sense of confidence. "Daily we see," said Aurelio in

---

meum Demostenem et Hortensium, cuius dicta ita mirabar, ita venerabar, ut semper ab ipsius ore penderem, penderent et consilia mea et omnes mee vite rationes." Ibid.

[360] "Me, me, Barbare, moriens exanimasti. Vita vitali digne, non morte, cum tuum spiritum illum nobilem amisisti, ad interitum pene me vocasti." Ibid., fol. 9ᵛ.

[361] This condition of vulnerability can be doubted in some individual cases. Cristoforo de Scarpis, for example, though he hopped from position to position, acquired considerable wealth; see A. Segarizzi, "Cristoforo de Scarpis." The general pattern, though, is otherwise. Note the examples, in addition to those already mentioned, of the insecurity of Giovanni Pietro Vitali d'Avenza (see G. Sforza, "Della vita e delle opere di Giovanni Pietro d'Avenza," and, in a later generation, of Giovanni Battista Egnazio (see Ross, "Venetian Schools," pp. 536ff.). Gilbert notes with regard to the rather successful teacher Marcantonio Sabellico "the low, or at least uncertain, position of a professional humanist in the Venetian social structure" ("Humanism in Venice," p. 16). There is a similar judgment by Pastore Stocchi, "La scuola e cultura umanistica," p. 104 and passim.

[362] Part Two, Preface, Section 13, for the office of secretary. In spite of their considerable influence on public affairs, however, the secretaries, like the teachers, were dependent on patrician favor. Ruggiero comments that they "subsisted at the mercy of the nobility" (*Violence*, p. 60).

[363] *De officio scribae liber unus, dialogus*, in *Opera*, fols. 115-17ᵛ. The following discussion summarizes this work.

the words given him by Sabellico, "the learned men of our order going forth with dignity on important legations to great princes and powerful kings—[an achievement] not to be expected from an ignorant man, who would lack both the learning and prudence [required]."[364]

Others, as well, perceived the cadre of secretaries as an "order," a clearly defined group. Francesco Contarini wrote that he was accompanied on his legation to Siena by Febo Capella, "from the order of scribes."[365] In a letter to the secretary Marco Basilio, Niccolò Sagundino sent regards from Rome to the "men of our order."[366] Marino Becichemo saluted, at the close of a letter to a friend, the "splendid college" of scribes, and consoled the government secretaries as a group for the death of their head, the grand chancellor.[367] The grand chancellor, chosen from among the secretaries, was one of the most revered men in Venice. No commoner could aspire to higher office—and it lent considerable status to a secretary that membership in the "order of scribes" entailed eligibility for that post. Giovanni Dedo was conscious of the plum he had earned when he was elected grand chancellor, though he attributed his election to divine will rather than his own merit. In thanking a friend for a letter of congratulations, he wrote: "you say that I was chosen for this office from among many worthy competitors because of my innate goodness, lofty learning, rare loyalty, virtuous life, wondrous diligence in attending to duties. . . . But I do not assume that I have been elected to this dignity from among so many excellent men because of my virtues, but rather by the highest and unitary will of the trinity."[368] When Dedo died, his eulogist praised that "prince of scribes" for his worthy origin, his devotion to Venice, and his love for the college of secretaries: his "rare benevolence toward

---

[364] "Quotidie praeterea videmus eruditos nostri ordinis viros amplissimas legationes apud summos principes potentissimosque reges cum dignitate obire; quod ab imperito homine quia eruditione ac proinde prudentia caret expectari non potest." Ibid., fol. 116ᵛ.

[365] ". . . e scribarum ordine." Contarini's *De rebus in Hetruria gestis*, p. 2.

[366] ". . . amicos omnes et ordinis nostri homines ad unum ex me salvere iube." Sagundino, *Epist. et opusc.*, fol. 72ᵛ.

[367] He salutes Niccolò Aurelio and the "splendidissimum Collegium scribarum" in a letter to Giovanni Battista Guielmo, and consoles that group (p. xxiv) at the close of the funeral eulogy for the Grand Chancellor Giovanni Pietro Stella (pp. xv-xxiv); in M. Becichemo, *Orationes duae*.

[368] ". . . ad id autem quod dicis me a pluribus competitoribus dignissimis hoc habuisse huiusque rei causa fuit innata bonitas, summa doctrina, fides singularis, vitae integritas, miranda in agendis rebus diligentia . . . . Noli igitur . . . mi arbitrari me in hanc dignitatem ex tot viris praestantissimis meis virtutibus electum esse sed pocius summe et individue trinitatis voluntate . . . ." Dedo's letter to Baptista Fregosus in the miscellany cod. Marc. Lat. XIV, 267 (4344), fols. 67ᵛ-68, at fol. 67ᵛ.

the whole of our order," to whom he was like a father.[369] An elite group of highly skilled men under the guidance of the chancellor, the "college of scribes" resembled the patriciate itself—privileged men grouped about a doge.

A reputation for learning and loyalty, the possession of discipline and skills, a tradition of reliable service, and perhaps, above all, access to the secrets of government councils and the ears of powerful men enhanced the status of these secretaries. Certainly they had the respect of patrician friends. Ludovico Foscarini turned to the secretary Giovanni Reguardati for advice about a letter he had written to a papal legate. Since he would rather be "timid than impudent," Foscarini asked the scribe to judge if the letter were worthy of a Venetian patrician and would meet the approval of the Council of Ten—the Council in which Reguardati was employed. Do so, he wrote, trusting the citizen with a sensitive problem "lest I unknowingly in any way injure public majesty, for the honor of which I shall not say what I have done, but I would think it beautiful and holy to die [for it]."[370] Even more revealing, perhaps, is Foscarini's relationship with the secretary and humanist Marco Aurelio, through whom he hoped to get the ear of the doge. He asked Aurelio to look for the optimal moment, then state Foscarini's case. "Since I do not dare to write to his excellency lest I be seen as importunate, and he will more willingly hear you than read what I write—for that is rather harsh, while you by your sweet speech will make it sweeter than honey."[371] Francesco Barbaro, too, wrote extensively and frankly to the secretary and humanist Febo Capella about political matters. On one occasion, relying implicitly on Capella's political judgment, he asked the secretary to

---

[369] ". . . singularem . . . erga universum ordinem nostrum benivolentiam." B. Comino, *Oratio pro funere Ioannis Dedi veneti scribae maximi,* fol. [4].

[370] "Scis et ego memoria teneo quid mihi fideliter et sapienter consulueris, sed quia in rebus p[ublicis] malo timidus quam impudens iudicari, iterum abs te peto epistolam nostram ad R.mum legatum legas acri rectoque ingenio non amico ut soles omnia iudices, antequam sequaris. Si eam dignam patricio veneto censebis decem virorum auctoritate firmes, ne publicam maiestatem inscius aliqua ex parte ledam, pro cuius dignitate quid egerim taceo, sed pulcherrimum sanctissimumque mori existimarem . . . ." Foscarini, *Epist.,* fol. 85.

[371] "Si tu qui gratissimus tua sapientia et virtutibus principi, novisti serenitatis sue ocia, quando libero animo aures adhibere volet, me illius sublimitati commendabis, spem desyderiumque nostrum vel universum vel in partes divisum prout tempus nactus [fueris declarabis]. [Quia] non audeo excellentiae suae scribere ne importunus videar, et te libentius audiet quam scripta nostra leget, que licet asperiora sint, tu eloquii suavitate melle dulciora reddes." Ibid., fol. 346; letters to Aurelio on fols. 345-46 (cited here), 347v-350. See also Foscarini's letters to Ulisse Aleotti, whom he asks to assist Senofonte Filelfo (son of Francesco) by introducing him to learned patricians; at fols. 174-75. Also letters to Alessandro de' Fornaci, fols. 21-25, 35v-37v.

report, "if you have time to breathe, not only what has been happening and what is happening, but even what you expect will happen."[372]

Secretaries were not only party to important information and close to some important members of the ruling elite, but were entrusted with important missions in Italy and abroad. Niccolò Sagundino—a figure to be looked at more closely later—was sent to describe Turkish military strength and culture to the pope in Rome and King Alfonso in Naples.[373] Marco Aurelio was sent to Rome to handle affairs during the sickness and subsequent death of the noble ambassador Leonardo Sanuto, and to Corfù to negotiate peace with the Turks.[374] Antonio Vinciguerra was sent on many important missions.[375] His mission to Veglia involved major responsibilities. He persuaded the Frangipane ruler to abdicate, ceding the island to Venice; he supervised the island as invaders were repelled, and was made in the end governor of the island. It was unusual for the latter post to be held by a nonpatrician; indeed, Vinciguerra's successor was noble. His thorough *relazione*, requested by the Senate, testifies to his clear-sighted management of a difficult situation, the outcome of which was advantageous to Venice.[376] Later, Vinciguerra was sent to arrange the hire of Venice's mercenary forces during the Farrarese war—a sensitive and important enterprise—and, after that war, was sent to negotiate with Roberto Sanseverino. Though it was thought in the Senate more appropriate to elect a nobleman, Vinciguerra was sent to Rome to recall the ambassador Antonio Loredan, suspected of sodomy. While in Rome, he was instrumental in arranging a peace treaty between Venice and the pope—during which negotiations he so impressed Innocent VIII that the pontiff wished to hire him. After a second assignment to Veglia, Vinciguerra was dispatched to Crema and Bologna. By the termination of his Bologna legation, Vinciguerra had accumulated an impressive record of more than twenty years of diplomatic service. The next few years he spent quietly in Venice, perhaps in the house of his patron Marco Giorgio, working on the vernacular poetic satires for which he is famous.[377]

---

[372] "Quare, si quod tempus habes respirandi, mihi significes non solum, quae gesta sunt et quae gerantur, sed etiam quae gerenda suspiceris . . . ." Barbaro, *Epist.*, ed. Quirini, p. 57. See also *Centotrenta*, ed. Sabbadini, pp. 42, 48, 49, 60, for letters to Capella.

[373] See F. Babinger, *Johannes Darius*, pp. 18ff.

[374] See Malipiero, *Annali*, pp. 242, 71.

[375] For these missions, see now the careful biography of Beffa, *Antonio Vinciguerra*, correcting della Torre's *Antonio Vinciguerra*.

[376] *Relazione sull'isola di Veglia.*

[377] For editions of the *Satire*, see Beffa, *Antonio Vinciguerra*, p. xiii. I have used the *Satire di Antonio Vinciguerra, Lodovico Ariosto, Ercolo Bentivoglio, Luigi Alamanni,*

Vinciguerra, whose whole life virtually from childhood was spent in republican service, was surely one of Venice's most loyal and trusted servants. The demands of his career and the discipline that Venice required must have left little opportunity or spirit for reflection. Yet his verse *satire*, orthodox in their political and religious perspectives, are at moments intensely personal. They reveal in Vinciguerra a consciousness of himself as an intellectual, subordinated to ignorant men, and as a poor man, surrounded by wealthy ones. His satire, for instance, *Against the Deadly Sins* is not only an ascetic treatise but a lament for the condition of learned men.[378] The poet grieves for the muses who work for money, for the wise subjected to the ignorant, for fine minds confined to low places, for the arts in ruins. The true poet must renounce the world. From lofty retreat, he looks down to see "the sceptre in the hand of ignorance, which has destroyed all good."[379] As a learned man and a poet, the author feels himself to be elevated above the vulgar masses, above those who pursue wealth. They think they can in a minute understand what must take a thousand years of learning and reflection. They prize their rich meals, proud palaces, soft vestments. But the poet rises above these, for his fame transcends centuries and distances. Though "on my lagoons," wrote the Venice-born Vinciguerra, my mind carries me to the shores of distant oceans.[380]

With Leonardo Giustiniani, the other major poet among our humanists, Vinciguerra speaks perhaps in the most natural voice of the century. And in speaking, he reveals himself not as, at heart, the servant of Venice—though patriotic sentiments fill his verse as well—but as a poet, rooted in an ancient tradition of learning, dazzled by but resistant to the dazzling wealth of the mighty of his age, austerely pious, and proudly independent. Perhaps because he was not a patrician, though he lived his life among the nobles of Venice and worked in their interests, he was able spiritually to detach himself from the narrow political realm and look more broadly at himself and the world. Yet he remained loyal to Venice and her rulers, and the political life infuses his work and language: he referred to heaven, for instance, as his

Lodovico Dolce. A. Sopetto publishes four not contained in this or other printed collections in *Le satire edite ed inedite di Antonio Vinciguerra.*

[378] The *Contra vitia capitalia*, in the *Satire di Antonio Vinciguerra*, pp. 16-30. See the discussion of della Torre, pp. 126ff.

[379] "il scettro in mano/all'ignoranza, ch'ha ogni ben distrutto." *Contra vitia capitalia*, p. 30.

[380] Quoted by della Torre from the *Contra falsum et imperitum vulgi iudicium*, in *Antonio Vinciguerra*, p. 139. The edition of the *satire* I have seen does not include this line.

"celestial *patria*." And in consoling a friend for the death of a virtuous daughter now surely in glory, he spoke of the blessed who cross this dark valley and become "true patricians" in heaven.[381] A citizen himself, Vinciguerra seems to project his profoundly rooted sense of caste into eternity and to long for that ennoblement.

Also a trusted secretary, employed often by the republic on sensitive and difficult missions, Niccolò Sagundino did not have Vinciguerra's gift of detachment. He struggled throughout his life for a secure and settled position in Venice for himself and for his family, barely united, it seems, in his adopted city when torn apart in a tragic shipwreck. In the midst of struggles and calamities, however, he remained a dedicated humanist. By birth Greek-speaking but expert in Latin, he wrote on rhetoric and theology, on the history of the Ottoman Turks—a topic of pressing interest in the latter part of the fifteenth century—and on philosophy.[382]

Living in his native Negropont, but in Venetian employ, Sagundino tutored Fantino Coppo, the Venetian governor, in philosophy. Later, on Coppo's request, Sagundino put his lessons in writing and dedicated them to that nobleman.[383] In his introductory words, Sagundino describes a charming scene. Coppo, wishing to relax in the leisure hours when public responsibilities did not press, turned aside from luxury and scurrilous jokes "or other things of this kind scarcely worthy of a free man," and from hunting or hawking, and applied himself to reading and literary study, knowing "that there could be collected and imbibed from these an honest and fruitful sweetness."[384] In this enterprise, he took Sagundino as his companion, choosing "me as the ally and partaker of your labor."[385] "And we did not lack, when public

---

[381] "chi con virtute in questa oscura valle/ Cercan farsi del ciel veri patrici." *Consolatoria de morte filiae*, to Giovanni Caldiera, pp. 31-45 in the *Satire di Antonio Vinciguerra*, at p. 45.

[382] For Sagundino's many works, see the thorough catalogue by P. D. Mastrodimitris, Νικόλαυς ὁ Σεκουνδινός, pp. 113-223 and 261-65; some works are also cited in the notes following and in the profile. Sagundino was famed for his displays of bilingualism at the Councils of Florence and Ferrara; note the accounts of Vespasiano da Bisticci in his *Vite di uomini illustri del secolo XV*, pp. 15, 26; also Pertusi, "L'umanesimo greco," pp. 217, 222.

[383] The *De origine et sectis philosophorum*, in Sagundino's *Epist. et opusc.*, fols. 25-36. The introduction (fols. 25-26) is summarized below.

[384] ". . . non ad luxum te neque ad iocos scurriles, caetera ve eiusmodi libero homine haud digna convertere consuevisse, neque ad venationes et aucupia . . . . Lenociniis et oblectamentis subinde posthabitis, lectioni confestim atque litterario studio incumbendum tibi, ac honestam et grandiferam inde suavitatem penitus colligendam atque adeo imbibendam existimabas . . . ." Ibid., fol. 25.

[385] ". . . tibi me comitem assumebas, et si vis socium et laboris participem adhibendum esse constituebas." Ibid.

responsibilities permitted, those rewards, that utility, that solace, which most pleasantly soothes the soul"; and they learned together to "instruct" and "mold" their lives to the standard of virtue.[386] Sometimes the two students would disagree, or pause while Sagundino explained terms or defined the various philosophical schools; "here I was useful to you because of my knowledge of Greek."[387] Coppo was eager to learn: "your heart wholly perceiving and drinking up [these ideas], your soul loftily imagining and absorbing, you seemed to burn with an incredible thirst of exploring them closely and accurately."[388]

The kinship forged by a mutual love of philosophy between the Venetian nobleman and the Euboean scribe is unique.[389] That relationship of equality did not persist into later years. After a gap of tumultuous years, Sagundino found himself in Venice—"in this city of kings, in this wondrous miracle of the whole world, in this brilliant and illustrious city of Venice, as though rescued from the waves I have found a port."[390] At last he had time to write a work examining the various philosophical schools, as Coppo had requested. But now Sagundino looked to Coppo as a patron who had aided him in the past and might again in the future. If the work satisfied the nobleman, Sagundino wrote, then "liberate me from my long-standing debt"; or if something were lacking, he would supply it, "for no duty more presses me . . . than that I try more abundantly to liquidate my debt to you."[391] Then he described his financial and domestic problems.[392]

Perhaps in response to this or a later plea, Coppo wrote Sagundino

[386] "Nec deesse videbantur nobis cum per publicas occupationes liceret, ea emolumenta, hi usus, ea solacia, quibus iocundissime animum relaxare, vitam denique ipsam et mores ad virtutis probitatisque normam ingenue instituere et praeclare formare possemus." Ibid., fol. 25ʳ⁻ᵛ.

[387] ". . . huc equidem in gratiam tuam per linguae graecae commoditatem et usum, rationem aliquam conabar afferre . . . ." Ibid., fol. 25ᵛ.

[388] ". . . toto percipienda ebibendaque pectore et animo altius figenda et inculcanda incredibili quadam videbare siti ardere horum explicatius accuratiusque disserendorum." Ibid.

[389] Later Sagundino described what he had written for Fantino Coppo as not so much a learned work "quam meae in Fantinum voluntatis argumentum et perpetuae animi observantiae testimonium." *Opusculum ad Petrum Molinum*, fol. 111.

[390] ". . . in hanc regum urbem, in hoc totius orbis insigne miraculum, in hanc clarissimam et inclytam urbem Venetam, velut in portum e fluctibus me recepi . . . ." *De origine*, fol. 26.

[391] ". . . benigne contentus superiore me debito liberaris; verum si quid tibi deesse sensero, quod a me addi insuper velis, quid tum agere debeam nescio, nihil enim amplius mihi virium superesse intelligo, quo tibi cumulatius debitum dissolvere queam." Ibid., fol. 35ᵛ.

[392] Ibid., fols. 35ᵛ-36. See also the lament in the *Epistola ad Bessarionem de naufragio suo [De naufragio suo]*, pp. 8ff. It was particularly hard to live in Venice because he was a "new man"—". . . et civitas sumptuosa novo praesertim homini difficilius . . . ." fol. 9.

assurances of love and esteem. Sagundino was grateful: "You can rightly be considered and called not only my patron and defender, but also in large part my creator."[393] In Naples on a mission for Venice, the length of which provoked many of the letters cited here, he begged Coppo to have him recalled: "among the other servants and ministers of so great an empire I cannot be thought totally worthless, detestable, and useless."[394] What was needed was not an expert in Latin or Greek, but someone who could speak the Neapolitan's barbarous language. Meanwhile, he hoped to bring his wife and remaining children— one son was already in Italy—to Venice where the family could be united.[395]

Sagundino also begged the patrician and humanist Domenico Morosini to intercede for his recall from Naples. How much I would like to be in Venice with you, wrote Sagundino, "where I would have the privilege of frequently visiting you, of speaking with you, chatting with you, of freely enjoying your most pleasant company."[396] But Sagundino was not free to do so: "For I depend on the will of those by whose aid I am duly sustained, by whose protection and beneficence I hope to feed not only myself, but a large circle of children."[397] He apologized for not writing more frequently. If his letters were sparse, it was not his fault, but the fault in part of his condition, "inborn and unchangeable," and in part of his burdensome responsibilities, "of unavoidable necessity and the force of pressing matters."[398] Be well, Sagundino urged in his closing words, "and love me, who am yours, as you do, and defend me while absent."[399]

Through patronal intercession, it seems, Sagundino was eventually recalled to Venice.[400] But his hopes of settling himself and his family were disappointed, as Sagundino reveals in a letter to Domenico Mo-

---

[393] ". . . non solum defensor et fautor, verum etiam auctor maxima ex parte haberi merito appellarique potes . . . ." *Epist. et opusc.*, fol. 119ᵛ. The letter to Fantino, fols. 119ᵛ-120ᵛ, is summarized here.

[394] "Dii faxint ut inter reliquos tanti imperii servulos et ministros, non admodum abiiciendus, non omnino aspernandus atque inutilis et ipse censeri queam." *Epist. et opusc.*, fol. 120.

[395] For Sagundino's paternal anxiety, see also *De naufragio suo*, pp. 8ff.

[396] ". . . saepius enim tui adeundi mihi daretur copia, te affandi, tecum fabulandi, consuetudine denique iocundissima tua utendi liberius . . . ." *Epist. et opusc.*, fol. 103ᵛ.

[397] "Nam de voluntate eorum dependeo, quorum ope honeste sustentor, quorum praesidio et beneficentia non modo me ipsum, verum etiam liberorum numerosam coronam spero nutritum iri . . . ." Ibid.

[398] ". . . et quidem non culpa mea, sed tum conditione irrefragibili et ingenita, tum necessitate indeprecabili et vi ingruentium rerum . . . ." Ibid., fol. 104.

[399] ". . . me tuum quod facis ama et absentem defende." Ibid., fol. 106.

[400] That of Giovanni Moro, "quo mihi bona senatus inclyti gracia redeundi decernatur potestas." Ibid., fol. 106ᵛ.

rosini.[401] He had returned during a bout of plague. The important men of the city had fled to find refuge but Sagundino was left there and, so far from being reunited with his family, forced to send the sons he had with him away for safety. Morosini's letter had arrived when Sagundino was most vulnerable. The nobleman had assured him of love and aid, to which the scribe responded gratefully. He described his unhappy situation: "I live alone at home with the company of one servant. Daily I go to the court, in case there is anything they wish me to do. Yet that happens rarely, for I am not one of those who is often commissioned to handle great or many matters. As far as I can, being energetic, in whatever time I have, I devote myself at home to reading Greek or Latin works, or spend some time writing."[402] He examined his conscience and sought to absolve his sins, so that "bound by the mercy of the ineffable creator, I freely give and commend myself to His mercy and immense goodness."[403] Now old, if he were to live longer, his only joy would be to impart some of his learning to his sons. And if he died, they would have a protector—not from among the Venetian nobility, in whom Sagundino seems to have lost hope— but in God: "they shall not . . . lack a protector, a helper, a lord, nor a father, and indeed One who is omnipotent."[404]

Despite his lofty independence here, however, where Sagundino trusted more in God than in patrician friends, he expressed fulsome gratitude to Morosini when that nobleman introduced him to Francesco Contarini. A practical man, Sagundino recognized the benefits that could accrue from that new connection. You have assisted me heretofore in many ways, Sagundino wrote Morosini, and now strive to win me the good favor of others: "and not of nobodies, but of those who by their authority, status, and greatness can perpetually aid me and advance me."[405] Contarini was so lofty that even a nod from him was a plum.[406]

[401] Ibid., fols. 47ᵛ-49ᵛ, summarized below.

[402] "Vivo solus domi unico puero comitatus. Accedo quotidie in curiam, si quid est quod meam desideret operam; quod tamen perraro evenit, neque enim is ego sum cui res vel magnae vel multae craebrius demandentur curandae. Id pro mea virili impiger suscipio quicquid superesse videtur temporis, domi id legendo tum graece tum latine, vel aliquid scribendi consumo." Ibid., fol. 49.

[403] ". . . ineffabili creatoris misericordia fretus, eius clementiae et immensae benignitati traditum commendatumque assercio." Ibid., fol. 49ʳ⁻ᵛ.

[404] ". . . non tamen . . . protector deerit filiis, non adiutor, non dominus, non denique pater, et quidem omnipotens . . . ." Ibid., fol. 49ᵛ.

[405] ". . . et non quorumvis, sed eorum qui auctoritate, gratia et amplitudine sua mihi usui et ornamento perpetuo esse possint . . . ." Ibid., fol. 58ᵛ.

[406] "Ea enim doctrina, eo ingenio, ea probitate vir est, eo ordine, ea denique dignitate, auctoritate et splendore familiae, ut vel tenui nutu mihi per grandi auxilio esse possit . . . ." Ibid. See also Sagundino's humble letter to Contarini, fols. 57ᵛ-58.

Sagundino lamented the circumstances of his life to peers as well as to patrons. From Naples, he wrote his fellow-secretary Marco Aurelio, asking him to intercede with Giovanni Moro (patron to them both) and the Senate for his return.[407] Once back in Venice, however, Sagundino's troubles multiplied—as has already been seen from his letter to Morosini. Giovanni Moro, his patron and Aurelio's, had died. "O, how unhappy and wretched we are," he wrote Aurelio, "to have lost such and so great a patron, who loved us each for a different reason: you for your merits and rare virtue, me far beyond merit on account of his generosity and great kindness."[408] He had been to us "new men" a "safe and tranquil port," a "firm and faithful hope, a certain refuge, an inviolable asylum."[409] I was in court when I heard the news, Sagundino wrote, rushed home, and groaned and called aloud: "I called to you, Marco, in my thought and soul I embraced you, I tried with you to recall our jewel from the grave, to release him from the dead."[410] From this climax of grief, Sagundino retreated to speak words of consolation and reflect on the necessity of death. "But if, though we grieve our calamity and bewail our fortune, we who have been orphaned of patron and foster father, deprived of such hope, defrauded of such expectation, yet it must be born temperately, placidly, moderately, civilly and, in sum, dutifully—especially by you, who in the flower of your age flourish rarely both in learning and intelligence, who by your virtue, probity and industry have won for yourself already many patrician friends."[411] Of his own fate, Sagundino seemed less confident.

Despite the efforts of patrons, despite his own considerable talents, Sagundino's career was destined for calamity.[412] Having finally gath-

---

[407] The request to approach Giovanni Moro, ibid., fol. 93ᵛ; to approach the Senate, fol. 102.

[408] "O nos infelices, o miseros tali tantoque destitutos patrono. Qui ut nos vehementer amabat, quamquam varia ratione: te scilicet tuis meritis proque tua singulari virtute; me suapte humanitate et egregia quadam benignitate ultro gratuitoque complexus." Ibid., fol. 53ᵛ.

[409] ". . . Marco mihique novis hominibus tutissimum et tranquilissimum portum, firmissimam et fidissimam spem, certissimum praesidium, asylum inviolabile . . . ." Ibid., fol. 54. An immigrant, Sagundino identified himself as a "new man." Marco, his relative, was probably an immigrant's son; see profile.

[410] ". . . te vocabam, Marce, te cogitatione et animo amplexabar, tecum decus nostrum ab interitu revocare, a mortuis excitare conabar." *Epist. et opusc.*, fol. 54.

[411] "Verum si casum dolemus nostrum et fortunam querimur nostram, qui tanto sumus orbati patrono et prope parente, tanta spe privati, tanta expectatione defraudati, at id temperate, placate, modice, humaniter tandem et officiose ferendum est—tibi praesertim, qui in isto flore aetatis tuae eruditione et ingenio singulariter vales, qui virtute, probitate et industria tua multos iam tibi patricios excitasti amicos." Ibid., fol. 55ᵛ.

[412] The following summarizes the events described in Sagundino's *De naufragio suo.*

ered his enormous family in Venice, he reluctantly accepted the office of chancellor of Crete—a secure position, but one far from the center of Venice's empire, and requiring the removal of his whole unwieldy clan. The decision made, wife, children, furniture, and a learned man's lifelong accumulation of books were loaded aboard a ship on a calm midsummer's day. The captain gave the order, the ship set sail—then, unexpectedly, began to sink. His wife called out to him before she was swallowed by the waves, which then seized two sons, then a daughter: "my daughter, the delight of her father, the image of my soul, fourteen years old; excellently endowed with intelligence, beauty, modesty, morals, learned deeply for her age and sex in Greek and Latin letters."[413] Later their dead bodies were seen floating on the surface: "the breathless body of my wife . . . the tender bodies of my sons . . . the corpse of my dear daughter."[414] Sagundino and his surviving children—one son and five daughters—were taken back in a small boat to Venice. He had lost wife, three children, and his possessions. "I lost my patrimony and all my fortune, carefully gathered and assembled through a long span of years marked by many dangers, with diligence, with constant and uncommon industry, with many labors."[415]

Always in difficulty, Sagundino was now poor indeed. Unable to support his household, he needed still to provide for a surviving son and to dower five daughters—an enormous liability. He approached the Cardinal Bessarion, whom he had known since childhood, for assistance.[416] He had some hopes of Zaccaria Trevisan the Younger.[417] Perhaps through Trevisan's intercession—for Sagundino had complained to him that the jealousy of the other secretaries was an obstacle—the Senate took action.[418] "Known to all of us is the horrible

[413] ". . . filiam patris delicias, effigiem animi mei, quartum jam, et decimum annum natam, ingenio, forma, pudore, moribus egregie praeditam, litteris cum graece, tum latine pro aetate et sexu ingenue eruditam." Ibid., p. 20.

[414] "Extitit super undas fluctibus agitatum exanimum corpus conjugis; apparuerunt subinde filiorum tenella corpora, et carae filiae cadaver prope exagitari conspectum est." Ibid., p. 22.

[415] "Amisi patrimonium, et fortunas omnes, longo curriculo et tempore, multis periculis aditis, assiduo studio, jugi, et non vulgari industria, variis laboribus . . . ." Ibid., p. 26.

[416] The whole De naufragio is a letter of petition addressed to Bessarion. Sagundino refers to Bessarion's lifelong support—"a teneris propemodum annis" (p. 40). The appeal apparently was successful. Sagundino's son, in his oration of petition to the pope (Epist. et opusc., fols. 151-53ᵛ), referred to Bessarion's protection of the family (fol. 152ʳ⁻ᵛ).

[417] Sagundino's plangent letter to Trevisan (Epist. et opusc., fols. 84ᵛ-87) indicates the patrician had already offered some encouragement.

[418] He complains of "nostri ordinis homines qui me persecuntur," fol. 86.

and miserable misfortune that befell our unhappy and unfortunate servant Niccolò Sagundino," reads the record of the Senate, "who lost before his eyes a pregnant wife, two sons and a daughter, with all his possessions, he himself scarcely in the end escaping with five daughters for the greater part grown and ready for marriage, and a son. And it befits the clemency and mercy of this state to show toward him and his offspring, the survivors of such an evil blow, that clemency and munificence that it has been customary to show toward many others in lesser and more tolerable difficulties."[419] Several provisions were made. Niccolò would remain in the post he had left to go to Crete. Since his poverty was so great that he was not able from salary alone to feed his family, other steps were taken. His son Ludovico, a youth of seventeen, would be given a government position from among the first to become vacant that was suitable for him, and would hold it for life. With his salary, he could then help his father, sisters—for whose dowries funds were also provided—and himself "in patiently bearing their miseries."[420]

The grant made Sagundino by the Senate was unusual indeed. It may have been greater than this document indicates. Pietro Perleone consoled his friend for his losses by stressing the extraordinary recompense he had been granted. Others were impoverished in the shipwreck, including some patricians, Perleone pointed out; yet the city received you "thrown naked on the shore," "responded to your disaster with such solemnity and sorrow, as though forgetful of all the other evils which occurred in that time, and . . . sympathizing with

---

[419] "Omnibus notum est horrendum et miserabile infortunium occursum infelici et calamitoso servitori nostro Nicolao Sagundino, qui in proprio conspectu amissa uxore gravida, duobus filiolis masculis, et una filia, cum tota eius facultate vix tandem evasit cum quinque filiabus pro maiori parte grandibus et viro maturis ac uno filio masculo. Et clementie ac mansuetudini tanti status convenit uti erga eum et eius creaturas, reliquias tante cladis et perniciei, illa clementia et munificentia, que erga complures in levioribus et supportabilioribus casibus uti consuevit." ASV, ST 4, c. 149, 10 July 1460; cf. Babinger, *Johannes Darius*, pp. 36-37. Provisions are given here for the outright gift and augmented salary that Perleone later alludes to.

[420] "Captum sit, quod Ludovico filio suo annorum circa XVII, iuveni optimorum morum et condicionis provideri debeat de aliquo officio in hac civitate nostra domini in vita sua, quo mediante iuvare possit patrem sorores ac se ipsum ad supportandum pacientius miserias suas. Et ut idem Nicolaus eius maximis filiabus suis supplicere possit, subveniatur de presenti de salario suo annorum trium ante tractum, ex computando et retinendo ei ducatorum XXV in anno, donec integram quantitatem predictam dominio nostro restituerit." ASV, ST 4, c. 149. These and further provisions were passed by a vote of 145/4/1. Nearly four years later, after Sagundino's death (22 March 1464), the provisions for Ludovico and his sisters were increased. The daughters were to be allowed dowries of 150 ducats each, and the son a salary of 120 ducats per year. The text of the act from ASV, ST 5, c. 73, 22 March 1464 (passed 93/37/10) in Babinger, *Johannes Darius*, pp. 44-45.

your calamity, considered you alone."[421] The Senate, the doge, and the whole Collegio granted, as Perleone puts it, six hundred gold ducats to Sagundino, and office for his son—though no one so young had ever been admitted to such a position. Sagundino, moreover, was restored to his office and given the large annual salary of two hundred gold ducats.[422] You are rich indeed, Perleone continued, with the city's good will. For Venice is a generous city, especially to learned men, who can on the basis of merit alone find preferment.[423] I also was in need, Perleone mused, but was assisted by powerful citizens; fortune has treated you worse than me, he wrote comfortingly, so that you could be made aware of the love the city bears you—"so that because of your calamity you might recognize clearly the love and benevolence of the whole city toward you."[424] That love is a treasure greater than the one Sagundino had lost. "For precious gems are purchased at great cost, so this immense treasure of such a republic was purchased by you with great expense, which treasure in its magnitude and amplitude exceeds all other things, and is so strong and solid and perpetual, that it can never be taken from you by any force, by any schemes, by any shipwreck, by any blow, finally, of fortune."[425] You are better off in the end: "You have lost what is doubtful, you have gained what is certain. You have lost what is perishable, you have gained what is perpetual."[426] Had you not been shipwrecked, you would not have

[421] ". . . te nudum, et ad littora ejectum, ita civitas excepit, ita casum tuum graviter ac moleste tulit, ut quasi caeterorum malorum, quae eo tempore acciderunt oblita et tuam calamitatem miserata . . . in te unum converteretur." Perleone, *Epistola [consolatoria] ad Nicolaum Sagundinum [Epist. cons.]*, p. 71.

[422] ". . . decreti sunt tibi sexcenti nummi aurei veneti; filio vero tuo adhuc adolescenti, publicum cum honore et commodo munus demandatum, quamvis nondum per aetatem liceret id muneris adire. Tibi praeterea in veterem locum, et dignitatem scribae reipublicae restituto annuum salarium decretum, aurei nummi Veneti CC." Ibid., p. 72. Two hundred ducats would have been an ample secretarial salary. These provisions in the acts discussed above, nn. 419, 420.

[423] "Quare cum tu is recte sis, cui quem in virtute, et doctrina conferamus, habemus profecto neminem, ac propterea minime dubitandum, quin si vel ignotus in urbem venires, posses cuncta tamen et dignitatis, et fortunae praesidia comperare." Ibid., p. 76. Compare Tito Livio Frulovisi's complaint in his *De republica* that Venice offered no reward to men of learning (*Opera*, ed. Prévité-Orton, p. 366).

[424] ". . . qua plane totius in te urbis amorem benignitatemque jactura perspiceres." *Epist. cons.*, p. 77.

[425] "Namque ut pretiosissimae gemmae non sine magno pretio comparantur; ita immensus hic tantae republicae thesaurus magna a te mercede emendus fuit, qui magnitudine atque amplitudine sua caeteras res omnes excedit, ita et firmus et rectus et perpetuus nulla vi, nullis insidiis, nullo naufragio, nullo denique fortunae impetu eripi tibi potest." Ibid.

[426] "Amisisti res dubias, parasti certissimas. Amisisti peritura, parasti perpetua . . . ." Ibid., p. 78.

gained the Senate's favor.[427] Do not go to Crete to live "ingloriously," where your learning and eloquence will count for nothing, Perleone closed, where you have no friends, where your children will receive a peasant's education, where you cannot have "your patrician friends, the princes of the earth and the protectors of all things . . . a fine, indeed, and precious inheritance, for parents to bestow upon children, first after virtue."[428]

Sagundino was to be consoled for the loss of half his family and all his fortune by the knowledge of patrician benevolence—a treasure more precious than all the goods he had lost. Even graced with that great gift, if we can read between the lines, Sagundino was inconsolable. He became ill and soon died, and his son, in Rome, pleaded poverty to the pope.[429] The Venetian bureaucracy, grinding no faster than others, still had not found him a job. But in the end, it did, and Ludovico appears in later years among the "order of scribes."[430]

Sagundino's misfortunes are richly documented. From his case, however idiosyncratic, can be had a glimpse of the struggle waged by members of the secretarial order for status and dignity. Because of their proximity to power, these men were privileged, in a position to render favors even to patricians. Conscious of that unique role, they perceived themselves as a special professional group—"our order," the "order of scribes." Yet their appointment to the secretariat, their salaries and pensions, their advancement, depended on the will of the Senate as shaped by patronal intercession. Despite his confidence that

---

[427] "Nec tu naufragium, clarissimum tui ingenii monumentum, scripsisses nec Senatum Venetum de te solicitum tibi uni, tuis rebus intentum, teque in sinum benigne excipientem atque amplexantem donisque ac muneribus et dignitate ac omnibus rebus te tuosque faventem expertus esses . . . ." Ibid.

[428] "Illud profecto certissimum in ea te urbe futurum fuisse, ubi tu inglorius vixisses, ubi tuo sublimi ingenio tuaque praestanti doctrina et facundia dignum ostendisses profecto nihil. Ubi sine suavissima familiarium, amicorum tuorum, praestantissimorumque civium consuetudine, quos hic pro tua virtute permultos habes, vitam molestam acerbissimamque duxisses. Ubi filii tui sine litteris, exuta urbanitate rusticitatem induissent. Ubi demum tu moriens, nec divitias ipsis ad usum, nec opes ad cultum, nec litteras ad maximum utriusque fortunae ornamentum et auxilium, nec amicos patricios Venetos, orbis terrae principes ad rerum omnium praesidium reliquisses, optimam profecto et pretiosam haereditatem ac in primis a parentibus post virtutem liberis tradendam." Ibid., p. 98.

[429] In the oration cited, *Epist. et opusc.*, fols. 151-53ᵛ.

[430] Ludovico appears in government documents from at least 1474, when he is listed among the notaries for a ducal election (ASV, MC—Regina, c. 142ᵛ, 5 December) until his death. On 29 April 1506, when he was "recently dead," provisions were made to promote in secretarial office his two sons, so they might support a large female household (ASV, CX—Miste 31, c. 16). Niccolò—one of those two sons—subsequently became grand chancellor of Venice (d. 14 April 1551). The Sagundinos had become a secretarial dynasty.

anyone of merit could find advancement in Venice, Perleone understood profoundly the importance of patrician friends who could pro-
cure for an aspirant "the benevolence of the whole city"—that is, of
its rulers.

13. THE STRATIFIED SOCIETY OF VENETIAN HUMANISM

The secretaries, with the physicians, the teachers, and wandering native-born clerics, form one stratum of the humanist elite of Venice.
They are united by their social condition. As commoners in a city
dominated by patrician rule, they either define their activity in terms
of the patriciate or absent themselves from the city in which they can
play no independent role. The physicians enjoy a high social position
and have easy converse with patrician friends. Yet they are conscious
of the void that separates them from men of noble status. Their daughters can marry into the nobility. Their sons can dress and behave like
patricians, but will never be ennobled. The natives who leave Venice
to pursue careers abroad do not forget their homeland and patrician
friends, but must seek others' favors to thrive. Among them some of
the most learned of our humanists, they are lured from Venice, perhaps,
in search of positions of greater independence than their own city
offers a native commoner. For though natives become doctors and
secretaries, they do not become teachers, or act in any capacity as
professional humanists within Venice.

The role one might expect citizen humanists to play was played, in
fact, by resident and transient foreigners. They taught the sons of the
patricians and, for the most part, they edited the books that rolled off
the early presses. Many came, but not many took up permanent residence. Perhaps they did not win the favor of patrician friends. Perhaps
they found the atmosphere of Venice inimical to professional humanist
activity, or the rewards insufficient. Those who did stay did so at the
will of patrician employers in their private and public capacity. The
secretaries, finally, for the most part a citizen group, were, despite
their position close to the center of power dependent, like the foreigners
on patrician support. Though all were trained in the *studia humanitatis*, by which training they were qualified for their posts, few were
humanist figures of any significance. Rare was Sagundino, who could
discourse in Greek or Latin on history, philosophy, theology, or rhetoric. Vinciguerra was perhaps unique; confident in the learning by
which he found kinship with the minds of "a thousand years," he
raised his sights beyond "his lagoons"; and confident, too, in God,
he hoped to join the ranks of the "true patricians"—the blessed—in

heaven. The patrician humanists form together a second stratum of the humanist elite. In nearly every case they were not only patricians but patricians among the most wealthy and powerful in the city. Thus they experienced an independence the other humanists did not know. But their independence was relative, not absolute. Political and social imperatives surrounded them. By their humanist training in their youth and their later achievements, they met the expectations of dynasty and class. In their public careers and in their humanist activity, they served—or were expected to serve—the republic. Their responsibilities (even when unfulfilled) to the nobility as a class and to the noble class as represented in the government of Venice dominated their lives: devoured their time, shaped their personalities, structured their thoughts.

Neither the commoner nor the patrician humanist in fifteenth-century Venice was a free man. Natives and foreigners were linked to the will and to the perspectives of noblemen. Noblemen, disciplined by their own assumptions, were tied to each other. These patterns of mutual reliance and obligation might be expected to lead to conflict, and undoubtedly did. But if so, hardly a whisper of discontent was heard in the works of the humanists. As they portrayed their world, all were content, all lived together on their lagoons in perpetual concord, fused into one personality, moved by a single will.

TWO

Themes: *Unanimitas*

UNANIMITY—the convergence of a multitude of wants and aspirations into a single will—is the central ideal of Venetian humanist culture in the fifteenth century. That ideal is the keynote of humanism's major works, colors the minor ones, and spills over the hazy boundaries of humanism to cognate disciplines.

Pervasive in humanist culture, the ideal of *unanimitas* was probably not realized in Venetian society. Ideals seldom are. Had it reached fruition, however, the achievement would have been applauded by the rulers of Venice. Nothing could more profoundly serve their needs than that the people of Venice should possess a single benevolent will in harmony—of course—with their own. It is not surprising that those among the rulers of Venice who acquired humanist skills should shape humanism to their needs. Nor is it surprising that humanists in Venice not of the ruling elite should concur in the ideal posed by patrician thinkers, or leave the city, or say nothing. Few murmured in dissent against the ideal of *unanimitas*. The condition axiomatically does not permit dissent.

The ideal of *unanimitas* has many facets that emerge as the themes of the major works of Venetian humanism. This chapter will examine fifteen critical works by seven authors. After relating those works of the broader expanse of humanist production, it will elicit some principal themes. Having outlined the themes that in their sum articulate the ideal of *unanimitas*, it will close by considering the phenomenon, slim and unsuccessful, of dissent. Discussion opens with the youthful Francesco Barbaro's *On Marriage*, the first major work of Venetian humanism and perhaps its most famous product.[1]

1. Francesco Barbaro on Marriage

Francesco Barbaro spent the summer of 1415 in Florence.[2] There he formed friendships with some leading figures of that city's humanist

---

[1] The *De re uxoria* [DRU]; Gnesotto's preface, pp. 6-22; text, pp. 23-105. Barbaro's work is, coincidentally, the earliest of the texts to be discussed; they are not, however, presented chronologically, but so as first to introduce the most fundamental themes.

[2] For Barbaro's trip to Florence and the circumstances of the composition of the DRU,

circles and with the wealthy and powerful Medici family, in whose house he was a guest. Lorenzo de' Medici, brother of Cosimo, Florence's future ruler, was shortly to be married to Ginevra Cavalcanti. Upon his return to Venice, Barbaro composed and addressed to Lorenzo the treatise *On Marriage*—a subject of which the young nobleman had no personal experience. Yet he could draw on the insights of the authors he had studied: the Latin works of Cicero and Augustine, among others, and, more recently, the Greek works of Plutarch and Xenophon. He drew, too, on the wisdom of his beloved mentor, the patrician and humanist Zaccaria Trevisan the Elder.[3] The substance of Trevisan's unwritten messages to Barbaro on marriage and other issues is lost to us. But surely it extended beyond the brief anecdotes attributed to Trevisan in the admiring author's work. Perhaps through the mature Trevisan's influence, as well as from Barbaro's own experience as the scion of a noble dynasty and observer of Venetian life, were formed the assumptions that undergird this remarkable work. For it is far from a naive patchwork of ancient tags on marriage, an amusing exercise and thoughtful wedding gift. It is a work of fundamental importance for the understanding of Venetian humanism, of Venetian culture, and perhaps of aristocratic consciousness in Europe for centuries to come. It defines as the object of marriage the preservation of the privilege and purity of noble families, giving self-conscious expression to principles long honored by the nobles who ruled Venice.[4]

The *De re uxoria* discusses the nature of marriage and the selection and duties of a wife. Marriage is, according to Barbaro, "a perpetual joining of man and wife, legitimately instituted for the purpose of procreating children and the avoidance [of the sin] of fornication."[5] From the outset, the author is concerned not only with the ample generation of children, but with their virtuous conception and education. Children born illegitimately and of passionate and forbidden embraces tend, necessarily, to sin. Those born of virtuous parents

---

see Gnesotto's, preface, pp. 10-15; B. G. Kohl, introduction to his translation (entitled "On Wifely Duties") of the preface and Book Two of DRU, in Kohl and R. Witt, eds., *The Earthly Republic*, pp. 180-82; R. Sabbadini, "La gita di Francesco Barbaro a Firenze nel 1415."

[3] In addition to works cited above, see P. Gothein, *Zaccaria Trevisan*, pp. 122ff., and Gothein, "Zaccaria Trevisan," pp. 51-52.

[4] This interpretation of Barbaro's work I have presented previously in my "Caldiera and the Barbaros on Marriage and the Family," pp. 31ff.

[5] "Est igitur conjugium viri et uxoris perpetua conjunctio procreandae sobolis vel vitandae fornicationis causa legitime instituta." DRU, p. 28. The following review of Barbaro's statements on the nature of marriage and selection of a spouse is based on DRU, pp. 28-53.

93

within the sacral limits of marriage have within them the seeds of virtue. Their parents' fineness, indeed, not only provides the context for the development of a fine child, but sets a standard short of which the sensitive child will not wish to fall. "The light of paternal glory," he writes, "does not permit the well-born to be mediocre; they understand that the image of their parents is more of a burden than an honor unless they prove themselves by their own virtue worthy of the dignity and greatness of their ancestors."[6] How swiftly paced is Barbaro's argument! His work barely begun, he has established that virtuous children—greatly to be desired for their usefulness to human society—are born only from the legitimate marriages of virtuous parents and, by extension, that the most worthy children are born of the most worthy parents. His defense of marriage has become, transmogrified, a defense of the principle of noble descent. He returns often to this theme.

The nobly born attain positions of honor in the republic more easily than the humble, Francesco observes approvingly. Even if they do not merit preferment in their own right, it is conceded to them on account of the merits of their progenitors (p. 42). In Venice, the honor due to heroes or benefactors of the state is also shown to their sons (p. 42). If good birth is not absolutely required for success, still it is difficult for new men to get ahead; they are feared like the wild dog who snaps and snarls as he walks, whereas the nobleman, a finely trained domestic animal, is trustworthy (p. 43). A nobleman is guarded from misfortune, because though all other things fail him, he can stand firm, affixed to the earth with long roots like an old tree, never bending or falling (p. 43). Secure against adversity, and virtuous because they come from virtuous stock, the nobly born are a natural political resource. They are the "walls," says Barbaro, of the city.[7]

In these and similar statements, Barbaro defends the principle of aristocracy: the well-born are leaders in the city because their origin provides them with superior qualities. Patrician dynasties must assume the responsibility of providing present and future rulers of the state. The dutiful family discharges its obligations by guarding the purity of its race. Thus the choice of a wife becomes a matter of profound significance. Her worthiness consists in virtue and good birth.

Virtue is so important that it alone suffices to make a spouse desirable, even if all other qualities are lacking (p. 32). Her virtue inspires

[6] "Honesto loco natos paternae gloriae lumen obscuros esse non patitur; qui parentum imagines sibi plus oneris quam honoris afferre intelligunt, nisi sua virtute majorum dignitati ac amplitudini responderint." DRU, p. 29.

[7] "Sic natos ad laudem moenia civitatis appellare poterimus." Ibid.

all other members of the family, who follow her example as citizens follow their rulers and soldiers their generals (p. 33). The diligence, frugality, and dignity of the wife inspires and instructs the family and renders it honest; and without the experience of ancestral virtues the city's leaders could not justly rule the republic (p. 35).

But if the quality of virtue is paramount because its purity purifies the race, nobility, which exalts it, is also sought in a wife. For the sake of posterity, one should marry a noblewoman, "for we see that those fruits are wondrous which are born of the best soil."[8] Indeed, the nobility of the woman seems possibly to be more important than that of the man in determining the status of offspring. Barbaro recalls Roman law, which declared a child free if born of a free mother, even though his father was a slave. And heroes, he adds, are considered gods if only their mothers were goddesses. Humble men, nevertheless, do not better themselves by marrying noble women. Like men who force their camels to kneel because they do not know how to mount, they do not raise themselves, but merely lower their wives (p. 43). But gentlemen who marry well-born women are made more worthy and beget worthier sons. Society itself benefits from the matching of aristocrats with aristocrats. Such marriages produce descendants ever more excellent both by nature and by education, whose domestic experience prepares them for glory (p. 44).

Virtuous and noble women make excellent wives, capable of engendering excellence in their progeny. Beauty may grace these preeminent qualities, but is not to be sought in itself. Neither is wealth required in the ideal spouse. Only poor and ignoble men seek wealthy wives, just as ignorant men buy bad books in splendid bindings (p. 51). Wealth is useful, of course. It permits liberality to friends and all of humanity, writes Barbaro, and the instruction of our children in the liberal arts (pp. 49-50). It sustains human society. But a woman's wealth is unimportant. If she brings wealth to the household, it is reckoned as her husband's in any case, just as wine, if mixed with water, is still called wine. Not she who brings a fortune with her, but she who can better serve the family, should be chosen as a wife (p. 50). Her wealth contributes nothing, whereas her goodness and nobility enrich the family.

Having outlined the main requirements to be sought in a good wife, Barbaro pauses to address the anticipated argument that only the wealthy and well-born were in a position to follow his advice. Not all men are Lorenzos, he concedes, referring to the wealthy bridegroom

---

[8] "Mirificas fruges esse perspicimus, quas optimae segetes pariunt." Ibid., p. 41.

to whom his work is addressed (p. 54). Humbler men must adjust their sights to their condition, counsels the nobleman. It is absurd that poor and low-born men should aspire to wives "in whom is found every principle of perfect and consummate worthiness"—who are, that is, virtuous and noble.[9] Rather, all men must seek a wife of their own class. "For what is more fair, what more appropriate, than that one obtain a wife equal to oneself?"[10] A reasonable guideline indeed—but one that would if obeyed ensure the perpetuation of a pure noble class invulnerably distinct from the nonnoble population.

The wife whom the nobleman chooses—for it is he, in fact, of whom Barbaro speaks—must next be instructed in her duties, by which she upholds the honor of the family and insures the worthiness of the children.[11] Her first duty is to love her husband. "Let her be so close to him that nothing seems good or pleasant to her without her husband." The love between man and wife, if it is heartfelt, creates "a pattern of perfect friendship."[12] Yet, though their affection is mutual, Barbaro does not perceive man and wife as equals. The woman is to be wholly obedient to her husband. With that end in view, Barbaro advised the selection of a young wife who, like soft wax that is easily impressed, can be molded to her husband's views, desires, and shifting moods.[13] The husband commands, and the wife complies without comment. His wrath should be quietly tolerated, and his behavior, however suspicious, never questioned. Her own behavior should be impeccable. Observing the rule of moderation at all times, wives must strictly control body and mind. They should "preserve an evenness and restraint in the motions of the eyes, in their walking, and in the movement of their bodies; for the wandering of the eyes, a hasty gait, and excessive movement of the hands and other parts of the body cannot be done without loss of dignity, and such actions are always joined to vanity and are signs of frivolity."[14] Wives must avoid excessive laughter and unnecessary speech, dress simply, in accord with the family's wealth, and appropriately for the occasion. They may wear jewels: "for such adornments are the sign of a wealthy, not a

---

[9] "Ita ridiculi merito videbunter, qui tenues et abjecti magno studio quaerunt uxores, in quibus omnis ratio perfectae et consummatae laudis invenitur." Ibid., p. 54.

[10] "Quid enim aequabilius, quid commodius, quam aequalem sibi mulierem asciscere?" Ibid., p. 55.

[11] The account of wifely duties that follows is based on DRU, pp. 62-100. Quoted passages are given in Kohl's translation in Kohl and Witt, *Earthly Republic*, pp. 189-228.

[12] Kohl, p. 196.

[13] Gnesotto, preface, p. 37.

[14] Barbaro, trans. Kohl, p. 202.

lascivious woman, and are taken as evidence of the wealth of the husband more than as a desire to impress wanton eyes."[15]

The same moral expectations hold in the administration of the household, the governance of servants, and the care of children. Though husbands are responsible for the tasks that require great strength—"they provision their homes by their labor, industry, and willingness to undergo hardships"[16]—women, being weaker, are responsible for the household. No wifely duty is more serious than that of her children's education. It begins with nursing, which the mother should undertake herself. Her milk is most appropriate for the child born of her body, and naturally shapes "the properties of body and mind to the character of the seed."[17] If she cannot suckle her own child, a nurse of good birth and high morals must be chosen, for spiritual qualities are transmitted to the infant through the nourishing milk. "But if, as often happens, mothers cannot for compelling reasons suckle their own children, they ought to place them with good nurses, not with slaves, strangers, or drunken and unchaste women. They ought to give their infants to the care of those who are freeborn, well-mannered, and especially those endowed with dignified speech. In this way the young infant will not imbibe corrupt habits and words and will not receive, with his milk, "baseness, faults, and impure infirmities, and thus be infected with a dangerous degenerative disease of mind and body."[18] The child's moral education thus begun in infancy continues, under the mother's guidance, until a pious, dutiful, and self-restrained young person is prepared for intellectual training under his father's direction.

The preservation and continuation of the patrician family, alone capable of supplying men to lead the republic, is the imperative that structures Barbaro's *On Marriage*. Given his object, he rightly focuses on the selection and duties of a wife. Through her, the stamp of nobility descends to the child, and through her mind and body the potential for sound character. She is both the precious jewel of the family, radiant with the promise of descendants yet unborn, and its willing tool—an unprotesting servant to husband and child, sober, still, and silent. But if she is their servant, they, too, have an overriding master: the dynasty itself, for the honor and perpetuation of which their lives are shaped. Marriage, Barbaro understands all too well, is an institution for the legitimate procreation of children: it is an institution

---

[15] Ibid., p. 208.
[16] Ibid., p. 215.
[17] Ibid., p. 223.
[18] Ibid.

indifferent to the present, in bondage to the future. As such, it is the focal institution of the patrician class and of the republic.

2. Giovanni Caldiera: A Trilogy and a Concordance

As obscure as Barbaro was famous, the citizen Giovanni Caldiera understood as well as had the noble statesman the moral and institutional underpinnings of Venetian culture. In two elaborate and lengthy works, he reinforced that culture's central values twice over. He integrated them with a philosophical vision sanctioned by the authority of Aristotle, the Church, and the University of Padua. And he transmitted to those values the granite hardness of his preferred intellectual traditions. The first of these sturdy dissertations is actually a trilogy of works, each representing a different field of moral philosophy. They define in turn the ideal individual, the ideal family, and the ideal state, explicitly identified with the real city of Venice.[19] Preserved in a unique Oxford manuscript, this trilogy constitutes a monumental summa of Venetian attitudes and values.

In *On the Moral and Theological Virtues*, the first work of the trilogy, Caldiera defines an ideal for the individual as though living alone, his domestic and political responsibilities aside: the "monastic" ideal. The work is closely modeled on Aristotle's *Nicomachean Ethics*, leavened by scholastic and patristic learning and concepts inherited from the medieval Christian tradition. After a definition of virtue, it proceeds to a conventional discussion of the moral and theological virtues almost unalloyed by reference to observed behavior in the real world.[20] Faith is not understood in human terms at all; it is a mode of the awareness of truth that is midway between knowledge and opinion, and in matters of doctrine has greater authority than reason. Hope is defined as hope for salvation, and is discussed in the context of the doctrine of grace. Charity is described by rhetorical devices more to be expected from a preaching friar than a fifteenth-century

[19] The *De virtutibus, De oeconomia,* and *De politia.* The following discussion draws substantially on my "Personal, Domestic, and Republican Values in the Moral Philosophy of Giovanni Caldiera." An extended analysis appears in my dissertation, "Venetian Ideology and the Reconstruction of Knowledge" pp. 234-471. Caldiera's three works parallel the three works commonly considered in that author's milieu to be fundamental to moral philosophy: Aristotle's *Nicomachean Ethics;* the pseudo-Aristotelian *Economics;* and Aristotle's *Politics;* see King, "Values," p. 540 n. 15. The trilogy was actually written later (1463) than the concordance (by 1457), yet logically precedes it for the purpose of this discussion.

[20] The following summary is based on fols. 25-37 of the *De virtutibus.* Note the mix of Aristotelian and Christian conceptions: Caldiera's definition of virtue is strictly Aristotelian, but when he moves to a discussion of specific virtues, he turns first to those of the Christian tradition.

humanist: it is likened "to gold which is proven in the furnace of tribulation . . . to the spouse who is virtually and indissolubly joined to God . . . to the supreme firmament dividing the waters of pleasure from the waters of eternity"; it is "a reddening rose watered by a gracious moisture, by which it is nourished, conserved, and increased."[21] Turning to the four moral or cardinal virtues, Caldiera continues to reiterate long-established truths. Temperance consists in the avoidance of superfluous desire for the pleasures derived from sensuous things. Fortitude consists in the fearless confrontation of danger and the forbearance of the good and adverse effects of Fortune. Prudence is defined through the definition of its component parts: intelligence, foresight, and memory. Justice is lauded and its origin in Natural Law demonstrated.

The author's exposition of the seven sins, still conventional, is more heated than his exposition of the virtues.[22] The key to the avoidance of sin is ascetic self-denial. Pride, the greatest of the sins, most flagrantly violates this principle. Pride is defined as a perverse appetite for greatness, a love of one's own excellence. Contemptuous of God, the proud man turns away from the Creator and toward the pursuit of lower things. Evil in itself, pride increases the malignancy of other sins. Envy derives from pride, because the man who is proud of his own possessions and achievements begins to resent those of other men. Anger turns men into beasts and dissipates in them the image of God. The pursuit of wealth, which a citizen of Venice's merchant economy might be expected to sanction, is roundly condemned in an attack on avarice.[23] A dishonest desire to acquire what should not be desired, avarice leads to simony, usury, theft, treachery, and perjury. The avaricious man seizes things for himself, depriving others: "so that by a certain insatiable cupidity, those things which are of no use to him he denies to those in need."[24] Men who have made themselves rich through their avaricious quest for wealth naturally fall prey to the sins of gluttony, lechery, and *accidia*. Those who have fed their stomachs too richly will afterwards be deprived of celestial bread. Immoderate sexuality is a "sweet poison," "an importunate plague," "a pernicious potion," and "a petulance of the flesh" that debilitates the body and erodes the

---

[21] ". . . auro . . . quod in tribulationis fornace probatum est . . . et sponse quae deo virtualitere indissolubiliter coniungitur . . . supremo firmamento . . . a quo aquae voluptatis ab aquis aeternitatis dividuntur [*ms.* dividenti]." *De virtutibus*, fols. 29ᵛ-30.

[22] This summary is based on *De virtutibus*, fols. 49ᵛ-55ᵛ.

[23] Later in the *De politia*, however, he will often speak approvingly of Venice's wealth and commercial activities.

[24] ". . . ut insaciabili quadam cupiditate, que nullo sibi usui sunt aliis egentibus prohibet." *De virtutibus*, fol. 52ᵛ.

virile strength of the soul. Men who have fallen prey to *accidia*, lacking the desire to work and be useful evident in the rest of nature, become impotent, dissolute, and sick, and are tormented by the memory of past sinful pleasures that they are no longer able to pursue.

Turning from the traditional seven virtues and vices to the virtues of social life defined by Aristotle, Caldiera no longer addresses himself, it seems, to mankind in general, but to that sector of the Venetian population whose behavior might affect the successful operation and honor of the republic: the patriciate or wealthy citizen class.[25] The virtue of magnificence, for instance, as Caldiera defines it, could pertain only to a member of a privileged ruling class. A magnificent man is expected to support a variety of projects that, even when performed for private reasons, cast glory upon the city and its rulers. "Hence the magnificent man is called magnificent because of 'doing great things' [*magna faciens*] in those situations for the performance of which not all men have sufficient wealth, as in the celebration of weddings, which should be celebrated with the greatest expense, and the more worthily because they occur rarely. Similarly, the splendor of the magnificent man appears also in the construction of homes, fortresses, and cities, which are intended to endure perpetually; and also similarly in the building of churches, in which divine offices are to be performed with the greatest devotion."[26] Moreover, the man whose wealth is inherited and is also a member of the dominant social group is considered more obligated in this regard than the man whose wealth is earned by labor: "And indeed, those who have received wealth from their parents and without labor can easily spend it. For one more carefully conserves that wealth which is achieved laboriously than that which is obtained with no labor."[27]

Magnanimity is another virtue that relates to the public life of the nobleman rather than to the inner worth of the individual. The foundation of magnanimity, Caldiera claims, is virtue itself, because it is

[25] These virtues of liberality, modesty, mildness, magnificence, and so on, are described generally in the same order and in the same way as Aristotle presents them in Book IV of the *Ethics*. Discussion of the virtues of magnificence and magnanimity is based on *De virtutibus*, fols. 38ᵛ-40.

[26] "Propterea magnificus quia magna faciens, quibus non omnes sumptus sufficiunt sicut in celebrandis nuptiis, que plurimis diviciis celebrande sunt, et quia rarius fiunt, eo dignius celebrentur. Similiter etiam . . . in edificatione domorum, castrorum et civitatum, quae sunt perpetuo duraturae, in quibus magnifici splendor apparet. Similiter etiam et in edificatione templorum, in quibus divina officia maxima cum devotione [celebrentur]." *De virtutibus*, fol. 39.

[27] "Et immo qui pecunias facile a parentibus acceperunt ipsas etiam facilius elargiuntur. Nam servare studiosius quisque solet que laboriosius conquiruntur, quam ea que nullo labore accipiuntur." Ibid., fol. 38ᵛ.

virtue that merits honor. But the magnanimous man is more splendid if he is also wealthy, not because wealth is essential to magnanimity but because with wealth his virtue is more conspicuous, and he seems more greatly honorable in the eyes of the vulgar. Liberality and magnificence are thus concerned with the accumulation of honor based upon economic behavior alone. Magnanimity, on the other hand, seeks the accumulation of honor through generous giving, but also requires something more: "Therefore these are the characteristics suitable to the magnanimous man, that for the great good and health of the republic, and for the honor of divine worship, he exposes himself to labors and dangers. Also that in the achievement of these things he would prefer death rather than commit any unworthy or shameful deed. ... The worthiness of the magnanimous man is most clearly seen in this, that he seems to require no rewards from other men, which he would not seek and earnestly entreat even if he were in genuine need, but he liberally and promptly succors those whom he knows to be in need or poor."[28]

Caldiera's *On the Virtues* is thus two-faceted. On the one hand, he prescribes to universal mankind the observance of the usual virtues for the usual reasons, and the avoidance of the usual vices. On the other, implicitly redefining his audience, he recommends to the upper classes of his city that they display through just beneficence their wealth and status. By the first series of prescriptions, the author seems to deny the complexities of personal existence and to impose constraints on all unruly tendencies of attitude or behavior. By the second, he encourages the rulers of the city to express through their deeds not their individual personalities but their consciousness of power.

The second work of Caldiera's trilogy, the *De oeconomia veneta (On the Venetian Household)*, describes the proper behavior of all members of the family and the proper function of the family as a whole.[29] The elements of the family are the father, the wife, children, servants, and domesticated animals. The family is a social system in miniature, each member of which plays an appropriate and indispen-

---

[28] "Proprietates itaque quae magnanimo essentialiter conveniunt sunt, ut pro magno bono, pro rei publice salute, pro observando divino culto, se [*ms.* sed] laboriosis periculis exponat. Ittem quod se rebus maximis exponens mortem preeligat, ne indignum aut turpe aliquid facinus profiteatur. ... Quod vero magnanimi dignitatem amplius ostentat ut nullis aliorum meritis indigere videatur, quibus etiam si caruerit vix petit vixque indigens exposcit, sed quos egere vel inopes novit his liberaliter et prompte succurrit." Ibid., fols. 39ᵛ-40.

[29] Once again, he relies on the Aristotelian tradition, but more freely in this case: the pseudo-Aristotelian *Oeconomia*, particularly 3:1343b-5:1344b and 6:1345a-1345b, and Aristotle's *Politics*, 1. The following definition of family members is based on the *De oeconomia*, fols. 82-89, 90ᵛ-99.

sable role, as do the separate members of a healthy body: "Hence if any of these fail in health the whole body sickens, yet more or less depending whether any more principal part is affected. The economy, similarly, or any domestic system, should have its principal and less principal parts. And indeed all should be sound, for if any one part is weak, they all perish, and the entire household is destroyed."[30] Of this perfect domestic coordination, the *paterfamilias* is likened to the head. His vigor rests in his intellect, or in prudence. He is required to be just and temperate, diligent in the acquisition of wealth, kind to his wife, dutiful and mild to his children, and merciful to his servants, whom he should keep amply supplied with food and clothing, and to his chattel: "likewise horses, cows, donkeys, birds, and other animals and inanimate things inhabiting the house demand their just right and portion."[31] Women, the second in dignity of the family members, must be utterly obedient to their husbands, sober, constant, and prudent. They follow their husbands' model with regard to the rule of the household, and nourish their children and instruct them in good morals. Children are to be reverent and obedient to their parents, from whom they obtain being, nourishment, reputation, and the privilege of citizenship. Servants, finally, must be always busy and prompt, and above all, loyal.

Caldiera here views the family as a perfectly equilibrated hierarchical system comprised of clearly articulated and seemingly inalterable personal relationships. Though his depiction of family structure is void of an understanding of individual psychological phenomena, however, it is not without an element of real social content. The pattern of family organization that emerges from his writings is patently aristocratic. It is a family so affluent that its breadwinner's just pursuit of wealth is not only encouraged, but moderated; in which the abundance of spiced foods and wines must be shunned for the sake of health; in which the *paterfamilias* must consider it among his duties to give his wife valuable jewels, which are not only beautiful in themselves but also bring honor upon the household.[32] The family's wealth and status is further indicated by the presence of servants and domestic animals, and by the care taken for the education of the children in the

---

[30] "Quare si ipsarum aliqua a sua valitudine dilabatur corpus omne egrotare dicetur, magis tamen aut minus secundum quod principalior aliqua pars amplius dilabetur. Iconomia similiter et communicatio quam domestica suas principales et minus principales habere partes debet. Et quidem omnes incolumes, ne si aliqua una depereat, universa etiam domus diruat." *De oeconomia*, fol. 99.

[31] "Item equi, boves, aseli, aves, et cetera animata et inanimata domui famulantia sua iura suasque portiones exposcunt." Ibid., fol. 99r-v.

[32] Ibid., fols. 83, 82v.

seven liberal and mechanical arts. Finally, the impressive construction of the house, the family's physical shell, as described by Caldiera, reveals that he is concerned only with families of substance. Their houses, located in the best neighborhoods and built with "zealous genius and the greatest and most excellent artistry," are equipped with broad portals and luminous inner courtyards.[33] But extravagant display should be avoided, the author cautions, reminding a proud nobility of its civic responsibility. "Homes should not be built by citizens according to the abundance of their wealth but for the sake of the dignity of the city, and according to the merits of the persons." Magnificence is appropriate in public buildings, but in private houses, utility and not splendor is fitting. "The householder should rather make himself worthy of admiration because of the virtue by which he excels than because of the sumptuous home by which he has desired to be conspicuous. Not the house but virtue makes men immortal and equal to the gods."[34]

Caldiera's assumptions are aristocratic, as well, as he describes the role of the father and social structure of the family. The father is to have absolute rule in the household. Just as the architect is the one supremely necessary ruler or principle (*principium*) of the construction of the material house, the *paterfamilias* is the one necessary ruler or principle of the household, alone having the experience of virtuous life, the knowledge of good morals, and the prudence necessary to provide for the future. Every household, therefore, requires a single ruler. In this requirement, the domestic household resembles the rest of nature, for in nature, too, all things are subjected to one first principle of their kind: efficient or mobile things are traced to a first cause; forms are resolved into one principal form; all matter is subordinate to one material essence. Thus there is one God, who is the first agent, the first form, the first end, to whom all things are subordinated either efficiently or materially. In the city, there is one prince by whom all things are ruled. In the home, necessarily, there is one *paterfamilias*, who is supreme among the members of the family.

[33] "Domus ergo melioribus civitatis locis sitae solerti ingenio, maxima praeclaraque arte struantur. Primumque patentes fores habeant, ut cum introeuntes postes subierint et extranei et [*ms.* extraneis at] domestici, ipsorum praecognoscant adventum. ... Patentia enim intrinsecus loca esse debent. Item sole luminosoque coelo coperta, ne latens introitus latentem fraudem pariat." Ibid., fol. 90.

[34] "Domus enim non pro divitiarum copiis a civibus formande sunt, sed pro decentia Civitatis et meritis personarum. ... Magis et enim se dignum admiratione faciat iconomus pro virtute qua prestat quam pro sumptuosa domo qua precellere curavit. Non domus sed virtus immortales homines et diis pares facit." Ibid., fol. 91. Talking of houses, Caldiera here echoes the "walls of the city" theme discussed above; see Introduction.

CHAPTER TWO

Along with the necessity of absolute rule in any group, small or large, Caldiera accepts the inevitability and permanence of social class distinction. His hierarchical vision of family structure is compatible with assumptions of class stratification. Just as there are understood to be various concentrations of virtue and power in the different categories of family members, there are assumed to be diverse concentrations of moral qualities and mental capacity in different social categories. Caldiera's pursuit of the hierarchical model is relentless. Coolly he follows the chain of being downward, from father, wife, and child, through the servant class and into the category of nonhuman and even inanimate existence: the ox, the ass, the horse, and household tools.[35]

Whereas servants are seen as a necessarily inferior class, useful to the functioning of the household if perfectly obedient but in nature only slightly more elevated than chattel or household implements, children, their immediate superiors in the family hierarchy, are understood as having the capacity of assuming a higher rank and dignity. Parents, Caldiera urges, should occasionally allow worthy children to direct the household—including, of course, the servants—so that by practicing this form of leadership, like princes whose sons practice kingship so as to be fit for succession, they may become habituated to ruling and make themselves worthy of their elders.[36]

Women, like servants, constitute a class by nature inferior to that of the male ruler of the family. Whereas the husband's role is moral and intellectual, the woman's is biological.[37] Superior in the family hierarchy to children, if only by reason of the latter's immaturity, the woman is subordinate to the *paterfamilias*, and must obey him. Wifely virtue consists in perfect chastity and "unanimity" to the will of the husband.

Caldiera's relegation of women to a social category inferior to and

[35] "Non enim servi instrumenta tantummodo domibus sunt, sed animata, pro quo et seipsis, et cum superioribus paruerint [*ms.* paruerit], ad omnia domus praesidia sufficere posse videntur. . . . Preter servos sunt et alia instrumenta etiam animata domuis servientia ut bos, aselus, et equus. Multa etiam preter hec domui necessario et instrumentaliter servientia quae ab ipsis domesticis humanisque servis reguntur." Ibid., fol. 88[r-v]. Cf. Aristotle, *Politics* I:3:1253b-4:1254a.
[36] Caldiera's advice to parents that children should be prepared to carry family responsibilities in the future is phrased in explicitly political terms (*De oeconomia*, fol. 88[v]): "Postea vero filiis, qui suorum parentum vices gerunt, quibus magis aut minus parendum est, secundum quod a parentibus benemeriti iudicantur. *Et sicut in principatu sapientia principis adnotatur, ita etiam principatus dignitas suos principes erudit, et ipsos principatu dignos reddit*" (emphasis added). Cf. Aristotle, *Politics* VII:14-1332b.
[37] This is made clear mainly in regard to the rearing of children (*De oeconomia*, fol. 87[r-v]): fathers are concerned with the practical and scientific education of their children, women with their prenatal nurture and physical requirements in infancy.

104

essentially distinct from that occupied by men, together with his assertion of the unquestioned authority of the *paterfamilias*, and his
acceptance of class stratification as natural and invariable, constitute
attitudes consistent with the advocacy of an authoritarian state and
society. Indeed, these social attitudes are not merely consistent with
such political views, but are seen by the author himself as having an
explicitly political reference. Political values thoroughly permeate Caldiera's exposition of the science of domestic administration. Far from
unconscious of the similarity of his domestic and political views, he
argues eloquently the parallelism of the family and the state. "And
just as every economy resembles a polity, so also the home is in the
likeness of the city."[38] The family is a cell, containing on a microscopic
scale the genetic material determining the existence of the political
body, not only because its structures are similar to those of the state,
but because it is an instrument of socialization: the virtues to which
children are habituated in their youth are displayed by them when
adult, and the behavior learned in the family assures appropriate civic
behavior in the future. The attitudes that Caldiera expresses, therefore,
in his analysis of the family unit, may be expected to be transferred
to the state when he turns his attention to the larger group. An authoritarian state is founded on an authoritarian family.

In the third work of his trilogy, *On the Excellence of the Venetian
Polity*, Caldiera does not create a science of politics, nor guide the
creation of an ideal political system, but describes one that had already
achieved the furthest limits of excellence. His systematic exposition of
the excellence of Venice in the seven mechanical arts, the seven liberal
arts, and the seven virtues closes with a survey of Venetian government
councils and a eulogy of the institution of the *dogado*. Thus interlacing
objective descriptions of Venetian life and achievements with a triadic
system of timeless philosophical and theological categories, Caldiera
mythologizes Venice, lending her real civic existence the tonalities of
perfection. This imposition of the ideal upon the real is most conspicuous in Caldiera's discussion of Venice's excellence in the first
three of the seven virtues, and in his description of the Venetian government.[39]

Merely personal virtues, performed for the sake of one's own soul,
are brushed aside as Caldiera opens the last book of this work. Virtue

---

[38] "Et quia omnia Iconomia Policie assimilatur, et domus etiam civitatis similitudinem
gerit." *Ibid.*, fol. 89ᵛ. Caldiera makes this likeness explicit. Monarchy, aristocracy, and
"timocracy," the three modes of rule encountered in states, are encountered within
families as well: fols. 81ᵛ-82.
[39] The analysis below based on *De politia*, fols. 133-39ᵛ, 146-48ᵛ.

105

is only profoundly virtuous when it has a republican, or civic, or social reference. No one can be considered virtuous unless he behaves virtuously toward the republic. Only those men are considered worthy before God, the Stoics said, who had served and profited the republic: "for which they awarded themselves also the title of patrician, and after their deaths moreover would be made divine."[40] Here the object of virtue is not God, but the state. This transposition of values can be seen, to take one example among many, in Caldiera's exposition of the three theological virtues, from which he creates a trinity of republican values. Devotion to the republic is related to devotion to God in his discussion of faith, the first of these three virtues. "Just as a man is constrained to preserve inviolate faith toward God, and so to compel his intellect to the belief in all things which are of God, so also he should show a similar faith in the republic, which merits all our talents, and from which we hope to have all merits and all supreme rewards."[41] Faith in the republic gives rise to a number of different fidelities, so that anyone who excels in *civilitas*, civic virtue, also easily fulfills these other responsibilities. Devotion must be shown to parents and familiars, to citizens, and rulers, and all others who are raised to the principal magistracies of the city. The citizens of Venice, whose "civility" cannot be doubted, so love the republic that they spare no labors, no expense, not even their lives for its protection. "Whence, just as we hope to see at a future time God through faith, so equally do we judge that we are not satisfied, unless we have manifestly embraced the supreme felicity of the republic."[42] Thus the immortal life of heaven and fulfilled republican existence are made rhetorically to converge. "Whereby the mutual faith existing among its members renders the republic immortal."[43] Without faith, moreover, all republican activities would languish. Trade would decline, and public and private laws would lose their dignity. Faith in the republic, therefore, is treasured more than life itself, so that if men of any order abandon it, they are rendered utterly inhuman.

The parallelism between religious and republican values is continued

[40] "Ex quo sibi etiam Patricii nomen promeruissent, postea vero et celites fierent." Ibid., fol. 134.
[41] "Sicut enim quisque inviolatam servare deo fidem tenetur et suum intellectum taliter coercere ad credendum omnia que dei maxime sunt, ita et quisque similem praestare fidem debet rei publice que omnes nostras partes promeretur, et a qua merita omnia maxima habituros [*ms.* habituri] speramus." Ibid.
[42] "Ex quo sicut deum per fidem nos visuros aliquando putamus, ita pariter nobis satisfactum minime existimamus, nisi supremam rei publice foelicitatem manifeste comprehenderimus. . . ." Ibid., fol. 134ᵛ.
[43] "Quare mutua inter collegas fides rem publicam immortalem reddit." Ibid.

in the discussion of charity, the second of the theological virtues. Charity consists in love of God and of neighbor on account of God. But this charity is to be extended to citizens and to the republic. For the republic seeks the benevolence of the citizens, and they consider themselves to be obligated to the republic. Responsibility is owed toward the republic—indeed it is demanded by a "most worthy kind of coercion"—which results in the perfect conjunction of the citizens in love.

The *scuole* (charitable institutions of a type general in Italy but that developed a unique importance in Venice) are presented as exemplifying the kind of charity existing among the citizens of Venice. In their *scuole*, the men of Venice are held together like loving brothers under one ruler, enjoying a perfect security.[44] These are the institutions that bind the men of Venice in civility and charity. The men are also related by ties of class into charitable communities. Most loving of all are the nobles, who are considered noble because of their social background, their marriages, their magistracies, their ruling of the republic. As rulers, they coerce with public laws those delinquent in love toward the republic. Men of inferior social orders are also united in love. Even foreigners residing within the city, although they had come from other more dissident cities, are rendered pacific by the morals of the city of Venice, and learn to behave virtuously. The purpose of republican charity is the same as that of republican faith: to cement the obedience of the citizen to the city, and thus to maintain harmony.

If the force of love binds the Venetian population together, its absence produces civil rebellion. Cities that cannot command the love of their citizens are destroyed: "wherefore their fortresses fall, likewise their towers and walls as well, likewise the homes constructed with the greatest artistry are utterly dissolved and perish; likewise the men are incapable of erecting them again."[45] The exiled, displaced by civic ruin, flow to Venice "from all parts of the world" and find a safe domicile.

Just as faith in God is associated with faith in the republic, and Christian charity with the mutual love of the citizens, the Christian hope for beatitude, the third of the theological virtues, is associated with the striving for republican honors. Princes and citizens have often

---

[44] The *scuole* (*scolae*) assisted with burial costs or otherwise tended the needs of members, their widows, and orphans. For these institutions, see B. Pullan, *Rich and Poor in Renaissance Venice*, Part I.

[45] ". . . quia ipsarum delabuntur castra, item etiam turres et moenia. Item etiam domus maxima arte constructe dissolvuntur et pereunt. Item etiam homines ab aliarum erectione deficiunt." *De politia*, fol. 132.

risked danger and death in order to serve the republic. None would have performed these deeds if they did not have some hope of future rewards, just as none would be virtuous if they did not hope for eternal beatitude on account of their merits and the grace of God. There has never been a city that inspires hope as great as does Venice, which rewards deserving citizens in infinite ways. "Just as God shows Himself infinitely generous to those with a good hope, so also citizens in every polity are granted excellent rewards for their merits."[46] It quickly appears, however, that although the republic may reward all according to their merits, both merits and rewards are firmly determined by class lines. Caldiera takes this opportunity, under the rubric of republican "hope," to expound his perception of the Venetian class system. Just as, in the Christian universe, some are born to salvation and some to damnation, in Venice, some are born to rule and some to serve.

Each social class has within its boundaries a different goal that represents the summit of what is attainable by its particular population.[47] Foreigners who have demonstrated their talents and worthiness are admitted to public positions. Even more do members of the citizen order expect to be rewarded for their merits with prestigious offices, and with the respect of their fellows: "So that according to their merits, they are made the heads of charitable institutions, and for their sanctimony they are esteemed; and thus because of their age, because of their merits, they obtain in every magistracy the supreme parts of honor and glory."[48] Thus both foreigners and citizens strive to achieve an office appropriate to their status. But they still have no access to the political offices that yield not only honor in Venice, but power as well. These are reserved for members of the nobility.

The patriciate was created, Caldiera explains, because certain men, inspired by hope of due reward, had served the republic and thereby merited honors that became hereditary. "Those . . . who are counselors of the prince, such as the procurators, *avogadori*, and all the order of the *savi*, and others who have won for themselves some kind of honor

---

[46] "Nam sicut deus infinita largitione bene sperantibus se praebet, ita et civibus in omni genere politie pro ipsorum meritis praeclaris muneribus donantur." Ibid., fol. 139.

[47] Caldiera discusses foreigners, citizens, and patricians; the *popolo*, except in one case, is omitted from his purview. In that exceptional case, Caldiera referred (ibid., fol. 139ᵛ) to the admission in 1381 of thirty *popolano* families to the nobility as a reward for service to Venice in the War of Chioggia. By "foreigners," Caldiera follows normal usage and intends not only non-Italians but anyone not born in Venice or holding citizen status.

[48] "Sunt et aliorum ordinum cives quibus differentes maximique magistratus pro ipsorum meritis conferunter, . . . ut pro ipsorum meritis principes scolarum habeantur, et pro ipsorum sanctimonia deligantur et sic pro etate, pro meritis hominum supremas honoris et gloriae in omni magistratu partes accipiunt." Ibid., fol. 138.

or utility, arrived at that end by following some form of hope; so that if they had greatly benefited the republic, the honors and the utility of their positions are transmitted also to their descendants."[49] Not birth but merit wins them standing in the republic; but thereafter their standing permits their descendants to accede to the same dignity as they had originally possessed as a reward for meritorious action. The patriciate is by this argument created and justified at the same time by circular argument: privilege is granted in perpetuity on account of merit; if patricians had not merited the privileges they now enjoy, it follows, they would never have received them. Once admitted to the political sphere, furthermore, through hereditary right, noblemen may climb as high in the magisterial hierarchy as their capabilities warrant: "If . . . they are from the senatorial order, they are granted by the Senate the honors and magistracies of the republic, according to the degree in which they deserve them (which is determined by the deliberation of the Senate); and so from inferior dignities they are extolled as high as they are judged deserving."[50] At the peak of the ladder of republican honors sought by the patriciate is the *dogado*. Since any magistracy is conferred by the Senate as the reward of virtue, the doge, awarded the highest attainable republican office, is by definition the most virtuous member of the patrician order, itself created for its innate excellence. Like pure gold that contains no baser element, the Venetian doge chosen by the wise Senate is unblemished by any vice.

The Venetian system of government that Caldiera perceives bears an uncertain relation to the one which in fact existed. Whereas the Venetian government consisted of a series of administrative, judicial, legislative, and advisory councils of overlapping responsibility, variable effectiveness, and uncertain correlation between function and prestige, headed by a doge whose powers were theoretically restricted, Caldiera describes a monarchy ruled by a doge superior to the law on account of his virtues, and assisted by a series of councils functioning as consultative bodies subordinate to the dogal will.[51] A government

---

[49] "Qui . . . consultores principis, item procuratores, advocatores, et omnes ordines sapientum, et coeteri qui sibi aliquid honoris vel utilitatis praefixerunt ad eam aliquo spei genere praecurrerunt. Quod si magis de re publica bene meriti fuissent, etiam ad coeteros omnes posteros sui feruntur honores suaque fertur [*ms.* finitur] utilitas." Ibid., fol. 139r-v.

[50] "Si vero ex senatorio fuerint ordine, ita a senatu traduntur honoribus et rei publice magistratibus quantum consulte promereri creduntur; et sic ab inferioribus dignitatibus tanto altius extolluntur quantum etiam ipsarum benemeriti existimantur." Ibid., fol. 138.

[51] For the government councils, G. Maranini, *La costituzione di Venezia dopo la serrata del Maggior Consiglio*; more briefly, see A. da Mosto, *L'Archivio di Stato di Venezia* [da Mosto, *Archivio*], vol. I; for the Senate, E. Besta, *Il senato veneziano*.

is better ruled by good men than good laws; in Venice, that good man is the doge.[52] "Splendid like the sun," the doge of Venice so excels in wisdom, justice, and prudence, Caldiera explains, that he is capable of ruling without assistance. But not wishing to appear arrogant, and acceding to law, he consults his colleagues in the Senate before arriving at a decision; or, if the matter is difficult, other bodies are consulted, so that the best decision may be reached by their "multiplied and proven minds."[53]

The ducal counselors, the three *capi* or chiefs of the Council of Forty, the three groups of "sages" (the *savi grandi*, the *savi di terra-ferma*, and the *savi agli ordini*), the Council of Ten, the three censors of morals, and two Councils of Forty (concerned with civil and criminal law, respectively), the Senate, and the Great Council are described in turn; with one notable exception, these bodies are described as being subject to the commands of the doge, or, less frequently, the Senate, and their function is in most cases defined as advisory—they "consult" among themselves; they advise (*consulunt*) the doge; they act on the advice (*consulto*) of some other body (*consulatu*).[54] The exception is

---

[52] Caldiera may have known of this Platonic question (whether it is better to have a virtuous ruler capable of interpreting the laws, or, in the absence of such a virtuous man, laws to which even the ruler is subject) from Plato's *Laws* IV:709a-715d (translated and dedicated to the doge of Venice by George of Trebizond in 1462). Plato believes that such a virtuous lawmaker could not in fact exist; Caldiera sees just such a figure in the Venetian doge.

[53] *De politia*, fol. 147. The notion that decisions are made in Venice by a process of consultation arriving at consensus seems implausible and naive. But it is not peculiar to Caldiera, as will be seen below in discussions of Lauro Quirini and Domenico Morosini.

[54] The counselors (see da Mosto, *Archivio*, I, 21) are described as advising the doge where it is necessary for the better operation of the republic (*De politia*, fol. 147ᵛ). The three *capi* (da Mosto, loc. cit.) decide which matters are to be put before the prince (*De politia*, loc. cit.). The *savi grandi* (da Mosto, *Archivo*, I, 22) supervise the execution of decisions as advised by the Senate (*De politia*, loc. cit.). The *savi di terraferma* (da Mosto, loc. cit.) are seen as carrying out Senate commands in matters of war and peace (*De politia*, loc. cit.). The *savi agli ordini* (da Mosto, *Archivo*, I, 22-23) advise on naval matters (*De politia*, fols. 147ᵛ-148). For the Council of Ten (da Mosto, *Archivo*, I, 52-55; *De politia*, fol. 148) see the next note. The censors advise the prince about actions to be taken to prevent shame from befalling the citizens and the republic (*De politia*, loc. cit.); a group of censors were charged after 1517 with preventing *broglio elettorale* (Besta, *Senato*, p. 269; da Mosto, *Archivio*, I, 77), and it is possible that an earlier attempt at a magistracy of this sort was in effect at the time that Caldiera wrote, and was later dissolved and reconstituted. The Councils of Forty (da Mosto, Archivo, I, 63-64) are seen as advising about civic or financial matters, or violent and criminal acts (*De politia*, loc. cit.). Caldiera mentions two such councils, although at this time there were three. The Senate (da Mosto, *Archivo*, I, 34-38) is convened by the prince and advises on the most important and controversial matters (*De politia*, loc. cit.). The Great Council (da Mosto, *Archivo*, I, 29-33) advises on matters in its jurisdiction, and its "judgment" cannot be overruled (*De politia*, loc. cit.).

the Council of Ten, which is seen—clear testimony of Caldiera's concern for the problem of social control—to act quite aggressively: "So great is the authority and power of these ten men, that they tolerate nothing threatening to the republic, and not only those who act evilly, but also those who speak evilly, and even those who think evil thoughts are severely punished, so that they are in no way allowed to contaminate or infect the republic."[55]

Aside from the ominous description of the functions of the Ten, however, Caldiera's description of the councils creates the illusion of the uniformity of function of these government agencies, minimizing their diversity and, in some cases, their power. He distorts the real structure of government function in Venice, attributing to the doge exaggerated authority and to the councils, seen as helpful but not essential to the administration, an ambiguous and primarily advisory role. This alteration of political reality betrays the authors' theoretical preference for a system unified through hierarchy and authority. In describing the councils as a series of assemblies of "wise men" advising the doge in different areas, he avoids the appearance of conflict between agencies or among persons that did in fact exist, and magnifies the appearance of unanimity and obedience. At the same time, in exaggerating the role of the doge, he asserts that the same hierarchical pattern of rule exists in Venice as in the order of nature, as he knew it, and is concordant with the will of God. As such, clearly, it can neither possess imperfection nor be denied obedience. Thus Caldiera renders rebellion unthinkable.

Not only does Caldiera impose upon the complex government structure of Venice the simpler and more imposing pattern of universal hierarchy, but he attempts to provide it with an astral parentage and a divinely sanctioned immortality.[56] Empires, kingdoms, princes, cities, armies, homes, and men are all subjected to the determining movement of the heavens. They all have a beginning, augmentation, a period of stability, and a decline, until they cease from being entirely. Thus first Babylon, then Athens, then Rome, all began, grew, held sway, and declined. Venice had been particularly favored by the stars, however, and while their influence might cause the city to weaken at some future time, still its superior political structures will permit it to endure per-

---

[55] "Horum decemvirorum tanta est auctoritas atque potestas, ut nihil violentum rei publice patiantur, et non solum qui male agunt, sed et qui mala loquuntur, *etiam qui mala cogitant*, gravius puniantur, tamquam nulla ex parte fedari se sive infici rem publicam patiatur" (emphasis added). *De politia*, fol. 148. Compare this with the statements of Domenico and Paolo Morosini about the Council of Ten, below, in Sections 5 and 4, respectively.

[56] The following summary based on *De politia*, fols. 102-103, 145-46.

petually. Immune, therefore, from the usual pattern of growth and decline, Venetian institutions can ensure Venice's supremacy. Finding the city's efficient cause in God and in the stars, is material cause in the sea and the resources of the earth, its formal cause in the aristocratic mode of rule, Caldiera declares that the final cause of the city of Venice, the purpose for which it exists, is that it might excel throughout the earth and proffer wisdom and assistance to the whole globe. Its destiny is imperial.

The individual, or "monastic" life had for Caldiera entailed the observance of conventional moral imperatives. Within the family, the individual takes on new moral responsibilities and is introduced to a social system reflecting in miniature the polity later to be described, hierarchical in structure and authoritarian in mode. Within the polity of Venice, the individual's moral responsibilities once again expand. He acquires obligations of love, loyalty, and obedience to his city and its rulers, for the faithful performance of which, within his own social class, he may confidently expect due rewards. Caldiera's Venice—the city, its families, the hearts of its people—rigidly structured, tautly controlled, blandly unchanging, in return for the surrender of individual freedoms of thought and behavior promises perfect harmony and endless peace.

In a second major work, Caldiera again poses a hierarchical model of the universe that in its solemn and relentless grandeur engulfs all that is merely human.[57] In the *Concordance of the Poets, Philosophers, and Theologians*, however, he focuses not on the relations of moral and social existence, but on the relations between modes of knowledge. Poetic knowledge, vague and shifting, nevertheless gives access to the ultimate truth that is seen as the goal of all forms of knowledge and the source of their perfect concord. The liberal arts, including some of the disciplines of the *studia humanitatis*, are ranked higher, but still subordinate to philosophical knowledge, to which they are preparatory. Philosophical knowledge, practical and speculative, is loftier still, and launches the knower on his journey toward theological knowledge and the direct contemplation of truth. This curious and problematical work thus illuminates the role of humanism in Venice. For Caldiera's humanism—and in this regard, though he is more complete and systematic than other Venetians, his thought is representative of the movement—does not vaunt the secular imagination over religious vision, the *studia humanitatis* over academic philosophy, civil over other-

[57] The *De concordantia poetarum, philosophorum et theologorum [Concordantia]*, cited here in the ms. version Vat. Urb. Lat. 1178. An extended discussion of this work appears in my "Venetian Ideology," pp. 92-233.

worldly existence, or this world over the afterworld, but embraces all forms of thought and existence in one pyramidal whole that dignifies an authoritarian state and culminates in the *visio dei*.

The lengthy first book of the *Concordance* presents a series of mythological images and episodes drawn ultimately from ancient poetry, and translates them into analogous Christian images and doctrines. The second book, less discursive, describes otherworldly realms of philosophy and the journey to God. His work thus embraces a reality extending from phantasms of the mind to the ultimate truth, remote and fixed, of eternity.

The first book presents, typically, a three-level interpretation of myth: the literal (simple narration), the moral (or natural-philosophical), and the spiritual (in which the events or figures of the myth are reduced to theological categories). Caldiera applies this format with varying consistency to thirty-seven mythic images or episodes, producing a compendium of mythographic interpretation too vast to be more than glanced at here. But the most important features of the method may be noted.

In presenting myth at the literal level, Caldiera fractures the plasticity of the classical image, reducing it to a rubric to which acceptable meanings may be assigned. In describing the goddess Minerva, for instance, he so fragments the figure that it is removed from the naturalistic classical world that gave it origin, and becomes an invariable and absolute pattern.[58] She has an iron helmet and a cap on her head, while her face is uncovered; a crest tops her helmet; her breastplate is ornamented. In her right hand she holds a lance with a sharp three-pointed blade; in her left, a crystal shield in which her face is reflected; on her feet are golden sandals. Her face is young and virginal, but on her chestplate is the image of the Gorgon. Dissolved into its parts, the image of Minerva is easily layered with abstract significations, causing the substantial reality of the goddess to recede yet further. At the moral level of interpretation, for instance, Minerva wears a helmet by which to defend wisdom, housed in the head, and her helmet sports a varicolored plume to signify the eminence, glory, and diversity of wisdom. Her lance is reason's weapon against false opinions, and is triangular in form to signify three kinds of argumentation or of syllogism by

[58] Part of the blame here lies with the medieval mythographers from whom Caldiera borrows this image. Yet it is significant that he chose to consult those authorities when humanist exploration of the classical tradition had already made available more sinuous images of the ancients. See the discussion of Caldiera's sources in "Venetian Ideology," pp. 139ff. The image of Minerva and interpretative commentary is in the *Concordantia*, fols. 10ᵛ-14.

113

which logical errors are overcome. At the spiritual level of interpretation, her headgear becomes a helmet of sobriety and temperance, and her weapon the lance of rectitude and justice, "through which we measure the altitude, latitude and profundity of God."[59] The moral and theological analogues closely resemble each other, but are distant indeed from the goddess of wisdom Homer had envisioned, and whom some humanists and artists of the Renaissance chose to recapture.[60]

In many other cases, moral or spiritual analogues of ancient myths jar strangely with the originals. Where Paris, asked to judge among three goddesses, awards the golden apple to Venus, Caldiera sees the apostle Paul presented with the three theological virtues, choosing love. Daphne, abducted by Jove from a fortress tower in a golden cloud, is made the Virgin Mary seized from her virginity (the tower) and impregnated by God. The trident carried by Neptune signifies three kinds of waters: the springs, which are the waters that flowed from the side of Christ on the Cross; the rivers, which are the waters of baptism; the sea, which is the holy water contained in the fonts of churches for the cleansing of sins. Jove's seduction of Leda, wife of King Tyndar, is seen as Christ's wresting of the holy church of God from its union with the Old Law. He appears as a swan, to signify that his nature was at once wholly spiritual (like a bird) yet joined to the pure principle (symbolized by whiteness) of humanity. The egg born of the union of Christ and the church—from which, in the ancient myth, Helen, Castor, and Pollux were born—symbolizes the Eucharist: its white representing Christ's divinity, the yolk, the human veil of flesh in which He appeared.[61]

Caldiera is no impassioned reader of classical literature who, like his compatriot Gregorio Correr, ravished by beauty, would weep over Virgil.[62] He regards the myths of the ancients as figments of human imagination, irrational and immoral, in which, nevertheless, reside

[59] "Dextera manu lanceam tenet rectitudinis et iustitiae per quam mensuramus altitudinem, latitudinem et profunditatem dei." *Concordantia*, fol. 13.

[60] According to Erwin Panofsky (*Renaissance and Renascences in Western Art*), the Renaissance view of classical antiquity differs essentially from the medieval view in that it sees the classical world in perspective and at a distance, thus regaining the wholeness and plasticity of the image with which it was conceived by the ancients themselves. Jean Seznec remarks similarly: "the Renaissance appears as the reintegration of antique subject matter within the antique form: we can speak of the Renaissance from the day Hercules resumed the athletic breadth of shoulder, his club, and his lion's skin." *The Survival of the Pagan Gods*, p. 211. Caldiera does not wish or does not succeed in viewing the classical image with this detachment.

[61] The myths of the judgment of Paris, *Concordantia*, fols. 5-8; Daphne, fol. 35ᵛ; Neptune, fols. 66-71ᵛ; Jove and Leda, fols. 35ᵛ-40ᵛ.

[62] See Correr's *Epistola ad Caeciliam virginem*, pp. 213ff.

scintillae of the divine. Pagan myths are understood to hold a reflection of truth, just as inanimate matter, the furthest substance from God in Caldiera's hierarchical universe, shares, though remotely, in His radiance. His aim is more to rescue from the dross of ancient imagery the pure kernel of moral and spiritual truth than to safeguard pagan imagination from clerical censors. In so doing he imprisons the sensuous imagery of the ancients in moral and theological categories as surely as, in *On the Virtues*, he confines the human being to a stern corset of seven imperious virtues.[63]

Far closer to divinity are the arts and sciences, modes of knowing vastly more worthy than the murky intuitions of the poets. In Book II of his *Concordance*, Caldiera journeys in a dream vision through the circles of the super-planetary world.[64] There he meets, in order of ascending importance, emblematic figures of the seven liberal arts: grammar, logic, rhetoric, arithmetic, geometry, music, and astrology. These modes of knowledge cannot provide true enlightenment but can point to a further path. The voyager plunges with difficulty past dark forests and across a treacherous river to the island of Philosophy, ringed by marble walls signifying the power and splendor of distilled philosophical truth. There he encounters the shades of Epicurus, Socrates, Seneca, Plato, and Aristotle. Flanked by these last two, he is led to the majestic presence of Philosophia herself, who discourses upon the branches of philosophy (in order of ascending dignity, moral, natural, and metaphysical), the liberal arts, and the philosophical schools. She then invests him with the insignia of wisdom—helmet, breastplate, sandals, shield, and lance, previously seen on Minerva— in a ritual reminiscent of knighthood. Aristotle escorts Caldiera to a place from which he may seek the other half of the island, walled like an enormous temple. In a final salute, he urges his charge not to neglect the external life to which philosophy pertains as much as to the life of the mind.

That other island realm is the home of practical knowledge as the first had been of speculative. There Caldiera encounters emblematic figures of the mechanical arts, the disciplines useful to those who lead a civic existence, just as the liberal arts are fundamental for the philosopher. Before him now rise in the distance golden towers. To reach them, he traverses lakes and swamps and turbulent seas, and comes

---

[63] In this he is distinguished from such defenders of the classical tradition as Boccaccio, Salutati, and Ficino. See Charles Trinkaus' discussion of the tradititon of *theologia poetica*, with a somewhat different evaluation of Caldiera's role, in *In Our Image and Likeness*, II, 683-721.

[64] The summary below based on the *Concordantia*, fols. 156-207ᵛ.

at last to a splendid city, resembling in all of its attributes Venice. On a throne before him sits the female personification of Respublica. At her feet sit a throng of excellent men, and first among them Francesco Foscari, the doge of Venice. After him, in their official order, are the *consiglieri*, the *savi*, and other members of the *Collegio*—the composite ranks of Venetian government. Inspired by this vision, Caldiera delivers an eloquent oration to Respublica, pledging his loyalty to his *patria* and promising to manifest his devotion by writing incessantly in her praise. The doge greets him, welcomes him to the city, and launches himself in an oration praising Venice's greatness in the liberal and mechanical arts. But no wit or power of eloquence can fully describe Venice's achievements in all these arts, he remarks, nor the beauty of the city adorned with gold and gems and splendid with wealth, nor the greatness of her aristocracy, "which resembles supercelestial government and imitates the form of divine institutions."[65]

Now a veteran of two symmetrical zones of the island-temple (those of contemplative and practical knowledge), Caldiera rushes to the highest point, where planets and stars splendidly shine. There he encounters a "supercelestial army" of Biblical characters escorting the Virgin Mary to the presence of God: Adam and Eve, Noah and his sons, patriarchs and kings, and John the Baptist. The Baptist is followed by a carriage bearing the theological virtues, the Virgin herself, the four evangelists, and the figure of Theologia, drawn by a griffon, symbolic of Christ, bleeding from diverse wounds. Theologia instructs Caldiera—as had Philosophia and Respublica—in the meaning of all he sees—for he is now in the realm of theological knowledge, the summit of the life of the mind, and the analogue to the zenith of the real universe. She prepares him for the divine vision by reviewing from its beginnings the whole history of the world. The procession, meanwhile, which has forged ahead as she spoke, reaches the boundary of heaven. The griffon casts off his yoke, and assumes the form of the Divine Word. The divine throne, the hierarchy of angels, the ranks of the saved are revealed. Christ presents the Virgin to the Father, and the three angel choruses sing, respectively, the Sanctus, the Benedictus, and the Gloria.

What is to be made of this curious work, this amalgam of Boccaccio and the medieval mythographers, of Dante and Boethius, of the academic curriculum and the church triumphant? It is an encyclopedia encompassing the whole of human and divine knowledge, and within

---

[65] ". . . et aristocratiam nostram non admiratur quae supercelesti regimini morem gerit et divinarum institutionum formam imitatur." Ibid., fol. 184ᵛ.

that compass, humanism and civic existence. It assumes a universal ontological hierarchy, as do the works of the Oxford trilogy examined earlier, radiating downward from God, and buttressed by both philosophical and Christian traditions. At the same time, it describes a congruent hierarchy of modes of knowledge, ranging from the poetic (inferior) through the rational (better) to the divine (promising the immediate apprehension of God). Poetry and the classical studies beloved of so many humanists Caldiera admits to this universe but does not revere. It is a lesser language, to be translated into the higher meanings of other disciplines. The passions and desires, self-knowledge and self-regard, the heroic and creative force of the human individual that poetry describes are suppressed as a purer meaning is abstracted and distilled. Civic existence, however, typically honored in Italian humanism, is honored here, indeed, and praised in rhetorical speech, the natural language of that movement. But it is honored not as an autonomous phenomenon but as part of a system that dwarfs it, and is subordinated to the greater truth of the Church.

Caldiera is the most prolific author of this era of Venetian humanism. His Oxford trilogy and the *Concordance* are among the most massive works in its whole corpus.[66] Substantial in length, they are uniquely comprehensive in range. Caldiera is a commoner, not a nobleman, yet a Venetian citizen profoundly accepting of his city's regime and self-image; he is a physican, trained in the arts and philosophy curricula of the University of Padua, and a Christian, the author of pious and theological works. His perspective is unique among the authors examined here. He brings to his labors, certainly, the professional's taste for systematization and completeness, and, possibly, the enthusiastic citizen's awed but distant respect for the city and its rulers. His works are *summae* of the vision of Venetian humanism, presenting in dry and heavy sequence assumptions about the individual and society, about knowledge and existence also met outside his works, but never with such relentless cohesion.

[66] The works examined in this chapter of Francesco Barbaro, Lauro Quirini, Paolo Morosini, and Ermolao Barbaro V are all brief in comparison to Caldiera's. Pietro Barozzi's (on factions) and Ermolao Barbaro G's (on celibacy) are perhaps of equivalent length, but neither approaches Caldiera's in range. Domenico Morosini's is lengthy but disorganized and repetitious, features disguising a certain lack of substance. Francesco Negri's on aristocracy is substantial, but is only in part his; in large part it plagiarizes della Porcia's *De reipublicae venetae administratione*. The collections of the letters of Francesco and Ermolao Barbaro G and Pietro Dolfin are also substantial, but not comparable. No other contemporary Venetian humanist has left us two works of this magnitude.

3. LAURO QUIRINI ON THE ARISTOCRATIC REPUBLIC

The Florentine humanist Poggio Bracciolini wrote in 1440 one of those
key works that encourage readers to see in humanism the gateway to
modern liberalism. His dialogue *On Nobility* challenged the traditional
notion implicit in the social systems prevalent in the Europe of his day
that nobility was acquired by birth.[67] For Poggio, nobility was a matter
not of blood, but of soul. Only a wise and virtuous man was truly
noble. His views provoked some discussion. Popular with many humanists, they were objectionable to the spokesmen for the hereditary
aristocracies of Italy. In Venice, the nobly born found a champion in
Lauro Quirini. He addressed a letter in defense of nobility (in his own
name and those of two friends) to Pietro Tommasi, citizen, humanist,
physician, and friend of the inimical Poggio.[68]

At the Rialto a few days ago, Quirini wrote, the subject of Poggio's
work on nobility arose, provoking such a passionate response that the
rest of the day passed in animated conversation (p. 67). The Greeks,
the Germans, the Genoese, were incensed. The Neapolitans were ready
to challenge Poggio to a duel, convinced that his resentment against
genuine nobility stemmed from his own low birth: "Nor did they think
that any other motive led Poggio to writing except that, as they themselves said, having been humbly born of an unknown father, he hoped
his book on ignobility which so slanders nobility would win for him
what neither his parents nor he himself could attain—nobility."[69] The
Venetians alone remained calm, though they were perplexed as to why
Poggio had so maligned their nobility and their city (p. 70). In the
end, wrote Quirini, we decided that the Florentine's assault was in-
tolerable: "For we who certainly both are and wished to be respected
as noble could no longer stomach it that that ancient foundation of

[67] *De nobilitate*, in Bracciolini's *Opera omnia*, I, 64-83. The work is also translated
(as "On Nobility") by R. N. Watkins (with D. Marsh) in *Humanism and Liberty*.

[68] The *Epistola ad Petrum Thomasium* [*Epist.*] (written c. 1446). A summary of the
work follows. Specific passages alluded to will be indicated in parentheses. For the
tradition of humanist treatises on nobility and the cirumstances of the composition of
Quirini's work, see Kristeller's introduction, pp. 33-41. Tommasi, who was frequently
in contact with non-Venetian humanists, and a friend of Poggio's, was a logical candidate
for spokesman and mediator. It does not appear, however, that he ever wrote, as Quirini
requests him to do in this letter, in defense of the Venetian nobility. The nobleman
Gregorio Correr did assail Poggio's views in a letter now lost, the substance of which
can be inferred from Poggio's courteous and conciliatory reply (in his *Epist.*, ed. Tonellis,
I, 223-28).

[69] "Nec ullam aliam causam esse arbitrabantur, que Poggium ad scribendum indu-
xisset, nisi quod, ut ipsi dicebant, vix ille infimo loco natus et cuius pater omnibus
incognitus esset, speraret eo de ignobilitate libello cum tanta nobilitatis vituperatione
sibi nobilitatem, quam neque parentes sui neque ipse consecutus essete, facile vendi-
caturum." Quirini, *Epist.*, p. 68.

nobility our progenitors bequeathed us and which has now become the private property of our families, of which we have now long held possession, should be investigated anew by him."[70] But you, Quirini continued, addressing Tommasi, know the nature of true nobility, and can respond to Poggio's arguments in a dialogue modeled on his. We trust in your loyalty, since "we know that you have undertaken greater tasks for our *patria* and for us, and so executed them, that all rightly judge that you have served us splendidly. On the basis of this record we are yours, who always wish to be the spectators not only of your professional but also of your literary skills. . . . Hence we cannot doubt that as you always strive so diligently to cure our bodies, so also you will in no way neglect those things which pertain to the deepest urging of our soul, and what you might perhaps deny to others, you will surely grant to us, your sons."[71]

Quirini's request is odd, plausible only in the cultural setting of Venice. Three young noblemen, proud of their ancestry, tenacious of the privilege of their class, without irony or malice turn for aid to a prominent member of the citizen class. Tommasi had served their republic well in "great tasks," unnamed, and had as a physician served their families. Now he must serve their social interests as well (betraying—unknowingly?—his own) by defending to a man of no social status but of high intellect and great reputation the Venetian noblemen who were his masters.

A few years later, Quirini, unforgiving, wrote a second work against Poggio and in defense of nobility. His *On Nobility* is a substantial treatise, unhesitantly focused on the central issue of that controversy.[72] Where Poggio contended that nobility derived from virtue, Quirini contends that nobility is grounded in nature. The two humanists—one Florentine, one Venetian—confront each other starkly, challenging

[70] "Non enim ulterius pati potuimus nos, qui certe et esse et dici nobiles volumus, quod antiquissimus nobilitatis fundus a progenitoribus nostris relictus et iam familiarum nostrarum peculiaris effectus, in cuius possessione iam dudum mansimus, novam quandam questionem subire incipiat." Ibid., p. 72.

[71] ". . . scimus te pro patria nostra et nobis quoque maiora opera esse aggressum et ita, ut non immerito omnes te de nobis optime meritum arbitrentur. Ex his enim tui sumus, qui non tantum negotii, sed etiam otii tui spectatores semper esse desideramus et propter accuratissima tua publica studia medicine et tuorum operum singularia et prestantia iuvamenta, que in nos nostrasque familias diu atque quotidie experti fuimus, quid private agas attendere et tempora ab aliis neglecta, que colligis, observare conati sumus. Quo fit, ut dubitare nequeamus, quod si nostra corpora tanta diligentia semper curare studeas, que ad animi nostri affectionem maximam pertinent, te nullo pacto neglecturum esse et, quod aliis fortasse negares, nobis nempe filiis tuis procul dubio concessurum." Ibid., p. 73.

[72] The *De nobilitate* [DN] (written c. 1449). The following paragraphs summarize this work.

the modern scholar of humanism to account alike for the pioneer champion of human equality and the conservative spokesman for aristocratic privilege. Quirini opens by reproving Poggio: "For in that book which you recently published about nobility, or I should say rather, against nobility, you employed such intemperate learning and such immoderate language especially against the noblest nations, the finest peoples, worthy republics, which both are and wish to be regarded as noble, that all wonder greatly by what right Poggio, departing entirely from the normal and common path, assaults them all with his sniping words and snaps at them with angry speech—particularly those to whom he owes much."[73] He will oppose the Florentine's attack, moved by the exhortations of his friends and the precepts of his ancestors, and by nobility itself, which cries out for a protector (p. 76). He will prove by means of philosophy—a subject of which Poggio, he says, is ignorant—that nobility is real and exquisite, the most beautiful of all things, superior to all other goods (p. 76). He will defend nobility, moreover, in the calm and temperate language befitting a nobleman, in contrast to Poggio's querulousness.

Quirini amicably concedes at the outset that nobility consists in virtue; but while Poggio denies, he affirms that it is transmitted by descent from noble parents (p. 78). Nobility may be defined as the conspicuous excellence found not only in human beings, but in any part of creation: "This nobility, that is, exceptional excellence, exists not only in men and in other animals, but also in the whole universe. . . ."[74] The perfection of the whole universe consists in its order. The first among all beings, "the greatest, most eminent, most perfect and most noble" is the first cause; from that highest cause, all other created species decline through a universal hierarchy to the basest substance.[75] The hierarchical principle prevails throughout the whole universe of nature and supernature. The first intelligence is superior to the second, superior in turn to the third. The rational soul is nobler than the

[73] "Nam eo in libello, quod nuper de nobilitate vel, rectius ut dicam, contra nobilitatem edidistit, usque adeo intemperata quadam sapientia immoderataque eloquentia usus fuisti presertim contra nobilissimas nationes, generossissimos populos, ingenuas res publicas, que et sunt et dici volunt nobiles, ut non parva admiratio omnes teneat, quo pacto Poggius extra omnino publicam et tritam viam ambulans universas petulantissimis verbis ledat et molestissimo sermone insectetur, eas presertim, que optime de Poggio merite sunt." Ibid., p. 74.

[74] "Hanc ergo nobilitatem, id est prestantiam atque excellentiam, non modo in hominibus et ceteris animalibus, sed in toto quoque universo existere . . . ." Ibid., p. 79.

[75] "Primum entium summum atque eminentissimum atque perfectissimum atque nobilissimum est prima causa . . . ." Ibid., p. 80. Quirini's vision of a hierarchical universe derives from the tradition of Aristotelian metaphysics taught at Padua where Quirini had been a student and teacher. The same vision is implicit in Caldiera's works.

sensitive, the sensitive than the vegetative. Among animals, the lion is superior to the wolf, the wolf to the fox. Among the elements, fire is more excellent than air, air than water, water than earth. Not only are there gradations of excellence between species, but within the same species: one lion is finer than another, or a dog or a horse may each surpass in excellence others of its kind. For Quirini, the universe is one continuous array of nobler and lesser substances. Some men, as well, it clearly follows, are nobler than others: "This natural excellence which is seen in all things, most evidently also appears among men; which, good Poggio, we have agreed to call excellence and nobility of birth."[76]

Indeed, an unbridgeable gap separates ordinary people from nobles. "Those, therefore, who by nature excel by a certain loftiness of excellent soul and a temperate and harmonious composition of body, we call noble by nature." They are, according to Aristotle, born to rule: "they are able to rule, govern, and protect both themselves and the republic."[77] These men who are born to rule, who "whether they apply their minds to administering the business of the republic or to examining the nature of things, are so brilliantly radiant with virtues and accomplishments that they are truly called most noble."[78] So much do I honor the excellence that is in nature, Quirini admonishes Poggio, "that I even affirm that no one can aspire to the nobility of virtue, unless noble nature has first transmitted to him the capacity for and, as it were, the seeds [of nobility]."[79] The great deeds of virtue which all admire are deeds of nobility. "Virtue is born of nobility as much as nobility of virtue."[80]

As nobility is inherent in nature conceived as a continuous hierarchy of substances, so nobility is conferred by nature. Those nobly born, having inherited from noble parents minds and souls finer than those

[76] "Hec itaque nature prestantia, que in omnibus rebus videtur, evidentissime in hominibus quoque apparet; quam, Poggii bone, generositatem et nobilitatem generis appellari diximus." Ibid., p. 82.

[77] "Hos itaque, qui natura prestant excellenti quadam animi generositate corporisque temperata et concordi compositione, nobiles natura dicimus, prevalentes ingenio et rerum eventus a longe prospicientes, quos Aristoteles ad regendum natos affirmat, quod consiliis et sese et rempublicam regere, gubernare tutarique possunt." Ibid.

[78] "Hi igitur, quos natos ad principandum dicimus . . . cum tamen vel ad rei publice negotia administranda vel ad rerum naturam rimandam animum applicuerint, adeo illustres profulgent virtutibus rebusque gestis, ut vere nobilissimi appellentur." Ibid., pp. 82-83.

[79] "Proinde ausculta, Poggii, quantum huic generose nature tribuam, ut etiam affirmem neminem ad nobilitatem virtutis aspirare posse, nisi generosa natura initia et quasi semina tradiderit." Ibid., p. 83.

[80] "Idcirco non minus affirmaverim virtutem ex nobilitate, quam ex virtute nasci nobilitatem." Ibid., pp. 83-84.

born of common stock, perform virtuous deeds by which their nobility is known. "For what else are noblemen but the truly live and vital images of illustrious men, what else indeed a noble heritage but the effulgence of virtue?"[81] For if nobility is inborn by nature, which lends those so born an inclination to greatness and virtue, "who would be so ignorant as to deny that they more easily and aptly proceed to virtue and great deeds by their nature, who emanate, if I may so speak, from the same fount of virtue, than those who burst forth from some stormy and fetid sewer?"[82] Quirini leaves no hope here for the person of common origin. Born of turbulence and fetor, his future is sealed. Just as the parents' bodily form, gestures, and voice are replicated in their children, so also are temperaments and characters transmitted through birth. "From noble and excellent parents, noble and excellent children are necessarily born."[83]

Nobility derives not only from one's parents, but from one's city. In antiquity, for instance, the Romans were more noble than the Campanians, Athenians, and Thebans (p. 87). Florence, to some extent, but more notably Venice, according to Quirini, had inherited the grandeur of Roman nobility. Today, the patricians of Venice are recognized as possessing "Romulean souls."[84] Indeed, the Venetian nobles are direct descendants of the Romans who fled from the menace of Attila to her lagoons (p. 88). They formed a government, guided still by the memory of Rome. Carefully excluding from their number the crowds of foreigners who subsequently thronged to Venice, they guarded the purity of their ancient nobility. Thus Venice conserved Rome's ancient liberty, "without sect, without faction, without any division. No other republic ever, no empire, no kind of city, so long endured as a harmony of minds of one accord (*concors unanimis*), if I may so speak, without domestic discord, as long as has excellent Venice. For now for more

---

[81] "Quid enim aliud sunt nobiles, quam vere vive animateque imagines virorum illustrium, hereditas vero nobilitatis quid aliud, quam gloria virtutis?" Ibid., p. 84.

[82] ". . . quis adeo rerum ignarus est, qui neget eos potius et aptius ad virtutem et res bene preclareque gerendas suapte natura procedere, qui ab ipso, ut sic dixerim, fonte virtutis emanant, quam illos, qui a turbulentissima et fetida quapiam cloaca erumpunt?" Ibid.

[83] ". . . ex nobilibus generosisque parentibus nobiles generososque filios necesse est provenire." Ibid., p. 85. There are some exceptions. The well-born sometimes degenerate from the standard of their ancestors. The low-born occasionally shine: "sed perraro id quidem" (p. 87).

[84] "Videre enim licet in nostra felicissima Veneta re publica patricios viros inclitas Romuleas animas possidentes." Ibid. Quirini probably knew Leonardo Bruni's *Panegyric to the City of Florence*, in which that humanist ascribed to Roman roots the greatness of modern Florentines; see Kohl's English translation in Kohl and Witt, *The Earthly Republic*, pp. 121-75. Note the similarities of Quirini's historical analysis linking primal liberty and preserved nobility to Paolo Morosini's, below, Section 4.

than one thousand years, the gods willing, she has ruled in just empire with virtue and dignity the greater part of Italy and nearly the whole of the Mediterranean Sea."[85] Venice's triumphant and unprotested power and awesome harmony is here ascribed to her nobility, descended by blood from patrician Romans whose "liberty" they had preserved.

Having established that nobility is implicit in the nature of the universe, and transmitted by natural succession from noble progenitors to noble offspring, born to rule and inclined to virtue, Quirini responds to some of Poggio's arguments against nobility. Of these responses, one in particular goes beyond what has already been said. If "nobility" were a real and solid concept, Poggio had objected, then all nations would agree on what nobility was.[86] In fact, they do not. Venetian noblemen, for instance, departing from all custom, engage in commerce. The opportunity for virtuous deeds, Quirini replies, lies in the administration of the republic (p. 91). Each city, however, has its own unique needs. For a maritime city, commerce is vital. To engage in it is not ignoble. "That should be considered neither vice nor virtue which is done purely by the persuasion of nature for the preservation of the human race."[87] In this way, Quirini justifies the mercantile activity of Venetian patricians, the source of all their power, which so distinguished them from other aristocracies.

Urging his opponent to the closer study of Aristotle, Quirini closes his defense of nobility, which "has as many enemies," the Venetian remarked unkindly, "as there are ignoble men, born of common parents to a low station."[88] Writing on nobility from the perspective of a nobleman, Quirini shields Venetian society, as it then existed, by means of humanism's linguistic tools and Aristotelian metaphysics against a "low-born" Florentine challenger. In so doing, he identifies the hierarchical social structure of his city with the hierarchical struc-

---

[85] "Libertatem ergo Romanorum felicissima Venetia conservat sine secta, sine factione, sine divisione aliqua. Immo nulla umquam res publica, nullum imperium, nullus urbis status concors unanimis, ut sic dixerim, sine domestica discordia tam diu stetit, quam diu inclita Venetia. Iam enim ultra millesimum annum diis bene iuvantibus cum virtute et dignitate maximam Italie partem et totum fere mediterraneum mare iusto regit imperio." DN, pp. 88-89.

[86] "On Nobility," passim. Niccolò Niccoli remarks: "If nobility is really something, standing, as it must, on a definite rational basis, it ought to be one and the same thing for all people" (p. 124). Again: "Nobility must be a fixed reality" (p. 125). A survey of different conceptions of nobility follows.

[87] "Nec vitio igitur nec virtuti datur, quod natura suadente incorrupte fit ad conservationem humani generis." DN, p. 92.

[88] ". . . nobilitatem tot hostes habere, quot ignobiles vili loco sordidisque parentibus nati." Ibid., p. 98.

tures of nature culminating in an eternal first cause, and has transferred to the former the majesty, certainty, and perpetuity of the latter.

Quirini's *On the Republic*, written at about the same time as *On Nobility*, presents the same themes on a broader canvas.[89] Here aristocracy (defined as political rule by that social class within human society characterized by its innate capacity for virtue) is shown to be the optimal form of government. As Quirini had claimed for his *On Nobility* a basis in Aristotelian metaphysics, he claims for *On the Republic* the authority of Aristotle's moral philosophy.[90] Indeed, Quirini's work closely draws on Aristotle's *Politics*, while deliberately modifying it to suit the author's purpose: "reorganizing Aristotle's statements at will and arriving at a clearer sense (which statements I have so disposed that it appears to be virtually a new work), adding also many of my own ideas and those of others, and particularly in the second book in which by my will and judgment I have founded and established a city according to my desires."[91] Thus shaping Aristotelian political theory to his own tastes—Venetian and aristocratic—Quirini created a work appropriate for Venice, and appropriately dedicated it to her doge. An architect of the city's imperial thrust landward, Doge Francesco Foscari was also learned. A wise ruler, fulfilling Plato's dream, he effectively ruled a fortunate city.[92]

Book One of *On the Republic* discusses the nature of human society,

---

[89] *De republica* [DR] (written c. 1449-1450); introduction, pp. 105-20.

[90] Moral or "human" philosophy Quirini sees as one of the two branches of philosophy, "divine" philosophy being the other. Of the three sorts of moral philosophy—ethics, economics, and politics—the last is most excellent, and can make the whole city blessed (DR, p. 123). These statements are similar to Caldiera's in both his trilogy and the *Concordantia*.

[91] ". . . Aristotelis sententias nostro arbitrio disponentes et sensum clariorem efficientes, quas ita disposuimus ut penitus aliud opus esse appareat, multa etiam nostra et aliena adicientes, potissimumque in libro secundo in quo nostro arbitrio iudicioque urbem pro votis condidimus et civitatem instituimus." Ibid., p. 124. Quirini reduces Aristotle's eight books to two, commenting modestly, "id est in luculentam reduximus consonantiam."

[92] Plato had called those blessed which are ruled by wise men: *Republic* V 473d. Seno in his introduction (pp. 109-16) speculates that the dedication to the doge suggests Quirini's association with a dogal party—a hypothesis that seems to conflict with another he proposes, that Quirini subsequently left Venice because of official displeasure aroused by critical statements in the DR. I see little evidence for either hypothesis. To dedicate a work to a ruler did not normally presuppose a political link, and it is far more likely that Quirini left Venice because he found there small opportunity for the pursuit of intellectual interests than because of political difficulties. See also the comments of B. Marx in her review of LQU in *Paideia*, pp. 48-49. I see no basis for Labalme's interpretation (*Bernardo Giustiniani*, pp. 94-95 n. 21) of Quirini's words to Francesco Barbaro as "joking" when he complained of official disapproval of his open-air teaching of Aristotle. Ermolao Barbaro G. complains unsmilingly of the same phenomenon a generation later; see his *Epist.*, ed. Branca, I, 79-80.

analyzes the possible forms of political rule, and argues the superiority of aristocratic government.[93] Human society is distinguished from the societies of all other living creatures by the capacity for reason (pp. 126ff.). Human beings alone are able to plan for and cooperate toward the fulfillment of their needs, for which purpose they alone have developed a language capable of indicating such needs (for other creatures can only cry out in pleasure or pain). But human society evolved not only because it was useful; it was also necessitated by nature. For the many offspring of the natural matings of men and women occupied houses and villages, and eventually, so great were their numbers, towns and cities. Thus human society finds its natural culmination in cities, for which man, a social animal, is suited by nature.

Thus Quirini establishes that civil society is a product of human calculation on the one hand and of natural evolution and inclination on the other—circumstances which, in both cases, sanctify it. Next he defines the "parts" of the city. These are the households, each composed in turn of the husband and master, or "lord," wife, children, and servants (p. 128). A serious issue emerges from this seemingly innocuous description: are the "lord" and servant distinct by nature, or accident? By nature, Quirini responds; some men are born to rule, and some to serve. Throughout the whole order of nature are visible patterns of domination and subjugation, exemplars of such patterns in human society. "And nature herself, that greatest craftsman of all things, teaches that lordship and servitude are naturally distinct in many things. For the soul naturally commands the body despotically, while the mind controls desire by a just and regal rule. Any thing is naturally a ruler which knows and provides and for which it is rather useful to rule; that serves indeed which is rude in soul and strong in body, so that what the lord commands the servant executes, and for which it is better to be ruled than to rule—which arrangement is beneficial both to lord and servant."[94]

Within each household, each atom of the city, therefore, the natural right of lord to rule servant (and, in modified forms, wife and chil-

---

[93] The following paragraphs summarize Book One, pp. 126-45.

[94] "Et natura ipsa optimus rerum opifex docet naturaliter distingui dominia et servitutes in plerisque rebus. Anima enim praeest naturaliter corpori despotico principatu, mens vero cupiditati politico ac regali praeest imperio. Illud itaque naturaliter dominatur quod sapit et providet cuique potius regere prodest; servit vero quod animo est indocili, corpore robustum, ut quod providit dominus exequatur servus, cuique regi quam regere praestat, propterea idem prodesse domino servoque videtur." DR, p. 128. Quirini's vision of lord-servant relationships as composing a continuous hierarchical structure extending from the material to the immaterial resembles Caldiera's.

CHAPTER TWO

dren),[95] reflects structures implicit in nature and prefigures as well the structures of civil society, where class dictates to class. For Quirini's discussion now advances from the part to the whole, from the household to the city. Defined as the jealous association of "true" citizens only, the city can be ruled by one man, or a few men, or many.[96] It is a monarchy, an aristocracy, or a democracy (131).

In a true monarchy, Quirini explains, the king is "a good man elected by the multitude on account of outstanding virtue for the sound administration of the city."[97] Chosen for his merit, not birth, he is the city's guardian, not its master. He exhibits three qualities: friendship—the city's "greatest good"—toward all; power to repel an enemy; virtue, particularly justice, by which each man receives what is due him. He is not superior to laws which, not subject to passion, are more to be relied upon than any man (p. 133). Tyranny is that form of rule which perverts the order of true monarchy just described. The tyrant rules according to his own pleasure, the just monarch according to his prudent sense of public utility. The tyrant erodes, moreover, the dignity of his subjects, and poisons their relations. "He makes the citizens distrust each other, loves no one, rewards no one, tries to subject all to his yoke; he hates wise men, neglects and stifles prudent ones."[98] Learned men are driven out when he comes to power, the rich and poor are exiled, their goods seized (p. 135).

Quirini's images of limited monarchy and hateful tyranny both show him to be sceptical of regal power. He prefers aristocracy, the rule of the "few but elect" (*paucorum sed electorum dominium*).[99] The poor and many, unable to agree among themselves, concede power to a few virtuous men. The result is a true republic, where the leadership of a qualified elite is sanctioned by the conscious will of the whole. "For the people largely distrustful of each other or also quarrelsome among themselves elect those prudent ones who with the best advice

[95] Ibid., p. 130: His authority over his wife is "political" or republican, subject to laws (of matrimony); his authority over his children is "regal."
[96] Ibid. The "true" citizen is one having the capacity—apparently a mental capacity—to participate in political processes; foreign and low-born persons do not possess it. "Est ergo civitas communicatio civium gratia dandi et capiendi ut bene vivant. Civitatis enim finis non est vivere, sed bene vivere. Quocirca et civis erit is qui tali societati communicare poterit principatu consiliativo vel iudicativo pro tempore vel saltem contractivo. Ex quo fit ut neque advenae et peregrini neque adventicii neque servi sint cives, quoniam nec principatu nec contractibus civilibus communicare possunt."
[97] "Est itaque rex vir bonus a multitudine electus ob virtutis excellentiam ad bonam civitatis administrationem." Ibid., p. 132.
[98] ". . . studet cives ad invicem diffidant, neminem diligit, neminem extollit, cunctos sub iugo deprimere conatur, sapientes odio habet, prudentes negligit et deprimit." Ibid., p. 134.
[99] "Est igitur aristocratia paucorum sed electorum dominium." Ibid., p. 136.

126

administer the city. Hence these few also make laws, confirmed by the people, and execute justice and well and readily guide the republic. For their tested virtue and prudence raises them worthily and meritedly to the peak of the highest power. Thus by this mechanism of consent that multitude tolerates aristocratic rule which is born to accept many legitimate and virtuous rulers."[100] Though there is a perverted form of aristocracy—oligarchy—it cannot long continue, since it is not tolerated by the people. But a genuine republic endures, anchored by the virtue and accompanying wealth of the noble class: "Nobility . . . consists in ancient wealth and as it were hereditary virtue. For they seem to be noble in whom are found the virtue and wealth of their ancestors."[101] An aristocratic republic, governed by a hereditary nobility with the consent of the multitude, strikes a mean between oligarchy (in which a few rich men selfishly rule) and a democracy (in which the vast numbers of the poor rule without wisdom).

In a democracy, all are equal, regardless of status: "A just democracy considers [people] equal according to number and not according to status."[102] As a result, the poor outnumber the rich. Rulers are chosen by lot in a democracy, whereas in an aristocratic republic, they are chosen "by election and debate." The two regimes are based on fundamentally different values: for democracy, that value is liberty; for aristocracy, virtue.[103] Like an aristocracy, a just democracy is long-lived, and like an aristocracy, it is perverted when some among the rulers seek excessive power.

Having described in the abstract three "pure" forms of political rule, Quirini turns to consider the problem of the best state. That city is best which is happiest, and the city's happiness depends on the happiness of its individual citizens: "Cities . . . were founded for this end, that we might live well and happily, associating [freely] among

---

[100] "Plebs enim plerumque sibi diffidens seu etiam sibi dissona prudentes eligit qui optimo consilio civitatem administrent. Itaque hi pauci et iura confirmante populo condunt et aequitatem exercent et reipublicae bene ac expedite consulunt. Spectata enim virtus atque prudentia ad fastigium summae potestatis digne et merito erigit. Quapropter et ea multitudo aristocratiam patitur quae ferre nata est quamplures legitime et cum virtute regentes." Ibid., p. 136.

[101] "Est . . . autem nobilitas antiquae divitiae et virtus quasi hereditaria. Nobiles enim illi esse videntur quibus progenitorum virtus divitiaeque existunt." Ibid., p. 137.

[102] "Iustum enim democraticum est habere aequalem secundum numerum et non secundum dignitatem. . . ." Ibid., p. 138.

[103] "Est autem democratiae proprium sorte singulos ad magistratus exercendos creare, rei vero publicae electione atque consilio: huic enim virtus terminus est, democratiae vero libertas." Ibid. Democracies thus choose rulers by what we would call election; aristocracies, guided by a principle of excellence, select the best candidate among the group by a consensual process.

ourselves."[104] Just as the individual's happiness depends on goods of both body and soul, so also must the city's. Virtue is that chief good of the soul from which principally derives the city's happiness. But virtue must have a bodily instrument, a material good that, though inferior, supports it. Wealth is this "instrument of virtue." The ideal city, therefore, will be amply supplied with the wealth and virtue that assure its felicity.

By this standard, Quirini evaluates the three forms of government to determine which will prevail in an ideal city. Monarchy is rejected because it rests on the fallible principle of rule by one man (p. 141).[105] A single man can be overcome by his passions and act unwisely or unfairly. Even if his mind is undisturbed by passions, moreover, he still cannot arrive at appropriate judgments, not having the perspective of many minds or the grasp of detail. Nor is it natural, when a city is made up of many individuals of similar condition, that one should be elevated above the others. If a monarchy can not provide happiness for its citizens because of the fallibility of one man, a democracy can do no better, because of the fallibility of the multitude. "The nature of the people is in itself fluid, having no clear direction, wherefore vulgar souls are also called mutable. Moreover, the multitude is not easily brought to order. . . . Finally and most importantly, the ignoble people wins its bread by illiberal arts, which can never wisely guide and govern a city. For only those can govern well and wisely make judgments who have been liberally educated, who strive intently not for bread but for honor and glory."[106] The shiftless, changeable, undisciplined populace, narrowly concerned with the means of survival, cannot have the vision of those who, raised on lofty thoughts, do lofty things. Without that higher vision and plunged in chaos, the numerous multitude, in a democracy, fatally outweighs the slim minority of the wise (p. 142).

A republic, therefore, which Quirini always defines as aristocratic in mode, is the best form of government, capable of providing the city with happiness. Nobility chooses the proper course, the people confirm

---

[104] "Civitates igitur ob id conditae sunt ut bene ac feliciter vivamus ad invicem singula communicantes." Ibid., p. 139.

[105] Using the same sources and dealing with the same arguments, Quirini here disagrees with Caldiera, who saw the rule of a good man as superior to the rule of good laws; see above at n. 52.

[106] "Est item natura plebis per se mobilis, nil firmi propositi habens, unde et mutabiles vulgi animi esse dicuntur. Multitudo insuper haud de facili in ordinem redigitur. . . . Praeterea, quod principalissimum est, plebs ignobilis artibus illiberalibus victum parat: quae nequaquam regere urbes, civitati consulere potest. Regere enim et recte consulere liberaliter instituti solum valent qui non victu sed de honore et gloria intentissime student." DR, p. 141.

their choice, liberty is conserved, and all in turn rule and are ruled. "Liberty, therefore, in the republic exists in that the noble rule, but the people confirm their choices: in a certain sense, they rule, although they do not hold office."[107] Ruling with the consent of the people, virtuous noblemen violate no individual's rights, but exercise the wisdom that only superior souls can nurture.

But to engage in government is to choose an active life over a life of philosophical contemplation, Quirini points out in an interesting digression on an ever-popular issue. The active life gives occasion for discord, death, the loss of liberty. Those who perform the greatest deeds become arrogant, provoke envy, trigger discord: "envy is considered the foul companion of honor and glory, as those who cannot imitate virtue hurl disparagements and ill will. Who therefore . . . can be so crude and insensitive as not to disdain and spurn and abjure this kind of unstable life in which the arrogance of citizens prevails, and the irrationality of fortune?"[108] The political life is problematic. In it are the seeds of danger, the possibility of discord. The contemplative life—though it, too, has its defects—is essentially superior, in that through it man is closer to God. Yet a middle way must be found. The active life is preferable in matters pertaining to mankind, he concludes, the contemplative in matters pertaining to the truths of nature and eternity (p. 145).

Book Two of Quirini's *On the Republic* presents miscellaneous recommendations for the creation of an ideal city, most of which can be quickly scanned.[109] The author suggests an ideal site and size, and urges close supervision of the food supply, essential to the city's survival.[110] He sketches the class system, at the summit of which are the patricians, distinguished by their total devotion to the *patria* (p. 149). They are followed by a second class of soldiers, and subsequently, in descending order, by merchants, artisans, farmers, and shepherds.[111]

---

[107] "Libertas igitur in republica est tam etsi generosi dumtaxat regunt quod plebs illorum electiones confirmat: hoc enim quodammodo regere est quamquam non exerceat magistratum." Ibid., p. 143.

[108] ". . . laudis et gloriae foeda comes habetur invidia, ut quos virtute imitari nequit, obtrectatione et malivolentia insectatur. Quis igitur . . . tam hebes et obtusi animi esse potest qui non dedignetur ac spernat et negligat huiusmodi instabilem vitam in qua temeritas civium dominatur et casus atque fortuna?" Ibid., p. 144.

[109] The following paragraphs summarize Book Two, pp. 146-61.

[110] He recommends a site removed some distance from the sea—quite unlike Venice's (Ibid., pp. 146-47)—both for ease of defense and because merchants are not fit for civic rule. But Venice, an excellent republic located close to the sea, is exceptional: "Quae sane sententia quamquam vera sit, a Venetis tamen elegantis ingenii viris sive usu sive natura superata est. Hi enim in mari habitantes et mercaturae acrem operam dantes optime admodum rempublicam administrant." Ibid., p. 147.

[111] In this sketch of the class system, the aristocrat Quirini alters Aristotle, placing

The patricians rule by establishing just laws, the systems of which are reviewed (p. 150). The citizens as a whole should strive for moderate wealth for the sake of the city's tranquillity (p. 151). Neither rich men nor poor make good citizens, and where there are great differences in wealth, discord arises. The city must strive for virtue, not wealth. Whenever dissension arises, it must be stamped out. "Therefore [the citizens] shall strive above all to remain in concord and harmony, since concord preserves the city, discord corrupts it."[112] Just as in music a harmony of different sounds is sought, "so from the [counterpoint of] highest, lowest, and intermediate [social] orders, just like sounds, a well-ordered city achieves harmony by means of the agreement of dissimilars, and what musicians call harmony in song, is in a city concord."[113]

The ideal of concord does not entail the elimination of social differences. Quirini makes this clear as he argues against the notions of the community of women and the community of property.[114] The chief arguments against the former are these: it would lead to unrestrained libidinousness, the neglect of children, the undermining of the family (p. 153). More, it would disrupt the city's harmony, which must be achieved by the consonance of diverse things, and is dissolved by the socialization of what should be private: "thus would be corrupted the harmony and consonance of the city."[115] Even more objectionable is the possibility of common ownership of possessions, or the notion that all citizens have equal wealth (p. 154). An equal distribution of wealth might discourage sedition, but it would blunt the spirit of industry. The better solution for great inequalities in wealth is that the wealthy freely bestow gifts on the poor. Rather than limit the sum of wealth any individual may acquire, the greed for possessions should be restrained through a careful education in virtue.

Quirini closes *On the Republic* with a detailed survey of such an

---

in the higher ranks patricians, soldiers, and merchants. In Quirini's social world, the latter two groups often held noble status, as well.

[112] "Igitur studebunt permaxime concordes et concinni semper manere, quoniam concordia civium urbem perpetuat, discordia corrumpit." Ibid., p. 151.

[113] ". . . Sic ex summis et infimis mediis interiectis ordinibus ut sonis moderatam ratione civitatem consensu dissimillimorum concinnere, et quae harmonia a musicis dicitur in cantu eam esse in civitate concordiam." Ibid., p. 152, based on Cicero, *De republica* II 69. Quirini's notion of concord is also closely related to hierarchical structure, two images of which immediately follow this passage. In the first, the republic is compared to a body in which the prince is the head, the senate the heart, and so on. In the second, the three kinds of people in the republic are related to the three functions of the soul (taken from the discussion in Plato's *Republic* beginning at IV:435c): rational, appetitive, irascible.

[114] These are recommended by Plato, *Republic* V:457c-d.

[115] "Corrumpetur enim sic concinnitas et consonantia urbis." DR, p. 153.

education. It is in fact, though not identified as such, a now-familiar prescription for the moral and intellectual training of a nobleman.[116] Since prenatal influences are of great concern, advice is given about the choice of a wife, as of a sober regimen of sex, food, and drink (p. 155). Breast-feeding is recommended, and an early solicitude about moral character in infancy and childhood (pp. 156-57). In adolescence, moral instruction is particularly important: "For youth is prone to sin, and unless good morals have been mastered [the young] are easily corrupted."[117] The young man should be guided to love for God, reverence for his elders, moderation in food and drink, control of anger, restraint in speech, and chastity. The desire should be awakened in him to imitate great men, whose deeds he knows from history and the other *studia humanitatis* (p. 159). Having by this regimen been made a good man, he may now become a good citizen, undertaking in due course his political career. Under the rule of such men, the city will find happiness. "By this means when they have become good and noble and have embraced the sacred chorus of virtues, and have acquired prudence so that they may guide the city well, modesty so that they are not corrupted by libidinous passions, justice so that the whole city may shine with the sun's radiance, when they will have preserved liberty inviolate and unshaken, rejecting avarice and laziness and intestine discord which like poison corrupt cities, our sacred city, living in peace and tranquillity—for they wage no wars but pious ones—happy and blessed, will flourish for eternity."[118]

In these three works, the patrician humanist Lauro Quirini defines nobility as the natural and innate superiority of one fraction of the human race, which holds the same position in the hierarchy of human excellence as the regal lion among animals, the noblest tree among vegetables, or God Himself in the sacred order of the universe. By their virtue, noblemen are recognized as the finest members of their species. That virtue descends in the blood and through nurture to their offspring, uniquely suited by their ancestral and personal qualities to rule the state. One may doubt the goodness of a monarch who, being

[116] See Chapter One, Sections 4 and 5.

[117] "Iuventus enim prona est ad peccandum, ac nisi boni mores accesserint penitus corrumpuntur . . . ." DR, p. 159.

[118] "Hoc igitur pacto cum boni et generosi evaserint virtutumque sanctissimum chorum amplexi fuerint, assecuti prudentiam ut civitati bene consulant, modestiam, quo non libidinibus corrumpantur, iustitiam quo urbs tota resplendeat instar solis radios, libertatemque inviolatam et inconcussam conservaverint abiecta avaritia et desidia et intestina discordia quae ut venenum civitates corrumpit, in pace et tranquillitate degentes—bellum enim nullum nisi pium suscipient—felix atque beata nostra civitas sacratissima in aeternum vigebit . . . ." Ibid., p. 161.

human and subject to passions as much as the many he rules, may easily fail in wisdom or honesty. One should doubt, likewise, the abilities of a multitude attempting democratic rule, for in their freedom they are disorderly, undisciplined, and prone to dissent. But one may trust in the aristocracy that governs a republic; uniquely gifted in virtue, they can wisely govern a well-ordered city with the sanctioning consent of the populace.

Quirini's uncompromising advocacy of a hierarchy of social classes is consonant with the works by Barbaro and Caldiera previously examined. He shares with Barbaro an understanding of the ruling noble class as innately virtuous and capable of transmitting that rare and exclusive virtue to posterity. He shares with Caldiera (both imbued with a contemporary understanding of Aristotelian metaphysics) a hierarchical vision of the universe and all its component parts. For both, the innate superiority of the nobleman merely repeats a pattern continuous in nature whereby in every species there is one individual that is best. For both, conformity to these hierarchical patterns ensures harmonious and eternal existence.

A theoretical framework of Venetian humanist views of their society is established in these works. The three figures to be considered next are more practical. As firm in their defense of Venetian society, they are concerned less with abstract statements of its relations with universal patterns, more with history, experience, and fact. Though Paolo Morosini, ironically, reveals himself elsewhere as profoundly knowledgeable in philosophy and theology,[119] his three works in defense of Venice exemplify this more practical approach.

4. PAOLO MOROSINI IN DEFENSE OF VENICE

When the Turks stormed Constantinople in 1453, Italy trembled. The destruction of that last outpost of ancient Rome threatened the Christian church and endangered European borders. During the years which followed, cities and nations exhorted each other to defend civilization against the Turkish menace. But fear could not galvanize concerted action among these jealous and quarrelsome states. Mutual exhortations gave way to mutual accusations of cowardly inaction and indifference to religion. Venice, that powerful city which had moved so swiftly earlier in the century to conquer half of northern Italy, was perceived as slow to assume responsibility in the struggle against the Turks. Paolo Morosini, one of the architects of Venetian policy on the

---

[119] He wrote two substantial works in these genres: *De fato seu praescientia divina et liberi humani arbitrii libertate* and *De aeterna temporalique Christi generatione*.

Turkish question, wrote three works in his city's defense. The need to defend Venetian motives at a particular juncture occasioned a profound if partisan exploration of the city's history, social structure, government, and values.[120]

Morosini's *Defense of the Venetians to the Princes of Europe against Her Detractors* is addressed to Marco Barbo, cardinal of the Church, favored relative of the pope, and Venetian loyalist. Well-situated in Rome, Barbo would have been in an excellent position to champion Venice's cause, as Morosini exhorts him to do: "I have decided to direct, therefore, to your wisdom and fairness this well-merited defense of Venice, so that you who are stationed in [Rome] to which, like a common *patria* all come, and who are judged to be loyal to your own *patria*, if you chance to hear anyone uttering false accusations against Venice, may by the assertion of the truth—if you are not able to lead them to love of Venice—at least teach them to abandon their unjust hatred, lest to the detriment of their souls they are led by lying sophistries to hate the Venetians."[121] Such "lying sophistries" Morosini intends to confute with a series of truths about Venice's rare virtues:

[120] Morosini's works are: *Defensio venetorum ad Europae principes contra obtrectatores* [DVEP]; *De rebus ac forma reipublicae venetae* [DRF]; *Lettera a Ciccho Simonetta* [*Lettera*]. For Venice's emerging policy against the Turks and Paolo Morosini's role, see especially G. B. Picotti, *La Dieta di Mantova e la politica dei veneziani*. The weight of Morosini's particular role is inferred from the direction to him by Ludovico Foscarini and Lauro Quirini of letters urging decisive action: those of the former in Picotti, *Dieta*, pp. 444-46, 457-59; that of the latter in the "Epistole storiche sulla caduta di Costantinopoli," ed. Pertusi, pp. 258-59.

Morosini's works respond to criticism generated by Venice's unpopular policies which intensified around mid-century; see the discussion in Chapter Three, Section 4. Both Poggio Bracciolini (in his *De nobilitate*) and Enea Silvio Piccolomini accused the Venetians of a vulgar mercantilism (*Opera inedita*, ed. J. Cugnoni, pp. 507, 512-13, 541-44). Perhaps such humanist accusations also underlay Morosini's response, as well as the nasty gossip of Francesco Filelfo that provoked the DVEP and the *Lettera*; cf. G. Fasoli, "Nascita di un mito," p. 478; M. Foscarini, *Della letteratura veneziana ed altri scritti intorno essa*, p. 310. The dating of Morosini's works is uncertain and is not clarified by data about their dedicatees. The DVEP is dedicated to Cardinal Marco Barbo, who became cardinal in 1467 (but may have been written earlier, since the title might have been added by a later scribe); for Barbo, see profile. The DRF is dedicated to Gregor Heimburg, for whom see Morimichi Watanabe's "Gregor Heimburg and Early Humanism in Germany." Morosini may have met Heimburg around 1430 at Padua. The *Lettera* is addressed to Cicco Simonetta, secretary and counselor to the dukes of Milan from c. 1448 until his execution by il Moro in 1480. A brief discussion of these Morosini works appears in F. Gaeta, "Alcune considerazioni sul mito di Venezia," at pp. 61-62.

[121] "Tuae igitur sapientiae et aequitati meritam Venetorum defensionem destinandam decrevi, ut qui in urbe moram trahis, in quam communis patriae gratia omnes conveniunt, et qui patriae haud immemor propriae judicaris, falsis suggestionibus quemquam Venetis improperantem audire contigerit, veri assertione, si non in Ventorum amorem adducere poteris, ab iniusto tamen odio discedere doceas; ne animarum suarum detrimento falsis cavillationibus odisse venetos eligant . . . ." DVEP, p. 191.

a unique and long-lived nobility; a long history unmarred by impiety, but marked by loyalty to the pope, helpfulness to Christians and militance against the enemies of Christianity; a record of avoidance of conquest, but of willing protection of dependent cities in need of her aid.[122]

The work thus proudly introduced opens cautiously with an explanation to the author's audience of "popes, emperors, cardinals, kings, and princes." He does not mean to stir up controversy, but only to defend Venice modestly and calmly against unjust but unnamed accusers.[123] Two types of criticism had been made: accusers had, first, denigrated the Venetian nobility, and, second, accused her, in pursuing her political and military strategies, of greed, ambition, and impiety.

The noblemen of Venice, as Morosini reports the arguments of their detractors, are fishermen, low-born, and soiled by their engagement in commerce (p. 192). The noblemen of Venice, Morosini responds, challenging spokesmen for other aristocracies to defend their own as well, are hardly low-born, but descended by pure and traceable lineage from the noblest men of antiquity. The first group of immigrants to help form the nobility of Venice were the Paphlagonians, the defeated heroes of Troy in whom there lingered a love of *patria* and zeal for liberty. Settling in the north of Italy, they called their lands Venetia. When the Gauls later invaded Italy during the Roman period, remembering the example of their ancestors and the principle of liberty, they fled to the sea, where cities stood amid the waters, and began a new life: "where, having abandoned their own homes, they chose to lead

---

[122] The issues Morosini chooses to address place his work squarely in the tradition of those creating the "myth of Venice," for which see below, Section 9, especially n. 231. These themes recur frequently in Venetian chronicles from the Middle Ages forward; see especially Muir, *Civic Ritual*, pp. 65ff.; the essays in Pertusi, ed., *La storiografia veneziana fino al secolo XVI*; F. Gaeta, "Storiografia, coscienza nazionale e politica culturale nella Venezia del Rinascimento"; also E. Cochrane, *Historians and Historiography in the Italian Renaissance*, pp. 60ff. They appear more pertinently in the important history of Morosini's contemporary Bernardo Giustiniani (*De origine urbis venetiarum*) and the minor one of his contemporary Michele Orsini (*De summa venetorum origine*). They are repeated by Marcantonio Sabellico; cf. F. Tateo, "Marcantonio Sabellico e la svolta del classicismo quattrocentesco," pp. 45ff. Even closer to Morosini's work in form and substance, though briefer, is Girolamo Donato's *Contra calumnias apologia*. The relationship between the two is close enough to suggest Donato's knowledge of Morosini's work, and make redundant an analysis of the former's. A summary of Morosini's DVEP follows.

[123] This audience of great men is addressed not because they are at fault, but because they are gifted with justice, and will recognize as unjust the accusations made against Venice (DVEP, p. 191). Morosini repeatedly states that his motives are not to engender hostility, but only modestly to state the truth so that it may be recognized and accepted by any fair judge.

their lives in the sweetness of liberty."[124] A new invasion of barbarians under Attila forced another group of mainland Veneto noblemen, committed as firmly to the preservation of liberty, to flee to Venice. They constituted a second immigration, or first addition to the Venetian nobility. A third and final immigration of noblemen from the mainland was provoked by the devastations of Totila. Furious with the Venetians for aiding Narses, the Emperor Justinian's general who liberated Rome from the barbarians, that Gothic king had tried to discourage such "friendship" with his enemy. Mainland leaders escaped to Venice. Thus three groups of noblemen of ancient origin and unblemished devotion to liberty had chosen the barren islands of Venice as a refuge, Morosini argues, from violence and tyranny. "This is the origin of the Venetian nobility; thus came the Venetians, in those times, to this place."[125]

The essential excellence of the Venetian nobility—that quality which makes them noble—Morosini understands as having two roots. The first is the essential excellence of the races from which they biologically descend. The second is liberty, a property linked to nobility, that spritual quality which they carefully preserve. Now the nature of this "liberty" which Morosini defines as essential to "nobility" deserves some reflection. It is certainly not comparable to what we know as liberty: an inner freedom in spirit, possessed by all human beings by natural right, transcending material circumstances and, sometimes, permitting their transformation. It is not even quite the same as what was often meant by liberty in the language of the Italian communes: autonomous civic existence in the absence of foreign domination. Rather, it connotes freedom from *servitude*, the condition of being subject to another's will, the condition of servility. The condition of liberty in this sense is transmitted from one generation to another. The noblemen of Venice were determined never to submit to the powerful Gauls, Morosini writes, so that they might continue to defend their long-cherished liberty; and so that *no one ever in the future might presume* to violate that nobility, only those legitimately born from sound stock were admitted to noble rank.[126] The nurture of liberty

[124] ". . . ibique, propriis relictis sedibus, dulcedine libertatis, vitam ducere decreverunt." Ibid., p. 193.

[125] "Hinc venetae nobilitatis origo; hisque temporibus, et in has sedes Venetos venisse constat." Ibid., p. 194.

[126] "Sanxere namque, a sui adventus primordiis, cum primum in has sedes declinarunt, ne scilicet praepotentioribus Gallis servire cogerentur, et eotenus servatam libertatem, quam vitae cunctisque opibus praeferendam decreverant, tutarentur: ut nemo usquam in posterum nobilitatis specimen violare praesumeret, ne quis nisi ingenuis legitimisque uxoribus natus in suae nobilitatis consortium posset adscribi . . . ." Ibid. Morosini's

and the pure descent of noble dynasties are identified, making it clear that this is an aristocrat's definition of liberty. No commoner can possess it. It inheres in the blood.

No finer spectacle can be seen anywhere than that of the Venetian nobility, rhapsodizes Morosini, departing from his historical scheme: "who are so grand indeed when in assembly, so vast in procession, that nowhere else in the whole of the earth can there be found such and so great a panoply of nobility."[127] Those who marvel when they come to Venice at its wondrous site, size, and beauty "which are recognized as the creations of lofty genius and spirit,"[128] marvel too at the vast array of her assembled nobility.

On their sea-beaten and uncultivated islands, continues Morosini in his historical account, those early noblemen who had chosen liberty over possessions lived an austere life (p. 195). Never injuring anyone else, because they wished to leave to their posterity no inheritance of enmity, they eked out by great industry the necessities of life. The unyielding soil made them turn to the sea, to shipbuilding and commerce. In so doing, they did not compromise their glorious nobility. For they engaged in trade not out of vulgar greed, but from the need to feed themselves and their families. Faced by the "necessity of place" with a choice between commerce and plunder, they "consulted among themselves" and "unanimously" decided to live by their own labor rather than by harming others.[129] The presence of compulsion and the collective nature of the decision-making process both remove these worthy Venetians from direct or personal responsibility for their actions: nature and circumstance make decisions for them, which a group soberly reviews and acknowledges. They act not from aggression or greed, but a considered acceptance of reality. They exercise their will only to lessen the burden on others of necessary actions. They established laws, for instance, which prohibited piracy or by any means causing injury to others in the course of trade—but which permitted just and necessary defense against aggressors.

The effects of the self-restraint and zealous labor of these original

---

DRF [discussed below] also relates liberty to the condition of serving no one (p. 232). At both points, the role of the monarch is to assure the observation of the laws so that liberty is not violated: ". . . ut nusquam ab aequissimis suis legius recedendo libertatem amitterent cives." DVEP, p. 194.

[127] ". . . cujus quidem tantus est in unum conventus, tantus adeuntium redeuntiumque conspectus, ut nusquam pene toto orbe terrarum tantus tamque illustris nobilitatis concursus valeat reperiri." DVEP, p. 195.

[128] ". . . quae altioris ingenii ac spiritus esse noscuntur." Ibid.

[129] Morosini uses these phrases in the same manner as Caldiera; see above, Section 2. A similar defense of the commercial role of the nobility appears in Niccolò Barbo's description of Luca Contarini; cf. Chapter One, n. 131.

Venetians is now clear, writes Morosini. Obedient to sacred laws, they built in that lone and barren place a city of great wealth, the center of the world's goods. "For just as the center of the circle is equally distant from the circumference at all points, so also is Venice established in this place that circled around by outlying regions of the world she abundantly furnishes necessary and also beneficial things, which from whatever extreme zones of the world, by appropriate kinds of boats and galleys, from nearly all encircling shores, at her own cost and peril, she transports home to a port safe and opportune for all; for at certain times innumerable fleets of ships and triremes travel nearly all the seas, and carry such a great quantity of all things, so that of those imports and exports no one ever grieved that there was ever lacking not merely anything necessary and useful, but neither anything pleasant or frivolous."[130] At the center of the world's commerce, Venice is helpful to all, and injures none. She is compelled to find elsewhere her own "victus ac vestitus"—food and clothing, necessities of life; barren herself, she is necessary to all other regions. She supplies them with necessary goods. She acts, again, from necessity—and thus without responsibility for overt actions—and again, with benevolent intent.

In terms quite different from those of Caldiera or Quirini, Morosini defends the Venetian nobility from aggressive opponents without recourse to philosophy, but by a historical narrative shaped to his ideological position. The noblemen of Venice are not low-born, he claims, but the pure descendants of an ancient nobility distinguished by its unyielding commitment to liberty. They are not crude fishermen and shopkeepers, but proud men who, adapting of necessity to a harsh environment, obedient to justly established regulations, have by their earnest labors acquired innocent wealth. The populace of Venice, those unnamed hands who assisted her patricians in their journey toward abundance, do not exist for Morosini. They are not among the city's noble founders, nor among their posterity whose processions fill the piazza. They are invisible.

[130] "Nam velut centrum circumferentiae aeque distans, omnibus circuli partibus indifferens esse conspicitur, ita in hoc loco Venetia condita circumquaque iacentibus orbis regionibus necessaria simul et conferentia abunde suppeditat, quae undique ab extremis orbis climatibus, opportunis navium triremiumque generibus, cunctis pene lustratis littoribus, suis sumptibus ac periculis in patriam, tutum cunctisque opportunum devehit locum; singulis namque temporibus innumera navium triremiumque classe cuncta pene maria lustrant, tantamque rerum omnium deferunt quantitatem, ut ingredientium egredientiumque nemo ne dum necessaria aut opportuna sed nec iucunda et quae ad voluptatem conferre possent unquam defuisse doluerit." DVEP, p. 197. State-owned Venetian fleets sailed to specific Mediterranean locations at regular intervals; see the chapters on the organization of sea power in F. C. Lane's *Venice: A Maritime Republic*.

In acquitting Venice of the charges of greed, ambition, and impiety, Morosini adopts again a historical approach. He presents a long series of anecdotes demonstrating his city's generosity, modesty, and piety.[131] From the sixth century, when Venetians aided at great risk the imperial forces under Narses, until the more recent years of struggle against the Turks, Venice had always acted not to extend its power, but to defend itself, aid other cities, and protect the Church. Had the Doge Pietro Orseolo not assisted, "moved by reverence for the pope and prayers of the people," Bari would have been lost in 1000, for example, to a besieging Saracen navy.[132] In 1178, the Doge Sebastiano Ziani reconciled Pope Alexander III and Emperor Frederick Barbarossa, divided by a long and bitter enmity (p. 204). In 1204, a Venetian fleet under Doge Enrico Dandolo warred "with anger and in hope of glory" against the schismatic Greeks, replacing on the throne the legitimate ruler of Constantinople.[133] Later that century, Venice pledged herself to a perpetual war against the Turkish enemies of the faith, who had just begun their incursions of the Mediterranean (p. 211). In 1463, Venice entered into a glorious league with Burgundy and the pope, prepared to fight, as she had for 200 years, not from necessity, but from zeal, faith, and piety.[134] On land as well as at sea, Venice's record was one of unblemished magnanimity toward cities that looked to her for protection. She conquered only for the benefit of oppressed citizens, or for the welfare of the church. Her true ideal has always been to stay within her own limits, and harm no one: "This indeed is their ideal and immutable position, which can rightly be argued a sign neither of ambition nor insensibility; this constant position they have held from their earliest history, and transmitted inviolate to their posterity: to contain themselves within their own limits, to be content with their own boundaries, to cause injury to none, [but] to resist the invader, repel an assault, always to be moderate."[135] Those who doubt the nobility of Venice's rulers, Morosini closes after a full recapitu-

---

[131] The examples (DVEP, pp. 198ff.) that follow are but a few of an extended calendar of Venetian benevolence. Morosini's dates are inaccurate; I have corrected them or supplied approximate dates.

[132] "... pontificis reverentia populorumque precibus." Ibid., p. 201.

[133] "... gloriae spe iraque in Schismaticos perciti." Ibid., p. 205.

[134] "Nullis ergo causis praeter quam fidei fideliumque zelo ac pontific[i]um suasionibus ...." Ibid., p. 215.

[135] "Haec profecto mens immutabilisque eorum sententia, quae nec ambitionis nota, nec insensibilitatis merito argui potest, haec constans opinio ipsis ab incunabulo orta, in posterosque per manus tradita inviolata servatur, suis se limitibus contineri, suis contentos finibus esse, nulli iniuriam ferre, inferenti resistere, illatam repellere, saepius parcere." Ibid., p. 225.

lation, or accuse her of ambition, or doubt her Christian zeal, do not equal Venice in nobility or piety and are not free of ambition.

Morosini's vernacular *Letter to Cicco Simonetta* and formal *On the Substance and Form of the Venetian Republic* repeat many of the arguments of the *Defense of the Venetians*, and require only brief comment. The former work, written at the express wish of the Senate,[136] deals with the charge that Venice, swollen with ambition, sought domination of all of mainland Italy. Carefully, Morosini explains the just causes of Venice's acquisition of Padua, Treviso, Verona, Vicenza, the Friuli, Cremona, Brescia, Bergamo, and other states, insisting throughout that Venice never waged war except for the sake of peace. Always modest and restrained, Venetians were "not greedy for power but avid for peace and content with her own boundaries."[137]

The second of these works is broader in scope. Here Morosini intends to satisfy the curiosity of the German jurist and humanist Gregor Heimburg, to whom the work is addressed. He had wondered, according to our author's report, how the Venetian empire had originated and flourished, subject to none, oppressing none, and how it could at once be a republic and a monarchy. Morosini will gladly satisfy Heimburg's curiosity as best he can—for no learned man had ever dared to undertake so great a task as the description of that city's greatness—so that the German citizen may come to love Venice and imitate her example.[138]

Since Venice's uniqueness is best seen by examining her origin, Morosini opens, as in the *Defense*, with the history of her first noble settlers. Founded by noblemen fiercely committed to ancestral liberty, and ruled by a prince subject to their laws, Venice grew in wealth and extent, acquiring new lands not from ambition, but at the request of the oppressed who sought her milder domination (pp. 241ff.). If the history of her growth shows Venice's unaltering devotion to liberty, the history and structures of her government reveal her commitment to justice. There follows a full account of the components of Venice's government: the doge, Great Council, counsellors and sages, *avogadori*, members of the Councils of Ten and Forty, the Grand Chancellor, the Senate, and a multitude of lesser offices. Amid the descriptive details, Morosini's key themes are heard again: the modesty of individuals, the worthiness of the nobility, based in its long and legitimate

---

[136] *Lettera*, fol. 1r-v.

[137] ". . . non cupidi de stado ma avidi de pace et contenti de termini suoi." Ibid., fol. 13.

[138] These paragraphs rapidly review the contents of the DRF: the historical sections, pp. 231-43; the analysis of the government, pp. 243-61.

CHAPTER TWO

descent, the authority of law. The doge, noble and virtuous, elected by the noblemen from among their number, is a "lover of peace and tranquillity."[139] At his death, the "orphaned city" mourns in solemn ritual, and the patricians select his successor by a ritual far more intricate—"lest anyone succeed in attaining or possessing the *dogado* by any craft or cleverness."[140] Assuming the ducal insignia, the nobleman thus elected ceases to be a citizen and becomes a prince, but a prince subject to laws—the father, not tyrant of his city. Though a ruler, he is subject to the will of the whole nobility, and cannot rule by self-interest or caprice. The city's nobility assembled in the Great Council are the image of the ancestors from whom they have legitimately descended over fifteen hundred years (p. 247). The *avogadori* are charged to "contain" the city with laws, and to punish the delinquent.[141] The Council of Ten harshly disciplines those who scheme against the city's welfare; their grave judgment arouses in all "extreme terror."[142] Glorious in origin, splendid in function, pure of motive, perfect in obedience, the aristocratic republic of Venice can in no way be impugned.

5. DOMENICO MOROSINI ON THE WELL-MANAGED REPUBLIC

Domenico Morosini was as experienced in Venetian government and policy-making as his namesake Paolo.[143] He drew on that experience of public life in constructing his model of an ideal republic described in his work *On the Well-Managed Republic*.[144] His perspective, unlike

[139] "Est princeps qui non genere vel origine, ne voluntatis aut naturae monumento a recto rationis tramite declinaret, sed optimatum primorumque electione ex ipsis nobilibus meritis ac virtutibus pollens, pacis ac quietis amator et auctor constitutus eligitur, et sublimatur . . . ." Ibid., p. 243.

[140] ". . . ne quis arte ulla versutiave principatum attingere aut consequi valeat." Ibid., p. 244.

[141] ". . . hoc est oppressorum omnium tocius principatus fautores et advocati, quibus civitatem legibus continere, delinquentesque arcere supliciis datum est." Ibid., p. 248.

[142] "Maximo itaque terrori omnibus exstat consilii huius tremenda sententia . . . ." Ibid., p. 259.

[143] There was no close relationship between Domenico and Paolo.

[144] The *De bene instituta re publica* [DBIRP]; Finzi's introduction, pp. 1-56; text, pp. 71-250. This is an unfinished work begun by Morosini in 1497 and still in process at his death. It is a working version, containing several versions of the same passages and marginal notations. Morosini's son Lorenzo collected and copied the notes without editing them in 1512; he is perhaps responsible for some of the grammatical and orthographical errors. See Finzi's description of this truly chaotic text, which he calls a "marasma," pp. 13ff. See also Cozzi's criticism of Finzi's failure to discipline the text in his "Domenico Morosini e il 'De bene instituta re publica,' " pp. 408-409 n. 14. Since the work is highly disorganized, the following discussion extracts central concepts from scattered loci (identified in the notes) rather than following the author's order of presentation. My interpretation parallels Cozzi's, and is particularly indebted to his

140

Paolo's, is universal, in spite of frequent allusions to specifically Venetian circumstances. Yet though his ideal republic is not identified as Venice, the resemblance is close, departing from the example mainly to reinforce the authority of the ruling class whose exclusive power was already the chief characteristic of Venetian politics. For Domenico Morosini, without attempting to prove the legitimacy of patrician rule through historical or philosophical demonstration, insists upon it for moral and prudential reasons. The rulers of his ideal republic come from that social class which alone is free of any trace of self-interest and thus capable of providing for the welfare of all the citizens.

Any state, Morosini asserts, has three social classes: that of great men, that of men of middling condition, and that of small or poor men.[145] These classes are differently defined according to the specific nature of each city. However defined, though, both great men and small men should be completely excluded from government. The poor, who greatly outnumber the best citizens, are prone to corruption and depravity, the seeds of faction and sedition (pp. 118, 245). The great men are no better, for, concerned to preserve the wealth and power they have attained, they are ambitious, factious, hostile, and dissident (p. 118). Neither group being eligible for power because of their proneness to faction among themselves, their presence in the city poses further the constant threat of strife arising from inevitable mutual resentment: "for this contagion of envy in every free city between the poor and rich citizens greatly flourishes, gradually stealing into the souls of men raging with such poison that sometimes it leads the whole city to destruction if it is not extinguished utterly by prudent and sober management."[146] Both groups are dangerous to the city whose population they largely compose.

Yet they are useful to the city. The wealthy, whose possessions and homes arouse great admiration (p. 206), help the city thrive through

---

analysis of Morosini's critical intent. I cannot accept Finzi's assessment of the work as uniquely practical, as an attempt "di passare dalla pratica alla dottrina, dottrina che deve però essere fondata sulla tradizione e sulle condizioni obiettive dello Stato" (p. 16).

[145] DBIRP, pp. 73ff. Here and throughout his work, Morosini borrows from Aristotle's *Politics*—the same work that underlay Caldiera's and Quirini's political analysis, and that will be fundamental for Pietro Barozzi, below. For this conception of class structure and the motivations of poor and rich, see the *Politics*, esp. III:6-13; IV:11-13; V:1-8.

[146] ". . . quoniam in omni libera civitate inter pauperes cives et locupletes hec invidie contagio, magnopere viget, serpitque interdum in animos hominum tanto veneno estuans ut aliquando usque ad interitum totam civitatem inficiat, nisi prudenti consilio et gravi penitus de medio tollatur, et in pace quidem latet in latebris hominum non extiguitur sublata omni oportuna ocasione prodeundi." DBIRP, p. 208.

their commercial activities, tax payments, and lavish spending, contributing "to the public advantage of cities and the comfort and utility of the private citizens."[147] They should be cherished and their fortunes protected "if they behave modestly and justly, injure no one, and curb their insolence."[148] The poor, too, have a useful function. Spending all they have for food and necessities, they do not enrich the city, "yet even they are a certain part of the city, without which the city could not exist."[149] Essential as they are, the poor should be treated well, their needs provided for. By such tender nurture, they will be taught to love and obey their rulers: "For there is nothing which more draws close the plebs in love and benevolence to their rulers than that by the careful attention of those magistrates to their needs they cause [the people] to think themselves beloved by those who so nourish them."[150] To win the citizens' love, rulers must ensure that the whole economy thrive: "that the city abound with imported goods, that they seek that the goods manufactured in the city be transported elsewhere for others' advantage and use, that agriculture be protected, crafts supported, the poor fed, the rich defended, that care and diligence be bestowed upon all, to each according to his need what can comfortably be done."[151] The poor are made obedient, the wealthy "great" men kept docile by such care and attentive supervision. All the citizens are placated, moreover, by the steady administration of justice. "Since indeed nothing more greatly furthers the concord of the citizens than justice and equity toward all and particularly in the zeal and concern shown by the city for the needs and profit of each [citizen's] fortune."[152] "The concord of the citizens is preserved when all are equal before just laws, and no exception is made for fortune or person, but justice alone reigns."[153]

---

[147] ". . . ad emolumentum publicum civitatum et privatorum concivium comodum ac utilitatem." Ibid., p. 207.

[148] ". . . si modeste et recte vivunt, si nemini inferunt iniurias, si non insolescunt in alios . . . ." Ibid., p. 208.

[149] "Sunt enim et ipsi pars aliqua civitatis, sine qua civitas non potest consistere." Ibid., p. 150.

[150] "Nihil enim est quod magis conciliet plebem amore et benivolentia magistratibus, quam magistratuum impensa cura comodis eorum existimant quidem se amari ab his qui eos colunt . . . ." Ibid., pp. 150-51.

[151] ". . . ut civitas rebus importatis habundet. ut que in civitate per artifices fiunt asportari alio questu et utilitate queant, ut agricultura colatur, artificia substententur alantur pauperes, divites protegantur cunctis cura et studium impartiatur unicuique secundum exigentiam suam quod fieri comode poterit . . . ." Ibid., p. 167. Morosini also advises a tax policy that arouses no hatred (p. 201) and the avoidance of war (pp. 158ff., 241).

[152] "Siquidem nulle res magis prosunt ad concordiam civium quam iustitia et paritas tum in omnibus tum vel maxime in studio et cura a civitate habita pro utilitatibus et emolumentis cuiusque fortune." Ibid., p. 151.

[153] "Concordia civium servatur cum iustis legibus omnia equantur, et nulla fit fortune aut personarum exceptio sed solum iustitia superat." Ibid., p. 213.

Small and great men alike, though prone to sedition, can be tamed by policies of benevolent nurture and unfailing justice, and the city blessed with perfect concord.[154]

The city's rulers are perforce those men capable of providing such benevolent and just government. They come from the "mediocre" class within the city, men neither swollen with ambition nor reduced by poverty to crass selfishness (pp. 73ff., 119, 219). The republic is best ruled, he advises, by the "middling citizens who are the health of the republic."[155] Since the city is as great as the greatness of its rulers, they should be wise, good, and learned, for knowledge is even more important to the city than wealth (pp. 80-81). An understanding of history is particularly important. History frees "the soul from that opacity by which it was befogged [and], the shadows lifted, as it were, restores it to perspicuity and clarity."[156] Since what has happened will happen again, moreover, history is a practical guide to current policy: "for time revolves in a kind of circle, so that what was the case before, later after a certain interval of time has elapsed, will occur in the same way or very like it again."[157] Not only a theoretical knowledge of history is required, but, alongside it, a vast fund of practical experience. "For experience and history teaches what should be done in any time or place and with what fortune and what we should be aware of in the future, which if any one lacks it, he is like a pupil . . . without a master."[158] Such experience comes only with age. For while young men can be intelligent, learned, and eloquent, "there are no wise men who are not old, and even then, very few."[159]

Learned and wise, the gerontocrats of Morosini's republic are public, not private persons: "Tend to public business for the sake of the public utility, not your own," Morosini commands, "for to this end you were made a magistrate and honored, and to this end the republic was

---

[154] The bishop of the city is also entrusted with responsibility for maintaining civic concord (ibid., pp. 190-91). Here Morosini's conception resembles Barozzi's, discussed below.

[155] ". . . mediocres cives quod est salus civitatis." Ibid., p. 119.

[156] ". . . tantum lucis addideris historie, ut illud opacitatis quo anima videbatur offusa quasi excusis tenebris ad perspicuitatem limpiditatemque redditum esse videatur . . . ." Ibid., p. 129.

[157] ". . . hoc seculum tanquam aliquo circulo ducitur, ut quod prius fuit postea aliquo elapso temporis intervallo aut idem aut prope simile reppetatur." Ibid.

[158] "Experientia enim et historia est magistra nobis quid quoque loco et tempore quaque etiam fortuna agere et quid in futurum prospicere debeamus qua qui caret sic se habet sicut discipulus . . . sine doctore . . . ." Ibid., p. 128.

[159] "Sapientes non nisi senes et illi perpauci." Ibid. Similar statements at pp. 107, 118, 156. A recommendation that rulers be advanced in age is found also in Paolo Morosini, DRF, p. 249. The Morosinis' statements reflect a cultural preference; see Finlay, "The Venetian Republic as a Gerontocracy." Domenico Morosini was himself a very old man when he wrote this work.

commended and committed to you, that you serve the common utility of all, not your own."[160] Such rulers win the obedience of their subjects, and the whole city prospers. "Wherefore if those who rule devote themselves to the public utility with one soul, and all consent with one soul and will, and for it labor and exert themselves, then that city to which this has happened, enriched with all good things, will with peace, tranquillity, and great happiness flourish, which happiness indeed also will redound to all private citizens, for the good health of the body extends to all its individual parts."[161]

The ideal system of government that is selflessly administered by the rulers of the city's "middling" class is described only vaguely.[162] Three general strata of government rule are discussed. First is the "General Council," which corresponds roughly to Venice's Great Council. Second are the magistracies, the various offices and councils manned by the ruling class just described. These are discussed in general terms, particular attention being given to the Senate and *Collegio*, censors, *avogadori*, and Council of Ten. Third is the prince, the city's ultimate ruler who by his single presence fuses the citizenry into a single *persona*.

Admitted to the Great Council are the young men of the ruling class, not yet sufficiently matured in judgment for more important offices, and a few categories of citizens from the groups normally debarred from political life.[163] Workers such as butchers, fishermen, carpenters, and the like may not attend, "lest their filthiness befoul civil and urban decency."[164] Those wealthy merchants may, however, who approach

[160] "Cura publicas res ad publicam omnium utilitatem non ad privatam tuam. ad hoc enim factus es magistratus ac insignitus honore et ad hoc res publica tibi tradita et comendata ut comuni omnium utilitati inservias non tua." DRF, p. 133. Also p. 179: "... quoniam publica tibi mandanda sunt, ut ea tantum a re publica gubernes privata ita tibi permissa ut ea privatim tantum modo curis nulla societate ac coniunctione rerum publicarum ...."

[161] "Quod si qui presint vacent utilitati publice unoque animo ad hoc omnes ac voluntate consentiant et ad hoc invigilent et incumbant, tunc illa civitas cui hoc contingit omnibus bonis aucta cum pace otio et plurima felicitate florebit, que quidem felicitas etiam ad privatos omnes cives redundabit nam corporis bona valitudo ad singula queque membra permanant fortuna." Ibid., p. 133.

[162] Both Caldiera and Paolo Morosini have given more detailed analyses. Domenico appears to describe an ideal city, not Venice. Yet his analysis of his mythical government discusses offices and councils recognizably Venetian.

[163] Ibid., pp. 119, 134. Morosini's broadening of the Great Council contradicts absolutely contemporary Venetian practice, which permitted entry only to members of the nobility. Morosini's essential aim, however, is consistent: to provide in the Great Council access to lesser offices for a fairly large group of persons who might thereby feel rewarded by the government and be disinclined to express discontent. See R. Finlay, *Politics in Renaissance Venice* for a similar understanding of the Maggior Consiglio in early sixteenth-century Venice.

[164] "... ne eius sordities fedet civilem et urbanam honestatem." DBIRP, p. 134. The poor are excluded for the same reason.

in dignity the city's rulers—wool and silk merchants, for instance—
as may the learned men. This body of young men of the political class,
wealthy merchants, and *litterati* convenes to elect some magistrates
and to supervise building activities, and such projects as the repair of
fortifications and drainage systems: "For diligence in these matters is
not very expensive but greatly adorns and dignifies the city."[165]
Authority is concentrated not in the broad population of the Great
Council, but in the magistracies. Although these are many and distinct,
having the same end in view they are perceived as a whole: "yet all
come together into one, since any one among them appears to act for
all."[166] Given his perception of Venetian offices and councils that must
underlie this statement, it is not surprising that Morosini does not
clearly designate specific functions even for the few that he names.
The Senate, its members elected for life from among the "best citizens,"[167] has particular responsibility for preserving the city's traditions and well-being: "this perpetual senate is the guardian of public
liberty, the patron of laws, a pillar of justice, the constant and unfailing
means of preserving and perpetuating [the city's] welfare."[168] Thus
entrusted, they are required to have a profound and practical knowledge of the city's physical, economic, and social structure.[169] Other
offices enforce public obedience, aiming to achieve that concord in
which consists the city's happiness. The state attorneys are specifically
responsible for protecting the laws of the city by assuring that they
are obeyed. Officials not previously known in any republic, nor envisioned by the philosophers, they keep the city "in security and equality and the observance of the laws."[170] The censors are vigilant lest
the citizens tend to immortality, a threat to civic unity.[171] The Venetian

[165] "Nam hec dilligentia non magnam exigit impensam sed magnum prebet civitati
ornamentum et decorem." Ibid., pp. 134-35.

[166] ". . . ut quamvis magistratus sint plures et inter se distincti, ipse tamen omnes in
unum cogere, unus eis siquidem et omnes gerrere videatur . . . ." Ibid., p. 93.

[167] The phrase "best citizens" is intriguing; here Morosini does not as elsewhere
designate the "middling" or "mediocre" class, and may perhaps intend, consistent with
Venetian practice, that the Senate be drawn from an elite subgroup of the ruling class.
His wishing them appointed for life strengthens this hypothesis that he envisioned an
exclusive body—one more so than the Venetian Senate, to which persons were appointed
for one-year terms.

[168] ". . . hec senatoria perpetuitas custos est publice libertatis, patrona legum, iustitie
columen, constans et firma ratio perpetuande ac conservande salutis . . . ." DBIRP, p.
124.

[169] These duties are closely detailed ibid., p. 105.

[170] ". . . in securitate ac equalitate et legum observantia continet, quem magistratum
nulla unquam res publica habuit neque ulla philosophorum traditio meminit." Ibid., p.
101.

[171] Ibid., pp. 94, 247. Morosini distinguishes the "censors" from the Council of Ten,
as, curiously, does Caldiera (*De politia*, fol. 148)—curiously, since a magistracy of
"censors" does not seem to have been instituted in Venice until the sixteenth century

145

Council of Ten, to which Caldiera had ascribed guardianship even of private thoughts, and whose power Paolo Morosini had described as "terrifying," is much admired by Domenico Morosini.[172] "This council has provided many benefits in our city: peace, tranquillity, and concord of the citizens, and the eternity of liberty. . . . From which Council so many and such great goods derive indeed that the perpetual tranquillity of our city and the continuation of our liberty can be in large part attributed to this council."[173] In the ideal republic, as in Venice, the Council of Ten handles all dissent, and disheartens would-be rebels, ensuring social cohesion and perfect obedience.

But even more essential to civic harmony in Morosini's republic is the prince.[174] Elected from among the "best citizens," that ruling class constituted by "middling" men, the prince, like them, is just and virtuous, but to an even greater degree: "for he who will rule all should be also more excellent than all."[175] No tyrant, he governs not by his own will but with the advice [consilio] of other leaders, in obedience to the law, and with a view to public utility. "Thus let our prince revere justice, guard the public utility, defend decency, grant what should be granted, deny what should be denied, and do these things openly to all, so that he not fail in any regard, granting privileges to some he denies to others, but be always the same, constantly just and sober, and faithfully rule the republic."[176]

His most serious role, however, is through his unitary person, in which culminate all the forces and elements of the city, to inspire and enforce the unity of the people. Not a private person but a whole

(Finzi in DBIRP, p. 23 n. 72; Besta, *Senato*, p. 206). Perhaps such a council existed informally in their lifetimes; more probably they are referring to the members of the Council of Ten.

[172] For Caldiera's and Paolo Morosini's comments, see above at nn. 55 and 142, respectively. Domenico Morosini remarks, as he did of the *avogadori*, that the institution of the Council of Ten had never before existed in any city (DBIRP, p. 195).

[173] "Hoc consilium multa bona nostre peperit civitati pacem tranquilitatem ac concordiam civium, et diuturnitatem libertatis . . . . A quo consilio tot et tanta bona profecta sunt ut tranquilitas perpetua nostre civitatis et diuturnitas nostre libertatis ex magna parte huic consilio possit ascribi." Ibid., p. 196.

[174] Like Caldiera, Domenico Morosini exalts the figure of the doge; see above, at nn. 51-53. Like Quirini and Paolo Morosini, he stresses the doge's subordination to law; above, at nn. 97-98 and 139-140, respectively. For the symbolic role of the doge in Venice, see Muir, *Civic Ritual*, pp. 203-204, 260ff.

[175] "Et enim qui prefuturus est omnibus, omnibus quoque debet excelentior esse." DBIRP, p. 85.

[176] "Itaque noster iste princeps colat iustitiam, tueatur utilitatem publicam, defendat honestatem, que concedenda sunt concedat, que neganda sunt neget, hecque faciat sincere cum omnibus, ut non claudicet, aliquibus aliqua concedens eadem aliis negans sed semper sit idem iustus et gravis perseverans ac magna fidutia rem publicam gerrat . . . ." Ibid., pp. 90-91.

public organism, "he speaks to all the people on any issue, he pronounces justice, and as one man governs the whole *imperium*."[177] All acquiesce to his single lordship, knowing that he is the representation of the public good: "since all obey and honor him, and if anyone hesitates, he is quickly dispatched and with public consent, since all love the general good, and it pleases all that it is protected and defended, with all understanding that in the common good of all is protected also his own private good."[178] As a public figure and symbol of the general good, the prince can quell all dissidence: "And since there are always diverse views among the citizens, quarrels and dissent, he takes care to quell and extinguish them, unite the dissident, reunite the disputants with love and benevolence."[179] He need not even speak. His public appearance, adorned with the signs of majesty and power, silently and effectively compels unity and obedience. That spectacle alone "wins the reverence of the people and attracts their respectful regard."[180]

That spectacle alone can cure the disease of faction. Morosini prescribes one other medicine for that disease: building. "The wealth and abundance of the city," he argues, "is better spent on [public] buildings than on depraved customs, on *clientelae*, clubs, and sodalities."[181] Self-indulgence weakens the citizens, and the formation of subgroups threatens the unitary allegiance of citizens to the republic and leads to rebelliousness. Not only wealth but time, as well, is absorbed by such activities—time that otherwise might be dangerously employed. But healthful "*occupatio*" preserves the city. Citizens should therefore be employed in the construction of private and public buildings, drainage, irrigation, and sewage systems, and the repair of walls, fortifications, and streets.[182] Such projects bring great honor to the city,

[177] "Denique populis cunctis de quacumque re respondet ius dicit et imperium unus totum gerrit." Ibid., p. 193.

[178] ". . . quoniam omnes ei cedunt ac parent, et si reluctetur quisquam e vestigio obruitur consensuque populari quoniam publicum bonum omnes amant ac cunctis placet illud protegi atque defendi intelligentibus in comuni bono omnium custodiri quoque privatum et suum." Ibid., p. 194.

[179] "Et quoniam inter cives semper sunt diversitates sententiarum emulationes disidiaque ipse ea tollere ac extinguere curet. disidentes uniat, emulantes amore benivolentiaque conglutinet . . . ." Ibid., p. 91; similar statements at pp. 104, 112.

[180] ". . . quod vendicat reverentiam a populis et omnium in se oculos conspectumque cum quadam veneratione converti." Ibid., p. 139.

[181] ". . . opes ac divitie civium melius quidem in ista hedifitia quam in pravos mores in clientelas amicicias sodalitatesque profundantur . . . ." Ibid., p. 84; similar statements at p. 116.

[182] "Quare aliis fosiones agri tuendi causa comitantur, aliis curationes fluminum, aliis rivuli et aque ductus ad aquandos agros ad impinguandam terram colendamque traduntur. Nec uni omnia sed singulis singula demandentur in civitate vero cloache eluende

CHAPTER TWO

impressing admirers and daunting enemies, expressing in enduring
stone its invincible wealth and power. So vital are buildings, monuments both real and symbolic of the city's unified strength, that the
duty to supervise such matters is assigned to the Council of Ten, that
stern guardian of civic concord. Just as the citizens are to be all of
one mind in the ideal republic, the façades of all the buildings should
so harmonize according to one grand plan.[183]

Morosini perceives dissidence and faction as the greatest possible
threat to the republic. Accordingly, he recommends that the city be
ruled by a class of men characterized by their lack of self-interest, their
emotional restraint, and unfailing commitment to the public good. To
these moral qualities, moreover, they add as well intellectual attainments and the wealth of experience gathered over long years. They
govern providently and benevolently, avoiding the entrapments of war,
administering impartial justice, diligently fostering the city's trade for
the sake of both poor and wealthy citizens. By such policies, they win
the people's loving allegiance, which is further monitored and enforced
by magistracies within the government specifically entrusted with that
task. Finally, they elect a prince who in his person encompasses and
unites all the functions of the republic, by his acts inspires unity, and
in his symbolic presence compels it. This ruling class Morosini sees
recruited from among the "mediocre" or "middling" citizens—a curious notion to be posed by a nobleman who had for the span of a
lifetime exercised the prerogatives and enjoyed the privileges of his
rank. The possibility may be ruled out from the start that Morosini
is a democrat who wishes the ideal republic to be ruled by members
of what today would be called the "middle class." What, then, did he
intend by this curious and often reiterated injunction?

The notion that political rule is most successful where the "mediocre" rather than the "great" or "small" men have power Morosini
borrows from Aristotle. That philosopher was well-known to educated
Venetians, and his *Politics* was immensely popular. The intellectual
climate of Venice made it quite natural for a learned politician seeking
theoretical guidance to turn to Aristotle. Aristotle's own political predilections also makes his work most congenial to a Venetian reader.

mundandeque, reparanda menia, sternende vie complanande aree, expedienda itinera
dilatandaque et in eis domus ad equalitatem reducende ac artifitia singula iuvanda si
ita opus erit, amplianda si fieri poterit, sin minus in sua firmitate conditione servanda."
Ibid., p. 148; similar statements at pp. 83-84, 134-35.
[183] "Privata vero ne una domus alterum progrediatur nec in via una ab altera referratur
sed omnes una paritate et ut ea uno ordine construantur . . ."; they should see "quod
edibus civium letum habent prospectum et civitatem luminosam atque spatiosam red-
dunt . . . ." Ibid., pp. 98, 99.

148

He values stability, as had the Venetians for centuries, approves of aristocracy, and devotes much energy to the problem of avoiding revolutionary disturbance. With that object in view, he recommends middle-class rule, a reasonable recommendation to make to a fourth-century Greek audience.[184]

Although Morosini adopts Aristotle's recommendation, however, the Venetian does not have the same class of men in mind, nor does he address the same audience—though he cherishes the same ultimate goal of civic tranquillity. His audience is that of the Venetian noblemen and those few citizen commoners who share their outlook. The "middling" citizens that he believes should rule are, in fact, not commoners of modest wealth, but noblemen of modest temperament. The group he excludes from his republic are two: first, like Aristotle, the poor—of course; second, not the nobility as a whole but those swaggering and haughty aristocrats who had in recent years lured Venice into military adventurism and to the edge of disaster.

Morosini's social vision is perhaps more generous than that implied in Venetian practice. He admits to the Great Council persons not of noble descent—wealthy merchants and the learned—where the Great Council of Venice enfranchised only the nobility, as indeed its membership was coincident with the nobility by law. Morosini's intention here is limited, however. He may wish to broaden the circle of those in contact with political rule, or to steady the nobility by encouraging in them, through greater propinquity, the influence of worthy commoners. But he does not admit even these very responsible commoners to serious political power. With the younger scions of noble families they are delegated housekeeping chores.

The real business of government is handled by upper councils: the Senate, the state attorneys, the Council of Ten. These bodies are staffed by the "best citizens": not the young, and not the vulgar, but the old and experienced nobility. The ambition and arrogance of the nobility is to be restrained, in Morosini's view, by a high cultural valuation of moderation (*mediocritas*) and by contact with wealthy commoners. But it is they, in the end, who rule—or at least the most sober and prudent among them, men, in fact, very like Morosini himself. Eighty when he began the DBIRP, Morosini had witnessed Venice's growing involvement in the miasma of terraferma politics, and on the brink of

---

[184] Reliance on Aristotle's *Politics* has already been seen in the works of Caldiera and Quirini, and will shortly appear in Barozzi's. For Aristotle's valuation of stability and consequent preference for the rule of "middling" men, see especially IV:11-13 and V:1-8. His faith in those of mediocre wealth does not contradict his view that aristocracy is the most perfect form of government; see especially IV:1-2, 7-8.

the next century, sniffed the debacle to come. Not a democrat—enfranchising a middle class—or a revolutionary—repudiating an aristocracy—not even a conservative, Morosini is a reactionary. He wishes to return to the days, now forgotten by those obsessed with power, when Venice's main purpose was to seek and accumulate wealth. He staffs the council halls of his ideal republic, the image of Venice in all but a few regards, with noblemen too old to thirst for blood, and wise enough to share his vision.

Morosini's covert intention is now revealed. He recommends government by "middling citizens," the mask of the older and wiser nobility, and the exclusion from power of the younger noblemen (anyone under eighty?) whose expansionist policies had landed the city on a dangerous path. He is, in fact, in the guise of a description of ideal government, a utopia, directing severe criticism against a current ruling clique. Obedient to the ideal of unity so deeply revered in Venice, he voices his criticisms through indirection and allusion. Had he been querulous or outspoken, he would have been guilty of the very sin he so deplored: vaunting himself too highly and betraying the community in which his identity was rooted, and which required of him self-discipline, self-sacrifice, selfless, sober stillness. Only thus could he merge facelessly into the whole of that nobility ruling a republic where the citizens were all of one mind and even the buildings, sternly marshaled, formed of their diverse façades one wall.

6. PIETRO BAROZZI ON ROOTING OUT FACTIONS

Whereas Domenico Morosini designs an ideal city resistant to faction and dissent, the Bishop Pietro Barozzi advises the incoming podestà of faction-ridden Bergamo, his friend Bernardo Bembo, how to quell the rebelliousness of his subjects. The learned cleric is well aware of the historical origins of political faction. Yet his analysis identifies chiefly moral and spiritual causes of that civic ailment, and prescribes apposite remedies. *On the Extirpation of Factions and Recalling and Compelling the Citizens to Obedience* is a peculiar mix of traditional piety, philosophical precept, and political realism.[185]

The treatise, as Barozzi explains to Bembo with characteristic lu-

---

[185] Barozzi's *De factionibus extinguendis et civibus in gratiam pristinam revocandis continendisque* [DFE]; Gaeta's introduction, pp. 7-47; text, pp. 49-157. The work was written in 1489, probably between the time of Bembo's election to the podestariate (29 April) and his assumption in July of the office of Savio di Terraferma. For the motivating circumstances of Bergamese civic strife, see Gaeta, pp. 14ff. An analysis of the text also appears in R. Abbondanza's review of Gaeta's work in BIS.

cidity, has three books.[186] The first reviews the development of the Guelph and Ghibelline factions, whose offspring still convulse Bergamo. The second examines the nature of factions "according to the views of the philosophers, to the first of whose ranks you belong."[187] The third seeks the judgment of Scripture. The first discusses factions by focusing on the people whom they enmesh; the second is written from the perspective of the ruler who must deal with them; the third from the perspective of the bishop who must judge them. The first addresses the ignorant; the second, the learned; the third, the religious. The order of Barozzi's work, reminiscent of Caldiera's massive and awkward symphonies, thus embodies a set of coincident hierarchies. A social hierarchy is explicit: the people at the base, the class of rulers more elevated, the bishop and the ecclesiastical order he represents at the peak. It mirrors an implied universal hierarchy based in mundanity and ascending to divinity. It is paralleled by a hierarchy of modes of knowledge: historical, philosophical, and theological. The advice Barozzi provides is also threefold and of intensifying value: Book One defines a problem, but offers no remedy; Book Two offers sound moral solutions; Book Three offers sounder spiritual ones.

As a Venetian—since Venice had long gloried in its freedom from civic strife—Pietro Barozzi recognizes factionalism as a fundamental evil: "certainly there has been in Italy, as long as men can remember, no plague more pernicious."[188] In the first book of *On the Extirpation of Factions*, he draws especially on the jurist Bartolus' *De guelphis et gebelinis*, but also on chronicles and histories to survey the origins and consequences of the party divisions that had tormented Italy for centuries: "such that there was no city in all of Italy, no town, no village, no community, indeed no house that was not split in two."[189] At first parties, respectively, of the Church and Empire, Guelphs and Ghibellines had become identified with the governments of certain cities or groups within them. What had begun as a pattern of just allegiance to a sovereign lord and benefactor had become an excuse for the expedient pursuit of interest, as Ghibellines or Guelphs by birth or inclination shifted their loyalty in search of greater advantage. In

---

[186] DFE, pp. 50-51 for the plan of this work.

[187] ". . . secundum philosophorum sententias, inter quos tu principatum obtines." Ibid., p. 50.

[188] ". . . certum est nihil ea peste post hominum memoriam in Italia pernitiosius extitisse." Ibid., p. 52.

[189] ". . . ut nulla in tota Italia civitas foret, nullum oppidum, nullus vicus, nullum rus, nulla postremo domus, quae in duas partes non scinderetur . . . ." Ibid., p. 51. Barozzi's discussion of factions is found on pp. 51-67. For sources, see Gaeta's introduction, pp. 40ff., and Abbondanza's, review, pp. 243ff.

fifteenth-century Bergamo specifically (although this reality does not enter Barozzi's work, general in scope, it was known, surely, to him as to Bembo) the Guelph party, loyal to Venice, was opposed by Ghibellines allied with Milan. Factionalism was a political problem for Venetian rulers, who discouraged all parties. For Barozzi it was more: a moral and spiritual disease of the people, requiring the lofty medicaments of secular and ecclesiastical authority.[190]

Book Two, directed to a learned governor, is analytical, rather than historical in approach.[191] It seeks cures for factions by first investigating their causes. That investigation requires an understanding of social structure. Every republic has three classes of men always at odds with each other: the "small" or poor men, who are very numerous: the "great" or wealthy men, who are few; and the "middling" or "mediocre" men.[192] The small men strive unceasingly to become the equals of the great men. The great men strive unceasingly to maintain their superiority to all. The small man's greed and the rich man's pride are two of the fundamental causes of faction. The third is envy, the resentment one man feels for another's good fortune. From these three vices originate nine others that are the immediate causes of faction. In addition to these nine ordinary causes of faction, there are several other extraordinary ones, related to place, social condition, change of fortune, and so on. To eliminate factions, action must be taken to neutralize the vices and conditions that caused them. Each problem or circumstance has a corresponding remedy. Barozzi's set of prescriptions is summarized in Table 1.

Barozzi's scaffolding of ailments and remedies is elaborate. Beneath a proliferation of antinomial states of mind, however, a main theme emerges. The city is and should be a whole and perfectly balanced organism, a *"consensus partium"* (p. 103). It includes rich and poor, foreigners and natives, all essential parts of the whole (pp. 102, 107). Not even in the smallest degree should that balance be disturbed: "the city is one body and old and new, noble and ignoble, poor and rich ... should know themselves to be members of this body, and no more shall seek disproportionate aggrandizement than to have a nose, elbow,

---

[190] Even in this first book, where Barozzi's discussion is historical, his examples are all drawn from Scripture. He is determined even here to anchor all historical and seemingly adventitious events to a providential framework.

[191] The following is a summary of Book Two, pp. 69-114.

[192] Like Domenico Morosini, Barozzi derives these concepts from Aristotle's *Politics*; see above, n. 184, and the discussion below. Barozzi dwells more than Morosini on the emotional behavior of rich and poor; indeed, it is his analysis of emotional states that form the substance of this book. For the relations of Barozzi's work to his Aristotelian model, see also Gaeta, introduction, pp. 26ff. and Abbondanza, review, pp. 246ff.

TABLE 1. On the Extirpation of Factions

Ordinary Causes of Action			
Category of Vice	Cause of Faction	Remedy	Countervailing Virtue
cupiditas (greed)	metus (fear)	give no cause for fear	liberalitas (liberality)
	pusillitas (status anxiety)	equalize citizens' condition	
	negligentia (negligence)	arouse citizens' trust	
superbia (pride)	contumelia (arrogance)	remove arrogant men	humilitas (humility)
	verecundia (dishonor)	reward merit	
	contemptus (scorn)	admit all citizens to power	
invidia (envy)	praepotentia (presumption)	suppress ambitious men	caritas (charity)
	incrementum immoderatum (immoderate aggrandisement)	advanced depressed social groups, limit rising ones	
	peregrinitas (marginality)	absorb foreigners, discourage transgressions against natives	

Extraordinary Causes of Faction	
Cause of Faction	Remedy
situs (site)	guard streets, bridges, etc.
conditio (social condition)	equalize social conditions
casus (accident)	take advantage of good fortune
vis et dolus (violence and pain)	as for "negligentia"
parificatio (attempt to equalize)	[none]
perfidia (perfidy)	repress
ambitio (ambition)	repress
injuria (injury)	as for metus and contemptus
delinitio (enticement)	as for ambitio
exclusio (exclusiveness)	as for contemptus and praepotentia
prodigalitas (prodigality)	bar from office

neck, five feet long; but there will be such concord between them that no more will the new wish to displace the old, the ignoble the noble, [or] the poor the rich, than the foot wishes to be made a hand or the ear an eye."[193] Those citizens who strive to attain more wealth and

[193] ". . . civitatem corpus unum et antiquos ac novos, nobiles atque ignobiles, egenos ac divites . . . huius esse corporis membra intelligant, nihilo magis incrementum capere immoderatum volent quam nasum, cubitum, collum quinque pedes longum habere; verum tanta inter ipsas est futura concordia ut non aliter novi veterum, ignobiles no-

status than they have should be suppressed (p. 103). Those who are insolent in their wealth and power should be isolated, and kept out of government (pp. 100ff.). Class distinctions are inevitable, though they may, perhaps, through careful policy be moderated, but the tensions they cause must not be allowed to disrupt the city, to which—and not to class—allegiance is directed. The role of the ruler is to arouse no hostility that might unsettle the city's delicate equilibrium (pp. 98ff.), to remain himself unassuming, disciplined, and faceless (pp. 101ff.), but to be vigilant in preserving in eternal suspension a social hierarchy in which the wealthy are permitted wealth but not arrogance, and the poor are sympathetically aided but not permitted greatness (p. 104 and passim). Enduring harmony is thus attained through the benevolent power of the ruler and the mutual love of the citizens, carefully trained in the appropriate civic virtues: "so should men be trained to civic discipline from their early youth that they may know and do those things . . . by which they may preserve the present condition of the republic as long as possible."[194]

Barozzi finds the inspiration for his vision of civic harmony in Aristotle's *Politics*.[195] There the tripartite nature of the city's social structure is presented, and the source of strife located in the attempts of small men to rise, and of the wealthy and powerful to maintain and increase their position. But Barozzi's emphasis on the need for equilibrium and harmony is more marked than Aristotle's. More strikingly, his analysis of the causes of faction is far more intricate. Indeed, although he reveals at points a shrewd insight into the psychology of ruler and ruled, Barozzi's message is on the whole frigidly abstract. Aristotle speaks of the psychological states of the small men or great caught up in political conflict, but names only a few. Barozzi in contrast isolates and enumerates twenty different causal factors—mental states (*pusillitas, contemptus, praepotentia, ambitio,* and so on), modes of behavior (*negligentia, prodigalitas*), social and physical conditions (*peregrinitas, situs, conditio*). Many of the causes of faction that he defines with excessive refinement amount, in effect, to the same thing.

---

bilium, egeni divitum invadere locum velint, quam pes, manus aut auris oculus fieri . . . ." DFE, pp. 105-106. Barozzi speaks of the city, but his imagery is from I Corinthians XII:12-26, where Paul describes the harmony that should prevail among members of a Christian community; this is suggestive, for Barozzi's ideal of community thus acquires a sacral quality. Barozzi's antipathy to change of any sort is evident elsewhere, as well: for instance, at p. 99 he cautions that "tunc est rei publicae immutatio, etiam in minimis quibusque rebus, fieri prohibeatur . . . ."

[194] ". . . sic ad civilem disciplinam ab ineunte adolescentia homines erudiri ut ea sciant et faciant . . . per quae praesentem rei publicae statum quam diutissime firmum conservent." Ibid., p. 113.

[195] See above, n. 192.

The line of distinction is pale, for instance, between the problems of "arrogance" and "scorn," or of "presumption" and "immoderate aggrandizement." Barozzi himself has difficulty, at times, making such distinctions. For the remedy for "delinitio," he refers us to the recommendation made about "ambitio," admitting, in effect, that the terms are synonymous: for "vis et dolus," he directs us to "negligentia." The tendency to pose precise definitions of very similar mental states or other conditions is Aristotelian; but Barozzi exceeds his master.[196]

The impression of abstractness in Barozzi's analysis is also strengthened by the importation of Christian categories. Superimposed on the twenty terms labeling the causes of faction is a triadic structure of vices and virtues derived from the religious, not the philosophical tradition.[197] At the core of the factious spirit lie three of the seven deadly vices: greed, pride, and envy. They are countered by a symmetrical triad of virtues: liberality, humility, charity. Encased in this moral framework ranked in threes of trinitarian resonance, Barozzi's philosophical analysis is subsumed by a religious one. The effect is reinforced by the dense carpet of scriptural references that provide—rather than anecdotes of contemporary political life—the only examples of factional behavior and appropriate antidotes. In the end, *On the Extirpation of Factions*, written by one experienced ruler to another in an age that saw the dawn of realistic political analysis, belongs, as one critic has commented, not to that genre but to scholasticism.[198]

[196] Abbondanza remarks that it is in Barozzi's delineation of an ideal city and of the qualities required in its rulers that one finds "un certo sapore di concretezza" (p. 247). The same critic sees Barozzi's adhesion to the Aristotelian model "strettissima" as he delineates the causes of faction (p. 247). But I find Barozzi's elaboration of abstract categories more striking than the concreteness of political analysis, and far in excess of Aristotle's. I have been unable to locate a precise source for Barozzi's terms—not even for the set of nine terms intriguingly generated as three triads from the vices of *cupiditas, superbia,* and *invidia*. Some of them derive from the *Politics*, but are not there presented in the pattern Barozzi devises. For that pattern he may have found inspiration, though not a direct source, in the *Rhetoric*, where at II:2-11 a sequence of pairs of antithetical moral states is presented. At II:2:1378b-1379a, Aristotle distinguishes three aspects of the emotion of "slighting" (contempt, spite, insolence) in a manner suggestive of Barozzi's distinction of the three aspects of "pride" (arrogance, dishonor, scorn). I have used here the translation of W. Rhys Roberts in Vol. XI (Oxford, 1924) of *The Works of Aristotle*, edited by W. D. Ross. A consequence of the intricacy of Barozzi's system is the difficulty of translating his terms. Both Gaeta and Abbondanza avoid doing so; the latter notes the difficulty of the philosophical vocabulary (p. 247).

[197] Of the six major categories of virtues and vices, all but one (*liberalitas*) are essentially Christian. Barozzi's superimposition of Christian categories here is reminiscent of Caldiera in the *De virtutibus*.

[198] Contrasting Barozzi's work with several more realistic and practical contemporary

The Christian tonalities of Barozzi's philosophical analysis of factionalism in Book Two become dominant in Book Three. There the problem posed is not the cause of faction, but the means of restoring concord to the troubled city. The responsibility rests squarely on the bishop, a powerful figure in these northern Italian communes, who is to summon the citizens to observance of the eternal law of love which embraces all the other commandments.[199] Drawn into a loving concord, possessed of one heart and one soul, they are secure against the hate-born temptations of faction.[200] The ultimate and surest cure for sin—a civic sin made mortal—is in the greatest of the virtues, commanded by Christ Himself. The chill refinement of philosophical definitions presented earlier is canceled by the rhapsodic warmth of this final chapter.

Unlike the authors considered heretofore, Barozzi is not primarily concerned with the nature of the ruling class, nor with specifically Venetian circumstances. He is concerned not with the orchestrations of Venetian government or the providential destiny of that city but abstractly with the roles of a city's governor and bishop to prevent in the citizenry the stain of faction. Yet in assuming that lofty viewpoint, he does not shed concerns sensed by other Venetian writers. He distrusts, as does Domenico Morosini, the great and proud men whose unregulated wills might rend the delicate fabric of civic concord, and like him hopes to reinforce that concord in part through the benevolent nurture of the poor. With both Morosinis, he sees the rulers of the city as passionless servants of the public good. With Barbaro and Quirini, he stresses the need for education in civic virtue. He shares with Caldiera a vision of the city as a system, an integral machine of tightly coordinated parts whose end is to endure; and views, like Caldiera and Quirini, the city and its denizens as parts of a universal hierarchy, formed in its pattern, and ascending by sure steps to knowledge of its final truth. With Ermolao Barbaro the Elder, finally, whose work is next before us, he shares a moral vision. The worlds of politics

---

works, Abbondanza calls it a political treatise "di stampo spiccatamente scolastico . . . ." (p. 256).

[199] The important role accorded the bishop is not unusual in Venetian culture, or explainable simply by the fact that Barozzi himself was a bishop. Compare the importance accorded that figure by the humanist Gasparo Contarini in his work on episcopal responsibility: the *De officio episcopi* in Contarini's *Opera*, for which see G. Fragnito's comprehensive "Cultura umanistica e riforma religiosa."

[200] Barozzi frequently draws on Pauline imagery of the unity of the Church (as at DFE, pp. 105-106 and 155, based on the same passage from I Corinthians) to describe the ideal unity of the city. The imagery of one heart and one soul is from Acts IV:32 quoted at DFE, p. 52: "multitudinis credentium erat cor unum et anima una."

and learning are not exempt from moral laws. There, as throughout the universe, vice must be fought with virtue and thus vanquished.

7. ERMOLAO BARBARO THE ELDER ON THE DANGERS OF POETRY

Alone of the authors considered in these pages, Ermolao Barbaro does not write explicitly on the republic or its ruling elite. Yet he shares with those authors a moral concern that appears to be, as much as the social and political issues which they had addressed, central to Venetian humanism. Giovanni Caldiera showed in his moral philosophical trilogy how the loftier edifices of family and polity rest on the sturdy base of the individual's strict observance of virtues meticulously defined. Francesco Barbaro, Lauro Quirini, and Paolo and Domenico Morosini each in different ways grounded the nobleman's right to rule in his possession of superior moral qualities. Pietro Barozzi presented an elaborate system of moral failings as the causes of political unrest, for each of which he prescribed as a remedy the appropriate virtue. Ermolao Barbaro, finally, condemning as immoral the whole of poetic activity, describes poetry as inimical to the welfare of the republic and the majesty of God. It threatens the well-ordered universe he knew and shared with his fellow Venetians.

His attack is articulated in two *Orations against the Poets* (actually small treatises) dedicated to his compatriot, Cardinal Pietro Barbo.[201] Barbo, himself a humanist of austere temperament, was an appropriate audience for Barbaro's diatribe against an activity on the whole cherished by contemporary humanists.[202] In the first oration, Barbaro demonstrated that poetry was antipathetic to civic life, and for that reason had never been honored in the great ages of antiquity. In the second, responding specifically to a defense of poetry directed to him by a fellow cleric, Barbaro demonstrated that poetry conveyed through its figments and fables no divine truth. Consisting of immoral tales told

---

[201] *Orationes contra poetas*, published with the *Epistolae* [OCP], texts pp. 81-142; discussion of the text, pp. 14-22. For Barbo, see the appropriate profile. The orations (written in 1455) are dedicated to Barbo by an introductory letter (pp. 83-84), but are in fact addressed to Bartholomaeus Lendinariensis, a learned Franciscan, to whose arguments in defense of poetry Barbaro responds. Ronconi points out that though Barbaro condemns poetry, he approves of rhetoric and grammar where they are consonant with Christian aims. Ronconi's introduction also relates Barbaro's work to the broader context of the defense of poetry (and attack against it) that starts with Mussato and appears in Petrarch, Salutati, Boccaccio, and others.

[202] Poetry was one of the five disciplines comprising the *studia humanitatis*. For the austere quality of Barbo's humanism, see Chapter One in R. Weiss, *Un umanista veneziano*.

by immoral men, poetry was harmful to the republic and useless in the quest for truth.

The first oration traces the history of poetry during Greek, Roman, and early Christian antiquity in order to show that poets, far from being revered, had always been condemned by the wise: "since I deem that there never was an age in which, I do not say ... they were considered neither divine nor theologians, but never achieved so long as they lived any kind of honor; but that moreover they were always rather held in contempt, always spurned, always rejected, with only the exception of those few who were favored by either the benignity of the time, or the absolute power of one man, or the depraved morals of a city which delighted in vain pastimes and silly songs and theatrical displays."[203] The early Romans had expelled poets from the city (p. 87). Even at her height, Rome had never accorded any great honor to poets (p. 94). Cato, that foe of Carthage, saw the lures of poetry as a threat to the military spirit of Roman youth. No city, even if its dominion spread, could be successful if it failed in moral strength: "nor did he think the art of poetry invented for any cause but the corruption of the city and the seduction of the young."[204] The wise men of antiquity joined in condemning poetry. Plato ordered that poets be expelled from his ideal republic (pp. 95, 103, 106). Cicero considered comedy and tragedy alike flagitious, and other forms of poetry likely to excite selfish passions (pp. 102, 106). Varro labeled works of poetry crimes against the gods (p. 103). The Christian authors Athanasius, Augustine, and Jerome agreed, finding poetry immoral (pp. 98ff.); for Paul, it was idolatry (pp. 99ff.). Dangerous to all spectators and readers, the lascivious antics of the poets' creatures were most injurious to the young. "For what adolescent has been so well-trained by nature that, when he reads about the adulteries of those gods and their grotesque fornications, which the poets celebrate, as well as the detestable vices of all the others, would not be moved to lust, not excited to frenzy, especially since that age is by nature

---

[203] "... cum nullam umquam fuisse aetatem existimem in qua non dico non divini aut theologi ... haberentur sed nec ullum umquam honoris gradum quoad vixerint sint consecuti; quin immo potius semper contempti, semper spreti, semper abiecti, praeter paucos admodum, quibus aut benignitas temporis favit aut summa in uno homine potestas aut perditi unius civitatis mores, quae vanis quibusdam studiis inanibusque cantilenis et theatricis ludis delectarentur ...." OCP, p. 85. The first oration, summarized below, appears on pp. 85-107.

[204] "... neque existimabat poeticam artem inventam fuisse nisi ad corrumpendam civitatem et ad libidinem iuventutem provocandam." Ibid., p. 94.

prone to vice nor capable in itself of controlling adolescent yearnings without the powerful grace of God."[205]

It is poetry alone, however, and not learning in general, that corrupts men and cities. The Romans held the other arts in great reverence (p. 101). Eloquence, indeed, is a worthy art, in contrast to poetry, and greatly useful to the republic (p. 105). And philosophers, unlike poets, do not construct vain fantasies, but teach sound moral and civic virtues: "they applied themselves . . . to teaching morals and to investigating the things of nature and to explaining the art of living, by which mortals might understand for what purpose they had been born and revere justice and virtue, and rightly govern their cities."[206]

The inferiority of poetry to other liberal studies, and particularly to theology, is the theme underlying Barbaro's second oration.[207] His opponent had presented the case, heard also elsewhere in this century, that the poets were prophets, inspired theologians, who encased their sacred truths in the lovely shell of beautiful and intricate language.[208] Barbaro responds that the poets are ordinary men, uninspired by divinity, creators of fictions concealing no truth, but bearing the germs of corruption.

The creativity of poets cannot be divinely inspired, begins Barbaro, because inspiration is provided by the Holy Spirit, of whom the poets know nothing (pp. 109ff.). Scripture records the appearances of the Holy Spirit. The grace accorded Moses and the apostles was not accorded poets who write of heathen gods. It is absurd to think that lies and fictions can come from divine inspiration. "Neither the gift of poetry nor its fervor, therefore, can proceed in any way from God, but rather a certain inventive capacity of the human mind, more apt . . . to lasciviousness and lust than to virtue."[209] Had the poets been inspired by God, they would have been moved to virtue and the desire

---

[205] "Quis enim adolescens tam bene a natura institutus qui, cum legerit deorum illorum adulteria insanosque concubitus qui a poetis decantantur, tum etiam ceterorum omnium detestanda flagitia, non commoveatur ad libidinem, non concitetur ad insaniam, et praesertim cum ea aetas a natura proclivis sit ad flagitium nec per se satis ad comprimendas adolescentiae cupiditates sine multa divinitatis gratia?" Ibid., pp. 100-101.

[206] ". . . se contulerint . . . in edocendis moribus investigandisque naturae rebus ac tradenda vitae disciplina, quibus mortales intelligerent ad quam rem nati essent colerentque iustitiam et virtutem, ac civitates recte administrarentur." Ibid., p. 105; see also pp. 106-107.

[207] The following summarizes the second oration, pp. 108-42, altering for greater clarity the order of Barbaro's presentation.

[208] For the tradition of *theologia poetica*, see above, n. 201.

[209] "Non erit igitur neque gratia poesis neque fervor qui procedere ex Deo quovis modo possit, sed potius inventio quaedam humani ingenii magis ad lasciviam . . . et libidinem quam ad virtutem comparata." OCP, pp. 112-13.

for truth; for His Spirit is "fire and warmth and fervor, by which the souls of mortals are aroused to piety and to faith and to charity and continence and chastity and constancy, and the power of every virtue, and inflamed to the cognition and worship of the true God."[210]

The poets, however, do not seek virtue, but their own fame (pp. 130ff.). Fame does not figure among the goods that the human soul can possess, according to the peripatetics, and cannot be the *summum bonum* which, Barbaro's opponent had claimed, inspired poets gained. There is a kind of fame that rewards an innocent and honest life: "that is the true fame which is born from virtue, not from the enticements of fables or the charm of song. . . . For not in the enjoyment of pleasure but in the performance of labor and tolerance of torment is all virtue, and from virtue is all honor and glory achieved."[211]

Ordinary men, without divine inspiration, the poets cannot teach us the truth. Having no experience of God, they do not know His true nature (pp. 120ff.). Having no great knowledge, they are unable to teach about Him—unlike the philosophers, who "in scope and excellence of learning and the cognition of God exceeded the poets."[212] They are unable to communicate to us timeless truth, because that truth is rooted in God (pp. 127ff.). What they do teach is turpitude. Their theology is "false, base, and vicious."[213] Whether he was a god ("incredible") or man ("absurd"), Jove was never "turned into a bull, nor liquefied in a golden rain, nor poured into a fountain, but all these things are poetic fictions . . . yet in the end it seems that he, whom they call the highest and greatest of the gods, was a famous fornicator and rapist and adulterer and polluted with every sin."[214] His opponent had claimed that these fables contained truth within their shell; but

[210] "Non distabit igitur poesis a Spiritu Dei, si ipsa fervor est qui procedat ex Deo, cum nihil amplius dici de spiritu possit, quandoquidem et ipse ignis sit et calor et fervor, unde mortalium animi et ad fidem et ad pietatem et ad caritatem et continentiam et castitatem constantiamque ac fortitudinem totius virtutis incenduntur atque ad veri Dei cognitionem et cultum inflammantur . . . ." Ibid., p. 111.

[211] ". . . ea est vera fama quae de virtute nascitur, non quae a lenociniis fabularum aut carminum venustate exoritur . . . . Non enim in percipienda voluptate sed in sustinendo labore perferendisque cruciatibus omnis virtus omnisque de virtute laus ac gloria perficitur." Ibid., p. 134.

[212] ". . . et doctrinae magnitudine et excellentia et de Deo cognitione poetas omnes anteierent . . . ." Ibid., p. 117.

[213] "Nam, quomodo Deus cognosci potest ex ea theologia quae mendax est, turpis ac flagitiosa?" Ibid., p. 120.

[214] "Sane nec me fugit omnia aliud significare neque umquam Iovem, sive is deus fuerit, quod minime credendum est, sive homo, quod etiam absurdum, in taurum fuisse conversum, neque umquam liquefactum in aureum imbrem neque umquam defluxisse per impluvium, sed omnia esse conficta poetica . . . ; verumtamen satis constat illum, quem summum ac maximum deorum appellant, illustrissimum quendam moechum et stupratorem et adulterum pollutumque omni labe fuisse." Ibid., p. 114.

Barbaro counters that that shell is shameful, and the nugget within contains nothing true or useful (p. 134). And his opponent had claimed, too, that the fruits of poetry—the accounts of the deeds of great men—were sweet and nourishing. Barbaro commented trenchantly on the value of such examples to youth: "How great a detriment would adolescents suffer if they were not taught what were Hercules' labors, nor knew that he snatched Cerberus from hell and overwhelmed Antaeus and Geryon and defeated the Erimanthine beast and stood his pillars in the Atlantic? Nor knew that Theseus freed his country and destroyed Ariadne, and with Hercules subdued the Amazons or with the Argonauts captured Troy; or if they were ignorant that Jason with those same Argonauts sailed to Colchis, seized the golden fleece and abducted Medea, witch, prostitute, and parricide?"[215]

Not such knowledge, but the knowledge of theology is valuable to mortal men. Why search further? "Why do I," complained Barbaro, "immersed in so vast a bucket of pitch, fish for one minuscule philosophical insight, and especially when there stretches before me so great an expanse of sacred letters in which there is no utterance, no phrase, no passage, which does not breathe forth the highest charity, highest wisdom, highest sanctity, highest learning, highest art, and finest pattern for a worthy life?"[216]

Thus poetry is condemned, morality protected, faith professed, and authority affirmed. In an age of broadening horizons, Barbaro turns his head. His inner eye is fixed on the truth that used to be, certain that it should exist and confident that it will endure.

8. An Overview

The corpus of Venetian humanism contains (as do most other Italian humanisms of this era) religious, philosophical, rhetorical, and other kinds of works, as well as those on social and political issues. And it contains works in many genres: the treatise, the oration, the epistle,

---

[215] "Quidnam existimas detrimenti adolescentes pati si a poetis non erudirentur quales fuerint Herculis labores, neque scirent ereptum ex inferis ab eo Cerberum et superatum Anthaeum et Geryonem et erimanthaeam feram devictam ac positas in Atlantico columnas? Neque scirent liberatam a Theseo patriam et ereptam totiens Adrianam et devictas cum Hercule Amazones aut captam cum Argonautis Troiam, aut ignorarent Iasonem cum ipsis Argonautis Cholchidem adnavigasse et aureum eripuisse vellus et Medeam magicam meretricem ac parricidam abduxisse?" Ibid., p. 139.

[216] ". . . cur ego, in tam vasto immersam bitumine, unicam philosophiae sententiunculam piscabor, et presertim cum adeo pateat sacrarum litterarum planities in quibus nulla est dictio, nulla oratio, nulla compositio quae non redoleat summam caritatem, summam sapientiam, summam sanctitatem, summam doctrinam, summam disciplinam ac verae vitae institutionem?" Ibid., p. 140.

and so on. This study has been based on a reading of most of these works: on various subjects, in many genres. The aim has been to locate the characteristic themes of Venetian humanism. The analyses presented in Sections 1-7 help to do just that. The works by seven authors just reviewed form together only a small part of the whole production of the Venetian humanists. Yet that fraction of the whole that they constitute is weighty. They are among the most substantial of that category of works—the treatises—in which authors' perspectives on the universe, on society, and on the human condition are most often explicitly stated. Several of these works have a specifically political purpose. Others, although verging on political or social issues, draw heavily on philosophical and religious traditions (and are in fact works of moral philosophy); this a tendency typical of Venetian writing. The perspectives these authors offer are, in fact, as it will appear in Section 9, central to Venetian humanism.

It is insufficient, however, merely to assume such significance for these works without placing them in the context of the wider range of Venice's humanist literature. A review of that literature will provide such a context, and suggest the continuity of themes between the major works already examined and the works, major and minor, of the same and other humanist genres.

The classification of humanist works is imprecise. For the purposes of this analysis, the term "treatise" will denote any independent prose work of at least the length of a long essay that is not a dialogue, a history or biography, or a translation of or commentary upon another text. "Opuscula" will denote shorter works that are yet sufficiently formal in structure and cogent in theme to be considered autonomous: long letters or orations, in effect, which amount to small treatises. The categories of history, biography, translation, commentary, edition, and poem are used without implication of length or substance; each may embrace a great variety of works. Unless noted, the works surveyed here are in Latin.[217]

Of the humanist treatises, dialogues, and *opuscula* authored by Venetians of the core group, few approach in scope or importance those examined in Sections 1 through 7 of this chapter. Among those that deal directly with the organization of society is Ermolao Barbaro the Younger's brief work on the office of the ambassador—the *De*

---

[217] This review searches for the most conspicuous features of Venetian humanist literature. It is not complete, and the supporting bibliography does not constitute a catalogue (such a work would be useful, but is impossible here) of the whole corpus of that literature. The profiles of individual figures provide guidance to more complete bibliographical information.

officio legati—which he himself found so irksome. Two others of substantial range stand out: Tito Livio Frulovisi's *On the Republic (De republica)* and Francesco Negri's *On Aristocracy (De aristocratia),* both written by commoners while outside of Venice, and reflective of Venetian culture only obliquely. The former, written for a non-Venetian audience, entertains concepts of political life inimical to Venetian rulers. The latter, written to flatter an audience of patricians, both defends the legitimacy of aristocratic rule and recommends social policies concordant with those in effect in Venice. Girolamo Donato's small *Apology* for Venice directed to the King of France (*Contra calumnias apologia*) is a work of quite another character, close in substance and mode of argument to Paolo Morosini's DVEP examined earlier. Marcantonio Sabellico's series of works describing the site of Venice and the duties of her magistrates, governors, and secretaries (*De situ Venetae urbis, De venetis magistratibus, De oratoris officio, De officio scribae*), flatter (as does the work of his friend Negri) the patricians to whom they are directed while praising the qualities revered in Venice of loyalty, prudence, and obedience. The letters of Lauro Quirini (his "Epistole storiche") and Niccolò Canal (*Epistola ad cardinales*), urging action against Turkish aggression, are political works of microscopic scale, as is Quirini's lament for war-torn Italy (*De pace italiae*). Candiano Bollani's unusual *Trialogus* looks ahead to future political events, plangently.[218]

The *opuscula* not concerned with political and social matters fall into three main categories: moral, rhetorical, and philosophical. Dealing with moral questions are the dialogues of the commoners Filippo Morandi da Rimini, Pietro del Monte and Niccolò Sagundino, respectively, on poverty, on vice and virtue, and on moral "ends" (*Symposium de paupertate, De vitiorum inter se differencia et comparatione, Dialogus de finibus*). Especially concerned with the celibate or solitary life is Ermolao Barbaro the Younger's substantial treatise *On Celibacy (De coelibatu),* and Gregorio Correr's brief but impassioned *Soliloquy (Soliloquium)* and exhortatory letters to Cecilia Gonzaga and an unnamed Carthusian novice (*Epistola ad Caeciliam virginem, ad novitium Cartusianum*). In the same category of moral works also falls consolatory literature of widely varying scope by Pietro Barozzi

[218] In addition to such works as presented here, there are official or semi-official works by the humanists: among these, prologues to legal statutes by Francesco Diedo and Leonardo Giustiniani; vernacular *relazioni* (of which many must have been written though few preserved), such as those by Zaccaria Barbaro, Francesco Contarini, and Francesco Diedo; or letters written on behalf of the republic, such as those of Sebastiano Badoer to the duke of Milan. For these vernacular works, see profiles and bibliography.

(three *consolationes*), Niccolò Leonardi (*Oratio in funere magistri Andreae Phisici venetiarum*), Pietro Marcello the Elder (*Epistola consolatoria* to Fantino Dandolo), Michele Orsini (*Epistola religiosae sorori*), Pietro Perleone (*epistolae* to Niccolò Sagundino and Jacopo Antonio Marcello), and Sagundino (*Consolatio* for Valerio to the same Marcello). Works on rhetorical matters include three interesting ones by the commoners Filippo Morandi da Rimini (*Invectiva in vanissimos oratores*), Pietro del Monte (*Invectiva adversus ridiculum quendam oratorem*), and Marcantonio Sabellico (*De reparatione latinae linguae*), inveighing against enemies of the *studia humanitatis*, praising the genuinely learned and dignifying the role of eloquence. Narrower in purpose but related in theme are invectives by Francesco Contarini (*Invectiva in ignavam poetam [Danielem de Porcilis]* and *in Marinum Baduarium*), Francesco Diedo (*In Franciscum Barocium Invectiva lacessiti iniuriis apprime*), Giorgio Merula, and Lauro Quirini (*Epistola Laurentio Vallensi*), and the eulogy (a laudatory *epistola*) of Ciriaco d'Ancona by Jacopo Zeno. The third category includes Francesco Contarini's eulogy of philosophy (*Proemium in disputatione de philosophia*), Lauro Quirini's imagined dialogue with the shade of Aristotle (his philosophical *dialogus* addressed to Andrea Morosini), Niccolò Sagundino's and Lorenzo Zane's discussions of philosophical schools (respectively the *De origine et sectis philosophorum, De difficillimae doctrinae palma capescenda*), and Niccolò Leonico Tomeo's dialogues concerned with the nature of the soul and other metaphysical and moral questions (*Dialogi*). Not easily classified are Girolamo Donato's and Niccolò Sagundino's accounts of their tragic adventures (respectively the *Epistola ad Petrum Contarenum de terremotu Cretensi, De naufragio suo*), Bernardo Bembo's personal journals (notably the London *Zibaldone*), and dialogues by Francesco Contarini and Lauro Quirini in imitation of Lucian (respectively the *Dialogus* and *Dialogus in gymnasiis fiorentinis*).[219]

Venetian humanists were highly productive of works, both massive and slight, that belong to genres usually considered to belong to professional disciplines and to lie outside of humanism: philosophy, theology, medicine, and law. Among the works of philosophy are two by Paolo Morosini and Andrea Contrario that deal with controversies of concern to humanists as well: those regarding fate and free will, and the relative merits of Plato and Aristotle (*De fato seu praescientia*

---

[219] Filippo's work is especially interesting for seeing eloquence as having an essentially civic role; see the speech of Eloquentia cited in my "Study in Venetian Humanism," Part One, p. 87 n. 27. For Merula's literary quarrels, see Gabotto and Confalonieri, "Vita di Giorgio Merula," first part, pp. 293ff.

divina et liberi humani arbitrii libertate, Reprehensio sive objurgatio in calumniatorem divini Platonis). The many religious works by these humanists present a more complex pattern. Marco Dandolo's *Celebration of the Holy Cross (Praeconium sanctissime crucis)*, humanist in style and deeply personal in tone, focuses on the image of crucifixion and touches closely on an evangelical notion of justification by faith. Other works also document the importance to humanist discussion of miscellaneous religious issues: Pietro Bruto's exhortations against the Jews (*Epistola* and *Victoria contra Iudaeos*), Pietro Dolfin's dialogue against Girolamo Savonarola (*Dialogus in Hieronymum Ferrariensem*), Girolamo Donato's defense of the primacy of the Roman See and the procession of the Holy Spirit (*Apologeticus ad Graecos de principatu Romanae sedis* and *De processione Spiritus Sancti contra Graecum schisma*)—both against believers in Greek Orthodoxy, Paolo Morosini's exposition of the two natures of Christ (*De aeterna temporalique Christi generatione*), Paolo Ramusio's discussion of fasting (*De ieiuniorum observatione*), Niccolò Sagundino's of the trinitarian nature of God (*De deo, de unitate essentiae eius, et de trinitate personarum*), and Fantino Vallaresso's historical survey of church councils (*Libellus de ordine generalium conciliorum et unione Florentina*). Both Dandolo and Caldiera compiled expositions of the Psalms (respectively, the *Catena seu expositio graecorum patrum in psalmos*, an arrangement of passages from Greek expositors translated by the author, and the *Expositio in psalmos*), and Candiano Bollani expounded three chapters of Genesis (*In tria priora capita Genesis*; note also his *Tractatus super canticum gloriosissimae virginis Mariae*). By Pietro Barozzi, Domenico Bollani, Domenico de' Domenichi, Ludovico Donato, and Pietro del Monte we have strictly systematic works of theology and canon law (Barozzi's *Repertorium* of Gratian's *Decretum*, Bollani's *De conceptione gloriosissime virginis Mariae*, de' Domenichi's *De reformationibus romane curie* and *De sanguine Christi*—among many others, Donato's *Praefatio in theologicarum textum sententiarum novo ordine dispositum*), and by Barozzi and Fantino Vallaresso, instructional and devotional works directed toward priests and parishioners (the former's *De modo bene moriendi* and *officia*, the latter's *Compendium Catholicae fidei*). Noteworthy here also are the "Orationes" (sermons) of Ludovico Donato (*pro annuntiationis solenitate; pro gloriosissimi doctoris Augustini celebritate; pro epiphaniae festivitate*), Giovanni Lorenzi's sermon *De passione domini oratio*, and sermons by Fantino Dandolo and Ermolao Barbaro the Elder. On medicine and astrology we have several works by Giovanni Caldiera (*Aphorismi, Liber canonum astrologiae, Consilia medica*)

CHAPTER TWO

and Pietro Tommasi (*Consilium medicum, Consilium de universali praeservatione contra venena, Excerptum de astrologica inspectione*) of an academic and professional nature.[220]

Returning from these excursions into other disciplines to forms more typical of humanist production, attention may be turned to history, a genre much favored in Venice. Foremost here is Bernardo Giustiniani's *On the Origin of the City of Venice (De origine urbis venetiarum)*, a testimony to the author's judicious and critical use of sources. In its concern with the city's founding and early development, moreover, and stress on the spirit of cooperation and love of justice that had always informed Venetian life, Giustiniani's work is reminiscent of the major works examined earlier by Paolo Morosini. Also concerned with origins is Michele Orsini's minute *De summa venetorum origine*. Vaster in scope than Giustiniani's monumental work is Marcantonio Sabellico's popular narrative of Venice's existence from its founding to the present (*Rerum venetiarum ab urbe condita*); that prolific author also wrote a universal history (the *Enneades sive rhapsodia historiarum*) and a history of Aquileia (*De vetustate Aquileiensis patriae*). Less ambitious but highly interesting are accounts by participants of contemporary events to a politically aware audience: Francesco Contarini's of Venice's Tuscan war (*De rebus in Hetruria a Senensibus gestis*), Filippo Morandi da Rimini's of the fall of Constantinople (*Excidium Constantinopolitanae urbis que quondam Bizantium ferebatur*), Niccolò Sagundino's of Ottoman origins and advance (*De familia otumanorum*), and Jacopo Zeno's of a Paduan rebellion (*Descriptio coniurationis patavinae*). Antonio Vinciguerra's vernacular *Relazione sull'isola di Veglia*, which provides a remarkable history of that Venetian possession, may be numbered among the eyewitness reports. Not a participant, Pietro Cirneo was a contemporary of those who fought in the war against Ferrara (about which he wrote the *Commentarius de bello ferrariensi*); as a Corsican, he wrote with considerable intensity the *De rebus Corsicis*. Pietro Marcello the Younger and Antonio Donato (very economically) wrote with far less

[220] Included with Morosini's and Contrario's works might be Giovanni Caldiera's *Centiloquium de causis et causalis*. Pietro Marcello V's short *Principium Monasterii Montis Vendae* might also be noted among works on religious matters. Theological works by Domenico Morosini are known to have been written but seem to be lost; see his profile under "Works." These works have not been seen: Barozzi, *Repertorium* (Padua, Bibl. Capitolare, cod. B 42); Dandolo, *De sacramentis* (Vat. Ottob. Lat. 2094; cf. Kristeller, *Iter*, II, 421); Donato, *Praefatio* (cf. *Iter* I, 372); the sermons of Fantino Dandolo and Ermolao Barbaro V (the former: Padua, Bibl. Capitolare, cod. C. 46, cf. *Iter*, II, 5; the latter: London, Brit. Mus., cod. Add. 14785, cf. OCP, ed. Ronconi, 20 n. 64).

verve on the city's rulers: respectively, the *De vita, moribus et rebus gestis omnium ducorum venetorum,* and *Vitae ducorum venetorum,* sparse chronicles rather than biographies.[221]

With the major exception of Jacopo Zeno's biography of his grandfather Carlo Zeno (*Vita Caroli Zeni*)—an elaborate apology for a man who had at times in reality placed self-interest before duty—the biographies written by Venetian humanists pertain to religious figures. Among these is Bernardo Giustiniani's tribute to his uncle, the holy Lorenzo, which may perhaps be considered, like Zeno's, a family memoir (*Vita beati Laurentii Justiniani Venetiarum protopatriarchae*). But no such explanation can be given for Zeno's lives of the popes or of the Cardinal Albergati (*Vitae summorum pontificorum, Vita B. Nicolai Cardinalis Albergati*), or the saints' lives by the lay and clerical authors Pietro Barozzi (*Sermo de moribus virtutibus et miraculis Sancti Petri Acotanti nobilis veneti, Vita B. Eustochii virginis paduanae*), Ludovico Foscarini (*Gesta martyrum Victoris et Coronae*), and Bernardo Giustiniani (*De divi Marci Evangelistae vita, translatione, et sepulturae loco*); the tiny *Sermo de Sancto Romualdo,* perhaps by Niccolò Barbo, should be noted here. Related are accounts of the translation and burial of saints' bodies: Ermolao Barbaro the Elder's *Vita S. Athanasii Alexandrini episcopi, cum translatione eius corporis,* and Pietro Dolfin's *Epistola de translatione corporis S. Romualdi Fabrianum.* Just as Venetian humanist authors often focused on philosophical and theological matters in their other works, in biography (though not in history, where more practical concerns prevailed) they tended to religious subjects.[222]

Humanist translations, typically from Greek to Latin, evidence the same spectrum of interests evident in the treatises and *opuscula,* histories and biography. They consist largely of translations from religious and philosophical works on the one hand, and from rhetorical works providing models of civil or military behavior on the other. In the first category, notable are saints' lives, once again: Barbaro's life of Athanasius (named above), Pietro Barozzi's of St. Basil the Great, Francesco Diedo's of San Rocco, Leonardo Giustiniani's of Bishop Nicholas of Myra; Lauro Quirini's translation of the *Narratio de*

---

[221] Latin histories of Venice by Domenico Bollani and Pietro Contarini are at present lost; see Pertusi, "Inizi," pp. 305 and 318, respectively.

[222] I have not seen these works: Zeno, *Vitae summorum pontificorum* (Vat. Lat. 5942, Vat. Chig. F VIII, 198; cf. *Iter,* II, 336, 474; Zonta, ed., Zeno's *Vita Caroli Zeni,* vii n. 1); Barozzi, *Vita B. Eustochii virginis paduanae* (Padua, Museo Civico, cod. BP 1273; cf. *Iter,* II, 22); Dolfin's work on the translation of St. Romuald's body (cf. Mittarelli, *Bibl. codd. mss.,* col. 317ᵛ). See profile for the attribution to Barbo of the *Sermo de Sancto Romualdo.*

sacerdotio Jesu Christi (falsely attributed to Suidas) is a related project. In this same category are the translations of patristic and philosophical works: of such authors as Chrysostom, Aristotle, Themistius, Alexander of Aphrodisias, and Galen. Such works are too numerous to list, but translators include Ermolao Barbaro the Younger, Barozzi, Girolamo Donato, Giovanni Lorenzi, Niccolò Leonico Tomeo and Giorgio Valla. In the second, works of Plutarch (translations by Francesco Barbaro, Leonardo Giustiniani, Lorenzi, Niccolò Sagundino) and Isocrates (by Diedo, Bernardo Giustiniani, Pietro Perleone) dominate. To these may be added translations from Dio Cassius by Quirini (Caesar's oration), from Demosthenes (three orations) and Onosander (*De optimo imperatore eiusque officio*) by Sagundino, and from Aesop by Ermolao Barbaro the Younger and Gregorio Correr. From the Italian (to Latin), Barozzi translated a Petrarch *canzone*, Diedo a Boccaccio *novella*. Jacopo Antonio Marcello supplied prefaces to works translated by others, among them those to Quirini's *Narratio*, to Chrysostom's *De tollerandis calamitatibus* by an anonymous translator, to Guarino's translation of Strabo.[223]

Humanist editions and commentaries upon texts also tend to moral or religious, and scientific or philosophical subjects. Included in the first category are two commentaries on the Psalms and one on Genesis, all three works by laymen (Caldiera, Marco Dandolo, Candiano Bollani, whose works were noted above). In the second are found editions of and commentaries upon Aristotle and Pliny (notably by Ermolao Barbaro the Younger, whose *Castigationes plinianae et in Pomponium Melam* is famous). Benedetto Brognoli edited Diogenes Laertius in the translation of Ambrogio Traversari. Commentaries on and editions of Latin classics—Cicero, Juvenal, Plautus—are numerous, such as those from the hands of Giorgio Merula and Giorgio Valla, resident foreigners working for printers in the latter third of the century. Pietro Dolfin composed a summary of the arguments of Cicero's orations (*Argumenta in Ciceronis orationes*), and Candiano Bollani a commentary on Cicero's rhetorical work (*In rhetoricorum novorum Ci-*

---

[223] For direction to the literature on translations by our humanists of patristic and philosophical works, see the "Works" section in these authors' respective profiles. I have not seen some of the works listed. For Lorenzi's Plutarch trans., cf. *Iter*, II, 358. Sagundino's third Demosthenes translation in Vat. Lat. 1732, fols. 15-19ᵛ, 70-116ᵛ, 117-21 (cf. *Iter*, II, 432; Mastrodimitris, Νικόλαος ὁ Σεκουνδινός, pp. 163-64, 214-16). For Barbaro's and Correr's Aesop translations, see J. R. Berrigan, "The Latin Aesop of Ermolao Barbaro," and Berrigan, "The *Libellus Fabellarum* of Gregorio Correr." Barozzi's Petrarch trans. is appended to *A Maria vergine e madre canzone di Messer Francesco Petrarca e Laude di Fra Jacopone da Todi*, translated by A. Piegadi (Venice, 1861); not seen.

ceronis librum primum commentum). A concern with the discipline of rhetoric is evident in several grammatical works and handbooks of composition useful for the instructional and editorial tasks central to humanism. These include Francesco Negri's *Modus epistolandi* and *Grammatica*, Sagundino's *De epistolari dicendi genere*, Valla's *Rhetorica*; interesting also is Maffeo Vallaresso's precocious *Regule*.

Related to the activity of editors and commentators is that of encyclopedists, compilers of digests of knowledge garnered from mostly ancient texts. Examples of this genre are the works of Niccolò Leonico Tomeo, historical and mythographical in focus (*De varia historia libri tres*), and Giorgio Valla, universal in scope but strongly colored by mathematical and scientific models (*De expetendis et fugiendis rebus*). Even Ermolao Barbaro the Younger's *Castigationes plinianae* are encyclopedic in range and erudition. Also worthy of attention here is Giovanni Marcanova's important collection of classical inscriptions: the *Antiquitates*.[224]

In the oration, the genre perhaps most typical of humanism, converge an interest in rhetoric and a concern with the social arena. The genre flourished in Venice, where the political and academic activity of patricians provided ample opportunity for oratorical display. The substance of these orations has concerned us already in Chapter One. Here it will be sufficient to review the main categories of oratorical composition. Orations to foreign rulers or visiting dignitaries were sometimes mere courteous eulogies of a friend or potential ally. Among these are Marco Dandolo's to Ladislaus, king of Bohemia and Hungary, or to Ferdinand of Aragon, king of Sicily; two by Pietro Molin to Emperor Frederick III; Girolamo Donato's *In obedientia oratio* to Pope Julius II. Others, delivered mainly by noblemen charged with diplomatic missions, were vehicles for the articulation and promotion of Venetian policies. These include Paolo Barbo's *Oratio in traditione*

---

[224] For Barbaro's works on Aristotle, see most conveniently E. Bigi in DBI, VI (1964), 99. See profile for guidance to Merula's many editions of and commentaries upon Latin texts (Cicero, Ovid, Pliny, Plautus, Varro and Columella, Virgil, etc.). For those of Valla (who also commented upon and edited scientific and philosophical works), see most conveniently the listings of G. Gardenal, "Cronologia della vita e delle opere di Giorgio Valla" and J. L. Heiberg, *Beiträge*, pp. 36-41; most notable is his *De expetendis et fugiendis rebus*, an encyclopedia of commentaries. Benedetto Brognoli also edited modern works: George of Trebizond's *Rhetorica* (cf. G. Castellani, "Giorgio da Trebisonda") and Bernardo Giustiniani's *De origine urbis venetiarum*. Many other authors commented upon or edited classical texts in Venice in this period, but they were transient foreigners not included in this survey. For them see the Preface to Part Two, Section 9. For the encyclopedic character of Barbaro's *Castigationes plinianae*, see V. Branca, "L'umanesimo veneziano alla fine del Quattrocento," p. 151. I have not seen Marcanova's *Antiquitates*; see his profile under "Works" for guidance to many manuscript versions.

insignium Bartholomeo de Colionibus, Bernardo Giustiniani's *Oratio pro militia*, Niccolò Sagundino's oration to King Alfonso of Aragon on the nature of the Turkish threat, and Zaccaria Trevisan the Elder's to Pope Gregory XII, against the Schism. Ludovico Foscarini's impressive address to the Diet of Mantua defending Venice's strategy with regard to Turkish advance has been lost.[225]

Orations delivered in university, school, or guild settings to honor individual achievement for a particular profession or branch of knowledge also ranged from purely formal to serious and substantial. Typical are the several *orationes* of Giovanni Caldiera, Marcantonio Sabellico's orations *De origine et incrementis philosophiae, De cultu et fructu philosophiae* and *De usu philosophiae*, and Pietro Tommasi's *Oratio pro collegio phisicorum*. Among the most interesting of the school orations are those which, in sketching the career of the person honored, describe a cultural ideal of piety, discipline, and self-sacrifice. These include Niccolò Barbo's for Francesco Contarini, Antonio Bernardo's *in doctoratu Albertini Baduarii* and *pro doctorato Jacobi Molini in gymnasio patavino*, Francesco Diedo's *Oratio de laudibus Bartholomaei Paierini*, Marco Donato's for Zaccaria Trevisan the Younger. Funeral orations for prominent individuals often served the same function. Among these: Pietro Contarini's for Marco Corner; Andrea Giuliani's for Chrysoloras; Bernardo Giustiniani's *Oratio funebris habita in obitu Francisci Fuscari Ducis*; Filippo Morandi da Rimini's for Francesco Barbaro; Sabellico's *Oratio in funere Zachariae Barbari*. Outside of these categories altogether are Pietro Marcello the Elder's mock orations "Aeschines," "Demades," "Demosthenes," and "a certain Athenian."

The letters of the Venetian humanists, written for a variety of purposes in tones of greater or less formality or intimacy, have survived with diverse success. Many, presumably, are lost; some have survived by happenstance; some were collected with care by the authors or sympathetic contemporaries. The collections, greater and smaller, more and less complete, are of the letters of Ermolao Barbaro the Elder and of his younger namesake, of Francesco Barbaro, Niccolò Barbo, Andrea Contrario, Marco Dandolo, Ludovico Foscarini, Bernardo Giustiniani, Leonardo Giustiniani, Pietro del Monte, Filippo Morandi da Rimini, Pietro Perleone, Marcantonio Sabellico, Niccolò Sagundino, Pietro Tommasi, Maffeo Vallaresso, and of the exchange between Marco Barbo and Giovanni Lorenzi. The genre is, on account of its inconsistencies, difficult to analyze with precision. Present in the letters, however, to hazard a minimum description, is most conspic-

[225] For Foscarini's oration, cf. G. B. Picotti, *Dieta di Mantova*, p. 181.

uously a concern also encountered in other types of humanist composition: a concern with the welfare of the republic and the nature of the citizen's duty to it, seen particularly in the letters of Francesco Barbaro and Leonardo Giustiniani. Letters also discuss the business of daily life: the management of a monastery or bishopric, or a commercial enterprise, or the struggle to gain and keep employment or status. Problems of daily management are often discussed by the busy bishops Pietro Dolfin and Maffeo Vallaresso, whereas commercial concerns occasionally surface in the correspondence of the two Giustinianis; Lorenzi and Marco Barbo discuss incessantly the affairs and policies of the Curia. The concern with status and employment is heard in the letters of Contrario, del Monte, Morandi, Perleone, Sabellico, and Sagundino. Somewhat less prominent is the discussion of literary affairs, which constitutes a major theme in the letters of only a few figures. They are discussed amid other matters in the letters of Francesco Barbaro, Foscarini, Dolfin, and Vallaresso, but are more central to the correspondence of Leonardo Giustiniani, Leonardi, Tommasi, and above all Ermolao Barbaro the Younger. Although ties of friendship among the humanists, finally, were extensive, in only a few cases does that intimacy receive in the letters a passionate expression. The most moving expressions of friendship are found in the letters of Niccolò Barbo, and again, Leonardo Giustiniani and the younger Ermolao Barbaro.[226]

The poetic compositions of Venetian humanists include a scattering of efforts in the usual categories: epigrams and epithalamia, verses in praise of great men or rulers, of Venice and her possessions, of a beloved. Representative of these are the epigrams of Filippo Morandi da Rimini, the *Ad Gelliam elegiarum libri tres [Elegiae]* of Pietro Contarini, and the *Epithalamion sive oratio in nuptiis Ludovici Draconis veneti* of Francesco Contarini. The poetic production of the Venetian humanists also includes an important early tragedy by Gregorio Correr, and famous early comedies of Tito Livio Frulovisi. Perhaps the single most conspicuous feature of Venetian poetics, however, is a tendency toward moral and religious themes, such as in the work of the high-minded bishop Pietro Barozzi (*Versuum atque hymnorum libri III*). The impression of the importance of such themes is heightened by the dramatic renunciation by three of the poets of youthful, or secular, or merely immodest compositions. Gregorio Correr renounced his youthful secular poetic works, and wrote some moral and

---

[226] See the profiles of these figures (categories of "Works" for the major collections, "Correspondence" for the partial and fragmentary ones) for manuscripts and editions, collections not seen, and discussions; complete citations of collections seen are in the Bibliography. See Chapter One for the content of the letters in general.

religious verse. Leonardo Giustiniani turned from his popular youthful compositions to intense spiritual *laudi*. Antonio Vinciguerra's *satire*, pious lamentations of the morals of his age, were irreproachable; but youthful and less modest works may have been among those he ordered in his will to be burnt.[227]

This review of the literary production of Venetian humanists may close by a look at the nonexistent. What kinds of works did they not author? What problems did they conspicuously fail to address? The Venetian corpus includes, to my knowledge, no works challenging economic or social assumptions: none, that is, like Poggio Bracciolini's discussion of alternative models of just economic behavior, or assessment of the notion of hereditary claims to nobility.[228] It contains, to my knowledge, no works critically examining received religious or philosophical traditions: none, that is, analogous to Valla's challenge to ecclesiastical authority and medieval systems of thought, or Bruni's reevaluation of Aristotle as a philosopher of civic existence, or Pico's or Ficino's generous eclecticism, which incorporated academic philosophy as part of a broader intellectual vision.[229] It contains, finally, to my knowledge, no works elevating the human being: none celebrating the dynamic will or the profundity of the interior life, or the heroic struggle of the individual against the malicious whims of fortune, or contrasting human freedom and creativity with the passive and circumscribed natures of beast, stone, or angel.[230] The distinctive themes of Venetian humanism are found elsewhere.

[227] For discussions of Morandi's epigrams, Correr's tragedy, and Frulovisi's comedies, see the relevant profiles under "Works." For the renunciations of secular poetry, see profiles and Section 6 in Chapter One.

[228] His *Historia disceptativa de avaritia* and *De nobilitate*, respectively.

[229] Allusions are to such of Lorenzo Valla's works as the *De vero falsoque bono*; see also Trinkaus' analysis, *In Our Image and Likeness* I, Part I, Chapter III. Leonardo Bruni's philosophical writings, edited by H. Baron, are in *Humanistisch-philosophische Schriften*; see also the analysis of E. Garin, *Italian Humanism*, pp. 41-43. The works of Giovanni Pico della Mirandola: see especially the works *De hominis dignitate, Heptaplus*, and *De ente et uno*. The works of Marsilio Ficino are in his *Opera omnia*. For the synthesis of philosophical traditions in the outlooks of Pico and Ficino and others, see Kristeller's many pertinent works, especially *The Philosophy of Marsilio Ficino*; "Giovanni Pico della Mirandola and His Sources," with a rich bibliographical appendix; and the relevant chapters in *Eight Philosophers of the Italian Renaissance*.

[230] For the works of Renaissance humanists and philosophers on the theme of human dignity, see especially Trinkaus, *In Our Image and Likeness*, Parts II and III, and Kristeller's many relevant studies, most conveniently in the collections *Renaissance Concepts of Man and Other Essays, Renaissance Thought: The Classic Scholastic, and Humanistic Strains, Renaissance Thought II: Papers on Humanism and the Arts, Renaissance Thought and Its Sources*, and *Studies in Renaissance Thought and Letters*. Note that the Venetian tradition of this period includes no works of a strictly personal nature (personal or family memoirs) such as were common in Florence; for these, see C. Bec, *Les Marchands écrivains à Florence, 1375-1434*.

The following analysis of those themes requires an understanding of the relations between the works by Caldiera, Quirini, Barozzi, the Morosinis, and the Barbaros studied closely in the first part of this chapter and the full spectrum of Venetian humanist production just reviewed. Since it has not been feasible in this single volume to examine in detail the whole of that body of literature, or even its most important works in every category, an intense focus on a few works of particular significance can more easily provide the main material for an analysis of themes. But it can do so legitimately only if those works are representative of the wider literature. It can be argued that they are.

The perceptions of social and political life evident in the treatises studied are consistent with those explicit in several treatises and *opuscula* of lesser scope, and implicit in the histories authored by humanists, and in the translations, orations, letters, and poems that address themselves to these matters. These perceptions are supported, moreover, in the treatises themselves, by philosophical, religious, and moral assumptions that are also conspicuous in nearly every category of Venetian humanist activity, even where they are not considered in the context of individual or social existence. Some of the *opuscula* are preoccupied with moral, religious, or philosophical issues, whereas the biographies and poems are often concerned with religious subjects, and many of the orations sketch an ideal of human personality somberly moralistic in tone.

At the same time, moral and religious, scientific and philosophical texts are conspicuous among works edited, commented upon, translated, or obtained and placed in humanist libraries, whereas humanists composed many works in the related disciplines of philosophy, theology, and canon law. Social and political matters, on the one hand, finally, and moral, religious, and philosophical issues on the other, are the dominant concerns of Venetian humanism. Some small works discuss the ideal of eloquence and some editors and commentators deal with classical texts—but these efforts in rhetorical humanism constitute a subordinate element in this intellectual movement. Even in the correspondence of Venetian humanists, literary matters are only a secondary focus, and a personal voice is interjected only here and there to betray the individual concerns of those who have learned to subordinate their own to others' interests. No major currents of thought or feeling other than those expressed in the treatises examined earlier, it can therefore be argued, are articulated in humanist works of other types.

The treatises studied, then, are thematically consistent with the general patterns of Venetian humanist production. That continuity of themes and the fact that they are among the most substantial works of that corpus permits them to be considered representative works of Venetian humanism. That representativeness will be confirmed in the analysis of the prominent themes of Venetian humanism which follows. It is based on the reading of these treatises and supported by due reference to many other works from the full range of the Venetian humanist corpus.

9. THEMES OF UNANIMITAS

The vision of Venice presented in the works of Venetian humanism is their most striking feature. Founded on the principles of liberty and justice, the city is viewed as intrinsically righteous. Favored by providence, she is sure to endure forever, just as she has already long endured. Her nobility, chosen originally from the best citizens and conferring their peculiar virtue to generations of descendants, serve the city without thought of self. Her doge, the best man of that corporation of good men, rules without ambition and subject to law. Her people, amply provided with necessary goods and confident in a just government, don't even think of rebellion. The city enjoys perfect tranquillity, and provides a refuge to the exiled and homeless victims of the discord that rakes other less fortunate cities. Venetian humanism, in brief, perpetuates the "myth of Venice," that amalgamation of ideas that has so provoked scholarly interest. Though these themes are familiar, the role played in the mythic tradition by humanist authors is not widely recognized. In the fifteenth century, humanists articulated the vision of Venice that had appeared in medieval chronicles and would become in the sixteenth century the common property of Europe.[231]

[231] The myth of Venice is surely the concept most strenuously discussed by modern students of the period. Some works concerned with the myth: W. Bouwsma, "Venice and the Political Education of Europe"; A. Buck, " 'Laus Venetiae' und Politik im 16. Jahrhundert"; F. Chabod, "Venezia nella politica italiana ed europeo del Cinquecento"; G. Fasoli, "Nascita di un mito"; F. Gaeta, "Alcune considerazioni sul mito di Venezia"; E. Gianturco, "Bodin's Conception of the Venetian Constitution"; F. Gilbert "The Venetian Constitution in Florentine Political Thought"; M. Gilmore, "Myth and Reality in Venetian Political Theory"; L. J. Libby, "Venetian History and Political Thought after 1509"; E. Muir, *Civic Ritual*, especially Chapter I; R. Pecchioli, "Il 'mito' di Venezia e la crisi fiorentina intorno al 1500"; D. Queller, "The Civic Irresponsibility of the Venetian Nobility"; idem, "The Myth of the Venetian Patriciate"; D. Robey and J. Law, "The Venetian Myth"; E. Rosand, "Music and the Myth of Venice"; C. Rose, "Marc Antonio Venier, Renier Zeno, and the 'Myth of Venice.' " For the myth in Venetian historiography, see esp. Gaeta, "Storiografia, coscienza nazionale"; Muir, *Civic Ritual*, pp. 23ff.; and the essays in A. Pertusi, ed., *Storiografia veneziana*. The question of the myth of Venice is not easily circumscribed; it underlies or enters into many other major and minor works not specifically directed to it: among others, S. Chojnacki's

Fifteenth-century humanist works do more, however, than perpetuate a mythic vision already established in Venice's literary tradition. They also elaborate a body of perceptions of the universe, of society, of its place in that universe, and of the individual and his place in the social and universal systems. This set of perceptions—the themes of *unanimitas*—underlies the mythic vision of Venice as it appears in humanist literature. The perceptions provide, in effect, an armature, a context, a metaphysics for that mythic vision in the language and forms of humanism. For the world they perceive is sturdy, ordered, balanced, a pyramid of crystal abstractions—and provides a setting for the jewel of Venetian perfections far more suitable than the world of a Petrarch, a Bruni, a Poggio, a Valla, a Pico, a Ficino: shifting, restless, multivalent.

Venetian humanists reveal in their works distinctive attitudes toward the self and the world. They subordinate the individual to the group, and place both in a timeless hierarchical universe, inherited from their ancestors and sanctioned by the authority, as they knew it, of Aristotle and Christ.

The individual must be sternly restrained, Venetian humanists advise, from destroying the community.[232] His passions are disruptive. The rich man is driven by greed or pride, the poor man by desire or resentment, the woman or young man by sexual urgings.[233] Rulers are counseled how to manage the vices of "cupiditas" and "superbia": the benevolent provision of goods and opportunities removes the causes of greed or resentment, while firm control prevents abuses of pride.[234] The engagement of citizens in large public works, moreover, diverts them from more dangerous uses of their leisure.[235] Diligent

---

studies of the patriciate ("In Search of the Venetan Patriciate"; "Crime, Punishment, and the Trecento Venetian State"); R. Finlay's of government process (*Politics*, especially pp. 27ff.); Logan's of the relation between culture and society (*Culture and Society*, Chapter I); the studies of G. Cozzi, Gilbert, R. Mueller, and B. Pullan of the interaction between society and politics (see the works of these authors listed in the Bibliography). For a theory similar to mine of the relationship of humanist activity to myth-building, see also B. Marx, "Venedig—'Altera Roma,' Transformationen eines Mythos."

[232] The fear that the social fabric is vulnerable to the wayward passions of the individual—which are prompt to erupt if not restrained by education and sound policy—is fundamental to Ermolao Barbaro V's OCP. Bernardo Giustiniani similarly finds moral explanations for social success and decay. See the discussion of his *De origine urbis venetiarum* in P. H. Labalme, *Bernardo Giustiniani*, pp. 279ff., 313ff.; and note the moralistic interpolations present in his translation of Isocrates' *De regno* quoted by Labalme, pp. 99ff.

[233] See D. Morosini and Barozzi on the rich and poor, above, Sections 5 and 6, respectively; F. Barbaro on women, Section 1; E. Barbaro V on the vulnerablility of youth, Section 7.

[234] See Barozzi's recommendations for managing greed and pride, above, Section 6.

[235] D. Morosini at nn. 181-83 above for the benefits of public works projects.

and relentless instruction in good morals and the *bonae artes* stem the tide of adolescent passions.[236] Youths are kept, as well, from the seductions of pagan literature and dramatic spectacle, and women kept at home, soberly dressed and carefully regulated in diet and sexual activity.[237]

Indeed, the emotional life of each individual is closely guarded. A strict moral code is imposed, couched in the language of Aristotle's ethics but intoning clerical prescriptions from more recent centuries. The seven virtues are sent forth on parade, abstractions of excellence, remote from the real world in which ethical choices are made. The seven vices follow, stilted parodies of the states of mind inhabiting those who have fallen from grace. This ordering of good and evil in two parallel litanies of instruction denatures each, and limits the individual.[238] His emotional range corseted by moral injunctions and by domestic and political management, the individual is subject as well to the scrutiny of censors.[239]

Only those persons who are superior by natural heredity, excellent training, and rich experience can be considered fit to guide a community of the irrational and passion-ridden. Nobly born, liberally educated, and matured by time, such men are passionless. They require no external controls because they have disciplined themselves in-

[236] Quirini at nn. 116-17 above for the restraint of adolescent passion by a disciplined pedagogy. See also Chapter One, Section 1 for the same point made by Francesco Negri and in humanist orations. This moralistic emphasis contrasts with the pedagogy favored by Florentine merchant humanists, who seem more concerned with freeing than constraining personal feeling and expression; see Bec, *Marchands écrivains*, pp. 290, 297.

[237] Ermolao Barbaro V, Section 7, especially nn. 204-205; F. Barbaro, at nn. 14-15 above.

[238] Caldiera, Section 2 above. The parade of the virtues is common in the Venetian tradition. It is seen in such varied works as the medieval panegyric of Henry of Rimini (see Robey and Law, "Venetian Myth," pp. 52-56) and the *De coelibatu* of Ermolao Barbaro G, pp. 143ff. Although the sixteenth-century humanist Giovanni Battista Egnazio sheds the specifically Christian framework, his eulogy of great men is also organized according to a scheme of virtues; see his *De exemplis illustrium virorum Venetae civitatis*.

[239] For censorship (sometimes but not always identified with the function of the Council of Ten), see Caldiera (at nn. 54-55 above), Domenico (nn. 171-73) and Paolo Morosini (nn. 141-42), respectively. Note also Ludovico Forscarini's encouragement to Paolo Barbo upon his appointment as a member of the Council of Ten: "Nulla ambitione rempu[blicam] a pernitiosorum insidiis tueberis, et facinora ulciscendo bonis favendis optimorum arcem munies, malorum cupiditatibus resistes, improborum perfugia obstrues; eadem tibi cura erit et publice libertatis et bonorum dignitatis." *Epist.*, fol. 248. Related to the censorship function is the prosecution of "speech crimes" in Venice, studied by Ruggiero alongside the crimes of violence. Verbal assaults on individuals or the state itself received heavy penalties, and indicate how seriously such acts were regarded in Venetian culture; see his *Violence*, especially Chapter VIII.

wardly, curbing all hint of self-interest with the weapons of self-effacement and self-sacrifice. The nobleman does not strive for himself—
even when he strives for wealth or power—but for the general good.[240]
He is rewarded for his altruism by public memory awakened by immaterial words, not by stone memorials.[241] His commitment is total
and inescapable.[242] He yearns to be nothing in himself, but a part of
the whole: "a member, not a body."[243] He becomes a "public" person,
impassive like one whose will is shaped by forces outside himself. In
government councils, he forms no personal judgment: the whole body
of selfless and faceless men "consult" among themselves, producing a
pure judgment of the group unsullied by the urgings of single wills.[244]

Moved by the nobleman's example, or constrained by the strategies
of moral control already noted, or compelled by the "necessity of
place," or beguiled by the ruler's benevolence, or fired by love, hope,
and faith, the personalities of all Venetians likewise tend to yield to
the personality of the group.[245] Paolo Morosini's notion of the "ne-

---

[240] D. Morosini at nn. 160-61 above. See also Chapter One Section 7 for the noblemen's sense of subordination to the needs of the commonweal. Note also the words of
Francesco Barbaro to his nephew, begging the latter to work for the cause of peace: I
cannot restrain myself from speaking of politics, he wrote, ". . . quia non solum nobis
nati sumus, et quia nunquam a nobis alienum putavi quod cum communi utilitate
coniunctum esset . . . ." *Centotrenta*, ed. Sabbadini, p. 83.

[241] For the Venetian tradition of funeral orations, see Chapter One at nn. 214-15.
The only major biography of a nonreligious figure in this period is Jacopo Zeno's of
his grandfather Carlo, the *Vita Caroli Zeni*. The private individual, even if a powerful
nobleman, is not impressively memorialized in Venice. Sometimes he does not even
receive a verbal tribute. Giovanni Caldiera had always declined to celebrate private
individuals, he wrote, since in such an "infinity" of noble and eager servants of Venice,
no individual's achievements stood out: ". . . me a privatorum hominum laudibus prorsus abstinere suaxeram, cum infiniti prope numero cives sint qui maxima vestre rei
publice merita obsequia [contulisent?] impavidique pro civitate tuenda [et] augenda
omnia discrimina mortemque subis[sent] . . . ." *Oratio in funere Orsati Justiniani*, fol.
91.

[242] Bernardo Giustiniani reminds Pietro Barbo on accession to the papacy of his duty
to Venice: "Licet enim ecclesia te puerum a nobis abduxerit, adolescentem Cardinalem
fecerit, nunc denique creavit summum pont[ificem]. Natale tamen solum, et illa prima
cunabula ubi natus, altus educatusque es *negare non potes*. . . . Sit Roma tibi cara, ut
esse debet, sit [*ed.* sic] romana ecclesia sponsa tua, filia tua. Istis illa nominibus contenta
sit. Dum patriae nomen Venetiis tuis relinquat." *Orat. et epist.*, sig. G; emphasis added.

[243] Jacopo Zeno attributes to his grandfather these words in addressing the Senate:
"Intelligebam equidem Senatui in hac urbe suppremum pacis ac belli, vitae ac necis
potestatem esse: me civem esse non dominum. In hac re publica *membrum esse non
corpus*." *Vita Caroli Zeni*, p. 63; emphasis added.

[244] For the theme of "consultation" to arrive at consensus, see Caldiera, above, at
nn. 51-54; P. Morosini, Section 4, especially at n. 129.

[245] For the strategy of benevolence, D. Morosini at nn. 177-81 above; for the repub-
licanized virtues of love, hope, and faith, Caldiera at nn. 41-46; for the "necessity of
place," P. Morosini at n. 129.

cessity of place"—that Venice's setting conditioned her people's behavior—is noteworthy, and had a real basis in fact. A collective mentality may have been encouraged by a history of collective action.
From its beginnings, Venice's success depended on the cooperation of
her peoples (a point that had been made by Bernardo Giustiniani in
his history of the city). The constant need to clear the lagoon and
related tasks of water management imposed on Venice by her unique
topography required an early and vigilant attention to the welfare of
the community. In later years, the mechanisms Venice developed to
deal with the sea, necessary to her for sustenance, required communal
efforts unique in medieval Europe. Her Arsenal became the first great
state industry of modern times, the womb of her state-owned galleys
that sailed in state-managed fleets. The habit of collective thought that
may have been nurtured by the "necessity of place" is described by
Poggio Bracciolini: "There is no discord among those who administer
public affairs, no dissension; . . . individuals all think alike and all
concur in spirit in regard to the public safety . . . . Thus diversity of
opinion is brought back to concord and not prolonged by compact
or civil conspiracy. For by this agreement you could say all are made
one in mind, will, spirit, and counsel."[246]

Thus the Venetians, as viewed by their humanists (and outsiders),
do not act as individuals but as a unity. The whole community, acting
as a single personality, acquires the moral characteristics of its most
virtuous citizens. Though one person die, the community survives
intact.[247] Where one individual is praised, the whole community is

[246] Poggio's *In laudem rei publicae venetorum*, in his *Opera omnia*, II, 928, 933,
given here in the translation of N. Struever, *The Language of History in the Renaissance*,
pp. 174-75. S. Troilo describes this collective mentality particularly well: "l'individuo
tende a scomparire nell'azione complessa dello Stato: la Repubblica cercava di ridurre
le tendenze dei singoli ad un fascio compatto di forze, di limitare quanto più fosse
possibile la personalità individuale e di assorbirla in quella tipica personalità collettiva
che fu per lei coefficiente di potenza, pei governanti coscienza di collaborazione, ma
causa di adequazione a un livello politico commune, dal quale non era dato a nessuno
di sollevarsi granfatto." *Andrea Giuliano*, p. 42. See also Finlay, *Politics*, pp. 55ff. for
the use of the term *terra* to describe the collectivity of all Venetians. For the history of
economic cooperation which may have engendered such attitudes see G. Luzzato, *Studi
di storia economica veneziana*, especially "Per la storia delle costruzioni navali a Venezia
nei secoli XV e XVI," and "Navigazione di linea e navigazione libera nelle grandi città
marinare del Medio Evo"; also F. C. Lane, *Venice*, Chapters x-xii. For Giustiniani,
Labalme, *Bernardo Giustiniani*, pp. 263ff.

[247] Consider, for example, the message of consolation Pietro Barozzi offers his fellow
cleric Pietro Foscari on the death of Foscari's brother. Though the *patria* grieved the
loss of a loyal servant, it now required all the more the services of the surviving brother.
He, for the sake of his country, must now put off mourning and resume the task of
winning for Venice the pope's love. *Consolatorius ad Petrum Fuscarum*, in *De modo
bene moriendi*, fols. 170ᵛ-171ᵛ.

honored. The whole community, joined in mutual love, raises its collective voice to celebrate its victories and acclaim its heroes.[248] The whole community, with unprecedented unity, chooses its doge.[249]

The doge himself is the symbol and culmination of the fused personality of the whole community: "because the whole republic is one, it culminates in the unity of one doge."[250] Not a tyrant, but an instrument of the community himself, "a member, not the body," he, too, as an individual is without power or will. His is subject to law. His pronouncements and decisions are not his own, but the product of that process of "consultation" by which rulers think as a group, impervious to the acid of individual preference.[251] Yet he is not superfluous, but profoundly necessary to the community whose flawless consensus cannot be expressed by multiplicity—even one of passionless men—but only in a unity.[252] In Venice, as the humanists depict her, the potentially dangerous individual is absorbed into a collectivity, the unity of which is in turn symbolized in the figure of the doge, powerful as a symbol, but selfless as man.

Thus the individual is subordinated to the welfare of the whole community. But a nameless "member" of the "body" of his city, he is but a meaningless atom in a vast pyramidal universe founded in

[248] Consider for example, Caldiera's perception that all the citizens rejoiced on the appointment of a worthy candidate to captain general *del mar*: "a veneto Senatu aureo splendentique vesilo omnibus supremi et inferioris ordinis civibus comitantibus delatum vidimus." *Oratio in funere Orsati Justiniani*, fol. 91ᵛ. Or Jacopo Zeno's report of the applause that greeted Carlo's appointment as naval leader: "Quo quum Senatus, plebs, clerique et omnium ordinum ageretur concursus frequens, haud impar festo, dies ingenti applausu celebratus est. Fereque populi totius voces, in Caroli gloriam resonabant." *Vita Caroli Zeni*, pp. 55-56.

[249] See Bernardo Giustiniani's description of the election by the city as a whole as well as by noble electors of Doge Tommaso Mocenigo: "Incredibili itaque civitatis studio summa electorum concordia . . . electus est." *Orat. et epist.*, sig. B4ᵛ. And Candiano Bollani's of the election of Doge Cristoforo Moro: "Ad te quasi ad commune refugium concurrerunt omnes, quasi nostrorum vulnerum praecipuum medicum, navis nostrae gubernatorem saluberrimum salutisque portum tranquillissimum atque exoptatum." *Oratio gratulatoria de creatione Christophori Mauri*, at fol. 86. It had been customary in the Middle Ages for the people to assemble and approve the election of a doge. By the time of Moro's election, that practice had ceased.

[250] ". . . et quia tota respublica unum est, quod unum ad ducem veluti aliquid unum refertur . . . ." Pietro Barozzi, *Oratio ad Christophorum Maurum*, p. 133. See also D. Morosini at nn. 177-78 above.

[251] For the limits placed on dogal power through the obligation to consult with patrician counsellors, see Caldiera at n. 53 above; L. Quirini at nn. 97-98; P. Morosini, discussion of the DRF, Section 4.

[252] For the necessity of the doge to the city, note the lament of B. Giustiniani for Francesco Foscari: "Nos te iacentem erigere non possumus. O tenues vires nostras, o generis humani fragilem et imbecillem conditionem: ubi nunc devictae urbes? ubi maria pacata? ubi consilia sapientiae plena? Ubi denique vox illa, quae saepius huic urbi opitulata est?" *Oratio funebris habita in obitu Francisci Fuscari Ducis*, sig. Dᵛ.

matter and culminating in God.[253] That cosmos imprints its vertical forms not only on nature and supernature but on social structures. The republic, a term within this hierarchy situated midway between man and God, is made in its image. For just as the doge represents in a horizontal direction the unity of all the people, embodying their homogeneous and collective will, he stands also at the apex of a vertical social system congruent in form and function with the divinely ruled system of the universe. He is selected for his excellence from among the most excellent men of the city. In his figure, therefore, at the zenith of the social hierarchy, is concentrated a principle of excellence—just as God, in the divine order, is that Being than Whom there is no greater.[254] Immediately beneath him is the group of selfless aristocrats graced with virtue and born to rule.[255] Beneath that aristrocracy is the population at large, rich and poor, all the other who, remote from the pure excellence at the peak of the social hierarchy, are unexceptional

[253] The hierarchical vision of the universe is fundamental in the works of Caldiera, Quirini, and Barozzi; see Sections 2, 3, and 6 above.

[254] For the transcendent excellence of the doge, see above, Caldiera at nn. 50-53, P. Morosini in the discussion of the DRF, Section 4, and D. Morosini at nn. 174-76. For assumptions of social stratification and thus a hierarchical vision of society, see Caldiera at nn. 44-50 and D. Morosini, especially at n. 145; Barozzi, Section 6 and especially n. 192. The assumption of social hierarchy is the thematic core of Quirini's DN, discussed in Section 3.

[255] For the innate virtue of patricians and consequent license to rule, see above F. Barbaro in Section 1, Quirini in Section 3 and especially nn. 74-83; P. Morosini, discussion of the DVEP, Section 4. Consider also Barozzi's razor-sharp explanation: "Ignobiles autem hoc loco intelligo non eos minus qui nihil ipsi quod ex eis est bonae frugis attulerunt, quam eos qui infimo loco nati moribusque infimi sunt. Nam eos qui summo genere orti nihil his unde orti sunt dignum habuere ignobiles et identidem eos qui humilibus nati parentibus ipsi non humiles evasere, nobiles jure optimo dixerim. Verum (uti de hoc etiam aliquid enucleatius disseramus) illi mea quidem sententia ignobilissimi sunt, qui humilibus orti parentibus vitiis atque sceleribus generis turpitudinem augent: et nobilissimi illi, qui summo loco nati virtuibus et bonis artibus domesticum splendorem illustrant. Nam etsi multo difficilius sit hominem humili genere ortum virtutibus clarum emergere atque ob eam rem ejus, qui talis emerserit, major esse nobilitas videatur, et quamvis multo facilius sit eum, qui claris est natalibus genitus, in virum praestantem evadere, iccirco quod si talis evaserit, minor fuisse probitas praedicetur; vulgo tamen cernere est ad summam illam veramque nobilitatem nescio quod et humilitate generis impedimentum et domestica gloria additamentum afferri; propter quae studio atque industria comparatus hic splendor et in illis tamquam nube soli objecta obscurior et in his velut luce luci apposita clarior habeatur. Contra vero quanquam longe difficilius sit hominem nobili genere ortum, vitiis atque sceleribus inquinari et propterea ejus qui, talis cum esset, inquinari sustinuit major fuisse improbitas videatur: et licet longe illud facilius ut qui infimo natus est loco vitiis ignobilior fiat atque ideo, si talis fiat, minus fuisse improbus aestimetur: illud tamen manifestum est infimo huic atque abjectissimo ignobilitatis generi et nobilitatem nonnihil obstare et ignobilitatem accessionem quamdam praebere; ut luxu atque inertia turpitudo quaesita in illis quidem, velut majorum nobilitate contecta, minus appareat; in his vero tamquam umbrae accedentibus tenebris omni genere obscurior fiat." *Oratio pro Francisco Scledo vicentino rectore juristarum Patavii*, pp. 122-23.

and undistinguished. Yet they, too, are necessary, as the ruled are to those who rule, and must be cherished. Each stratum of the social order performs its role well and is duly honored and rewarded.[256] A perfect concord results, deriving not from the bland equality of all people but from the resolution of inequalities, the more subtle and beautiful harmony of separate parts: "no musical harmony," remarked Marcantonio Sabellico, "is so concordant."[257]

That perfect harmony of parts, that tranquillity, is a quality unique to Venice.[258] It fears and resists all change. Motion threatens its perfect balance, and is seen as discord. Even liberty, though valued and carefully preserved, is suspect; the free citizens of a democracy are prone to dissension, which the aristocrats of Venice, born and trained to virtue, resist.[259] For dissension is abhorred as the diabolic enemy of Venice's sacred peace.[260] In Venice, an earthly city partakes in the flawless equilibrium of the exemplary heavens.

Venice's perfect concord is unmoved as well by time. She has endured longer than other cities, and, transcending natural limits, will endure perpetually.[261] Exempt from the law of time, she has had a past, but will see no growth; for she is unchanging, and her past, her present, her future are one. Her noblemen have always ruled, preserving liberty, defending themselves while injuring no one, assisting their neighbors, protecting the church.[262] Venice's history, like the city herself, is un-

---

[256] Little is said of the poor. Calidiera does not even mention them in his breakdown of social classes. D. Morosini and Barozzi compare their psychology to the very rich, while advising the exclusion of both from rule; above, Sections 5 and 6 (Morosini, especially at nn. 145-46). For the need to cherish the poor, see D. Morosini at nn. 149-50. For the rewards granted each social stratum, see Caldiera at nn. 46-48.

[257] "Nulla in musicis armonia tam sibi ex omni parte respondet quam nostrae civitatis diligens administratio . . . ." *De venetis magistratibus*, fol. 94ᵛ. Sabellico's statement recalls L. Quirini's musical analogies; see nn. 112 and 113 above.

[258] Guarino Veronese says concord is the "peculiar ornament" of Venice (*Oratio funebris in Georgium Lauretanum venetum*, at fol. 40). Zaccaria Trevisan V calls the zeal for concord "inborn" (*ingenitus*) in Venice (*Oratio* to Pope Gregory XII, p. 37). B. Giustiniani's words claiming a long and unique tradition of concord are characteristic: ". . . ut nullius civitatis extet memoria, quae majore civium concordia constantiori gubernandi disciplina tot saecula transmiserit." *De origine urbis venetiarum*, p. 118.

[259] See Quirini, especially at nn. 103 and 106 above.

[260] Consider the imagery of P. Barozzi of a diabolic force within the city arousing dissension and inciting war: "Non jam vel Fossae vel Propugnacula clausos/ Alta tegunt; ipsa interius certatur in Urbe,/ Et bellum in nobis geritur civile forisque." *Versuum atque hymnorum libri III*, p. 232. The need to avoid dissension is the urgent concern motivating Barozzi's DFE, and a primary concern in D. Morosini's DBIRP; see discussions in Sections 6 and 5, respectively.

[261] See Caldiera, above at n. 56; Quirini at n. 118.

[262] The theme of P. Morosini's DVEP, *Lettera* and DRF (see above, Section 4), and of G. Donato's *Apologia* and recurrent themes in B. Giustiniani's *De orgine urbis venetiarum* and other histories.

moving. It is a history without time or will, a description of excellence fulfilling the innate promise of its principle, limited by natural necessity by unaffected by chance. The historian's task is not to explain her evolution, but to display her perfection, which, like the perfection of God, has always been and will be.[263]

The humanists viewed their city and the people who composed it in terms of the hierarchical universe in which both participated. That universe they had inherited from the philosophers and theologians of their own and past centuries, recent and remote.[264] They never shed structures of thought honored by earlier generations of thinkers. At the same time, they welcomed new ideas—selectively. The ideas received from the arts faculty of the university in nearby Padua, creative new offspring of an ancient tradition of Aristotelian thought, they readily absorbed, for these reinforced the traditional model of a hierarchical universe. The ideas embedded in the corpus of literature the humanists studied they anchored firmly to inherited intellectual traditions that had a closer affinity to the cultural values they espoused. Other ideas they admitted and permitted to proliferate, but only in such form that they posed no challenge to traditional culture.[265]

Venetian humanism bears everywhere the imprint of Aristotle. Aristotelian concepts of the different forms of government, of social structure, of domestic administration and the relation of family to state, of friendship, of virtue as the mean between vicious extremes, are pervasive in humanist treatises and *opuscula*. Less frequent but still conspicuous are those drawn from Aristotelian metaphysics and physics. Nor do Aristotelian principles appear only sporadically, as quotations or anecdotes within a broader discourse; they often provide the whole armature of a humanist work. Aristotelian perspectives intermix with humanist and theological statements alike. The authors of such marriages perceive no incompatibility. Indeed, the interpenetration of Aristotelian and humanist traditions in Venice was the product of no superficial eclecticism, but was a profound fusion culminating, during the period here studied, in such figures as Girolamo Donato and Ermolao Barbaro the Younger, Niccolò Leonico Tomeo, and Giorgio Valla.[266]

---

[263] For the study of history as reverence for the past, see especially Ludovico Foscarini's letter to Girolamo da Ponte, *Epist.*, fols. 215ᵛ-219.

[264] The persistence in Venice of the hierarchical vision of the whole universe is documented by the heroic work of the theologian Francesco Giorgi, a later near-contemporary of our humanists: the *De harmonia mundi totius cantica tria*.

[265] A discussion of the traditional roots of Venetian humanist culture appears in Chapter Three, Section 1.

[266] An Aristotelian model is seen in the works of Caldiera, Quirini, D. Morosini, and

A deep-rooted reverence for philosophy as a branch of knowledge
made that fusion both possible and necessary. Philosophy was not
regarded in Venice as a useful discipline, valuable in its own right,
entailing a vision alternative to that of the *studia humanitatis*. Instead,
it was regarded as a fundamental intellectual discipline that embraced
the studies of human life and communication as one part of its sum,
just as the heavens embraced and surpassed human society. Grammar
and rhetoric, taught by humanists in public and private schools
through the medium of ancient historical and literary works, were
clearly considered to be subordinate and relatively elementary disciplines. Philosophy, an advanced and honored discipline, was taught
in Venice (notably at the famous Rialto school) mostly by noblemen
and to a largely aristocratic audience.[267] The relative valuations of
these two schools express in the structures of institutional organization
the relations perceived generally and articulated often between the
studia humanitatis and philosophy. The former were seen still as fixed
among the disciplines of the trivium and quadrivium categories of the
medieval arts curriculum which was a preparation for the study of
the latter. They were the stepping stones to the several branches of

P. Barozzi examined above; of those, all but Morosini's DBIRP directly borrow principles
of organization from Aristotle's *Nicomachaean Ethics* and *Politics*. Caldiera and Barozzi
both intermingle Christian and Aristotelian notions. Thus, among the most substantial
works of Venetian humanism the influence of Aristotle is conspicuous; no other single
author exercised a remotely comparable influence. Even where Aristotelian models are
not directly imitated, Aristotelian assumptions about the moral and physical world are
pervasive. The same observations apply more broadly to the whole Venetian humanist
corpus. The figures named applied humanist skills in translating, editing, and commenting upon works by Aristotle and his followers, joining the "new philology" with
the Venetian Aristotelian tradition; see here especially Branca, "L'umanesimo
veneziano."

[267] For the schools of rhetorical and philosophical studies, see Chapter One n. 96,
and Chapter Three, Section 3. J. Monfasani persuasively reconstructs the relations of
the two (later three) schools in his *George of Trebizond*, pp. 297ff., when headed by
George and Paolo della Pergola, respectively. It was perhaps, I suggest, the climate of
intense regard for Aristotelian philosophy that may explain George's conversion to it
from Platonism; see Monfasani, pp. 16ff. For assumptions of the superiority of philosophical to rhetorical studies, see Marco Donato's description of Zaccaria Travisan
G's education. After the youthful study of the humanities he proceeded to philosophy
under Paolo della Pergola ("phylosophum ceterarum artium dominam celo mortalibus
infusam"; *Oratio in laudes Zacharie Trivisani*, fol. 162ᵛ) and ultimately to law at the
university (fols. 162ᵛff). Niccolò Barbo's description of Francesco Contarini's education,
in contrast, sees his studies with the two masters as comparable in importance: ". . .
sub hoc clarissimo et praestantissimo philosopho Paulo pergulense dyalecticam didi-
cisset, navare quoque statuit opera aliquam oratoriae facultati et in ea cognoscenda
egregium ac excellentissimum virum Georgium Trapezuntium praeceptorem meum in
suum deligere doctorem, qui posset etiam sicuti desiderabat eum aliquantulum litteris
graecis instruere." *Oratio in laudem Francisci Contareni*, fols. 74ᵛ-75. Certainly, Venetians saw no inherent contradiction in the combined studies of letters and philosophy.

philosophy that were organized in a hierarchy of disciplines, the *si-mulacrum* of the universal hierarchy, ascending from ethics to mathematics and natural science to climax in metaphysics, vaguely linked to theology—the goal of knowledge, as the *visio dei* was the goal of life.[268]

Aristotelianism, familiar though still evolving in new directions at nearby Padua, was a comfortable intellectual habit for learned Venetians, many of them humanists. Its success among Venetian humanists was not due alone, however, to its traditional authority but also to its congruence with their perceptions of their society. Aristotle's systematic approach to reality was congenial. His tendency to subdivide and define every element or moral, social, and political life was imitated and even exceeded by the humanists, for whom, perhaps, the exhaustive anatomization of their cultural world made it manageable, stable, invulnerable to dissent. His comprehensive vision of a purposeful universe also suited their perceptions of the world. The family, the polity, the natural, and the supernatural were viewed as continuous manifestations of the same truth, operating in similar ways, obeying the same laws; such confidence, once again, reinforced a belief in the permanence and grandeur of Venice. Aristotle's acceptance of class divisions in society and approval of the accumulation of modest wealth also appealed to the humanists, who willingly espoused the notion that some men were naturally superior to others. Aristotelian ethical, political, metaphysical thought provided, in brief, legitimation for Ven-

---

[268] For the perception of the liberal arts as lesser than but fundamental to philosophy (with ethics or the "active" aspect of philosophy seen as the equal of metaphysics, its "contemplative" aspect), and philosophy as subordinate to and lesser than theology, see the discussion of Caldiera's *Concordantia* above, Section 2. Marcantonio Sabellico assumes the superiority of philosophy to the supporting disciplines of the liberal arts in his two orations *De origine et incrementis philosophiae* and *De cultu et fructu philosophiae*; Giorgio Valla does so in his *De expetendis fugiendisque rebus*; Ermolao Barbaro's *De coelibatu* (discussed below, Section 10), is a celebration of celibacy as the ideal setting for philosophical reflection. It dismisses the first three liberal arts (grammar, rhetoric—that humanist mainstay—and dialectic) as lesser disciplines, or useful mainly in social and political life; poetry is scorned. More highly valued are natural and moral philosophy. But the true goal of the contemplative man is the discovery of truth, which is discovered through philosophy, and ultimately the veneration of God (*De coelibatu*, pp. 131-48). A particularly clear statement of the hierarchical order of knowledge is given by Francesco Pisani, a figure of a later generation. He employs the image of a mountain. At the base are the four arts (expanded from three) of grammar, poetry, rhetoric, and dialectic. Higher up are history, oratory, and the more worthy forms of poetry. Higher than these are the four arts of the quadrivium. The student then ascends to the higher reaches of philosophy: first moral, then natural, then metaphysical. By these stages he reaches the temple at the peak: perfect beatitude and the knowledge of God; *Oratio de universae philosophiae ornamentis*, pp. 247-64. A similar but less elaborate presentation is found in Jacopo Boldù's *Oratio de laudibus totius philosophiae*, delivered in 1498.

ice's highly stratified, rigid, and authoritarian society.[269] The human-ists, who in large measure profited from that social order, happily wedded their humanism to that philosophical vision.

Venetian humanism also made a marriage with Christianity. Just as Aristotle's four causes, or ethical mean between extremes, or three forms of rule, are ubiquitous in Venetian humanist works, so are the trinity, the seven virtues and seven vices, the prayers and vigils and sufferings of saints and martyrs.[270] Scripture and the church fathers are frequently cited, even in nontheological works. And the number of the theological works written by humanists, including those who were not professionally religious, is striking.[271] Notable, too, is the conservative tendency of these works considered as a whole. Scriptural commentaries, lives of saints, defenses of papal power or Roman Cath-olic orthodoxy, anti-Semitic diatribes, aids to devotion are frequently encountered, whereas criticism of church institutions or clerical prac-tices is scarcely heard, and few nods are given to changing directions in Christian thought: seldom is there expressed yearning, for instance, as occasionally elsewhere in humanism, for a closer relationship with the divine, a deeper experience of faith, or greater freedom of the will.[272] The humanists themselves, moreover, seem to be seriously pious. Their piety is seen not only in their frequent attention to the-ological subjects, but by their behavior as well: they establish hostels, abjure or burn the impious products of their youthful studies, seek the advice of holy men, great and humble, when pained by headache or contemplating a journey.[273]

[269] So did Plato's *Republic* and *Laws*, although these works were not nearly so often read and commented upon in Venice. See F. Gaeta, "Giorgio da Trebisonda," especially pp. 482ff.

[270] For the scaffolding of virtues and vices, see the discussions of Caldiera and Barozzi, Sections 2 and 6 above. For saints and martyrs, see Chapter One, Section 6. The symbolism of the trinity may lie behind the tripartite divisions of some works—see for example the pattern of Pietro Barozzi's DFE. Note also Caldiera's likening to the holy trinity of the alliance against the Turk of the pope, the duke of Burgundy, and the doge of Venice: "Quare cedant [*ms.* credant] amicitiae omnes que perpetua memoria cre-debantur, et hanc solam trium divissimorum Principum amicitiam mererentur, que in teris similitudinem gerit tribus divinis personis que maximo et indissolubili perpetuoque amore iunguntur." *De virtutibus*, fol. 68ᵛ. Articulating most clearly what many scholars have observed, Weiss has noted the "religious-ascetic" character of fifteenth-century Venetian humanism: *Un umanista veneziano*, p. 12.

[271] See above, Section 8, discussion of theological works by humanist authors.

[272] Exceptions: Antonio Vinciguerra criticizes in his *Satire* the corruption of the clergy; see, for example, the *Contra mores huius seculi*. Marco Dandolo, among our humanists, speaks passionately of Christian faith in his *Praeconium sanctissime crucis*. The early sixteenth-century sees an outburst of evangelical fervor among some young patricians, including the humanist Gasparo Contarini; see Chapter Three, n. 87.

[273] See above, Chapter One, Section 6.

Venetians had long prided themselves on their loyal Christianity, and believed that their city enjoyed to a peculiar degree the benevolence of providence.[274] The humanists who incorporated into their works traditional pieties or the categories of theological thought no doubt shared this pride and faith. But they surely also found in religion, as in Aristotelianism, matter legitimating their perceptions of the human world. As yet untransformed by the Protestant or Catholic evangelism of the next century, the Christianity they inherited reinforced their understanding of the role of the human being in society and in the universe. It urged reverence for authority, strict observance of adamantine moral laws, firm commitment to doctrinal norms, and thus, in short, the acquiescence of the individual to standards established by others and beyond control.

Venetian humanism is thus thoroughly integrated with both philosophical and religious modes of understanding the world. It picks no quarrel with disciplines rooted in the past—for the humanists of this city, numbering among them so many noblemen, sought to find their own origins in a distant past. It poses no challenge to systems of thought that affirm principles of authority, obedience, and stability, and link them to moral excellence. Given this, it is no surprise that humanist libraries in Venice, if weak on the classics, are rich in academic works of systematic thought. It is no surprise that humanist works sometimes speak the language of philosophy and theology, and are sometimes forgetful of the ideal of eloquence Petrarch had revived.[275]

Not only philosophical and religious, but also legal and medical and scientific knowledge was absorbed complacently by Venetian humanism—although these latter disciplines did not in our period stand in the forefront of the humanist synthesis. Curiously, while deeply conservative at its core, humanism in Venice was in fact generously

---

[274] See below, Chapter Three, Section 1.

[275] An excellent mirror of the diversity of Venetian humanism, which embraced alongside the rhetorical tradition—and perhaps even before it—the philosophical and Christian, is found in Filippo Morandi's *Symposium de paupertate*. There, within the context of a humanist dialogue, the case for poverty is made by a spokesman of each tradition in turn, with the honor of last place going to the advocate of Christian poverty. See my "A Study in Venetian Humanism," especially Part Three, pp. 39ff. For deprecations of eloquence vis-à-vis philosophical truth, see Lauro Quirini's letter to Isotta Nogarola in E. Abel's edition of Nogarola's *Opera quae supersunt omnia*, II, 9-22, now translated in King and Rabil, *Her Immaculate Hand*, pp. 112-16. But see also the famous letter of Ermolao Barbaro G to Pico insisting that philosophical truth be expressed in eloquent language: in Barbaro's *Epist.*, ed. Branca, I, 84-87 (and other editions by E. Garin and Q. Breen; see profile). I see Barbaro's position here as a logical outgrowth of the Venetian cultural situation, which accepted humanist style and philosophical substance as complementary.

receptive, accommodating new trends, new persons, new objects, new books. All branches of knowledge were jammed side by side in encyclopedic works. Wealthy collectors indulged in a hectic antiquarianism. Foreign writers and litterati slipped in and out of the city. Patricians took time out to witness dissections or build mathematical models. The presses produced an enormous variety of books. All this ferment occupied great numbers of people, but did not alter Venetian humanism at its heart. Exposed to a wide range of perspectives, it pursued its own: those which encompassed a well-ordered universe, a concordant republic, an obedient humanity. Secure at its center, Venetian humanism could easily risk a generous welcome to a marketplace of ideas which in their very profusion, their contradictions, their thinness posed no real threat. Indeed, they may have inhibited reflection upon potentially disruptive ideas—the seeds of which were present in Italy. Just as an allegiance to traditional intellectual modes colored Venetian humanism, so eclecticism armored it from the thrust of rebellious thought.[276]

For the task of Venetian humanism was to affirm, not challenge, Venetian culture. Critical in their reading and emendation of texts, Venetian humanists are in a broader sense uncritical: uncritical of inherited intellectual traditions to which they fuse their humanist learning, uncritical of institutions, of rulers, of their past or their present, of the patterns of thought and actions that limit individual freedom. They refrain from judging a world which, to their eyes, is not subject to judgment: for it is already perfect, its monumental stillness undisturbed by the raucous and dissonant voices that have all been resolved in sublime harmony. Venetian humanism achieves the *unanimitas* in its products that it seeks and finds in its nurturing culture: all share one will, acquiesce in one vision of the universe, embrace the same ideas.

For Venetian humanism, though humanism without a doubt, is humanism in a particular form. It lacks as an ingredient the concept of individual freedom, the assumption of the "psychological importance of liberty," notions incompatible with the ideal of unanimity.[277] The

---

[276] For the openness of humanist culture during the later phases of its fifteenth-century development, see below, Chapter Three, Section 5. For the eclecticism of cultural life, see especially A. Chastel, "Art et humanisme au Quattrocento," and R. Palluchini, "L'arte a Venezia nel Quattrocento," p. 152. Both these scholars speak specifically of artistic styles, but the analogy to intellectual styles is patent. For the concept of a protective conservatism or "anachronism," see G. Piovene, "L'anacronismo della Venezia quattrocentesca," especially p. 15.

[277] The phrase is R. Witt's; see his "The *De tyranno* and Coluccio Salutati's View of Politics and Roman History."

individual is viewed as limited: he is not free to vent his passions, but must suppress them, or suffer them to be suppressed. He does not possess freedom of choice, but his will is merged with the will of the group. He cannot shape his own destiny in a social world where all are destined by birth to one particular place in a rigid hierarchy. He cannot construct new institutions or foster new visions in a culture that resists change and denies motion. He cannot pose new ideals or shed old values, but must hone and sculpt his new percepts to accord with existing conceptions. In exchange for these limits on his freedom, he inherits a culture self-confident of its truth, justice, ease, and eternity. His culture's ideal, and his own, is unanimity.

That ideal affects also the humanist's vision of civic life, and helps differentiate Venetian humanism, even with its strong imperative of republican service, from the "civic humanism" encountered elsewhere in the Quattrocento and most patently in Florence.[278] Venetians treasured their liberty, for them an ancestral tradition. Occasionally, they spoke of the necessity of the "liberty" of their city to the "peace" of Italy. But there was in Venice no awareness of a new awakening, as in Florence, that encouraged a search for fulfillment in the civic life. That commitment to the civic life had been valued and encouraged in Venice well before the age of humanism, and in works not humanistic in nature. Humanist literature followed the lead of the poetry and history of prior generations, expressing old concepts in new forms. Civicism in Venice, moreover, as it was strongly tied to past and continuing ideals, was closely linked to systematic philosophy and to

---

[278] Some scholars have likened Venetian civicism to "civic humanism" on the Florentine model. G. Zippel argues that the patrician humanists active in terraferma conquest shape, in their discussions of Venice's duty to preserve the principle of liberty, a modern conception of the autonomy of politics; see his "Lorenzo Valla" and "Ludovico Foscarini." N. Carotti argues a similar thesis with regard to Francesco Barbaro, whom he presents as a modern man, a political realist, who has thrown aside medieval pieties; see his "Politico umanista." C. Seno has argued that Venice develops a "self-conception of liberty" similar to Florence's and expressed in the works of Lauro Quirini; see his preface to Quirini's DR in LQU, pp. 105-20. (P. O. Kristeller, however, notes the dissimilarity between Quirini's political outlook and that of Florentine "civic humanism"; see his "Il codice Plimpton 187 della Columbia University Library," especially p. 211.) W. Bouwsma in his Venice and the Defense of Republican Liberty indicates the development of a modern and secular political vision similar to Florence's, but places it in the sixteenth century. But I argue that although Venetian authors undoubtedly speak of liberty and write of the "pace d'Italia," their rhetoric does not in itself constitute evidence of a modern or secular or activist outlook—which the evidence elsewhere belies. The rhetoric of liberty is heard in Florence, Venice, Milan, and other cities in this century, where "liberty" signifies the freedom of a locality from foreign domination. It did not necessarily entail our notions of human rights or equality, and not everywhere in the Renaissance did it entail a notion of inner human freedom, although it may have done so for some authors. It did not in Venice.

religion. Humanists in Venice embraced the whole range of academic philosophy and read the *Ethics* and the *Politics* squarely in the context of Aristotle's physical and metaphysical works. And although they well understood the benefits of wealth and its origins in human activity, they accorded at least equal honor to the contemplative as to the active existence.[279] Related to their appreciation of the contemplative life was their personal piety, which had an impact as well on their social vision. The political life was not seen as a secular arena in which to unleash human energies striving for a secular perfection. It was seen as nurtured by the benevolence of God and the saints and serving a holy destiny.

Some scholars have viewed the philological activities of Venetian humanism as a counterpart to the fascination with rhetoric in other humanist centers, and as indeed the heart of humanism in Venice.[280] But in this realm, as well as in that of civic humanism, the Venetian case is distinctive. Certainly the fervor of textual criticism that peaked in late Quattrocento Venice paralleled philological enthusiasm elsewhere in Italy. Surely no other city in those years surpassed Venice in the pursuit of Greek learning, one of the activities for which Renaissance is renowned. Rhetoric was taught in Venice both privately and publicly, and the composition of histories, treatises, and orations obeyed new rhetorical principles there as elsewhere. Yet the philological movement in Venice was not preceded or accompanied by zeal for rhetoric such as was often characteristic of Italian humanism. There is little discussion in the lagoon city of the power of language to arouse passions and persuade to action, little fascination with the subtlety and expressiveness of language. Venetian Latin tends to dryness and conventionality, and more flexible expression was discouraged by a sustained devotion to the academic Aristotelianism of Padua. A critical perspective, finally, the companion of the reexamination and reeval-

[279] Even in the sixteenth century, less conservative theologically than the fifteenth, the humanists do not vaunt the active over the contemplative life, but arrive at a balance between the two; see Logan, *Culture and Society*, Chapter IV.

[280] This is the position V. Branca expresses in several works; see especially his "Ermolao Barbaro and Late Quattrocento Venetian Humanism"; "Ermolao Barbaro e l'umanesimo veneziano"; and "L'umanesimo veneziano alla fine del Quattrocento." It is shared by P. G. Ricci, "Umanesimo filologico in Toscana e nel Veneto." The primacy of the philological component (especially its Greek dimension) for D. Geanakoplos is evident in his discounting of Venetian humanism before the last two decades of the century; see his *Greek Scholars in Venice*. A. Chastel places the beginnings of Venetian humanism in the same decades, and ties them to philological activities and the book trade, in his "Art et humanisme au Quattrocento." Garin sees philological interests as central to Venetian humanism and sees in them the link to Florentine culture; "Cultura filosofica toscana e veneta nel Quattrocento."

uation of language, is also lacking in Venetian humanism. The tend-ency that has been noted in the preceding discussion to affirm rather than question inherited institutions, values, and ideas is a hallmark of that city's humanist culture and reflects its dedication to an ideal of unanimity. The benevolence and sublime destiny of Venice, the sanctity of Christian doctrine, the wisdom of Aristotle were assumed without scrutiny. Critical techniques were exercised to uncover the true and original Aristotle, or Cicero, or Juvenal. They were not applied to analyses that could challenge assumptions fundamental to the culture.

The ideal of unanimity that lends Venetian humanism its distinctive character is most particularly the ideal of the patrician humanists. For it constitutes an ideology useful to the city's ruling elite. A set of ideas that encourages self-control and self-sacrifice, acquiescence to the will of the whole community, faith in the timeless stability of the city, unquestioning loyalty to traditional values, suited the needs of that small group of noblemen at the center of power. Imported to Venice by visitors and teachers and well-traveled noblemen, humanism was turned to the advantage of these rulers, it seems, by the learned and agile minds among them. Rid of the potentially corrosive notions of individual freedom, attitudinal openness, cosmic dynamism, it became the vehicle of accepted values and familiar ideas shaped to new pre-cision, vested with new elegance, pronounced more boldly to larger audiences at home and abroad. To strangers, it presented the bland face of propaganda. Venice, it assured an Italy fearful of Venetian aggression, was pure of greed or ambition, and waged only just wars. To natives, it compelled acquiescence, for how is it possible to protect against an order that is righteous and synchronous with a heavenly order of ineffable perfection?[281] To the powerful patricians from whose caste so many of the humanists came, it promised secure dominion and ease of conscience at but a small price: that of free self-knowledge and expression.

Thus patrician intellectuals guided the formation of a humanist culture that would help protect patrician hegemony by anticipating any challenge to it. They pursued in the realm of ideas a strategy pursued also in other areas of Venetian culture. Benevolent social practices and policies encouraged a passive and faceless population not to disturb the city's tranquil stability: the provision of even-handed justice, the prudent administration of grain, water, and wood supplies, the thoughtful administration of charity. The privileges allowed the

---

[281] Obedience can be compelled by the presentation to subject peoples of an appear-ance of benevolent justice; see B. Moore, Jr., *Injustice*, especially, pp. 79ff. for this notion and an outline of mechanisms of control.

institutions of guilds and *scuole* permitted the expression of interest without intrusion upon the authority of the ruling class. The nobility meanwhile managed itself: by extending the privilege of office holding to all its members, broadly defined, it removed prime causes of discontent; and it instituted constitutional machinery designed to prevent the expression of factional interest, and quietly and swiftly to punish its exercise. Benevolent policies and constitutional structures alike served as prophylaxis against social unrest. By preventing the sources of unrest, Venice's rulers were able to avoid the painful costs of suppression.[282]

In Venice, then, humanism successfully serves as a means of prophylaxis analogous to these others and useful, like them, to the ruling elite whose political power extends into the realm of culture. Meanwhile, that smaller group of humanists who were not patricians either gladly or reluctantly adopted, or at least did not oppose, that patrician ideology. They had no other choice: the shape of Venetian humanist culture was determined by the patricians, dominant because of their numbers, their awesome status, their power as individuals or statesmen to hire or appoint, their influence, and their wealth.

But as an intellectual movement, humanism could only create an ideal. It could not create a reality. To what extent did the ideal of unanimity voiced by the humanists affect the behavior of individuals poor and rich, native and foreign, noble and citizen? The answer to this most provocative question is perhaps unreachable. To attain it, much more would have to be known about how ideas expressed in an esoteric language were transmitted—if they were—to the general culture; about the degree to which all Venetians conformed to the humanists' injunctions; and about the possible causes—other than humanist indoctrination—of their conformity or nonconformity. This study will confine itself to questions that can be answered. The hu-

---

[282] For this interpretation of strategies of benevolence, see especially R. Mueller, "Charitable Institutions, the Jewish Community, and Venetian Society"; Mueller, "The Procurators of San Marco in the Thirteenth and Fourteenth Centuries"; Pullan, *Rich and Poor in Renaissance Venice.* See, among humanist authors: D. Morosini's recommendation for the nurture of the poor, above at nn. 149-50; Caldiera's description of the city's careful management of food and fuel supplies, *De politia,* fols. 104^{v}ff.; Negri's recommendations that the city see to these needs, *De aristocratia,* fols. 109^{v}ff. For the nobility's self-policing, see especially Lane, *Venice,* pp. 109ff., Chojnacki, "Crime," pp. 186ff. and Ruggiero, *Violence.* Note also J. C. Davis' judgment of the patriciate's unique capacity to coordinate its efforts to achieve a common purpose: *The Decline of the Venetian Nobility as a Ruling Class,* p. 25. By pursuing strategies of prophylaxis, Venetian rulers avoided the need to pursue repressive measures, such as the censorship measures they felt reluctantly compelled to adopt after the middle of the sixteenth century; for these, see P. F. Grendler, *The Roman Inquisition and the Venetian Press, 1540-1605.*

manists enunciate an ideal to which they themselves, on the whole, are committed.[283] Even among themselves, there is rebellion against the oppressive rule of unanimity. But that dissent is so limited and so muted that it poses no true threat to the norm. The dissenters conform in time, or are expelled, or are destroyed.

10. DISSENT

The heroic individual—the antithesis of a good citizen joined to the single will of the community—strides across the stage of Venetian humanism in the early years of the Quattrocento: but only briefly.

God created man, said Zaccaria Trevisan the Elder in his oration in honor of Pietro Marcello, so that there might be someone worthy— a "divine animal"—to admire the splendid works of his creation.[284] He joined to the "divine minds" of his new creation a fragile and mortal body. The human soul was meant not to serve that mortal body, nor to spurn it, but to rule it freely, creating through it things useful and beautiful. Those creative tasks fulfilled, the soul lifts itself again to the heavens and, insouciant, to the contemplation of God.

Trevisan's vision of the noble human soul, uniquely graced, wondrously inventive, earnestly seeking higher illumination, has to my knowledge no successor in the generations of Venetian humanism considered here. Its inspiration is not Aristotelian but Platonic (Trevisan apparently knew the *Timaeus*). Its message is freedom, not restraint. It points to the works on human dignity found elsewhere in Renaissance humanism, perhaps even to Pico's famous oration.[285] In Venice, though that path is opened, it is not pursued. The theme of the nobility of the free human spirit in its pure utterance is not heard again, and does not compete with the emerging and prevalent theme of *unanimitas*.

Even here, however, the message of *unanimitas* is challenged only in part. Trevisan's "divine animal," though a splendid creature undoubtedly, has some peculiarly Venetian traits. Though created "free," he is charged with serious duties. He is commanded to strive for higher, never lower things: to assume, in effect, the full burden of morality. His eloquence is exercised to hold human society together: "as though to join all humankind into one body."[286] His creations are the laws

[283] Here I concur with F. Gaeta that the myth is not simply a self-serving "elaborazione" of the ruling class, but of "una speranza e credenza" ("Alcune considerazioni," p. 59)—a cherished self-image and perhaps self-deception.
[284] In Gothein, "Zaccaria Trevisan," pp. 47-49.
[285] Giovanni Pico della Mirandola's *De hominis dignitate*.
[286] Trevisan in Gothein, "Zaccaria Trevisan," p. 48.

and customs that perfect human society and preserve it for future centuries. He is, in fact, not an ordinary member of the human race, but a ruler, undoubtedly Venetian, and of noble birth. Trevisan describes the whole universe, but gives it his own face.

If the image of a restless, dynamic, self-willed individual, however, poses no significant threat to the ideal of *unanimitas* in Venetian culture, the delinquency of some real figures, among them humanists, may have done so. How are their words to be believed, if they themselves violated fundamental principles of loyalty and decorum?

Vitale Lando and Lorenzo Zane, for instance, related by marriage to each other and to the then-reigning pope, were convicted of betraying state secrets, and exiled.[287] The doge's son Jacopo Foscari, in perhaps the most famous case of the century, was convicted of the same charge three times, and died, still young, in exile.[288] Niccolò Canal, no criminal, was tried and sentenced for defending with insufficient zeal the island of Negropont, the loss of which was disastrous for Venice.[289] From Milan, Francesco Filelfo chided the Venetians for their condemnation of the learned Canal: people will think, he warned, "that you are moved more by your grief than by justice, and value tranquillity more than truth."[290] But in Venice, no one protests the public vengeance taken on a leading citizen.

As ambassador to Florence, Bernardo Bembo did not hesitate to seek financial advantage from his friendship with the Medici, the city's rulers and bankers; perhaps this conduct explains in part the dissatisfaction of the Signoria with his diplomatic performance.[291] Pietro Barbo, the pope's choice for the vacant bishopric of Padua, refused to yield, in spite of Venice's urgent commands, to that city's candidate, Jacopo Zeno. Miffed, the Senate ordered their two ambassadors to the Diet of Mantua held that same year—Paolo Barbo (the delinquent's own brother) and Ludovico Foscarini, both men of exceptional reputation—to have no intercourse with him. Foscarini, encountering the

---

[287] See the account in Malipiero, *Annali*, pp. 668-70.

[288] A judicious account appears in Romanin, *Stor. doc.*, IV, 265ff.

[289] For Canal's tragedy see *ibid.*, pp. 337ff.

[290] "Haec ipse quottidie audiens divulgari per omnem Italiam, non poteram pro mea erga vos pietate non angi animo [*ed.* animi] atque cruciari, veritus in id iam calamitatis [*ed.* calamitas] florentissimam vestram rempublicam incidisse, ut plus apud vos valere coepisset perturbationis fluctus quam iustitiae atque rationis tranquillitas." *Epist. fam.*, fol. 231ᵛ, from the first of two letters to Ludovico Foscarini discussing Canal's condemnation: fols. 231ʳ⁻ᵛ and 250, dated 22 May 1471 and 5 May 1472, respectively.

[291] For Bembo's financial dealings with the Medici, see Pintor, "Le due ambascerie," pp. 78ff., 793ff.; for the Senate's dissatisfaction, pp. 801ff., 810. Full documentation will be given by Nella Giannetto in *Bernardo Bembo: umanista e politico veneziano*, in press (Florence, Olschki).

bishop in the street, bowed; the Senate subsequently punished, and eventually forgave, both Foscarini and his colleague for this act of forbidden courtesy.[292]

Some disobeyed their city's written and unwritten laws, putting self-interest before duty. Others chafed at its restrictions and demands. But such cases of "civic irresponsibility" do not disprove the existence or the effectiveness or even the sincerity of an ideal of *unanimitas*. Even a delinquent may genuinely espouse a cultural ideal that he has heedlessly or flagrantly betrayed.[293] There is no need to delve into the past: our own civic experience bears witness.

No fundamental alienation, similarly, from the framework of values constituting the ideal of *unanimitas* is implied by the criticism of councils, peers, or populace sometimes uttered by Venetian humanists in private correspondence. Ludovico Foscarini was often bold enough in his private correspondence to excoriate public policy, as was Francesco Barbaro. A critical view of the current state of things is inferred, similarly, from the work of Pietro Barozzi and Domenico Morosini, writing late in the century, where descriptions of an ideal society mutely suggested the presence of flaws in the real one.[294] But such readiness to quarrel suggests, in fact, more commitment in all these cases to high standards of political behavior than a dissatisfaction with the city's underlying cultural assumptions.

Fundamental rebellion against the ideal of *unanimitas* can be found, however, in the works of Tito Livio Frulovisi, a resident foreigner and naturalized citizen. His impudent comedies, performed publicly in Venice, mocked the city's proud aristocrats. His *On the Republic* is so broad and generous in its consideration of possible political structures that it denies implicitly the absolute and immaculate legitimacy of Venice's.[295] For him, the political body is forged by human hands, unguided by divine providence. Religion, indeed, is seen cynically as a tool usefully manipulated by rulers: Aristotelian categories of gov-

---

[292] For this incident, see especially G. Zonta, "Un conflitto tra la repubblica veneta e la curia romana per l'episcopato di Padova (1459-60)," and Picotti, *Dieta di Mantova*, pp. 308ff., 322ff., 497ff.

[293] Here I depart from Queller ("Civic Irresponsibility," "The Myth of the Venetian Patriciate"), who sees delinquent behavior as invalidating an ideal; and from the views of P. Herde ("Politik und Rhetorik in Florenz am Vorabend der Renaissance"), who considers stated beliefs insincere when belied by actions.

[294] See the discussions of Barozzi's and Morosini's works above in Section 6 and 5 respectively; also Cozzi, "Domenico Morosini." Bernardo Giustiniani indirectly criticizes Venetian society in the same way; see Labalme, *Bernardo Giustiniani*, pp. 311-12.

[295] See profile for Frulovisi's career and direction to works analyzing his comedies and *De republica*.

ernment, beloved by many Venetian humanists, are familiar to Frulovisi, but considered irrelevant. History and circumstance, more than fine abstractions, suggests this young realist, determine the nature of a state. Frulovisi's views, so radically at odds with the prevailing Venetian outlook, aroused the ire of powerful men. Frulovisi anticipated public action against him, and fled. He returned only years later, chastened.

Distinct from those who were disobedient to Venice in large or small matters are those who, while remaining committed and obedient, felt oppressed by the extraordinary demands made upon them by their city. Although any nobleman significantly involved in government might resent these demands, the issue was particularly poignant for the humanists, who yearned for the leisure for study. Leonardo Giustiniani, for example, complained to Pietro Tommasi of the many public occupations that beset him and from which he could find no respite, while he craved peace: "For there is no need in all of life either more difficult, or more greatly worthy of man, than either that he should suffer no passions, or, already perturbed in soul, and fragmented far and wide, that he should be able to collect himself and arrive in a safe and tranquil port."[296] Don't imagine, therefore, he said with some asperity, that I am translating Greek, though I yearn to have time for study: "There is nothing, believe me, that I crave so powerfully, nothing that I more utterly desire from my soul, than that I might collect my thoughts in peace, and in these noble literary studies. By this one desire I am nearly tortured."[297]

Leonardo's son Bernardo experienced the same problem. "You ask me" he wrote George of Trebizond, "if I have written anything in prose or verse. Would that I had been able to! But my occupations, both private and public, do not permit it. Scarcely do I have time to read; none is left me to write."[298]

---

[296] "Nullum est enim in omni vita opus neque difficilius, neque homine maximo dignius, quam aut non moveri, aut turbatum jam animum, et longe, lateque disjectum colligere facile, et tuto, tranquilloque portu posse." In G. B. Contarini, *Anec. ven.*, I, 74.

[297] "Nihil est, mihi crede, quod tam vehementer exoptem, nihil prorsus quod magis ex animo cupiam, quam me in ocium et in haec me nobilia literarum studia colligere. Hoc uno desiderio pene discrucior." Ibid., p. 75. Giustiniani makes similar laments to Palla Strozzi and Francesco Filelfo (in B. Giustiniani, *Orat. et epist.*, sigs. K and K^v, respectively, in both cases referring to the interruption of his studies when he undertook an adult career. Indeed, much of the patrician humanist's most productive work was accomplished during youth.

[298] "Petis a me tibi significari si quid aliud scripsi vel prosa vel versu. Utinam possem. Sed non sinunt occupationes cum private tum publicae. Vix tempus ad legendum supetit, nedum ad scribendum supersit." *Orat. et epist.*, sig. K6^v.

Gregorio Correr had recognized as a young man, then intoxicated with secular literature, the weight of public duties. He felt that for him an ecclesiastical career, though it did not otherwise interest him, would permit freedom for study: "My soul recoiled then from nothing so greatly as the clerical life, but I feared that in a secular career I would have to abandon the literary studies which I greatly loved. For the state of my affairs so dictated, and I hoped to be able in the clerical life to find eventually some kind of quiet refuge."[299] Lauro Quirini also may have resisted the burdens of public office because of his desire to pursue a normal academic career.[300]

Although Correr and Quirini chose to avoid, it seems, the pressures of public life, and did so in great part from a desire to continue literary studies, most patrician humanists persevered in their public careers, pursuing their studies as best they could. Invited by the noble Ermolao Donato to assist him in his studies, Filippo Morandi da Rimini showed that he well understood the limits of patrician time and temperament. Filippo "burned" with desire, he replied, to join Donato in study for whatever moments the nobleman could snatch from business, and congratulated him for devoting, in imitation of Caesar, energy to literature as well as to war.[301] Perhaps no nobleman more successfully combined the two occupations than Girolamo Donato, a humanist of major importance. He, too, felt the voracious demands of a patrician's career. Enviously Donato wrote to the Florentine Angelo Poliziano, whose letter had borne witness to an abundance of studious leisure: "But we are torn by both public and private obligations, and ours are not really studies, but moments snatched from time."[302] Yet Donato stole heroically from his time, and continued to write seriously and assiduously during an active and productive political career, among the most remarkable of his generation. He so married his learning to republican service, wrote his son Filippo years after Girolamo's death, "that neither at home nor abroad did he ever interrupt his studies of the best arts."[303]

[299] "Nihil tunc magis ab animo meo abborebat, quam vita clericalis, sed angebat animum quod in vita saeculari studia litterarum, quae multum amabam, deserenda essent; sic enim ratio rerum mearum poscebat: et sperabam in vita clericali posse aliquando in portum aliquem quietius confugere . . . ." *Soliloquium*, p. 15.

[300] Thus one might infer from the career record; see Quirini's profile and n. 92, above.

[301] Filippo's words in my "A Study in Venetian Humanism," Part One, p. 81 nn. 8, 9.

[302] "Nam nos et publica et privata distringunt, et nostra fere sunt temporis furta, non studia." Angelo Poliziano, in his *Opera omnia*, I, 25-26.

[303] "Haec enim duo ita coniunxit, ut nec domi nec foris unquam studia optimarum artium intermiserit." Filippo Donato's introductory letter to Pope Clement VII (fols. i-iv), fol. i, in G. Donato's *Apologeticus ad Graecos*.

It was this exceptional man who was sent to Rome in 1491 to recall to Venice and to obedience his best friend, Ermolao Barbaro the Younger, scion of a dynasty of heroes, whose commitment to the life of the mind led to his outright defiance of his city and her laws. Barbaro's tragic figure towers over the last years of our period, which closes with his disobedience and death. The story must be told from the beginning of his rebellion, profound and doomed, against Venetian values and the humanists' own code of *unanimitas*.[304]

At age eighteen, Barbaro addressed to his father Zaccaria his work *On Celibacy*.[305] The counterpart of his grandfather Francesco's *On Marriage*, which had called on man and woman alike to subordinate themselves to the requirements of a noble dynasty in a patrician republic, Ermolao's treatise defends that individual who chooses not to shoulder such responsibilities. It is a remarkable work for a young nobleman to have written. Nor does it bespeak a mere passing adolescent rebellion against the awesome standard set by father and grandfather, for its themes reappear in later years. The young man, simply, enjoyed philosophy, never cared for the destiny that Venice and the Barbaro clan had prepared for him, and wished to relieve himself of the responsibilites implicit in his exalted social position. *On Celibacy* is the quiet but potent manifesto of Venetian humanism's most genuine rebel.

On Celibacy rejects the ideal of domestic life not because that life is unworthy in itself, but because it is vexatious.[306] It not only subjects the individual to the demands posed by wife and children but, more importantly, it coerces him to assume political responsibilities. Hence the man who wishes to devote himself to the pursuit of wisdom must free himself from family ties in order to free himself from republican obligations. Chastity becomes, to the mind of this troubled Venetian youth and heir to an oppressive tradition of state service, the only possible foundation for freedom.

Though Ermolao accepts his grandfather's defense of marriage, he is more struck by the anxieties than by the joys of family life. A wife,

[304] This interpretation of Ermolao Barbaro G's role in Venetian culture substantially follows an earlier version presented in my "Caldiera and the Barbaros," pp. 35ff.

[305] The *De coelibatu.*

[306] Ermolao discusses the goods of marriage in the *De coelibatu*, pp. 68-72. He even approves of women (pp. 59-60, 154-55). In a letter to Arnold of Bost in 1486, he answers the latter's inquiry about his marital status: "Quaeris an sim maritus. Non sum, uxorem ne cogito quidem; satis mihi rerum est ac negotii cum litteris; alioquin eae non litigant. . . . Itaque carendum uxore duxi, non tanquam flagitio, sed tanquam molestia; non enim facit uxoria vita noxios, facit obnoxios." *Epist.*, ed. Branca, I, 96. Branca discusses Barbaro's views on marriage as expressed in his letters in "Un trattato inedito di Ermolao Barbaro," p. 93.

whatever her virtues, will rob her husband of possessions, time, and pleasure. Children require even more attention. The pursuit of truth, which requires stern concentration, cannot progress in the family. It is worse if we love our wives, for the very force of that emotion distracts us from contemplation (p. 72). Study requires solitude; those who can free themselves from family affections can love themselves (p. 66).

While family life is an obstacle to the man who devotes his life to contemplation, it is unquestionably suited to a man involved in civic life. Those who occupy themselves in public and commercial affairs should marry (p. 58). Indeed, the procreation of children is a civic duty. Marriage serves to perpetuate the species, to enhance the glory of the republic, and to assure the survival of the empire; it was not established to gratify the individual, but to benefit the city (pp. 77-78). But it is precisely this civic utility of marriage that concerns Ermolao, who doesn't wish to lead a useful life, but one suited to his inclinations. "We openly admit," he writes, "that the assumption of this responsibility is necessary for those who are the leaders of cities and who are chosen to direct the governing of the republic or the extension of the empire. But at the moment we are not seeking to know which life is more useful, but which is more pleasant and more joyful."[307] Barbaro here concedes that marriage and family are institutions necessary to the welfare of the republic, and recognizes that the city's rulers should assume such responsibilities—but though this life is useful, it is unpleasant, and he wishes no part of it.

Not only does family existence, then, make the contemplative life impossible, but it coincides with the political life, which is even more an impediment to pure thought. But how is Barbaro to reject the ideal of an active life, so honored by other humanists in this century, so lauded by Aristotle and Cicero, and so revered by his peers in Venice? To argue against the active life, Ermolao complains, is to argue against diligence and excellence; and to defend the life of contemplation is to praise inertia and ignobility (p. 61). Barbaro must forge a new vision of the ideal life that would be met with public applause, not condemnation: such a life would be nonpolitical on the one hand and nonmonastic on the other.

The life of the man who has chosen celibacy, not from religious conviction but from the need to avoid domestic and civil entaglements,

---

[307] "Haec autem nos adeo esse concessa volumus, ut aperte fateamur necessarium esse hanc curam adhibere eos qui civitatibus praesunt quique ad gubernandum rei publicae statum et amplificandum imperium principes deliguntur. Nos autem non id quaerimus impraesentia ut utra sit utilior sed utra iocundior vita et alacrior sit sciamus." *De coelibatu*, p. 70.

constitutes this new ideal. Divorced from the world of action, the celibate's talents, interests, and virtues are fundamentally different from those of the man who has chosen to lead a civic life. Men active in the republic must be tough and vigorous.[308] They have a range of talents: some are suited for military activities, some for governing, some for navigation. But nothing could be less desirable in those who choose a contemplative life than this energy and variety. Calm and stable, the celibate has no ambition for glory and does not defile himself with cares about human and passing things. If he is commanded to undertake a busy task, he does it badly, is careless of the common good, and destroys himself with efforts alien to his nature (surely Barbaro here is speaking of himself). But though his attempts to engage in active tasks weaken him, his energy for study is boundless, and he is dejected when called away from studious pursuits. Few are capable of the contemplative life, which requires a mental constitution so different from that of the active man.[309]

Thus the personality of the celibate is unlike that of the man suited for public service. His education must also be different. The man destined for a civic life will study the disciplines that prepare him for the business of government, whereas the celibate will avoid those very areas of knowledge.[310] Specifically, the celibate should avoid grammar, which is considered a base study not suitable for a gentleman; eloquence, because it is useful for republican oratory but not for private contemplation; poetry, because it arouses impure thoughts; and that part of dialectic which involves disputation because, once again, it is appropriate to the civic sphere. Geometry, music, arithmetic, astrology, and the various branches of philosophy, including natural philosophy and the theoretical branch of medicine, are suitable studies for the celibate.

Unlike the man engaged in public life in character and education, the celibate must also cultivate the virtues appropriate to his isolation rather than the civic virtues of the active citizen. Even the virtues that appear to be civic by nature can be accommodated to the ideal of celibacy.[311] Justice, for instance, as a civic virtue, pertains to decisions

[308] The following comments summarize Ermolao's discussion of the different natures of the man destined for action or contemplation, ibid., pp. 93-96.

[309] Those who merely incline to studies, without wholly committing themselves to the isolation that such studies demand, are better suited for republican existence. Two such, Barbaro suggests, were Demosthenes and Francesco Barbaro.

[310] The disciplines appropriate and inappropriate for a celibate life are discussed on pp. 136-43.

[311] The virtues befitting the celibate are defined on pp. 143-53. Contrast Barbaro's contention that virtues can be performed by the private man as well as the citizen with

made in government and commerce. How then can the man devoted to a contemplative life be just? Inasmuch as justice is a virtue that serves the public good, Ermolao responds, the contemplative man is assuredly just; for filled with goodness and holiness, he stands closer to God than other men and is able more easily to intercede with Him. Thus no one is more a servant of the public good than the celibate (pp. 144-45). Similar reasoning is applied to courage, the virtue of heroes: the celibate is courageous in that he fears nothing but that which is antipathetic to truth, and is strong in that he is close to God, from Whom all strength derives (p. 146). Thus the celibate, though inactive, does not lack the virtues most prized in the leading citizens of the republic.

The celibate's life is presented as the obverse of the life of the man committed to civic action. Where the latter's character is vigorous, flexible, and multifaceted, the celibate's nature is steady and tranquil; while the active man studies the disciplines most useful to the city, the celibate is devoted to philosophy. The active man, if virtuous, is just and brave in government, in business, and in war, whereas the celibate is just and brave in his unwavering devotion to truth and to God.[312]

Although the ideal of life of celibacy is deliberately defined as non-political, it is not, in spite of its Christian tonalities, a monastic ideal. Its object is not self-sacrifice, but self-discovery. "Not they who hide within domestic walls, fearing the light and the rays of the sun, nor they who in the manner of beasts lead their lives in darkness and shadows are . . . considered to be contemplative, but they who remove themselves from the favors of the people, so that they might be freed from heavy cares and so that in the diligent quest for truth they might live blessedly and happily."[313] Seclusion in itself has no value and is not to be confused with contemplation. Contemplative existence is secured by two means: first, by the decision to abdicate from worldly concerns—and this entails a decision for celibacy, since the repudiation of city and family go hand in hand; and second, by the unfailing and

---

Caldiera's insistence on the greater merit of virtues performed in the civic arena; see above at n. 40.

[312] Unlike the active citizen, moreover, the celibate is not able to pursue wealth, and should thus be born wealthy. Wills were invented so that fathers who had labored for their sons while alive might after death make them free: "Neque viventibus viventes praestare solum id velint, verumetiam et si forte prius sit sibi moriendum plurimum studere debent ut post mortem quoque sine molestia et lite filii relinquantur." *De coelibatu*, p. 87. Affluence is shown to be desirable for the celibate, pp. 85-87.

[313] "Contemplatores autem illos existimari voluerunt, non qui se intra domesticos parietes lucem et radium formidantes continerent aut qui vitam in tenebris et latebris more ferarum exigerent, sed qui se a popularibus auris secernentes et curis gravioribus liberarentur et veritatis solicita inquisitione beatius et felicius viverent." Ibid., p. 63.

fervent desire to know the truth (p. 100). The distinction thus made between a selfish, mindless seclusion and a proud repudiation of public life for the sake of the mind is fine, but serious.

Released from obligations to the public and confident that his solitude is just, the celibate has attained freedom. Liberated from human concerns so that he may pursue the divine, he needs nothing from the city and is subject to no one (p. 66). He is not to be considered human, but as a God, since he has raised himself beyond the condition of humanity[314]—in part because of the divine nature of his studies, but in part, too, because he has shed the public responsibilities that are the lot of ordinary mankind, masking his irrevocable act of civic irresponsibility by identifying it with the virtue of celibacy. For sexual purity is basic to Barbaro's notion of the contemplative life. Barbaro is repulsed by sexuality[315]—by nature and as a result of Christian training, certainly, but also perhaps because sexual activity is associated with the family and its concomitant burdens that are the real enemies of his freedom.

Barbaro's motives for preferring the contemplative to the active life are complex: he is in search not only of the leisure necessary for study, but also of a rationale for the repudiation of the social responsibilities, domestic and political, which constrained him. In Venice, where membership in a patrician family with a tradition of public service imposed the obligation to participate in civic life, an individual so constrained, and who was also devoted to the pursuit of knowledge, had only one clear alternative. That alternative was to refuse to sustain the dynastic tradition, to refuse to marry, and to refuse to participate in public affairs. Ermolao's defense of celibacy is thus a plea for individual self-determination in a social context where family and state limited the possibilities for self-determination.

Though he remained celibate and untrammeled by familial cares, the adult Barbaro was not able in the years that immediately followed wholly to free himself from public obligations. Again and again, he found himself enmeshed in political affairs for which he had no taste, and he yearned for leisure and for study. The conflict between the personal independence Barbaro craved and the public obligations he

[314] Since man *is* a social animal, Ermolao reasons, accepting Aristotle's principle (*Politics* I.2.1253a), then the celibate is not human: "non esse igitur hominum numero aggregandum" (*De coelibatu*, p. 63). If he is not human, however, it is because he is superhuman.

[315] He regrets, for example, that absolute purity cannot be observed in infancy, since children must suck the breast (*De coelibatu*, p. 81). For Branca's comment on Barbaro's notion of purity, see "Trattato inedito," pp. 94-95.

resented is evident in many of his letters during these years.[316] In one of several, for instance, Barbaro defends himself to Antonio Calvo, who was distressed that his friend had willfully deserted his republican obligations when he fled to Padua, ostensibly to escape the plague. Barbaro will miss standing by Calvo's side in the Senate, he replies, but the Senate itself he does not regret.[317] Calvo is angry with him for deserting the republic in a time of need, when he had only recently been made a Senator, on the trivial pretext of the fear of plague. Had the republic really needed his services, Barbaro assured his friend, he would not have left. And if the city condemns him for his insolence and negligence, he has the means by which to console himself: in letters. Nor will he in the future, as some, Calvo among them, have predicted, abandon his studies for the sake of public office—for within these forty days since he left, he had accomplished more in solitude than during two years amid the press of business. Months later, back in Venice, he still sought solitude: "In this populous city," he wrote to Pontico Faccino, "I delight in a wondrous solitude and a silence truly vast and religious .... Others marvel at the multitude of men who have thronged here for the sights: I [seek] solitude."[318] During this period of abhorrence for public office and quest for healing solitude, Barbaro taught Aristotle in his own house, without pay, and was, as he lamented to the philosopher Nicoletto Vernia, accused of ambition. The city's patricians, his own friends among them, wished him to conform to a respectable norm of behavior: the relinquishment, at an appropriate age, of intellectual pursuits, and the assumption of a political role. Barbaro resisted.

Sent as ambassador to Milan in 1488, Barbaro put to good use the leisure that such missions seem to have afforded. He pursued his literary studies and engaged in literary conversation and reflections.[319] After his return from Milan in April 1489, but before his departure in May 1490 on his fateful mission to Rome, he composed a second treatise entitled *On the Office of Ambassador*. Unlike his *On Celibacy* or his impassioned letters of the mid-1480s, this work not only accepts the concept of a nobleman's responsibility to serve his republic, but

[316] See especially his *Epist.* I, 54-55 (to Giorgio Merula), 60-62 (to Pontico Faccino), 62-64 (to Antonio Calvo), 79-80 (to Nicoletto Vernia), 83-84 (to Faccino), and 99-100 (to an anonymous correspondent).

[317] The following summarizes the *Epist.* I, 62-63.

[318] "Amabam in civitate populossissima solitudinem admirabilem et silentium paene vastum religiosumque .... Mirabantur alii multitudinem hominum qui confluxerant ad spectandum, ego solitudinem." *Epist.* I, 83. The comment to Vernia that follows is at I, 79-80.

[319] See *Epist*, II, 14-15, 17-22; also, *De officio legati*, pp. 163-64.

ceaselessly praises as most essential in an ambassador one virtue in particular central, as well, to an ideal of *unanimitas*: the virtue of obedience.[320] The ambassador must diligently obey those who have appointed him, writes Barbaro. His purpose is to "do, say, advise, and think those things which they judge might possibly pertain to the best condition and maintenance and amplification of their city."[321] He must follow orders unquestioningly, never holding himself superior to those who have instructed him: "It is the height of madness, and a sin nearer to a crime than to folly, I do not say to exceed or to disobey, but even grudgingly or negligently to obey the commands of the government . . . ."[322] Such injunctions are particularly weighty in Venice, he warns, where an ambassador's actions are carefully scrutinized: "nowhere is there less delinquency, but nowhere is delinquency more odious."[323] In executing his duty of perfect subordination to the will of his masters, it is helpful if the ambassador be of only middling intellect (p. 161), guarded in speech (pp. 163, 164), and modestly self-deprecating when praised (p. 164).[324] In brief, he must serve not himself, but his *patria*—particularly if he is a Venetian, "since the greatness of our empire has germinated, grown, endured for no reason so great as the concord of its citizens: he who hates this concord, does not hate merely those he hates, but plainly hates the republic herself."[325]

Ermolao Barbaro, a profound individualist and impassioned thinker of far from middling intellect, a rebel from adolescence against Venetian cultural expectations, here praises the faceless citizen praised by

---

[320] My interpretation of this work differs from Branca's, who sees in it an explanation of how profound individualism may be realized and satisfied in the context of the state; see his "Ermolao Barbaro e l'umanesimo veneziano," p. 207. M. L. Doglio's "Ambasciatore e principle" follows Branca's lead, and relates the *De officio legati* to similar prescriptive works on the prince. The following discussion summarizes the whole of this work.

[321] "Finis legato idem est qui et caeteris ad Rempublicam accedentibus; ut ea faciant, dicant, consulant et cogitent, quae ad optimum suae civitatis statum et retinendum et amplificandum pertinere posse iudicent." *De officio legati*, p. 159.

[322] "Extrema dementia, et propius sceleri quam dementiae peccatum, non dico praeterire aut in contrarium ire, sed aut malignius aut negligentius obire mandata curiae . . . ." Ibid., p. 160.

[323] ". . . praesertim in nostra civitate, ubi nihil severius expenditur, quam aut factum aut dictum legati: nulla parte delinquitur minus, nulla parte delinquitur odiosius." Ibid., p. 161. See also Barbaro's detailing of other requirements of the ambassador that appear to have a distinctively Venetian flavor: he must be particularly sensitive to the republic's honor (p. 162); he must not accept gifts from foreign princes (p. 164).

[324] Yet Barbaro enjoyed the praise of admirers in Milan (pp. 163-64). The ambassador must also refrain from crime and self-indulgence (pp. 165-66).

[325] ". . . cum haec dignitas imperii non alia tam ratione coaluerit, creverit, duraverit, quam civium inter se concordia; hanc qui odit, non eos odit, quos odit, sed ipsam plane Rempublicam odit." Ibid., p. 165.

other humanists whose destiny is to obey the general will and fuse
with that amoebic concord on which was based Venetian greatness.
He adopts here, in short, the perspectives of *unanimitas* shown earlier
to be characteristic of Venetian humanism, and has suspended his
dissent from those values. But he has not wholly accepted them, in
spite of his words: they are, perhaps, signs of his intention to conform
to a patrician norm still inimical to him, or they may be, perhaps,
insincere. Within two years of the time he wrote on the ideal ambassador, Barbaro would break spirit and letter of the law of obedience
he had defined, and would dramatically and finally renounce the obligations that he had inherited as a member of the patrician order.[326]

Barbaro arrived in Rome by June 1490 as Venetian ambassador,
proceeding, as in Milan, to devote leisure hours to his literary interests.
On 2 March 1491, the patriarch of Aquileia, the pious Venetian nobleman Marco Barbo, died in that city. On 6 March, the ambassador
Ermolao Barbaro appeared before the pope, requesting that he wait,
as was routine, for word from Venice before making a new appointment. On that very occasion, the pope appointed Barbaro to the post.
Obedient to the pope, but in grave defiance of Venetian laws, Barbaro
accepted. He informed the Senate—which had already nominated a
different candidate—of these events, signing himself boldly but con-
fusedly, "doctor and knight, ambassador, and patriarch of Aquileia,
if it pleases you."[327] They were not pleased. From Rome, Barbaro
wrote his friends of the profound joys of the priesthood he had so
suddenly acquired, permitting leisure for his studies and for meditations on salvation.[328] In Venice, there were rumors of treason. Barbaro's friend Girolamo Donato was sent to Rome to rebuke and replace him; his father Zaccaria was ordered to persuade his son to
return. But Ermolao would not leave Rome, where in the midst of
despair, resentful of the republic for its cruelty, anguished by his betrayal of his family's honor and hopes of him, he labored on the corrupt

---

[326] The following account of Barbaro's last years is drawn from P. Paschini, *Tre
illustri prelati del Rinascimento*, pp. 19-39; see also Ferriguto, *Almorò Barbaro*. A brief
summation of the events appears in Branca's edition of the *De officio legati*, pp. 21-23
n. 2.

[327] ". . . doctor et miles, orator et patriarcha Aquileiensis si vobis placet." Quoted in
Paschini, *Tre illustri prelati*, p. 26.

[328] Consider his words to Jacopo Antiquario: "Scito me, Antiquarie, illo ipso die,
quo sacerdotio intratus sum, volente atque adeo iubente Deo, fortiorem una hora factum
fuisse quam per annos viginti quibus philosophiae studia exercui. Hoc argumentum
habeo voluntatis et vocationis Dei, quod commoda sacerdotii possum contemnere,
sacerdotium nec possum nec volo. Vivo hilaris, vivo liber, vivo litteris . . . ." Barbaro,
Epist. II, 65. See also his letters to Ugolino Verino (pp. 65-66); Antonio Calvo (pp. 66-
67, 69-72, 81-82), and again to Antiquario (pp. 72-77).

text of Pliny.[329] Not yet forty years old, he died of the plague in 1493, less than a year after the death of his heartbroken father, just over two years after his acceptance of the patriarchate and defiance of the Venetian Senate. The liberty he had sought in his *On Celibacy* he obtained at great cost in the last two years of his life. In one decisive act he had repudiated the claims of family and state. It was a difficult task for a Venetian nobleman whose family origins committed him to public service.

With the tragic figure of Ermolao Barbaro the Younger, this discussion of the values of *unanimitas* and their opponents may close, as does the era in which the principal motive of humanism in Venice was the articulation of those values.[330] His conspicuous dissent from the norm stated and observed, on the whole, by other humanists, does not deny but highlights the severity of the constraints on the individual in Venetian culture. Barbaro had resisted, but not destroyed them. For three generations, the humanist movement, firmly directed by the patrician majority within its ranks, had acquiesced to, digested, and published the values of *unanimitas* implicit in Venetian culture: that the individual be subordinate to the group, that perfect and timeless concord prevail, that traditional intellectual and cultural values be sustained and defended with new cannonades of words. Those values had preexisted the age studied here, and will survive it, though in different form. The career of humanism changes course, as well.

[329] For Barbaro's expressions of resentment and anguish, see the *Epist.* II, 69 and 73ff. The *Castigationes Plinianae* were dedicated to Pope Alexander VI on completion early in 1493. (The dedicatory letters, reprinted from the original Roman edition, appear also in the *Epist.* II, 82ff.)

[330] Also viewing Barbaro's experience as tragic are Ferriguto, *Almorò Barbaro*, pp. 10, 88, 424ff. and, more recently, B. Marx in her review of LQU, p. 50.

THREE

Choices: *Moenia civitatis*

By 1407, the Great Schism of the church had scandalized a generation of Europeans. Secular and ecclesiastical leaders pressed for a resolution of the crisis. On December 19, the Venetian Senate instructed two ambassadors to exhort to unity first the one, then the other pope, as each journeyed by a separate road to meet with a council of the whole church: "so that the Schism . . . be ended and wholly eliminated, that there might be one flock and one Shepherd, and that the Christian people, divided by their shepherds' perversity, be recalled to union and the right way."[1] On December 31, the Venetians addressed their countryman Pope Gregory XII: Zaccaria Trevisan the Elder in the Latin oration that made him famous, Marino Caravello in the vernacular. The Tuscan humanist Leonardo Bruni, then with the Curia, described the speakers to his Venetian friend Pietro Miani:

The Roman curia has for a long time heard no finer display of oratory than that performed by the voice of that excellent man, your—or indeed rather my—Zaccaria. For his remarkable virtues cause me to love him as much or nearly as much as you do. When he made his public appearance before the pope, the reverend cardinal fathers of the holy Roman church in attendance, and a dense multitude of clerics and laymen ringed around, he spoke so that in his words the vigor of a strong man, the prudence of a learned one, the elegance of an eloquent orator conspicuously appeared. I wish that you had witnessed how attentive was his audience; for in that great crowd not even a breath could be heard, so awesomely were their spirits soothed by his majestic delivery, his fertile thought, his rich abundance of elegant words. That worthy man Marino Caravello spoke thereafter, and he also with great spirit, nor with less dignity, who even though he spoke not in Latin but in the vernacular, yet did not go unpraised, and his nature was clearly seen to be lofty and sincere.[2]

---

[1] ". . . quod scisma . . . removeretur et tolleretur ex toto, itaque fieret unum ovile et unus pastor, et quod populus christianus, quem sciderat pastorum perversitas, ad unionem rectamque revocaretur ad viam . . . ." Gothein, "Zaccaria Trevisan," p. 31. For a discussion of Trevisan's embassy, see Gothein's later *Zaccaria Trevisan*, Chapter Five.

[2] "Iamdiu nichil magis oratorium Curia Romana audivit, quam vocem praestantissimi viri Zachariae tui, immo potius nostri. Ego enim propter maximas ejus virtutes amori erga illum tuo aut nichil aut non multum concedo. Qui cum a Pontifice maximo publice audiretur astantibus Reverendissimis Patribus Sanctae Romanae ecclesiae Cardinalibus,

Trevisan's performance was exceptional. Caravello's was merely sound. Caravello spoke as an intelligent and informed Venetian statesman. Trevisan, a Venetian statesman, spoke as a humanist. He was learned as well as informed, eloquent as well as intelligent. He represents a new phenomenon in Venetian intellectual life—not wholly unprecedented, since all human phenomena have histories in which they are prefigured, but perceptibly new.

With Trevisan, whose adult career begins some few years before 1409, a distinctive phase in the evolution of Venetian humanism begins. It will end—not abruptly, but unmistakably—by the opening of the century's last decade, when a new era in the intellectual culture of Venice unfolds. During the years from 1400 to 1490, the same noblemen who ruled Venetian society—though they were mainly amateurs—dominated the society of humanists. Their concerns invaded humanist discourse, paired with the concerns of those others who wished to please them. The major themes of Venetian humanism reflect the perceptions and the interests of the noblemen who shaped it, are in accord with the city's intellectual traditions, and reinforce cultural assumptions during an era when Venice joined to her maritime empire an empire on land. At a critical point in history, humanism challenged Venetian culture. The same men who ruled the city assumed control over humanism, transformed it, and turned it to advantage.

The patrician appropriation of humanism at the turn of the century constitutes a cultural choice. The patrician relinquishment of humanism at the end of the century constitutes another. At each of these moments, the culture was pregnant with different possibilities for development. Of many fertile seeds, some were chosen. These choices were made—clearly—by no single act of will, but by a complex of individual decisions and events acting together with sufficient force as to compel a shift in cultural patterns. These decisions and events, these shifting patterns, these choices now confront us. The development of Venetian humanism will be traced from fourteenth-century origins, through the three generations of Quattrocento humanism of central

---

et frequentissima cleri populique multitudine circumfusa ita locutus est, ut in verbis ejus robur fortissimi viri, prudentia doctissimi hominis, elegantia disertissimi oratoris perfacile appareret. Vellem aspexisses, quanta cum attentione auditus est, ut in tanta multitudine ne respiratio quidem alicujus sentiretur, majestate orationis, ubertate sententiarum, copia optimorum verborum mirum in modum animos demulcentibus. Dixit praeterea fortis vir Marinus Caravellus, et ipse quoque magno cum spiritu, nec minori cum majestate, qui etsi non latino, sed patrio sermone in dicendo uteretur, tamen nec sua caruit laude et alti ac sinceri animi haud dubie apparuit." Bruni, *Epist.*, ed. Mehus, I, 51.

concern here, to the aftermath of that movement in the late fifteenth and sixteenth centuries.

1. Prelude: The Fourteenth-Century Background

A hundred years before the century of patrician humanism, Venice was aleady rich, powerful, and old.[3] By 1300, she had long enjoyed a major share of Mediterranean trade, and had developed advanced shipping and commercial techniques. She possessed an empire of maritime colonies and protectorates—vast holdings for an island city, if not, perhaps, the *quartus et dimidius* of ancient Rome boasted by her doges. She had not yet reached her peak. The next two centuries would see further growth of wealth and empire, and greater refinement of already-established social structures and institutions. Two series of developments would have a particular impact on her intellectual culture: the emergence of the patriciate as a legally defined and cohesive class, and the turn from an essentially maritime orientation to a policy of terraferma domination. The second, a process largely of the fifteenth century, will be of concern shortly. The first, a process largely of the fourteenth, provides the context for the study of the Trecento shaping of Venetian humanism.

Before 1297, a patriciate of wealthy merchants ruled Venice and identified its interests with their own.[4] But not until the famous and paradoxical "closing" of the Great Council that began in that year and continued for a generation did she acquire a legally defined nobility uniquely privileged with access to political power. By a slow process of definition, continuing even after that date, the nobility came to "coincide" with the state.[5] Once defined, the class was consummate.

[3] Examining chronologically the course of Venetian humanism necessitates some repetition here of material treated thematically in Chapter One and Two.

[4] The following brief sketch of Venice's situation on the brink of and during the fourteenth century relies upon many studies, especially R. Cessi, *Storia della Repubblica di Venezia*; G. Cracco, *Società e stato nel medioevo veneziano, secoli XII-XIV*; F. C. Lane, "The Enlargement of the Great Council of Venice"; Lane, *Venice*; G. Luzzatto, *Storia economica di Venezia dall'XI al XVI secolo*; Luzzatto, *Studi di storia economica veneziana*; G. Ruggiero, *Violence*. See also (and throughout this chapter) the general works on Venice's history by Hazlitt, Kretschmayr, Musatti, and Romanin.

[5] The figure is Collodo's in his "Temi e caratteri della cronachista veneziana in volgare del Tre-Quattrocento (Enrico Dandolo)," p. 147. Lane, in his "Enlargement," shows that Great Council membership actually expanded before it became "locked in" and exclusive, and describes the gradual process, extending well into the next century, by which the members of the Great Council became a solid ruling class. For this process, see also Ruggiero, *Violence*, Chapter Four, and S. Chojnacki, "In Search." The definition of Venice's noble class had a clarity unique in Italy; see in contrast the situation described by J. K. Hyde, *Padua in the Age of Dante*, pp. 60ff. For general discussions of the Venetian nobility and its relation to the state, see in addition to the sources already

Thenceforth, only descendants of the families denoted as noble were to be admitted to the councils that ruled the city. And with the important exception of the thirty families admitted for their extraordinary service following the war of Chioggia (1381), that principle of exclusiveness was respected until the seventeenth century, an era beyond the range of this study. For about three centuries, political power descended by blood. Thus already a republic because of her conciliar form of government, and a monarchy by reason of her doges, Venice became an aristocracy, as well—a befuddling constitutional array whose ambiguities bothered no Venetian, and later won the admiration of Europe.[6]

Aristocracy, not oligarchy. Many but not all aristocrats were wealthy; many but not all of the wealthy were aggregated to the nobility by the constitutional measures of the Serrata. The main characteristic of the Venetian noble class was neither its monopoly of wealth—for it had none—nor its narrowness—for it was fairly broad—but its quality of closure.[7]

The laws that created a class defined by heritable political privilege where none had previously existed could not create a unified social group.[8] Antipathies expressed themselves as factions within the new class and between its members and those newly excluded from the political realm and its perquisites. Unrest disturbed the city that had always presented to the world a face serene and impassive as a block of granite.[9] The early years of the century saw the Quirini-Tiepolo insurrection. In the middle years, factional struggle involved the Doge Marino Falier, who became its notorious victim.[10] As the role of the nobility coalesced and clarified in the late Trecento, however, its consciousness matured, as well. It developed a greater sense of cohesion, of commitment to a common purpose, as the small inner circle that

---

cited, G. Cracco, "Patriziato e oligarchia a Venezia nel Tre-Quattrocento"; J. C. Davis, *The Decline of the Venetian Nobility*; M. Merores, "Der venezianische Adel."

[6] Venice was widely admired for her so-called "mixed" constitution. See the literature on the myth of Venice cited in Chapter Two, n. 231, esp. W. Bouwsma, "Venice and the Political Education of Europe."

[7] The principle that the patriciate was unified not as an economic but as a political class is stated by G. Luzzatto, "Les activités économiques du patriciat vénitien (X^e-XIVe siècles)," in his *Studi di storia economia veneziana*, pp. 125-65. A similar argument is given by B. Pullan, "Poverty, Charity and the Reason of State," pp. 28ff.

[8] In addition to the sources already cited, this account of social conflict and eventual consolidation relies on S. Chojnacki, "Crime" and "In Search"; Collodo, "Temi"; G. Pillinini, "Marino Falier e la crisi economica e politica della metà del '300 a Venezia."

[9] I allude to Cracco, *Società e stato*, pp. 270-71: "Venezia era . . . un blocco granitico, dove la comunità, non il singolo, aveva valore."

[10] Pillinini's interpretation ("Marino Falier") abandons the image of Falier as an ambitious conspirator.

mastered the central machinery of government imposed a collective discipline upon the whole class, and stamped as essentially aristocratic the character of the maritime republic of Venice under its resplendent doge.[11]

Confronting the troubled social world of Venice at mid-century, the Doge Andrea Dandolo turned chronicler himself. He called for moral regeneration, summoning the nobility to its historic task of self-abnegation for the greater welfare of the whole city.[12] The damage caused by the uncontrolled pursuit of self-interest would be repaired under a worthy doge, ally of the people and symbol of their unity. His implicit criticism of a factious patriciate and exaggerated hopes of the dogado did not diminish the overall effect of his chronicle: the celebration of Venice. Dandolo epitomizes a historiographical tradition that had begun well before his lifetime and was to long survive him. Its consistent aim was apologetic.[13] The city was lauded for its extraordinary origins, its crusading zeal, its perfect justice, its exemplary rulers. Unpleasantnesses past and present were ignored, for the story of Venice's development was perceived, in Doge Dandolo's words, as a long road "from the good to the better."[14] Along that road, Venice had unfailingly followed the standard of virtue. A pure devotion to liberty stirred her founders. An absolute perfection of moral virtue characterized her perfectly faceless doges. Unerringly loyal to the church in the battle against heresy and paganism, Venice remained true to the Christian mission, buoyed by her own apostolic tradition and precious store of relics, even when the church herself deserted it and foundered in vice. United in their commitment to the good, the people of Venice never quarreled, nor disobeyed their leaders to policies always righteous and wars invariably just. These historiographical staples appeared in an abundance of chronicles written in the Latin of scholars and clerks or in courtly French, and circulated widely to an audience of socially elevated, well-educated readers cut of the same cloth as their authors,

[11] For the ascendancy of a small elite within the aristocracy, see especially Chojnacki, "In Search," and Cracco, *Società e stato*, pp. 450, 453.

[12] This interpretation of Dandolo's message to the patriciate is Cracco's in *Società e stato*, pp. 401ff.; but see also the qualifications of G. Arnaldi, "Andrea Dandolo doge-cronista."

[13] The conclusion of A. Carile, "Aspetti della cronachista veneziana nei secoli XIII e XIV," especially pp. 84-85: "tale volontà apologetica è una costante nella cronachista veneziana." His view is shared by Cracco, among others, in *Società e stato* and "Il pensiero storico di fronte ai problemi del comune veneziano," and by Pertusi, "Inizi," especially pp. 270-71. For the major themes of the works of the medieval chroniclers described below, see G. Fasoli, "I fondamenti della storiografia veneziana"; also E. Cochrane, *Historians and Historiography*, Chapter Three.

[14] Cited by Carile, "Aspetti della cronachista veneziana," p. 89.

close to centers of wealth and power.[15] This idealized vision of Venice's past favored by her rulers and their spokesmen is noticeably akin to some of the themes of *unanimitas* discussed in the preceding chapter. Indeed, the two traditions of pre-Renaissance Latin historiography and Renaissance humanism are continuous, as will soon more clearly emerge. Patrician humanism would absorb the rhapsodic vision of medieval historians, expand it, and refurbish it to suit a new age. But in both traditions, the aim would be the same: to describe a society as perfect even if it were flawed, as just even if unjust, as harmonious even if turbulent, in order best to protect the interests of the rich and powerful.

In the turbulent fourteenth century, not all historians adhered to this Latin tradition. Wielding the vernacular, a language more suited to the presentation of personal or unorthodox viewpoints than was the conventional Latin of court and church, several frankly described the events produced by social conflict.[16] Or, less ingenuously, they portrayed events so as to justify the interests of one faction over another, their partisanship betraying their discontent with the present, their words laden with a "sediment of bitter preoccupation."[17] Still the dissident voice of the vernacular chronicler in the fourteenth century spoke not for the people at large, but for a segment of the economically or politically privileged. This counter-tradition of vernacular history would also survive into the age of humanism. There it sometimes met with repression, and sometimes lapsed into diaristic anecdote, personal but trivial, always subordinate to the public intellectual tradition that spoke, for the moment, in Latin.[18]

In the vernacular, like these chronicles, but a vernacular sparked with tuscanisms, the poetry of the Venetian Trecento constitutes another and distinct tradition of intellectual life. The poetry was mostly didactic, dealing with matters religious (such as the verse homogenization of the four gospels by Jacomel Gradenigo) or historical (such as Pietro Natali's *terza rima* account of the legendary peace of 1177).[19]

[15] For the social status of the chroniclers and their readers, see Carile, "Aspetti," especially pp. 83-84 and 116ff., and Pertusi, "Inizi," p. 270.

[16] This analysis of vernacular historiography follows Carile, "Aspetti," pp. 97ff., and Collodo, "Temi."

[17] Carile, "Aspetti," p. 100.

[18] A remarkable case of repression is seen in the order to destroy the scandalous chronicle of Antonio Morosini in 1418 (cf. F. Gaeta, "Storiografia, coscienza nazionale," p. 16 n. 47; Cochrane, *Historians and Historiography*, p. 63 and n. 10). The diaristic tendency is seen in such fifteenth-century chronicles as those of Giorgio and Pietro Dolfin and Domenico Malipiero, and culminates in the famous multi-volume diaries of Marino Sanuto: *I diarii di Marino Sanuto, 1496-1533 [Diarii]*.

[19] This review of the fourteenth-century literary tradition is based primarily on

Even the *Leandride*, Gian Girolamo Natali's famous relation of the classical romance of Hero and Leander, provides the context for a sober discussion of ancient and modern authors. The narrator of that literary survey is Dante, whose influence on the forms and language of the Venetian literature of this period is strikingly evident, and whose works were copied and circulated widely in that city.[20] These poets, most of them patricians, imitated, along with Dante, also Petrarch and Boccaccio.[21] Their openness to literary currents from the mainland marks a new phase in the evolution of the city's intellectual culture, pointing to the following century, when Venetian humanists would discourse with humanists throughout Italy, and to the century after, as well, when the patrician Pietro Bembo would make the language of Dante, not the Latin of Cicero, the literary language of the nation not yet formed.[22]

The poets' readiness to absorb Tuscan culture and groom their language to the standard it set was not matched, as has been seen, by the historians. In their more ancient tradition, the focus remained strictly Venetian and local, even when the chronicler broadened his range to universal history. But it was paralleled by an openness to the Aristotelian tradition in philosophy, only recently imported from France and grafted upon the medical faculties of Italian universities, and longer-established traditions of law and theology. Venice's professionals and university-trained intellectuals (doctors, civic and canon lawyers, theologians, and the professors of these and their supporting disciplines) were products of this academic culture, as were the patricians and affluent citizens whose university studies had no professional goal. Though the neighboring University at Padua did not have

---

A. Viscardi, "Lingua e letteratura"; analysis of content at pp. 195ff. See also V. Lazzarini, *Rimatori veneziani del secolo XIV*. The *Leandride* is the subject of much discussion: see R. Meneghel, "La 'Leandride' di Giovanni Girolamo Nadal," and now L. Lazzarini, "Nuovi documenti su Giovanni Gerolamo e la Leandride." E. Cicogna wrongly attributes this work to Leonardo Giustiniani, but his analysis of the poet's language, imitative of Dante and Petrarch, is still valuable: see his "Della Leandreide, poema anonimo inedito." L. Lazzarini contributes greatly to an understanding of the poetic tradition, which he perceives as largely patrician. See his *Paolo de Bernardo e i primordi dell'umanesimo in Venezia*, especially pp. 121ff.

[20] For the influence of Dante, see in addition to works already cited, V. Branca and G. Padoan, ed., *Dante e la cultura veneta*, esp. G. Fasoli, "Veneti e veneziani fra Dante e i primi commentatori," and G. Folena, "Il primo imitatore veneto di Dante, Giovanni Quirini"; also V. Lazzarini, "I più antichi codici di Dante."

[21] See A. Medin, "Il culto el Petrarca nel Veneto fino alla dittatura del Bembo," and Medin, "Per la storia della fortuna del Boccaccio nel Veneto." The main example of Boccaccio imitation is actually a prose work: Sabelio Michiel's *Il vago Filogeo*.

[22] Their receptivity is particularly striking because it is so early; see Viscardi, "Lingua e letteratura," p. 204. It is paralleled by a receptivity in other areas of culture: see G. Volpe, "L'Italia e Venezia," and L. Coletti, "Le arti figurative."

the massive influence on Venetian culture in the fourteenth century that it was to have later, nevertheless Venetians appear in these years among the rolls of students and teachers there, as at other universities. Whether inherited from Padua or Bologna or Pavia, or even Paris or Oxford, the scholastic tradition of medieval universities was well rooted in the lagoon city, which was not during the Renaissance to have a university of its own.[23] It would flourish even more vigorously in the fifteenth century.

Belonging to this vital tradition were the four visitors—two patricians, one merchant, and a physician—who offended Petrarch, then resident in Venice, and sparked his famous invective *On His Own Ignorance and That of Many Others.* In that work, Petrarch attacked not merely his Venetian friends but the Aristotelian tradition they represented. That tradition, he argued, entailed an unbridled confidence to human reason's capacity to explore and know the natural world, and consequent blindness to the inner self and its relations to God and nature, better understood through the thinkers of Christian and pre-Christian antiquity. His eloquent diatribe can be viewed in retrospect as a manifesto of the moral philosophical concerns of humanism as opposed to the assumptions of scholasticism.[24] Though

[23] For the influence on Venice of Aristotelian philosophy in this period, see especially P. O. Kristeller, "Il Petrarca, l'umanesimo e la scolastica a Venezia," "Petrarch's 'Averroists.' " Kristeller's exceedingly lucid *La tradizione aristotelica nel Rinascimento* places Italian Aristotelianism within its broader context. A. Poppi's *Introduzione all'aristotelismo padovano* and C. B. Schmitt's *A Critical Survey and Bibliography of Studies on Renaisance Aristotelianism, 1958-1969* capsulize modern understandings of the importance and evolution of Aristotelianism at Padua and elsewhere. In spite of qualifications reported there, J. H. Randall, Jr.'s *The School of Padua and the Emergence of Modern Science* remains important. See also now Randall, "Paduan Aristotelianism Reconsidered." For the early development of Paduan philosophy, see N. G. Siraisi, *Arts and Sciences at Padua.* For intellectual trends there in the late Quattrocento, see the studies in A. Poppi, ed., *Scienza e filosofia all'Università di Padova nel Quattrocento.* For an overview of Padua in the fifteenth and sixteenth centuries, see F. Dupuigrenet Desroussilles, "L'università di Padova dal 1405 al Concilio di Trento."

For the participation of Venetians as students and teachers of civil and canon law at various universities, see Agostini, *Notizie,* I, i-lviii, pp. viiiff., and M. Foscarini, *Lett. ven.,* pp. 15ff. Although the information available is sketchy, both Agostini and Foscarini are able to trace the history of that involvement to the fourteenth century. Agostini's reviews of the early development in Venice of philosophy (pp. xlviiff.) and medicine (pp. xlixff.) are relevant here. Venetians frequently appear among those fourteenth-century figures named as present at the university in Padua by J. Facciolati, *Fasti gymnasii patavini [Fasti gymn. pat.],* Vol. I, Part I; J. F. Tomasini, *Gymnasium patavinum;* A. Gloria, *Monumenti della Università di Padova, 1318-1405;* L. Gargan, *Lo studio teologico e la biblioteca dei Domenicani a Padova nel Tre e Quattrocento;* N. Papadopoli, *Historia gymnasii patavini [Hist. gymn. pat.].* That upper-class Venetians acquired university education without becoming professionals is evident from Petrarch's experience; see below.

[24] For this incident, see especially Kristeller, "Il Petrarca" and "Petrarch's 'Averro-

Petrarch's anger against his detractors may have been just, yet the picture he paints of the Aristotelian tradition in Venice is not wholly fair. In the lagoon city, that pervasive tradition coexisted with both piety and humanism. In the fourteenth century, indeed, there is encountered a phenomenon that continues, as has been seen, into the fifteenth: the figure of the physician-humanist, by professional training an Aristotelian, by avocation a lover and student of the classics.[25]

But the main locus of Venice's early humanism was in the circle of notaries and scribes employed by the government.[26] That this would be so is entirely understandable, and conforms to a pattern seen elsewhere in Italy. As city governments became more complex, they required larger secretarial staffs to handle correspondence, compose official documents, record deliberations and laws. This army of secretaries required instruction in Latin language and rhetoric, a training provided by increasingly larger squadrons of grammar teachers. From the fourteenth century on, these teachers probed more deeply into the corpus of ancient literature for models of style and form, acquiring a love for classical expression and a taste for the values and outlook of classical authors that they transmitted to their students. Here lie the origins of Italian humanism, whose main practitioners were to remain, alongside a few wealthy amateurs, secretaries and teachers. The presence of humanists in the Venetian chancery in the second half of the Trecento is paralleled elsewhere: in neighboring Padua, for instance, there was Giovanni Conversino da Ravenna; at Bologna, Pellegrino Zambeccari; at Florence, Coluccio Salutati.[27]

---

ists,' " and L. Lazzarini, "Francesco Petrarca e il primo umanesimo a Venezia." Petrarch's work is available (translated by H. Nachod) in E. Cassirer et al., eds., *The Renaissance Philosophy of Man*.

[25] The Venetian physician Gabriele Dondi, whose more famous father and brother were among the major figures of Paduan culture in this period, belonged to the humanist circle that was to form around the grand chancellor and was learned in classical literature; see L. Lazzarini, *Paolo de Bernardo*, pp. 112ff. The type of physician-humanist reappears in the fifteenth century in Pietro Tommasi, Niccolò Leonardi, Giovanni Caldiera, and Giovanni Marcanova; see profiles.

[26] This account of early Venetian humanism follows L. Gargan, "Il preumanesimo a Vicenza, Treviso e Venezia," and several works of L. Lazzarini: "Francesco Petrarca" and *Paolo de Bernardo*; " 'Dux ille Danduleus,' Andrea Dandolo e la cultura veneziana a metà del Trecento"; and "Un libro su Francesco Barbaro."

[27] For Conversino, see especially B. G. Kohl's article in DBI, XXVIII (1983), 574-78, and his introduction to Conversino's *Dragmologia de eligibili vite genere*, and his "The Manuscript Tradition of Some Works of Giovanni da Ravenna"; for Zambeccari, see the edition by L. Frati of his *Epistolario*; for Salutati, R. Witt's monumental *Hercules at the Crossroads*. In seeing humanism as developing because of the need felt in Italy's urban centers of experts able to communicate effectively and to teach others to do so, I follow Kristeller's views articulated in many works; see titles in the Bibliography.

Venice's humanists formed around the Doge Andrea Dandolo, not a humanist himself, but trained in law and an author, as seen earlier, of Latin works. Dandolo's chancellor, Benintendi de' Ravagnani, did belong to the humanist movement, which was strongly influenced by Petrarch, his friend and correspondent. Paolo de Bernardo, Ravagnani's notary, Raffaino de' Caresini, his successor as chancellor and historian, and Lorenzo de' Monaci, another historian and most famous of them all, also belonged to this chancery humanism.[28] Yet beyond these names, though the influence of humanism seems to have been diffuse in their circle, few individuals in fact stand out. The emphasis in Venice was on the practical goal, the mastery of technical skills, rather than on broader cultural exploration.[29] Perhaps this emphasis explains to some extent the disillusionment of the chancery humanists in the last years of the century. They shied away from the public arena and its routine labors, seeking the warmth of friendship in Latin letters clouded with Senecan thoughts.[30]

Venice's chancellors and notaries might have continued to lead the humanist movement. Had they done so, Venetian humanism might well have developed in a pattern more closely resembling that of other Italian cities. But they did not. By the last decades of the century, patricians had come into contact with humanism. Those holding political office would have regularly encountered the notaries attached to the various government councils. The correspondence that survives between the Natali brothers, noblemen and poets, and Paolo de Bernardo, one of the learned notaries, suggests the existence of other cases of this kind of interaction.[31]

At the same time, a generation of young patricians from the inner circle of the exclusive ruling class had felt the lure of humanism. During these years, they received their education from the grammar teachers

[28] For Petrarch's influence, see in addition to the works by Lazzarini already cited his "Amici del Petrarca a Venezia e Treviso," and N. Mann's two studies, "Benintendi Ravagnani, il Petrarca, l'umanesimo veneziano," and "Petrarca e la cancelleria veneziana." For Ravagnani, see also Agostini, *Notizie*, II, 322-31; for de' Monaci, see A. Pertusi, "Le fonti greche del 'De gestis, moribus et nobilitate civitatis venetiarum' di Lorenzo de Monacis, cancelliere di Creta (1388-1428)"; M. Poppi, "Un'orazione del cronista Lorenzo de Monacis," and Poppi, "Ricerche sulla vita e cultura del notaio e cronista Lorenzo de Monacis, cancelliere cretese (ca. 1351-1428)"; also Agostini, *Notizie*, II, 363-71. De' Monaci, who survived well into the fifteenth century, had a particularly strong impact on humanists of the first generation of that period.

[29] Lazzarini, *Paolo de Bernardo*, pp. 94-95, and "Francesco Petrarca," p. 85; Cracco, *Società e stato*, p. 452.

[30] Lazzarini, "Francesco Petrarca," pp. 86-87.

[31] For that correspondence, see Lazzarini, *Paolo de Bernardo*, p. 122, and the comments of Meneghel, "La 'Leandride,' " pp. 170ff.

who were numerous in Venice—important transmitters of humanist learning to young patricians as well as to the young natives who aspired to secretarial appointments.[32] Thus acquainted with learned men, these noblemen acquired a culture that was fascinating in itself as a program of study, seductive in offering a mode of communication with friends which, however conventional, permitted a new range of emotional expression, and appealing as a vehicle for the celebration of their city and the articulation of the values of their class. For this generation born in the late Trecento had as children witnessed the consolidation of the city's ruling class. At this critical moment in their history, they intercepted and appropriated the humanist movement. Humanism would reinforce and express the newly healed consciousness grafted on the inherited values of that class, which they identified with the interests of their city. They would launch the next century's dominant and most characteristic intellectual movement: patrician humanism.

That humanism descended logically but not inevitably from the various intellectual traditions of the late Trecento. The vernacular tradition in literature and history subsided, although it did not disappear, as the classicizing Latin of the humanists asserted itself, incorporating or coexisting with the medieval Latin of the chroniclers and university-trained professionals. The academic disciplines of law, theology, and medicine retained the respect of the humanists, who remained receptive, as well, to the perspectives and methods of Aristotelian philosophy. The vision of Venice lodged in the Latin chronicles was transmitted to the new humanist elite, and found expression as a pervasive theme, as has been seen, not only in the histories they produced but in their treatises, letters, orations, as well. As humanism passed from the notaries to the patricians, it welded to itself as much of the Venetian intellectual heritage as it could usefully and profitably accommodate.[33] That heritage was precious to a ruling class which claimed a thousand-year history. It did not relinquish the past as it

[32] For the role of teachers in Venetian culture in the late fourteenth century, see Lazzarini, *Paolo de Bernardo*, pp. 115ff.; B. Cecchetti, "Libri, scuole, maestri, sussidii allo studio in Venezia nei secoli XIV e XV"; and M. Pastore Stocchi, "Scuola e cultura." Giovanni Conversino da Ravenna, the Trecento humanist pedagogue who survived into the fifteenth century, had during his Venetian residence a particularly weighty influence on the young patricians of the first generation of Quattrocento humanism; for him, see above, n. 27.

[33] Patrician humanism absorbed, as well, attitudes of piety embedded in a literary tradition not belonging to the culture of the learned, and excluded for that reason from this review; see G. de Luca, "Letteratura di pietà," and his *Letteratura di pietà a Venezia dal '300 al '600*.

embraced the new learning that captivated the young intellectuals of an elite which felt itself born to rule.

2. Three Generations of Patrician Humanism

On January 1, 1380, Carlo Zeno appeared with his fleet out of nowhere—so it seemed—to assist his besieged compatriots unloose a Genoese stranglehold. A few months later, the decisive triumph at Chioggia ended Venice's long struggle against her maritime rival, boosting morale and liberating energies for the approaching challenges of Ottoman advance and mainland opportunity.[34]

Venice recovered sturdily from the shock of war. Her merchants, noble and commoner, resumed their Mediterranean trade, enriching a citizenry drained by wartime expenses and affirming a maritime empire which, in spite of some losses agreed to at the 1381 Peace of Turin, was still growing. Blinded, perhaps, by their love of dominion— for to the East frightened cities, seeking protection, surrendered to Venice—the city's rulers viewed the aggression of the Ottoman Turks with insufficient alarm. As Turkish pressure mounted on the seas, Venice's rulers turned westward at the opening of the fifteenth century to the terraferma, the mainland of Italy.

The independent mainland cities of northeastern Italy had been for centuries a valuable resource to Venice. Their farmers and merchants provided foodstuffs and other basic goods Venice could not herself produce and did not wish to import at great expense from more distant ports. Through their territories, moreover, traveled the caravans that brought merchandise from over the Alps to Venice and back again to Germany and beyond. The city's governors had previously shown no taste for territorial conquest as a goal in itself, as their outlook was above all maritime and commercial. At the turn of the century, however, they sensed their interests to the west threatened by mainland

---

[34] The following account relies upon these studies in addition to those already cited: F. Babinger, "Le vicende veneziane nella lotta contro i Turchi durante il secolo XV"; G. Luzzatto, "L'economia veneziana nei secoli '400 e '500"; M. Mallett, "Venice and Its Condottieri, 1404-54"; C. Manfroni, "La battaglia di Gallipoli e la politica veneto-turca (1381-1420)"; C. G. Mor, "Problemi organizzativi e politica veneziana nei riguardi dei nuovi acquisti di terraferma"; R. Mueller, "Effetti della guerra di Chioggia sulla vita economica e sociale di Venezia"; P. Prodi, "The Structure and Organization of the Church in Renaissance Venice"; B. Pullan, "The Occupations and Investments of the Venetian Nobility in the Middle and Late Sixteenth Century"; N. Rubinstein, "Italian Reactions to Terraferma Expansion in the Fifteenth Century"; A. Tenenti, "The Sense of Space and Time in the Venetian World of the Fifteenth and Sixteenth Centuries"; N. Valeri, "Venezia nella crisi italiana del Rinascimento"; A. Ventura, *Nobiltà e popolo nella società veneta del '400 e '500*; S. J. Woolf, "Venice and the Terraferma."

signori with imperial ambitions. A generation after Chioggia they sent out a mainland army, and over the two-year period from 1404 to 1406 absorbed Padua, Vicenza, and Verona. Along with little Treviso, acquired in 1339, these cities formed the basis of Venice's terraferma empire. Its continued growth throughout this period fundamentally changed life in Venice.

The Veneto, the Serenissima's mainland dominion, produced rich revenues that by the end of the century amounted to more than a quarter of the total.[35] It provided, moreover, an opportunity for land investment to wealthy Venetians. Though they remained, for this century at least, committed on the whole to commercial activities, their terraferma properties became extensive in this period and were to become more so in the next. The absorption of mainland cities provided not only opportunities for investment, but employment, as well. Although the Serenissima permitted the subject cities a large measure of self-government, it assigned to each one Venetian civil and military administrators—the *podestà* and *capitano*, respectively—in addition to a large number of other functionaries, noble and commoner, who formed the bureaucracy by which Venice managed her new empire.

Mainland matters, naturally, increasingly occupied the councils in Venice. By 1440, Senate deliberations pertaining to terraferma issues became so massive that they were recorded in a series of documents separate from deliberations regarding the *cose del mar*. To deal with terraferma issues, five new *savi* (sages) were created to join eleven others in the Collegio, the doge's advisory body. More profoundly than these institutional changes indicate, Venice's political life was transformed by her terraferma acquisitions. She had become a mainland power. She would have to develop a new range of expertise, a new mentality, and a new military presence to support her new position. She armed herself accordingly, and began to participate in the struggles, verbal and bloody, that marked the years leading to Italy's downfall at the end of the fifteenth century.

The ruling class of Venice had only begun to consolidate under the guidance of a small elite shortly before it undertook a program of mainland expansion. The hierarchy within that nobility rigidified in the years which followed. Primarily from its higher strata were drawn the men who performed the missions of mainland domination: the ambassadors to Milan, Florence, Naples, and the pope; the governors of Padua, Vicenza, Verona, Brescia, and Bergamo; the *savi* and terraferma counsellors who most greatly influenced policy, among others.

[35] See the table in Lane, *Venice*, p. 237.

From their numbers, too, were chosen whenever possible the bishops of the subject cities. Venice had always maintained a certain independence in ecclesiastical matters; she extended her self-declared right to appoint into her new dominion. Her bishops, like her *podestà* and *capitani*, served as her governors. Charged with such responsibilities, these noblemen who were the privileged masters of Venice perceived themselves as her loyal and self-sacrificing servants. The patrician consciousness of unity in commitment to the republic that had gradually developed in the fourteenth century was affirmed and renewed by the challenges the fifteenth century presented.

The terraferma conquests had inevitably an impact in the realm of culture.[36] Constantly in contact with mainland social and intellectual elites, Venice profited from the acceleration of the process begun in the Trecento. The city developed a greater openness to Italian currents of thought and expression, and learned eagerly from those it had conquered. At the same time that it acquired a humanist culture from mainland teachers and associates, it employed that new culture as a weapon of mainland expansion. Patrician governors introduced to the aristocrats of subject cities not only the values implicit in Venetian laws and practice of government, but those expressed in the works of Venetian humanism. The conquest of the terraferma was cultural as well as military. Coming increasingly into conflict with other Italian powers, moreover, Venice would learn to defend its policies with what was then the lingua franca of political confrontation: humanist rhetoric. The same rhetoric was a rallying cry to those members of the aristocracy who were both rulers and learned. Wielding it, they clarified their sense of public responsibility and private self, alike affected (though not basically altered) by a westward orientation. As a consequence of terraferma activities, Venetian culture was reshaped.

3. The First Generation

Born in the late Trecento, the first generation of fifteenth-century humanists witnessed as adults the early stages of Venice's terraferma expansion. And they saw, after the election of the hawkish Doge Francesco Foscari in 1423, the outbreak of mainland wars that would continue with brief interruptions for the remainder of their lives. Yet

---

[36] For astute perceptions of the relations between humanist culture specifically and terraferma expansion, see G. Cozzi, "Domenico Morosini"; O. Logan, *Culture and Society*, Chapter Three; Pastore Stocchi, "Scuola e cultura"; G. Zippel, "Lorenzo Valla e le origini della storiografia umanistica a Venezia"; and Zippel, "Ludovico Foscarini ambasciatore a Genova." I disagree, however, with Zippel's interpretation of the effect of that "crisis" on humanism; see above, Chapter Two, n. 278.

these years were buoyant with expectation. The mainland beckoned, cloudless.[37]

The humanists of this generation were mostly patrician, and drawn from that inner circle of the nobility which ruled Venice.[38] As such, they were not only aware of the city's mainland ventures, but actively involved in them. Lawyers and clerics alike were among those who guided Venice's destiny and shared their perceptions. The three Venetian-born commoners who were significant figures in the humanism of these years, moreover, were closely attached to aristocratic circles. Thus related, they probably identified their own interest with those of patrician friends and acquaintances to some extent, and shared the perceptions of that group. Even if they did not, still their insignificant number and the nature of their humanist activity could not have overridden the effects of patrician leadership in culture or establish an independent tradition. Patricians of high position and authority, very simply, directed the formation of humanist culture in critical years when its essential character was determined.

They could not do so unaided. They required instruction in the philological tools basic to humanism, and intercourse with professional humanists more learned than they and more actively in pursuit of intellectual goals. These services were performed by a great number of foreigners, largely from the Italian mainland, who flowed through Venice but did not make it their home. Barzizza and Vittorino, Filelfo and Guarino, George of Trebizond and Cristoforo de Scarpis came and left.[39] The companions of noblemen and teachers of noblemen's sons, they were the catalysts of Venetian humanism. Their presence allowed patrician amateurs to take direction of the humanist movement. Their impermanence assured that not they but their noble patrons and students would have a decisive impact on that movement.

The transiency of these foreign humanists is a phenomenon important to understand. They won the respect of the patricians. In some cases, they developed affectionate relations with those noblemen which continued after they had left Venice, and even to a second generation.[40] Patricians, whether humanists themselves or patrons not active as

[37] The conservative warnings of Doge Tommaso Mocenigo against mainland adventurism were not heeded; see the text of his "Farewell Address" in Marino Sanuto, *Vitae ducum venetorum* at cols. 958-60.

[38] See the generations of core group humanists and explanation of their analysis according to a generational framework in Part II, Preface, Sections 5 and 10, and Tables 2, 7, and 8.

[39] See the discussion of transient foreigners in Part II, Preface, Section 9.

[40] See the cases of Guarino and Filelfo described in Chapter One, Section 8, and J. Monfasani's comments, *George of Trebizond*, p. 25 n. 4.

humanists, valued the latter's skills as teachers of Latin and Greek and transmitters of classical learning, assisted their studies and provided employment, deplored their departure from Venice but promoted their careers elsewhere in Italy.[41] Since they were warmly received in Venice, the foreigners' motives for leaving invite speculation.[42] Perhaps they were insufficiently rewarded as private teachers in Venice, and found the security of communal or university appointments in other cities attractive enough to lure them from supportive patrician circles. Perhaps the opportunities available to them as professional humanists in Venice were inadequate, their ambitions for advancement or self-expression exceeding the limits drawn by patrician rulers. Perhaps they were congenital wanderers. Of these explanations, the first and second are most plausible. The patricians who managed the city's intellectual culture (a subset of the patriciate which made law and set policy) welcomed and embraced the foreign humanists as bearers of the new learning. But at the same time, they discouraged and demoralized these learned men who were at once their teachers and their clients. No professional humanist became a major voice of Venice's humanist culture in this period because, perhaps, to state the matter simply, none was allowed to do so. At this stage of the evolution of humanism in their city, Venetians would not permit themselves to be controlled or even affected seriously by the outlook of foreign humanists. Perceiving the Venetian environment as comfortable but ultimately barren, the foreign humanists moved on.

When they did so, they left behind them as a heritage a knowledge of and love for the *studia humanitatis* embodied in the young men they had taught or the mature men with whom they had conversed.[43] The absorption of humanist learning by patricians is the most con-

[41] Note, for example, the efforts made by Leonardo Giustiniani for several foreigners (see P. H. Labalme, *Bernardo Giustiniani*, Chapter Three) and by Francesco Barbaro especially for George of Trebizond (Monfasani, *George*); also above, Chapter One, Sections 8 and 9.

[42] For this problem, see esp. Pastore Stocchi, "Scuola e cultura"; also Labalme, *Bernardo Giustiniani*, especially pp. 11ff. and 34, and Monfasani, *George*, pp. 24ff.

[43] It is not suggested that the creation of a humanist culture in Venice is due exclusively to their influence. A role was played, too, by the native humanism of the Trecento described earlier, centered in the chancery. Venice's direct contacts with Greek culture, moreover, particularly by way of Crete, where there was a colonial government staffed by Venetians, also had an impact on the development of Venetian humanism. The acquaintance with Greek sources of Lorenzo de' Monaci, chancellor of Crete for much of his lifetime, has been demonstrated by Pertusi in "Le fonti greche." Of the first generation of humanists, several lived in Crete for brief periods as governors or prelates, merchants or bureaucrats: Giovanni Corner, Fantino Dandolo, Pietro Donato, Marco Lippomano, Zaccaria Trevisan V, and Fantino Vallaresso (consult the appropriate profiles).

spicuous feature of this period of Venice's intellectual life. Those noblemen of earlier generations who inclined to the life of the mind had
written verse or studied law or philosophy. Now they collected Greek
and Latin books, sought copies of newly recovered texts, and affirmed
in their spoken and written discourse the merit of ancient wisdom.[44]
Mutual enthusiasms fueled enduring friendships among patricians, and
between them and the small group of native commoners who shared
their passion for learning. Humanism provided for intelligent noblemen a refuge not merely from political and social responsibilities, but
from the psychic strain the noble class imposed as a discipline upon
itself as a price of power: the strain of seeming faceless, passionless,
selfless. In the alien languages and conventions of the *studia humanitatis* that they made personal and their own they found release from
the strict conventions that bound their public lives.[45] These patrician
amateurs were as ardent lovers of learning as were their more productive professional counterparts.

   In their enthusiasm for the *studia humanitatis*, however, learned
patricians did not fail to guide the development of humanist culture
in directions appropriate to the interests of their class. Previously in
Venice, historical writing had defended the aristocracy, representing
as identical its aims and the welfare of Venice, portraying its activity
as virtuous and benign. Now humanist works, histories among them,
would convey the same message, whether authored by patricians themselves, by commoners who were their friends or servants, or by foreigners in their employ. Not every humanist work written in this period

   [44] Patricians of this generation pursued manuscripts with diligence: some are noted
in Chapter One, Section 1. An appreciation for humanist learning was so clearly enun-
ciated as to become a declaration of a new cultural program in two of the most famous
orations of the period, both by and for important men. The first of these was Andrea
Giuliani's 1415 *Funebris oratio* for Manuel Chrysoloras, the Byzantine nobleman who
died at the Council of Constance after having accomplished much for the appreciation
of Greek antiquity in Italy. The second was Leonardo Giustiniani's 1418 *Funebris oratio*
for Carlo Zeno, the disgraced hero of Chioggia who in his late years became an ardent
patron and student of the humanities. For these, see also Chapter One, Section 1. A
survivor of a much earlier generation, who had experienced a great deal in his lifetime,
Zeno prefigured in his last decades the type of the patrician humanist.

   [45] This dimension of humanism (which explains, I suggest, the popularity of that
intellectual movement among members not only of Venice's patriciate but also of other
ruling elites) has not been adequately explored. Friendship occurs when conventions
are suspended and the real self exposed: thus the patron-client relationship may be
viewed as a socially imbalanced tie of friendship; see, for instance, G. Suttles, "Friendship
as a Social Institution," and E. R. Wolf, "Kinship, Friendship and Patron-Client Relationships in Complex Societies." It is possible that the novel conventions of humanist
discourse provided a mode of communication of the warm emotions of friendship that
could develop only when the strict norms of Venetian patrician culture could be laid
aside.

assumes this ideological mission—when are the products of intellectual culture ever so uniform in purpose?—but many of the most interesting and significant do. They are sufficient to make this tendency within the humanist culture of the first generations representative of the whole.

Among the earliest humanist works explicitly concerned with the celebration of Venice and her benevolent nobility are two by commoners. Pier Paolo Vergerio wrote the *De republica Veneta*, he stated, because Venice did not have authors of her own.[46] The elderly Lorenzo de' Monaci delivered on the occasion in 1421 of Venice's legendary millennium a major oration justifying terraferma conquests as an aspect of Venice's destined responsibility to the oppressed.[47] But even before that date, the patrician Zaccaria Trevisan (the Elder) had shown himself in several orations to be a prime architect of Venetian humanism. The special destiny of Venice, the unique creativity and responsibility of those who found cities, the narrow universal hierarchy that embraces human society as a mirror of a more perfect order are among the fundamental themes there articulated, which become familiar in later products of this culture.[48] More than any other single figure, Trevisan is the link between Italian humanism and the particular ideology of the Venetian patriciate, committed to their city, jealous of their prerogatives, loyal to a traditional metaphysics that dwarfs human society and individual existence but that supplies the order and eternity they valued.

Directly influenced by Trevisan was his young friend Francesco Barbaro, the intellectual giant certainly of this generation, and (rivaled only by his own grandson and the son of his friend Leonardo Giustiniani) perhaps of the whole course of fifteenth-century humanism.[49] From his hands, the patrician humanism of Venice receives its legiti-

---

[46] P. 38; a similar comment in his *Epist.*, ed. Smith, p. 103. See also the discussion of F. Gaeta, "Storiografia, coscienza nazionale," pp. 7ff. The observation that Venice did not have her own apologists is interesting, and relates to the condition of Venetian humanism before its Quattrocento development; see the discussion of D. Robey and J. Law, "Venetian Myth," pp. 31-32.

[47] The oration is published in Poppi, "Un'orazione del cronista Lorenzo de Monacis," pp. 483-97. In the introduction, the author discusses the millenarian tradition and de' Monaci's approbation of a westward orientation. For the former, see also V. Lazzarini, "Il preteso documento della fondazione di Venezia e la cronaca del medico Jacopo Dondi."

[48] These themes are encountered in Trevisan's orations to Pope Gregory XII, Pietro Rimondo (Arimundus), and Pietro Marcello (in P. Gothein, "Zaccaria Trevisan," pp. 34-42, 28-30, and 47-49, respectively). For Trevisan, see profile. For the themes of *unanimitas* named here, see also above, Chapter Two, Section 9.

[49] The links between Zaccaria Trevisan and Francesco Barbaro are traced by Gothein in several works; see especially his *Zaccaria Trevisan*, pp. 122ff.

mation: the *De re uxoria*. It is no mere coincidence that the first major work of Venetian humanism consists of a defense of nobility and a program for its perpetuation. Barbaro's contribution to the development of Venetian humanism does not, of course, end there. His letters urge directly and indirectly the application of classical learning to the practical business of running the state and waging war. His translations from Plutarch (like those of his lifelong friend Leonardo Giustiniani) are not mere exercises in Greek, but portraits of aristocratic leadership. His whole life is a testimony to the marriage of word and act.[50] By the efforts of Barbaro and Trevisan and their contemporaries, Venetian humanism assumed the ideological mission it would not abandon in the coming years.[51]

Nor did it abandon its traditional allegiances to Aristotelian philosophy and Christian piety.[52] In both these tendencies, the humanists were participating in Venetian traditions that extended beyond humanism. These first three decades of the fifteenth century saw the failure of the zealous *Bianchi*, led by Giovanni Dominici, suppressed by the Senate in spite of broad popular support, and the success of a monastic reform movement closely linked to the nobleman Ludovico Barbo. It saw and heard the charismatic San Bernardino da Siena. And to this generation belonged Lorenzo Giustiniani, brother to the humanist Leonardo, a pale and forceful ascetic who would become Venice's first patriarch, ultimately her saint.

Alongside the classical learning of the patrician humanists and the fervent piety of populace and nobles alike, flourished the study of philosophy. Venice's receptivity to scholastic philosophy was already evident in the Trecento, as has been seen, and was institutionalized early in the new century in the school of philosophy established by the will of Tomà Talenti.[53] Soon after, the Venetian conquest of Padua

[50] For his translations, see profile. Passages from his letters are drawn on throughout Chapter One. N. Carotti stresses Barbaro's political role in "Un politico umanista del Quattrocento," understating, I believe, Barbaro's role as humanist and his religious sentiment.

[51] At about the time it does so, themes of the myth of Venice begin to appear in vernacular literature, and reach an audience significantly larger than that of the humanists; see A. Medin, *Per la storia della Repubblica di Venezia nella poesia*. The simultaneous projection of these themes in two literary traditions is more than coincidental.

[52] For the piety and philosophical tastes of the humanists, including members of this generation, see, respectively, the discussions above in Chapter One, Section 6, and Chapter Two, Sections 8 and 9.

[53] For the founding of the school, B. Nardi, "La scuola di Rialto e l'umanesimo veneziano," pp. 93-95; for its subsequent development, see the same work and Nardi's "Letteratura e cultura veneziana del Quattrocento," both reprinted in Nardi's *Saggi sulla cultura veneta del Quattro e Cinquecento*; and F. Lepori, "La scuola di Rialto."

would lead, in the realm of intellectual life, to the Paduan "conquest" of Venice. The university at Padua continued to develop under Venetian supervision in the fifteenth century as a flourishing seat of Aristotelian philosophy. At the same time, it became Venice's university.[54] Her subjects were allowed to study nowhere else. The Venetian graduates of Padua's arts curriculum (many patricians and humanists among them) absorbed an Aristotelian conception of the universe so absolute that other intellectual images and notions, if entertained, were subordinated to that one.[55] The launching of patrician humanism in Venice coincided with, and did not succeed or replace, the intensification of the tradition of Aristotelian philosophy.

By the end of the first phase of its evolution, Venetian humanism had developed under patrician guidance a distinctively Venetian profile. A generation of humanists had absorbed the new learning, opening to it their libraries, their houses, their purses, and their minds. They had at the same time accommodated the *studia humanitatis* to Venetian circumstances in two main areas. First, they had assured that their humanism would coexist with their traditional Christian piety and their inherited and intensifying Aristotelianism. Second, they had applied the resources of humanist rhetoric to the celebration of Venice and her aristocracy and the values supportive of both. In these two directions, and faced by new challenges, the humanists of the next generation would continue to progress.

4. THE SECOND GENERATION

The first generation of patrician humanists in Venice projected the concerns of their class upon the *studia humanitatis*. In so doing, they expressed with the tools of the new learning a patrician consciousness already forming in the late Trecento before they had reached adulthood, which was boosted by the experience of terraferma expansion of the early Quattrocento. The second generation would have known as children the first moments of westward expansion. But their main experience as adults would be of unrelenting war on the mainland until the fall of Constantinople forced the Italian states to reach a truce; then, as a consequence of that same event, they would face

---

Pastore Stocchi comments that it is significant that Venice's first-formed public school lay outside the humanist tradition: "Scuola e cultura," p. 109.

[54] The point is effectively made by J. Le Goff, "Dépenses universitaires à Padoue au XVᵉ siècle." See also the general works cited above, n. 23.

[55] See the profiles under "Education" for the university careers of our humanists. Of ninety-two, fifty-one attended that institution (of these, four cases are merely probable). For the culture of the university, see above, n. 23.

impending war at sea. In the early years of the century, Venetians' perception of their own benevolence soared unchallenged. In these middle years, Venice met with hissing rebuke for her actions on the mainland, while her policies with regard to the Ottoman threat provoked criticism from outsiders and doubts from within when Christian zeal and commercial interests unhappily collided.[56]

These pressures weighed upon the rulers of Venice, and among them the learned patricians who dominated the society of humanists. Keenly aware of such public events, these men were poised to respond to them, securing by words the status in the world Venice had won through arms and policy. The relative weight of patrician participation in humanism in this generation is not quite so great as in the first. Yet the presence among the patrician humanists of so many men of major political and military importance makes their participation particularly striking. In the middle years of the century, a large fraction of Venice's political elite were humanists.

Meanwhile, the participation of commoners increased. But that participation, as before, could not challenge the patrician leadership of Renaissance culture. Only one among the commoners (a citizen physician graced with patrician friends) resided in Venice free of direct patrician patronage. The others were either salaried during their Venetian careers by the government or by patrician employers, or they spent a major portion of their careers outside of Venice. As before, commoner humanists, while in Venice, probably by preference shared, or else by compulsion adopted, patrician perceptions of Venetian society and the world order.

As in the first generation, foreign humanists continued to flow through the city, contributing richly to its intellectual resources but not residing there long enough to alter the nature of Venice's distinctive humanist culture: among them, Giovanni Pietro Vitali d'Avenza (da Lucca), Giovanni Mario Filelfo, Gregorio Tifernate, and again, George of Trebizond.[57] But the importance of the transient humanists seems to recede somewhat in this period as patrician leaders found other means to fulfill the needs they had met. Natives and resident foreigners, both professional and amateur, now engaged in discourse with learned patricians, and taught their sons and the sons of citizens who were to

---

[56] For the criticism of Venice that increased from the middle years of the century, see especially N. Rubinstein, "Italian Reactions"; for the formation of Venice's Ottoman policy, R. Cessi, "La caduta di Costantinopoli nel 1453," and G. B. Picotti, *Dieta di Mantova*. For the impact on the patriciates of Venice and the Veneto of terraferma conquests, see A. Ventura, "Il dominio di Venezia nel Quattrocento."

[57] For these figures, see Part II, Preface, Section 9.

fill the ranks of the secretaries. Humanism had taken root in Venice, and provided from its own substance the means of perpetuation and growth.

One sign of the rootedness of humanist culture in the city was the creation by the Senate in 1446 of a public school at San Marco.[58] It was intended to train young citizens destined for the secretariat in the skills basic to humanism. A counterpart to the Rialto school of philosophy established nearly forty years earlier, it represents the commitment of the republic to the *studia humanitatis*. That commitment was admittedly limited: the utility of the humanities, rather than their ability to inform and illuminate human existence, was clearly the paramount concern of the school's creators.[59] Thus the public and institutional role of humanist culture was constricted at the same time that it was allowed an unprecedented place in the city's life. Despite these limitations, the impact of the school on intellectual life was considerable. The teachers chosen to staff it—of foreign origin in these years—tended to become long-term residents of Venice.[60] Unlike the transient humanists, they had a sustained influence on the development of humanist culture, and were resident long enough to adopt to some extent the values and perceptions of their hosts. Though none possessed the stature or intellectual range of Guarino Veronese or Francesco Filelfo (transients of the previous generation), they nevertheless taught during their respective tenures of the San Marco position a solid number of young men. These included, alongside those who would hold secretarial positions, many patricians whose families took advantage of the institution even though it was founded not for general education but for vocational training. By no means all of those educated in the *studia humanitatis* during these years attended the San Marco school. But its existence in the city (and the presence of its respected teachers drawn from foreign cities because native talent could not be found or would not be tolerated) lent prestige to humanism, and coincides with the time when humanism became the culture of the ruling class.

[58] Of a large literature on the San Marco school, see especially B. Nardi, "Letteratura e cultura"; J. B. Ross, "Venetian Schools"; A. Segarizzi, "Cenni sulle scuole pubbliche a Venezia nel secolo XV e sul primo maestro d'esse"; and Pastore Stocchi, "Scuola e cultura."

[59] In this circumscription of the role of the humanities, the Senate was adhering to the fourteenth-century tradition of chancery humanism. A limited commitment to the San Marco school, particularly in relation to the commitment to philosophical training, has been noted by P. H. Labalme, *Bernardo Giustiniani*, pp. 91ff.; J. Monfasani, *George of Trebizond*, pp. 297ff.; and B. Nardi, "Scuola di Rialto," pp. 98ff.

[60] Giovanni Pietro Vitali d'Avenza (da Lucca) stayed seven years. Filippo Morandi da Rimini and Pietro Perleone became residents and citizens.

That ruling class would harness humanism in its service even more aggressively in this generation than in the first. In innumerable orations delivered at foreign courts, noble humanists and commoners speaking for them employed their skills to state Venice's position and persuasively argue her cause. Their orations at home, meanwhile, for deaths or graduations, elaborated the ideal of the aristocrat: strong, virtuous, learned, and anonymous. Their letters, where they survive, continue to dwell on political themes, defending Venetian policy as benevolent, pursuing their city's best interest, urging her to the right course. Their treatises and small works were more often apologies for Venice and her nobility than anything else. From this generation come the works of Lauro Quirini, Giovanni Caldiera, and Domenico and Paolo Morosini, four of the seven authors discussed in Chapter Two as articulating the themes of *unanimitas*. As before, the choice of translations from the Greek in this generation often reflected an apologetic motive: Niccolò Sagundino's translation of Onosander's work, and Bernardo Giustiniani's of Isocrates' oration *ad Nicoclem* portray ideal rulers acceptable by Venetian standards.[61]

In this period, moreover, history takes its due place in Venice's humanist movement.[62] Several patricians of this generation actively tried to persuade commoners, transient and resident, to write histories of the city that would embody both the elegance of humanist style and the truisms of Venice's historiographical tradition. Flavio Biondo, Lorenzo Valla, Jacopo Ragazzoni, Porcellio Pandoni were approached. Each, for one reason or another, either never wrote, or did not write in a manner that was pleasing to their patrician judges, who had adopted humanist concepts of eloquence without accepting wholeheartedly, perhaps, newly stringent humanist standards of evidence.[63] Meanwhile, Venetians themselves wrote history in a humanist genre:

[61] Consult the profiles of the second-generation humanists for the titles of their many orations; also the brief analysis in Chapter Two, Section 8. For the works delineating an aristocratic ideal, see also Chapter One, Sections 4 and 5; Chapter Two, Sections 2, 3, 4 and 5, for the works of Caldiera, Quirini, and Paolo, and Domenico Morosini, respectively.

[62] G. Cozzi points out in "Cultura politica e religione nella 'pubblica storiografia' veneziana del '500," p. 218, the intensification of interest in historical writing during the fifteenth century, when the availability of humanist techniques and the pressures of the terraferma expansion coincided. But this intensification belongs particularly, a scanning of the key participants reveals, to the second generation of Quattrocento humanism. For the historiography of this period, see especially F. Gilbert, "Biondo, Sabellico"; F. Gaeta, "Storiografia, coscienza nazionale"; A. Pertusi, "Inizi"; and G. Zippel, "Lorenzo Valla."

[63] Labalme (*Bernardo Giustiniani*, p. 300) suggests that the patrician patrons of a Venetian history may have found the works of these foreign authors too critical.

Michele Orsini, a native cleric closely linked to noble families, and the patricians Francesco Contarini, Antonio Donato, and—masterfully—Bernardo Giustiniani. True to Venice's traditions, their histories were celebrations of the city, as were the medieval chronicles that preceded them.

In sum, these works amount to an explosion of humanist effort in defense of Venice and the policies, interests, and values of her rulers. This militant humanism had been prepared for, certainly, in the preceding years and is the predictable expression of a group of authors whose links to power were secure. But it was triggered by the immediate experience of these years. Venice had to be explained to the Italian world at large, with assurances of its benevolence, piety, reverence for peace, and love of tranquillity, precisely when its aggressive terraferma policies and sluggish response to the Turks most exposed the city to criticism. And even if the outside world was not persuaded, Venice had to explain itself to itself. The authors of these apologetic works wrote to persuade a patrician audience that, appearances to the contrary, all was well, and justice reigned. Venetian humanism became increasingly ideological and apologetic as it applied itself more energetically to the task of self-defense.

While humanism's potential as a medium of propaganda was exploited to the fullest, its potential as a stimulus to spiritual liberation was carefully controlled. The enthusiastic classicism of the previous generation was tempered. Although books continued to be sought and circulated, taste continued to lean toward the more sober historical, philosophical, and scientific texts, as sentiment grew among the Venetians against what they perceived as the immorality of some classical literature. Ermolao Barbaro the Elder wrote heatedly against the ancient poets, as has been seen. Both he and Gregorio Correr chose to translate as youths not the seductive fictions of the poets, but the moral tales of Aesop. After renouncing some of his youthful compositions not known to us, Correr's interests remained deeply and sternly moral. Giovanni Caldiera, in order to save the ancient myths, interpreted them as static allegories of Christian or philosophical doctrine, with some eerie results. Thus allegorized, they lost their potential to provoke the imagination to lust or waywardness; they were Venetianized.[64]

Suspicion of the classical tradition coincided with continued and

[64] For the works of Barbaro and Caldiera, see Chapter Two, Sections 1 and 2, respectively. For rejection of worldly literature by Correr and others, see Chapter One, Section 6.

even increased attention to religious and philosophical genres. Caldiera and the two patricians Candiano Bollani and Domenico Morosini wrote religious works atypical of the essentially lay humanist movement, but logical and even predictable in the context of the Venetian version of that movement: cautious, austere, and pious. Meanwhile, two commoner humanists and clerics, Domenico de' Domenichi and Pietro del Monte, pursued simultaneously humanistic activities and the writing of systematic works informed by academic theology and canon law on papal authority and matters of doctrine, while a third, Pietro Bruto, employed his rhetorical skills in vituperation against the Jews. Anti-Semitism, indeed, formed a conspicuous strain of Venetian piety. Harsh in Bruto's works and in the letters of Ludovico Foscarini, it is couched in cool and rational form by Paolo Morosini. The well-rounded Morosini also wrote on providence and free will, continuing to this generation the Aristotelian tradition of a work of pure philosophy. Free will did exist, he maintained, but it only operated in accord with the direction indicated by providence—a Venetian solution, indeed, that both affirms orthodoxy while upholding free will and constrains the individual by denying its effectiveness.[65]

The humanists of this second generation, in sum, resisted certain ideas and tendencies implicit in the classical literature on which humanism depended: the freedom of the individual, the worthiness and diversity of human affects. At the same time, they defended orthodoxy, religious and philosophical, respected the authority of the church, feared and rejected outsiders, feared and condemned immorality. This conservative component of Venetian humanism coexisted with its other main purpose: the celebration of Venice. The two tendencies, indeed, were coordinated. As humanism developed under patrician leadership, its resources were actively applied to the task of defending the interests of Venice and its rulers, while its potential for challenging other rooted traditions, pious and scholastic—vital elements of that city's system of values—was sternly restrained. Building on the achievement of the first generation of humanists who had, as they embraced the new learning, domesticated it, the second generation constructed a massive and integrated humanist culture, nimble in performing its ideological mission, sturdy in its support of established intellectual traditions and moral values. A third generation of hu-

[65] For these works of Caldiera, Bollani, D. Morosini, de' Domenichi, del Monte, Bruto, and P. Morosini, see the overview of works on religious themes in Chapter Two, Section 8. For anti-Semitism as a strain of Venetian piety, see Chapter One, Section 6.

manists would permit greater diversity—perhaps this was, willynilly, inevitable—while extending the achievements of their predecessors.

5. THE THIRD GENERATION

The generation of humanists born in the years following 1430 inherited a world whose boundaries were established by their elders.[66] They were born into a society ruled by a cohesive elite drawn from a well-defined noble class. They knew as children an Italy dominated by a few principal powers, among whom Venice numbered conspicuously. They had seen the Mediterranean arena imperilled by the advance of the Ottoman Turks, and before the eldest of them reached maturity, they would experience the trauma of Constantinople's fall. As adults, they would live within these structures and suffer the consequences of these events. The nobility would expand in number, dominated, as before, by an inner elite. Mainland possessions already secured would continue to be competently governed, and extended a little toward the end of this period as a consequence of the unfortunate war of Ferrara. That war provoked (as did Venice's diplomatic maneuvers in the difficult years of the "Italian League") a barrage of anti-Venetian criticism, a continuing stimulus to the rhetorical defenses of the city. A sixteen-year battle against the Turks, the first phases of the long process of the erosion of Venice's sea empire, would result in a pruning of maritime colonies but the salvaging of trade privileges. No new paths opened to present either glorious opportunity or insuperable difficulty. Morale, on the whole, was high, revenues sound, building boomed.

The Venetian humanists of this third generation were fewer than before, and the political activity of the patricians among them somewhat less important. To the extent that humanism in Venice was shaped by its principal leaders to wage ideological battles, to defend the city and its rulers, it would flourish in proportion to need. Perhaps these years when the challenge of mainland expansion was no longer fresh, with success no longer easy and the defense of maritime hegemony steady and unexhilarating, did not inspire young intellectuals as greatly as earlier ones. Moreover, the task of domesticating the humanist movement in Venice was already accomplished. That challenge met, perhaps fewer natives of any class felt the lure of studies. Those

---

[66] In addition to sources already cited, see also for this period especially R. Cessi, "La 'Lega italica' e la sua funzione storica nella seconda metà del secolo XV"; R. Lopez, "Il principio della guerra veneto-turca nel 1463"; M. Mallett, "Preparations for War in Florence and Venice in the Second Half of the Fifteenth Century"; and A. Wyrobisz, "L'attività edilizia a Venezia nel XIV e XV secolo."

who did, on the whole, were further from the centers of power than those in the previous generation. Of the patricians, few were figures of major importance, true soldiers of Venice's diplomatic political and military enterprises of the sort who appear frequently among the humanists of the preceding generation. Yet the patricians remain the dominant group within humanist society. Of the commoners, the participation of several was weakened because of long absence from the city during their adult careers. The others were in the direct pay of the government, and were unlikely to have articulated views in friction with the prevailing patrician culture.

That picture of patrician dominance is modified, though not essentially changed, when the frame of vision broadens to include the transient foreigners.[67] These were numerous during this third stage of the evolution of fifteenth-century humanism in Venice, their emphatic presence pointing to the next period, when they would crowd the stage even more. They came, in part, for the same reasons as before: to provide companionship to learned nobles and to teach noblemen's sons. But in this period, they began to come with a new motive: to staff the printing presses that would erupt in Venice in the last three decades of the century.[68] They corrected and edited classical and contemporary texts, or supervised the publication of their own works. They came and went rapidly, as need or opportunity dictated. To some extent, they developed ties with resident humanists, common and noble. But they were also able to maintain a certain independence—unprecedented in earlier generations of transients—since they drew their sustenance not directly from the patricians in their palaces or council halls, but from the printers, businessmen with low status and only short roots in Venetian society.[69]

Even before the advent of the press, humanism in Venice had broad-

[67] The transient foreigners of this generation include Giovanni Aurelio Augurello, Girolamo Bologni, Filippo Buonaccorsi, Coriolano Cippico, Giovanni Mario Filelfo, Paolo Marsi, Gregorio Tifernate, and Raffaele Zovenzoni. See the discussion of transients in Part II, Preface, Section 9.

[68] Of the extensive literature on the early history of printing in Venice, see these works and studies there cited: L. V. Gerulaitis, *Printing and Publishing in Fifteenth-Century Venice*; M.J.C. Lowry, *The World of Aldus Manutius*; E. Pastorello, *Bibliografia storico-analitica dell'arte della stampa a Venezia*; and N. Pozza, "L'editoria veneziana da Vindelino ad Aldo Manuzio."

[69] Raffaele Zovenzoni epitomizes this new breed of transient. For the relative independence of the printing enterprise from patrician supervision and involvement, see M.J.C. Lowry, "Two Great Venetian Libraries," and Lowry, *World of Aldus Manutius*, passim. Although patricians such as Bernardo Giustiniani clearly approved of printing (Labalme, *Bernardo Giustiniani*, pp. 239ff.), others, like Marco Dandolo, bitterly resented the vulgarization they felt it entailed; see A. Medin, "Gli scritti umanistici di Marco Dandolo," p. 346.

ened to permit a greater emphasis on the word. Rhetoric was every-where one among the disciplines called the *studia humanitatis*; in Venice, however, in earlier stages of the development of humanism, the study and use of rhetoric had been narrowly channeled. In the San Marco school, rhetoric was taught as a preparation for secretarial service. Among patrician humanists, rhetorical expression was largely devoted to the celebration of Venice or affirmation of aristocratic values. In 1460, with the institution of a third public school, the study of rhetoric as a discipline intrinsically worthy of attention was given legitimation and prominence.[70]

Soon, however, the nature of the study of rhetoric at the second San Marco school and within Venetian humanist culture changed again. The chair of eloquence remained vacant for several years after it had been held briefly by two transients—Giovanni Mario Filelfo and George of Trebizond—both expert rhetoricians with longstanding ties to Venice. When the position was filled in 1468, its new occupant, Giorgio Merula, would lead the attention of Venetian humanists away from a broader interest in rhetoric as a means of persuasive com-munication to a narrower and more technical concentration on phil-ology.[71] In the coming years, the philological focus advocated by Me-rula flourished, and coincided with the explosion of the printing industry. The science of the precise reading, interpretation, and emen-dation of texts embodied in Merula and his successor Giorgio Valla became the ideal companion of the business of printing. Both these teachers, with their colleagues in the first San Marco school—Bene-detto Brognoli and Marcantonio Sabellico—participated in the edi-torial activity of the presses, alongside the transient foreigners drawn to the new enterprise. And although that activity mostly involved commoners, native and foreign, resident and transient, it involved some patricians, as well. Throughout the century, native and foreign humanists had dedicated their works to patricians. But now as the presses churned out more books more rapidly, some patricians were

---

[70] For the school of rhetoric, see the sources cited above, n. 58. In 1468, a few years after the founding of the school, Cardinal Bessarion donated his library to Venice. That donation may serve as another symbol of the city's commitment to the study of classical antiquity. Yet its influence was limited: see Lowry, "Two Great Venetian Libraries," pp. 133ff.

[71] Merula's key role in the new philological trend of Venetian humanist culture has often been highlighted by V. Branca: see especially "Ermolao Barbaro and Late Quat-trocento Venetian Humanism," pp. 219ff., "Ermolao Barbaro e l'umanesimo vene-ziano," pp. 196ff., and "L'umanesimo veneziano," pp. 157ff.; also P. G. Ricci in "Uma-nesimo filologico in Toscana e nel Veneto." For the idea of a shift in the orientation of Venetian humanism from rhetorical to philological, see Gilbert, "Biondo, Sabellico"; Gilbert locates that shift in the early sixteenth century.

named repeatedly in dedicatory letters that suggest their role as promoters of publication.[72] Indeed, many patricians henceforth would become satisfied with this relatively passive patronage role, and fewer would themselves engage in writing humanist works or directly guide the development of humanist culture. Others would remain active and, like those remarkable friends, Ermolao Barbaro the Younger and Girolamo Donato, become philologists themselves and engage at the highest level in the study and criticism of texts.[73]

Philological interests and the business of printing thus converged in these years, giving a new focus—though not an exclusive one—to Venetian humanism. They spurred increased attention to areas of classical literature avoided by the morally austere and practically oriented humanists of earlier generations. At the same time, they continued to attend vigorously to those aspects of the classical and Christian tradition which had particular appeal for Venice's sober audience: science and mathematics, architecture and agriculture, history and law, philosophy and theology.[74] In all, the philological and editorial activities of this period constitute an independent tradition within Venetian humanism complementary to its main tendencies.

The main tendencies of Venetian humanism—its allegiance to Aristotelian philosophy and traditional Christianity and its preference for apologetic themes—continued to this generation largely in the hands of patricians, aided by commoner intellectuals. Ermolao Barbaro and Girolamo Donato have already been noted as philologists. They applied their philologists' skills not to literary texts, however, but to works by Aristotle or authors in the Aristotelian tradition. Their efforts evidence again in this generation the links between patrician humanism and the Paduan and scholastic tradition of philosophy. That link is seen to be even more concrete in the figure of Niccolò Leonico Tomeo, a native commoner, who became the first expositor at Padua

---

[72] Frequently so named, for instance, are Marco Dandolo, Girolamo Donato, Marcantonio Morosini, Paolo Pisani, Daniele Renier, Marco Sanuto, and Jacopo Zeno.

[73] Barbaro's preeminent role in forging the "new philology" of the late fifteenth century is a theme of Branca's many works on that remarkable patrician; see especially "L'umanesimo veneziano." There Branca also assesses the roles of Donato (pp. 166ff.), Merula (pp. 157ff.), and Valla (pp. 161ff.). Barbaro's philological orientation is strikingly seen to contrast with his grandfather's less critical approach to an Aristotelian text; see P. O. Kristeller, "Un codice padovano di Aristotile postillato da Francesco ed Ermolao Barbaro," pp. 346ff.

[74] Gerulaitis (*Printing and Publishing*) sees a tendency away from publication in the classics to a concentration on these subjects more appropriate to professionals than to amateurs. Philological skills were applied to the latter subjects (above all to scientific and philosophical texts) as well as to the former; for which note the roles of Ermolao Barbaro, Girolamo Donato, Niccolò Leonico Tomeo, and Giorgio Valla discussed below.

of Aristotle's works in the original Greek.[75] Barbaro, meanwhile, evinced a more general interest in science, as well, rather than in metaphysics, in his critical emendation of the Roman natural historian Pliny. A broadening of the Venetian blend of humanism and philosophy to include science and mathematics was furthered significantly by the foreigner Giorgio Valla. Digesting his vast knowledge of these subjects into a modern encyclopedia, he reaffirmed Venetian traditions first hallowed by patrician humanists: a commitment to system and to a vision of the universe as a whole and immense machine in which the life of the individual human being played a small and prescribed part.[76]

Several patrician humanists of this generation, both clerical and lay, affirmed another tradition, that of Christian orthodoxy. They followed the example of their forebears in writing religious hymns and meditations, saints' lives, moral laments, works on problems of church history, or systematic theology.[77] Like those of earlier generations, finally, humanists of the third generation wrote or encouraged the composition in appropriately laudable form of Venice's history. The first three contenders for the chair of eloquence were expected as part of their duties to compose such a history, and a later occupant of that chair, Marcantonio Sabellico, subsequently did so, to the great delight of the Senate. The defense of Venice was pursued, as well, in genres other than history. Both Ermolao Barbaro the Younger (reluctantly, it seems), and Pietro Barozzi wrote works that defend the values central to the patrician ideal of *unanimitas*. But only one patrician humanist of this generation wrote forcefully in defense of Venice: Girolamo

[75] For guidance to the scientific and philosophical work of Barbaro, Donato, and Tomeo, see their respective profiles. At Padua itself, a philological orientation in which these Venetians participated was evident at this time. See A. Poppi, *Introduzione all'aristotelismo padovano*, pp. 26ff. For philological and printing activity in general with regard to Aristotelian texts, see L. Minio-Paluello, "Attività filosofico-editoriale aristotelica dell' umanesimo."

[76] For Valla, see his appendix profile and works there cited. For Valla's fusion of humanistic with mathematical, scientific, and philosophical interests and his key role in Venetian culture, see especially P. L. Rose, "Bartolomeo Zamberto's Funeral Oration," pp. 299-310, and Rose, "Humanist Culture and Renaissance Mathematics," pp. 91ff.; for his scientific work specifically, see the studies of G. Gardenal, P. L. Ruffo, and C. Vasoli in V. Branca, ed., *Giorgio Valla tra scienza e sapienzia*; also Branca, "L'umanesimo veneziano," pp. 161ff. Valla's influence was exerted already in the decade of the 1480s, although his major work was published later. For Ermolao Barbaro's relation to scientific currents of Venetian culture, see Branca, "L'umanesimo veneziano," and A. Ferriguto, *Almorò Barbaro*.

[77] See the discussion above of the works in this genre in Chapter Two, Section 8. Third-generation authors of such works include Pietro Barozzi, Marco Dandolo, Francesco Diedo, Pietro Dolfin, Girolamo Donato, Ludovico Donato, Giovanni Lorenzi, Paolo Ramusio, and Antonio Vinciguerra.

Donato, in many regards the most perfect exponent in its third generation of the phenomenon of patrician humanism.[78]

For patrician humanism, that synthesis of humanism and the values of the Venetian aristocracy, was beginning to fade. Its sturdy tradition would continue into the next generation and through the next century, as so many things Venetian have the knack of survival. Yet it lacked in this era the vitality seen in the philological/editorial movement fueled by the printing presses. Nor was that movement fully successful: it lacked not energy but a moral dimension. There seemed to be embedded in the intellectual movement of those dissectors and correctors of words no broad conception of the world, of society, of the place and depths and stature of the human being. Though they produced useful texts, forged invaluable tools of knowledge, their zeal was sterile. Their words, bloodless, do not live.

Venetian humanism, not yet old, had begun to exhaust itself by the end of this period. Harbingers of a new era appeared. The unruly monk Francesco Colonna wrote the *Hypnerotomachia Poliphili*—that disorganized, fanciful, sensuous *pasticcio* of a romance, a shattered mirror of Venetian taboos and verities. An arrogant bronze condottiere on his swaggering horse exploded on a gray Dominican square. A printer with hopes of glory—Aldo Manuzio—took the road to Venice. The young aristocrat Ermolao Barbaro, rebellious in his soul, would soon contemplate an act of disloyalty to his country and his ancestors, and would soon act.[79]

The stern discipline that had characterized intellectual life through most of the fifteenth century would dissolve as the patricians who had imposed it put down their reins.

6. AFTERMATH

An Italy shocked by the threat from the Turkish East was ravaged in 1494 by an invader from the north.[80] The swift conquest and retreat

[78] For expectations of the contenders (Pietro Perleone, Giovanni Mario Filelfo and George of Trebizond), see Gilbert, "Biondo, Sabellico." For discussions of Barozzi's DFE, see above, Chapter Two, Section 6; of Barbaro's *De officio legati*, Section 10. Donato's *Contra calumnias apologia* is similar in content to Paolo Morosini's defenses of Venice discussed in Chapter Two, Section 4; see also Donato's orations listed in his profile.

[79] For Colonna and his work, see especially M. T. Casella and G. Pozzi, *Francesco Colonna, biografia e opere*; also A. Chastel's evaluation of it as a fantastic summation of the spirit of Venetian humanism in his "Art et humanisme au Quattrocento," p. 404. The equestrian Colleoni of Verrocchio is known to travelers to Venice. For the printer Manuzio, see below. Barbaro G's disloyalty and other "delinquents" are discussed in Chapter Two, Section 10.

[80] In addition to general sources already cited, this account relies on F. Braudel, "La

of the French King Charles VIII was a stern warning of trials to come. At first, Venice remained aloof and secure in her lagoon. In time, she could not escape the battles that ripped Italy apart, fought by Italian rulers at odds with each other and in league with dangerous foreign allies. By the League of Cambrai of 1508, France, Spain, and the Empire joined the pope against Venice. Venice could not withstand such massive pressures, and suffered a catastrophic defeat at Agnadello in 1509. But the republic rallied, encouraged by the demonstrated loyalty of its mainland cities. In 1511, the city joined the Pope Julius' Holy League, a crusade to drive the French "barbarian" out of Italy; in 1513, it defected to France. By 1516, the city was out of danger, and able to tend her wounds. It would retain its position as a major power in the years to come. But in a Europe of increasingly powerful nations, its role became relatively less significant than it was in the splendid fifteenth century.

During that century, the aristocracy of Venice had increased in size at the same time that a narrow group within it retained a monopoly of major political offices. Competition for all offices was intense. Perhaps related to these trends, a malaise affected the noblemen of Venice at the turn of the century. Demoralization gave way after Cambrai to a new unity, a stern discipline, that accompanied and informed post-war recovery.[81] But the slow decline of the Venetian nobility as a

---

vita economica di Venezia nel secolo XVI"; F. Chabod, "Venezia nella politica italiana ed europea del Cinquecento"; G. Cozzi, "Authority and Law in Renaissance Venice"; R. Finlay, "Venice, the Po Expedition, and the End of the League of Cambrai, 1509-1510"; F. Gilbert, "Venice in the Crisis of the League of Cambrai"; F. C. Lane, "Naval Actions and Fleet Organization, 1499-1502"; P. S. Leicht, "Ideali di vita dei veneziani del Cinquecento"; F. Seneca, *Venezia e Papa Giulio II*; and U. Tucci, "The Psychology of the Venetian Merchant in the Sixteenth Century." A succinct account of the French invasion and consequent political disarray in L. Martines, *Power and Imagination*, pp. 277ff.

[81] See Gilbert, "Venice in the Crisis of the League of Cambrai," esp. (in the Hale edition) pp. 277ff. Both Gilbert and Cozzi ("Domenico Morosini," "Authority and Law") indicate a significant change in patrician culture, both psychological and institutional, from the late fifteenth to the early sixteenth century, linked to the experience of Cambrai. It should be noted, however, that neither the tendency to reinforce the monopoly of an inner oligarchy nor that toward the consolidation of patrician consciousness was new; both were evident in the fourteenth century with consequences extending through the fifteenth, as has been seen. These early sixteenth-century developments should be viewed as a renewal and intensification, provoked by a particular set of experiences, of tendencies already well rooted in Venetian culture. W. Bouwsma in his massive *Venice and the Defense of Republican Liberty* attributes to the Cambrai crisis an even more dramatic importance, seeing it as the catalyst of a modern secular political consciousness in Venice. L. Libby presents a similar argument in his "Venetian History and Political Thought after 1509." Both Bouwsma and Libby liken Cambrai to the crisis that, according to H. Baron, triggered civic humanism in Florence; see especially his *The Crisis of the Early Italian Renaissance*, a culmination of earlier studies.

ruling class had already, if just a little, begun. In the coming years, wealthy noblemen would tend increasingly to mainland investments and the stable, leisurely life they afforded, leaving the risks of commerce to newer men and citizen merchants. Yet Venice remained prosperous, sustained as always by her maritime commerce, and now also by her newly vigorous industries.

Among these was the printing industry, which would have in the next generations an immeasurable impact on intellectual life not only in Venice but throughout Italy and Europe.[82] Already two decades old and highly successful in 1490, Venice's printing enterprise entered another and distinctive phase under the leadership of Aldo Manuzio. A Roman pedagogue with a faith in the power of classical literature to perfect humanity, he published pure texts unencumbered by commentary—first mainly Greek, then mainly Latin—in readable and affordable editions.[83] From his arrival in 1491 until his death in 1516, humanism in Venice centered about Aldo. In his shop worked a team of correctors and editors, nameless and illustrious, native and foreign. Around him and his assistants flocked the humanists of Venice, pedagogues and secretaries, university professors and physicians, young or leisured noblemen. Their skills, their libraries, their learned conversation all served as a resource for the printer. Thus not only a businessman but an intellectual himself, Aldo forged a program valid in its goals and far-reaching in its effects.

Despite the presence of some patricians in the Aldine circle, and the funding or business involvement of others, most of Aldo's associates were commoners.[84] They continued the philological tendency within

[82] For the Venetian press in this period, see the following in addition to sources cited above, n. 68: C. Dionisotti, "Aldo Manuzio umanista"; P. F. Grendler, The Roman Inquisition and the Venetian Press; Lowry, "The 'New Academy' of Aldus Manutius: A Renaissance Dream"; and Lowry, "Two Great Venetian Libraries." The materials on Manuzio are vast; the works of Dionisotti and Lowry provide guidance.

[83] Aldo's Greek focus was intentional and was his own, but it was certainly facilitated by the abundance of Greek texts in Venice and by the city's tradition of Greek scholarship. V. Branca demonstrates a relation between Ermolao Barbaro G's Greek scholarship and Aldo's: "L'umanesimo veneziano," pp. 156-57. For Greek learning in Venice, see A. Pertusi, "L'umanesimo greco," which updates and corrects D. Geanakoplos' Greek Scholars in Venice. In his focus on immigrant scholars of the late fifteenth century, Geanakoplos may undervalue earlier stages of the development of Greek erudition and the role played by native scholars.

[84] For its beginnings, as has been repeatedly demonstrated, Venetian humanism was a complex movement involving different cultural tendencies, usually related to the social position of the participants simultaneously in play. By the late fifteenth and sixteenth centuries, the humanist culture of commoners and patricians became notably distinct, even though the two tendencies naturally overlapped. For perceptive studies from different vantage points of this diversity in humanist culture, see especially Gilbert, "Biondo, Sabellico," and Lowry, "Two Great Venetian Libraries." O. Logan also re-

Venetian humanism, given impetus in the previous generation, especially by Giorgio Merula and Giorgio Valla, the younger Ermolao Barbaro and Girolamo Donato. At the same time, they continued to perform the useful functions performed everywhere by humanists in the employ of the wealthy and powerful. They delivered orations as required, wrote elegant letters, composed testimonies to the greatness of patrician patrons or their ancestors, and taught patrician sons. These were the most active humanists in the decades following 1490, competing for position, thronging the printing houses, contending with each other in oral disputation and angry print, seeking patrons. But at its heart, their humanist culture had become narrow and technical, concerned with the bare mechanism of language at the very time when Aldo nurtured hopes of the liberating power of the pure word.[85]

Meanwhile, patrician humanists, often of less illustrious family or lesser wealth than their mid-fifteenth century predecessors, tended to take spectator roles. They gathered for intellectual conversation in their palaces and, after a while, at their quiet terraferma villas. They spoke not only about the classics central to humanism, but about philosophy (its companion in Venice) and mathematics, science and medicine, and law. In these matters, their approach was less literary than encyclopedic. They were an audience for the flourishing Venetian press, and to some extent supported more directly the work of the printers. They collected manuscripts and printed books reflecting their broad interests. In addition, they collected antiquities—works of art, coins, and medals surviving from a distant past. At the same time, they patronized the writers and artists of their generation. These activities created in Venice an openness to humanistic, literary, scientific, and artistic expression. But they reflected rather than forged the diverse aspects of an intellectual heritage and of ongoing intellectual life. Such cultural activities, too broad and unfocused to be genuinely productive, became an adornment of the life of wealthy patricians, not a vehicle, as in the Quattrocento, for the expression of a recently formed and powerful self-consciousness.[86]

---

marks on the difference in the culture of the plebeian and patrician humanists: *Culture and Society*, p. 90.

[85] Typical of these humanists were such figures as Giovanni Battista Egnazio, Vettore Fausto, Marco Musuro, Giovanni Battista Ramusio, and Raffaele Regio; for these see Part II, Preface, Section 10. Particularly vivid images of their struggle to gain and keep positions are offered by A. Medin, "Raffaele Regio a Venezia, epigrammi per la sua morte," and J. B. Ross (dealing with Egnazio), "Venetian Schools," pp. 536-56.

[86] For the humanist culture of the patricians, see especially Logan, *Culture and Society*, Chapter Five and Eight. Logan notes a tendency in their activities toward "unreflective erudition" (p. 90), a "compendious accumulation of knowledge devoid of ultimate philosophical or ethical purpose," an atmosphere of "intellectual caution" in which

That strong sense of self in commitment to a class that had claimed
the helm of the city seems to have weakened by the late fifteenth
century. The previous generation had produced in Ermolao Barbaro
the Younger a brilliant but fatefully irresponsible humanist. After
1490, the figure of the nobleman seeking refuge from public responsibility becomes increasingly common. Escape could be found in the
Church, in leisure, and in the self. At least some of the disenchanted
noblemen of the early sixteenth century shed the "awesome discipline"
of their class to find freedom in the inner life: in the monastery, in
contemplation, in communion with God sealed by the assurance of
salvation. Piety had always thrived among the Venetian patriciate. But
here that piety deepened, inspiring not only the observance of traditional rituals and the veneration of saints and charismatic holy men,
but also the search for a spiritual home within newly receptive souls.[87]

"while enquiry was restricted, erudition boomed" (p. 88). I concur in his judgments.
But where he ascribes these tendencies to the ethos of the Counter-Reformation, which
inhibited "the development of an ideology out of classical humanism," I would like to
point also to the long history of Venetian humanism reviewed in the preceding pages.
For an older but similar vision of intellectual life, primarily patrician and humanistic,
see P. Molmenti, *La storia di Venezia nella vita privata* [Molmenti, *Vita privata*], II,
Lo splendore, Chapter Seven and Eight, treating subjects he also deals with in a series
of articles. For the *convegni* and academies, see P. L. Rose, "The Accademia Venetiana."
For the scientific orientation of patrician culture, see additionally Rose, "Bartolomeo
Zamberti's Funeral Oration" and "Humanist Culture and Renaissance Mathematics,"
and R. Massalongo, "Alessandro Benedetti e la medicina veneta del Quattrocento."
G. Cozzi sketches one member of this late patrician humanist culture in "Federico
Contarini, un antiquario veneziano tra Rinascimento e Controriforma."
   [87] Vincenzo (Pietro) Quirini and Tommaso (Paolo) Giustiniani, young and learned
patricians, sought religious solitude. Gasparo Contarini, the giant of this generation,
thought tempted to follow the example of his friends, stayed in the world first as layman,
then as a religious, having first explored deeply his own relation to God. Pietro Bembo,
the central figure of Venice's literary movement in the early sixteenth century, became
a cleric without experiencing any spiritual conversion, and avoided Venice and her
demands as much as possible. For guidance to the literature on Bembo, see C. Dionisotti
in DBI, VIII; for that on Contarini and his circle, Ross, "The Emergence of Gasparo
Contarini"; Ross, "Gasparo Contarini and His Friends"; S. Tramontin, "Cultura monastica," pp. 453ff. Ross ("The Emergence") has noted a common tendency in these
patrician circles to reject public and social obligations. For Contarini in particular, see
also G. Fragnito, "Cultura umanistica e riforma religiosa"; F. Gaeta, "Sul 'de potestate
pontificis' di Gasparo Contarini"; the several studies by F. Gilbert: "Contarini on
Savonarola," "Cristianesimo, umanesimo e la bolla 'Apostolici Regiminis' del 1513,"
"The Date of the Composition of Contarini's and Giannotti's Books on Venice," and
"Religion and Politics in the Thought of Gasparo Contarini"; by H. Jedin, especially
"Contarini and Camaldoli," "Gasparo Contarini e il contributo veneziano alla riforma
cattolica," and "Ein 'Turmerlebnis' des jungen Contarini." The experience of some of
these young patricians may be related to a peculiarly Venetian spirituality, as some
scholars have argued; see, for instance, I. Cervelli, "Storiografia e problemi intorno alla
vita religiosa e spirituale a Venezia"; R. Cessi, "Paolinismo preluterano"; E. Pommier,
"La société vénitienne et la réforme protestante au XVIᵉ siècle." See also P. Grendler's
challenge to W. Bouwsma's image of "Venetian evangelism" in his *Roman Inquisition*,

CHOICES: *MOENIA CIVITATIS*

Amid these tendencies toward absorption in the self, rejection of social responsibilities, display of wealth in patronage and acquisition, dilettantism and unfocused eclecticism, the patrician humanism that had been born in the Quattrocento foundered. Yet it survived. The social and political pressures that may have triggered demoralization or tense interiority on the one hand, fostered on the other, particularly in the wake of the War of the League of Cambrai, a reassertion of patrician discipline and a renewed self-consciousness within some circles of patricians. The fifteenth-century tradition of patrician humanism flourished in this moral climate, and found such famous sixteenth-century spokesmen, both laymen and clerics, as Gasparo Contarini, Daniele Barbaro, Agostino Valier, Paolo Paruta, and Niccolò Contarini. Among these and other patricians who participated actively and significantly in humanist culture, enthusiasm waned for the classics and the rhetorical dimension of humanism (which had not since the first generation of fifteenth-century figures been a principal, and never a paramount concern of the Venetian form of the movement). The philosophical and religious concerns, however, so typical of Venetian humanism in the fifteenth century were also central in the sixteenth. Aristotelian philosophy still provided a metaphysical framework for these thinkers, not relinquished even when Platonic outlooks became popular, as well. The contemplative ideal was still cherished, even by those who were themselves to lead very active lives. Commitment to the Church and to established religion was still strong. Personal religious experience was expressed, as before, in prose and verse. As then, humanist outlooks were formed and expressed within a context of profound allegiance to inherited Christian and academic traditions.[88]

---

pp. 26-27 n. 4. Despite Grendler's cautions, there does appear to be a strong current of Venetian spirituality, a blend of inner piety and external orthodoxy, evident in pious literature and the work of religious reformers from the Trecento at least through the late years of the republic; for the later period, see A. Vecchi, *Correnti religiose nel Sei-Settecento veneto.* The Quattrocento humanists shared in it.

[88] For the philosophical and religious concerns of these figures and the sixteenth-century Venetian resolution of the dilemma of the competing claims of the active and contemplative life, see Logan, *Culture and Society,* Chapter Four. Excellent portraits of particular figures in whom religious, philosophical, political, and social concerns intermingle without apparent contradiction (in a manner found here to be characteristically Venetian and prepared for by the experience of Quattrocento humanism) are provided by Gilbert, "Religion and Politics"; P. Paschini, "Daniele Barbaro, letterato e prelato veneziano nel Cinquecento," and "Gli scritti religiosi di Daniele Barbaro"; A. Tenenti, "Il 'De perfectione rerum' di Nicolò Contarini." Bouwsma finds the mix of philosophical abstraction and political analysis in Gasparo Contarini "slightly jarring," and deplores that author's "weak excursions into systematic thought" (*Venice,* p. 147). That mixture of perspectives, however, may be no eccentricity of Contarini's, but an

At the same time (and as in the previous century, once again) these patrician humanists were concerned in their works with the life and history of their city. History became the special province of the patricians as commoner humanists tended more intently to philological tasks. The position of official historiographer, created early in the sixteenth century, was held in these years by a series of patrician writers whose outlook on the past became increasingly rational and critical. History would become during the century a practical tool for policy makers rather than an opportunity for the rhetorical celebration of the past. Political analysis evolved in the same way.[89] Despite the more rational description of past and present politics in humanist works, however, the task of celebration was not abandoned. For this was, indeed, the great age of the Venetian myth. Enshrined in some of the most interesting works of the century were the notions that had roots in the Middle Ages and that were first wedded to humanism by Quattrocento authors: the eternity of Venice, the perfect balance of her governmental system, her historic commitment to liberty, the harmonious cooperation of her social classes encouraged by a just distribution of duties and rewards, her benevolent doge subject to law, her nobility's selfless devotion to the common welfare. These notions traveled far in the sixteenth century, no longer addressed by Venetians primarily to each other in reinforcement of common values, but more to the outside world, which was eager to hear of them.[90]

Thus patrician humanism survived into the sixteenth century, marked by its peculiarly Venetian balance of universal vision and local civic responsibility, and by its expression of the themes of *unanimitas* fundamental to the city's myth. Yet it constituted but one tendency of sixteenth-century humanism, which included, as well, the technical and routinized culture of the philologists and encyclopedists, the mediocre classicism of teachers and secretaries, the book talk and trading

---

established tradition in Venetian thought. The interpolation of religious concerns in intellectual life may also have been further encouraged in the sixteenth century by the increased participation of clerics in intellectual life; see C. Dionisotti, "Chierici e laici nella letteratura italiana del primo Cinquecento." Of the figures named, for example, the first three were clerics for at least part of their careers.

[89] For discussions of the development of historiography and political writing in the sixteenth century, see especially the works of Gilbert: "Biondo, Sabellico," "The Date of the Composition of Contarini's and Giannotti's Books on Venice," and "Venetian Diplomacy before Pavia." Also Logan (*Culture and Society*, pp. 57ff.) distinguishes between the "starkly factual history" written by statesmen and the moralistic, perhaps regressive, historiography of more humanistically oriented writers. See also G. Cozzi, *Il doge Nicolò Contarini*, Chapter Two and Five; the studies cited in the profile of M. A. Sabellico; and the prefaces of Apostolo Zeno to the various histories in his edition of *Istorici*.

[90] The myth of Venice again; for which see Chapter Two, n. 231.

generated by the presses. And it constituted but one strand of Venice's intellectual culture in this century, and neither the primary nor most characteristic one. For the foci of Venice's culture in the sixteenth century, and perhaps the true glories of her Renaissance, were not in humanism at all, but in vernacular literature and the arts.[91]

Under the leadership of the patrician Pietro Bembo, Venetian authors, mostly commoners, many foreign by origin, in large measure shed the armor of Latin that had cooled and controlled poetic and prose expression. They shed at the same time other restraints operative in Quattrocento humanism. The sensuality prohibited by humanist arbiters of taste exploded into view. A diversity of themes and sentiments appeared that had not been possible within the contours of humanist culture neatly dictated by the assumptions of scholastic philosophy and Christian orthodoxy. A critical voice, which the Latin prose of the humanists had stifled, became audible. In a parallel development, the visual arts at about this time abandoned the conservative canons of form followed strictly during most of the fifteenth century and embraced the language of color. With that revolution, a whole new expressive range of softness, sensuality, and drama became available. In literature and the arts, in contrast to the Quattrocento culture integrated by patrician humanists, a new stage of Venetian culture emerged: the first sternly moralistic, the second sensual; the first rational, the second emotive; the first focused on the political arena, aiming mainly to instruct and to command, the second adrift from that arena, aiming mainly to please and intrigue. Though much of the fifteenth-century tradition was inherited by the culture of the sixteenth, the balance had shifted. A cultural choice had once again been made.

Oddly, though, there was still no place for the strong and self-sufficient individual in the new Venetian culture that began to form in the years following 1490. The Quattrocento ideal of *unanimitas* yielded in the new age to whim and self-indulgence without a pause for the discovery of the dignity of man. The Venetian Renaissance bequeathes to the proud heroes of the modern world no ancestral model.

[91] For this judgment, see especially Dionisotti's three studies, "Il Fortunio e la filologia umanistica," "Niccolò Liburnio e la letteratura cortigiana," and "Pietro Bembo e la nuova letteratura"; W. T. Elwert, "Pietro Bembo e la vita letteraria del suo tempo" and *Studi di letteratura veneziana*; three works by P. F. Grendler: *Critics of the Italian World, 1530-1560*, "Francesco Sansovino and Italian Popular History, 1560-1600," and *Roman Inquisition*; and Logan, *Culture and Society*, Chapter Six.

7. CONCLUSIONS

Venetian humanism in the period 1400 to 1490 was essentially ideological. It was conspicuously stamped by the values, the perspectives, the concerns of that cohesive class which played so large a role within it. This contention is grounded in the evidence presented in previous chapters and in Part II. Chapter One has shown that the relations among the humanists, even those directly pertaining to intellectual life, were at all levels deeply colored by social origin and position. Chapter Two has shown that an ideal of *unanimitas*, expressed in a variety of related motifs, was fundamental to much of humanist production in Venice, and that it was an ideal profoundly in accord with the city's inherited culture and values and with the interests of the ruling class. Part II (in the profiles and analytical preface) demonstrates the numerical and social dominance of patricians among the Venetian humanists.

This chapter has traced the process by which patricians placed their seal upon humanist culture and subsequently—though the stamp remained indelible—receded, along with humanism itself, from center stage. Patrician humanism emerged from a fortuitous confluence in the late Trecento and early Quattrocento of three major developments. One was the maturation of the patriciate as a class, entailing the creation within it of a narrow elite with privileged access to power. A second, following soon upon the first, was the embarkation on a program of terraferma expansion under the leadership of that elite. A third development, simultaneous with these social and political processes, was the availability to that elite, through the agency of resident teachers and publicly employed scribes, of the knowledge and perspectives basic to humanism. A ruling class that wished to defend its policy, affirm a self-image of sobriety, benevolence, and prudence, and thereby command the allegiance of the population at large, found in humanism an adequate means to do so.

Patricians appropriated the leadership of humanist culture—a first cultural choice—about the turn of the fifteenth century. A first generation of humanists, patrician and commoner, absorbed the classical tradition thirstily, while a few among them began to shape the new learning to accord to the values and traditions of their city and its ruling class. A second generation, fully equipped with a humanist education, actively defended Venetian policies and principles. A third generation continued that mission, while a new fascination developed, particularly among commoners, and encouraged by the new industry of printing, with the philological dimension of humanism. In the last years of the fifteenth century and early years of the sixteenth, finally, while this humanism of earlier generations survived, patricians became relatively less important within humanism, and humanism itself played a smaller role in Venetian culture. The effects of this shift of equilibrium, constituting a second cultural choice, were already evident in the years following 1490 in the activities of Aldo's printing shop (a magnet for diverse intellectual energies), in vernacular literature, and in the visual arts. Such developments were notably free of the sober discipline of the ideal of *unanimitas*. Though they did not challenge patrician cultural hegemony, neither did they, as had the humanism of the Quattrocento, directly promote it.

By the turn of the sixteenth century, the circumstances that had encouraged the development of patrician humanism no longer existed or interacted as they had at the turn of the fifteenth. The patrician role in society was long established, mainland involvement was an old story, and the humanist education of members of the aristocracy was routine. Meanwhile, the threat to Venice's power at sea, and the history of mainland affairs leading up to the war of the League of Cambrai were demoralizing to a patriciate disrupted from within, as well, by the pressure of its own expanding numbers. As demoralization and disunity grew, discipline relaxed. The task of defending patrician policy and shaping civic consciousness was left to those humanists who wished to assume it, and did so admirably. And it was performed, and perhaps more effectively, by other media: by the ritual processions that frequently filled the piazza, and in the broad canvasses that displayed in form and color the myth of Venice, and compelled belief.[92]

This interpretation of the evolution of humanism in Venice has embraced the whole of intellectual culture and at times the whole of Venetian life. It has not argued that Venetian humanism mimicked humanism elsewhere, but that a particular society will generate a characteristic form of any intellectual movement. It has not assumed *a priori* that a few well-known figures are "typical" or "representative" of Venetian humanism, but has spoken of ninety-two concrete personalities named by plausible guidelines as members of the humanist circle. It has not simply asserted that social origin affected the behavior and production of intellectuals engaged in humanism, but has pointed to documented cases of such influence. It has not put faith in conclusions drawn from the reading of a few works but has tested them in many drawn from the whole of humanist production. It has not rashly claimed novelty or singularity for Quattrocento humanism, but has

---

[92] See Muir, *Civic Ritual*; in shorter compass, his "Images of Power."

been alert to Trecento origins and Cinquecento departures. Finally, it has eyed the social environment of humanism, seeking not immediate causal links between society and expression so much as the slow and intricate molding of that expression through interaction with a series of conditions and events. It has located the distinctiveness of Venetian humanism in the distinctive social organization of the humanists, the filter through which the perspectives and interests of the city's ruling elite converged with the ideas articulated in humanist works. Such an explanation seems better to accord with the known phenomena of Venetian culture than one keyed to bright moments of political or military crisis or simple vectors of economic interest. It also seems more successful than would be the attempt to account for those phenomena by the strict attention to the transmission and elaboration of ideas apart from social context. Indeed, the history of Venetian humanism makes hardly any sense at all when viewed as a problem of purely intellectual type.[93]

In this resistance of the phenomena of Venetian humanism to an explanation independent of societal context consists a reminder to scholars—if another reminder were still required—of the need everywhere to examine the experience of humanism from the perspective of society. A rich man is not a poor man, a young man not an old one, a native not a foreigner, a ruler not a subject, a woman not a man, a Venetian not a Florentine. Though the humanists shared a common educational program and a preference for the models of classical antiquity, they were a remarkably diverse group. A different constellation—a shifting one at that—is found in each center. Venetian humanism, therefore, distinctive precisely because of the role played by patricians within it, contrasts variously with the humanism of other Italian cities.[94] It is less purely literary, for instance, than the humanism

[93] Gilbert ("Humanism in Venice," p. 19) has called for a large study that takes into account the social context of Venetian humanism. In attending to that matter, I also find myself in accord with current tendencies in intellectual history; see, for instance, R. Darnton, "Intellectual and Cultural History," and P. Burke, "Back to Burckhardt." Many recent works on the history of the Renaissance link culture and society, among them H. Baron, Crisis of the Early Italian Renaissance; C. Bec, Marchands écrivains; P. Burke, Culture and Society in Italy, 1420-1540; Hyde, Padua; Logan, Culture and Society; Martines, The Social World of the Florentine Humanists; and Martines, Power and Imagination (especially Chapter Eleven for the relationship of humanism to the culture of Italy's ruling classes). See also titles cited in next note.

[94] For a survey of humanism in various settings, see F. Tateo, La cultura umanistica e is suoi centri; still necessary are the classic works of Monnier, Rossi, and Voigt. Martines' recent overview is sensitive to the differences in cultural style that emerge in different settings: see his Power and Imagination, Chapter Eleven. Some studies have focused on particular centers: for Rome, see J. F. d'Amico, Renaissance Humanism in Papal Rome, E. Lee, Sixtus IV and Men of Letters, Rome, and J. W. O'Malley, Praise

of Rome, where a series of popes encouraged the reading, translation, and diffusion of the works of classical antiquity. It was less purely literary, also, than the humanism of those courts—Milan and Naples, Ferrara and Urbino, among others—where the creation of elegant works by courtier intellectuals was considered an appropriate celebration of a monarch's glory. It was more aggressive in the defense of intellectual traditions and civic values than the humanism of Veneto cities—Verona, Vicenza, Padua—even though in those centers members of the magisterial class, as in Venice itself, were active as humanists. It was less fluid, less imaginative, less original than the humanism of Florence. That city's patriciate was dynamic and fluid, both in composition and outlook. Faction-ridden and accustomed to commercial ventures more turbulent than those undertaken by Venetian merchant-nobles, Florentine patricians contributed to the formation of a consciousness more open than others to new percepts.[95] Florence's particular social history permitted humanism to reach there in the Quattrocento more than in any other single setting its classic and perhaps most genuine expression.

The uniqueness of Venice's social experience encouraged the development of the unique humanist culture that has been judged by many modern scholars as, at one level at least, a failure. Venice had a head start in the fourteenth century, as J. K. Hyde points out. With Venice's greater closeness to the monuments of antiquity, it is puzzling that Florence was able to annihilate its lead. Venice failed to develop, Lino Lazzarini remarked, even granted so dynamic a figure as Francesco Barbaro, a humanist culture comparable to its political greatness. Undaunted, likewise, by the extraordinary image of Leonardo Giustiniani, Aldo Oberdorfer judged the output of Venetian humanism to

---

and Blame in Renaissance Rome; for Milan, E. Garin, "La cultura milanese nella prima metà del XV secolo," and "La cultura milanese nella seconda metà del XV secolo." Florence has been studied even in general works, where Florentine humanists often take center stage; but see especially Bec, *Marchands écrivains*; A. Brown, *Bartolomeo Scala, 1430-97*; and Martines, *Social World*. The collection of essays on humanism edited by A. Rabil, Jr. (*Renaissance Humanism*, to be published by the University of Pennsylvania Press) will contain several on specific Italian centers (Florence, Milan, Naples, Rome, Venice).

[95] Martines' analysis in his *Social World*. For a portrait of the Florentine patriciate in the early fifteenth century, see G. Brucker, *The Civic World of Early Renaissance Florence*, Chapter Five, and for the relationship between the emergence of that patriciate and the development of humanism, his "Humanism, Politics and the Social Order in Early Renaissance Florence." For the social organization of humanism in Florence and the "merchant spirit" (Bec's phrase), see Bec, *Marchands écrivains*, and Martines, *Social World*. For older but broader speculations on the culture of the Florentine patriciate, see F. Antal, *Florentine Painting and Its Social Background*, and A. von Martin, *Sociology of the Renaissance*.

be insignificant. There was in Venice, Berthold Fenigstein observed in his work on the same patrician humanist and poet, no class of humanists who sought wisdom for its own sake. Georg Voigt had already noted, in his analysis comparing "Spartan" Venice to "Athenian" Florence, the absence of a class of litterati, the varied quality of the participation of patricians in humanism, the paralyzing effect of insecurity on non-Venetian participants. Philippe Monnier, also noting the major presence of patricians, characterized humanism in Venice as "luxury," an amusement for a leisured elite. Not only the patricians but even the citizen humanists of Venice, distracted by other occupations, according to Pier Georgio Ricci, were not fully devoted to studies, and thus produced a culture focused on practical matters, stressing technical skills.[96]

While Ricci saw political and other involvements as a distraction, Antonio Carile saw the solidity of political life, Venice's "politica culturale," as an impediment to the development of subtlety in historical writing. Guido Piovene observed, similarly, that the responsibilities to the state felt by patrician humanists discouraged free expression, inhibiting exploration of the "revolutionary potential" of the word. Manlio Pastore Stocchi, deploring the repressive effects of aristocratic interest upon the development of pedagogy not only in Venice but in the Veneto, pronounced that Venetian humanism was in fact excluded from the most brilliant achievements of contemporary Italian humanism. Without indicating the suffocating effect of Venice's "political culture," David Chambers remarked on the lack of a self-critical perspective in Venetian humanism. William Bouwsma linked the insufficiency of Quattrocento humanism to political life, but saw it as merely anachronistic, not fateful; in the next century, inspired by an experience of crisis to a renewed appreciation of its own liberty, Venice would produce a full-blown Renaissance humanism. Carlo Dionisotti, viewing the lush terrain of sixteenth-century Venetian literature, dismissed the preceding Latin culture of humanism as uncreative. Hubert Jedin diagnosed the lack of some vital quality, a "spiritual abstinence," as lying at the root of Venice's ceding leadership in humanist culture to Florence and Rome. More practically, Agostino Valier—not a modern, but the sixteenth-century heir of Quattrocento humanism—tactfully but pointedly observed that too exclusive a concern with pre-

[96] Hyde, review of L. Gargan, *Cultura e arte*, p. 96; Lazzarini, "Un libro su Francesco Barbaro," p. 97; Oberdorfer, "Di Leonardo Giustiniani umanista," p. 109; Fenigstein, *Leonardo Giustiniani*, p. 29; Voigt, *Risorgimento*, I, 410-11; Monnier, *Le Quattrocento* I, 168; Ricci, "Umanesimo filologico in Toscana e nel Veneto," pp. 161ff.

serving the learning of the past might discourage the formation of new perceptions.[97]

It is perplexing, indeed, that Venetian humanism is found to be by so many sound judges hollow at the core, even though humanism undoubtedly flourished there, scholars flocked there, and some men of vision or sensitivity or commitment to learning wrote there. Responsibility for the failure of Venetian humanism—if it was failure— must be laid at the door of the same patricians whose involvement lent it peculiar flavor. Their object, unknowingly, was control, not creation. They controlled intellectual life, permitting intellectuals not of their class to participate in some roles, not others, encouraging the expression of some ideas, discouraging others. Their intent is deduced from, as their success is evident in, the negatives of Venetian culture: the insufficiency of native intellectuals, particularly teachers, merchants, amateurs, and lawyers; the rapid circulation of commoner intellectuals as natives emigrated or foreign transients departed without becoming resident; the absence of a critical literature or an ideal of individualism; the reluctance to shed traditional modes of thought. Patrician humanists aimed, as well, at self-control, the discipline of their class. In their treatises, letters, and orations they described the ideal of the aristocrat. That ideal insisted that, unmoved by personal passions (which a humanist education was meant to suppress), they subordinate themselves to their family, their city, to history, to nature, to God. And patrician humanists aimed at social control. By describing Venice as having already achieved perfection, they forestalled unrest. If Venetian humanism lacked vitality and luster, it lacked these shining qualities not because of poverty of mind or exhaustion of energy: both mental acuity and well-focused energy were required to accomplish these tasks of cultural control. It lacked them because the patrician intellectuals who led the humanist movement—in yet another cultural choice—served the interests of their class and not of mind.

Having done so, they are recognized as distant from the modern type of the intellectual whose perspective is essentially critical. Intellectuals of any age or place have, perhaps, two tasks. The first is the transmission of inherited knowledge. The second (as the consequence

---

[97] Carile, "Aspetti della cronachista veneziana," p. 118; C. Piovene, "L'anacronismo della Venezia quattrocentesca," pp. 9-10; Pastore Stocchi, "Scuola e cultura," p. 121 and passim; Chambers, *The Imperial Age of Venice*, p. 154; Bouwsma, *Venice*, especially Chapter Two; Dionisotti, "Niccolò Liburnio," pp. 30-36; Jedin, "Gasparo Contarini," p. 105; Agostino Valier, *Epistola ad Philippum Mocenicum, Cypri archiepiscopum*, p. 280. Gilbert reports similar comments of Burckhardt and the Trecento notary Paolo de Bernardo in his "Humanism in Venice," p. 13. For Vergerio's assessment, see above, n. 46.

of their fundamental commitment to a realm of values that transcends their own time and culture, a loyalty, in effect, to the sacred as they perceive it) is the advancement of knowledge. In performing the first task, they affirm their culture's values and support the political authority characteristic of their society. In performing the second, they challenge that authority. Intellectuals thus stand in some tension with regard to authority, the more so the more their commitment to an absolute standard of truth compels the modification of received tradition. The creation of new perceptions may require, therefore, a group of intellectuals ready to pursue that commitment and free to challenge that authority—a group who are to some degree "classless." Though they have originated in one class, and identify their interests more or less consciously with the same or another class, yet they float, not firmly anchored in society, because of their commitment to extra-social truth.[98]

Such a "classless" intelligentsia—which may nowhere exist—is most likely to be found in Western European society in recent centuries. Here publishers, academies, and foundations have permitted intellectuals to support themselves and not to depend directly on the patronage of those having a deep stake in the social system. Such independence was not accessible to the intellectuals of early modern Europe or Renaissance Italy. Yet, even in these eras, adequate freedom existed for the exploration of ideas. Though the professional humanists of the Renaissance tended to depend on the oligarchs, aristocrats, monarchs who paid them, the genuinely original and significant ideas to emerge from the humanist movement cannot all be dismissed as mirroring the interests of the powerful. They may have done so, and yet still possess a deeper and enduring importance.[99] In Venice, however, the society of humanists poses a near antithesis to a modern intelligentsia. Far

[98] For this understanding of the role of intellectuals, I rely primarily upon E. Shils' articles: "Intellectuals" in the *International Encyclopedia of the Social Sciences*, "The Intellectuals and the Powers," and "The Traditions of Intellectuals." For similar understandings of the intellectual as having an essentially critical perspective, and as possessing a primary commitment to the realm of knowledge rather than to society, see also L. A. Coser, *Men of Ideas*; R. Dahrendorf, "The Intellectual and Society," T. Parsons, "The Intellectual"; and F. Znaniecki, *The Social Role of the Man of Knowledge*. For an understanding of intellectuals as forming a relatively classless group, see esp. K Mannheim, *Ideology and Utopia* and "The Sociological Problem of the 'Intelligentsia' "; also J. Schumpeter, "The Sociology of the Intellectuals." An interpretation at odds with all cited is in A. W. Gouldner, *The Future of Intellectuals and the Rise of the New Class*.

[99] Martines in his *Power and Imagination* tends, in my view, to undervalue the independence of the idea of tradition at the same time that he so valuably points out the close relations of Renaissance humanism to the interests and outlook of ruling classes.

from being classless, that humanist group was penetrated by the ruling class so deeply as to assure the absolute hegemony of that class in the realm of culture. Innovation would be admitted only insofar as it enhanced the power of the ruler over the ruled. Commitment to the sacred yielded to a commitment to another ideal: that of a harmonious society contentedly ordered under aristocratic rule.

Venetian humanists recognized that commitment and honored it diligently. Intercepting the new learning before its explosive potentiality could be explored or expressed, attaching it sturdily to honored intellectual traditions, to long-established social values, to the interest of the ruling class, they fostered the perpetuation of a benign, if stratified, society. This was their principal accomplishment, and it was an admirable one. They forged a culture efficiently in the service of their community: what an achievement! There is a cost in originality, in spontaneity, and in freedom; there is a benefit in solidarity, in comprehensiveness, in security. The Venetian humanists acted as the strong and trustworthy walls of their city, defending it from the ethereal dangers that waited without, and the potential for danger that hid, menacing, within.

Part Two

The Venetian Humanist Circle (1400-1490):
Definition of the Core Group

WHO WERE the Venetian humanists? If they had known who they were themselves, or had enrolled in a humanist society and properly paid their dues, author and reader would have been spared the heavy chain of reasoning that follows.

They did not know who they were. They did not constitute a professional group. Though numerous, they must be searched for, certified, and entered into our rolls, for they had none. And our rolls will not be complete or defensible at every point, but provisional. They will provide an approximation of the group of Venetian humanists active in the first nine decades of the fifteenth century. They define a core group of figures, selected from a much larger pool of candidates according to four criteria (which will be described after the discussion of sources immediately following).[1]

1. DEFINITION OF THE CORE GROUP: SOURCES

The definition of a core group of fifteenth-century Venetian humanists has required the examination of a literature that is vast but various, disorganized, and at times difficult of access.

Numerous monographs have been devoted to individual figures, both Venetian and foreign, members of the city's humanist circle or related to it. These include full-scale biographies like those of Percy Gothein and Patricia Labalme. And they include smaller but indispensable studies like those published over the last century by Ludwig Bertalot, Vittore Branca, Roberto Cessi, Paul Oskar Kristeller, Remigio Sabbadini, Giuseppe dalla Santa, and Arnaldo Segarizzi, among others; or recently by Daniela de Bellis, Paola Rigo, Gilbert Tournoy, or by the junior and senior collaborators on *Lauro Quirini umanista*. They swell the bibliography of this work. They often not only portray ex-

---

[1] Members of the core group are listed in full in Table 7, having been presented successively as subgroups in preceding tables. Bio-bibliographical profiles for each core group member follow this discussion and are the basis for the summary tables and analysis given here. Please refer to these profiles for documentation of career events wherever a core group member is named.

haustively one central figure concerned, but also provide important and discrete data about others with whom that central personality was in communication. This large body of monographs—which do not constitute even in their sum a full study of Venetian humanist culture—has opened many roads toward the understanding of that phenomenon.[2]

Standard references and general works (including contemporary chronicles and diaries) have provided additional information about the careers and works of individual figures, including those who have not yet claimed the attention of scholars for the purpose of a monographic study.

Among these are studies of Venetian literature and life (G. degli Agostini, *Notizie*; E. A. Cicogna, *Delle iscrizioni veneziane*; M. Foscarini, *Letteratura veneziana*); of Italian literature and history (G. Tiraboschi, *Storia della letteratura italiana*; A. Zeno, *Dissertazioni vossiane*); of Renaissance humanism (M. E. Cosenza, *Dictionary*; E. Garin, *Italian Humanism* and *Letteratura degli umanisti*; P. Monnier, *Le Quattrocento*; V. Rossi, *Il Quattrocento*; G. Voigt, *Risorgimento*). General but invaluable is the *Dizionario biografico degli italiani* [DBI], still in progress.[3] Of the many manuscript catalogues consulted in a search for works by our humanists, three in particular have been invaluable sources: the handwritten catalogue of Latin manuscripts (four volumes and two index volumes) of the Biblioteca Nazionale Marciana; P. O. Kristeller's *Iter Italicum*, which has made the uncatalogued manuscripts of European humanism more accessible than those previously catalogued; and G. Valentinelli's *Bibliotheca manuscripta*.[4] Useful for occasional details about particular individuals

---

[2] P. Gothein, *Francesco Barbaro (1390-1454)*; P. H. Labalme, *Bernardo Giustiniani*; D. de' Bellis, "La vita e l'ambiente di Niccolò Leonico Tomeo"; P. Rigo, "Per il carteggio di Girolamo Donato" and "Catalogo e tradizione degli scritti di Girolamo Donato"; G. Tournoy, "Francesco Diedo, Venetian Humanist and Politician of the Quattrocento." There are several titles each by Bertalot, Cessi, Kristeller, Sabbadini, dalla Santa, and Segarizzi: see Bibliography. LQU includes major works by Quirini with valuable introductory essays by the editors. Recall also the general studies of humanism listed in Introduction, n. 4.

[3] G. M. Mazzuchelli's *Gli scrittori d'Italia*, which proceeds no further than the letter "B," is less useful than those named. In the profiles, the standard and reference works named in these pages will be cited by author's name and short title or abbreviation (as indicated in brackets following the full title given in the Bibliography and listed in the Table of Abbreviations). P. O. Kristeller informs me that he learned from Dott.a Paola Rigo that valuable Agostini papers, including much material not included in his *Notizie*, and copies of works which may otherwise not be extant, are found in the library of the Museo Correr in Venice (mss. P. D. 792C-805C). I have not been able to see this source.

[4] For the Marciana manuscript catalogue (*Appendice, Codici Latini*) located in that library's *Sala di consultazione* and its relations to other catalogues, cf. P. O. Kristeller,

have been the modern histories of S. Romanin (*Storia documentata*, volumes IV and V), E. Musatti, *Storia di Venezia*, and P. Molmenti (*Vita privata*, II: *Lo splendore*) and contemporary or older sources by Domenico Malipiero (*Annali veneti*), F. Sansovino (*Venetia città nobilissima*), and Marino Sanuto (*Diarii*). Less useful are the contemporary histories of Marcantonio Sabellico, Pietro Bembo (*Historia veneta libri XII*), and Andrea Navagero (*Historia veneta ab origine urbis usque ad annum 1498*).

Works by the humanists themselves (Venetians and related foreigners)—examined, of cource, in their own right as objects of this study—have also proved a rich mine of information about our circle. The letters of Francesco Barbaro, Ludovico Foscarini, and Bernardo Giustiniani, among the Venetians, for instance, and those of Francesco Filelfo and Guarino Veronese, among the foreigners, have greatly illuminated the nature of the social relations among the humanists. An added benefit, in the case of modern editions, is the critical apparatus, such as R. Sabbadini provides for Barbaro's *Centotrenta lettere inedite* or for the *Epistolario di Guarino Veronese*.

Documents, finally, some published but most unpublished and in repository at the Archivio di Stato in Venice, have yielded information about the careers, especially of patrician humanists, not elsewhere available. More will be said about these later.

Investigation of these sources has yielded the names—without exaggeration—of hundreds of figures involved in the intellectual life of Venice in the fifteenth century: philosophers, theologians, lawyers, and humanists; patrons, dilettantes, and amateurs; citizens and other natives, visiting and resident foreigners. The following criteria have been devised to select a core group from this plethora so that meaningful analysis could be undertaken.

2. THE CRITERION OF ACTIVITY

The figures admitted to the core group were, above all, humanists: students and lovers of the *studia humanitatis*, a program of studies including grammar, rhetoric, history, moral philosophy, and poetry. Evolved from medieval intellectual traditions, this program represented a departure from the organization of knowledge usual in the Middle Ages. It both was stimulated by and furthered the ongoing exploration of the classical tradition, both Greek and Latin. It gave

---

Latin Manuscript Books before 1600, pp. 214-16. Kristeller's *Iter* is frequently cited in these pages, but not so often as it was actually used. I have indicated the catalogue—usually the *Iter*—by which I was guided to the manuscript works cited in the profiles that follow *only* when I have not actually seen the texts themselves.

rise quite naturally to outlooks and emphases different from those familiar in medieval culture, but generated no canon of beliefs or perceptions that scholars have satisfactorily defined as essentially humanistic.

Humanists in Venice, as elsewhere, wrote works (primarily Latin) in several genres that were the suitable vehicles of their main intellectual concerns. They wrote treatises and dialogues, forms permitting the free discussion—as opposed to the systematic discourse typical of scholastic writing—of moral, historical, and aesthetic issues, among others not easily classified. They wrote histories of great cities and biographies of great men. They wrote letters, often intended for formal publication in collections, dealing with these issues as well as with familiar or occasional matters. They wrote and delivered orations to honor dignitaries, to urge political or military action, to celebrate marriages, to commend academic achievement, to praise the dead. They wrote poems on all of these subjects. They taught the *studia humanitatis*, and composed the books that were their tools: grammars (Greek and Latin), lexicons, manuals of rhetoric. They sought out, collected, borrowed, lent, and read the classical texts—first in manuscript, later in printed versions—upon which the *studia humanitatis* were based. They translated Greek into Latin, Latin into Italian, and Italian into Latin, gaining new audiences for important or beloved books. They purged, annotated, glossed, and published ancient texts. They encouraged and reviled each other in the pursuit of these activities. They paid each other and were paid to accomplish them. They gathered in rooms and gardens now invisible to us to discuss them in words to us inaudible. Some were professional humanists, some joined humanist pursuits to other professions, some pursued humanist interests in their leisure. Some were born in Venice; some came to Venice from abroad and stayed; some, though native, left. Some were prominent figures who wrote works or engaged in activities of interest mainly to the historian. Some were minor, but their existence and activity still helped construct the landscape of Venetian humanist culture, and should be remembered.

3. THE CRITERION OF SIGNIFICANCE

The core group includes the humanists active at a certain minimum level. Had it been defined more narrowly to include only conspicuously important humanists, the following analysis would not yield conclusions about the representative group it is the object of this book to investigate. Such a core group definition would scarcely advance insight into Venetian humanism beyond the series of monographs on particular figures already available. Had the group been defined more broadly, embracing every figure known to have engaged in some humanist activity, it would become impossible to analyze. The numbers of occasional readers of the classics, ordinary teachers of rudimentary Latin, authors of one or two Latin letters would dwarf the relatively few humanists more seriously committed to a humanist program. Great distortions would have been introduced, moreover, as these lesser figures are easily missed; those included, almost whimsically, would be those who happened to survive in available documents, whereas as many figures of equal importance would be omitted. The aim here has been to define, therefore, a middle-range group of humanists.

Authors of substantial or many humanist works have been included without further reflection. Authors of minor or few works in humanist genres have been included where evidence pointed to their engagement in other humanist activities, as well: in discourse with other humanists, as witnessed in correspondence (even where the candidate's own letters are not known but are inferred from the correspondent's) and conversation; in the acquisition of a reputation for learning; in participation in literary affairs inferred from the dedication to them of works by other humanists; in patronage of known humanists; in the seeking, exchange, and collection of humanist texts. Some figures not known to be authors of any works, finally, have been included if they were conspicuously engaged in these activities of discourse, patronage, and collection.

For it has not been possible to draw a line cleanly around the written word, to embrace authors and cast out nonauthors. Humanism was notably a movement of spoken words and shared enthusiasms. In Quattrocento Venice, it is simply untrue that authors universally were more important in humanist culture than nonauthors. (Indeed, a case might be made that the most important category of humanists were the collectors of manuscripts—among whom figure several nonauthors.) Of sixty-four core group patrician humanists, fifty-two authored orations, treatises, or other typical humanist works, but twelve did not; nor did two of twenty-eight commoners. But all of those twelve did engage in correspondence with humanists on literary subjects, and were engaged in the exchange of ideas in important ways. They included several figures (Pietro Miani, Barbone Morosini, Daniele Renier, for example) of great significance in humanist culture—of an importance exceeding that of some authors of short or minor works. It would be odd to exclude figures of this stature on the technical question of authorship, a concern really less appropriate to the fifteenth century than our own. The issue of authorship, moreover, is cloudy in that era of manuscript publication, since the record can never be complete: those previously thought to be nonauthors constantly enter the ranks of authors as new manuscripts are discovered and identified.

4. THE CRITERION OF RESIDENCE

Foreigners thronged fifteenth-century Venice.[5] They came to trade, to find refuge, to look, to work, to study. They passed through, or stayed for a few years, or stayed for many. Among the foreigners who came to Venice were humanists, and among those humanists were some whose impact on the city's culture was decisive. The core group, however, does not include all these figures. Their exclusion from this sample does not deny their great influence, particularly as teachers and editors, on the development of Venetian humanism. Due attention has been given to their role (in Chapter Three; see also the discussion of transient foreigners in Section 9, below). To include in our sample transient figures the main part of whose careers transpired elsewhere would be to examine not so much Venetian humanism as the culture of the Italian humanists momentarily in Venice. They are excluded here, therefore, because of the particular goal of this chapter: to examine the social organization of Venetian humanism as a tool for understanding the distinctive features of that culture. Ideally, the phenomenon of Venetian humanism should be envisioned as a core group of Venetians and resident foreigners vigorously acted upon and responding to a large peripheral group of transient foreigners.

In addition to native Venetians, therefore, the core group is restricted to foreigners who became permanent or long-term residents of the city, a substantial part of whose careers ran their course in Venice. Included are those who lived several continuous years in the city and pursued an important phase of their careers there. Most arrived already adult; one came as a child. Most stayed to die in their adopted city; one left, after a long residence, some years before his death. These resident foreigners not only influenced the development of Venetian humanism but were, presumably, to some extent formed by the culture of their adopted city.[6]

[5] For the overwhelming presence of foreigners in early sixteenth-century Venice—a period adjacent to that considered here—see R. Finlay, *Politics*, pp. 17-18. For the diverse groups of foreigners, see G. Fedalto, "Stranieri a Venezia e a Padova."

[6] Resident foreigners, like other core group members (see below, "Criterion of Generation") are required to have been born by 1370 but before 1460, or to have reached

Of native-born Venetians, in contrast, long-term adult residence in the city has not been required. Indeed, several humanists have been included in the core group who were born and raised in Venice but who spent many adult years abroad and there met their death. Having received their intellectual formation in Venice, however, they have been assumed to be the products of the Venetian cultural milieu in a way that transient foreigners could not be. Moreover, many of these humanists pursued clerical or political careers that took them out of Venice for long periods but did not imply the severance of Venetian ties. Their cases may be distinguished only with difficulty from those who (happily or not) exiled themselves from Venice and sought employment in foreign cities. The period of their actual absence from the city may have been as long as that of the voluntary exiles. The exclusion of these latter figures would have resulted in considerable distortion of the sample of humanists studied.[7]

5. THE CRITERION OF GENERATION

Not every humanist active at some point in Venice from 1400 to 1490 is numbered in the core group. For the aim is not to construct a neutral catalogue of all humanists identified, but to understand the culture of a particular era, its makers, and its progeny. The core group has accordingly been restricted to those who reached maturity during the bracketed years, and who were therefore the creatures of similar circumstances and the principal shapers of humanist culture in this period. Three thirty-year generations of humanists reached maturity in the ninety-year period considered here. Since maturity is considered here to begin at age thirty, their dates of birth, to the best knowledge available, also span a ninety-year period. Those in the first generation were born by 1370 but before 1400; those in the second by 1400 but before 1430; those in the third by 1430 but before 1460. Dates of death have been ignored as criteria for inclusion in our core group. They tell us little. Some very early thinkers who had been born well before our period lived into the fifteenth century, longer than core group figures who belong to the era of humanism. Some late figures predeceased our Quattrocento humanists. The dates of death of our

maturity by 1400 but before 1490. The generation of Venetian humanism to which they are assigned is determined neither by date of birth nor of maturity, but by the period of their Venetian residence.

[7] Domenico de' Domenichi and Pietro del Monte, for example, spent the largest parts of their careers outside of Venice, though they remained Venetian by self-identification and outlook. Their cases can hardly be distinguished from those of Andrea Contrario and Francesco Negri, for example, whose years outside of Venice were spent in search of adequate employment.

TABLE 2. Core Group Generations

Maturity: First: 1400-1429   Second: 1430-1459   Third: 1460-1489

1370   1400   1430   1460   1490   1520   1550

First generation: births, 1370-1399
First births: Zaccaria Trevisan V (c. 1370)
  Giovanni Corner (c. 1370)
Last birth: Jacopo Ant. Marcello (1398 or 1399)
First death: Zaccaria Trevisan V (1414)
Last deaths: Jacopo Ant. Marcello (c. 1464/1465)
  Jacopo Languschi (after 1465)

Second generation: births, 1400-1429
First births: (c. 1400) G. Caldiera, T. L. L. Frulovisi, P. del Monte (or 1404), P. Perleone
Last birth: Lorenzo Zane (1429)
First deaths: Jacopo Foscari (1457); Barbone Morosini (1457/58)
Last deaths: Taddeo Quirini (1508); Domenico Morosini (1509)

Third generation: births, 1430-1459
First births: (c. 1430) M. Aurelio, A. Bernardo, L. Donato, P. Foscari, G. Merula, P. Molin
Last births: Marco Dandolo (1458); Daniele Renier (c. 1458)
First death: Francesco Barozzi (1471)
Last deaths: Marco Dandolo (1535); Daniele Renier (1535)

core group figures span a period of 121 years, whereas their literary activities commence before the first death and have largely ceased decades ahead of the last. By those late years, the youthful works of new generations of thinkers had already set a different tempo.[8] In view of these overlappings, the generational framework sketched in Table 2 has been adopted. It permits analysis to focus on those who received their cultural formation and made their initial commitments to humanism under similar historical circumstances, and who were as adults positioned to direct the course of humanism in the period under study.[9]

The four criteria just reviewed define a group of fifteenth-century Venetian humanists and permit the analysis that follows. This array of figures is perhaps as defensible as any could be where neither the nature of the phenomenon nor the nature of the evidence allows honed certainty. The patterns that emerge upon analysis, moreover, are broad and conspicuous. Only a substantial redefinition of the group based on a different set of assumptions would yield very different conclusions.[10]

6. EXCLUDED, MARGINAL, AND PERIPHERAL FIGURES

But boundaries are ruthless, excluding as they embrace, lending an appearance of absolute definition to a group that cannot be defined— as was confessed at the outset—absolutely. Some of the figures included in our sample can perhaps be challenged for their minor contributions to humanist culture or a misconstrual of dates of birth or Venetian residence. Others have been excluded according to the criteria drawn, but may perhaps have had as weighty an influence on Venetian

---

[8] Birthdates are not always known precisely. For many core group figures, an approximate date has been assigned based on career evidence. Such judgments are explained for each case in the profiles. Resident foreigners are expected to fall into one of the three generations as assigned here, and are further required to have begun and established the Venetian phase of their career—the initial date of which actually determines generational placement—within the 1400-1489 period; see above, n. 6. Marginal figures born slightly too early or too late to belong to our core group but whose careers overlap with those of core group humanists are discussed below.

[9] For the utility of studying cultural developments by focusing on the generation unit, see L. A. Coser, *Men of Ideas*, p. 127. Coser in turn draws on the definition of K. Mannheim in "The Problem of Generations," especially pp. 304ff. See also the valuable bibliographical survey in R. Wohl's *The Generation of 1914*, pp. 239-40 n. 3. A narrative organized by generation of the development of Venetian humanism in the fifteenth century is found in Chapter Three, Sections 2-5.

[10] Examination of the process of group definition in other similar studies suggests that the one undertaken here is adequately precise. See, for example, P. Burke, *Culture and Society in Italy, 1420-1540*; C. Dionisotti,"Chierici e laici nella letteratura italiana del primo Cinquecento"; J. J. Linz, "Intellectual Roles in Sixteenth- and Seventeenth-Century Spain."

humanist culture as some figures retained. Categories of excluded figures are described below. Fine distinctions have sometimes been drawn between the elect and nonelect.

7. EXCLUSION BY THE CRITERION OF ACTIVITY

Though prominent in Venice's Quattrocento intellectual life, some figures have not been included because the nature of their main intellectual activity falls outside the range of humanism. The philosophers and theologians Domenico Bragadin, Paolo Veneto, Paolo della Pergola, and Gasparino Borro are conspicuous in this category. Note should also be made of the reformers Ludovico Barbo and the patriarch and saint Lorenzo Giustiniani, author of a large corpus of works; the writers of religious or devotional works such as Antonio Grassello, Niccolò Manerbio (Malermi), and Moro Lapi; physicians such as Pietro Roccabonella, the volgare chroniclers Giorgio and Pietro Dolfin and Domenico Malipiero, and that unclassifiable author of the *Hypnerotomachia Poliphili*, Francesco Colonna.[11]

Several core group figures, however, do write on philosophical or theological subjects; but they also write humanist works, or write on those matters in a humanist style or demonstrate humanist interests. Many of our core group figures follow the latter pattern: Giovanni Caldiera, Fantino Dandolo, Domenico de' Domenichi, Ludovico Donato, Pietro Marcello the Elder, Fantino Vallaresso, among others.

[11] For Bragadin, see the article by G. Stabile in DBI, XIII; also F. Lepori, "La scuola di Rialto," pp. 571ff. For Paolo Veneto, see the monograph of F. Momigliano, *Paolo Veneto e le correnti del pensiero religioso e filosofico nel suo tempo*, and F. Bottin, "Logica e filosofia naturale nelle opere di Paolo Veneto," which throughly reviews biographical studies and works; for his relationship with at least two Venetian students, see. P. Gothein, "Paolo Veneto e Prosdocimo de' Conti maestri padovani di Lodovico Foscarini," and the studies of R. Cessi and A. Segarizzi on Pietro Tommasi. For Paolo della Pergola, see Lepori, "Scuola," pp. 541ff. For Borro, see Agostini, *Notizie*, II, 600-606, and the article by B. Recchilongo in DBI, XIII. For Barbo, see L. Pesce, *Ludovico Barbo vescovo di Traviso* and I. Tassi, *Ludovico Barbo (1381-1443)*; also S. Tramontin, "Cultura monastica," pp. 443ff., and the article by A. Pratesi in DBI, VI. For Giustiniani, see *San Lorenzo Giustiniani, protopatriarca di Venezia nel V centenario di morte: 1456-1956*; also Tramontin, "Cultura monastica," pp. 435ff., with bibliographical n. 30. A. Grassello wrote an *Opus de gratia recuperanda ad instantiam Angele sororis sue*, and an *Opus de eucharistia et de extrema untione*. For Manerbio (Malermi), vernacular translator of the Bible and Voragine's *Legenda aurea*, see Tramontin, "Cultura monastica," p. 447. Works of Moro Lapi (a Florentine monk at San Michele da Murano in Venice), including letters and translations, are cited in the Bibliography. For Pietro Roccabonella, see Facciolati, *Fasti gymn. pat.*, I, ii, 105; Molmenti, *Vita privata*, II, 217. For the two Dolfins, see M. Zannoni, "Le fonti della cronaca veneziana di Giorgio Dolfin" and "Giorgio Dolfin, cronista veneziano del secolo XV"; Pietro continued his father's famous chronicle. For Malipiero, see A. Sagredo's introduction to his *Annali*, pp. xiii-xxv; also Finlay, *Politics*, pp. 7-8. For Colonna, see among others M. T. Casella and G. Pozzi, *Francesco Colonna*.

8. Exclusion by the Criterion of Significance

Many figures have been excluded from the core group who, though native Venetian and born within the time span concerned, were only peripherally related to humanism. In this category fall such figures as Antonio Dandolo or Francesco Marcello, bishop of Trau; or Albano or Michele Morosini, or Jacopo Grasolari, who authored only one or two small humanist works, but whose careers otherwise do not suggest a pattern of humanist involvement. Also excluded here are persons who had some humanist contacts, but were not themselves active as humanists: Jacopino Badoer, for instance, a minor poet; Antonio Boldù, reputed as learned; Niccolò Michiel, a bibliophile; Francesco Minio, who encouraged Giorgio Merula and protected the secretaries Niccolò Sagundino and Marco Aurelio; Federico Contarini, Ermolao Donato, and Santo Venier, to whom Francesco Barbaro wrote letters, or Alessandro de' Fornaci and Girolamo da Ponte, to whom Ludovico Foscarini wrote, or Ludovico Barozzi, a correspondent of both major figures. Finally, there may be grouped the youthful Domenico Barbarigo, Fantino Giorgi, and Giovanni Barbo, known primarily for their relations to their teachers, and some collectors of books: Girolamo Molin, Guglielmo Quirini, and Gioacchino della Torre.[12]

---

[12] For Dandolo, see Agostini, *Notizie*, I, 509-14; A. Zeno, *Diss. voss.*, II, 58; he wrote a *Pro gymnasii patavini iuris scholasticis gratulacio* to Doge Pasquale Malipiero. For Marcello, see C. Cenci, "Senato veneto 'Probae,' " index; Cosenza, *Dict.*, III, 2164; his works consist of an oration (Marc. Lat. XI, 16 [4427], not seen by me; see Kristeller, *Iter* II, 238) and the *Libellus in quo excursus describit turcarum*, both to Doge Leonardo Loredan. (By extrapolation from Marcello's ecclesiastical career, I am assuming that he belongs to the last of the core group generations.) The two Morosini wrote an oration each. Grasolari, who published an *Oratio ad illustrissimum venetorum dominium in assumptione Reverendissimi Domini Ludovico Contareni ad Patriarchatum*, is also known to have studied with Giorgio Merula and with his assistance edited Quintilian (addressed to Cristoforo de' Priuli); see Cosenza, *Dict.*, II, 1665. For Badoer, see A. Segarizzi, *Jacopino Badoer rimatore veneziano del secolo XV*. For Boldù, see Cicogna, *Iscrizioni*, III, 107-108. For Michiel, see Cosenza, *Dict.*, III, 2308; B. Nardi, "Scuola di Rialto" [UEUV ed.], p. 127-28 n. 79; F. Pisani, *Oratio de universae philosophiae ornamentis*, p. 266; his testament (17 May 1518) in Venice, Bibl. del Museo Correr, cod. P.D.C. 2166/17, vol. II, cc. 27-29, c. 28ᵛ, 29. For Minio's relations with Merula, see F. Gabotto and A. Badini Confalonieri, "Vita di Giorgio Merula," first part, p. 285, and Cosenza, *Dict.*, III, 2321; with Sagundino and Aurelio, see the former's *Epist. et opusc.*, fol. 57. For Contarini, Donato, Venier, and Barozzi, see Barbaro's *Centotrenta*, ed. Sabbadini, indices; for Contarini, see also the comment of C. Bollani (*Trialogus*, fol. 7); for Donato, the letter of Filippo Morandi da Rimini discussed in King, "A Study in Venetian Humanism at Mid-Quattrocento," Part One, pp. 79-81. For de' Fornaci, see Foscarini's *Epist.*, fols. 21-25, 35ᵛ-37ᵛ, 47ᵛ-49ᵛ; for da Ponte, ibid., fols. 206ʳ·ᵛ and 209, and 225ᵛ-229; for Barozzi, ibid., fol. 141ʳ·ᵛ. For Barbarigo, see F. Filelfo, *Epist. fam.*, fols. 150-51ᵛ. For Giorgi, see the letters to him of Guarino (in the latter's *Epist.*, ed. Sabbadini, I, 677-79) and Cristoforo de Scarpis (in Segarizzi, "Cristoforo de Scarpis," pp. 218-20), and that of Francesco Barbaro to Vinciguerra Giorgi (not Giorgio Vinciguerra) on Fantino's death (Barbaro's *Centotrenta*, p. 63), and the comment of Poggio

The greatest difficulty in segregating those to be excluded from core group figures has arisen with regard to this criterion of significance. Here it has been necessary to compare unlike quantities and render Solomonic judgment: a figure with a lofty reputation for learning who has authored but one *opusculum* vis-à-vis another with three orations to his name but not otherwise a hint of relationship to learned circles, vis-à-vis another whose works cannot be assessed because they may not be extant. In general, the margins have been drawn broadly and generously. So many figures have emerged from obscurity because of serendipitous discoveries and chance survivals of correspondence or texts that it has been thought unwise to dismiss one whose profile is thin but who is still recognizable as one of our humanist circle.

Several patricians have been counted among the humanists although they wrote no works if their careers show evidence of engagement in humanist discourse, if they received letters from known humanists, if they possessed a reputation for learning, if they collected books. Included by these standards, with little hesitation, are Giovanni Corner, Jacopo Foscari, Barbone Morosini, Paolo Pisani, Daniele Renier, and Daniele Vitturi. More timidly, Domenico Giorgi and Antonio Calvo have been entered. (For nonauthors who have been included, see also Section 3 above.)

A similar situation arose in the case of figures who have written one or few or very small works. Where there is ample suggestion, in addition, of participation in discourse, correspondence, and so on, these have been duly included: Antonio Bernardo, Niccolò Canal, Antonio Donato, Marco Donato, Pietro Molin, and Marco Sanuto, for example. Others have been more grudgingly received: Francesco Barozzi and Fantino Vallaresso, for example. The case of Federico Corner has been distinguished, on the basis of his substantial letter to Leonardo Giustiniani and his clear reputation, from those of the other young scholars mentioned above—Barbarigo, Giorgi, and Barbo.

Three secretaries, finally—Ulisse Aleotti, Marco Aurelio, and Febo Capella—have been admitted to the core group although they composed no humanist works known to me. The latter two received the dedications of several humanist works as well as letters from prominent humanists. The case for the inclusion of the first is shakier: he

---

Bracciolini to Niccolò Niccoli in the former's *Epist.*, ed. Tonellis, I, 56-60, p. 57. For Barbo, see Kristeller, "An Unknown Letter of Giovanni Barbo to Guarino." For Molin, see B. Cecchetti, "Una libreria circolante a Venezia nel secolo XV." For Quirini, see G. dalla Santa, "Di un patrizio mercante veneziano," and S. Connell, "Books and Their Owners," p. 172. For della Torre, see Cicogna, *Iscrizioni*, III, 21; Pertusi, "L'umanesimo greco," pp. 261-62.

wrote a few *volgare* sonnets, and received letters from Ludovico Foscarini and Niccolò Sagundino, which have been taken as evidence of participation in intellectual life.

9. EXCLUSION BY THE CRITERION OF RESIDENCE

Foreigners appear in the core group when they have established a permanent presence in Venice. But many more have been excluded who merely visited, or who stayed briefly, or who resided in the city for several years but left without either having made a commitment to Venice or establishing an identity as Venetian. Foremost among these is Guarino Veronese, the teacher of many Venetians, active in our city from 1414 to 1419. Early in the century, Vittorino da Feltre (1416, 1422-1423), Cristoforo de Scarpis (intermittently, 1416-1425), George of Trebizond (intermittently, 1416-1437), and Francesco Filelfo (1417-1419, 1427-1428), were also drawn to Venice to teach or engage in discourse with learned patricians. Gasparino Barzizza, teaching in nearby Padua, visited friends and pupils during 1407 and 1408. Antonio Bartatella (c. 1418, c. 1427-1429), and perhaps Bartolomeo Facio (1426-1429) tutored Jacopo Foscari, the son of Doge Francesco. Around mid-century, teaching opportunities at the public schools lured Giovanni Pietro Vitali (da Lucca) d'Avenza (1450-1456), Giovanni Mario Filelfo (1460), and Gregorio (da Città di Castello) Tifernate (1462-1464). Flavio Biondo (c. 1423-1427), Girolamo Bologni (c. 1470, then 1510-1513), Paolo Marsi (intermittently, 1468-1473), and Girolamo Aurelio Augurello (1485) found employment as secretaries or companions to wealthy patricians (to Francesco Barbaro, to Lorenzo Zane, to Bernardo Bembo and Niccolò Canal, and to Niccolò Franco, respectively); Marsi also as tutor in the family of Marco Corner. The century's late decades (the trend continues and strengthens in the early years of the next) saw an influx of visitors from the nearby Veneto or further regions to print books or find employment at the presses. Of this crew (which flourished even more beyond our period, from the 1490s) Raffaele Zovenzoni (1470-1473, 1474-c. 1475) is perhaps typical. Luca Pacioli (1480s), the mathematician, and Urbanio Bolzanio (c. 1473), the Hellenist, both studied in Venice during our period, returning later to establish residence.[13]

---

[13] There is extensive information on some of these figures. The sources listed here and in the next note are particularly useful for their Venetian careers and relations. The dates given in parentheses in the text are those of the figure's presence in Venice during the period of concern. For Guarino, see especially C. de' Rosmini, *Vita e disciplina di Guarino Veronese e de' suoi discepoli*, and R. Sabbadini, *Vita di Guarino Veronese* and *La scuola e gli studi di Guarino Guarini Veronese*. For Vittorino, see especially de'

Girolamo Ramusio received perhaps part of his elementary education in Venice, where he was brought as a child by his brother in 1458, but soon after had moved to Padua, from where he fled on exotic and fateful travels. Urged by Marcantonio Morosini, Coriolano Cippico, a Dalmatian naval commander who served in the Venetian fleet from 1470 to 1474 under the captain general Pietro Mocenigo, wrote his *Petri Mocenici venetae classis imperatoris contra Ottomannum Turcarum principem rebus gestis libri III* before returning to his native Trau. Giannozzo Manetti and Filippo (Callimaco Esperiente) Buonaccorsi were sent as ambassadors to Venice from Florence (1448) and Poland (1476-1477, 1486) respectively. Ambrogio Traversari visited in 1433, when he examined some fine Venetian libraries; the

---

Rosmini, *L'idea dell'ottimo precettore*, W. H. Woodward, *Vittorino da Feltre and Other Humanist Educators*, and B. Nardi, "Contributo alla biografia di Vittorino da Feltre." For de Scarpis, see A. Segarizzi, "Cristoforo de Scarpis," and Labalme, *Bernardo Giustiniani*, pp. 29ff. For George, G. Castellani, "Giorgio da Trebisonda," F. Gaeta, "Giorgio da Trebisonda," J. Monfasani, *George of Trebizond*, and A. Pertusi, "L'umanesimo greco," pp. 225ff.; also several works by George to Venetians (and to him from them) in Monfasani, ed., *Collectanea Trapezuntiana*. For Francesco Filelfo, see especially G. Castellani, "Documenti veneziani inediti relativi a Francesco e Mario Filelfo," C. de' Rosmini, *Vita di Francesco Filelfo da Tolentino*, and G. dalla Santa, "Di un patrizio mercante veneziano." For Barzizza, see the article by G. Martellotti in DBI, VIII; also C. Colombo, "Gasparino Barzizza a Padova," D. Magni, "Gasparino Barzizza," Sabbadini, "Lettere e orazioni edite e inedite di Gasparino Barzizza" and "Delle nuove lettere di Gasparino Barzizza"; and DBI, VII. For Baratella, see Segarizzi, *Antonio Baratella*, and B. Ziliotto in DBI, V. For Facio, see P. O. Kristeller, "The Humanist Bartolomeo Facio and His Unknown Correspondence"; U. Mazzini, "Appunti e notizie per servire alla bio-bibliografia di Bartolomeo Facio"; and Sabbadini, "Bartolomeo Facio, scolaro a Verona, maestro a Venezia." For Vitali d'Avenza, see M. Cortesi, "Alla scuola di Gian Pietro d'Avenza in Lucca" and G. Sforza, "Della vita e delle opere di Giovanni Pietro d'Avenza"; also J. B. Ross, "Venetian Schools," App., for his term (1450-1456). For Giovanni Mario Filelfo, see L. Agostinelli and G. Benaducci, *Biografia e bibliografia di Giovan Mario Filelfo*; Castellani, "Documenti veneziani"; G. Favre, *Vie de Jean-Marius Philelphe*; and C. Monzani, "Di Guglielmo Favre e della vita di Gianmario Filelfo scritta da lui." For Tifernate, a teacher of Giorgio Merula, see A. Torrioli, *Publio Gregorio Tifernate*; also Tiraboschi, *Stor. lett. ital.*, III, 156, and Cosenza, *Dict.*, IV, 3412ff.; I have been unable to see F. Gabotto, *Ancora un letterato del Quattrocento (Gregorio Tifernate)*. For Biondo, see the article of R. Fubini in DBI, X; also F. Gilbert, "Biondo, Sabellico"; F. Gaeta, "Storiografia, coscienza nazionale," pp. 30ff. For Bologni, see the article of R. Ceserani in DBI, XI, and the profile in G. Pavanello, *Un maestro del Quattrocento (Giovanni Aurelio Augurello)*, pp. 152-57. For Marsi, see A. della Torre, *Paolo Marsi*. For Augurello, see Pavanello, *Maestro*, and R. Weiss in DBI, IV; he subsequently visited Venice also in 1499 and 1509. For Zovenzoni, see especially B. Ziliotto, *Raffaele Zovenzoni*. For Pacioli's work in relation to Venice, see Lepori, "La scuola di Rialto," pp. 597ff. and B. Nardi, "Scuola di Rialto" [UEUV ed.], pp. 101ff.; he had studied in Venice during his youth under Domenico Bragadin, later returning for visits and ultimately to reside (from 1508). For Bolzanio, who studied Greek from 1473 at San Niccolò before undertaking travels in the East, and who taught in Venice from after 1490 until his death in 1524, see G. Bustico, "Due umanisti veneti."

epigraphist Ciriaco d'Ancona, en route to the East, in 1443; Cardinal Bessarion, who had many Venetian friends, came in 1463, in order to encourage his pope's Crusade; Poliziano visited in 1480 and 1491, his later journey yielding contacts with Venice's "new philology," of great moment in his intellectual development.[14]

It has been necessary to handle the criterion of residence flexibly. Although it is easy to distinguish between a Filippo Morandi, who came to Venice as a youth and stayed more than sixty years until his death, and a Giovanni Mario Filelfo, who lived in the city barely six months, some other cases have presented muddier contours. Giorgio Merula lived in Venice for nineteen years, then left to spend his remaining eleven in Pavia and Milan. His final commitment was not to Venice, yet he passed the greatest part of his adult career there, and has been considered, for our purposes, Venetian. Tito Livio Frulovisi (a different but equally idiosyncratic case), though born in Ferrara, was resident in Venice from early childhood through adolescence. He was then intermittently absent from his adopted city until about age forty, then absent for perhaps sixteen years more. Though he left Venice readily and spent, in effect, many of his adult years abroad, he too has been considered Venetian. Pietro Perleone, finally, who spent only his six final years continuously in Venice, has been included due to a record of earlier extended stays.

10. EXCLUSION BY THE CRITERION OF GENERATION

Since it has been necessary to define our core group within certain boundaries of time, other humanists and related figures have been excluded whose maturity was reached in the generations preceding or

---

[14] For Girolamo Ramusio, see especially F. Flamini, "Girolamo Ramusio (1450-1486) e i suoi versi latini e volgari." For Cippico, see the article of M. Palma in DBI, XXV; also Cicogna, *Iscrizioni*, II, 134, and III, 515; Pavanello, *Maestro*, p. 99. For Manetti's presence in Venice, cf. LQU, p. 107 n. 7, and Barbaro's *Centotrenta*, ed. Sabbadini, p. 47. Manetti's letters from Venice are in cod. Vat. Pal. Lat. 931. For Buonaccorsi, see the article of D. Caccamo in DBI, XV; the 1486 embassy is described in the humanist's own *De his quae a Venetis tentata sunt, Persis ac Tartaris contra Turcos movendis*. For Ciriaco's relations with Leonardo Giustiniani, see especially B. Fenigstein, *Leonardo Giustiniani*, pp. 18, 47-50; for his Venetian connections, L. Bertalot and A. Campana, "Gli scritti di Jacopo Zeno e il suo elogio di Ciriaco d'Ancona." For Traversari's relations (most notably with Leonardo Giustiniani and Francesco Barbaro) see especially C. L. Stinger, *Humanism and the Church Fathers*, index. Bessarion was in contact with Francesco Barbaro, Ludovico Foscarini, Paolo Morosini, and Andrea Contrario among others, and ultimately willed his library to the city of Venice; see L. Labowsky in DBI, IX. For Poliziano's visits, see Branca, "L'umanesimo veneziano," pp. 128 n. 8, 144, 146; also Branca, *Poliziano e l'umanesimo della parola*, index. For visitors to Venice in general, see G. Fedalto, "Stranieri a Venezia"; for visitors of Greek extraction or specifically expert in Greek learning, see Pertusi, "L'umanesimo greco."

following those three central generations defined in this study. Significantly older than our figures are the secretaries Rafaino de' Caresini (b. c. 1314), Benintendi de' Ravagnani (1317-1365), Paolo de Bernardo (d. 1393), and Lorenzo de' Monaci (c. 1351-1428). They represent Venice's earliest humanism, heirs to the inspiration of the learned Doge Andrea Dandolo and his correspondent and guest, Francesco Petrarch, who was himself resident in the city from 1362 to 1368. Giovanni Conversino da Ravenna (1343-1408) taught in Venice in 1382, 1388-1389, and 1404-1406, and influenced some of our first generation of core group humanists, and Manuel Chrysoloras (1355?-1415), who had so great an impact on the Florentine intellectual circle in 1397 to 1400, also visited Venice several times between 1396 to 1408. Carlo Zeno (1334-1418), finally, who turned in his last years to humanist studies, is perhaps the eldest in the tradition of patrician humanists that came to typify the mid-fifteenth century.[15]

Humanists and related members of Venice's intellectual circles born in the generation immediately following the third of our core group generations (those having a birth date from 1460 to 1489 or establishing residence in Venice from between 1490 and 1519) are multitudinous; for the ranks of humanist circles are swelled by amateurs, patrons, collectors, printers' assistants, editors, translators, teachers of all kinds in the last decade of the century. This circle includes several prominent names alongside a bevy of minor ones: Pietro Bembo (1479-1547) and Gasparo Contarini (1483-1542), for instance, both thinkers and writers of exceptional importance who dwarf all but the most important of our core group figures, or Domenico Grimani (1461-1523), the learned Churchman, scholar, patron and bibliophile. Belonging to this generation of patrician humanists are also found Pietro Pasqualigo (1472-1515), an orator similar in type to many of our core group; Andrea Navagero (1483-1529), the public historiographer, and Andrea Mocenigo, author of the *Bellum Cameracense*; Ludovico Mocenigo, who, returning as ambassador to France in 1506, brought a manuscript of Pliny's letters for the press of Aldo Manuzio; and the churchmen Francesco Giorgi (1460-1540), Antonio Pizzamano (1462-1512), and Cristoforo Marcello (d. 1527), involved as well in the humanist circle of their era. The diarist Marino Sanuto (1466-1536)

---

[15] For this early proto-humanist circle in general, see Chapter Three, Section 1, and for specific figures the following. For Petrarch's influence on Venetian culture, see the studies cited in Chapter Three, nn. 24 and 28; for Ravagnani and de' Monaci, n. 28; for Conversino, n. 27. For Chrysoloras in this relation, R. Sabbadini, "L'ultimo ventennio della vita di Manuele Crisolora (1396-1415)." For Zeno, see Chapter One, n. 4. Philosophers, poets, and other learned men of these early generations have not been noted here.

looms large in the intellectual life of this generation. Such professional humanists as Giovanni Battista Egnazio (1473-1553), Vettore Fausto (1480-1551), and Giovanni Battista Ramusio (1485-1557) head the list of native Venetian commoners in this generation. Several resident foreigners appear as teachers in the public schools in the early sixteenth century: Giovanni Battista Scita (d. 1500) from Feltre; Gregorio Amaseo (d. 1517) from Udine; Niccolò Leoniceno (1428-1524) from Vicenza; Girolamo Masserio from Forli; Girolamo Calvo from Vicenza; Marino Becichemo (c. 1468-1526) from Scutari; Marcus Musurus (1470-1517) from Crete; Raffaele Regio (d. 1520) from Bergamo. Also foreign were Niccolò Liburnio (1474-1557) and Giovanni Francesco Fortunio, who alongside the native Bembo were leading literary figures of the age. Conspicuous among both foreigners and natives in this generation is the master printer Aldo Manuzio (1449-1516), active in Venice after 1491.[16]

[16] For Venetian intellectual life from the late fifteenth century, see Chapter Three, Section 6, and for specific figures the following. For Bembo and Contarini, Chapter Three, n. 87. For Grimani, see especially T. Freudenberger, "Die Bibliothek des Kardinals Domenico Grimani"; P. Kibre, "Cardinal Domenico Grimani, *Quaestio de Intensione et Remissione Qualitatis*"; M.J.C. Lowry, "Two Great Libraries"; P. Paschini, *Domenico Grimani, Cardinale di S. Maria (+ 1523)*; and M. Perry, "Cardinal Domenico Grimani's Legacy of Ancient Art to Venice." For Pasqualigo, see D. Weinstein, *Ambassador from Venice*, with his famous oration (facsimile of the edition of Venice, 1501) on pp. 33-42, translated, pp. 43-51; see also Agostini, *Notizie*, II, 303-13. For Navagero, see Cicogna, *Iscrizioni*, VI, 169-348 (I have been unable to consult Cicogna's *Della vita e delle opere di Andrea Navagero* [Venice, 1855]); also F. Gaeta, "Storiografia, coscienza nazionale," pp. 78ff. For A. Mocenigo, ibid., pp. 76ff. For L. Mocenigo, cf. A. Firmin-Didot, *Alde Manuce et l'hellénisme à Venise*, p. 304ff.; Cosenza, *Dict.*, III, 2329; also a capsule life in Cappellari, *Camp. ven.*, III, fol. 95. For Giorgi, see Agostini, *Notizie*, II, 332-62; also the brief notes in Kristeller, "The Contribution of Religious Orders to Renaissance Thought and Learning," p. 114, 140. For Pizzamano, Agostini, *Notizie*, II, 189-200; also cf. Freudenberger, "Bibliothek," p. 16. For Marcello, see Cicogna, *Iscrizioni*, II, 79-83. For Sanuto, the subject of many studies, see especially G. Cozzi, "Marino Sanudo il Giovane," and Finlay, *Politics*. Note should also be made of the patrician Antonio Giustiniani (1466?-after 1523) who combined his political career with that of philosopher and theologian rather like the patrician humanists of the preceding generation. For him, see Lepori, "La scuola di Rialto," pp. 591ff.; B. Nardi, "Letteratura e cultura" [CVQ edition], p. 118; and Nardi, "Scuola di Rialto" [UEUV ed.], p. 115; also Cosenza, *Dict.*, II, 1869. His exquisite *Quaestiones in secundum sententiarum* is an intriguing counterweight to his dispatches from his Roman embassy: *Dispacci di Antonio Giustiniani, ambasciatore veneto in Roma dal 1502 al 1505*. Perhaps not too distant from our concerns is also Donato da Legge (1479-1526), patrician author of the *Historia tuchesca*. For Egnazio, see J. B. Ross's exhaustive monograph in "Venetian Schools." For Fausto, see Agostini, *Notizie*, II, 448-72. For Ramusio, see Cicogna, *Iscrizioni*, II, 311-15, and V, 596; and A. del Piero, "Della vita e degli studi di Giovanni Battista Ramusio." For the several foreign-born teachers in the Venetian public schools in the early sixteenth century, see V. Branca, "L'umanesimo veneziano," pp. 126-27; F. Gilbert, "Biondo, Sabellico," pp. 281ff., Lepori, "Scuola," pp. 600ff., and Ross, "Venetian Schools," pp. 534ff. and Appendix. In addition, see specifically for literature on Leoniceno, or Leonico (not to be confused with Niccolò

Since the criterion of generation was established in order to demarcate a core group, the distinction between members of our core group and the adjacent generation have been clearly if artificially drawn. At the early end of our span of generations, the line of demarcation is unambiguous. At the late end, however, the delineation is fine: Domenico Grimani, for instance, born in 1461, has been excluded, but Marco Dandolo, born in 1458, is incorporated into our core group.

The framework of generations presents complexities. Some members of the generation previous to the earliest one of the core group survive into the main period. Yet they have been excluded. Lorenzo de' Monaci, for example, born too early to be enlisted in the core group, outlived by fourteen years Zaccaria Trevisan the Elder of the core group's first generation. Core group figures survive beyond the later boundary of the period under study, and produce some of their major works during the first generation following it—indeed, later in some cases than major works produced by members of a younger generation. Yet these latter have been excluded, as well. Domenico Morosini and Marco Dandolo, of the second and third core group generations, respectively, were still active when their younger contemporaries Pietro Bembo and Gasparo Contarini had already entered boldly upon the stage of intellectual life.

11. PERIPHERAL FIGURES

Other figures whose activity was related but peripheral to that of the Venetian humanist circle have also been excluded from the core group. These included prominent rulers or prelates to whom works were dedicated or letters addressed by our humanists (such as Doge Francesco Foscari, Cardinal Ludovico [Scarampo] Trevisan, Cardinal Francesco Condulmier); patrons and helpers of talented foreigners establishing themselves in Venice (such as Fantino Michiel, Paolo Zane, Marco Corner, Marco Giorgi, Fantino Coppo); physician and philos-

Leonico Tomeo), W. F. Edwards, "Niccolò Leoniceno and the Origins of Humanist Discussion of Method," the bibliographical n. 1 on p. 283; for Becichemo, the article by C. H. Clough in DBI, VII, and for his role as tutor to Girolamo Donato, Agostini, *Notizie*, II, 203, 214-15; for Musurus, see F. Foffano, "Marco Musuro, professore di greco a Padova ed a Venezia," and Geanakoplos, *Greek Scholars*, pp. 111-66; also Fedalto, "Stranieri a Venezia," pp. 507-508; for Regio, see Tiraboschi, *Stor. lett. ital.*, III, 250-51; Cosenza, *Dict.*, IV, 3017ff.; A. Medin, "Raffaele Regio a Venezia"; also Gilbert, "Biondo, Sabellico," p. 283. For Liburnio and Fortunio in the Venetian context, see the two studies by C. Dionisotti, "Niccolò Liburnio" and "Il Fortunio." Among many Manuzio studies, see especially Lowry, *The World of Aldus Manuzius*, and "The 'New Academy' of Aldus Manutius"; also Dionisotti, "Aldo Manuzio umanista"; E. Pastorello, *L'epistolario manuziano*; and Firmin-Didot's classic *Alde Manuce*.

opher friends, spiritual advisers, university professors of law, medicine, or philosophy (such as Giovannino Corradini, Francesco Trevisan, Prosdocimo de' Conti, Antonio Roselli); provincial humanists who came in contact with (mainly patrician) humanists from the core group in their own cities (such as Dante III Alighieri, Giorgio Bevilacqua de Lazise, Giovanni Jacopo Cane, Giovanni Michele Alberto da Carrara); prominent humanists, many from the Florentine circle, who came personally to know or corresponded with or engaged in controversy with our Venetians (Poggio Bracciolini, Leonardo Bruni, Marsilio Ficino, Giovanni Pico della Mirandola, Angelo Poliziano, Ambrogio Traversari, Lorenzo Valla).[17]

[17] To Doge Foscari, for instance, is dedicated Lauro Quirini's *De republica* [DR]. To Scarampo (for whom see A. Alcaro, *Lodovico Scarampo*, and P. Paschini, "Umanisti intorno a un cardinale"), Jacopo Zeno (cf. Zonta's introduction to the *Vita Caroli Zeni*, p. vii, n. 12) and Lauro Quirini (in the "Epistole storiche," pp. 234-40) addressed letters of a political nature; Francesco Barbaro corresponded with him extensively (see *Centotrenta*, ed. Sabbadini, indices). To Condulmier, Barbaro addressed several routine letters (ibid.). Note Pietro del Monte's deprecating assessment of Condulmier's learning in a letter to Bartolomeo Zabarella (cf. A. Sottili, *Studenti tedeschi e umanesimo italiano nell'Università di Padova durante il Quattrocento*, I, 77-79).

Michiel was on the verge of hiring Pietro Perleone as a tutor for his children when he died in 1434; George of Trebizond delivered his funeral oration (cf. Labalme, *Bernardo Giustiniani*, pp. 65-67; J. Monfasani, *Collectanea Trapezuntiana*, pp. 445ff.). For Zane's relationship to Guarino, see Sabbadini, *Vita di Guarino Veronese*, pp. 6, 11, 12, and Guarino's later letter to Paolo's son Marco in his *Epist.*, ed. Sabbadini, II, 611, with comment on III, 472. For Marco di Giorgio Corner's patronage of humanists, see della Torre, *Paolo Marsi*, pp. 193ff., and Gabotto and Confalonieri, "Vita di Giorgio Merula," first part, pp. 291-92. Giorgi was Antonio Vinciguerra's patron, to whom the poet dedicated his *Liber utrum deceat sapientem ducere uxorem*; see della Torre, *Antonio Vinciguerra*, p. 147. Sagundino's *De origine et sectis philosophorum*, addressed to Coppo, opens with introductory comments revealing the nature of their relationship. The physician Corradini was a friend of Francesco Barbaro and Guarino (Sabbadini, *Vita di Guarino Veronese*, p. 27); the former delivered Corradini's funeral oration (Quirini, *Diatriba*, pp. 155-60). To Francesco (or Giovanni Francesco) Trevisan, a Carthusian monk, both Francesco Barbaro (cf. *Centotrenta*, pp. 42, 50) and Ludovico Foscarini (*Epist.*, fols. 37v-39, 57-58v, 110v-111v, 166v-167v, 176-79, 194-96, 243v-250, 260-61v, 280-81, 329v-331) write warmly; Agostini (*Notizie*, I, 63, 79, 90-91) describes him as confidant of several noblemen. For the Paduan mathematician de' Conti, see P. Gothein, "Paolo Veneto e Prosdocimo de' Conti." The professor of law Roselli (1380-1466), under whom many of our Venetians received their degrees, is the author of the controversial *Monarchia seu tractatus de potestate imperatoris et papae*. P. Barozzi delivered in his honor the *Oratio in funere Antonii Roicelli Aretini*.

Dante III corresponded with Bernardo Bembo (see V. Cian, "Per Bernardo Bembo—II," p. 58) and addressed verse to Francesco Diedo (see G. Tournoy, "Francesco Diedo," p. 216 n. 82). Bevilacqua dedicated works to Marco Donato (the *De bello gallico*, for which see Abel's preface to Isotta Nogarola's *Opera omnia*, I, cix n. 33, and Kristeller, *Iter*, II, 294); to Zaccaria Barbaro (his *Flores ex dictis B. Hieronymi collecti*, see Zeno, *Diss. voss.*, II, 356); and to Jacopo Antonio Marcello (a consolatory epistle on the death of the Venetian's son Valerio), and wrote in Marcello's name the *Excusatio adversus consolatores in obitu Valerii*. To him was addressed Lorenzo Zane's *De difficillimae doctrinae palma capescenda*. Cane dedicated to Francesco Diedo his *De ar-*

12. Possibility of Distortion

The preceding pages have described the boundaries defining the core group. The extent of the discussion highlights what may have been apparent from the start: that the erection of such boundaries imposes structure on a human and elastic phenomenon, and is an intrinsically artificial enterprise. But it is necessary. Without the boundaries drawn, it would be impossible to go beyond vague impressions of the nature of Venice's humanist circle to focus on a concrete phenomenon.

But the possibility of distortion also arises from the erection of these boundaries. If errors have been made in constituting our core group, they are the more glaring because the neat structure suggests an unreal

---

bitriis, and included him as interlocutor in the dialogue *De Constantini donatione*; dedicated two legal works to Bernardo Giustiniani (see Labalme, *Bernardo Giustiniani*, p. 326); addressed to Ludovico Foscarini the verse *De ludo equestri Patavii* (ca. 1475?) and to Niccolò Canal a verse *epistola* (1485). Carrara, finally, dedicated works to Diedo (his *De pestilentia*, and verse; see Tournoy, "Diedo," p. 215 n. 50, and pp. 218-25); to Domenico Giorgi (the *Liber stromathum*, see Cosenza, *Dict.*, II, 1584); to Marcello (the *De bello in Italia gesto*); and addressed a letter with verse to Sebastiano Badoer (cf. Kristeller, *Iter*, I, 12) and verse to Candiano Bollani (*Iter*, I, 12, 15, 16).

Poggio wrote to several of our Venetians: to Pietro Barbo (*Epist.*, ed. Tonellis, III, 261-62); Pietro Donato (I, 120-26 and 143-44); Jacopo Foscari (II, 150-54, 177-78); Pietro del Monte (II, 119-21, 281-82; III, 82-83, 101-103, 115-16, 216-17). Del Monte also wrote Poggio; cf. A. Zanelli, "Pietro del Monte," 8, p. 114, #13, and the summary chart of the correspondence between Poggio and del Monte in the former's *Opera omnia*, IV, 738-39. See also L. Casarsa, "Gregorio Correr," p. 47 n. 50, and LQU, p. 38, for a letter to Correr, perhaps lost. Poggio dedicated to Francesco Barbaro his *De avaritia* and directed an invective against Jacopo Zeno. Bruni wrote letters to Jacopo Foscari (*Epist.*, ed. Mehus, II, 96-97, 109) and Pietro Miani (ibid., I, 51-56, 67-68, 83-84, 122; II, 184-85; and *Humanistisch-philosophische Schriften*, ed. H. Baron, pp. 107-108). He was impressed by the oratory of Zaccaria Trevisan V, as he wrote Miani (*Epist.*, II, 15), but quarreled with Lauro Quirini (cf. A. Segarizzi, "Lauro Quirini," p. 7, and Bruni's *Epist.*, II, 134-47). Ficino corresponded with Marco Aurelio, Sebastiano Badoer, Ermolao Barbaro G, Marco Barbo, Bernardo Bembo, Febo Capella, Girolamo Donato, Pietro Molin, and Antonio Vinciguerra, all of the core group, as well as other Venetian figures; see Chapter One, n. 50, and the relevant profiles; also discussion in Kristeller, "Marsilio Ficino e Venezia." Girolamo Donato and Ermolao Barbaro G corresponded with Pico and Poliziano: for the former, cf. Rigo, "Carteggio," pp. 533-35; for the latter, see in his *Epist.* the editor Branca's catalogue, II, 156 and 157, respectively. Poliziano also wrote Latin verse in praise of Bembo: cf. Cian, "Per Bernardo Bembo—II," pp. 51-52.

Traversari wrote letters to Federico Corner (*Epist.*, ed. Mehus, II, 326-28), to Fantino Dandolo (ibid., II, 97-99; *Epist.*, ed. Martène and Durand, cols. 611-12); to Marco Lippomano (cf. Stinger, *Humanism*, p. 147); several to Francesco Barbaro (cf. *Cento-trenta*, pp. 11-15, 19, 63; also a letter from Barbaro on p. 63); and exchanged several letters with Leonardo Giustiniani (cf. A. Oberdorfer, "L'epistolario, di Leonardo Giustiniano," pp. 8-13, 15). Valla quarrelled with Andrea Contrario (cf. Sabbadini, "Andrea Contrario," pp. 382-83) and Lauro Quirini (Quirini's letter to Valla in Segarizzi, "Lauro Quirini," pp. 23-24, provoked Valla's response in L. Barozzi and R. Sabbadini, *Studi sul Panormita e sul Valla*, pp. 112-13) and was defended against Poggio by Lorenzo Zane (cf. Agostini, *Notizie*, I, 180; R. Weiss, "Lorenzo Zane," p. 165; G. Zippel, "Lorenzo Valla," pp. 104ff.).

finitude and clarity. The reader, however, far from being misled, has been fully informed of the kinds of figures barely included or narrowly excluded. Some further comments should still be made.

It is perhaps the most vulnerable aspect of the construction of this core group that patrician dominance is susceptible to overstatement. Patrician humanists of minor importance may be more conspicuous and thus more likely to be included in our group than commoner humanists with equal attributes. Their accomplishments attracted greater attention than those of commoners. Privileged and wealthy, they had the means to hire humanist teachers, to acquire books or to commission works, or to gain access to learned men. As each decision of inclusion or exclusion is made, the implicit bias is strengthened.

To some extent, then, this distortion is inevitable; to some extent it is also acceptable. Venetian humanism is, it seems, naturally characterized by the participation at a modest level of a great many patricians whose main commitment is outside of intellectual life. It is not wholly a misrepresentation, therefore, to admit these figures, if due effort is also made to identify and include commoner humanists of similarly modest achievement.

Also susceptible to distortion are the criteria of significance and activity for the last twenty years of the period under discussion. During the 1470s and 1480s, the sheer sum of intellectual activity in Venice increased as foreigners and natives surrounded the new printers in circles perhaps similar to that which later crystallized around Manuzio. Much of this activity was minor. For this reason, and because it was chiefly characterized by the preparation of texts for printing—an activity not central to our concern—some of it has perhaps escaped notice here. This cultural phenomenon deserves a separate study, and will shortly receive one (by Martin Lowry). In the meantime, though some minor activity of Venetians in this category, and some major activity by foreign transients, has fallen outside the range of our core group, still the most important natives and resident foreigners thus involved have assuredly been included.

Another problem is implicit in this enterprise of defining a core group. How tightly or how loosely should the net be drawn? If the core group had been defined more narrowly, only major humanists would have been included. Many patricians would have dropped out of our sample—but also several minor figures among the clerics, physicians, and secretaries. The distinctiveness of the Venetian humanist circle would have been missed with the elimination of such critical and colorful figures as Marco Lippomano, Vitale Lando, Marco Sanuto, and Niccolò Leonardi, among others. Patrician participation would still be the dominant note, for Venice's most important and prolific humanists are indisputably patrician: the two Giustinianis, Bernardo and Leonardo; the two Barbaros, Francesco and Ermolao the Younger; Paolo Morosini, Lauro Quirini, and Girolamo Donato.

Defined more broadly, the core group would have eluded definition. It would include patrician patrons and readers and attenders of lectures, teachers and priests of all sorts, transient as well as permanently resident foreigners. Two main effects could perhaps be noted. First, the number of foreigners would swell relative to the whole group, since, particularly in the later years of the century, Venice was a magnet for foreigners wishing to work for the presses or edit or publish their own or others' works. Second, the patricians would still establish a dominant presence—for, indeed, that patrician prominence is a fact of Venetian humanist society, whether the eye is cast on giants alone, or on all participants.

The definition of our core group, therefore, like any definition, inevitably admits the possiblity of distortion. But it does not essentially misrepresent the Venetian humanist circle. An analysis of the core group as here defined may now be undertaken.

13. THE CORE GROUP ANALYZED

The humanists of early Renaissance Venice constitute a small society in themselves. They derive from different social classes, pursue a variety of occupations, belong to different generations. As they converse—rich and poor, powerful and insecure, young and old—their various conditions cannot fail to affect their thought and expression. To understand the nature of Venetian humanism, it is necessary to answer the question that opened this discussion: who were the Venetian humanists? To answer that question, it is necessary not only to name them, but to analyze their social organization.

The most important distinction of class in the society of Venetian humanists, as in Venetian society generally, is that between noblemen and commoners. The Venetian patriciate, unlike the patriciates of most late medieval or Renaissance cities, was a class precisely defined by law, possessing uniquely the right to rule and to transmit that right of access to power to legitimate descendents. Unlike the feudal aristocracies of most of Europe, the Venetian patriciate originally derived its wealth and ultimately its power not from land but commerce, and commerce remained in the fifteenth century its characteristic enterprise. Commoners were denied access to power and—though many were rich—only members of the small and elite class of citizens enjoyed the commercial privileges extended to all noblemen.[18]

Sixty-four members of the core group of humanists were patricians, twenty-eight were commoners. Patricians constitued 3 to 4 percent of the population of Venice. Patrician humanists constitued more than two-thirds of the population of Venetian humanists. Their massive presence among this small society of learned men is the most striking phenomenon that this analysis will note. It was to affect fundamentally, as earlier chapters have shown, the culture of Venetian humanism.

These figures are bold, but do not tell the whole story. Not only are the patricians the largest social group among the society of Venetian humanists. They also come overwhelmingly from the most privileged sector of that class. Though admitted by birth to the ruling class, not all Venetian noblemen pursued political careers. Many devoted their energies to commerce. Some joined the church, ascending to lower or higher ranks within that hierarchy. Among those who did seek office, moreover, most held minor offices. For by our period, the major offices of Venetian government and thus the helm of the republic were in the possession of a small elite within the patriciate. Among our core group patricians, eighteen are clergymen whose careers will be examined shortly. Nearly all of the forty-six laymen remaining derive from that inner circle of the Venetian ruling class.[19]

[18] This analysis of the social organization of the Venetian humanists significantly refines that in my "The Patriciate and the Intellectuals." Note that F. Gilbert's "Humanism in Venice" calls for a rigorous sociological approach to the problem (p. 19). For Venice's social structure in this period, see especially S. Chojnacki, "In Search of the Venetian Patriciate"; J. Davis, *The Decline of the Venetian Nobility*; Finlay, *Politics*, pp. 44ff. and passim; E. Muir, *Civic Ritual*, pp. 34ff.; G. Ruggiero, *Violence*, especially Chapter Four. For a sixteenth-century discussion of Venice's social structure, defined as consisting of nobles, citizens, foreigners, and the "popolo," see Donato Giannotti's *Dialogus de republica venetorum*, cols. 22-25. Ruggiero remarks that for contemporary chroniclers—less sensitive than Giannotti to the small but important groups of professionals and intellectuals—"the distinction between *nobilitas* and *populares* was the limit of social analysis" (*Violence*, p. 55). Some contemporaries omitted all mention of a lowest class of the "popolo." Pier Paolo Vergerio used the term "populus" to refer to the *nobles* of Venice, "plebs" for the privileged citizen class (D. Robey and J. Law, "The Venetian Myth and the 'De Republica Veneta' of Pier Paolo Vergerio," p. 16). Giovanni Caldiera defines the social classes of Venice thus: foreigners, citizens, nobles (King, "Personal, Domestic and Republican Values in the Moral Philosophy of Giovanni Caldiera," p. 562). S. Collodo observes the same prejudice in the vernacular chronicles: the "popolo" is scarcely mentioned, and their perspective is purely oligarchic ("Temi e caratteri della cronachista veneziana," p. 148).

[19] For the stratification of the patriciate and the existence of an elite within that elite, see especially S. Chojnacki, "In Search"; G. Cozzi, "Authority and Law in Renaissance Venice," pp. 297-98; Cozzi, "Domenico Morosini e il 'De bene instituta re pubblica,' " pp. 426ff.; J. Davis, *Decline*, pp. 21ff. and D. Queller, "The Civic Irresponsibility of

The bio-bibliographical profiles of these forty-six lay patricians will provide details of their political careers. This analysis will focus on ten major offices: those of *consigliere* (ducal counselor); *savio grande (del consiglio); savio di terraferma*; Consiglio dei Dieci, member; *avogador di comun*; ducal elector; ambassador; governor; military or naval leader; Procuratore di San Marco.

These offices are among the most important in Venetian government. The counselors, *savi grandi* ("great sages"), and *savi di terraferma* ("sages for the mainland") helped to guide policy. The Council of Ten—infamous for its silent and thorough investigations—was charged to protect Venice against political and moral crime. The *avogadori*, or public attorneys, investigated allegations of impropriety by government councils and officials. The ducal electors (nine sets of varying numbers) chosen in a series of ballots during the election of each doge, self-evidently had an impact on policy. The *procuratori*, who held a position considered to be second in importance only to the doge's, administered the affairs of the Church of San Marco and supervised the administration of charity to widows and orphans. The ambassadors for whom Venice is famous drew normally on their own fortunes to support the lavish missions in which they negotiated treaties and alliances. The military *provveditori* observed and directed the land wars fought by hired *condottieri* and inspected the systems of fortifications, and the naval *capitani generali* themselves headed the war fleets manned largely by native captains. To the cities Venice conquered on the land she sent governors and military leaders: *podestà* and *capitani*, in general, but to Friuli a *luogotenente* and to Ferrara— not a Venetian city—a *visdomino* to head the community of resident Venetians and to protect Venetian interests. To her maritime colonies, Venice sent governors, as well: a duke to Crete, and *capitani* elsewhere.[20]

---

the Venetian Nobility," p. 223-35. The distinction between layman and cleric has sometimes been unclear. Ermolao Barbaro G (included among the laymen), Fantino Dandolo, Taddeo Quirini, and (perhaps) Pietro Miani (included among the clerics) had pursued political careers before switching to ecclesiastical ones. They have been assigned to one group or the other according to individual circumstances, for which see the individual profiles. It is difficult in general to deal with the clergy as a social group because of their relations as individuals to other groups within the population; cf. Ruggiero, *Violence*, pp. 58-59.

[20] For a discussion of these offices, see especially G. Maranini, *La costituzione di Venezia dopo la serrata del Maggior Consiglio*, and the brief digest of da Mosto, *Archivio*; for the Senate, E. Besta, *Il senato veneziano*. See also the synopses in Chambers, *The Imperial Age of Venice*, pp. 73ff.; Finlay, *Politics*; F. C. Lane, *Venice: A Maritime Republic*, pp. 250ff.; O. Logan, *Culture and Society*, pp. 25ff. For the office of ambassador, see D. Queller, *Early Venetian Legislation on Ambassadors*. A discussion of the shift in the relative powers of the councils from the fourteenth to the fifteenth centuries is found in G. Cracco, "Patriziato e oligarchia a Venezia nel Tre-Quattrocento."

A record of whether and how often each of our lay patrician humanists held these office or categories of position is presented in Table 3. Table 4 summarizes the data presented in Table 3. It shows for each figure how many major offices were held repeatedly, twice, or once in the course of a career. In the absence of any record of major office-holding, it shows what noteworthy but lesser political office the figure is known (by me) to have held.

The regimentation of career data required in Tables 3 and 4 ignores to some extent the complex and nearly unmeasurable reality of Venetian politics. Some figures, for instance, who participated in several ducal elections did so in part by pure fate—doges died rapidly during the years of their political activity—while others who never did similarly had the ill fate to live earlier in the century when a single doge—Foscari—reigned for thirty-four years and vitiated the opportunity for participation in the election ritual. The offices of *provveditore* and ambassador were of irregular term, sometimes lasting many months or even years. Those of *consigliere, savio,* and member of the Council of Ten had regular terms, but figures were frequently elected to replace others for a fraction of the time. Governorships, normally held for a one-year term on the mainland, varied according to title and circumstances for the maritime colonies. The distinction between political and military offices has been made arbitrarily: that of *provveditore,* often only supervisory, has been considered military, whereas the captaincy of a city has been classed as a governorship. Occasionally these distinctions are awkward: Jacopo Antonio Marcello's captaincies, for example, were real military positions, as was Barbaro's heroic captaincy of Brescia during its defence against besieging Milanese forces. The two offices held by Pietro Contarini (*provveditore* of Coron and governor of Nisia) I have classed as military and political, respectively.

The figures who held major offices, finally, also held minor titles. These I have usually omitted, not only in the tables, but also in the biographical profile if the information does not significantly further illumine the character. Minor offices have, however, in Table 4 as in the profiles, been noted for figures who did not attain major ones.

Yet the discipline imposed upon career data in Tables 3 and 4 is necessary for the overview intended here, and does not misrepresent the intricate reality more fully presented in the profiles. Examination of these data shows that our patrician humanists participated in the political life of Venice to a very high degree, holding many major offices frequently over the course of their careers.

Thirty-eight of our forty-six lay patricians (82 percent) held repeatedly at least one of the offices designated here as major, and may

TABLE 3. Lay Patricians: Frequency of Office-Holding

	CONS	SAV GR	SAV TF	CONS X	AVOG	DUC EL	AMB	GOV	MIL	PROC
Badoer, Sebastiano	+	+	1	1	1		+	+		
Barbarigo, Girolamo	+	+	+	+	1	1	+	+	+	+
Barbaro, Ermolao G			1		1		+			
Barbaro, Francesco	+	+	+	+			+	+	1	+
Barbaro, Zaccaria	+	+	+	+	1	+	+	+	2	+
Barbo, Niccolò						1	2	1		
Barbo, Paolo	2		+	+	2	2	+	1	2	
Bembo, Bernardo	1		+	+	2		+	+		
Bernardo, Antonio			+			1		+		
Bollani, Candiano	2	+	+	+	+	+	+	+	2	
Bollani, Domenico			1		2	1	+		+	
Calvo, Antonio	1		1	+	1	+		+	1	
Canal, Niccolò	1	2	+	+	1	1	+	+	+	
Contarini, Francesco							+			
Contarini, Pietro								1	1	
Corner, Federico										
Corner, Giovanni							1			
Dandolo, Marco	2	+	+		1	2	+	2		
Diedo, Francesco		2	+	+		1	+	+		
Donato, Antonio		1	+	1	1	1	+	2	1	
Donato, Girolamo	2	1			1	1	+	+		
Donato, Marco	1		+	+			+	2		
Foscari, Giacomo										
Foscarini, Ludovico	+	+	+	+	+	2	+	+	1	+
Giorgi, Domenico	+	+	+	+	1	+		2	1	
Giuliani, Andrea	2		2	1		1	+	+	+	
Giustiniani, Bernardo	+	+	+	+	1	+	+	1	2	+
Giustiniani, Leonardo	1	+	+	+	+		2	1	1	+
Lando, Vitale	2	+	+	+	2	+	+	+	1	
Lippomano, Marco	+	+	+	+	1		+	+	1	
Marcello, Jacopo Ant	+		1	1		1	2	2	+	
Marcello, Pietro G										
Marino, Giovanni			2				+	1		
Molin, Pietro							+	+		
Morosini, Barbone			+	1			+	+		
Morosini, Domenico	+	+	2	+		+				+
Morosini, Marcantonio	2	+	+	+	+		+	+	+	+
Morosini, Paolo	2	+	+	+	1	+	+	+	+	
Pisani, Paolo	2	+	2	2	2	1	+	+		
Quirini, Lauro										
Renier, Daniele	+	+		+	2	1	1	1		+
Sanuto, Leonardo							1	1		
Sanuto, Marco	2	2	+		+	2	1	2		
Trevisan, Zaccaria V		+		2			+	+	2	
Trevisan, Zaccaria G	+	+	+	+	+	1	+	+		
Vitturi, Daniele	+	+	+	+	2	1	2	+	1	

NOTES:

CONS	Consigliere		DUC EL	Ducal elector
SAV GR	Savio grande		AMB	Ambassador
SAV TF	Savio di terraferma		GOV	Governor
CONS X	Consiglio dei Dieci		MIL	Military command
AVOG	Avogador di comun		PROC	Procuratore (held for life)

1 = office held once   2 = office held twice   + = office held three or more times (or for life)

TABLE 4. Lay Patricians: Summary of Office-Holding Frequency

	Major Offices Held			
	Repeatedly	Twice	Once	Other
Badoer, Sebastiano	4		3	
Barbarigo, Girolamo	8		2	
Barbaro, Ermolao G	1		2	
Barbaro, Francesco	7		1	
Barbaro, Zaccaria	8	1	1	
Barbo, Niccolò		1	2	
Barbo, Paolo	3	4	1	
Bembo, Bernardo	4	1	1	
Bernardo, Antonio	2		1	
Bollani, Candiano	7	2		
Bollani, Domenico	2	1	2	
Calvo, Antonio	3		4	
Canal, Niccolò	5	1	3	
Contarini, Francesco	1			
Contarini, Pietro			2	
Corner, Federico				Consiglio XL
Corner, Giovanni			1	
Dandolo, Marco	3	3	1	
Diedo, Francesco	4	1	1	
Donato, Antonio	2	1	5	
Donato, Girolamo	2	1	3	
Donato, Marco	3	1	1	
Foscari, Jacopo				Senate, Senate zonta
Foscarini, Ludovico	8	1	1	
Giorgi, Domenico	5	1	2	
Giuliani, Andrea	3	2	2	
Giustiniani, Bernardo	7	1	2	
Giustiniani, Leonardo	5	1	3	
Lando, Vitale	6	2	1	
Lippomano, Marco	6		2	
Marcello, Jacopo Ant	2	2	3	
Marcello, Pietro G				merchant?
Marino, Giovanni	1	1	1	
Molin, Pietro	2			
Morosini, Barbone	3		1	
Morosini, Domenico	5	1		
Morosini, Marcantonio	8	1		
Morosini, Paolo	7	1	1	
Pisani, Paolo	3	4	1	
Quirini, Lauro				auditor veterum sententiarum
Renier, Daniele	4	1	3	
Sanuto, Leonardo			2	
Sanuto, Marco	2	4	1	
Trevisan, Zaccaria V	3	2		
Trevisan, Zaccaria G	7		1	
Vitturi, Daniele	5	2	2	

be considered to have had political careers of major importance. Of these, four (approximately 9 percent of the whole group of forty-six) held eight major offices repeatedly; five (11 percent) held seven offices repeatedly; two (4 percent) held six; five (11 percent) held five; four (9 percent) held four; eight (17 percent) held three; seven (15 percent) held two; and three (7 percent) held one office repeatedly.

If those patricians who held each of between four and eight major offices repeatedly (three or more times) can be considered to have had political careers of exceptional importance—and I think that that judgment is fair—then 45 percent of our lay patrician humanists achieved that standing.

Less brilliant but still solid are the political records of those who held none of our major offices repeatedly but held at least one major office twice (only one figure falls into this category) or even once (as do three). These four together constitute less than 10 percent of our group of forty-six lay patrician humanists.

Only four members of that group held, to my knowledge, no major office as defined here. Their cases have idiosyncratic features. Lauro Quirini, a humanist of first importance, began his Venetian career as *auditor veterum sententiarum* in 1450; soon after, for reasons not certainly established, he retired not only from political life but from Venice, returning to the Venetian colony of Crete (his birthplace), where he successfully pursued a career as landed proprietor and entrepreneur. Jacopo Foscari had barely begun his political career when, accused of betraying state secrets, he was arrested and exiled. Both Federico Corner and Pietro Marcello the Younger may have had commercial interests. In the case of the former, these may have precluded a political career otherwise open to him, given his family's great wealth and prestige. In the case of the latter, whose activities—alone among the humanists—are so obscure as to suggest the obscurity of his branch of the powerful Marcello clan, I venture no such explanation. It is to be noted that he died rather young (at forty-eight), a circumstance that might help explain the obscurity of his record.

Among our politically active humanists, as well, circumstances occasionally terminated careers successfully begun. The delinquents Niccolò Canal and Vitale Lando were both banished after long and impressive careers; Domenico Bollani, younger but enterprising and already embarked on major achievements, was also banished for a crime against the state. Niccolò and Paolo Barbo, Francesco Contarini, Giovanni Marino, and Barbone Morosini all died relatively young (at forty-two, forty-six, thirty-six, thirty-seven [?], and forty-three or four, respectively), their propitious political careers perhaps curtailed by that decision of fate. Ermolao Barbaro the Younger, who had also attained several honorable offices before his nomination to the patriarchate at age thirty-seven, died three years later. Nor were commercial activities the exclusive reserve of the humanists who were less active politically. Candiano Bollani and Leonardo and Bernardo Giustiniani were humanists of first rank and politicans of first importance who also engaged in commercial ventures. Leonardo Sanuto, a figure of some interest though not so conspicuous in his achievements as these, was in commercial partnership with his brothers, and Giovanni Corner, an early collector of ancient manuscripts, traveled extensively in the eastern Mediterranean to administer family property.

These are the principal cases known to me where lay patricians engaged in commerce. To these might be added the incidents of land purchase by Bernardo Bembo and Ludovico Foscarini, and the possibility that Antonio Donato, who perhaps served once as a galley captain, may have engaged in trade. Evidence of wealth is a matter distinct from evidence of commercial activity. Domenico Morosini, prominent in both intellectual and political life, was a man of great wealth, and Marco Lippomano, equally prominent, probably a man of substance. Jacopo Antonio Marcello was able to reward the humanist Francesco Filelfo with a silver bowl of conspicuous value. The wealth of the fathers of Girolamo Barbarigo and Giovanni Corner was legendary. Bollani and Bembo were apparently poor (in the relative sense of poverty that can be used of these privileged individuals).

Information about the wealth and commercial activity of these figures is scarce and found only adventitiously. No tax records exist for this period to give full information. Occasional documents will reveal that a figure is engaged in ongoing commercial enterprises; these or a testament will note the size of a dowry. Assumption of ambassadorial duties suggests wealth, since these were expensive, with most or all of the costs, including those of display, assumed by the nobleman himself. Nor did the other major offices pay a salary. A patrician holding such offices, therefore, was relatively wealthy. The less affluent (and even the rich, at times) diligently avoided these responsibilities, while poor patricians sought minor bureaucratic positions that carried a stipend.[21]

Just as the majority of lay patricians attained high office in the Venetian government, so patrician clerics achieved high offices in the church. Table 5 summarizes their major positions.

Of our eighteen patrician clerics, fifteen attained the position of bishop or archbishop. Of these fifteen, three additionally attained the

[21] See D. Queller, "Civic Irresponsibility," p. 231 and passim.

TABLE 5. Patrician Clerics

	Major Positions	Minor Offices and Curial Titles
Barbaro, Ermolao V	bishop of Treviso (1443) bishop of Verona (1453)	apostolic protonotary, papal legate, papal governor (Perugia)
Barbo, Marco	bishop of Treviso (1455) bishop of Vicenza (1464) cardinal (1467) patriarch of Aquileia (1471) bishop of Palestrina (1478)	papal legate (repeatedly)
Barbo, Pietro	bishop of Cervia (1440) cardinal (1440) bishop of Vicenza (1451) bishop of Padua (1459) pope (1464)	archdeacon (Bologna), apostolic protonotary
Barozzi, Francesco	bishop of Treviso (1466)	canon (Bergamo), papal referendarius
Barozzi, Pietro	bishop of Belluno (1471) bishop of Padua (1487)	
Correr, Gregorio	abbot of San Zeno (1443) elected patriarch of Venice (1464)	apostolic protonotary
Dandolo, Fantino	archbishop of Candia (1444) bishop of Padua (1448)	[previous political career]; apostolic protonotary, papal governor (Bologna)
Dolfin, Pietro	abbot of S. Michele (1462) general, Camaldulensians (1480)	
Donato, Ludovico	bishop of Belluno (1462) bishop of Bergamo (1465)	apostolic protonotary; canon, Cathedral of Padua
Donato, Pietro	archbishop of Candia (1415) bishop of Castello (1425) bishop of Padua (1428)	apostolic protonotary, papal legate, papal governor (Perugia)
Foscari, Pietro	cardinal (1477) bishop of Padua (1481)	primicerius of San Marco, apostolic protonotary
Marcello, Pietro V	bishop of Ceneda (1399) bishop of Padua (1409)	canon, Parenzo; papal vicar, Ancona
Miani, Pietro	bishop of Vicenza (1409)	[previous political career?]
Quirini, Taddeo		[previous political career]; deacon (Candia), canon (Treviso and Brescia), vicar-general (Padua), archpriest (Padua)

TABLE 5 (*cont.*)

	Major Positions	Minor Offices and Curial Titles
Vallaresso, Fantino	bishop of Parenzo and Pola (1415) archibishop of Candia (1425)	papal legate
Vallaresso, Maffeo	archbishop of Zara (1450)	canon (Crete and Treviso); apostolic protonotary
Zane, Lorenzo	archbishop of Spalato (1452) patriarch of Antioch (1473) bishop of Treviso (1473) bishop of Brescia (1478)	apostolic protonotary; papal legate, governor (Cesena, repeatedly), treasurer-general, etc.
Zeno, Jacopo	bishop of Feltre & Belluno (1447) bishop of Padua (1460)	apostolic subdeacon, papal referendarius

NOTE: Ermolao Barbaro Giovane, listed among the lay patricians, was made Patriarch of Aquileia in 1491.

dignity of cardinal (the two Barbos and Foscari), and of these Pietro Barbo also ascended to the papal chair. Of the three remaining clerics, Correr and Dolfin both held the title of abbot, and were subsequently chosen for higher positions: the former, the patriarchate of Venice, a title that he never assumed because of his untimely death; the latter, the generalship of his order. Only Taddeo Quirini was limited to minor church positions. Several of these figures also attained lesser dignities and benefices, the most notable of which are indicated.

The fifteen patrician clerics who held bishoprics or archbishoprics were assigned mainly to Venetian-controlled sees, territorial or maritime (exceptions were Palestrina, Cervia, and Antioch). Indeed, they tended to specialize in certain sees. Three were archbishop of Candia in Crete—a fine location for amateurs of Greek literature. Three were bishops of Belluno, three of Vicenza, four of Treviso, and, remarkably, seven of Padua. The see of that university town and center of intellectual activity was held continuously by our humanists from 1409 through 1507.

The majority of Venice's patrician humanist clerics, in sum, attained high office with the Church, and in themselves constituted a significant fraction of the group of Venice's leading churchmen in the fifteenth century.

Members of the clergy presumably owed a primary allegiance to Rome. That situation did not exist purely in Venice, however, any more than it did in the feudatories of medieval Europe. The major ecclesiastical positions of the Venetian terraferma and maritime colonies were at least in part arms of the system of control that protected the Venetian empire. Candidates for these positions were presented to the Venetian Senate, which in turn selected among them the new dignitary. Though the Senate's choice often accorded with the wishes of the prelate's constituency (the monks of the abbey or the citizens of the city), often it did not. And often it clashed with the pope's own choice. The persons appointed to these lofty positions were normally, though not invariably, noblemen. The ecclesiastical offices of Venice's empire were consequently, like the empire itself, a province of the city's nobility. Members of the same families dominated Church and government offices.[22]

Not surprisingly, they played in some cases a political role. The bishop of a Venetian city was viewed as a spiritual governor, concerned with the souls of the citizens he guided while holding the interests of Venice firmly in view.[23] Other clerics were also expected to act upon Venetian loyalties as well as loyalty to Rome. Francesco Barbaro reminded both his nephew Ermolao Barbaro the Elder and his friend Pietro Donato to maintain an allegiance to Venice while serving the pope. Marco Barbo continued to pursue Venice's interest in the Ferrarese war, although the pope was the city's principal opponent. Pietro Dolfin, then abbot of San Michele di Murano, performed invaluable service as a spy.[24]

Some clerics, on the other hand, had weaker links to Venice—in-

[22] For a description of the steps by which Venice exerted control over ecclesiastical positions at home and on the terraferma, and the process of the selection of appointees, see C. Cenci, "Senato veneto 'probae' ai benefizi ecclesiastici," pp. 315ff. For the use made by the Venetian government of the ecclesiastical positions in its empire, see also Logan, *Culture and Society*, pp. 30ff., and P. Prodi, "The Structure and Organization of the Church in Renaissance Venice." A. Ventura points out that the acquisition of terraferma ecclesiastical benefices for the Venetian nobility, a consequence of conquest, resulted in the deflection to aristocratic purses of mainland wealth; see "Il dominio di Venezia nel Quattrocento," p. 180.

[23] Venice's humanist literature possesses two works that give an excellent portrait of the guiding role it was expected a bishop would play. The first is by Pietro Barozzi, a member of our core group: the *De factionibus extinguendis* [DFE], especially Book III; see the discussion of themes in F. Gaeta's introduction, pp. 35ff., and Chapter Two, Section 6 above. The second is by Gasparo Contarini: the *De officio boni viri ac probi episcopi*; see the discussion of themes by G. Fragnito, "Cultura umanistica e riforma religiosa," pp. 138ff. Both these works reveal that the office of bishop had considerable political importance. O. Logan's excellent review of the literature on the office of bishop in "The Ideal of the Bishop and the Venetian Patriciate" does not make full note of this expectation of political service from Venetian ecclesiasts.

[24] For Barbaro's advice, see his *Epist.*, ed. Quirini, pp. 109-10, and *Centotrenta*, ed. Sabbadini, pp. 71-72. For Barbo's loyalty, see Labalme, *Bernardo Giustiniani*, pp. 216-17, and P. Paschini, *Il carteggio fra il cardinale Marco Barbo e Giovanni Lorenzi*, pp. 42ff., especially Barbo's letter to the doge, pp. 79-80. For Dolfin's activities, see G. Soranzo, "Pietro Dolfin e il suo epistolario," pp. 158ff. and J. Schnitzer, *Peter Delfin General des Camaldulensenordens*, pp. 199ff.

cluding delinquent clerics (like the lay patricians already named) who publicly defied Venetian law and authority. Lorenzo Zane, raised in Rome and related to three fifteenth-century popes (all Venetians), notoriously declared himself by his actions a papal loyalist and was twice condemned by the Council of Ten. Pietro Barbo accepted papal appointment to the bishopric of Padua in 1459, spurning Venice's choice (Gregorio Correr). Later as Paul II, one of that triad of Venetian popes, he pursued policies often at odds with those of his native city. Ermolao Barbaro the Younger also defied the Senate to accept papal nomination as patriarch of Aquileia, winning the rebuke of friends and his father's disgrace.

In general, however, patrician clerics did not, because of their ties to Rome, cease to be strongly committed to Venice by sentiment and blood. Other members of their families remained at home, and some held important government positions. Family relations, indeed, soldered the patrician class, though its activities—political, clerical, mercantile—were diverse. Even among the small subgroup of the patriciate that the patrician humanists considered here constitute, links of blood united lay and cleric, generation and generation, core group figures with intellectuals of other periods or categories.[25]

The four Barbaros were close relatives; Francesco Barbaro was uncle of Ermolao the Elder, father of Zaccaria, and grandfather of Ermolao the Younger. Leonardo Giustiniani was father of Bernardo, and brother, incidentally, of that austere first patriarch of Venice, San Lorenzo. The Giustinianis were related, as well, to Carlo Zeno, grandfather of Jacopo, to the brothers Lauro and Taddeo Quirini, and to Marco Dandolo. Bernardo Bembo was father of the leading intellectual of the generation that lies just beyond this study's scope—Pietro Bembo. Candiano Bollani was father of the less eminent but erudite Domenico, and Giovanni Corner of the precocious Federico. Francesco Contarini was the son of the philosopher Niccolò. Antonio Donato was son of the learned Andrea, and Girolamo, more famous than father or grandfather, of Antonio. Ludovico and Marco Donato were cousins, and both were nephews of the bishop Pietro Donato. Leo-

---

[25] For the clan organization of the Venetian nobility generally, see especially S. Chojnacki, "In Search"; Chojnacki, "Kinship Ties and Young Patricians in Fifteenth-Century Venice"; and J. Davis, *Decline*. Molmenti remarked on the participation of whole families in humanist culture (*Vita privata*, II, 230). Logan (*Culture and Society*, pp. 76ff.) remarked on these and other relationships among intellectuals. For relationships of friendship were also pervasive among the noble humanists, and served further to consolidate that group. The individual profiles explain the family relationships sketched here; particularly intricate is the network of Barbo and related clans, for which see the profile of Pietro Barbo.

nardo Sanuto, uncle of Marco, was the father of the next generation's most remarkable intellectual figure, the diarist Marino; these Sanutos are related, as well, to Doge Cristoforo Moro. Zaccaria Trevisan the Elder, related as well by marriage to the brothers Pietro Marcello the Elder and Jacopo Antonio Marcello, was the father of his namesake whose birth he did not live to greet. Fantino Vallaresso was uncle of Maffeo, both clerics. The Camuldulensian General Pietro Dolfin was nephew of the chronicler of the same name, in turn the son of the chronicler Giorgio; our Dolfin was also cousin to the cousins Domenico and Marcantonio Morosini.

Jacopo Foscari—son of Doge Francesco—was cousin to the cardinal Pietro. Fantino Dandolo was grandson of the learned Doge Andrea, and son of that Leonardo who appeared unnamed as one of Petrarch's opponents in that poet's work *On His Own Ignorance and That of Many Others*. Vitale Lando married the sister of Lorenzo Zane, and Vitale and Lorenzo were implicated together through that connection in charges of disloyalty in 1478. Zane was a member of that extraordinary network of families—Condulmier and Barbo—to which belonged the three fifteenth-century pontiffs Gregory XII, Eugene IV, and Paul II (our Pietro Barbo), the patriarch Giovanni Barozzi, the cardinals Giovanni Battista Zeno and Giovanni Michiel. Among our humanists who also belong to this stem are the Barbo pope's brother Paolo (also father of Guarino's student Giovanni) and more distant Barbo relations Marco and Niccolò (these three all laymen), the abbot Gregorio Correr (nephew of Pope Gregory's nephew, Antonio Correr, and uncle of Pietro and Paolo Barbo), and the bishops Francesco and Pietro Barozzi, uncle and nephew, and, respectively, brother and nephew of the patriarch Giovanni Barozzi, brother and son of the learned Ludovico, the correspondent of Francesco Barbaro and Ludovico Foscarini.

Not only individuals, but families, it seems, engaged in the intellectual life of Venice. Ties of birth and interest—crossing the barrier of ordination—knit the patrician humanists together, perhaps even more intensively than they knit together Venice's wider ruling class.

The patricians thus dominate the core group of humanists in number. The great majority of them are powerful figures, the laymen directly committed to the service of Venetian interests, the clerics, in many cases, indirectly so committed, or minimally attached to Venice because of their membership in one of her powerful clans. Lay and clerical patricians alike joined their activities as humanists to their urgent political and administrative duties. They were amateur humanists, for whom the intellectual life complemented responsibilities unique to their class.

Core group commoners are not so numerous, nor so unified, nor so powerful. They are a disparate group, including persons of different social strata and professions. They can be recognized as belonging to the group one recent author names "important people."[26] The term is admittedly vague, its vagueness expressing the difficulty of categorizing this assemblage of petty communal officials, nonnoble merchants and boat owners, professionals and foreigners of social rank equivalent to these. Lying between *popolo* (laborers and marginal persons such as servants, beggars, and wanderers) and nobility in the Venetian social hierarchy, they are a conspicuously dutiful and hardworking group, more concerned to please the patricians upon whom they depended for economic welfare and political stability than to dream of competing with or challenging their proud masters. Core group commoners form a small subset of this larger group that may have constituted from 8 to 11 percent of the population in our century, and share their characteristics while presenting their own distinctive features.

Core group commoners include both natives and resident foreigners, citizens and noncitizens. The eighteen natives (defined as those born in Venice, whether of Venetian or foreign parents) are clearly distinct from the ten resident foreigners (defined earlier under "criterion of residence"). The distinction between citizen and noncitizen has been more difficult to define, because the nature of citizenship was not clearly established during the period under study. The restricted class of *cittadini originari*—or "citizens-by-birth"—would eventually receive precise legal definition as persons born of families long-established in Venice, with neither father nor grandfather who had practiced a mechanical trade. These privileged citizens possessed full trading rights, and were alone permitted access to secretarial positions within the government; their most successful members could strive for directorial positions in the charitable *scuole* and even for the lofty office of grand chancellor. They formed a kind of secondary nobility within Venetian society, their names recorded in a "silver," as were those of the nobility in a "golden" book.

But in our period, the class was still fluid. Some of our humanist figures came from families known to be already established and respected in Venice during our period: Aleotti, Bruto, Caldiera, Capella, Domenichi, Leonardi, del Monte, Orsini, Tommasi surely belong to

---

[26] See Ruggiero, *Violence*, especially pp. 59ff., 82ff.

this category. Others came from seemingly humbler native families: Lorenzi, Marcanova, Ragazzoni, Vinciguerra. Others of our group were born to immigrant fathers, or were themselves immigrants: Aurelio, Contrario, Negri, Ramusio, Sagundino. Yet all these family names—lustrous, humble, and new—appear on rolls compiled in later centuries of the *cittadini originari*. In time, the principle was established, as has been said, that the status of "original citizenship" was a prerequisite for entry to Venice's corps of government secretaries. But for our period that principle does not prevail, and does not assist the unraveling of the citizenship question. At least two of the eight core group humanists who held such positions were themselves immigrants, or sons of recent immigrants. Marco Aurelio (whose father Niccolò, brother Paolo, and son Niccolò were also secretaries) was probably the son of an immigrant, and a relative of Niccolò Sagundino, himself a native of Negropont (Euboea) in Greece. Members of successive generations of both families also served in the government secretariat. The secretary Jacopo Languschi was probably also the son of an immigrant. Paolo Ramusio, a Riminese by birth, served not as a secretary in the central Venetian councils but as assessor, "judge," and in other clerical capacities for Venetian governors and representatives in various Veneto posts. His son Giovanni Battista, however, did serve in the government secretariat, like those of Aurelio and Sagundino. One fifteenth-century grand chancellor—Francesco della Sega, not of our group—was himself an immigrant; yet the grand chancellorship would come to be considered a particular preserve of native citizens, the analogue for that social class of the *dogado* for noblemen.[27]

Another category of citizens in Venice beside the *originari* are "citizens by privilege." These foreigners were granted citizenship and con-

[27] For G. B. Ramusio, see E. A. Cicogna, *Iscrizioni*, II, 315ff. For Francesco della Sega, see Giovanni Caldiera, *De praestantia venetae politiae*, fol. 138, a passage reviewed in King, "Personal, Domestic and Republican Values," pp. 562-63. Caldiera writes as late as 1463. In the early part of our period, secretarial positions did not yet have as a prerequisite *cittadinanza originaria*, nor was that prerequisite established by the second half of the century, despite a 1478 law. The early genealogies and chronicles describe the institution of original citizenship as it later existed, not as it in fact was emerging in the fifteenth century: see, for example, the anonymous *Cronaca di famiglie cittadini originari veneti*, pp. 127ff., and the pertinent discussion of this work in R. Bratti, *I codici nobiliari del Museo Correr di Venezia*, p. 36; also in modern works the discussion of da Mosto, *Archivio*, I, 73ff.; Logan, *Culture and Society*, pp. 26ff.; B. Pullan, *Rich and Poor in Renaissance Venice*, pp. 101ff.; Romanin, *Stor. doc.*, IV, 468ff.; A. della Torre, *Antonio Vinciguerra*, p. 6. A comprehensive analysis of the development of Venice's chancery elite from the late fifteenth through the seventeenth centuries in relationship to the citizen class appears in G. Trebbi, "La cancelleria veneta nei secoli XVI e XVII."

TABLE 6: All Commoners

Clerics	Teachers and Professors	Secretaries	Physicians
Bruto, Pietro (N)*	Brognoli, Benedetto (RF)	Aleotti, Ulisse (N)*	Caldiera, Giovanni (N)*
Cirneo, Pietro (RF)**	Frulovisi, Tito L. (RF)**	Aurelio, Marco (N)*+	Leonardi, Niccolò (N)*
Contrario, Andrea (N)*+	Merula, Giorgio (RF)	Capella, Febo (N)*	Tommasi, Pietro (N)*
Domenichi, Dom. de' (N)*	Morandi, Filippo (RF)**	Languschi, Jacopo (N)+?	
Lorenzi, Giovanni (N)*	Perleone, Pietro (RF)**	Ragazzoni, Jacopo (N)*	
del Monte, Pietro (N)*	Sabellico, Marcant. (RF)	Ramusio, Paolo (RF)*	
Negri, Francesco (N)*+	Valla, Giorgio (RF)	Sagundino, Niccolò (RF)*	
Orsini, Michele (N)*		Vinciguerra, Antonio (N)*	
	Marcanova, Giovanni (N)*		
	Tomeo, Nicc. Leonico (N)+		

* Original citizenship held in the fifteenth century or gained for the family subsequently.
** citizenship by privilege.
+ son of immigrant.   N native   RF resident foreigner

comitant trade privileges after a residence of a certain period: citizenship status *de intus* after ten years, *de intus et extra* after twenty-five. Of the ten core group foreigners, four were granted citizenship. Their family names do not subsequently appear among the lists of *cittadini originari*. Other of our foreigners resided in Venice for long periods without receiving—and perhaps never applying for—the privilege of citizenship.

Table 6 indicates the status of the twenty-eight commoner humanists of the core group by denoting natives, and resident foreigners, family names eventually identified as citizen, figures who received grants of citizenship, and "new" natives, sons of recent immigrants. The commoner humanists of the core group are various by occupation as by social category, as the table shows. They include eight clerics, seven teachers, two university professors, eight secretaries, and three physicians. These identifications are not so neat as they appear, however. Some categories embrace a considerable range of career achievement, or include figures who practiced the indicated profession for only a part of their careers. The following discussion will describe these complexities.

The clerics form a substantial subgroup of the commoner humanists, about the same size in proportion to the whole of that class as is the subgroup of patrician clerics relative to the whole community of patrician humanists (approximately 28 percent). Yet the group is diverse. Careers do not conform to a clear pattern, as do those of the patrician clerical humanists, and they do not constitute a monolithic and independent bloc. Two among them pursued successful church careers, eventually attaining episcopal titles of great dignity, and curial offices that testify to the esteem they earned from Rome. Their careers, indeed, compare well in status to those achieved by most of our patrician clerics. Domenico de' Domenichi was made bishop of Torcello (in Venice) in 1445 and bishop of Brescia, a major Veneto see, in 1464. He attained the titles of apostolic protonotary and later *referendarius*, served as papal legate on various missions, and was made papal vicar of Rome in 1473. Pietro del Monte, Domenichi's predecessor as bishop of Brescia (which see he held from 1442) likewise held the titles of protonotary and *referendarius*, and served the pope as papal legate, collector (in England), and governor of Perugia. Both Domenichi and del Monte were humanists and theologians of considerable reputation. Like the patricians in the pattern of their careers, however, neither Domenichi nor del Monte behaved (as did most of their noble counterparts) like agents of Venetian policy. Both were ardent defenders of papal authority.[28]

Distinctly more modest than these are the records of Pietro Bruto and Michele Orsini. Yet both attained episcopal dignity. The former, made bishop of Croja (Epirus) in 1468, served as vicar general for the bishop of Cattaro (Dalmatia) before ascending himself to that see, probably in 1471. Still holding Cattaro, he served as first vice regent, then lieutenant to the bishop of more prestigious Vicenza, in which role he is best remembered. The latter, having served from 1449 as prior of San Antonio di Castello (in Venice), was made bishop of Pola (Istria) in 1475, and held the see until 1497, shortly before his death, when he resigned in favor of an impoverished but noble young relation. Still holding Pola, he served briefly (1483-1484) as vicar and suffragen of the bishop of Padua. The sees held by these four bishops were subject to Venetian domination. To some extent, therefore, as for patrician clerics holding Veneto sees, these clerics may be seen as agents of Venetian empire. But it should be noted that Bruto and Orsini held sees of minor importance—although Bruto's activities as proponent of official anti-Semitism in Vicenza had notable success.

The remaining four commoner clerics of our group acquired only small and precarious positions, and should be considered, perhaps, to have pursued clerical careers only in a technical sense. Of these, Giovanni Lorenzi, whose life was far from fortunate, achieved perhaps greatest success. An ordained priest and secretary to Cardinal Marco Barbo, whom he followed to Rome, this skilled Hellenist subsequently became papal scribe, secretary, and librarian. Pietro Cirneo (the only

---

[28] See del Monte's *Monarchia in qua generalium conciliorum materia de potestate prestantia et excellentia Romani pontificis et imperatoris plenissime discutitur* and de' Domenichi's *De non exigendis decimis a clericis sine licentia papae [et] sedis apostolice.*

foreigner among the clerics), Andrea Contrario, and Francesco Negri (the latter two both "new men") were also ordained as priests. But all devoted their main energies to—and apparently derived their sustenance primarily from—teaching and writing. The natives Contrario and Negri roamed Italy and beyond in search of patronage; the foreigner Cirneo attached himself in Venice to one noble house.

In their activities of teaching and writing (Contrario and Lorenzi also edited texts), these last figures in some way more nearly resemble the teachers—all professional humanists—shortly to be discussed than the ecclesiastical administrators de' Domenichi and del Monte, or Bruto and Orsini. They have been classed with the clerics for the sake of consistency, but because of their relations to other social groups, clerics elude strict classification.

The group of commoner clerics thus includes a range of persons of differing social rank which seems to correlate to some extent with the type of career attainments. The four bishops came from citizen families already well established in Venice in the fifteenth century. The four priests include one member of a humble native family (Lorenzi), two sons of immigrants (Contrario and Negri), and one foreigner (Cirneo). All, however, may have been citizens: Cirneo was granted citizenship by privilege, and the remaining seven family names appear on the citizen lists of a later generation.

Seven members of our core group commoners—all resident foreigners—were teachers for at least part of their Venetian careers. Morandi, Perleone, Brognoli, and Sabellico, in that order, taught at the San Marco school established by the Venetian government for the linguistic preparation of future notaries and secretaries. Merula, Valla, and Sabellico taught in turn at the equally famous school of rhetoric, also publicly founded. Prior to their public appointments, Brognoli and Morandi are known to have taught in local schools, as did Frulovisi who, a malcontent and notorious critic of Venetian patrician culture, never attained a public chair.

Though primarily identified as teachers, not all these humanists limited themselves to that activity during their years in Venice. Brognoli, Merula, Sabellico, and Valla, all professional humanists, engaged in the criticism or edition of texts and were linked to the printing industry that burgeoned in Venice during the late-century years of their major activity. Morandi served at different points in his career as Venetian chancellor of Corcyra, secretary to the bailo of Constantinople, and chancellor to the patriarch of Venice, Maffeo Gerardi. Frulovisi, in Venice, wrote Latin comedies for which he is justly famous; for many years abroad, he haunted noble courts, acquired a degree in medicine, resisted permanence and definition.

As teachers, these figures were dependent upon the favor of wealthy or powerful men for their appointment and advancement. The public school teachers were appointed by patricians in the Senate. It is less clear how local school teachers were appointed, but the influence of prominent men was likely to have been present. Private teachers and tutors were often employed by patricians, as well, as were Perleone, while teaching at San Marco, Pietro Cirneo of our core group clerics, and Paolo Marsi, for example, among the transient foreigners. Pay for teachers in Venice was relatively low, and so, perhaps in consequence, was their status. Their condition of dependency, moreover, was the more marked because they were unrooted, non-Venetian, "new men." Their position was precarious, and was recognized as such.[29]

The careers of Giovanni Marcanova and Niccolò Leonico Tomeo pose a contrast to those of the foreign teachers. Both were natives who left Venice to become professors at nearby Padua, spending most of their lifetimes there, where they acquired their wide reputation. The former, a doctor, philosopher, and antiquarian, was identified so closely with Padua that he has often been assumed to have been Paduan. The latter, a Hellenist and philosopher, was the first to teach Aristotle from the Greek text at the university. They were Paduan residents; the pattern of their careers more closely resembles those of clerics who also spent many years abroad than that of foreigners who taught at the elementary or secondary level in Venice.

The eight core group commoners employed as government secretaries were on the whole more solidly rooted in Venice than either the native-born clerics or the foreign-born teachers. The ducal secretaries (Aleotti, Aurelio, Capella, Languschi, Sagundino, and Vinciguerra) held great status, commanded good salaries, and exercised considerable authority when dispatched on foreign missions.

Members of the secretarial order—numbering perhaps as many as one hundred in the early sixteenth century—enjoyed a status so great as to call in time for the perquisite of original citizenship. Salaries were good. In 1454, Ulisse Aleotti had his salary raised to a "mere" fifty ducats annually, whereas teachers at the San Marco school were

---

[29] For a survey of the school appointments (with information about salaries, which ranged from 100 to 200 ducats annually) and relevant bibliography, see Ross, "Venetian Schools," pp. 521-36 and 561ff.; for salaries, see also Molmenti, *Vita privata*, II, 258. For the relatively low pay and status of teachers in Venice, see M. Pastore Stocchi, "Scuola e cultura umanistica fra due secoli," especially p. 104. For the insecurity experienced by some of the core group teachers, see the examples given in Chapter One, Section 11.

receiving 100 ducats annually, at the Rialto school 200. But in 1464, a salary of 120 ducats was thought suitable for the needy orphan of Niccolò Sagundino, and in 1498, Antonio Vinciguerra's reached 150 ducats, nearing the 200 ducats that the teachers of rhetoric (the second San Marco school) enjoyed at about the same time. Sagundino himself may have been granted the extraordinary salary of 200 ducats following his disastrous shipwreck. In the early sixteenth century, ducal secretaries earned 200 ducats, the grand chancellor 300 ducats annually.[30]

Members of the secretariat had in some cases frequent and easy relations with powerful patricians either in Venice itself in the course of government business, or in employment abroad. The great influence of such secretaries as Ulisse Aleotti, Marco Aurelio, and Febo Capella (of our core group) and of Alessandro de' Fornaci and Giovanni Reguardati (outside of it) are witnessed by Ludovico Foscarini's and Francesco Barbaro's letters begging favors, influence, or information. The entry of a member to the secretarial circle enhanced a family's status. Some new men found the opportunity while so employed to obtain posts for their children in the same bureaucracy, and to launch a citizen dynasty, as did Aurelio and Sagundino. Ramusio, who served as assessor and judge to Venetian governors in various terraferma cities, enjoyed a status similar to that of the secretaries, and his descendants, as well, achieved significant status in Venice as learned men. Capella in his own right attained the office, supreme for his class, of grand chancellor.[31]

The secretaries, nevertheless, appointed like the public teachers by government council, were dependent upon the good will of patricians

---

[30] For the linking of secretarial status to citizenship, see n. 27 above. For a description of the secretaries' number, organization, and appointment, see F. Babinger, *Johannes Darius*, p. 21 n. 1; this work examines one secretary and describes his considerable influence. See also F. Gilbert's discussion of the role of the grand chancellor (p. 505) and of the secretaries (pp. 506ff.) in his "The Last Will of a Venetian Grand Chancellor." His citation of a contemporary source estimating the size of the secretariat is repeated here. Its size in the fifteenth century is suggested by Maggior Consiglio lists of notaries assigned to record the results of ducal elections; see, for example, ASV, MC-Regina, c. 16. For Aleotti's raise, see CLN 9, c. 30, 20 Sept.; for teachers' salaries, cf. Ross, "Venetian Schools," n. 28. The provision for Sagundino's orphan in ST 5, c. 73, 22 March; for his shipwreck, see above, Chapter One, Section 13. See the profile for Vinciguerra. For sixteenth-century salaries, see Gilbert, "Will," 506ff.

[31] The Foscarini and Barbaro letters are cited frequently in Chapter One. See the secretaries' profiles for diplomatic activity; for an earlier example, see M. Poppi, "Ricerche sulla vita e cultura del notaio e cronista veneziano Lorenzo de Monacis." For the Aurelio, Sagundino, and Ramusio offspring, see the profiles. As an example of the enhancement of family status through advancement in the secretariat, see Francesco Negri's *oratio* for Girolamo Reguardati (in P. Verrua, "Cinque orazioni dette dall'umanista Francesco Negri nello studio di Padova," p. 211).

acting in a public capacity, and were anxious about their status and security. Although they belonged to Venice's elite secretarial corps, they did not thereby acquire independence. They had joined an army of skilled clerks within whose ranks they could progress; but they progressed without expectation, through that route alone, of entry to the prerogatives of power. There was in aristocratic Venice an un-bridgeable barrier between the commoner, however skilled, and the nobleman who had access to real authority. Contrast this situation with that in Florence, where "new men" or old would acquire, in the role of chancellor, considerable power.[32]

These humanists constitute, moreover, only a small fraction of that corps of skilled writers from whom a larger harvest of humanists might be expected. The humanists identified here were a minority within the extensive Venetian secretariat. And secretaries, just as surprisingly, perhaps, represent only a minority within the group of commoner humanists (29 percent), and an even smaller one (7 percent) within the whole core group.

Three physicians (Tommasi, Leonardi, and Caldiera) complete the ranks of commoner humanists and of the core group. All from *cittadino* families well established in the fifteenth century, they were affluent men employed in a highly honored profession, renowned for their skill and their learning.[33]

The commoner humanists, diverse in social condition, in occupation, and in experience, were not united by family relations, as were the patricians, nor by pervasive ties of friendship. The search has been futile for family networks among a group so small and diverse as this. Nor are these figures linked by extensive ties of friendship. Aleotti, Aurelio, and Capella were friends of Niccolò Sagundino, a foreigner who had been able to enter their secretarial order. The teacher Perleone, Sagundino's consoler, was also a friend. Andrea Contrario and Giovanni Caldiera may have known each other through the foreigner Filippo Morandi, who knew them both.[34]

---

[32] For secretaries' status and insecurity, see Chapter One, Sections 12 and 13. For the Florentine situation, see A. Brown, *Bartolomeo Scala*; the author calls Scala's history "the classic new man's story," p. vii; E. Garin, "I cancellieri umanisti della repubblica fiorentina da Coluccio Salutati a Bartolomeo Scala"; L. Martines, *The Social World of the Florentine Humanists*, especially pp. 147ff. and 165ff.

[33] For the status enjoyed by these physicians, see Chapter One, Section 10. Note that Caldiera also—perhaps informally—taught philosophy; he was the teacher of the secretary Antonio Vinciguerra.

[34] The only significant family relationships I can trace are these: Paolo Ramusio's descendants (Giovanni Battista, Paolo G, Girolamo) were learned men (see profile), as was to a lesser degree Niccolò Leonardi's son, the physician Girolamo (for whom see the oration by Lauro Quirini *In laudibus Jeronimi de Leonardis veneti*). Giovanni

More striking are the ties formed between some of these figures and patrician humanists. In some cases, the higher status of the latter made these not relationships of friendship but of dependency. Thus Contrario and Morandi were clients of Francesco Barbaro, Jacopo Ragazzoni of Ludovico Foscarini, and Giovanni Lorenzi—in Rome—of Marco Barbo. Brognoli, Merula, and Valla numbered Venetian noblemen among their admiring students. Niccolò Sagundino was in communication with many noblemen but never, it appears, intimately so; the same statement applies to Marcantonio Sabellico. Gingerly, Perleone and Sagundino offered to Jacopo Antonio Marcello consolation for his son's death; Michele Orsini, closely related to Marcello, also refers to him with awe. In the same mood of reverence, Paolo Ramusio wrote with pride of his role in the baptism of a nobleman's son.

In contrast, the doctors Leonardi and Tommasi (also close to Leonardo Giustiniani), and perhaps also Caldiera, had relationships to Francesco Barbaro close to egalitarian. The principal clerics among our commoners—Domenichi and del Monte—corresponded easily with such patricians as the Barbaros and Andrea Giuliani. Yet although some of the commoner humanists formed easy ties with patricians, Pietro Tommasi is the only one known to me to have developed an intimate relationship with patrician friends—and he, in a remarkable letter, was encouraged to familiarity by the patrician Leonardo Giustiniani who reproved his too great modesty. These commoner humanists, in sum, though not closely bound to each other, have significant relationships—ranging in quality over a spectrum from friendship to dependency—with Venetian patricians, and specifically with patrician humanists.

Now that the core group commoners have been introduced, they may be compared in terms of their social organization to the patricians, lay and clerical. Forty-two of forty-six patrician laymen, as has been seen, played political roles of some importance, and seventeen of eighteen patrician clerics attained church positions also of significance. They were powerful men. The group of commoners is more fragmented. Four of the commoner clerics achieved substantial church positions, but only two could be compared in achievement with the more powerful patrician clerics. The three physicians, substantial citizens, were amateurs of humanism in a manner similar to the patrician laymen whose society they desired, and to some extent came to enjoy. The

---

Caldiera's daughter Caterina was also learned, and the writer of saints' lives; see my "Personal, Domestic and Republican Values," pp. 537-38 n. 7. For the relationships among commoners and with patricians, see the profiles and Chapter One, Section 10.

TABLE 7. The Core Group: Generation, Class, Profession

	Patricians		Commoners			
Generation	Laymen	Clerics	Clerics	Teachers, Professors	Secretaries	Physicians
First	Barbaro, Francesco Corner, Giovanni Giuliani, Andrea Giustiniani, Leon. Lippomano, Marco Marcello, Jac. Ant. Trevisan, Zacc. V Vitturi, Daniele	Dandolo, Fantino Donato, Pietro Marcello, Pietro V Miani, Pietro Vallaresso, Fantino			Languschi, Jacopo	Leonardi, Niccolò Tommasi, Pietro
Second	Badoer, Sebastiano Barbarigo, Girolamo Barbaro, Zaccaria Barbo, Niccolò Barbo, Paolo Bollani, Candiano Canal, Niccolò Contarini, Fran. Corner, Federico Donato, Antonio Donato, Marco Foscari, Jacopo Foscarini, Ludovico Giorgi, Domenico Giustiniani, Bern. Lando, Vitale Marino, Giovanni Morosini, Barbone Morosini, Domenico	Barbaro, Ermolao V Barbo, Marco Barbo, Pietro Correr, Gregorio Quirini, Taddeo Vallaresso, Maffeo Zane, Lorenzo Zeno, Jacopo	Bruto, Pietro Contrario, Andrea Domenichi, Dom. de' del Monte, Pietro Orsini, Michele	Brognoli, Benedetto Frulovisi, Tito L. Morandi, Filippo Perleone, Pietro Marcanova, Giovanni	Aleotti, Ulisse Capella, Febo Sagundino, Niccolò	Caldiera, Giovanni

	Patricians		Commoners			
Generation	Laymen	Clerics	Clerics	Teachers, Professors	Secretaries	Physicians
(First, cont.)	Morosini, Paolo Quirini, Lauro Sanuto, Leonardo Trevisan, Zaccaria G					
Third	Barbaro, Ermolao G Bembo, Bernardo Bernardo, Antonio Bollani, Domenico Calvo, Antonio Contarini, Pietro Dandolo, Marco Diedo, Francesco Donato, Girolamo Marcello, Pietro G Molin, Pietro Morosini, Marcant. Pisani, Paolo Renier, Daniele Sanuto, Marco	Barozzi, Francesco Barozzi, Pietro Dolfin, Petro Donato, Ludovico Foscari, Pietro	Cirneo, Pietro Lorenzi, Giovanni Negri, Francesco	Tomeo, Nicc.Leon.	Merula, Giorgio Sabellico, Marcant. Valla, Giorgio	Aurelio, Marco Ragazzoni, Jacopo Ramusio, Paolo Vinciguerra, Antonio

TABLE 8. The Core Group: Summary of Generations, Classes, Professions

	Patricians		Commoners				
Generation	Laymen	Clerics	Clerics	Teachers, Professors	Secretaries	Physicians	Totals
First	8	5	0	0	1	2	16
Second	23	8	5	5	3	1	45
Third	15	5	3	4	4	0	31
Totals	46	18	8	9	8	3	92

four priests (for convenience to so designate the less eminent clerics), the seven teachers, the eight secretaries, are distinguishable from all these other figures. They inhabit a marginal social position and depend on the patronage of great men or government councils. Of our core group, moreover, they most nearly approach being professional humanists, for whom the study and discussion of literature are central concerns, and linguistic skills primary requirements of their work. The two university professors are similar to these. Both were professional men of learning, who combined humanist studies with their primary work in philosophy and medicine. And though they were not in the same way dependent upon patronage for their positions in society, both had left Venice to establish their careers in Padua, and did not occupy privileged positions in Venetian society.

The element of time has heretofore been disregarded in this analysis of the society of Venetian humanists. Core group humanists have been examined in subgroups of class and occupation, their generational affiliation, for the moment, set aside. Now it will be useful to call that factor back into play—for it was one of those by which the core group was defined—and consider the social organization of each generation of humanists. That task will be aided by the examination of Tables 7 and 8.

Proportions among classes and occupations represented, it appears from these tables, are fairly stable during three generations. Patricians dominate in each generation, although in declining proportions. In the first they are 81 percent of the whole; in the second, 69 percent; in the third, 65 percent; they constitute, overall, 70 percent of the entire core group. Within the patriciate, the relation between cleric and layman also shifts downward somewhat over the generations. In the first generation, clerics constitute 38 percent of all patricians; in the second, 26 percent; in the third 25 percent; and they constitute, overall, 28 percent of all core group patricians.

Greater variation is seen, as might be expected, among the commoners. Weakest in the first generation, as has been noted, they are stronger in the second and third. This shift follows the contours of even more powerful trends within the commoners' professional subgroups. Physicians make their strongest appearance at the beginning of our period, and vanish in the third generation. Clerics and teachers and professors are absent in the first generation, appear massively in the second and third, whereas secretaries make a stronger presence in each succeeding generation. The professional group that loses ascendancy over time (the physicians) is one made up of commoners who possess relatively high status and great independence in

Venetian society. Those professional groups that gain ascendancy among the humanists over the three generations, on the other hand, are those made up of persons more often dependent for patronage or salary on private figures or public councils. This statement gains force when two further points are noted (see Table 6): the commoner clerics of the third generation are all priests, the more successful bishops appearing all in the second generation; and the third generation commoners are nearly all foreigners or "new men" (eight of eleven), whereas foreigners are scarcer in the second generation (five of fourteen), lacking "new men."

The prominence of the second generation of core group humanists is striking. Nearly half (48 percent) of all patricians belong to the second generation, as do half of all commoners. The first generation is the smallest, just over half (51 percent) the size of the third, and 36 percent of the second. In all subgroups except those of secretaries and physicians, the middle generation is the most prominent, the first generation the weakest. The patrician clerics are as weak in the third generation as in the first. Physicians are too few to establish a clear pattern: numbering two in the first generation and one in the second, they disappear in the third. Secretaries, who are weak in the first generation, strengthen in the second and third when they are bolstered by "new men" and a foreigner. Although the weakness of the first generation is explainable—it is not surprising that the humanist movement required time before larger numbers of participants could be acquired—the relative weakness of the third is intriguing. The features that this study will define as typical of fifteenth-century humanism in Venice seem to have crystallized near mid-century, but to have already yielded by later decades to new patterns, a dynamic also remarked upon in Chapter Three.

14. Conclusions

The names and numbers presented in this chapter point to these brief conclusions.

Patricians dominate the core group of humanists in every one of its component generations. They dominate by their number, and by their leaden power; for most walked among the narrowest circle of Venice's jealous rulers. United by family links, ties of friendship, and common experiences, they constitute a formidable group capable of stern leadership in the cultural as well as the political realm. Among them are Venice's most famous and perhaps her greatest humanists.[35]

---

[35] These statements reinforce the perception of the patrician presence in Venetian

Commoners pose a lesser presence among the core group humanists. Not only are they relatively few in number but their ability to shape cultural direction is weakened by their precarious social condition. Many were absent from Venice for long adult years for the sake of careers as clerics or intellectuals that did not on the whole encourage them (as did those of many patrician clerics) to act consistently on the basis of Venetian loyalties. Others, born abroad and resident in the city, were without Venetian roots, and had to establish themselves as new men. In most cases, like some natives (the secretaries), these were dependent for employment and advancement on patrician patronage, private and personal, or funneled through government councils. Among the commoner humanists are a few figures of the first rank (Merula, Valla, Sabellico, Sagundino), rivaling, perhaps, but not exceeding the humanist giants among the patricians.

Patterns of absence can be as striking as patterns that were operative. The secretaries are few in relation to the whole core group, few even in relation to the group of commoner humanists. This fact is surprising; secretaries constitute one of the two major professional groups (teachers are the other) providing the humanists of the Italian Renaissance. Also surprising is the absence of practicing lawyers, since the legal profession was closely linked to Italian humanism, particularly at its inception. Many of our patrician humanists studied law at the University of Padua, but none is known to this author to have practiced law (except in performance of conciliar responsibilities). The tendency in Venice in general, moreover, was to bring from Padua a heritage of Aristotelian, not legal, thinking.[36]

The absence of a significant participation in intellectual life by mer-

---

humanism held by several scholars. See, among others, V. Branca, "Ermolao Barbaro and Late Quattrocento Venetian Humanism," pp. 218-19; N. Carotti, "Un politico umanista del Quattrocento," p. 27; B. Fenigstein, *Leonardo Giustiniani*, p. 31; A. Ferriguto, *Almorò Barbaro*, pp. 69-70; W. C. Hazlitt, *The Venetian Republic*, I, 965; Labalme, *Bernardo Giustiniani*, p. 15; L. Lazzarini, "Francesco Petrarca e il primo umanesimo a Venezia," p. 85; Molmenti, *Vita privata*, II, 229ff.; Monnier, *Le Quattrocento*, I, 168-70; Romanin, *Stor. doc.*, IV, 512; A. Segarizzi, "Niccolò Barbo patrizio veneziano del secolo XV e le accuse contro Isotta Nogarola," p. 41. F. Dupuigrenet Desroussilles notes the parallel situation of a high rate of patrician presence among Venetian students at Padua: "L'università di Padova."

[36] For the identification of secretaries and teachers as professional groups particularly productive of humanists, see Kristeller, *Renaissance Thought and Its Sources*, p. 24. Note for the relation of lawyers and humanists the significant participation of these professionals in Padua's proto-humanism sketched by J. K. Hyde, *Padua in the Age of Dante*, pp. 291ff. For the affinity of humanism with law, see Garin, *Italian Humanism*, pp. 31ff. For the importance of lawyers generally in the Renaissance—making the more striking the absence of professional lawyers from the rolls of Venetian humanists—see L. Martines, *Lawyers and Statecraft in Renaissance Florence*. For the Aristotelian cast of Venetian thought, see Chapter Two, especially Section 9.

chants is also notable. For the spirit of mercantile enterprise has been seen as related to the spirit of humanism in the Italian Renaissance.[37] Our humanists were not untouched by a concern with wealth or by involvement in commerce. The Venetian patriciate, as has been earlier said, was a merchant class, and the wealth of patrician humanists derived in most cases from commerce. But most of the lay patricians among our humanists were committed to political careers; commercial activities may have been carried on by other members of the family, perhaps, or passively, through agents, instructed from a distance by letters written between embassies or Senate sessions. Among the lay commoners, none is known to have had commercial careers. Tommasi and Leonardi, the physicians, and Capella, the secretary, were men of substance, and the bishop de' Domenichi possessed great resources; Ramusio, Tomeo, and Vinciguerra held property. Others—like Marcanova and Valla—evidently possessed the funds to amass libraries. None was a merchant. Many of our humanists (of all classes) were clerics—28 percent, a high figure for an intellectual movement often seen as the opening of a secular phase in culture. Few members, indeed, of the core group—considering natives and foreigners, commoners and patricians, clerics and laymen—were essentially merchants. The ghost of account books does not haunt Venetian humanism, possessed of no *esprit marchand*.[38]

Conspicuously poor, finally, in professionals, the group of Venetian humanists is, on the whole, a group of committed amateurs. The great patrician amateurs are the city's most famous and perhaps her greatest intellectuals: the Barbaros, the Giustinianis, Bernardo Bembo, Girolamo Donato, Ludovico Foscarini, Paolo Morosini, Lauro Quirini. Of the professionals only Giorgio Merula, Marcantonio Sabellico, and Giorgio Valla had comparable status. Not one was Venetian, nor even Veneto, by birth. The two occupational groups—teachers and secretaries—from whom professional humanists were most commonly recruited in the Italian Renaissance contributed only fifteen members to our core group (I exclude the two university professors), a mere one-sixth of the whole. Humanism in Venice was an amateur's game.

---

[37] See especially C. Bec, *Les marchands écrivains*; H. Baron, "Franciscan Poverty and Civic Wealth in Humanist Thought"; and A. von Martin, *Sociology of the Renaissance*. See also the discussion in chapter Three, Section 9.

[38] The term is Bec's in *Marchands écrivains*; see, for instance, p. 173. Ruggiero observes that Venetian nobility, despite its mercantile roots, was not possessed of a "bourgeois" outlook, but imitated feudal nobilities in prizing honor and the trappings of aristocratic privilege; at the very moment of their crystallization as a social class, "they styled themselves, arbitrarily, *nobles*" (*Violence*, p. 65). A nonbourgeois patriciate produced a nonbourgeois humanist culture.

Humanist amateurs who were at the same time the city's rulers diligently shaped her culture.

The humanists surveyed here have appeared in lists, tables, and catalogues. Though the face of the group has emerged, the faces of individuals have not. They appear in the narrative chapters of Part One and, comprehensively, in the ninety-two bio-bibliographical profiles that will follow this Preface. First, an explanation of format of the profiles is needed.

15. FORMAT OF THE PROFILES

The profiles are intended as a guide and supplement to materials already existing. They do not pretend to be exhaustive. The format of the profile has been designed to suit its restricted function.

At the head of each profile, the figure is identified—not always an easy task. The name is normally given in a conventional Italian form.[39] Variants of the family name—first Italian, then Latin—follow. Where place of origin is pertinent, or is a conventional accompaniment to the name, it too is given. The generation to which the figure belongs is indicated by a number (1, 2, or 3) between parentheses. After identification, titles of monographs and other studies dealing specifically with the concerned figures are presented in short form. In the ensuing summary, sources for specific data are provided in parentheses. Where no specific source is cited, the information derives from the major study or studies cited. Where several are cited, specific reference will be given, unless the information is of a general and widely acknowledged kind such as the birth or death date of a major figure.

The listing of monographs and studies is followed by a career summary. If the available studies are thorough and reliable, career information (stressing that fundamental to the preceding analysis) will be repeated without other documentation. Where the available studies are inadequate or incorrect, additional information is provided and the source duly noted in parentheses. Where there are no studies known to me devoted to the concerned figure, all the career information presented is accompanied by a notation of source. The effect of this method can be paradoxical: the careers of obscure figures will sometimes be presented in greater detail than those of prominent ones. Where possible, dates of birth and death and testament are provided. Site of burial and date of monumentary tribute have not regularly

[39] In some cases, the choice is arbitrary: Bartolomeo has been consistently used for Bartolommeo, Girolamo for Geronimo, Jacopo for Giacomo, Niccolò for Nicolò or Nicola. Elsewhere, the Italian has been preferred to *veneziano*: Ludovico to Alvise, Ermolao to Almorò, Giorgi to Zorzi, Donato to Donà, and so on.

been noted. In the career summaries, the Venetian careers or relations of natives who lived abroad or foreigners working in Venice are stressed. These biographical profiles are thus shaped to the specific purpose of this study.

After the career summary is a summary of intellectual activity under four headings: works, correspondence, discourse, education. Once again, where monographic studies adequately deal with these matters, a brief digest of information otherwise available has been considered sufficient. Where such studies cannot be relied upon, information is given in greater detail.

Each of the four categories of intellectual activity named presents certain peculiarities. Under that of "works" are listed works known to me by the concerned figure. Included are those that are known but that I have not myself been able to see—although I have seen the great majority—and those that are securely witnessed but perhaps not extant. Attributed works that are doubtful are also noted.[40] Works are listed selectively. To have aimed for completeness would have been inefficient as well as impossible. Instead, the aim has been to supplement, not to duplicate, the existing literature, and make it accessible.[41] Humanist works by core group authors (or works closely related to humanism and humanist circles) are listed, therefore, and the existence of nonhumanist works and the tools by which they are to be found are indicated. Where an author has not been studied in modern critical literature, a list complete (to the extent of my knowledge) is offered. Where an author has been studied but significant data can be added, the supplementary data is provided in detail, and the relevant studies are named which deal with the works already made known to the scholarly public. Where an author has been amply studied, only the most significant works (judged in the context of this study) are named, whereas those secondary works are cited which provide complete bibliographies and textual discussions. Once again, therefore, the presentation of evidence for minor or less-studied figures can occasionally

[40] The main source of doubtful attributions is Sansovino's *Venetia*, and that author's followers: G. Alberici, *Catalogo breve degl'illustri et famosi scrittori venetiani*; A. Superbi, *Il trionfo glorioso d'heroi illustri et eminenti di Venetia*; Pietro Angelo Zeno, *Memoria de' scrittori veneti patritii ecclesiastici et secolari*. For these, see Segarizzi's enumeration with comment in "Lauro Quirini" p. 16 and notes.

[41] My model is P. O. Kristeller's monumental *Iter Italicum*, cited many times in these pages. Kristeller performs the vital task of listing all uncatalogued manuscripts of a humanist nature known to him, while indicating the existence of poorly and incompletely catalogued manuscripts (with reference to other works that can assist the scholar in uncovering them) and signaling adequately catalogued collections. He thus supplements and completes the work of previous scholars. In a more modest way, I have tried to provide a tool supplemental to existing literature.

be more thorough than for major or better-known ones. In the case of no figure, however, do I suggest that my listing of works is complete.

Works are normally cited in the alphabetical order of their titles; sometimes, however, the presentation of works will follow the order of their appearance in a modern collection of the *opera*. The listing of works does not, therefore, obey a chronological principle and cannot be read as an intellectual biography of the author. Dates of works are given only when the dates are of particular historical significance. The dates of orations, therefore, which can illuminate the career record, are given when known. The dedicatees of works by the Venetian humanists are given when they are of special interest. Text editions for the press are cited under the "works" category only where the title clearly constitutes an original work of the figure concerned.

The category of "correspondence" has been deliberately separated from that of "works." In many cases, letters to a humanist survive, whereas letters from him to his correspondent, to my knowledge, do not. In those cases where the figure himself wrote a body of letters that survives, the information given here to some extent duplicates that given under "works." Here, however, correspondents are named, for the aim is to indicate participation in an important form of literary conversation as much as to prove authorship. In the case of major figures for whom a complete *epistolario* is available, only correspondents of particular concern in the context of this study are named. Letters directed to minor figures outside the Venetian circle, or those even to Venetians but without a literary or humanist focus have normally been omitted. For the major figures, correspondents of particular interest are simply listed. In other cases, all evidence of correspondence known and available to me is provided. In the case of these lesser figures, the extent of whose engagement in epistolary activity is not certain, distinctions are made: the phrase "exchange with" introduces persons to whom our correspondent wrote and from whom he received letters (not necessarily an immediate response), or vice versa; "letters from" or "letters to" introduce the names of persons appropriately so signified. Letters about a core group figure (allusion to a core group figure in an exchange between other persons) are not included. Dates of letters are not given. Often they are not known to me. Where known (usually for those authors whose letters have found modern editors), their inclusion would have greatly burdened the apparatus.[42]

---

[42] The letters of Francesco Barbaro, who corresponded with a wide circle, are frequently encountered in the profiles. Sabbadini's edition of Barbaro's *Centotrenta* is referred to in these cases rather than Quirini's edition. Sabbadini provides a catalogue of all the letters known to him to and from Barbaro, including those in Quirini's

The category of "discourse" includes a variety of activities important in establishing the nature of a given figure's role in the society of humanism. Here it is noted whether the concerned figure was reputed for his learning; whether he encouraged another's authorship, or whether there were addressed to him works by other authors; whether he edited works for printers; whether he was known to engage in conversation about literary matters; whether he patronized other figures, commanded any notable skills, or collected ancient manuscripts.[43]

How, where, or by whom our humanists were educated—to turn to the fourth category of "education"—has been surprisingly difficult to determine. Often where a teacher's name is known, it is known by sheer chance: a letter or oration survives in which the teacher is noted in passing. Education at the university level, postsecondary and usually peripheral to humanism, has been considered relevant, since humanist interests were blended with those characteristic of law, medicine, or philosophy. The record of university studies, however, is also elusive. For the period 1400-1450, the record is complete: G. Zonta and G. Brotto's *Acta graduum academicorum gymnasii patavini (Acta)* prints the relevant documents. For the earlier and later periods, however, other and less thorough sources must be relied on: especially J. Facciolati, *Historia gymnasii patavini*; A. Gloria, *Monumenti della Università di Padova*; and N. C. Papadopoli, *Historia gymnasii patavini*.[44]

The general format for the profiles of core group figures has just been outlined, but specific subgroups among the humanists have certain characteristics that affect profile organization and require more

---

Epistolae. Sabbadini's catalogue gives date and a capsule summary of letters, which can be read in full in Quirini. Sabbadini's work is also, of course, the only reference given if the letter is one of the 130 published by that scholar in the same volume.

[43] In establishing the reputation of a given figure, I have drawn on standard sources: Ciriaco d'Ancona's *Itinerarium*, Erasmus' *Dialogus cui titulus Ciceronianus sive de optimo dicendi genere (Il ciceroniano)*; Paolo Giovio's *Elogia virorum literis illustrium*; Marcantonio Sabellico's *De reparatione latinae linguae*; less frequently Candiano Bollani's *Trialogus* and Francesco Pisani's *Oratio de universae philosophiae ornamentis*. Many prominent figures, especially patrician governors or prelates, were also lauded in a plethora of orations on their entry to office or for official visits—but these have not normally been included unless information derived from them is specifically relevant to intellectual life.

[44] A. Riccobono (*De gymnasio patavino commentarium libri sex*) and G. F. Tomasini (*Gymnasium patavinum*) have been less useful. The university acts are not published for the period 1450 to 1500; degrees granted from 1500 to 1550 are published by E. Martellozzo Forin (*Acta graduum academicorum ab anno 1501 ad annum 1525; ab anno 1526 ad annum 1537; ab anno 1538 ad annum 1550*) but are not relevant for our figures. I have indicated for university careers the degree and the faculty. The term "law," unless otherwise indicated, signifies "both laws," canon and civil.

detailed discussion. For the clerics, both patrician and commoner, the reference sources by Eubel and Gams have been used to detail ecclesiastical careers where the monographs and studies cited do not adequately do so.[45] Major positions (bishoprics, archbishoprics, abbacies, cardinalates) have usually been given only for figures who did obtain high church position. But several of our figures had very minor clerical careers, which are noted when appropriate. The minor benefices that several accrued are not listed. Normally, only positions actually attained are indicated, although cases of failed attempts are occasionally noted.

Stress has been laid on the Venetian phase of the careers of resident foreigners, both in the career summaries and in the listing of works and pertinent monographs and studies. For the citizenship status of natives and resident foreigners—which in many cases remains obscure—the series of the *Privilegi* of the Senate and T. Toderini's *Genealogie delle famigle venete ascritte alla cittadinanza originaria* (*Genealogie*; both in the Archivio di Stato in Venice) have been useful. Native commoners have not systematically been labeled "citizen" or "noncitizen" given what I believe to be that term's imprecision for this period.

The careers of lay patricians have in most cases been illumined particularly by the examination of archival documents. But their cases, in general, present difficulties in presentation, and these documents, in turn, present difficulties of interpretation and notation.

A name often does not suffice to identify a Venetian nobleman. Since the number of noble clans was limited, and favored given names were often repeated even within one generation, several contemporaries could well bear the same name. To identify the figure of our humanists, therefore, the patronymic is given in each case after the name and notation of generation and orthographical varieties of the family name. Following the patronymic are the honorific titles—*doctor, miles*, or both—by which the figure is commonly denoted in the documents.

In some cases, though the patronymic has been determined, it has been difficult to distinguish our humanist from other contemporary figures bearing the same name. Due explanation is given where the problem of homonyms has been particularly trying. Useful but not

---

[45] C. Eubel, *Hierarchia catholica medii aevi [Hier. cath.]*, II and III; P. B. Gams, *Series episcoporum ecclesiae catholicae [Ser. episc.]*, with *supplementa*. Where Eubel and Gams differ, the data provided by the former appears first in the profile. These sources supersede F. Ughelli's *Italia sacra, sive de episcopis Italiae* and the derivative *Tiara et purpura veneta*. J. Trithemius (*De scriptoribus ecclesiasticis*) has not been useful. Cenci's compilation of Senate "Probae" has been cited where it supplements or clarifies Eubel and Gams, and for failed petitions.

always reliable for identifying our humanists and locating the patronymic have been two manuscript genealogical works: Marco Barbaro's *Arbori di patrizi veneti (Arbori)* and G. A. Cappellari Vivaro's *Campidoglio veneto (Cappellari, Camp. ven.)*. The latter provides brief biographical sketches often helpful in determining which of several figures was engaged in humanist activities.

The careers of those lay patricians who engaged in politics at a high level—and these constitute a large fraction of our sample—have been traceable in archival documents. Though the cost in time of doing so has been enormous, the investment has been well made. Archival research has permitted an accumulation of detail about these careers that was not elsewhere or easily available. Histories and chronicles will mention an occasional embassy or lofty attainment (as do also contemporary letters and orations). Marino Sanuto's *Diarii* can provide detailed and reliable information, but only from the late fifteenth century. Such a compilation as the Marciana *Libro dei reggimenti* also begins late (only the first volume is useful for our sample), and is, moreover, not accurate. The *Libri commemoriali (Comm.,* ed. R. Predelli) are an excellent source, but mainly for information about diplomatic activities. Chronicles and histories of other cities where our figures held office would have been sound and productive sources; but to consult those of all the cities in which our humanists did hold or were likely to have held office has not been possible. The Archivio di Stato in Venice, it became apparent from the first, was the best source of accurate information about the political careers of our lay patrician humanists, and from it has been reaped a rich harvest.

The Archivio holds no lists for this period of the series of persons holding major government offices. It has been necessary to read through whole series of a variety of documents to find our figures actively engaged in office. The *Segreteria alle voci*, recording election to office, is irregular and incomplete for this period. Not all offices are included, and none consistently over the whole span of time. Nevertheless, it has been possible from its record to note for some years who was elected to certain offices among those that primarily concern us here: those of *consigliere, savio grande,* and *savio di terraferma* (very sparsely), *Consiglio dei Dieci* (rarely), *avogador di comun,* rectorates of colonies on land and sea. From the *Notatorio* of the *Collegio* has come, rather unsystematically, information about embassies and rectorates, whereas the names of the reigning *consiglieri* frequently appear. The records of the *Consiglio dei Dieci* (the *Miste* and *Secrete,* successively, for our period) yield—again, in no systematic way—the names of the members of that body, as well as those of *avogadori* or *consiglieri* serving in the special *collegio* or subcommittee of that Council. These records also yield, occasionally, information about embassies, missions of *provveditori*, and rectorates, where these concern the Ten. The records of the *Maggior Consiglio* give us the names of ducal electors, and again, by happenstance, information about embassies or other offices when a pertinent matter has been brought before the body.

The three series of Senate documents consulted—the *Deliberazioni Miste* (to 1440), and *Mar* and *Terra* (after 1440)—yield occasional information about embassies, rectorates, and military missions somewhat more richly than the *Consiglio dei Dieci* or *Maggior Consiglio* records, and are the best and, for many years of the relevant period, the only source for the names of some important members of the *Collegio*—the *savi grandi* and *savi di terraferma*. The *Balla d'oro* of the *Avogaria di Comun*, finally, records the official presentation of young noblemen, presumably at the age of eighteen, to that body for competition for early entry to the *Maggior Consiglio*. These records are therefore often an excellent source of information of date of birth. Imprecise and fallible at times, however, these records are also incomplete; patrician clerics are not usually found there, and our eldest figures escape notice, since the earliest documents in regular form are from 1414. Consultation of the modern card index of testaments (the *schedario testamenti*) led me to wills for several figures, but that index cannot be presumed to be complete. The Archivio, finally, possesses later manuscript compilations of marriages and noble and citizen genealogies: Barbaro's *Arbori*, Toderini's *Genealogie* of citizen families, and G. Giomo's index of patrician marriages: the *Indice per nome di donna dei matrimoni dei patrizi veneti (Matrimoni)*.

There are, of course, many other series of documents that it would have been valuable to consult had time permitted. The most serious omission is that of the *Secrete* of the Senate. These provide detailed information about sensitive diplomatic and military missions, and would have yielded both greater insight into the political role played by some of our humanists, and greater precision about times of departure and return. But their very richness made them unmanageable for this project. It would have been necessary to consult numerous *registri* to scan the period in question. These documents would have been invaluable if our object were to reconstruct the diplomatic careers of a few figures; but their use was impractical for the object at hand. The vast fund of notarial materials, with the exception of the testaments, has remained untouched, once again because of the mammoth complexity of the task: they are unindexed.

The documents I have seen (listed in the Bibliography, with indication of the abbreviations by which they are cited in the profiles) were consulted in a series of visits to the Archivio di Stato: in 1973, 1974, 1976, 1977, 1978, 1980. As new figures were added to my provisional list, I was compelled to return to documents already consulted. For some figures, therefore, I have seen the same documents several times. For others, added later, I have seen the relevant documents only once. For a few stragglers, I have not had the opportunity to see all the pertinent documents, and have had to rely on Sanuto's *Diarii* and other sources. Such cases are indicated in the career summaries.

In the profiles of lay patricians, as in those of other core group humanists, a principal aim has been to digest pertinent information already available in secondary materials. In the career summaries of these profiles, therefore, data given with no indication of source derives in fact from the modern studies cited. Where my study of documents has required correction or has permitted me to supplement these data, the archival source is indicated. Where no adequate secondary studies exist, the career information derives primarily from archival materials, which are noted in every case.

The careers of lay patricians who had modest political records are described briefly. The careers of politically prominent figures are given more fully by a listing in paragraph form of (normally only) major offices. "Major offices" include those named and defined earlier in this discussion, the tenure of which indicates prominent position in the republic. In pinpointing these indices, some subtlety has been sacrificed. No distinction has been made between embassies of grave political import and those of an honorific nature, or of those to major and those to minor places; colleagues on the mission (whether one or twelve) are not named unless they, too, are core group figures. No indication has been made whether a ducal elector participated in that election during the relatively unimportant early stages or the critical last stages. No indication has been made as to whether a member of the Council of Ten held the title of *capo* of that body during his term, or how often. Participation in the *zonte* of the Council of Ten, or on any other special committee (and some figures, particularly Daniele Renier and Marco Dandolo, did so repeatedly) has not been noted. A review of the evidence has shown that for the immediate purpose these distinctions are fairly unimportant. Most of our ambassadors served, in fact, in major missions; most of our ducal electors participated at least when older in the later "hands" of the election; most of our *decemviri* served as *capi*, and more than once; most participants in special *zonte* or commissions also held other important offices. To have spelled out these points would have stretched the apparatus unnecessarily.

For figures whose record of major office-holding is weak, evidence of the tenure of some minor offices (indicated by italics) is provided. Occasionally, minor offices or special assignments are also so indicated for figures of more substantial achievement where the office itself is of particular interest or where it fills an otherwise perplexing gap in the chronological record. Explanations are provided where required for such gaps: if there is evidence of minor office-holding for years long before the commencement of a record of major office-holding, or if there is evidence of engagement in a commercial career. Available information about commercial activity and financial status is also supplied. Such evidence is sparse.

The information presented in the career lists is of three kinds: the year in which the office was held; the name of the office; the citation of source, if any. The year alone is given for the sake of clarity, rather than a more specific date. It is impossible, moreover, given the diversity of the kind of information yielded by the documents to date the tenure of these offices consistently. Sometimes the date available refers to an election, sometimes to a privilege connected with the office, sometimes to the figure's appearance mid-term in office, sometimes to the date of premature or regular termination; missions abroad are sometimes dated from designation to title, often months before departure from the city, and dates of return from such missions are seldom available. Dates have been converted from *modo veneto* (by which the year began March 1), as they invariably appear in the documents, to our calendar. An office is shown as extending from one year into the next only on clear evidence, and not merely on the presumption that the term of office was fulfilled; often it was not.

The names of the offices have been standardized and given in their simplest forms. Plain English equivalents—as for "ambassador," "captain," and "ducal elector" (abbreviated as amb., capt., duc. el.)—have been given when available; Italian or Latin forms would have seemed unnecessarily strained. Italian forms have been kept for *avogador di comun, consigliere, Consiglio dei Dieci, podestà, procuratore, provveditore, savio grande,* and *savio di terraferma* (abbreviated as avog. com., cons., Cons. X, pod., proc., prov., sav. gr., sav. tf), just as Italian rather than Latin forms of names have been preferred. Latin forms have been kept for the less well-known minor offices given (e.g., *gubernator introitum, auditor veterum sententiarum, visdominus fontici theutonicorum*); they are not easily recognizable by their Italian equivalents, and so have been given as they appear in the documents. *Savio grande* has been preferred to its alternative *savio del consiglio* in order to avoid confusion with the look-alike *consigliere*. The title *savio di terraferma* is used throughout, although when that office was new in the early fifteenth century, it was titled *savio de terris de novo acquisitis*.

The kinds of evidence derived from the documents consulted are varied. In some cases, the information is specific: a figure appears among a list of ducal electors on a particular date; or, as an ambassador or rector about to depart on his mission, he is granted a certain privilege; or he is elected to a stated office, or is noted as having assumed the duties of that office. In these cases, the documentary source of each datum is given in full. In many cases, however, the information is nonspecific: the figure's name appears among the *savi grandi* or *savi di terraferma* or *consiglieri* or members of the *Consiglio dei Dieci* several times during his term. Here only the name and *registro* number of the document are given. Peculiarly, the latter form of evidence is actually more precise. For it can be certain that the figure actually held the office, whereas in the case of information about election or entry to an office, it cannot be assumed on that basis alone that the office was in fact held, or held to the expiration of the term. Generally, however, data about election to office are confirmed by other sources, and notations often appear in the documents if the position had been refused or, if assumed, subsequently exited for another office. Where there is no contrary indication, the evidence of election in itself has been judged to signify that the office was held. Where there is indication of conflict or improbability, unconfirmed cases of election to office have either been omitted or noted as problematic.

Where date of entry to office is known as well as or rather than date of election, that date is given. The notation of "cancellavit," indicating that an office was exited, is usually undated; it seems generally to refer, however, to a date later than that of the election to office, and cannot be understood to mean that an office was not (if only briefly) undertaken. Where information shows only election to office and not subsequent tenure, but the author of a reliable source has indicated tenure of that office, the latter evidence has been accepted. In the case of no figure is the record of political activity significantly affected by this kind of evidential weakness; such weak links are offset by many stronger ones.

Citation of Sanuto's *Diarii* follows the pattern for that of documents. Where a figure appears in office repeatedly in the course of a volume, the volume number is given with no specific page numbers indicated.

When a figure is elected to office, volume and page number are given. When a figure's election or first appearance is so noted, and he subsequently appears in nonspecific instances, the page number of the first appearance is noted, followed by "etc." to indicate repeated subsequent appearances.

PROFILES

Aleotti, Ulisse. (2) Aliotti, Aliottus. Son of Graziadeo.

MONOGRAPHS AND STUDIES. P. Rizzi in DBI, II (1960), 155; A. Segarizzi, "Ulisse Aleotti, rimatore veneziano del secolo XV." See also the useful profile by Segarizzi, *Antonio Baratella e i suoi corrispondenti,* pp. 74-75, and the review of his works by G. dalla Santa, pp. 202-203.

CAREER. B. c. 1412 (hypothesized from career record). D. 1468 (Segarizzi, *Antonio Baratella,* p. 75; I find no evidence for Rizzi's date of 1488). Born to an established and affluent Venetian family (subsequently listed among the *cittadinanza;* see da Mosto, *Archivio,* I, 74) with a previous record of secretarial service, Aleotti's entire career was spent in that city's bureaucracy, in duties that often took him abroad on state missions. In 1424, Aleotti was one of the youths assigned in the Maggior Consiglio "ad portandum bussolos"; for that dignity, twelve was the minimum age. He appears in his role as secretary as witness to official acts from the 1430s through 26 April 1468 (*Comm.,* ed. Predelli, VIII, X, indices); after 1458, he was assigned to the *savi di terraferma* (see F. Babinger, *Johannes Darius,* p. 26). He was honored during his lifetime with the titles of *conte palatino* and Guardian of the *Scuola della Carità,* a lofty achievement for a member of the citizen class.

WORKS. Sonnets (note Segarizzi's comment, *Antonio Baratella,* 75 n. 6).

CORRESPONDENCE. Letters from Ludovico Foscarini (*Epist.,* fols. 174-175) and Niccolò Sagundino (*Epist. et opusc.,* fols. 81ᵛ-82ᵛ, 87-88ᵛ).

Aurelio, Marco. (3) Aurelius. Son of Niccolò.

CAREER. B. c. 1430 (based on the career record; Aurelio's career had barely been launched in 1456—cf. the letters from Niccolò Sagundino cited below—whereas he had a son Niccolò already adolescent in 1476; see CLN 12, c. 43, of 30 June, appointing Niccolò one of the youths *ad portandum bussolos* in the Maggior Consiglio). D. after 1478 (in which year he affixed his signature to a dogal letter; see *Iter,* II, 19). Aurelio's family stemmed ultimately from Negropont (Euboea)—like Niccolò Sagundino, with whom the Aurelii were related (*Genealogie dei cittadini veneziani,* Bibl. del Museo Correr, cod. Gradenigo Dolfin 158, II, c. 31ʳ⁻ᵛ, and T. Toderini, *Genealogie,* I, 149; Marco and his brothers Paolo and Pietro were sons of Niccolò Aurelio and a daughter of [presumably an elder] Niccolò Sagundino). The emigration had seemingly been recent, as our Sagundino refers to himself (foreign-born) along with the native-born Marco as "new men." The Aurelio family had with Marco's father

315

already established itself in the Venetian bureaucracy. Marco's brother Paolo was also a secretary, as was his father Niccolò and his son of the same name, subsequently grand chancellor; for the latter two figures, see in addition to genealogies cited, CXM 30, c. 141ᵛ and 35, c. 93ʳ⁻ᵛ. The Aurelio family appears among the *cittadino* families in da Mosto, *Archivio*, I, 74. Aurelio served in the Venetian secretariat from at least 1457 (as notary in the dogal election: MC-Regina, c. 16), was perhaps assigned to the Council of Ten in 1476 (see the Correr *Genealogie*, II, 31ʳ⁻ᵛ, not an entirely reliable source), and performed missions abroad: as Venetian secretary in Rome in 1473 and 1475 (Malipiero, *Annali*, p. 242, and SM 10, c. 32ᵛ), and as secretary for peace negotiations in Corfù in 1472 (Malipiero, *Annali*, p. 71). He appears with the title of ducal secretary as witness to official acts in the 1470s (*Comm.*, ed. Predelli, X, indices). His signature on dogal letters of c. 1474-1476 and 1478 are recorded by Kristeller, *Iter*, II, 19, 299.

CORRESPONDENCE. Letters from Marsilio Ficino (*Epist.*, pp. 757-60, containing dedications to Aurelio of six *opuscula*, pp. 771-72 [two], 801); Francesco Filelfo (*Epist. fam.*, fols. 184ᵛ, 185ʳ⁻ᵛ, 231; C. de' Rosmini, *Vita di Francesco Filelfo*, II, 282-83; Filelfo, *Cent-dix lettres grecques*, ed. E. Legrand, p. 132); Ludovico Foscarini (*Epist.*, fols. 345-46, 347ᵛ-50); Battista Guarini (see *Iter*, I, 381); and Niccolò Sagundino (*Epist. et opusc.*, fols. 53ᵛ-57, 59-60, 62ᵛ-66, 79-81ᵛ, 83ʳ⁻ᵛ, 89ᵛ-91, 93ʳ⁻ᵛ, 101-102ᵛ, 106ʳ⁻ᵛ; those to Marco's brother Paolo, fols. 73-76, 91ʳ⁻ᵛ).

DISCOURSE. A member of the circle of learned commoners that included Sagundino, Febo Capella, and Pietro Perleone (cf. Perleone's *Epistola consolatoria ad Nicolaum Sagundinum*, pp. 47-48). Learned men addressed works to him: Giovanni Calfurnio his editions of Horace and of Plutarch's *Problemata* (translated by Giovanni Pietro Vitali d'Avenza [da Lucca]), and his commentary on Terence (see Cosenza, *Dict.*, I, 336, 794); Francesco Diedo his translation from Boccaccio; Janus Pannonius his translation of Plutarch's *De capienda ex hostibus utilitate* and *De curiositate* (Cosenza, *Dict.*, I, 336); poems by Sebastiano Bursa (see *Iter*, II, 359), Christophorus Lanfranchinus (Cosenza, *Dict.*, I, 336) and Aurelius Trebanus (see *Iter*, I, 335). Domizio Calderini wrote in the dedicatory letter to Giuliano de' Medici that Aurelio had urged him to publish his commentary on Juvenal (Cosenza, *Dict.*, I, 336, and A. della Torre, "La prima ambasceria di Bernardo Bembo a Firenze," p. 264). Marcantonio Sabellico made Aurelio an interlocutor in his *De officio scribae*. Ficino sent Aurelio six small *opuscula* (see above and Kristeller, "Marsilio Ficino e Venezia," p. 482 and n. 41). Aurelio borrowed Gregory of Nyssa's *Life of Moses*, translated by George of Trebizond, from the library of Girolamo Molin in 1458 (B. Cecchetti, "Una libreria circolante a Venezia nel secolo XV," p. 165).

EDUCATION. With Guarino Veronese (R. Sabbadini, *Vita di Guarino Veronese*, p. 159).

PROFILES

Badoer, Sebastiano. (2) Badoero, Baduario, Baduarius. Son of Jacopo. Miles.

MONOGRAPHS AND STUDIES. G. Cracco in DBI, V (1963), 124-26.

CAREER. B. c. 1427. M. 1448, Caterina di Pangrazio Giustiniani (Giomo, *Matrimoni*, I, 506). D. 30 June 1498. Reconstructing Badoer's political and intellectual career has been made more difficult by the presence of one or two near-contemporary homonyms. Cracco states that the early sixteenth-century figure often referred to was in fact Giovanni, not Sebastiano, Badoer. There was, however, a Sebastiano Badoer who survived into the sixteenth century: Sebastiano di Giacomo di Marco, born c. 1454 (AC-BO 164/III, c. 8, presented 16 May 1472). It is probably this figure who appears repeatedly as the nominee for a series of minor offices beginning in the 1470s in SGV 6-9. After his appearance in the records, our Sebastiano is usually though not invariably distinguished by the title *miles*. It was perhaps this same Sebastiano di Giacomo di Marco to whom was dedicated Agostino Nifo's *De intellectu* in 1503 (Cosenza, *Dict.*, I, 362, and below). That identification would jeopardize the dedications to our Sebastiano of philosophical works by Faventino and Vernia (see below). But the Vernia connection is firm for Sebastiano. Vernia stayed in the house of a Sebastiano Badoer who was, like him, a student under Paolo della Pergola; since our Sebastiano was more nearly Vernia's contemporary than his homonym (Vernia received his doctorate in philosophy at Padua in 1458, not long after Badoer had launched his adult career; see B. Nardi, *Saggi sull'aristotelismo padovano*, p. 98), I infer he was Vernia's associate and the dedicatee of the philosopher's edition of Burley. I have discovered no record of Badoer's career between 1457, when he was ambassador as shown below and *savio agli ordini* (SM 6, c. 25ᵛ; ST 4, c. 52ᵛ) and 1469, when he was designated one of two *sapientes supra hereditatibus Taddei et Bertoldi d'Este* (ST 6, c. 64ᵛ). During the intervening years, Badoer may have engaged in commercial activities. Badoer's political career began as early as 1451, when he was elected to the *Quarantìa* (SGV 4, c. 141).

Offices. 1457, Amb. to Naples (Malipiero, *Annali*, 206); 1474-76, Amb. to Hungary; 1477, Pod. of Bergamo (SGV 6, c. 19); 1478, Pod. of Verona; 1479, Amb. to Rome; Capt. of Brescia (MC-Regina, c. 187ᵛ; SGV 6, c. 91); 1481-1482, Avog. (CLN 13; CXM 20; SGV 6, c. 7); 1482, Amb. to Rome (CLN 13, c. 15ᵛ; Malipiero, *Annali*, p. 283; P. Paschini, *Il carteggio fra . . . Marco Barbo e Giovanni Lorenzi*, p. 63); 1482-83, Sav. tf. (CLN 13; ST 8, c. 180, 9); 1483-84, Amb. to Emperor; 1484, Amb. to France (Malipiero, *Annali*, p. 290); Pod. of Verona (MC-Stella, c. 39); 1485-86, Amb. to Milan (MC-Stella, c. 64ᵛ); 1486, Cons. (CLN 13; CXM 23; MC-Stella, c. 64ᵛ and passim; ST 10); Amb. to Rome; 1487, Amb. to Milan; CX (CXM 23); 1487-88, Amb. to Rome (ST 10, cc. 72, 76ᵛ, 90ᵛ, 116ᵛ; in this embassy a colleague of Bernardo Bembo, who delivered three orations to Pope Innocent VIII, of which the first [24 Nov. 1487] is in Badoer's name as well); 1489, Cons. (ST 10); 1490, Capt. of Padua (SGV 6, c. 50ᵛ; Papadopoli, *Hist. gymn. pat.*,

I.i.84); 1492, Sav. gr. (ST 11, c. 130); Amb. to Rome; 1493-94, Cons. (CXM 26; SGV 7, c. 0; SM 14); 1494-95, Amb. to Milan; 1496, Sav. gr. (ST 12, c. 117ᵛ); Cons.; 1498, Sav. gr. (CXM 27, c. 143; ST 13).

WORKS. *Oratio ad Alexandrum VI Pontificem Maximum in prestanda Venetorum obedientia* (17 Dec. 1492); *Oratio ad Sixtum IV, Responsio ad pontificis responsionem*, not seen (in Lucca, Biblioteca Capitolare, cod. 544, fols. 507-508ᵛ; see *Iter*, I, 255-56). For Badoer's encounter with Sixtus IV, see Giovanni Lorenzi's letter to Marco Barbo of 20 Dec. 1482 describing the hostile reaction of pope and curia in P. Paschini, *Il carteggio*, p. 63. Thus the oration to Alexander VI is not Badoer's sole surviving work, as suggested in Cracco, p. 125. A printed volume of orations and epistles known to early authorities is not known to be extant; see Cracco, "Badoer," p. 124; F. Sansovino, *Venetia*, II, 585. Letters by Badoer also survive in a *Registrum litterarum magnificorum dominorum Sebastiani Baduario equitis et Benedicti Trivisano oratorum ad illustrissimum dominum ducem Mediolani* (1494-1495).

CORRESPONDENCE. Letters from Giovanni Michele Alberto da Carrara (see *Iter*, I, 12; with verse); Bernardino Gadolo (in his *Epist.*, pp. 325-28, and pp. 162-82, to Badoer along with Girolamo Giorgio and Marcantonio Morosini; see *Iter*, II, 500 for a published version of the latter, not seen by me); Marsilio Ficino (to Badoer and Bembo, *Epist.*, 866); Marcantonio Sabellico (*Opera*, fols. 9ᵛ-10).

DISCOURSE. Praised as among the learned men of Venice by Giovanni Morosini (cf. Nardi, "Scuola di Rialto" [UEUV ed.], p. 126), Francesco Negri (*De aristocratia*, fol. 144ᵛ), and Francesco Pisani (*Oratio de universae philosophiae ornamentis*, p. 266). One of those who engaged in literary conversation in the circle surrounding Filippo Buonaccorsi (see his *De his quae a Venetis tentata sunt* [1533 ed.], p. 84), and one of two interlocutors in Sabellico's *De venetis magistratibus*. Alessandro Benedetti concluded his *Diaria de bello carolino* (27 Aug. 1496) with a letter to Badoer and Girolamo Bernardo (D. Schullian, ed., pp. 198-99), while Antonio Cittadini of Faenza, a professor of medicine of Ferrara, dedicated to Badoer his paraphrases of Averroes (see *Iter*, I, 110), Giorgio Valla his edition of Eusebius (see Cosenza, *Dict.*, I, 362), and Nicoletto Vernia his edition of Burley's commentary on Aristotle's *Physics* (1482) (see E. P. Mahoney, "Philosophy and Science in Nicoletto Vernia and Agostino Nifo"; Nardi, "Ancora qualche notizia . . . su Nicoletto Vernia," pp. 115ff.). A manuscript note shows that Badoer had copied a work *De bello troiano* in 1439 (see *Iter* II, 241). Badoer's family patronized Vernia, whom Badoer had preceded as a student of Paolo della Pergola (F. Lepori, "Scuola di Rialto," p. 568). Cosenza, *Dict.*, I, 362, says that Agostino Nifo dedicated his *De intellectu* (written by 1498, first published in 1503) to Badoer; but our Sebastiano was already dead.

EDUCATION. With Paolo della Pergola at the Rialto school (Lepori, "Scuola di Rialto," p. 568; Nardi, "Scuola di Rialto," p. 126).

Barbarigo, Girolamo. (2) Barbadicus, Barbarigus. Son of Francesco "il ricco" (Cicogna, *Iscrizioni*, II, 54-55); brother of Doges Marco and Agostino; father of the learned Domenico (for whom see F. Filelfo, *Epist. fam.*, fols. 150-51ᵛ).

MONOGRAPHS AND STUDIES. G. Cracco in DBI, VI (1964), 66-67.

CAREER. B. c. 1402 (AC-BO 162/I, c. 18ᵛ [27 Nov. 1420]; Cracco gives c. 1410, for which I see no basis, but find the date of marriage consistent with that given). M. 1428, Cristina di Pietro Morosini (see Giomo, *Matrimoni*, II, 142). D. 1467 (poisoned in Ravenna while provveditore; for his tomb, see Cicogna, *Iscrizioni*, II, 55). His political career dates from at least 1437 (when on 19 Sept. he was elected one of the *savi agli ordini*: SM 60, c. 37), but he may have pursued a commercial career both before that date and during the 1440s. On 17 Feb. 1441, he was made captain of the second galley to Flanders (SM 1, c. 19ᵛ). Ludovico Foscarini alluded to his great wealth (*Epist.*, fol. 354ʳ⁻ᵛ).

Offices. 1448-49, Sav. tf. (SGV 4, c. 159; SM 3; ST 2); 1449, Cons. (CLN 8; CXM 13; MC-Ursa; SGV 4, c. 104; SM 3; ST 2); 1450, Sav. tf. (SGV 4, c. 159ᵛ; SM 3); 1450-51, Sav. tf. (SGV 4, c. 159ᵛ; SM 4; ST 2, c. 164ᵛ); 1451, Sav. tf. (SGV 4, c. 160; ST 2, c. 197ᵛ); 1451-52, Amb. to Genoa (MC-Ursa, c. 179ᵛ; for Fran. Barbaro's correspondence with powerful men in Genoa paving the way in this embassy see *Centotrenta*, ed. Sabbadini, pp. 54, 55-56); 1452, Cons. (CLN 8; CXM 14; MC-Ursa, c. 179ᵛ and passim; SM 4; ST 3); Capt. of Verona (SGV 4, c. 71ᵛ); 1453, Sav. tf. (SGV 4, c. 148; ST 3, c. 51ᵛ); Capt. of Brescia (SGV 4, c. 96ᵛ) and prov. in esercito (CXM 14, c. 142; ST 3, c. 54ᵛ); 1453-54, Prov. in Brescia (ST 3, c. 65, 99ᵛ, 100ᵛ); 1454, Sav. gr. (SGV 4, c. 148ᵛ; SM 5; ST 3, c. 106ᵛ); 1454-55, Amb. to Naples (MC-Ursa, c. 192; SM 5, cc. 60ᵛ-61; ST 3, c. 130ᵛ); 1455-56, Lt. in Friuli (SGV 4, c. 65ᵛ); 1457-58, Sav. gr. (SGV 4, c. 147ᵛ; SM 6; ST 4, c. 52ᵛ); CX (CLN 9, c. 175ᵛ; CXM 15, c. 137ᵛ; this and the previous office held concurrently); 1458, Amb. in obedientia to Pope Pius II; 1459, Cons. (SM 6); Sav. gr. (ST 4, c. 112); 1459-60, Avog. (CXM 15, 16); 1461, Sav. gr. (SM 6, 7); Cons. (CLN 10; MC-Regina; ST 4); 1462, Duc. el., Cristoforo Moro (MC-Regina, cc. 39, 40; Sav. gr. (SM 7; ST 5); 1462-63, CX (CXM 16, c. 77; this and the previous office held in part concurrently); 1463, Sav. gr. (SM 7; ST 5); 1464, Amb. to Milan (ST 5, c. 66ᵛ); *One of four special counsellors designated to accompany Doge Cristoforo Moro to launch a crusade from Ancona* (Malipiero, *Annali*, p. 23); Amb. in obedientia to Pope Paul II; Cons. (CLN 10; SM 7; ST 5); 1465, Sav. gr. (SM 8; ST 5, c. 117); 1465-66, CX (CXM 16); 1466, Sav. gr. (SM 8; ST 5; c. 153; this and the previous office held in part concurrently); 1466-67, Amb. to the Captain General at sea (CXM 17, cc. 1ᵛ and passim to 21ᵛ); 1467, Sav. gr. (ST 5, c. 189); Proc. di San Marco, for life (SGV 6, c. 86ᵛ); Amb. to the condottiere Bartolomeo Colleoni (ST 5, c. 194); subsequently prov. in the Romagna, for the defense of Ravenna and Cervia, in which office he died (Cicogna, *Iscrizioni*, II, 55).

CORRESPONDENCE. Letters to and from Pier Candido Decembrio (cf. V. Zaccaria, "L'epistolario di Pier Candido Decembrio," p. 112; Decembrio's letters are addressed to Barbarigo along with Zaccaria Barbaro G); letters from Francesco Barbaro (*Epist.*, ed. Quirini, App., pp. 30-33); Francesco Filelfo (*Epist. fam.*, fol. 187ᵛ); Giovanni Mario Filelfo (see *Iter*, II, 483; a poem to Barbarigo appears with the letter); Ludovico Foscarini (*Epist.*, fols. 80-82ᵛ; 329ʳ⁻ᵛ; 354ʳ⁻ᵛ); and Maffeo Vallaresso (*Epist.*, pp. 410-11).

DISCOURSE. Praised for his learning by Flavio Biondo (It. illus. [1510 ed.], fol. 101ᵛ) and Ciriaco d'Ancona (*Itinerarium*, ed. L. Mehus, pp. 18-19 and n. 1). With Ludovico Foscarini, involved in the quest for a Venetian historiographer; cf. A. Pertusi, "Gli inizi della storiografia umanistica," p. 301, and F. Gaeta, "Storiografia, coscienza nazionale," p. 40. Barbarigo with Barbaro had been instructed by Biondo to burn a historical work by the latter; see Barbaro's *Centotrenta*, ed. Sabbadini, p. 44, and *Epist.*, p. 123. Barbarigo's role as a patron can be inferred from the letters of Francesco Filelfo and Vallaresso, cited above.

Barbaro, Ermolao (Almorò) Vecchio. (2) Barbarus. Son of Zaccaria; nephew of Francesco, cousin of Zaccaria, second cousin of the younger Ermolao.

MONOGRAPHS AND STUDIES. G. degli Agostini, *Notizie*, I, 229-56; J. Berrigan, "The Latin Aesop of Ermolao Barbaro"; E. Bigi in DBI, VI (1964), 95-96; G. Ronconi, "Lettere di Ermolao Barbaro il Vecchio ai Gonzaga di Mantova"; Ronconi, introduction to his edition of Barbaro's *Orationes contra poetas, epistolae*, pp. 3-80. For further bibliography see Ronconi in the *Orationes contra poetas*, p. 3 n. 1.

CAREER. B. c. 1410. D. 12 March 1471. Before assuming the major offices given below, Barbaro held the title of apostolic protonotary as well as other benefices. His impatient uncle Francesco labored assiduously to advance Ermolao's ecclesiastical career. Yet Ermolao was not always fortunate, and his name appears as an unsuccessful candidate in *probae* for office; see C. Cenci, "Senato veneto 'Probae,' " p. 386, #93; p. 388, #96. In 1460, Barbaro served as papal legate to King Charles VII of France; in 1460-62, as papal governor of Perugia.

Titles. 1443— Bishop of Treviso; 1453— Bishop of Verona.

WORKS. *Epistolae*, ed. Ronconi; also *volgare* letters to the Marquis Ludovico Gonzaga; *Orationes contra poetas*, ed. Ronconi (pp. 9ff. for the surrounding controversy, pp. 23ff. for a complete listing of manuscript and printed versions); 76 *Sermones de tempore*, not seen (ibid., p. 20 n. 64); *Vita Sancti Athanasii Alexandri episcopi, cum translatione eius corporis*, with *prohemium* to the nuns of Santa Croce of Giudecca (ibid., pp. 74ff.); translation of some *Fables* of Aesop, with letter of dedication to Ambrogio Traversari (ibid., pp. 71ff., and Berrigan, "Latin Aesop"). R. Avesani has demonstrated in "Una 'Lectura' di Domenico da San Gemignano" that the *Lectura in decretales* attributed to Barbaro by Ronconi and predecessors was owned but not written by him.

CORRESPONDENCE. Ronconi notes letters from Francesco and Zaccaria Barbaro (V), Matteo Bosso, Domenico de' Domenichi, Francesco Filelfo, Ludovico Foscarini, Guarino Veronese, Timoteo Maffei, Pietro del Monte, Francesco Patrizi, Niccolò Sagundino, and Maffeo Vallaresso. To these may be added letters to and from Isotta Nogarola. Letters to Ambrogio Traversari, Francesco Condulmier, Antonio Donato Cavodasino, Teodoro de' Lelli, the nuns of Santa Croce, Alessandro Gonzaga, Flavio Biondo, Isotta Nogarola, Ludovico Gonzaga, and Celso Maffei are published in that order by Ronconi. For the letters to Barbaro, cf. Ronzoni, *Orationes*, p. 21 n. 65. The following information is supplementary. For Bosso's letters, see also G. Soranzo, *L'umanista canonico regolare Lateranense Matteo Bosso di Verona (1427-1502)*, p. 146 n. 5, 208 n. 30, 226 and n. 8, 227-28 and n. 15, 228-29 and n. 18, 255 and n. 139. Filelfo's letters are in his *Epist. fam.*, fols. 118^v, 115^{v}bis, 123^v, 125, 125^v, 217; Foscarini's in his *Epist.*, fols. 147^v-149, 152^v-59, 210^v-214, 297^v, 299^v, 302-304^v, the latter also printed in E. Abel's edition of Isotta Nogarola's *Opera omnia*, II, 181-82; Guarino's in his *Epist.*, ed. Sabbadini, I, 409-10, 473-74; Niccolò Sagundino's in his *Epist. et opusc.*, fols. 83^v-84^v; in addition to the pages of Vallaresso's *Epist.* cited by Ronconi, a letter to Barbaro appears on pp. 560-61. Nogarola's letter to Barbaro in her *Opera omnia*, I, 6-11; Barbaro's to her, ibid., II, 179-80. Nogarola also wrote an oration praising Barbaro; see below. Barbaro's letters to the persons named appear in Ronconi, *Orationes*, pp. 145-80, with a critical introduction to each, pp. 71-80. The letters to Traversari and the nuns of Santa Croce are, in fact, introductory to Barbaro's translation from Aesop and his *Vita Sancti Athanasii*, respectively. That to Nogarola—not in Abel—was known to Agostini (*Notizie*, I, 253) and listed as a separate work.

DISCOURSE. Barbaro was widely known for his learning, and was explicitly praised in an oration of Isotta Nogarola's (*Opera*, II, 267-75) and letters of Ludovico Foscarini (see the first and last of those cited above). Acquainted early with members of Florence's humanist circle (Agostini, *Notizie*, I, 231), he became as bishop the guiding figure of literary discussions among the learned in Verona (see Ronconi, *Orationes*, pp. 3ff.). Barbaro was also active in rebuilding and beautifying ecclesiastical monuments; see Agostini, *Notizie*, I, 239ff., 247, and the interesting letter of Maffeo Vallaresso in the latter's *Epist.*, pp. 308-310. Many learned men dedicated works to Barbaro, including Antonio Beccaria, Bartolomeo Cipolla, Giovanni Mario Filelfo, Battista Guarini, and Aleardo Pindemonti (Ronconi, *Orationes*, pp. 5ff. and notes). His important collection of manuscripts was noted by Foscarini (see the last of the letters cited above) and Ambrogio Traversari (Ronconi, *Orationes*, pp. 18 and n. 61).

EDUCATION. With Guarino Veronese and his uncle Francesco. Present at Padua from at least 3 March 1431 (Zonta and Brotto, *Acta*, p. 184, #819, and later acts), he received his license in law on 7 March 1436 (ibid., p. 243, #1091), for which event Giovanni Marino delivered his *Oratio in licentia Hermolai Barbari Romanae ecclesiae prothonotarii*.

Barbaro, Ermolao (Almorò) Giovane. (3) Barbarus. Son of Zaccaria; grandson of Francesco, second cousin of the elder Ermolao Barbaro. Doctor, miles.

MONOGRAPHS AND STUDIES. L. Banfi, "Ermolao Barbaro, Venezia, ed il patriarchato di Aquileia"; E. Bigi in DBI, VI (1964), 96-99; V. Branca, "Ermolao Barbaro in Francia," "Ermolao Barbaro and Late Quattrocento Venetian Humanism," "Ermolao Barbaro 'poeta' e la sua 'presentazione' alla corte degli Aragonesi," "Ermolao Barbaro e l'umanesimo veneziano," "Un trattato inedito di Ermolao Barbaro: il 'De coelibatu libri,' " "L'umanesimo veneziano alla fine del Quattrocento, Ermolao Barbaro e il suo circolo"; A. Diller, "The Library of Francesco and Ermolao Barbaro"; C. Dionisotti, "Ermolao Barbaro e la fortuna di Suiseth"; M. L. Doglio, "Ambasciatore e principe: l'*Institutio Legati* di Ermolao Barbaro"; A. Ferriguto, *Almorò Barbaro: l'alta cultura nel settentrione d'Italia nel '400, i "sacri canones" di Roma e le "santissime leze" di Venezia*; P. O. Kristeller, "Un codice padovano di Aristotile postillato da Francesco ed Ermolao Barbaro"; P. Paschini, *Tre illustri prelati del Rinascimento: Ermolao Barbaro, Adriano Castellesi, Giovanni Grimani*; G. dalla Santa, "Una vicenda della dimora di Ermolao Barbaro a Roma nel 1492"; J. T. Stickney, *De Hermolai Barbari vita atque ingenio*. Also Branca's editions of Barbaro's works. Further bibliography provided in the notes to these studies; see especially Branca, "Uman. ven.," pp. 128ff. n. 8, 147 n. 41; a career summary at n. 8.

CAREER. B. 1453/1454. D. 1492, perhaps July.

Offices. 1486, Amb. to Emperor Frederick III and King Maximilian, Belgium; 1488, Sav. tf.; 1488-89, Amb. to Milan; 1489-90, Sav. tf.; 1490, Avog. com.; 1490-91, Amb. to Rome; 1491, made Pat. of Aquileia by Pope Innocent VIII (6 March).

WORKS. *Castigationes plinianae et in Pomponiuim Melam; De coelibatu* and *De officio legati*, ed. Branca; the *Epistolae, orationes, carmina*, ed. Branca. The latter includes four orations: for the funeral of Niccolò Marcello; to René, duke of Lorraine; to his pupils; to the Emperor Frederick III and King Maximilian. Also works on Aristotle's ethics and natural science, on Dioscorides, and translations of Aristotle and Themistius. Comprehensive bibliography in Branca, "Uman. ven.," pp. 128ff. n. 8.

CORRESPONDENCE. With Jacopo Antiquario, Pietro Barozzi, Bernardo Bembo, Antonio Calvo, Marco Dandolo, Domenico de' Domenichi, Girolamo Donato, Pontico Faccino, Marsilio Ficino, Pietro Foscari, Elia del Medigo, Giorgio Merula, Domenico Morosini, Giovanni Pico della Mirandola, Angelo Poliziano, Marcantonio Sabellico, Giorgio Valla, Ugolino Verino, and Nicoletto Vernia, among others, in Barbaro's *Epistolae*; Branca catalogues Barbaro's correspondents in the *Epistolae* II, 130-62. Additional notes on correspondents in Branca, "Uman. ven.," pp. 143-44 n. 33. E. Garin publishes three letters of Barbaro's (to Donato, Arnoldo di Bost, and Pico) with Italian translation in his *Prosatori latini del Quattrocento*, pp. 837-63; the letter to Pico (with discussion of their controversy) also in Q. Breen, "Giovanni Pico della Mirandola on the Conflict of Philosophy and Rhetoric." See also the Greek letter to the young Barbaro from Francesco Filelfo in his *Cent-dix lettres grecques de François Philelphe*, ed. E. Legrand, pp. 188-90. For correspondence with Ficino, see Kristeller, "Marsilio Ficino e Venezia," pp. 483-86 and nn. 47-62.

DISCOURSE. A humanist of first importance, widely renowned in his age and thereafter, Barbaro is numbered among the group of late Quattrocentro giants—Poliziano, Merula—whose interests were primarily philological. His achievement epitomizes the characteristically Venetian synthesis of Paduan Aristotelianism and humanistic techniques and cultural tastes. Barbaro possessed an important library of ancient and modern, Latin and Greek works, including books of his grandfather Francesco (Diller, "The Library," and Kristeller, "Codice padovano").

EDUCATION. Elementary studies from 1460 in Verona with Matteo Bosso and his uncle Ermolao, bishop of the city, and in Rome in 1462 with Pomponio Leto and Theodore Gaza. At Padua from 1471 (a student of Nicoletto Vernia), he received his doctorate in arts on 12 Aug. 1474, in laws on 27 Oct. 1477.

Barbaro, Francesco. (1) Barbarus. Son of Candiano; father of Zaccaria, uncle of the elder and grandfather of the younger Ermolao Barbaro. Miles.

MONOGRAPHS AND STUDIES. G. degli Agostini, *Notizie*, II, 28-134; B. Bughetti, "Alcune lettere di Francesco Barbaro riguardanti l'Ordine Francescano"; N. Carotti, "Un politico umanista del Quattrocento: Francesco Barbaro"; A. Diller, "The Library of Francesco and Ermolao Barbaro"; P. Gothein, *Francesco Barbaro (1390-1454): Frühhumanismus und Staatskunst in Venedig*; C. Griggio, "Il codice berlinese lat. fol. 667: nuove lettere di Francesco Barbaro"; G. Gualdo in DBI, VI (1964), 101-103; M. L. King, "Caldiera and the Barbaros on Marriage and the Family"; P. O. Kristeller, "Un codice padovano di Aristotile postillato da Francesco ed Ermolao Barbaro"; L. Lazzarini, "Un libro su Francesco Barbaro"; G. Pillinini, "L'umanista veneziano Francesco Barbaro e l'origine della politica di equilibrio"; A. M. Quirini, *Diatriba praeliminaris* (Vol. I) to Barbaro's *Francisci Barbari et aliorum ad ipsum epistolae ab anno Christi 1425 ad annum 1453* (Vol. II); R. Sabbadini, ed., *Centotrenta lettere inedite di Francesco Barbaro precedute dall'ordinamento critico cronologico dell'intero suo epistolario*; Sabbadini, "La gita di Francesco Barbaro a Firenze nel 1415." See these studies for further bibliography. Gothein (pp. 330-41) and Sabbadini (in the *Centotrenta*, pp. 135-37) provide tabular chronologies upon which the following draws.

Career. B. 1390. M. 1419, Maria di Pietro Loredan. D. late Jan. 1454.

Offices. 1422-23, Pod. of Treviso; 1424, CX (CXM 10, c. 71; 1425-26, Pod. of Vicenza (CLN 6, c. 37v); 1426, Amb. to Rome; Sav. tf. (SMS 56, c. 65v); 1427, Cons. (CLN 6; CXM 10; MC-Ursa); 1428, Amb. to Florence (SMS 56, c. 184); Sav. tf.; 1428-29, CX (CXM 10); 1429, Sav. tf. (SMS 57, c. 123); 1430-32, Pod. and Capt. of Bergamo (SMS 58, cc. 79v, 133v); 1432-33, Cons. (CLN 6, c. 118v; CXM 11; MC-Ursa; SMS 58); 1433, Sav. tf. (SMS 58, c. 211 and passim); Amb. to Emperor Sigismund at Ferrara; 1434, Amb. to Ferrara; CX (CXM 11); Sav. tf. (SMS 59, c. 59v; held concurrently with preceding office); 1434-35, Pod. of Verona; 1435-36, Amb. to Ferrara and Florence; 1436, Cons. (CLN 6, c. 158v; MC-Ursa; SMS 59); Sav. tf. (SMS 59, c. 164); 1436-37, CX (CXM 11); 1437, Amb. to Bologna (CXM 11, c. 151v); 1437-40, Capt. of Brescia (during these years, Brescia was beseiged by Milan's army, and Barbaro led the valiant defense of the city); 1441, Sav. tf.; Prov. and vice-capt. in Verona; 1442, Sav. gr. (SM 1); Cons.; 1443, Sav. gr. (SM 1; ST 1, c. 93); CX (CXM 12); 1444, Amb. to Milan; Amb. to Ferrara; 1444-45, Sav. gr. (SM 2); 1445-46, CX (CXM 13); 1446, Sav. gr. (SM 2); Amb. to Ferrara; 1446-47, Sav. gr. (SM 2, 3); 1447; Sav. gr. (ST 2, c. 45v); 1448, Sav. gr. (SGV 4, c. 159; SM 3); 1448-49, Lt. in Friuli; 1449-50, Sav. gr. (SGV 4, c. 159v; SM 3; ST 2, c. 119); 1450, Sav. gr. (SGV 4, c. 160; SM 4; ST 2, c. 156); 1451, Sav. gr., 2 terms (SGV 4, cc. 160r,v, ST 2, c. 180v); 1452, Proc. di S. Marco.

Works. *De re uxoria* [DRU], ed. A. Gnesotto (see that editor's introduction, pp. 18ff., for other editions and mss.; this edition the basis of Gothein's *Das Buch von der Ehe* and B. G. Kohl's translation of the introduction and Book II—as "On Wifely Duties"—with preface, in *The Earthly Republic*, ed. Kohl and Witt, pp. 177-228); several orations, including most notably the *Oratio funebris pro Joannino Corradino*, published by Quirini in the *Diatriba*, pp. 156-61; trans., Plutarch's lives of Aristides and Cato the Elder to Zaccaria Barbaro V (for printed versions, see V. R. Giustiniani, "Sulle traduzioni latine delle 'Vite' di Plutarco nel Quattrocento," pp. 26-27; also A. Pertusi, "Umanesimo greco," pp. 195ff., 205ff.). Letters in *Epistolae*, ed. Quirini, and *Centotrenta lettere*, ed. Sabbadini, pp. 65ff., with a digest of all the letters known to Sabbadini, pp. 9ff., and indices of correspondents, pp. 139ff. Previously unedited letters are published by Griggio, "Codice berlinese," pp. 149-76. Griggio is preparing a comprehensive modern edition of the letters. For works not named here, see the studies cited, especially the *Diatriba*, and Gothein's *Francesco Barbaro*. The attribution to Barbaro of the letter to Jacopo Foscari published by K. Müllner, *Reden und Briefe*, pp. 201-10, is unlikely.

Correspondence. With most notably Ermolao Barbaro V, Zaccaria Barbaro G, Niccolò Barbo, Pietro Barbo, Gasparino Barzizza, Flavio Biondo, Poggio Bracciolini, Leonardo Bruni, Niccolò Canal, Febo Capella, Fantino Dandolo, Pier Candido Decembrio, Domenico de' Domenichi, Pietro Donato, Francesco Filelfo, Jacopo Foscari, Pietro Foscari, Ludovico Foscarini, George of Trebizond, Leonardo Giustiniani, Guarino Veronese, Niccolò Leonardi,

Marco Lippomano, Pietro del Monte, Filippo Morandi da Rimini, Barbone Morosini, Lauro Quirini, Taddeo Quirini, Ludovico [Scarampo] Trevisan, Pietro Tommasi, Ambrogio Traversari, Zaccaria Trevisan G, Lorenzo Valla, Maffeo Vallaresso, Daniele Vitturi, and Lorenzo Zane. For Barbaro's correspondents, see the *Centotrenta*, ed. Sabbadini, indices, and Griggio, "Codice berlinese." The Greek letters of Francesco Filelfo published by E. Legrand (*Cent-dix lettres grecques di François Philelphe*) include some to Barbaro; pp. 8-9, 46-47, 53-54.

DISCOURSE. Widely reputed at home and abroad for his learning and particularly for the DRU, diffused in many manuscript versions in Italy and Germany, and popular in later editions and translations. In close contact with Florentine humanists of the early Quattrocento, Barbaro participated significantly in the literary discourse of the age. He was the recipient of the dedications of humanist works by others (Poggio Bracciolini, for instance, dedicated to Barbaro his *De avaritia*), the subject of laudatory orations (notably those by the Venetians Lauro Quirini [*Oratio in laudem Francisci Barbari*] and Filippo Morandi da Rimini [*Oratio in funere Francisci Barbari*], and the patron of many figures, notably Flavio Biondo (note especially Barbaro's *prohemium* to Biondo's *It. illus.*, addressed to King Alfonso of Aragon, in Quirini, *Diatriba*, pp. 171-73) and George of Trebizond (see J. Monfasani, *George of Trebizond*, passim; Monfasani, *Collectanea Trapezuntiana*, pp. 198-206, reprinting and digesting texts to Barbaro; F. Gaeta, "Giorgio da Trebisonda, le 'Leggi' di Platone e la costituzione di Venezia") among the foreigners, and among the Venetians, Filippo da Rimini (see M. L. King, "A Study in Venetian Humanism at Mid-Quattrocento," Part Two, pp. 82ff.). He possessed an important library of Greek and Latin manuscripts (see Diller, "Library," and Kristeller, "Codice padovano").

EDUCATION. With Giovanni Conversino da Ravenna, Barzizza, and Guarino. He received his doctorate in arts at Padua, 1 Oct. 1412.

Barbaro, Zaccaria. (2) Barbarus. Son of Francesco; cousin of the elder, father of the younger Ermolao Barbaro. Miles.

MONOGRAPHS AND STUDIES. S. Borsari, in DBI, VI (1964), 118-19.

CAREER. B. 1422-23. M. 1449, Chiara, daughter of the future Doge Andrea Vendramin (Giomo, *Matrimoni*, II, 439). D. 29 Nov. 1492. For the circumstances of Barbaro's last months, during which he was tormented by clashing loyalties and the disobedience of his son, see especially the account of P. Paschini, *Tre illustri prelati*, pp. 26ff. Barbaro shows a record of minor officeholding from 1443, when he was elected one of the *advocati mobilium* (SV 4, c. 23). There are indications that Barbaro possessed considerable wealth: for surviving loan receipts of 1472, see *Iter*, I, 115; for a 1482 loan to the city of 3,000 ducats to support the Ferrarese war, see Malipiero, *Annali*, pp. 263-64.

Offices. 1459, Amb. to the King of Aragon (CLN 9, c. 161; ST 4, c. 112);

1462, Duc. el., Cristoforo Moro (MC-Regina, c. 39ᵛ); Amb. to the Pope; 1468, Sav. tf. (SM 8; ST 6); 1469, Amb. to the Emperor (Verona); Sav. tf. (CLN 11); 1469-70, Pod. and capt. of Ravenna (SGV 5, c. 5; 6, c. 22ᵛ; SM 9, c. 78ʳ⁻ᵛ); 1471, CX (CXM 17); 1471-73, Amb. to Naples; 1473, Sav. tf. (SM 9, c. 184; ST 7); 1473-74, CX (CXM 18); 1474, Sav. tf. (SM 10; ST 7, c. 42ᵛ); Duc. el., Pietro Mocenigo (MC-Regina, c. 143); 1475, Avog. (CXM 18, c. 105ᵛ; SGV 6, c. 7); 1475-76, Capt. of Verona (CXM 18, cc. 127ᵛ-128, 128ʳ⁻ᵛ; SGV 6, cc. 7, 16ᵛ; ST 7, c. 107ᵛ); 1476, Amb. to Milan; Amb. to Mantua; Capt. of Verona; 1477, Prov. in Friuli; 1478, Sav. gr. (SM 10; ST 8); Duc. el., Giovanni Mocenigo; 1478-79, Pod. of Padua (SGV 6, c. 50ᵛ; ST 8, c. 15ᵛ); 1479, Amb. to Ferrara; 1480, Sav. gr. (ST 8); 1480-81, Amb. to Rome; 1481, Cons. (CLN 12; CXM 20; SM 11; ST 8); 1482, Sav. gr.; 1482-83, CX (CLN 13, c. 14; CXM 20, 21; MC-Stella); 1482, Amb. to Robert Sansovino, Capt. Gen. of the army; 1483, Amb. to Robert Sansovino, Capt. Gen. of the army; 1483-84, Prov. in Brescia (CXM 21, cc. 120, 130); 1484, Cons. (CLN 13; CXM 21; SM 12); Amb. to the Papal Legate at Cesena; Sav. gr. (CXM 22, c. 87ᵛ); 1485, Sav. gr. (CXM 22, cc. 151, 160ᵛ; SM 12; ST 9); Amb. to Milan; Sav. tf. (ST 9); Duc. el., Marco Barbarigo, and corrector of ducal *promissio*; 1486, Cons. (CLN 13; CXM 23; MC-Stella; SM 12); 1487, Proc. di San Marco (R. M. della Rocca and M. F. Tiepolo, "Cronologia veneziana del Quattrocento," p. 234); 1488, Sav. gr. (SM 12; ST 10, c. 76ᵛ); Cons. (CXM 24); 1490, Sav. gr. (SM 13).

WORKS. A brief life of his father Francesco with dedicatory letter to King Ferdinand of Aragon (15 May 1472). See V. Branca, "Un codice aragonese scritto da Cinico," pp. 170ff. for the circumstances of this collection and Barbaro's humanist interests in general. Zaccaria also left in manuscript his *Dispacci da Napoli*.

CORRESPONDENCE. Letters to Ermolao Barbaro V (Quirini, *Diatriba*, pp. 337-38); Pier Candido Decembrio (see V. Zaccaria, "L'epistolario di Pier Candido Decembrio," p. 112); Francesco Loschi (see Mazzatinti, *Inventario*, III, 137); Lauro Quirini (*Diatriba*, pp. 520-21). Letters to and from Domenico de' Domenichi (in R. Sabbadini, "Andrea Contrario," pp. 431-33). Letters from Francesco Barbaro (*Centotrenta*, ed. Sabbadini, pp. 93, 96-100); Andreas Brentius (cf. Cosenza, *Dict.*, I, 412); Francesco Filelfo (*Epist. fam.*, fols. 265ᵛ-266); Maffeo Vallaresso (*Epist.*, p. 181).

DISCOURSE. Praised by Poliziano in a letter to Lorenzo de' Medici (see Branca, "Codice aragonese," p. 171), and by Marcantonio Sabellico in his funeral oration. Ermolao Barbaro G ded. to Zaccaria his *De coelibatu*, Giorgio Bevilacqua da Lazise his *Flores ex dictis B. Hieronymi collecti* (see Zeno, *Diss. voss.*, II, 356), Marino Sanuto his *Commentari della guerra di Ferrara* (see G. Cozzi, "Marino Sanuto," p. 337), and Andreas Brentius his trans. of Hippocrates' *De insomniis* (cf. Cosenza, *Dict.*, I, 412). Barbaro collected Greek and Latin manuscripts (Cosenza, *Dict.*, I, 412). He possessed a splendid manuscript containing works relating to Francesco Barbaro's heroic defense of

Brescia, 1439-40; these works in Marc. cod. Lat. XIV, 120 (4625), copied from Barbaro's original, as is evident from a note in the manuscript; see Valentinelli, *Bibl. man.*, VI, 188, and *Iter*, II, 235.

EDUCATION. Early humanist studies with Lorenzo Cesano (F. Barbaro's *Epistolae*, ed. Quirini, p. 74).

Barbo, Marco. (2) Son of Marino di Marco. Distantly related to Pietro and Paolo Barbo and their clan (clarification of this relationship in G. Zippel, ed., *Le vite di Paolo II di Gasparino da Verona e Michele Canensi*, pp. 173-74 n. 7). For the Barbo family relations, see the profile of Pietro Barbo.

MONOGRAPH AND STUDIES. G. Gualdo in DBI, VI (1964), 249-52; P. Paschini, "I benefici ecclesiastici del cardinale Marco Barbo" and *Il carteggio fra il cardinale Marco Barbo e Giovanni Lorenzi (1481-1490)*; G. Zippel, "La morte di Marco Barbo cardinale." Gualdo's digest has been relied upon below where other sources are not specifically noted. I have not seen P. Paschini, "Due cardinali mecenati nel secolo XV: Lodovico carmerlengo e Marco Barbo," in *Le conferenze del Laterano* (Rome, 1925), pp. 63-95.

CAREER. B. 1420. D. 2 March 1491. Barbo's testament has not survived, but it is clear from the actions of its executors that he died in relative poverty. Barbo was known for his austerity and piety, and had apparently distributed a large portion of his wealth to the poor. He had held, nevertheless, many lucrative benefices, having been favored not only by his relative and countryman Paul II, but by Sixtus IV and Innocent VIII, as well. For Barbo's benefices and minor offices, see Paschini, "Benefici ecclesiastici" and *Il carteggio*, pp. 1-12. From 1472 to 1474, he was papal ambassador to Germany, Bohemia, Hungary, Poland, and Scandinavia to urge union against the Turks. His ample report on this mission is perhaps to be identified with that cited below; an itinerary was composed by Paulus Sanctoninus (see *Iter*, II, 323, 583). In 1480-81, he performed a mission for the pope in Ancona to assess Adriatic defenses (his *relazione* of this mission cited below).

Titles. 1455-64, Bishop of Treviso (Eubel, *Hier. cath.*, II, 248); 1464-70, Bishop of Vicenza (II, 267); 1467— Card. (II, 15); 1470— Pat. of Aquileia (II, 92); 1478— Bishop of Palestrina (II, 15).

WORKS. Translations from the Greek: *Tractatus de fide catholica et responsiones ad quaestiones Mahumetis magni Turcarum imperatoris* by Gennadius, Pat. of Constantinople, and *Opusculum quoddam* of Dionysius the Areopagite, neither seen; cf. Gualdo, DBI, VI, 252. *Oratio in concistorio habita cum ex Hungarica legatione remearet* and *relazioni* of his missions to the north in 1472-74 (ibid.) and to Ancona in 1480-81 (Cicogna, *Iscrizioni*, II, 258). Correspondence with Giovanni Lorenzi, published in Paschini, *Il Carteggio*. A. Segarizzi ("Niccolò Barbo," p. 43) attributes the *Sermo* in praise of Saint Romuald (in Lapi's *Opera*, fols. 43^v-44^v) to Marco rather than Niccolò Barbo; see the latter's profile. The treatise *De coelibatu*, once attributed to Marco Barbo, is undoubtedly by Ermolao Barbaro G.

CORRESPONDENCE. Exchange with Giovanni Lorenzi (Paschini, *Il carteggio*), Card. Giacomo Ammannati Piccolomini (Gualdo, p. 252), and Maffeo Vallaresso (*Epist.*, pp. 15, 46-48, 62-63, 78, 137-78, 142-44, 218-19, 236, 312-13, 345-46, 352-53, 372-74). Letters from Matteo Bosso (cf. G. Soranzo, *L'umanista canonico regolare Lateranense Matteo Bosso di Verona [1427-1502]*, pp. 24 and n. 8; 135 n. 95, 247 and n. 95); Pietro Dolfin (*Epist. [1524]*, I, xlvi); Marco Donato (two, edited by J. Monfasani in *Collectanea Trapezuntiana*, pp. 419-21); Marsilio Ficino (*Epist.*, pp. 874, 875, 883, 892, 911; see also Kristeller, "Marsilio Ficino e Venezia," p. 481 and n. 38); Francesco Filelfo (*Epist. fam.*, fols. 187, 188ᵛ, 210ᵛ, 213ʳ⁻ᵛ, 236ᵛ, and C. de' Rosmini, *Vita di Francesco Filelfo*, II, 408-409); Moro Lapi (*Opera*, fol. Aʳ⁻ᵛ). A letter from Barbo to Benedetto Maffei acknowledging the dedication follows the latter's *De moribus nostrorum temporum*, fols. 36ᵛ-37.

DISCOURSE. To Barbo were addressed many humanist and other works and editions or translations of classical texts, of which the most interesting in this context are these: Ermolao Barbaro G's translation of Themistius' *De divinatione secundum quietem* (prefatory letter in Barbaro's *Epist.*, I, 6-7); Pietro Barozzi's *De modo bene moriendi*; George of Trebizond's Latin translation of his Greek treatise on the *filioque* and papal primacy (see J. Monfasani, *George of Trebizond*, p. 138); Moro Lapi's *Itinerarium Hierosolymitanum* (*Opera*, fols. 121-85ᵛ); Benedetto Maffei's *De moribus nostrorum temporum*; Paolo Morosini's *Defensio venetorum*; Matteo Palmieri's translation of Aristotle's *Meteora* (see E. Garin, "Le traduzioni umanistiche di Aristotele nel secolo XV," p. 100); and Aurelius Trebanius' *De felicitate libellus*. Barbo was highly reputed for his learning and looked to as a patron of letters and arts. Platina and Rodrigo Sanchez de Arevalo wished him to judge their debate on peace and war (cf. *Le vite di P Paolo II*, ed. Zippel, p. 159). The Palazzo di Venezia, Barbo's residence in Rome, was a gathering place for Rome's humanist circle (P. de Nolhac, "Giovanni Lorenzi, bibliothécaire d'Innocent VIII," p. 10). Barbo collected a significant library of some five hundred volumes, the fate of which is unknown. He placed his library at the disposal of friends and editors, supporting the new art of printing. He encouraged the arts by commissioning the building of numerous churches and monuments. He was a patron, above all, of Lorenzi; for their relationship, see Paschini, *Il carteggio* and "Un ellenista veneziano del Quattrocento: Giovanni Lorenzi"; and P. de Nolhac, "Giovanni Lorenzi."

EDUCATION. Law (perhaps earlier arts) at Padua (Papadopoli, *Hist. gymn. pat.*, II.i.25).

Barbo, Niccolò. (2) Barbus. Son of Pietro; distantly related to Pietro and Paolo Barbo and their clan (see the profile of Pietro Barbo).

MONOGRAPHS AND STUDIES. F. Gaeta in DBI, VI (1964), 252-53; A. Segarizzi, "Niccolò Barbo patrizio veneziano del secolo XV e le accuse contro Isotta Nogarola."

CAREER. B. c. 1420. M. 1453, Pellegrina di Tommaso Franceschi (Giomo, *Matrimoni*, I, 481). D. 1462, before 31 Aug. (the date of Maffeo Vallaresso's letter to Giovanni, brother of Niccolò, consoling the former for his death; *Epist.*, pp. 537-39). Barbo held a series of minor offices (*advoc. per omnes curias* and *super datio vini*, member of the *Consiglio XL, sav. agli ordini, iudex publicorum, auditor veterum sententiarum*) from 1441-57, for which see Segarizzi.

Offices. 1440, Amb. to Alessandria; 1448, Amb. to the Counts of Segna; 1450-53, Visdomino at Ferrara; 1457, Duc. el., Pasquale Malipiero (MC-Regina, c. 17).

WORKS. *Epistolae* (1438-42); *Oratio in laudem Francisci Contareni* (1442). For other manuscript versions of this important oration, see Gaeta, DBI, VI, 253. Barbo was probably the author of a brief *Oratio* that appears among his letters (fol. 101^{r-v}) and is headed: "has ineptias anno aetatis meae XV composui et egi, non sine gloriola ingenioli mei." He was perhaps the author of the *Sermo de Sancto Romualdo*, which Segarizzi and Gaeta attribute to Marco Barbo, but for which Cicogna (*Iscrizioni*, VI, 102) offers convincing evidence of Niccolò's authorship.

CORRESPONDENCE. In his *Epistolae*, letters to Andrea Trapesunzio (fols. 50-55^v), Paolo Barbo (56-59^v), Jacopo Rizzoni (60-61), Tommaso Pontano (70-75^v, 90-99, 102, 102^v), Isotta Nogarola (78-79^v), Antonio Beccadelli (Panormita) (82-85, 85-86); letters from Pontano (103-105) and Nogarola (105^v-108). Elsewhere, letters to and from Francesco Barbaro (cf. *Centotrenta*, ed. Sabbadini, pp. 55, 56, 60 and 62) and Nogarola, and from Guarino Veronese (*Epist.*, ed. Sabbadini, II, 534-37) and Maffeo Vallaresso (*Epist.*, pp. 192-94, 272-74). The correspondence with Nogarola (*Opera omnia*, ed. E. Abel, I, 177-98) includes two letters of Barbo's, one of which (pp. 192-98) does not also appear among his ms. *epistolae*, and one of Nogarola's (pp. 186-91).

DISCOURSE. Praised for his learning by Flavio Biondo (*It. illus.* [1510 ed.], fol. 101^v). With Francesco Contarini, participated in a controversy regarding nobility with Poggio Bracciolini of which the document is Quirini's *Epistola ad Petrum Thomasium*, signed by the three young men. Defended the Veronese humanist Isotta Nogarola against her anonymous accusers; see Barbo's *Epist.*, fols. 70-75^v and 90-99, letters responding to an attack published by Segarizzi (pp. 50-54), who also discusses the controversy (pp. 48-50).

EDUCATION. With George of Trebizond and Paolo della Pergola.

Barbo, Paolo. (2) Barbus. Son of Niccolò; brother of Pietro Barbo (Pope Paul II), and relative to several members of the Barbo clan (for which see the profile of Pietro Barbo). Father of Giovanni, a student of Guarino's (see Kristeller, "An Unknown Letter of Giovanni Barbo to Guarino"). Miles.

MONOGRAPHS AND STUDIES. S. Borsari in DBI, VI (1964), 254-55; G. degli Agostini, *Notizie*, I, 333-45.

PROFILES

CAREER. B. 1416, M. 1434, Ventimiglia della Vedova. Testaments, c. 1460 (AN, Cancelleria Inferiore, Misc. Testamenti, Notai Diversi, B. 31e, #3929, autograph; there his wife is named Ursa) and 14 Nov. 1462 (Procuratori di S. Marco di Citra, Testamenti, #231, not seen; see G. Zippel, ed., *Le vite di Paolo II*, pp. 72-73 n. 3). D. between 14 Nov. and 4 Dec. 1462. For contemporary homonyms, see DBI, VI, 255-57. Through 1447, Barbo resided at the papal court and performed military service for his uncle Pope Eugene IV, receiving many benefices and knighthood. He remained close to his brother, later Pope Paul II, named one of his *commissarii* (see wills cited above), whose accounts he administered until 1460 (Zippel, *Vite*, pp. 4 n. 2, 73-74 n. 2).

Offices. 1449, CX; 1450-51, CX (CXM 14; SGV 4, c. 140); Sav. tf.; Pod. and Capt. of Treviso; 1452, Amb. (among several) to honor Emperor Frederick III at Padua; Sav. tf. (SGV 4, c. x [= 48]; ST 3); Prov. in Verona (ST 3, c. 33); 1452-53, Cons. (CLN 8; CXM 14; MC-Ursa; SGV 4, c. x [= 94]; ST 3); 1453, Prov. with army in Lombardy; 1453-54, Sav. tf. (SGV 4, c. x [= 148]; SM 5; ST 3); 1454, Amb. at Lodi for signing of peace (Romanin, *Stor. doc.*, IV, 225; Zippel, *Vite*, p. 75 n. 2); Sav. tf. (SGV 4, c. x [= 148]; SM 5; ST 3); Amb. to Milan (ST 3, c. 130ᵛ); 1455, Sav. tf.; CX (CXM 15, c. 74 and passim; SGV 4, c. 156ᵛ); 1455-56, Cons. (CLN 9; CXM 15; MC-Regina; SGV 4, c. xᵛ [= 94ᵛ]; SM 5; ST 3, 4); 1457, Sav. tf. (SGV 4, c. 147ᵛ; SM 6; ST 4, c. 35 and passim); CX (CLN 9; CXM 15, c. 137ᵛ); Duc. el., Pasquale Malipiero; 1457-58, Avog. (CXM 15; SM 6; ST 4); 1458-59, *Exile, as punishment for not having persuaded his brother Pietro to renounce, as the Signoria demanded, the bishopric of Padua* (see especially Malipiero, *Annali*, pp. 652-53); 1460, Sav. tf. (SM 6; ST 4); 1460-61, CX (CXM 16, c. 14 and passim), 1461, Sav. tf. (SM 7; ST 4); 1461-62, Amb. to France (especially P. H. Labalme, *Bernardo Giustiniani*, pp. 157ff.; here Barbo delivered the oration to the king of France cited below); 1462, Duc. el., Cristoforo Moro; Avog. Com.; died in office.

WORKS. *Oratio in traditione insignium Bartolomeo de Colionibus* (Brescia, 1455); *Oratio ad imperatorem Federicum III* (Padua, 1452); *Oratio ad Ludovicum Francorum regem* (Tours, 8 Dec. 1461). The oration to Colleoni is a fragment of the whole as explained on fol. 26: "Oratiuncula ... que est particula excerpta ex parte prohemii et conclusionis alterius maioris ab ipso edite sed propter temporis brevitatem intermisse." It was given on the occasion of Colleoni's receiving from the Venetian ambassadors Barbo and Giovanni Moro the scepter of command. The previous attribution to Barbo of a funeral oration for Colleoni has confused the record, since Barbo predeceased the *condottiere*. This oration will probably be identified with the *Oratiuncula* at Brescia (see Borsari, DBI, VI, 255), not seen, and with the work Agostini describes (*Notizie*, I, 343).

CORRESPONDENCE. Letters from Niccolò Barbo (*Epist.*, fols. 56-59ᵛ), Andrea Fiocchi (in G. Mercati, *Ultimi contributi*, I, 121-29, with discussion, pp. 103ff.), Ludovico Foscarini (*Epist.*, fols. 201 and—mistakenly indicated as directed to Paolo Barbaro—250ʳ⁻ᵛ, 250ᵛ-253, 254ᵛ-255, 256ᵛ-257ᵛ, 257ᵛ-258,

261ᵛ-262ᵛ), and Maffeo Vallaresso (*Epist.*, pp. 9-10, 112-13, 171-77, 179-81, 182-83, 246, 345, 422, 520-21).

DISCOURSE. Praised for his learning by Flavio Biondo (*It. illus.* [Venice, 1510], fol. 101ᵛ), Poggio Bracciolini (see Agostini, *Notizie*, I, 336), Francesco Contarini (*De rebus in Hetruria gestis*, p. 17), and in two orations to Barbo's brother, Pope Paul II, by Bernardo Giustiniani (*Orat. et. epist., sig.* G) and Zaccaria Trevisan G (*Oratio habita ad Pontificem Barbum*, col. 1160). L. Trebanius Aurelius addressed to Barbo a dialogue *De libertate* (described by that author in the preface to Marco Barbo of his *De felicitate libellus*; see also *Iter*, II, 66), and Porcellio Pandoni some verse (see *Iter*, I, 164).

EDUCATION. With Andrea Fiocchi (see the letters from Fiocchi cited above).

Barbo, Pietro (= Pope Paul II, 1464-71). (2) Barbus. Son of Niccolò. Brother of Paolo Barbo, and relative to the many humanists and prelates of the Barbo clan. The Barbo family relations, which included Condulmier and Barozzi popes and prelates, are outlined in G. Zippel, ed., *Le vite di Paolo II di Gasparo da Verona e Michele Canensi*, p. 216. All related from among our core group are Pietro, Paolo, Marco, and Niccolò Barbo, Francesco and Pietro Barozzi, and Gregorio Correr. For the more distant Barozzi and Correr relationships, see also M. Bolzonella, *Pietro Barozzi, Vescovo di Padova (1487-1507)*, p. 25 n. 1, and L. Casarsa, "Contributo per la biografia di Gregorio Correr," p. 29 and n. 1.

MONOGRAPHS AND STUDIES. A. J. Dunston, "Pope Paul II and the Humanists"; R. Weiss, *Un umanista veneziano: Papa Paolo II*; Zippel, introduction (and annotated texts) to *Le vite di Paolo II*; G. Zonta, "Un conflitto tra la repubblica veneta e la curia romana per l'episcopato di Padova (1459-60)." See also L. Pastor, "Life of Paul II," in *History of the Popes*, IV.

CAREER. B. 23 Feb. 1417. D. 26 July 1471. During his early career Barbo held the titles of archdeacon of Bologna and apostolic protonotary. In 1459 he fell into conflict with the Venetian government over the appointment to the Paduan see; for this controversy, see especially Zonta, "Un conflitto." Later, when pope, he was also often at odds with Venetian policies; note the comments of Pietro Marcello G in his *Oratio in funere Andreae Vendrameni Venetiarum Principis*, p. 152 and Malipiero, *Annali*, p. 239.

Titles. 1440-51, Bishop of Cervia (Eubel, *Hier. cath.*, II, 126); 1440— Card. (ibid., II, 8; Pastor, "Life," IV, 14); 1451-64, Bishop of Vicenza (Eubel, *Hier. cath.*, II, 267); 1459-60, Bishop of Padua (ibid., II, 210); 1464— pope.

CORRESPONDENCE. Letters from Francesco Barbaro (cf. *Centotrenta*, ed. Sabbadini, 34, 62); Poggio Bracciolini (*Epist.*, ed. Tonellis, III, 261-62), Andrea Contrario (in his *epist.* in R. Sabbadini, "Andrea Contrario," P. 409), Francesco Filelfo (*Epist. fam.*, fols. 83, 166ᵛ-167, 184, 186ᵛ-187, 212ʳ-ᵛ, 216ʳ-ᵛ, 223ᵛ-224), Ludovico Foscarini (*Epist.*, fols. 350-51), George of Trebizond (in J. Monfasani, *George of Trebizond*, pp. 355-59), Pietro del Monte (in his

letters, ed. J. Haller, *Pier da Monte*, pp. 29-30, 38, 73-75, 76-77, 179-80),
Bartolomeo Pagliarino (see F. Diedo's *Oratio de laudibus Bartholomaei Paie-rini*, fol. 75), Maffeo Vallaresso (*Epist.*, passim).

DISCOURSE. Among the many works dedicated to the powerful and influential
Barbo while he was cardinal and pope, these are most pertinent here: Ermolao
Barbaro V's *Orationes contra poetas*; Francesco Filelfo's translation of Xenophon's *Cyropaedeia* (see Filelfo's *Epist. fam.*, fol. 217); Jacopo Zeno's *De
vita B. Nicolai Cardinalis Albergati* and *Vitae summorum pontificum* (for the
latter work, not seen, see *Iter*, II, 336, 474, and G. Zonta, ed., *Vita Caroli
Zeni*, vii n. 1). Notable also are the orations and *opuscula* of our humanists
directed to their compatriot: Pietro Barozzi's *Oratio in morte Johanni [Barocii]
patrui Patriarchae Venetiarum*; Bernardo Giustiniani's *Oratio ad Paulum II*;
Zaccaria Trevisan G's *Oratio habita ad Pontificem Barbum*; Jacopo Zeno's
Oratio ad Paulum Secundum (not seen; see *Iter*, II, 322, and Zonta, "Conflitto," iii no. 4). In addition to assisting in their careers a small army of
relatives (including our humanists Marco Barbo and Francesco Barozzi, for
whom see profiles), Barbo assisted the learned commoner prelates Domenico
de' Domenichi (see H. Jedin, *Studien über Domenico de' Domenichi [1416-
1478]*, pp. 23, 27ff.) and Pietro del Monte (see letters cited above), and the
nobleman Maffeo Vallaresso (see letters cited). He patronized Andrea Contrario (cf. Sabbadini, "Andrea Contrario," pp. 382, 386), Francesco Filelfo
(whom he rewarded for the *Cyropaedeia*; see the Filelfo's letter cited above),
and George of Trebizond (cf. Monfasani, *George*, pp. 34, 38, 97, and 179ff.).
Barbo was hostile to some tendencies within humanist thought, holding a
strictly moralistic position on classical studies; he was infamous for his dis-
solution of Leto's Roman academy. Yet he was an ardent lover of the arts
and of antiquities, restoring ancient monuments in Rome and acquiring a
valuable and massive collection of coins and medals. He was also a devoté
of historical and geographical studies, with exemplars of which he occupied
his leisure and enriched his important library of Latin prose authors. He
collected Greek texts, as well; see A. Pertusi, "L'umanesimo greco," p. 251.
In these predilections he was representative, if not of humanism in general,
certainly of Venetian humanism characterized by its austere religious and
historical orientation. (For this interpretation of Barbo's relations to Venetian
humanism, see Weiss, *Un umanista veneziano*.)

EDUCATION. Studied with Jacopo Rizzoni, Lotto degli Agli, and George of
Trebizond.

Barozzi, Francesco. (3) Baroccius, Barotius. Son of Benedetto; uncle of Pietro
Barozzi and related to the Barbo clan (for which see profile of Pietro Barbo).

CAREER. B. c. 1435 (AC-BO 163/II, c. 22; presented 27 Nov. 1453). D. 1471
(Eubel, *Hier. cath.*, II, 248; Gams, *Ser. episc.*, p. 804). The sixteenth-century
bibliophile Francesco Barozzi was far more prominent than ours, and is often
confused with him. Cappellari (*Camp. ven.*, I, 118ᵛ [119ᵛ] lists two Francesco

Barozzis, both sons of Benedetto: the first taught law, the second married and later turned to a clerical career, becoming bishop of Treviso. He has probably split a single figure in two. Certainly Agostini (*Notizie*, I, x) makes the canon lawyer who taught at Padua the same as the bishop of Treviso. Giomo does list two Francesco Barozzis, both sons of Benedetto, who married, respectively, in 1487 (*Matrimoni*, I, 22) and 1515 (II, 78); neither is easily identified with our figure, nor with the figure Cappellari perhaps created. I have assumed the existence of only one Francesco Barozzi in this particular generation, the son of Benedetto, the uncle of Pietro Barozzi, and a relative of Pope Paul II, who furthered his ecclesiastical career. From about 1458 to perhaps 1466, Barozzi taught canon law at Padua (A. Zeno, *Diss. voss.*, p. 57; M. Bolzonella, *Pietro Barozzi, Vescovo di Padova [1487-1507]*, p. 25 n. 1; Facciolati, *Fasti gymn. pat.*, I.ii.39). According to Facciolati (I.ii.39), Barozzi enjoyed in 1464 the substantial salary of 500 ducats, and was assigned—an honorable challenge— to teach in *concorrenza* with the illustrious Antonio Roselli. It was during Barozzi's Paduan career that Francesco Diedo launched his invective against him. G. Tournoy ("Francesco Diedo, Venetian Humanist and Politician of the Quattrocento," p. 202) refers to Barozzi as a philosopher and mathematician— that is, a student or teacher of arts, rather than law. Prior to his appointment to the see of Treviso, while teaching at Padua, Barozzi held the title of canon of Bergamo (*Vite di Paolo II*, ed. G. Zippel, p. 213). He was present in Rome on 26 June 1468, when the ambassador Paolo (not Pietro) Morosini took possession of the library of Cardinal Bessarion (*Comm.*, ed. Predelli, X, 197 [xvi, #22]).

Titles. 1466— papal *referendarius* (*Vite di Papa Paolo II*, ed. G. Zippel, p. 213; here also a general outline of Barozzi's role in the Curia); 1466— Bishop of Treviso (Eubel, *Hier. cath.*, II, 248).

WORKS. *Oratio pro doctoratu Jacobi Molini in gymnasio patavino; Oratio de laudibus Bonifacii Bonfilii et Iohannis Roti* (Padua, 14 May 1459); oration on death of Bertoldo d'Este (1463), not known to me to be extant (but its existence securely testified to by the author's nephew Pietro in his *Versuum atque hymnorum libri III*, 216). Sansovino (*Venetia*, II, 585) and his followers attribute to him a work *De cognitione iuris*.

DISCOURSE. Francesco Diedo attacked Barozzi in his *Invectiva lacessiti iniuriis apprime* (1458).

EDUCATION. Received his doctorate in law at Padua, a title which he held on 8 April 1466, when he was listed in the *proba* for bishop of Treviso (C. Cenci, "Senato veneto 'probae,' " pp. 400-401). He subsequently taught at Padua.

Barozzi, Pietro. (3) Baroccius, Barotius. Son of Ludovico; nephew of Francesco Barozzi and related to the Barbo clan (for which see profile of Pietro Barbo). Pietro's father Ludovico was also learned, and the correspondent of Francesco Barbaro and Ludovico Foscarini.

MONOGRAPHS AND STUDIES. R. Abbondanza, "Franco Gaeta 'Il vescovo Pietro Barozzi' e il trattato 'De factionibus extinguendis' "; M. Bolzonella, *Pietro Barozzi, Vescovo di Padova (1487-1507)*; F. Gaeta's introduction to Barozzi's principal work in *Il vescovo Pietro Barozzi e il trattato "De factionibus extinguendis"*; Gaeta in DBI, VI (1964), 510-12; E. Govi, "Petri Barocii bibliothecae inventarium"; G. de Sandre Gasparini, "Uno studio sull'episcopato padovano di Pietro Barozzi (1487-1507) e altri contributi sui vescovi veneti nel Quattrocento: problemi e linee di ricerca." I have not been able to see P. Gios, *L'attività pastorale del vescovo Pietro Barozzi a Padova (1487-1507)* (Padua, 1977); the work is reviewed and discussed by de Sandre Gasparini. See these studies for further bibliographical guidance.

CAREER. B. 1441 (all authorities; but Barozzi was presented to the AC in Nov. 1462—BO 163/II, cc. 22—suggesting a birthdate c. 1444). D. 1507. In Padua, Barozzi showed himself to be an effective and concerned administrator. He published the constitutions of the diocesan synod in 1488, instituted a *monte di pietà*, and concerned himself with overseeing monastic reforms. Upon him is based the ideal of the bishop presented in Gasparo Contarini's *De officio episcopi*; see also the discussion of O. Logan, "The Ideal of the Bishop and the Venetian Patriciate: c. 1430-c. 1630," 423ff.; de Sandre Gasparini, "Studio."

Titles. 1471-87, Bishop of Belluno; 1487— Bishop of Padua.

WORKS. Of special interest here: *De factionibus extinguendis* (DFE); *De modo bene moriendi*, to Marco Barbo, with *Consolationes* to Pietro Foscari and Giovanni Michiel (two), and three *officia; Orationes:* 1. *ad Christophorum Maurum Ducem habita quo die Joanni Barrocio Patriarcae Venetiarum obviam cum Senatu profectus est*, 2. *pro Francisco Scledo vicentino rectore juristarum Patavii*, 3. *in funere Antonii Roicelli aretini professoris juris civilis in gymnasio patavino*, 4. *in morte Johannis [Baroccii] patrui Patriarchae Venetiarum*, 5. *ad Marcum Cornarium, cardinalitium galerum suscipienti; Sermo perbrevis ac simplex de moribus virtutibus et miraculis Sancti Petri Acotanti nobilis veneti; Versuum atque hymnorum libri III; Vita B. Eustochii virginis paduanae*, not seen (Padua, Museo Civico, cod. BP 1273; see *Iter*, II, 22); trans., *Basilii magni vita*, from John Chrysostom. See the studies cited for minor works in manuscript, or scattered in printed editions, or perhaps lost.

CORRESPONDENCE. Ample correspondence with Pietro Dolfin (letters from Dolfin in latter's *Epist. CCXLII* and *Epist. [1524]*, passim, and J. Schnitzer, *Peter Delfin General des Camaldulensenordens*, pp. 342ff., passim, but the location of Barozzi's many letters to Dolfin is unknown to me; Dolfin intended to have transcribed those in his possession and instructed a scribe accordingly—*Epist. CCXLII*, 1180—but did not, to my knowledge, complete that project). Exchange with Giorgio Valla (J. L. Heiberg, *Beiträge zur Geschichte Georg Vallas*, pp. 83-85); letters from Giosafat Barbaro (in N. di Lennas, "Giosafat Barbaro [1413-94] e i suoi viaggi nella regione russa [1436-51] e nella Persia [1474-78]," p. 40), Ermolao Barbaro G (*Epist.*, ed. V. Branca, II, 10), Bernardo Bembo (see V. Cian, "Per Bernardo Bembo-II," p. 77), Matteo Bosso (see G. Soranzo, *L'umanista canonico regolare Lateranense Matteo Bosso da Verona*, pp. 94 and n. 5, 121 and n. 36, 132 and n. 80, 190-91 and n. 40, 254 and n. 136, 297), Bernardino Gadolo (*Epist.*, pp. 230-35, 328), Marcantonio Sabellico (*Opera*, fol. 11ʳ⁻ᵛ), and Leonardo Sanuto (cod. Marc. Lat. XIV, 267 [4344], fol. 58ʳ⁻ᵛ).

DISCOURSE. Widely reputed for his learning and piety, Barozzi is also known for his 1489 prohibition, as bishop of Padua and chancellor of the university, against the Averroist doctrine of the unity of the intellect (see E. P. Mahoney, "Philosophy and Science in Nicoletto Vernia and Agostino Nifo," p. 168 n. 85). Matteo Bosso dedicated to Barozzi his *Recuperationes Fesulanae* (see M. Foscarini, *Lett. ven.*, p. 384 n. 3, and Soranzo, *L'umanista canonico*, p. 93); Mauritius Hibernicus his *Castigationes* of Duns Scotus' *Quaestiones in Metaphysicam Aristotelis* (see Cosenza, *Dict.*, I, 430); Niccolò Leoniceno his translation of Ptolemy's *Harmonicorum liber* (ibid.); Jacopo Ragazzoni a poem on the death of Bertoldo d'Este (see Agostini, *Notizie*, I, 559; Agostini cites a Treviso ms. I have not found); Antonio Trombetta his *Contra averroistas* (see Bolzonella, *Pietro Barozzi*, p. 74). Barozzi collected an extensive library, subsequently dispersed, of 354 volumes, including juridical and theological works, Greek, Latin, and volgare classics, and humanist authors. He was reputed for his knowledge of mathematics as well as of the classics and theology; note Pietro Pomponazzi's praise, cited Foscarini, *Lett. ven.*, p. 384 n. 3.

EDUCATION. Barozzi studied with Pietro Perleone, and subsequently at Padua, where he received degrees in law and, apparently, theology, as the following data indicate. In *probae* for the bishoprics of Padua and Treviso in 1481 and 1485, respectively, Barozzi is listed with the titles of doctor of laws and professor of sacred theology (C. Cenci, "Senato veneto 'probae,' " pp. 411, #110; 419, #115). In *probae* for the archbishop of Nicosia and bishop of Bergamo, both in 1484, he appears with the title of doctor of laws (ibid., pp. 415, #113; 416, #114). In the *proba* for bishop of Padua in 1485 (in which Barozzi was the victor), he appears with the titles of doctor of laws and master of sacred theology (ibid., p. 422, #117).

Bembo, Bernardo. (3) Bembus. Son of Niccolò; father of Pietro. Doctor, miles.

MONOGRAPHS AND STUDIES. G. Baruffaldi, "Relazione, o sia esame d'un codice manoscritto del secolo XV, nel quale si contengono diversi opuscoli appartenenti, per qualche titolo, a Bernardo Bembo Cavalliere, e Senatore veneziano"; V. Cian, "Per Bernardo Bembo-I: Le sue relazioni coi Medici" and "Per Bernardo Bembo-II: Le relazioni letterarie, i codici e gli scritti"; C. Frati, "Un codice autografo di Bernardo Bembo"; N. Giannetto, "Un messaggio autografo di Bernardo Bembo a Baldassar Castiglione" and

"Un'orazione inedita di Bernardo Bembo per Cristoforo Moro"; C. Grayson, "Alberti, Poliziano, e Bernardo Bembo" and "Un codice del 'De re aedificatoria' posseduto da Bernardo Bembo"; E.-G. Ledos, "Lettre inédite de Cristoforo Landino à Bernardo Bembo"; E. Levi, "Lo zibaldone di Bernardo Bembo"; E. Narducci, "Intorno all'autenticità di'un codice Vaticano contenente il trattato di Boezio 'De consolatione philosophiae' scritto di mano di Giovanni Boccaccio, seguita da un'appendice di documenti riguardanti le ambascerie di Bernardo Bembo"; G. Nielson, "A Venetian's Commonplaces"; F. Pintor, "Le due ambascerie di Bernardo Bembo a Firenze e le sue relazioni coi Medici"; P. Rajna, "Il codice Vaticano 3357 del trattato 'De vita solitaria' di Francesco Petrarca"; A. della Torre, "La prima ambasceria di Bernardo Bembo a Firenze"; A. Ventura and M. Pecoraro in DBI, VIII (1966), 103-109. The career summary below is based on Ventura and Pecoraro unless otherwise noted. Nella Giannetto's *Bernardo Bembo: umanista e politico veneziano* is now (1985) in press (Florence, Olschki). I am deeply in debt to the author for her kind assistance to me.

CAREER. B. 19 Oct. 1433. M. 1462, Elena di Matteo Morosini (Giomo, *Matrimoni*, II, 144); Elena Marcello. D. 28 May 1519. Several Bernardo Bembos appear in the relevant archival documents. A Bernardo di Pietro, in particular, holds high offices in the 1470s and 1480s. I have offered from archival sources no positions for which the identity of our Bernardo has not been securely established. Bembo held minor political offices from as early as 1455, when he was a member of the congratulatory embassy to Pope Calixtus III in Rome (Giannetto, "Orazione inedita," p. 261 and n. 10). Bembo's pecuniary difficulties are suggested by his need at various points in his career to fund loans (see, for example, Cian, "Per Bernardo Bembo-II," p. 355); he did, however, possess land in Paduan territory on the terraferma (V. Lazzarini, "Beni carraresi e proprietari veneziani," p. 281).

Offices. 1468-69, Amb. to Castille (accompanied by the poets Paolo Marsi and Antonio Vinciguerra, the latter as one of his staff; see A. della Torre, *Paolo Marsi*, pp. 149ff.); 1471-74, Amb. to Burgundy; 1474, Amb. to Austria (uncertain; Ventura and Pecoraro, p. 104); Duc. el., Pietro Mocenigo (MC-Regina, c. 143); 1475-76, Amb. to Florence; 1476, Amb. to Ferrara (ST 7, c 132ᵛ); 1477-78, CX (CXM 19); 1478-80, Amb. to Florence; 1481-83, Pod. and Capt. of Ravenna (where Bembo restored Dante's tomb; see below); 1483-84, Amb. to England and/or France;* 1485, Amb. in obedientia to Pope Innocent VIII; 1486, Avog. (CXM 23; SGV 6, c. 112); 1487, *tried for fiscal improprieties by the CX; acquitted 22 October* (CXM 23, cc. 131, 135, 136ᵛ, 137); 1487-88, Amb. to Rome (on which mission he delivered the three orations to Pope Innocent VIII cited below); 1489-90, Pod. of Bergamo; 1494-95, Avog. (MC-Stella, c. 136; SGV 6, c. 132; SGV 7 già 12, c. 2ᵛ); 1496-97, CX; 1497, Visdomino in Ferrara; 1499-1500, CX (CXM 28); 1500, Avog. (MC-Stella, c. 169); 1501, Duc el., Leonardo Loredan; 1501-2, CX (CXM 28); 1502-3, Pod. of Verona; 1502, Amb. to King Louis XII in Pavia and Milan (performed while holding the office of pod.); 1504-5, Avog.; 1505,

Amb. in obedientia to Pope Julius II; 1505-6, CX; 1509-10, Avog.; 1510-11, Cons.; 1512-13, Avog.; 1513-14, CX.

Note: It is unclear whether Bembo ever went to England. Giving the year as 1484 (conflicting with archival evidence), Malipiero says he was sent to England (*Annali*, p. 290). Seven months after Bembo was granted admission to the Senate so that he might be informed about England, he was elected ambassador to France. The acts referring to the English and French appointments, respectively, dated 13 July 1483 and 13 Feb. 1484, in ST 9, cc. 14, 54ᵛ-55. The brief elapsed time between them could suggest that Bembo never left for England. Ventura finds no further evidence of that journey (p. 105). It is also uncertain whether he ever went on the mission to France.

WORKS. *Gratulatio ad Christophorum Maurum pro clarissimo divini atque humani iuris scolasticorum ordine Patavini habita* (1462); *Oratio in adventu Cardinalis Sancti Angeli Legati Apostolici*; *Oratio in adventu Jacobi Zeni [Episcopi Patavini]* (1460); *Oratio in funere Bertholdi Marchionis Estensis* (1464), with *consolatio* to his widow Jacoba; three *orationes ad Innocentium VIII* (1487-88); *Zibaldone* (see Levi, "Lo zibaldone"; Nielson, "A Venetian's Commonplaces").

CORRESPONDENCE. Exchange with Dante III Alighieri (see Cian, "Per Bernardo Bembo-II," p. 58) and Marcantonio Sabellico (*Opera*, fols. 45ᵛ, 49ʳ⁻ᵛ). Letters to Pietro Barozzi (see Cian, "Bembo-II," p. 77); Lauro Quirini (perhaps; ibid.); Lorenzo de' Medici (see Pintor, "Due ambascerie"; for other letters to the Medici and Gonzaga, see Cian, "Bembo-II," p. 77); Jacopo Zeno (see G. Zonta, introduction to the *Vita Caroli Zeni*, p. v n. 8). Letters from Ermolao Barbaro G (*Epist.*, ed. Branca, II, 12-13, 36); Pietro Bembo (in among other editions his *Opere in volgare*, ed. M. Marti, pp. 700, 701-703); Marsilio Ficino, Francesco Filelfo (*Epist. fam.*, p. 153); Cristoforo Landino (see E.-G. Ledos, "Lettre inédite," and P. de Nolhac, *La Bibliothèque de Fulvio Orsini*, p. 240); Antonio Vinciguerra (vernacular letter in the Pierpont Morgan Library's collection of autograph manuscripts, dated 25 May 1498). Letters from Ficino in his *Epist.*, pp. 652, 654, 688-70, 722-23, 730, 739-40, 748-49, 753, 761, 771, 772, 777, 782, 787, 794, 799, 801, 803, 807, 810-11 (with Antonio Vinciguerra), 821, 826-27, 828, 829, 833, 842, 843, 880, 907-908, 957; and see P. O. Kristeller, "Marsilio Ficino e Venezia," pp. 477ff. The letters from Books I, III, and IV are translated in *The Letters of Marsilio Ficino*; see indices. Bembo probably wrote many letters, now lost. For his correspondence in general, see Cian, "Bembo-II," 76ff. Vernacular letters in Cian, "Pietro Bembo e Isabella d'Este Gonzaga."

DISCOURSE. A humanist of great importance (P. Monnier ranks him with Girolamo Donato and Ermolao Barbaro G: *Le Quattrocento*, I, 173; O. Logan sees that same triad as the major representatives of late-century humanism: *Culture and Society*, pp. 50ff.), Bembo was even more active as a participant in the society of the learned than as an author in his own right. He was perhaps

more than any other Venetian humanist (Francesco and Ermolao Barbaro G,
Girolamo Donato, and Antonio Vinciguerra are his closest competitors) aware
of the currents of Florentine culture in which he mixed during two long and
important missions to that city. For Bembo's Florentine missions and literary
relations while there, see especially Cian, "Per Bernardo Bembo-I"; Pintor,
"Due ambascerie"; della Torre, "Prima ambasceria." Giannetto's "Un messaggio autografo" shows that Bembo was also in contact with Baldassar
Castiglione, later the literary colleague of Bernardo's more famous son Pietro.

Many contemporary humanists dedicated works to Bembo, not only to
honor him, but to seek his criticism (see della Torre, "Prima ambasceria," p.
260). Of this large literature, particularly noteworthy are the works of the
Venetians Pietro Barozzi (De factionibus extinguendis), Francesco Contarini
(De rebus in Hetruria gestis), Giorgio Merula (commentary on Cicero's Pro
Ligario, see F. Gabotto and A. B. Confalonieri, "Vita di Giorgio Merula,"
first part, p. 286, and translation of three sermons of John Chrysostom, in
Ferrara, Bibl. Comunale Ariostea, cod. II 162, fols. 28ᵛ-36; see della Torre,
Paolo Marsi, p. 15); and Antonio Vinciguerra (two satire; see d. Torre, An-
tonio Vinciguerra, pp. 109ff.); Paolo Marsi also addressed an epigram to
Bembo, in his Elegiae, fol. 42. Works by several foreigners and Venetians were
gathered by Bembo himself in a unique manuscript: the famous Ferrara codex,
cited above, containing works dedicated to Bembo by Battista Mantovano,
Marsilio Ficino, Filippo Morandi da Rimini, Cristoforo Landino, Benedetto
Maffei, Paolo Marsi, and Giorgio Merula, Angelo Poliziano, and two dialogues of Cane's (one dedicated to Francesco Diedo) in which Bembo is an
interlocutor (fols. 60-94ᵛ). For discussion of this unusual manuscript, see
G. Baruffaldi, "Relazione," and Kristeller, Iter, I, 58-59. For Battista, see Cian,
"Bembo-II," p. 55, and Cosenza, Dict., I, 489. For Landino, see d. Torre,
"Prima ambasceria," 301ff.; Landino also gives a sketch of the august Bembo
in his De nobilitate (cf. V. Branca, "Ermolao Barbaro e l'umanesimo veneziano," p. 209). For Poliziano, see Cian, "Bembo-II," pp. 51-52. Ficino dedicates to Bembo the fifth book of his Epist.; see p. 782; for Bembo's relations
with Ficino, see Kristeller, "Marsilio Ficino e Venezia."

To the delight of the Florentines (see Landino's appreciative letter, Ledos,
"Lettre inédite"), Bembo ordered restored in Ravenna in May 1483 the tomb
of Dante, and composed an epitaph for the Tuscan poet. He joined in the
circle of scholars around Aldo Manuzio in the 1490s. In 1509, the Senate
asked Bembo as censor to screen for publication Pietro Cirneo's De rebus
corsicis (G. dalla Santa, "Un testamento ed alcune note biografiche di Pietro
Cirneo, prete, storico, umanista," p. 164). Bembo was a patron of Giovanni
Aurelio Augurello (G. Pavanello, Un maestro del Quattrocento, p. 91); Jacopo
da Udine (d. Torre, Paolo Marsi, p. 50); Paolo Marsi (ibid., pp. 149ff. and
passim); Pietro Pomponazzi (d. Torre, "Prima ambasceria," p. 283); Antonio
Vinciguerra (d. Torre, Antonio Vinciguerra, pp. 36, 40ff., 46ff., 49ff.; also
served Bembo on occasions by state appointment). Bembo's famous library,
which included several important manuscripts written or glossed in his own

hand, passed to his illustrious son, the Cardinal Pietro, and ultimately enriched the Vatican and other libraries (see especially de Nolhac, *Bibliothèque de Fulvio Orsini* and C. H. Clough, *Pietro Bembo's Library as Represented Particularly in the British Museum*; also Cian, "Bembo-II," pp. 66ff.; R. Sabbadini, *Le scoperte dei codici latini e greci*, I, 146ff.; Frati, "Un codice autografo"; Grayson, "Alberti, Poliziano"; Grayson, "Un codice"; Narducci, "Intorno all'autenticità"; Rajna, "Il codice Vaticano").

EDUCATION. Bembo studied at Padua, receiving his doctorate in arts under Gaetano da Thiene on 10 Nov. 1455 (Giannetto, "Orazione inedita," p. 259 n. 5). He continued to study law, and was still a student (with Francesco Diedo, under Angelo Ubaldi) when he gave on behalf of the law students a congratulatory oration to Doge Moro in 1462 (see G. Tournoy, "Francesco Diedo, Venetian Humanist and Politician of the Quattrocento," p. 201, and the oration for Moro cited above). Doctorate in law granted 1456 (Giannetto, "Orazione inedita," p. 259 n. 5).

Bernardo, Antonio. (3) Bernardus. Son of Andrea. Doctor, miles.

MONOGRAPHS AND STUDIES. M. Caravale in DBI, IX (1967), 304-305.

CAREER. B. c. 1430. M. 1462, Elena di Carlo Quirini (Giomo, *Matrimoni*, II, 288). D. after 5 May 1504 (when listed in the *scrutinio* for Proc. di San Marco; Sanuto, *Diarii*, VI, 19), and before 23 June 1512 (CXM 35, c. 39). Bernardo's three brothers were presented to the AC in 1453, 1454 and 1459 (BO 163/II, c. 108ᵛ), and his two sons in 1487 and 1490 (BO 164/III, c. 60ᵛ). These data, with those regarding marriage, first election (as *advoc. proprii*, 1 Sept. 1454; SGV 4, c. 19), and university career, suggest the birthdate given. Before and after 1471, Bernardo may have engaged in commerce or held minor offices. Some early years were spent at Padua.

Offices. 1471, Duc. el., Niccolò Tron (MC-Regina, c. 102); 1484-86, Pod. of Vicenza (CXM 22, c. 104ʳ⁻ᵛ; SGV 6, c. 56; notoriously expelled the Jews [Agostini, *Notizie*, I, 499-501, and Caravale, p. 305]); 1489, Pod. and Capt. of Treviso; 1495-96, CX (CXM 26, c. 184ᵛ and passim and 27; SGV 9 già 13, c. 8); 1497-98, Capt. of Bergamo (SGV 6, c. 19 and 8 già 7, c. 56ᵛ; Sanuto, *Diarii*, II, 74); 1499-1500, CX; 1501-2, CX (CXM 28, 29).

WORKS. *Oratio in doctoratu Albertini Baduarii; Oratio pro doctoratu Jacobi Molini in gymnasio patavino.* Bernardo may have delivered the funeral oration for the Doge Cristoforo Moro; cf. Cappellari, *Camp. ven.*, I, 157ᵛ.

DISCOURSE. Bartolomeo Pagello wrote an elegy to Bernardo (cf. B. Marx, *Bartolomeo Pagello*, p. 91). Alessandro Benedetti dedicated to him, Giorgio Corner, and Ludovico Venier the second book of his *Diaria de bello carolino.*

EDUCATION. Taught civil law at Padua in 1462, where he had previously been a student.

Bollani, Candiano. (2) Pollani, Bolanus, Bollanus. Son of Maffeo; father of Domenico.

MONOGRAPHS AND STUDIES. G. Pillinini in DBI, XI (1969), 287-89; G. degli Agostini, *Notizie,* II, 157-67.

CAREER. B. c. 1413. M. 1438, Lucrezia di Pietro Marcello (Giomo, *Matrimoni,* II, 42). D. August 1478 (Pillinini, DBI, XI, 287). That date of death is consistent with Malipiero's report that Bollani died of the plague in autumn 1478 (*Annali,* p. 670). He was still alive and reporting to the Senate on the Turkish assault on Scutari in the summer of that year (P. Dolfin, *Epist.* CCXLII, 1041-42, letter of 5 Aug.). The evidence which follows that Bollani died earlier is probably erroneous. Girolamo Bollani appears in the *proba* for Bishop of Trau of Nov./Dec. 1483 with this comment indicating that Candiano died in 1478, while provveditore in Friuli: "filius . . . ser Candiani Bollani, illius qui ob honorem patriae, post multa magna facinora, legatus in patriam Fori Iulii missus, inde finem invenit morte apreciandissima, dimissis liberis ob virtutem maximam suam in summa paupertate" (C. Cenci, "Senato veneto 'Probae,' " p. 413). Bollani held minor political posts from 1438, when on 17 Aug. he was elected to the *Tabula exitus* (SGV 4, c. 45^v). His involvement in commercial activities is suggested by the privilege granted him to mine precious and other metals in the vicinity of Brescia and Bergamo (ST 6, cc. 178^v and 181, 12 Sept. and 6 Oct. 1472, respectively). Yet he was not wealthy, if we can believe his son Girolamo.

Offices. 1452, Amb. to Ferrara; Amb. to Istria (SM 4, c. 163^v); 1455, Amb. to Pordenone, representatives of Emperor Frederick III; 1456, Sav. tf. (SGV 4, c. 147; SM 5; ST 4); 1458, Sav. tf. (SGV 4, c. 147^v; SM 6; ST 4, c. 71); 1460, Sav. tf. (SM 6; ST 4); Pod. and Capt. of Belluno; 1462, Duc. el., Cristoforo Moro; Sav. tf.; 1463, Sav. tf.; 1464, Pod. of Vicenza; 1465, Sav. tf. (SM 8; ST 5); CX (CXM 16; held concurrently with the previous office); 1466?, Capt. of Crete (SGV 6, c. 80; elected 8 May 1466, Bollani may have returned shortly before 11 Nov. 1469, when he appears "olim Capitanus Crete": SM 9, c. 22^v; perhaps he served in this position considerably longer than the normal term, or perhaps he did not assume office until some time after his election); 1469, Cons. (CLN 11; CXM 17; MC-Regina; SGV 6, c. 1; SM 9; ST 6); 1469-70, Avog. (CXM 17; SGV 6, cc. 1, 7; ST 6); 1471, Capt. of Brescia and prov. (SGV 6, c. 91; ST 6, c. 116^v); 1472, Avog. (SGV 6, c. 7; held position concurrently with others while also on CX); Amb. to Ferrara (ST 6, c. 174^v; performed mission while also on CX); Sav. tf. (SM 9; held position concurrently with others while also on CX); 1472-73, CX (CXM 17, 18; while holding other positions concurrently); 1473, Sav. gr. (SM 9; ST 6; held position concurrently with others while also on CX); Avog.; Duc. el., Niccolò Marcello; 1474-75, Capt. of Verona; 1475, Sav. gr. (ST 7, c. 84^v); CX (CXM 18); Amb. to Milan, then to Malpaga, the deathplace of the condottiere Bartolomeo Colleoni, as one of those elected to insure the inheritance for Venice; 1476, Duc. el., Andrea Vendramin; Cons.; 1477, Sav. gr.

(CLN 12; SM 10; ST 7); 1477-78, CX (CXM 19; held concurrently with previous position); 1478, Duc el., Giovanni Mocenigo; Sav. gr.; Prov. in Friuli.

WORKS. *Libri XVIII in tria priora capita Genesis* (1466); *Oratio gratulatoria de creatione Christophori Mauri; In rhetoricorum novorum Ciceronis librum primum commentum; Tractatus super canticum gloriosissimae virginis Mariae; Trialogus in rebus futuris annorum XX proximorum* (Bollani appears as an interlocutor; for his authorship, see A. Segarizzi, "Jacopo Languschi," p. 181 and n. 6); translation with preface to Pope Eugene IV of George of Trebizond's commentary on the Magnificat to John Cuboclesios (Bollani's preface in J. Monfasani, ed., *Collectanea Trapezuntiana*, pp. 260-61). I have not been able to see the *Oratio de laudibus Francisci Sphortiae Mediolanensis ducis* or the *Oratio de invidia* (cf. Agostini, *Notizie*, II, 166; mss. formerly in the collection of Giulio Saibante). For Bollani's works now in the British Museum (the translation of George of Trebizond and the youthful *tractatus*), see J. Monfasani, *George of Trebizond*, p. 23 n. 102. On fol. 24ᵛ of the commentary on the Canticum is read the following remark: "Est satis quid puerile"; and on fol. 39: "Explicit super cantico, et satis ineptum est. Nam anus garulavit, ignorans scripturam."

CORRESPONDENCE. Letters from Ludovico Foscarini (*Epist.*, fol. 204ʳ⁻ᵛ continued on fol. 203) and Maffeo Vallaresso (*Epist.*, pp. 395-97, 421, 429-31, 436-37, 515).

DISCOURSE. Praised for his learning by Flavio Biondo (*It. illus.* [Venice, 1510], fol. 101ᵛ). Domenico de' Domenichi dedicated to him his *Quaestio de nominibus his quidditas et essentia*, and Giovanni Michele Alberto da Carrara addressed poems to him (see *Iter*, I, 12, 15, 16).

EDUCATION. A student, perhaps with Ludovico Foscarini, of George of Trebizond (Monfasani, *George of Trebizond*, p. 23). Foscarini notes Bollani as a co-student—whether with George or another teacher—in the letter cited above.

Bollani, Domenico. (3) Bolani, Polani, Bollanus. Son of Candiano. Doctor, miles.

MONOGRAPHS AND STUDIES. DBI, XI (1969), 289-90 [no author named]; G. degli Agostini, *Notizie*, I, 521-32.

CAREER. B. c. 1445 (thus the principal studies; but Bollani was presented to the AC on 26 Nov. 1465 [BO 164/III, c. 31], indicating a 1447 birthdate). M. 1475, Elena di Michele Boldù (Giomo, *Matrimoni*, I, 131 gives Isabella). D. perhaps 1496. The problem of homonymns has been difficult; see Agostini I, 528ff., and G. Pillinini on Domenico di Francesco in DBI, XI, 290-91. It was certainly the latter who served as duke of Crete, 1494-96 (SGV 8 già 7, c. 100). It was probably not our Domenico to whom Marsilio Ficino addressed his letter (*Epist.*, p. 812; see Kristeller, "Marsilio Ficino e Venezia," pp. 480-81 nn. 33 and 36).

Offices. 1474, Sind. and prov. in Dalmatia and Albania (SM 9, cc. 191ᵛ, 195-97); 1476, Castellan of Belluno; 1477, Sind. and Prov. in Dalmatia and Albania (SM 10, cc. 144, 178-81ᵛ, 184ᵛ); 1478, Duc. el., Giovanni Mocenigo (MC-Regina, cc. 177ᵛ, 178); 1478, 1479, Amb. to Mantua (ST 8, cc. 14, 67); 1479-80, Amb. to Spain (SM 11, cc. 19ᵛ, 23ᵛ, 63); 1480, Sind. and Prov. in eastern Mediterranean (SM 11, cc. 81, 85); 1481-82, Amb. to Hungary; 1483-84, Sind. in eastern Mediterranean (SM 11, cc. 194, 199ᵛ-202); 1487, Amb. in Dalmatia (SM 12, cc. 107, 117); Avog. (CXM 23); 1488, Amb. in Dalmatia (ST 10, c. 85ᵛ); 1489-90, Amb. to Hungary; 1491, Sav. tf.; 1492-93, Avog. (CXM 25, 26; SGV 6, c. 132; ST 11, 12); 1493, *Accused before Senate for acceptance of bribes; fled, and was exiled in his absence to Crete* (the eloquent condemnation in ST 12, cc. 21-22ᵛ).

WORKS. *De conceptione gloriosissime Virginis Mariae.* Perhaps no longer extant are his *Venetarum rerum historia* (known to Sebastiano Manilio, editor of Petrarch's *Familiares,* which had been based on Bollani's exemplar; see DBI, XI, 290), and funeral orations for the Doges Niccolò Marcello (1474; noted by Malipiero, *Annali,* p. 664) and Pietro Mocenigo (1476).

DISCOURSE. Publicly recited the congratulatory oration for Doge Cristoforo Moro composed by his father Candiano (see a note on the manuscript of the oration, Marc. cod. Lat. XIV, 252 [4718], fol. 85). Domenico's codex furnished the basis for the *editio princeps* of Petrarch's *Epistolae familiares,* published in Venice by Giovanni e Gregorio de' Gregoris, 1492; Sebastiano Manilio, who edited the work, dedicated it to him in gratitude (see DBI, XI, 190).

EDUCATION. After elementary studies with his father, Bollani received a doctorate in arts at Padua, and perhaps continued there afterwards to study theology.

Brognoli, Benedetto. (2?) Brunulus, Prunulus.

MONOGRAPHS AND STUDIES. E. Mioni, in DBI, XIV (1972), 501-503. See also Giovanni Quirini's *Consolatoria oratio pro obitu eximii ac integerrimi viri Benedicti Brugnoli utriusque preceptoris,* to his co-student Girolamo Raimundo. Giovanni Battista Egnazio's funeral oration for Brognoli (Venice: Aldo, 1502) I have been unable to see.

CAREER. B. Legnago, 1427. D. 7 July 1502. Early in the 1450s, Brognoli came to Venice to study. By 1 June 1466, when he was appointed to the public position of teacher of humanities at the San Marco school, Brognoli had already "long taught" in Venice. The document of appointment thus describes Brognoli's previous Venetian career: "qui iam diu in hac urbe venetiarum cum summa omnium laude et commendatione docuit" (CLN 10, c. 146ᵛ, published A. della Torre, *Antonio Vinciguerra,* p. 15 n. 1, and A. Segarizzi, "Cenni," p. 645 n. 1; see also n. 38 on p. 92 of the first part of M. L. King, "A Study in Venetian Humanism"). He had served for nearly ten years as the assistant of one of his predecessors in that post, Giovanni Pietro Vitali d'Avenza (da Lucca). He continued to hold that position for an unparalleled term of thirty-six years, until his death (J. B. Ross, "Venetian Schools," Appendix). From the 1470s, Brognoli was also active in the career of early printing as a corrector for the presses of Jenson and others. Other Brognolis, but not Benedetto, received citizenship grants during this period; Toderini, *Genealogie*, III, Appendix.

WORKS. *Oratio super Ethicis Aristotelis* (7 Aug. 1494), not seen; trans., Libanius, declamation XXVI, not seen (Verona, Bibl. Capitolare, cod. CCXXVII [354], with other miscellaneous works; cf. *Iter*, II, 295); nine *epistolae*. For these works, see Mioni, DBI, XIV, 502. The *Oratio* on Aristotle and letters in Belluno, Bibl. Lolliniana, cod. 22. A microfilm of fols. 127-41^v, containing the letters, was generously obtained for me by Martin Lowry.

CORRESPONDENCE. Letters to, most notably, Filippo Buonaccorsi (16 Oct. 1488; in Marc. Lat. X, 125 [3247], fols. 137-41) and Lorenzo di Bernardo Giustiniani (in J. G. Graevius, ed., *Thesaurus antiquitatum et historiarum Italiae*, V, Part I, cols. 3-4, amid the material introductory to Giustiniani's works). Both these letters are also in the Belluno codex cited above, respectively on fols. 127-29^v and 135-41.

DISCOURSE. Among the works he edited for the Venetian presses are Priscian's *Institutiones grammaticae*, George of Trebizond's *Rhetorica*, Lorenzo Valla's translation of Herodotus' *Histories*, Ambrogio Traversari's translation of Diogenes Laertius, Bernardo Giustiniani's posthumous *History of the Origin of Venice*, works of Cicero, and a new edition of Niccolò Perotti's *Cornucopia* (see Mioni, DBI, XIV, 502-503; for the publication of Giustiniani's work, also P. H. Labalme, *Bernardo Giustiniani*, pp. 256-57, and the letter to Lorenzo cited above). A member of Buonaccorsi's circle during that humanist's residence in Venice in 1486 (see the latter's *De his quae a Venetis tentata sunt* [1533], p. 88, and the letter cited above), Brognoli was praised for his learning by Quirini and Egnazio in the orations cited and Francesco Negri (*De aristocratia*, fol. 98^{r-v}), Marcantonio Sabellico (*De rep. lat. ling.*, fol. 109^v), and Marino Sanuto (*Cronachetta*; the relevant passage translated and published in J. B. Ross, "Venetian Schools," p. 557). He numbered among his pupils Quirini and Egnazio again (ibid., p. 536), Domizio Calderini, Pietro Cirneo (G. dalla Santa, "Un testamento ed alcune note biografiche di Pietro Cirneo"), and Daniele Renier (Sabellico, *Opera*, fol. 51^v).

EDUCATION. With Ognibene da Lonigo (Leoniceno), George of Trebizond, and Giovanni Pietro Vitali d'Avenza (da Lucca).

Bruto, Pietro. (2?) Brutus.

MONOGRAPHS AND STUDIES. G. degli Agostini, *Notizie*, I, 495-508; F. Lepori in DBI, XIV (1972), 735-37.

CAREER. B. probably by 1430 (based on the career record; Lepori suggests the first decades of the fifteenth century, based on Bruto's 1486 statement that he was "aetate iam ingravescente"). D. after 12 Oct. 1492 and before 16 Aug. 1493 (Lepori, 736-37; on the latter date, Bruto had been replaced as bishop of Cattaro, for the ornamentation of whose church he had bequeathed funds: Agostini, *Notizie*, I, 502). Born to an established native Venetian family, Bruto, an ordained priest, held the title of *piovano* in the Church of S. Agata in Venice, and rector of schools in the district of San Marco. In Vicenza in later years, he was famed as a leader of civic action against the Jews, provoked by the alleged murder in Trent of a Christian child (the beatified Simon) and resulting in their expulsion by the Venetian podestà Antonio Bernardo in 1486. (For Bruto's crusade against the Vicentine Jews, see also B. Marx, *Bartolomeo Pagello*, p. 90). This controversy occasioned two of Bruto's works cited below. Bruto may have resided only sporadically in Croia or Cattaro, and may never have entered the former see. Bruto appears among the *cittadino* families named by da Mosto (*Archivio*, I, 74).

Titles. 1468-74, Bishop of Croia (Albania); ?-1471?, *Vicar Gen. for Marco Negro, B. of Cattaro*; 1471?— Bishop of Cattaro; by 1477, *Vice regent and lieutenant to Giovanni Battista Zeno, Bishop of Vicenza.*

WORKS. *Epistola contra Judeos; Victoria contra Judaeos*, to the Vicentine nobility. The *Victoria* opens with a prefatory letter to the Mantuan Giovanni Bonavita (Benavides), and closes with a letter on the same anti-Semitic theme to Pope Innocent VIII and an oration to the Vicentines. A work *De virtute amplectenda*, known to Agostini (*Notizie*, I, 508), is perhaps lost.

CORRESPONDENCE. Letters to Oliviero d'Arzignano (see Agostini, *Notizie*, I, 507ff. and Cosenza, *Dict.*, I, 725) and to and from Barnaba Celsano (see Agostini, *Notizie*, I, 505ff., Cosenza, *Dict.*, I, 725, and Marx, *Pagello*, pp. 57-58 n. 17).

DISCOURSE. Bruto was among the few Venetians of our group who knew Hebrew, which he employed in the sacred studies given rich but hostile voice in his works. He taught Francesco Negri (see G. Mercati, *Ultimi contributi*, II, 38). D'Arzignano dedicated to Bruto his commentaries on Valerius Maximus (Agostini, *Notizie*, I, 496, 507; also D. Schullian in CTC, V, forthcoming).

EDUCATION. Elementary studies followed by a university degree in arts, perhaps at Padua.

Caldiera, Giovanni. (2) Calderia, de Calderiis.

MONOGRAPHS AND STUDIES. G. degli Agostini, *Notizie*, II, 411-19; J. C. Hill in DBI, XVI (1973), 626-28; M. L. King, "Caldiera and the Barbaros on Marriage and the Family" and "Personal, Domestic, and Republican Values in the Moral Philosophy of Giovanni Caldiera"; C. Trinkaus, *In Our Image and Likeness*, II, 704ff.

CAREER. B. c. 1400. D. by 1474. Born to a wealthy and established Venetian family, Caldiera first studied, then taught medicine at Padua in the 1420s and 1430s. He subsequently returned to Venice to undertake the practice of medicine, achieving in later years the dignity of prior of the Venetian College of Physicians.

WORKS. Of Caldiera's many works, especially noteworthy here are: the *De concordantia poetarum philosophorum et theologorum*, to his daughter Cataruzza (ms. versions cited in King, "Personal, Domestic, and Republican Virtues," p. 538 n. 9, are superior to the printed version [1547]); a trilogy of moral philosophical works comprising: 1. *De virtutibus moralibus et theologicis*, 2. *De oeconomia veneta*, 3. *De praestantia venetae politiae, et artibus in eadem excultis tam mechanicis quam liberalibus [et] de virtutibus quae maxime reipublica[e] veneta[e] debentur*, dedicated to Doge Cristoforo Moro, the cleric Tommaso Gradenigo, and the secretary Antonio Vinciguerra, respectively (I have seen the Oxford ms. cited in the bibliography and late Venetian copies, but have not located the 1830 fragment published by E. A. Cicogna); *Oratio in funere Orsati Justiniani Sancti Marci Procuratoris ad senatum populumque; Oratio habita in collegio phisicorum Venetorum pro principio prioralis*; also several university *Orationes*. To the record of Caldiera's works given in "Personal, Domestic and Republican Values," p. 538 n. 9, see also the note in "Caldiera and the Barbaros," p. 23 n. 9. P. O. Kristeller has alerted me to these additional works: *Centiloquium de causis et causalis*, and the commentaries *Liber de physico auditu* and *Liber metaphysice* (not seen; in Poppi, Bibl. Comunale, cod. 144, see Mazzatinti, *Inventario*, VI, 140). He evidently wrote others which are not to my knowledge extant; see his own detailed catalogue of *opera* on fols. 100-101 of the *Oratio in collegio phisicorum*.

DISCOURSE. Respected in Venice for his learning and particularly for his skills in astrological prediction. Caldiera privately taught Antonio Vinciguerra, the dedicatee of his *De praestantia venetae politiae*. He appears as an interlocutor in Filippo Morandi da Rimini's *Symposium de paupertate* (see King, "A Study in Venetian Humanism at Mid-Quattrocento," Part One).

EDUCATION. Present at Padua from at least 1417, Caldiera received his doctorates in arts and medicine in 1420 and 1426, respectively.

Calvo, Antonio. (3) Calbo, Calvus, Calbus. Perhaps the son of Ludovico; identity uncertain. If our Antonio was the son of Ludovico, he was considerably older than his friend Ermolao Barbaro G. The latter's letters to Calvo suggest, however, a near contemporary. V. Branca makes that assumption in his notes on Calvo in Barbaro's *Epist.*, II, 139. I have found the traces of no other Antonio Calvo in the Avogaria di Comun. That document, however, does list a Marcantonio, son of Girolamo, born approximately in 1458 and thus a close contemporary of Barbaro (BO 164/III, c. 88; 1 Dec. 1476).

Cappellari, furthermore, names an Antonio Calvo di Girolamo as a nephew of Antonio Calvo di Ludovico (*Camp. ven.*, I, 214, 214ᵛ). Perhaps it is this Calvo who is Barbaro's correspondent. If so, I have been unable to trace his political career. It is unlikely that Barbaro's correspondent was a clergyman. The information given in the career table pertains to Antonio Calvo, son of Ludovico, who remains the most likely candidate for identification with our humanist. Olivieri gives a biography of this Calvo that partly harmonizes with the data I have located for the same figure. Olivieri does not mention, and may not be aware of, any connection between this Calvo nor any other with Barbaro, although that connection is the main basis for including Calvo among our humanists. He does, however, note that while holding the office of count of Sebenico, Antonio di Ludovico read deeply in that locale's history; the anecdote suggests a learned man who could be identified, if the chronology were more favorable, with Barbaro's correspondent. I have repeated Olivieri's data about principal offices in the career summary, supplementing that record from archival documents. An asterisk indicates that the datum given is merely probable; otherwise, the identification is certain.

MONOGRAPH AND STUDIES. A. Olivieri in DBI, XVI (1973), 476-77.

CAREER. B. c. 1439. The birthdate from AC-BO 163/II, c. 149; presented 14 June 1457. Here I depart from Olivieri (DBI, XVI, 476), who follows Priuli in saying Calvo was born c. 1450. Olivieri himself finds Calvo in minor political offices in the 1460s, an impossibility for an adolescent, and as *savio agli ordini* in 1471, unlikely for a young man scarcely past twenty. D. 1505, from Olivieri. Calvo had held a series of minor political offices beginning as early as 1466, when he was elected to (and subsequently refused) the office of the *advocator per omnes curias* (SGV 6, c. 25).

Offices. 1473, Duc. el., Niccolò Marcello (MC-Regina, c. 122ᵛ); 1474, Duc. el., Pietro Mocenigo (MC-Regina, c. 143); 1486-89, Count of Sebenico; 1495-96, Capt. of Bergamo; 1497, CX (CXM 27; SGV 9 già 13, c. 10ᵛ); *1498, Sav. tf. (CXM 27, c. 179ᵛ; SM 14); 1498-99, Avog. (CXM 27, 28; SGV 6, c. 132 and 7 già 12, c. 2ᵛ); *1499-1500, CX (CXM 28, c. 32 and passim); 1501, Duc. el., Leonardo Loredan (MC-Stella, cc. 187, 188); *1502, CX (CXM 29); 1503, Cons. (CXM 29; MC-Deda; SGV 7 già 12, c. 1ᵛ; ST 14); 1503-5, Lt. di Friuli; died in that office.

CORRESPONDENCE. Letters from Ermolao Barbaro G (*Epist.*, I, 62-64, 74-75; II, 17, 64, 66-67, 69-70, 71-72, 81-82) and Giorgio Merula (on the recent death of Barbaro; in A. Zeno, *Diss. voss.*, II, 394-95).

DISCOURSE. Regio addressed to Calvo a letter at the end of his *Ducenta problemata* in Quintilian's *De oratore* (fols. 35ᵛ-36), noting Calvo's approving comments on his public disputation on the subject. Calvo was one of several patricians who witnessed a demonstration by Alessandro Benedetti of anatomical dissection at the University of Padua (R. Massalongo, "Alessandro

Benedetti e la medicina veneta del Quattrocento," p. 248). He collected ancient manuscripts (Cosenza, *Dict.*, I, 797).

Canal, Niccolò. (2) da Canale, Canalis. Son of Vito (Guido). Doctor.

MONOGRAPHS AND STUDIES. A. Ventura in DBI, XVII (1974), 662-68.

CAREER. B. 1415, M. 1438, Orsa di Giorgio Soranzo. D. 12 May 1483.

Offices. 1442, Amb. to Ferrara (ST 1, c. 51ᵛ); 1442-43, Amb. to Francesco Sforza (SM 1, cc. 136, 142ᵛ); 1444, Amb. in Florence and Perugia; 1444-45, Sav. tf. (SM 2; ST 1, c. 140ᵛ and passim); 1445, Amb. to Portugal; 1446, Sav. tf. (SM 2; ST 1, c. 177 and passim); CX (CXM 13); 1447, Sav. tf. (SM 3; ST 2, c. 26 and passim); 1448, Amb. to Florence (MC-Ursa, cc. 164, 165; ST 2, cc. 69, 85ᵛ, 88); CX (MC-Ursa, c. 165; SGV 4, c. 136ᵛ); Sav. tf. (SGV 4, c. 159; SM 3; ST 2); 1449, Sav. tf., two terms (SGV 4, c. 159; SM 3; ST 2, cc. 98ᵛ, 112ᵛ and passim); CX (CXM 13; SGV 4, c. 136ᵛ; held part of the time concurrently with the preceding office); Amb. to Florence; 1449-50, Amb. to Rome (MC-Ursa, c. 171ᵛ; ST 2, cc. 121, 123, 128ᵛ, 131, 140); 1450, Sav. tf. (SGV 4, c. 159ᵛ; SM 3; ST 2); Amb. to Constantinople; Amb. to Morea (CLN 8, c. 130); 1451, Sav. tf. (SGV 4, c. 160; ST 2, c. 180ᵛ); Prov. in campo, after having brought *bastone* of command to condottiere Gentile da Leonessa; 1451-53, Capt. of Brescia; 1453-54, Sav. tf. (SGV 4, c. 148; SM 5; ST 3, passim and c. 106ᵛ); 1454, CX (CXM 14; SGV 4, c. 148; for part of the term, held concurrently with the preceding office); Amb. to the Diet of Ratisbon and Emperor Frederick III; Amb. to Milan; 1455-57, Capt. of Bergamo (CLN 9, c. 49; CXM 15, cc. 39ᵛ, 136ᵛ; SGV 4, c. 98ᵛ; *Comm.*, ed. Predelli, XI [= VI], 293 [xxiii, #62]; Ventura gives 1457 as terminal date); 1458, Capt. of Brescia (CLN 9, c. 126ᵛ; CXM 15, cc. 153ᵛ, 156ᵛ); 1460, Sav. tf.; Amb. to Turks at Constantinople (elected; mission perhaps not executed); 1461, Sav. tf.; 1462, Duc. el., Cristoforo Moro; Sav. tf.; Amb. to Duke of Milan; 1463, Prov. in Morea (CLN 10, c. 87); 1463-64, Amb. to France; 1464, Sav. tf. (ST 5, c. 84); 1465, CX (CXM 16); Amb. to Rome (CXM 16, cc. 168, 171, 177, 177ᵛ; MC-Regina, c. 59; SM 8, c. 44ᵛ; ST 5, cc. 110, 112, 115, 122, 139); 1466, Sav. gr. (SM 8; ST 5); 1466, Avog. (CXM 16, 17; SGV 6, c. 7); 1467-68, Prov. in Negropont; 1468, Amb. to Bartolomeo Colleoni, Venetian Capt. Gen. against the Turks in Albania; Sav. gr. (SM 8; ST 6); Cons. (MC-Regina; SGV 6, c. 1; SM 8; ST 6, c. 33 and passim); honorary Amb. to Emperor *en route* to Rome; 1469-70, Admiral of the Aegean fleet; 1470, *Recalled, tried and condemned for failure to save Negropont; confined to Portogruaro, where he died* (see also Agostini, *Notizie*, II, 161-62, Romanin, *Stor. doc.*, IV, 337ff., and the letters of Francesco Filelfo to Ludovico Foscarini bemoaning the verdict: Filelfo's *Epist. fam.*, fols. 231ʳ⁻ᵛ, 250).

WORKS. *Epistola ad cardinales* (9 June 1470).

CORRESPONDENCE. Letters exchanged with Francesco Barbaro (see *Cento-trenta*, ed. Sabbadini, pp. 52, 53, 56, 57, 59), and from Francesco Filelfo

(*Epist. fam.*, fols. 97, 108ᵛ, 109ᵛ, 198ᵛ, 199, 200ᵛ, 203ᵛ-204, 204ʳ⁻ᵛ, 204ᵛ-205, 220) and Ludovico Foscarini (*Epist.*, fols. 137ᵛ-139; 173-74; 200-201; 233ʳ⁻ᵛ; 236ᵛ-237ᵛ). In his letter consoling Canal, whose sister had died, Foscarini refers to Canal's learning and wisdom: "Non discedas a tuae vitae institutionibus, non divertas a dignitate doctrinae, non recedas a splendore sapientiae; constantis robustaeque mentis tuae est necessitati parere" (fol. 233).

DISCOURSE. Praised by Flavio Biondo (*It. illus.* [1510 ed.], fol. 101ᵛ; see also Foscarini's comment given above). Giovanni Jacopo Cane addressed a poem *Clarissimo iurisconsulto D. Nicolao Canali universae classis in Turchos imperatori designato* (see A. della Torre, *Paolo Marsi*, p. 172). Patron of Francesco Filelfo and Paolo Marsi. Canal asked Filelfo to transcribe and dedicate to him a copy of that humanist's translation of Xenophon's *Cyropaedeia* so that he might take it on his fateful mission to the East (ibid., p. 173; for an extant version of this work with the ded. to Canal, cf., *Iter*, II, 388). On that same journey, he also took with him the poet Marsi, who wrote an elegiac poem describing the course of battle to Canal's son Giovanni (d. Torre, *Paolo Marsi*, p. 176; the elegy pub. ibid., pp. 287-95). D. Torre comments: "E quale cosa di più corrispondente al suo secolo che questo generale, il quale, partendo per una difficile impresa, voleva con se un libro di filosofia e un poeta umanista?" (p. 174). Canal also took with him to France in 1463 the physician Pietro Roccabonella; cf. P. Verrua, "Cinque orazioni dette dall'umanista Francesco Negri nello studio di Padova," p. 229.

EDUCATION. Doctorate in arts, Padua, 11 Jan. 1434; later a student of law; doctorate in laws on 11 March 1439. Canal taught law in the ensuing months, appearing among the *promotores* in acts through August of that year.

Capella, Febo. (2) Cappella.

MONOGRAPHS AND STUDIES. S. Prete in DBI, XVIII (1975), 470-71.

CAREER. B. c. 1420 (based on career record). D. soon before 12 May 1482 (documents alluding to Capella's recent demise and calling for the election of a new grand chancellor: MC-Stella, c. 23, 12 May 1482; CXM 20, c. 142ᵛ, 5 July 1482). Born to an established Venetian family (subsequently listed among the *cittadini originari*, cf. da Mosto, *Archivio*, I, 74), Capella served as a Venetian secretary from at least 1442, when he appeared as ducal notary and chancellor in Cattaro in Dalmatia (see F. Babinger, *Johannes Darius*, p. 26); in 1443-44, he was secretary to Francesco Barbaro on his legation to Milan (Prete, DBI, XVIII, 470, and S. Connell, "Books and Their Owners in Venice," p. 172). Capella was subsequently assigned to the *savi di terraferma* (Babinger, *Johannes Darius*, p. 26) and the Council of Ten (among other instances, CXM, 16, c. 126; 17, cc. 151ᵛ, 177; 18, cc. 38, 71, 76; 19, c. 180), and performed several missions abroad (Prete, DBI, XVIII, 470): to King René d'Anjou in 1455, to the Emperor Frederick III in 1459, to Florence in 1460. He appears with the title of ducal secretary in official acts from the 1450s through 1480 (*Comm.*, ed. Predelli, X, indices), and was elected grand chancellor in 1480 (28 May; MC-Stella, cc. 2^v, 23). His affluence is suggested by his 1,000-ducat loan—no small sum—for the dowry of his daughter (Cicogna, *Iscrizioni*, IV, 605).

CORRESPONDENCE. Letters from Francesco Barbaro (see *Centotrenta*, ed. Sabbadini, pp. 42, 48, 57, 60), Marsilio Ficino (*Epist.*, pp. 717-20 [the same as the *Quid sit lumen*, referred to below], 806, 854 [two]), and Francesco Filelfo (*Epist. fam.*, fols. 43, 107^v-108, 198^v, 225, 237^v). Cosenza (*Dict.*, I, 837) also cites a letter from Antonius Rubeus.

DISCOURSE. A member of the circle of learned commoners of his generation, including Marco Aurelio, Pietro Perleone, and Niccolò Sagundino (see Perleone's *Epist. cons. ad Nicolaum Sagundinum*, pp. 47-48, and Sagundino's letter to Marco Aurelio in the former's *Epist. et opusc.*, fol. 80^v). Several learned men dedicated works to Capella: Marsilio Ficino his philosophical letter *Quid sit lumen in corpore mundi, in angelo, in Deo* (*Epist.*, pp. 717-20; see above); Niccolò Leonico Tomeo his dialogue *Phoebus, sive de aetatum moribus* (*Dialogi*, fols. 68ff.); Sagundino his *De deo, de unitate essentiae eius, et de trinitate personarum* (*Epist. et opusc.*, fols. 121-130^v, with letter of dedication, fol. 132^{r-v}); Marino Becichemo, chapter 68 of his *Epistolicarum quaestionum centuria* (Cosenza, Dict., I, 837). In 1443, then in Milan as secretary to Francesco Barbaro, Capella was requested by Guglielmo Quirini to purchase on his behalf several classical works in good manuscript versions (G. dalla Santa, "Di un patrizio mercante veneziano," p. 75). Capella requested from Ficino in 1477 a copy of the latter's Latin translation of Plato, and Ficino sent him, in February 1482, his *De stella magorum* (Kristeller, "Marsilio Ficino e Venezia," p. 482 and n. 40). Verse to Capella by Naldo Naldi and others: see Prete, DBI, XVIII, 471.

Cirneo, Pietro. (3) Cirneus, Cyrneus. Son of Picino Felce (Filice).

MONOGRAPHS AND STUDIES. G. dalla Santa, "Un testamento ed alcune note biografiche di Pietro Cirneo, prete, storico, umanista." A DBI article should appear soon. E. Cochrane's comments (*Historians and Historiography in the Italian Renaissance*, pp. 82-83) should be read in the light of evidence presented here.

CAREER. B. Corsica, 9 Nov. 1447. Testament, 17 April 1493. D. after 31 March 1509. Already a priest, Cirneo came to Venice after 1475, and undertook a long course of study with Benedetto Brognoli from 1480. During those years, he tutored the children of Andrea Capello (until at least 1493, when Andrea died); Capello also arranged, so that Cirneo could supplement his meager salary, for a position in the local church of S. Maria Mater Domini. Made a citizen *de intus* by Senate privilege on 6 Oct. 1489, Cirneo journeyed in 1493 to his homeland Corsica, whose history he was writing, returning after a few months, and then left the city again briefly to escort home from Rome the orphaned child of his patron who had been serving as Venetian ambassador to the pope. On 31 March 1509, Cirneo was granted permission by the Council of Ten to print his history of Corsica following its screening by Bernardo Bembo. For Bembo's role, see also V. Cian, "Per Bernardo Bembo-II," p. 63. But the history, in spite of this privilege notable as an early instance of official censorship, was not printed at this time.

WORKS. *Commentarius de bello Ferrariensi ab anno MCCCCLXXXII usque ad annum MCCCCLXXXIV; De rebus Corsicis libris quattuor a temporibus romanorum usque ad annum MDVI.*

DISCOURSE. Despite his slim resources, Cirneo acquired a rich library of ancient classical and some contemporary humanist works, subsequently dispersed. By his 1493 will, made obsolete by Brognoli's death in 1502 and perhaps revised in later years in a version not now known, Cirneo left his books to Brognoli, and requested the latter to correct for publication his history of Corsica.

EDUCATION. With Brognoli.

Contarini, Francesco. (2) Contareno, Contarenus. Son of Niccolò (who had studied philosophy in Padua and was reputed as learned). Doctor.

MONOGRAPHS AND STUDIES. A. Segarizzi, "Francesco Contarini, politico e letterato veneziano del secolo XV"; A. Zeno, *Diss. voss.*, I, 189-96.

CAREER. B. c. 1424. M. 1447, Contarina di Giovanni Contarini. D. c. 1460. Segarizzi, ("Francesco Contarini," pp. 273-74) offers three possible birthdates: 1421, 1423, and 1424. I offer the latter date, which is not contradicted by the evidence of Contarini's presentation to the Avogaria di comun on 1 Dec. 1441. Segarizzi places the date of death after 1460 but before 1475 (p. 277), offering no evidence for either date. I follow A. Pertusi, "Gli inizi della storiografia umanistica," p. 304 in giving the date of death as c. 1460: Contarini's active political, academic, and literary careers, which left many traces before then, all cease by that date. The reconstruction of Contarini's life has been bedevilled by homonyms. For a contemporary homonym (di Bertuccio) at the University of Padua, see Segarizzi, "Francesco Contarini," pp. 286-87. Archival documents list sons of Pietro, of Giovanni, of Marino, and of Angelo for the same and adjacent periods (SGV 4, passim; ST 3 and 4, passim).

Offices. 1451, Amb. to Bologna; 1454-55, Amb. to Siena; commander of Venetian expedition; 1458, Amb. in obedientia to Pope Pius II.

WORKS. *Dialogus; Epithalamion in nuptiis Ludovici Draconis veneti* (4 Jan. 1440); invectives *in ignavum poetam [Danielem de Porcilis]* (1450) and *in Marinum Baduarium* (1450); *Oratio in conventu Iordani de Ursinis* and *Oratio habita in suo conventu (in law)* (1453); *Proemium in disputatione de philosophia* (1438; an oration to Demetrius, brother of the Byzantine Emperor John Paleologus); *De rebus in Hetruria a Senensibus gestis.* Not seen by me: an oration on a philosophical subject (1439) and *Novella di Tedaldino e Monna Rosa* (see Segarizzi, "Francesco Contarini," pp. 278 n. 4 and 284ff.);

carmina (Marc. Lat. XII, 113 [4444]). Contarini also left vernacular *Dispacci* from his Siennese mission. For additional printed and ms. versions of the *De rebus*, see Segarizzi, "Francesco Contarini," p. 280; the critical edition he describes has not since appeared. One of the mss. on which it was to be based is cod. Vat. Lat. 3365, an autograph of Bernardo Bembo completed in 1460, containing Contarini's dedicatory letter to Bembo; cf. *Iter*, II, 318; P. de Nolhac, *Bibliothèque de Fulvio Orsini*, pp. 240-41.

CORRESPONDENCE. Letter from Niccolò Sagundino (*Epist. et opusc.*, fols. 57ᵛ-58).

DISCOURSE. Praised for his character and learning on the occasion of receiving his doctorate in arts by Niccolò Barbo (*Oratio in laudem Francisci Contareni*) and an anonymous orator (*Oratio in laudem domini Francisci Contareni*), and on the occasion of the doctorate in law by Antonio Roselli (Segarizzi, "Francesco Contarini," p. 275); praised as both learned and powerful by Niccolò Sagundino in a letter to Domenico Morosini (Sagundino, *Epist. et opusc.*, fols. 58-59). With Niccolò Barbo, he joined Lauro Quirini in signing the letter the latter had written in defense of the Venetian nobility against Poggio Bracciolini (the *Epistola ad Petrum Thomasium*, 1446; see Kristeller's introduction to Quirini's *Tre trattati sulla nobiltà*, pp. 31-32).

EDUCATION. With Paolo della Pergola and George of Trebizond (F. Lepori, "Scuola di Rialto," p. 553; Segarizzi, "Francesco Contarini," p. 273; also Contarini's references to his teacher della Pergola in the *Proemium in disputatione de philosophia*, cited above). Present as a student in arts from at least 24 March 1436 at Padua (Zonta and Brotto, *Acta*, pp. 244, #1094; 330, ##1610, 1611; 344, #1692), attaining his license and doctorate in arts on 14 and 26 May, respectively, of 1442. A law student from at least 18 March 1443, he received his doctorate on 5 Sept. 1453 (Segarizzi, p. 275 and nn. 5, 7). Taught philosophy in 1458, substituting for Gaetano da Thiene (ibid.).

Contarini, Pietro. (3) Contarenus. Son of Adorno.

MONOGRAPHS AND STUDIES. None, but see the miniature profile in A. Medin, "Gli scritti umanistici di Marco Dandolo," p. 378-79 n. 1.

CAREER. B. c. 1446 (AC-BO 164/III, c. 64ᵛ; presented 27 Nov. 1464). M. 1483, daughter of Pietro Gradenigo. D. April 1495 (see the letter of Marco Dandolo to Filippo Buonaccorsi reporting the event, in Medin, "Gli scritti," pp. 377-79). The record of Contarini's political career is particularly hard to reconstruct because of the presence in the documents of a number of contemporaries who bore the same name, and the absence in many cases of a patronymic. Only positions known to have been held by the correct Pietro Contarini are listed below. During the years unaccounted for, Contarini may have pursued a commercial career, or held other minor political offices not known to me.

Offices. 1468, *Advoc. per omnes curias* (SGV 6, c. 25); 1487, one of five *sapientes in Rivoalto* (SGV 6, c. 119ᵛ); 1489-90, *Prov. of Coron*; 1494-95, *Gov. of Nisia*; died in office.

WORKS. *Ad Gelliam elegiarum libri tres; In funere Marci Cornelii oratio* (Venice, Church of Santi Apostoli, 27 Aug. 1479). Possibly also a Latin history, now lost; see Foscarini, *Lett. ven.*, p. 255; A. Pertusi, "Gli inizi della storiografia umanistica," p. 318. Both note Buonaccorsi's comment (*De his quae a Venetis tentata sunt* [1533 ed.], p. 85) that Contarini was a historian, "accuratus et prudens."

DISCOURSE. Paolo Ramusio praised him as a poet (in the codex containing Contarini's elegies, Marc. Lat. XII, 234 [4219], fol. 43), and Filippo Buonaccorsi as a historian (*De his*, p. 85). Contarini belonged to the circle of learned men known to Buonaccorsi during his 1486 stay in Venice, including Marco Dandolo whose letter to Buonaccorsi (see above) reported Contarini's death. Contarini's elegies were addressed mainly to a wide range of patricians, among them the learned Benedetto Sanuto and Marcantonio Morosini (fols. 13 and 40, respectively).

Contrario, Andrea. (2)

MONOGRAPHS AND STUDIES. G degli Agostini, *Notizie*, I, 420-32; R. Sabbadini, "Andrea Contrario."

CAREER. B. before 1410. D. 1473. Born in Venice of a Ferrarese family, Contrario was an intimate of the learned circle around Francesco Barbaro, and a friend of Filippo Morandi da Rimini, Niccolò Sagundino (perhaps his teacher), and Pietro Tommasi. (For the status of Contrario's family, see Agostini, *Notizie*, I, 420.) He is not closely related to the Uguccione de Contrariis ennobled in 1411. The Contrario name subsequently appears among the citizen families of Venice: da Mosto, *Archivio*, I, 74. Having previously entered the priesthood, Contrario left Venice in 1453 to establish himself in Rome, moved to Naples after the death of Pope Nicholas V, and returned to Rome in 1457. In 1459, he transferred to Bologna, in 1461 to Florence, in 1463 to Siena. He returned to Rome in 1464, where he enjoyed the favor of Pope Paul II until the latter's death in 1471. He then moved, as before, to Naples, where he received a stipend from Alfonso, duke of Calabria, and participated in the Accademia Pontaniana, dying soon afterwards. Although a priest (unsuccessful alike in obtaining and retaining benefices), Contrario was a professional humanist supported variously by the labors of teaching and writing and patronal support. Absent from Venice during the last decades of his life, he continued to have relations with several Venetians of our group.

WORKS. *Epistolae*, with orations and related documents published by Sabbadini in the work cited, are largely printed from the valuable Siena manuscript (Biblioteca Comunale degli Intronati, cod. H VI 32), which is cited additionally henceforth where Sabbadini's version is condensed or fragmentary. The addressees of the letters are given in part below; Agostini supplies an index of all the letters in the Siena codex (I, 429ff.). The Sabbadini collection also includes notably, among other materials, an *Exhortatio* to Cosimo de' Medici on behalf of the Olivetan monks (pp. 423-24; Siena, fols. 1-7); an invective against Lorenzo Valla in the form of a letter addressed to Niccolò Barbo and Ermolao Celso, elsewhere entitled "Mamurcha" (thus referred to by Agostini, *Notizie*, I, 429-30, whose identification of "Paleo" with "Barbo" is accepted by A. Segarizzi, "Niccolò Barbo," p. 42 n. 4; Sabbadini retains "Paleo" and argues [pp. 382-83] that the target of this invective is Valla) and rededicated to Niccolò Sagundino (pp. 402-409); orations to King Alfonso, against the Turks (pp. 398, 399; Siena, fols. 32ᵛ-33, 35-44), and to Pope Nicholas V (p. 393, Siena fols. 44ᵛ-46). Elsewhere is Contrario's important *Reprehensio sive objurgatio in calumniatorem divini Platonis*. Other works, not seen by me, include an *Oratio in laudem Bartholomaei Storladi* (known to Agostini: *Notizie*, I, 431), and a translation of Eusebius' *De praeparatione evangelica*, an emendation of George of Trebizond's (dedication published by Sabbadini, pp. 395-96).

CORRESPONDENCE. Contrario's *Epistolae* contain letters to, among others, Pietro Barbo, Domenico de' Domenichi, Teodoro Gaza, Isotta Nogarola, Niccolò Sagundino, Pope Nicholas V, Pope Pius II (several), and a collection of love letters from Maia Isotta, a nun. See Sabbadini's edition for references to other manuscript and printed versions of the letters he publishes. Elsewhere are found letters to George of Trebizond (in J. Monfasani, ed., *Collectanea Trapezuntiana*, pp. 108-13), Guarino Veronese (*Epist.*, ed. Sabbadini, II, 344) and from Filippo Morandi da Rimini, with verse (see Bibliography).

DISCOURSE. Highly regarded by contemporaries for his learning, Contrario was praised by Lorenzo Valla (see his verse published by Sabbadini, "Andrea Contrario," pp. 391-92) and Giovanni Pontano (ibid., p. 387), and patronized by Francesco Barbaro, King Alfonso of Aragon, and Pope Paul II. He was active in learned circles in Venice, Rome, and Naples. Testimony of his activity in the first of these cities is his appearance as an interlocutor in Filippo Morandi's *Symposium de paupertate*; of that in Rome are his quarrels with Valla (for which see the invective cited above) and George of Trebizond (see J. Monfasani, *George of Trebizond*, especially pp. 127-55, 228-29); of that in Naples, his introduction as an interlocutor in the dialogue *Antonius* by Giovanni Pontano (in *I dialoghi*, pp. 57ff.). For Contrario's existence in Naples and relations there with the Barbaro family, see also V. Branca, "Un codice aragonese scritto dal Cinico."

EDUCATION. Possibly with Niccolò Sagundino (Sabbadini, "Andrea Contrario," p. 380; A. Pertusi, "Umanesimo greco," p. 212 n. 132, thinks it unlikely).

Corner, Federico. (2) Cornaro, Cornelius. Son of Giovanni.

CAREER. B. c. 1401 (AC-BO 162/I, c. 36; presented 29 Nov. 1419). M. 1439 (see Filelfo's congratulatory letter, *Epist. fam.*, fols. 18ᵛ-19ᵛ). D. c. 1455.

Elected to the Consiglio di XL in 1455, a notation next to the name indicates that Corner left that office to become Consigliere; but I find no record of him in that position, normally well documented in contemporaneous sources. I assume he died in that year or soon after. The more famous homonymn Federico di Francesco had a major political career from the 1460s to the early sixteenth century. This figure also had intellectual interests; it is probably he who encouraged Pietro Dolfin (the chronicler) to transcribe Appian's history in 1469 (see *Iter*, I, 415), and to whom is addressed a letter in the Sanuto miscellany Marc. cod. Lat. XIV, 267 (4344), fol. 76. Since the career information given is drawn entirely from SGV, it is not certain that Corner indeed held the offices indicated. In any case, his political role was minor.

Offices. 1447, *Consiglio di XL* (SGV 4, c. 131); 1450, *Consiglio di XL* (c. 141); 1452, *Consiglio di XL* (c. 145); 1455, *Consiglio di XL* (c. 156).

CORRESPONDENCE. Letters to (Vat. Pal. Lat. 492, fols. 188^v-93; cf. A. Oberdorfer, "Epistolario di Leonardo Giustiniani," p. 15) and from (in G. B. Contarini, *Anec. ven.*, pp. 77-78) Leonardo Giustiniani. From Gasparino Barzizza (in L. Bertalot, "Die älteste Briefsammlung des Gasparinus Barzizza," p. 77, and Barzizza's *Opera*, ed. J. A. Furiettus, pp. 153-54), Francesco Filelfo (*Epist. fam.*, fols. 3, 18^v-19^v), and Ambrogio Traversari (*Epist.*, ed. Mehus, II, 326-28).

DISCOURSE. Praised for his learning by Antonio Baratella (*Policleomenareis*, fol. 14^v), and called by Traversari in a letter to Francesco Barbaro a "most famous youth" (Traversari in his *Epist.*, ed. E. Martène and U. Durand, III, 560).

EDUCATION. With Facino Ventraria (c. 1408/11-1416), Guarino Veronese (1414), and (advanced studies) Giovanni Romano in Padua (see C. Colombo, "Gasparino Barzizza a Padova," pp. 1ff., 17-18, 23-24, 26).

Corner, Giovanni. (1) Cornaro, Cornelius. Son of Federico (Ferrante); father of Federico.

CAREER. B. c. 1370 (hypothesized from career record). M. 1395, Francesca di Filippo Corner (Giomo, *Matrimoni*, I, 311). D. after 10 Sept. 1452 (date of election to the Senate). The reconstruction of Corner's career has been bedeviled by homonyms. During the relevant period, SGV 4 and 5 list Giovanni di Andrea, di Giovanni, di Ludovico, di Marco, and di Niccolò, as well as figures holding that name not identified by patronymics. Cappellari (*Camp. ven.*, I, 323^v) further lists for the early fifteenth century Giovanni di Francesco. Our Giovanni was both the son and father of Federico; see C. Colombo, "Gasparino Barzizza a Padova," and AC-BO 162/I, c. 36 (presentation on 29 Nov. 1419 by Giovanni Corner di Federigo of his son Federigo). Corner's father, Federico of San Luca, had been the richest nobleman listed in Venice's 1379 census, his wealth derived from commercial enterprises pursued with his brother Fantino (G. Luzzatto, "Les noblesses," p. 33); the family possessed a fief in Crete. Corner pursued a commercial career in his youth, traveling largely in the eastern Mediterranean. For his involvement with the family's Cretan interests, see *Comm.*, ed. Predelli, VII [= III], 12, #51; 210-11, #36; 248, #71. Corner's experience in the East would have enabled him to collect his rich library. Since the information about Corner's political career is entirely from SGV, it is not certain that he indeed occupied the offices indicated. His political role, in any case, was minor.

Offices. 1433, Amb. (one of twelve) to the Council of Basel (A. Gatari, *Diario del Concilio di Basilea*, pp. 379 and 431 n. 6); 1438, *Zonta to Sen.* (SGV 4, c. 97); 1440, *Zonta to Sen.* (c. 103); 1443, *Zonta to Sen.* (c. 122); 1444, *Sen.* (c. 124); 1445, *Zonta to Sen.* (c. 115ᵛ); 1446, *Zonta to Sen.* (c. 130); 1447, *Zonta to Sen.* (c. 132ᵛ); 1449, *Zonta to Sen.* (c. 137ᵛ); 1450, *Zonta to Sen.* (c. 140ᵛ); 1452, *Sen.* (c. 146).

CORRESPONDENCE. Letters from Gasparino Barzizza (*Opera*, ed. J. A. Furiettus, pp. 209-10; L. Bertalot, "Die älteste Briefsammlung des Gasparinus Barzizza," pp. 94-95; Colombo, "Gasparino Barzizza," pp. 17-18, 22-24, 25-26), Francesco Filelfo (*Epist. Fam.*, fols. 21ᵛ, 29ᵛ).

DISCOURSE. Praised for his learning by Flavio Biondo (*It. illus.* [1510 ed.], fol. 101ᵛ) and Ciriaco d'Ancona (*Itinerarium*, ed. L. Mehus, p. 18). Ciriaco dedicated to Corner his translation of Gregory Nazianzen's *De septem spectaculis mundi* (*Iter*, I, 115, and II, 308, 438; CTC, II, 61ff., III, 414), while Pietro Perleone dedicated to him a translation from Plutarch (see Filelfo's *Epist. fam.*, fols. 13ᵛ-14). Corner was a patron of Filelfo (see the latter's letter to Federico Corner in *Epist. fam.*, fol. 3), recommended Perleone as a tutor to the sons of the patrician Fantino Michiel (P. H. Labalme, *Bernardo Giustiniani*, pp. 66, 67), and hosted the Sicilian humanist Antonio Cassarino, stopping in Venice on his return from Greece in 1438 (see Cassarino's letter to Isotta Nogarola in her *Opera omnia*, ed. E. Abel, I, 143). On Barzizza's advice, Corner hired Facino Ventraria as tutor to his son Federico (Colombo, "Gasparino Barzizza," pp. 1ff., and Barzizza's letters cited above). With Fantino Dandolo, he showed Ambrogio Traversari the sites and holy places of Venice in 1433 (*Hodoeporicon*, ed. L. Mehus, p. 64; R. Sabbadini, *Le scoperte dei codici latini e greci*, I, 95). On that occasion, Traversari saw Corner's splendid palace and precious library, its Greek manuscripts remarkable particularly for their physical beauty. Corner's copy of Cicero's *De oratore*, emended and ordered by Barzizza, passed into the family collection and is now in Milan's Bibl. Ambrosiana (ibid., p. 81, and "Codici latini posseduti, scoperti, illustrati da Guarino Veronese," pp. 397-98). The Venetian lent Barzizza his copy of Pliny's *Natural History* and other books, and helped him obtain a valuable manuscript of Livy (Colombo, "Gasparino Barzizza," pp. 4ff., 7ff.).

Correr, Gregorio. (2) Corraro, Corrarius. Son of Giovanni; uncle of Pietro and Paolo Barbo; nephew of Cardinal Antonio Correr and of Giovanni Barozzi, Patriarch; related to other members of the Barbo clan (for which see profile of Pietro Barbo).

PROFILES

MONOGRAPHS AND STUDIES. L. Casarsa, "Contributi per la biografia di Gregorio Correr," an exhaustive study providing guidance to other bibliographical resources (see especially p. 29 n. 2). Among these, see especially G. degli Agostini, *Notizie*, I, 108-34; J. R. Berrigan, "The *Libellus Fabellarum* of Gregorio Correr"; W. Cloetta, *Beiträge zur Literaturgeschichte des Mittelalters und der Renaissance*, I: *Die Anfänge der Renaissancetragödie*, "Gregorio Correr."

CAREER. B. 14 Sept. 1409. Testament 29 Nov. 1464 (Casarsa, "Contributi," p. 55 n. 80). D. 30 Nov. 1464. After studies with Vittorino da Feltre, Correr moved in the entourage of his uncle, Cardinal Antonio Correr, who was closely attached to the papal curia. He held the title of apostolic protonotary from 1433, and in 1433-34 attended the Council of Basel, where he delivered the oration hostile to papal authority to Emperor Sigismund (cited below) which may in part explain the failure of his later ecclesiastical career (for this speculation, see G. B. Picotti, *Dieta di Mantova*, p. 122). After the cardinal's death in 1445, Correr competed unsuccessfully for several major ecclesiastical posts.

Titles. 1443— Abbot of the monastery of San Zeno, Verona (in residence from 1448); 1464— elected Pat. of Venice; died before assuming office.

WORKS. *Epistola ad Ceciliam virginem de fugiendo saeculo; Epistola ad novitium Cartusianum de commodis vitae regularis; Hymnus ad pueros et virgines*, to Pope Martin V; *Liber satyrarum; Oratio ad Sigismundum Romanorum imperatorem* (Basel, 1433); the tragedy *Progne*, not seen; *Quomodo educari debeant pueri*, to his brother Andrea; *Soliloquium ad Deum de vita sua et de vita et obitu beatae memoriae Antonii episcopi Ostiensis et cardinalis patrui sui* (I have seen the edition cited in the Bibliography; the recent edition in G. Musolino, A. Niero, and S. Tramontin, eds., *Santi e beati veneti: quaranta profili* [Venice, 1963], pp. 329-41, I have not found). Also *Carmina et epigrammata*. Casarsa discusses these works extensively and provides in her notes listings of alternate manuscript and printed versions. She is preparing a critical edition of the *Progne*. For that tragedy, see pp. 35ff. and n. 16; also Cloetta, *Beiträge*, and Berrigan, "Latin Tragedy of the Quattrocento," pp. 2-7; Casarsa's study "La Progne di Gregorio Correr," in the *Atti* of the conference *La Rinascita della tragedia nell'Italia dell'Umanesimo, Viterbo, 15-17 June 1979* (1980), pp. 119-34, I have not been able to see. For other works, not seen by me, see Casarsa, "Contributi," pp. 35 n. 15; 40 n. 32; 41, nn. 33, 35; 45 n. 44. Some youthful works were burned; ibid., pp. 40ff. n. 32.

CORRESPONDENCE. Letters to Giovanni Tortelli (15, in Casarsa, "Contributi," pp. 58-63, 64-85; cf. pp. 45, 52ff. and n. 63), Pope Nicholas V (ibid., pp. 63-64), and Vittorino da Feltre (ibid., p. 46 n. 47). Letters from Girolamo Aliotti (see ibid., p. 48 and nn. 52, 53; 52 n. 62), Poggio Bracciolini (regarding Correr's protest against the former's work on nobility, see ibid., p. 47 n. 50, and LQU, p. 38), and Lapo da Castiglionchio (see Casarsa, "Contributi," p. 46 and n. 46). There are also volgare letters to Ludovico Gonzaga published by Casarsa at pp. 86-88.

DISCOURSE. Praised for his learning by Flavio Biondo (*It. illus.* [Venice, 1510], fol. 101ᵛ) and Vespasiano da Bisticci (*Vite di uomini illustri*, pp. 149ff.). Lapo da Castiglionchio dedicated to him two translations from Lucian (see Casarsa, "Contributi," p. 46 n. 46). He participated in humanist circles around the papal curia in Rome and Florence.

EDUCATION. Correr studied with Vittorino da Feltre at the latter's famous school in Mantua, as well as earlier, perhaps, in Venice.

Dandolo, Fantino. (1) Dandulo, Dandulus. Son of Leonardo. Leonardo, son of the learned fourteenth-century doge Andrea, was himself learned and now identified as one of the opponents of Petrarch remembered but unnamed in the *De sui ipsius et multorum aliorum ignorantia*. Miles, doctor.

MONOGRAPHS AND STUDIES. G. degli Agostini, *Notizie*, I, 1-44. I have been unable to see D. Cortese, "Francesco della Rovere e le orationes sull'Immacolata del vescovo di Padova Fantino Dandolo," *Il Santo*, 12 (1977), 197-225.

CAREER. B. 1379. D. 17 Feb. 1459. Until 1431, Dandolo pursued a political career; thereafter an ecclesiastical one.

Offices. 1405, Amb. to accompany Cardinal Filargo to Lombardy for peace negotiations with Milan; 1407, Prov. in the Veronese; 1408, Cons.; 1409, Amb. to Milan; 1410, Cons. (CLN 4; CXM 9; MC-Leona; SMS 48); 1410-11, CX (CXM 9); 1411, Amb. to the dukes of Austria in Trent; 1412, *Savio di guerra* (SMS 49); 1412-13, Pod. of Padua (CLN 5, c. 9; SMS 49, cc. 132, 145); 1414, Pod. of Verona; 1415-16, CX (CXM 9); 1416, Amb. to Lombardy for peace negotiations; 1417-18, CX (CXM 9); 1418, Cons.; Pod. of Padua; 1420, *Savio di guerra* (later tf.) (SMS 53, c. 32; Senato-Secrete 7, c. 145); Sav. gr. (SMS 53, c. 80 and passim); 1420-21, CX (CXM 10); 1421, Amb. to Rome (Senato-Secrete 7, c. 203; 8, cc. 5ᵛ-6 and passim); 1421-23, Avog. (CLN 5, c. 183ᵛ; CXM 10; SMS 54); 1423, Duc. el., Francesco Foscari (MC-Ursa, cc. 49ᵛ, 50); 1423-24, Cons. (CLN 5; CXM 10; MC-Ursa; SMS 54); 1424-25, Amb. to King Alfonso of Aragon; 1425, Sav. gr. (SMS 55); 1425-26, Amb. to Rome; 1426, Avog.; Sav. gr.; Cons. (CLN 6; CXM 10); *Plenipotentiary (in Venice) for signing of alliance with Savoy and Florence* (Romanin, *Stor. doc.*, IV, 117; *Comm.*, ed. Predelli, VIII, 75-77 [xi, #232]); Amb. to the Marquis of Ferrara Niccolò d'Este; 1427-28, Prov. of Brescia (SMS 56, cc. 69ʳ⁻ᵛ, 110ʳ⁻ᵛ; 57, c. 15ᵛ; *Comm.*, X, 21-22 [xiv, #471]); 1428, Sav. gr. (SMS 57, c. 45ᵛ); Amb. for peace negotiation in Milan; 1429, Amb. to Florence; Amb. to Emperor (SMS 57, c. 96); Cons.; Sav. gr. (SMS 57, c. 160ᵛ); 1430, Sav. gr. (SMS 57, c. 206; *Comm.*, VIII, 160 [xii, #132]); 1430-31, Avog. (CXM 11); 1431, Amb. in obedientia to Pope Eugene IV.

Dandolo remained in Rome. By September of 1431 he had been made apostolic protonotary and papal governor of Bologna. In that month, Leonardo Giustiniani commented on Dandolo's new appointments in a letter to Ambrogio Traversari (A. Oberdorfer, "Epistolario di Leonardo Giustiniano," p. 11). Dandolo's ecclesiastical career was exemplary: he was particularly active in monastic reform (Agostini, *Notizie*, I, 24ff.; L. Pesce, *Ludovico Barbo*, pp. 160, 181); he contributed generously of his own wealth for ecclesiastical construction (Agostini, *Notizie*, I, 26); he gave generously to the poor (ibid., I, 25, 33). From 1437, he held in *commenda* the abbey of S. Stefano di Carrara in Padua.

Titles. 1444-48, Archbishop of Candia [Crete] (Eubel, *Hier. cath.*, II, 139); 1448— Bishop of Padua (ibid., II, 210).

WORKS. *Compendium Catholicae fidei; Sermo de laudibus philosophiae*, not seen (see Cicogna, *Iscrizioni*, IV, 655); sermons, not seen (Padua, Bibl. Capitolare, cod. C. 46; see, *Iter*, II, 5; list of contents in Agostini, *Notizie*, I, 36-42, who also notes [I, 42] a codex of six letters, as does Mittarelli, *Bibl. codd. mss.*, col. 310). Kristeller further notes eighteenth-century mss. containing, respectively, *epistolae* by Dandolo, an *epistola* and sermons, and a collection of sermons (*Iter*, II, 206, none seen by me). Dandolo also authored a collection of *Constitutiones* of the Paduan church; see Agostini, *Notizie*, I, 42. The *Compendium Catholicae fidei* published under Dandolo's name is actually by Fantino Vallaresso. See V. Peri, "Tre lettere inedite a Fantino Vallaresso ed un suo catechismo attribuito a Fantino Dandolo," pp. 57ff. and 66. Sansovino (*Venetia*, II, 576) and his followers attribute to Dandolo two works, *De beneficiis* and *Opusculum de responsis*.

CORRESPONDENCE. Exchange with Francesco Barbaro (see *Centotrenta*, ed. Sabbadini, pp. 47, 48). Letters to Pietro Tommasi (in A. Segarizzi, "La corrispondenza famigliare di un medico erudito del Quattrocento," pp. 242-43) and from Antonio Baratella (in Segarizzi, *Antonio Baratella*, p. 98), Giovanni Conversino da Ravenna (see B. G. Kohl, "The Works of Giovanni di Conversino," p. 363), Sicco Polenton (in *La Catinia*, ed. Segarizzi, pp. 106-109, 114-16), Ambrogio Traversari (*Epist.*, ed. Mehus, II, 97-98, 98-99, and *Epist.*, ed. Martène and Durand, cols. 611-12), and Maffeo Vallaresso (*Epist.*, p. 87).

DISCOURSE. One of Venice's early enthusiasts of humanist studies, esteemed by contemporaries for his learning (see M. Foscarini, *Lett. ven.*, p. 56; also Candiano Bollani's inclusion of Dandolo among those who defended learning [*Trialogus*, fol. 7], and Flavio Biondo's tribute in his *It. illus.* [1510 ed.], fol. 101ᵛ). Pietro Marcello V addressed to Dandolo a consolatory letter on the death of his father, and Giovanni Conversino da Ravenna his *Conventio inter podagram et araneam* (see the introduction by B. G. Kohl to the former's *Dragmalogia de eligibili vite genere*, p. 29). With Giovanni Corner, Dandolo showed Ambrogio Traversari the sights and libraries of Venice in 1433 (see the latter's *Hodoeporicon*, ed. L. Mehus, p. 64). He collected a notable manuscript library (Foscarini, *Dei veneziani raccoglitori di codici*, p. 535). That Dandolo exchanged books with humanist friends is evident from his correspondence with Traversari, cited above. Jacopo Zeno acquired two books from Dandolo's collection, including a biblical concordance and Dandolo's own sermons (E. Govi, "La biblioteca di Jacopo Zeno," pp. 51, 89). Dandolo's executors attempted in 1459 to recover some books from the collection that had been dispersed (CLN 9, c. 151ᵛ, 27 Feb.), perhaps indicating the fate of the collection.

EDUCATION. Dandolo studied at the universities of Bologna and Padua, receiving a doctorate in law from Padua on 8 Aug. 1401; thereafter he taught civil law (briefly) and (after 1433) took up sacred studies (Agostini, *Notizie*, I, 1-3, 19; A. Gloria, *Monumenti della Università di Padova, 1318-1405*, I, 217).

Dandolo, Marco. (3) Dandulo, Dandulus. Son of Andrea; grandson of Bernardo Giustiniani (cf. Ermolao Barbaro G, *Epist.*, ed. Branca, II, 48-49). Doctor, miles.

MONOGRAPHS AND STUDIES. A. Medin. "Gli scritti umanistici di Marco Dandolo"; G. degli Agostini, *Notizie*, II, 281-93.

CAREER. B. 25 March 1458. M. 1485, Laura di Marco Corner, the sister of Caterina, Queen of Cyprus; 1491, Nicolosa di Pietro Loredan; 1521, a sister of Gasparo Contarini. D. 15 May 1535. Dandolo's first wife was the daughter of the wealthy patron. Agostini reports a 1485 marriage (*Notizie*, II, 281), but Medin ("Scritti umanistici," p. 349) saw a 1483 contract providing the large dowry of 4,500 ducats. For the second marriage, see also Giomo, *Matrimoni*, I, 606. For the third, see Sanuto, *Diarii*, XXX, 29 (16 March 1521): "Se partì questa matina ser Gasparo Contarini, va orator nostro al Serenissimo re di Romani, et la commission se li manderà drio; el qual ha indusiato fin hora per aver maridato una so' sorela, in questi zorni, in sier Marco Dandolo dotor et cavalier, con dota di ducati 8000 [enormous!] in tutto." The following archival documents were not seen in assembling Dandolo's record: CLN for 1511-35; CXM for 1513-24; SM for 1512-35. The omission is compensated for by Sanuto's *Diarii* for the period until late 1533.

Offices. 1492-93, Amb. to King Ladislaus VI of Bohemia and Hungary; 1496-97, Amb. to Duke Ludovico Sforza of Milan; 1498, Amb. to Pope Alexander VI; 1501, Sav. tf.; 1502-4, Amb. to King Louis XII of France (CXM 29, cc. 97, 164; ST 14, c. 194; 15, c. 1ᵛ; Sanuto, *Diarii*, IV, 269 etc. and V); 1504, Sav. tf. (ST 15); 1505, Sav. tf. (Sanuto, *Diarii*, VI, 117—election only); 1506, Sav. tf. (MC-Deda; ST 15; Sanuto, *Diarii*, VI, 360 etc.); Avog. (Sanuto, *Diarii*, VI, 412); 1506-7, Amb. to Naples (ST 15, c. 151; Sanuto, *Diarii*, VI, 441, and VII); 1507-8, Sav. tf., two terms (CXM 31; SM 16; ST 15; Sanuto, *Diarii*, VII, 134 etc., 241 etc.); 1508-9, Capt. of Brescia (SGV 8 già 7, c. 50ᵛ; Sanuto, *Diarii*, VII, 374 etc., and VIII); 1509-1513, *captured and brought to France, where imprisoned*; 1513-15, *released from prison, made Amb. to King Francis I of France*; 1515, *upon return from France, permitted as recompense for his hardships to keep the golden chain given him by King Francis I* (ST 19, c. 59; Sanuto, *Diarii*, XXI, 360); 1515-19, Capt. of Candia [Crete] (MC-Deda, cc. 110ʳ⁻ᵛ; SGV 8 già 7, c. 100ᵛ; Sanuto, *Diarii*, XXI, 362 [election], XXIII, 14 [departure, 1516], 559 [arrival, 1517], XXIV-XXVII); 1521, Duc. el., Antonio Grimani (MC-Deda, cc. 186ʳ⁻ᵛ; Sanuto, *Diarii*, XXX, 438); 1522-

23, Amb. in obedientia to Pope Adrian VI (Sanuto, *Diarii*, XXXIII, 420, 496-97, and XXXIV, 23 etc.); 1523, Duc. el., Andrea Gritti (MC-Diana, c. 25ᵛ; Sanuto, *Diarii*, XXXIV, 151); Sav. gr. (ST 23; Sanuto, *Diarii*, XXXIV, 303 etc., and XXXV); Amb. in obedientia to Pope Clement VII; mission not completed; 1524-25, Cons. (MC-Diana; SGV 7 già 12, c. 29ᵛ; ST 23; Sanuto, *Diarii*, XXXVI, 189 etc., and XXXVII); 1528, Sav. tf.; Sav. gr. (MC-Diana; ST 25; Sanuto, *Diarii*, XLVII, 160 etc., XLVIII, XLIX); 1529, Sav. gr. (ST 25; Sanuto, *Diarii*, L, 502, etc.-LII); 1530, Amb. (his plea to be excused denied) to the Pope and Emperor in Bologna (ST 25, cc. 204ᵛ, 205; Sanuto, *Diarii*, LII, 396 etc., LIII); 1530-31, Cons. (CXS 2; MC-Diana; SGV 10 già 14, c. 1ᵛ; ST 26; Sanuto, *Diarii*, LIII, 78, etc., LIV); 1531, Sav. gr. (ST 26; Sanuto, *Diarii*, LIV, 620, and LV); Amb. to the wedding of the Duke of Mantua (Sanuto, *Diarii*, LV, 234).

WORKS. *Catena seu expositio graecorum patrum in psalmos: in Psalterium expositionum collectio e graeco in latinum versa; Praeconium sanctissime crucis*, written in captivity in France, published thereafter by Lefèvre d'Etaples; 15 *epistolae*, and orations to Ferdinand of Aragon, K. of Naples, and Ladislaus, K. of Hungary.

CORRESPONDENCE. Letters to Filippo Buonaccorsi (Medin, "Scritti umanistici," pp. 377-79), Girolamo Donato (pp. 365-67, 381-82); Battista Guarini (pp. 364-65, 374-76); Bartolomeo Pagello (p. 384); Paolo Pisani (pp. 371-72, 382-83); among others and from Ermolao Barbaro (*Epist.*, ed. Branca, II, 14-15, 24-25, 48-49; also Medin, "Scritti umanistici," pp. 399-402); Pietro Bembo (*Lettere di M. Pietro Bembo*, II, 149-51 [in volgare], in *Opere del Cardinale Pietro Bembo*, VI), and Bartolomeo Pagello (*epistolae* in B. Marx, *Bartolomeo Pagello*, pp. 254-55).

DISCOURSE. Celebrated by Marino Becichemo (oration to Doge Andrea Gritti, in *Orationes duae*, fol. viiᵛ); Girolamo Bologni (Agostini, *Notizie*, II, 284), Buonaccorsi (*De his quae a Venetis tentata sunt* [1533 ed.], p. 85), Raffaele Regio (Agostini, *Notizie*, II, 282), Marcantonio Sabellico (*De reparatione latinae linguae*, fol. 109ᵛ). Pietro Niccolò dal Lino's dialogue *De generatione formarum naturalium* (2 March 1483) were dedicated to Dandolo (see *Iter*, II, 303), as were fifteen chapters of Becichemo's *Centuria epistolicarum quaestionum* (Chapters 17 to 29 of Becichemo's *Centuria*, published with his *Panegiricus*). Regio dedicated to Dandolo, along with Girolamo Donato and Paolo Pisani, his dialogue on four passages from Quintilian (Medin, "Scritti umanistici," p. 335). A patron of Marino Becichemo, whom Girolamo Donato on departing for Crete in 1506 commended to Dandolo: Agostini, *Notizie*, II, 292; A. Zeno, *Diss. voss.*, II, 414-15.

EDUCATION. With Battista Guarini (Medin, "Scritti umanistici," p. 338) and Giorgio Merula (Agostini, *Notizie*, II, 282). Studied arts (under Pietro Roccabonella) and law at Padua, where he attended from 1471 to at least 1489; the doctorate in philosophy granted 1481 (Agostini, *Notizie*, II, 282; P. Verrua, "Cinque orazioni dette dall'umanista Francesco Negri nello studio di Padova,"

p. 229, and "L'università di Padova circa il 1488 nell' 'Opusculum scribendi epistolas' di Francesco Negri," p. 188). The years of captivity were also devoted to study.

Diedo, Francesco. (3) Diedus. Son of Ludovico (Alvise). Doctor.

MONOGRAPHS AND STUDIES. G. Tournoy, "Francesco Diedo, Venetian Humanist and Politician of the Quattrocento," thoroughly studies the life and works. See also F. Fossati, "Sulla partenza degli oratori Leonardo Botta da Venezia e Francesco Diedo da Milano."

CAREER. B. c. 1433 (Tournoy's estimate; on 2 Dec. 1465 and 23 Nov. 1474 [BO 164/III, fols. 131, 131ᵛ], Diedo presented his younger brothers Domenico and Girolamo to the AC). M. 1465, Elena di Antonio Erizzo (Giomo, *Matrimoni*, I, 437). D. 25 March 1484.

Offices. 1464-65, Amb. to Austria; 1467-68, Amb. to Hungary; 1469-70, Amb. to Savoy; 1470, Capt. of Vicenza; 1472, CX (CXM 17); Sav. tf.; Amb. to Urbino; 1473-74, Pod. and Capt. of Ravenna; 1474, Sav. tf.; Duc. el., Pietro Mocenigo (MC-Regina, c. 143); 1474-75, CX (CXM 18); 1475, Capt. of Bergamo; 1477, Sav. tf.; 1478-79, Capt. of Brescia; 1479-80, Amb. to Milan; 1480, Sav. gr.; 1480-81, CX (CXM 20; MC-Stella, c. 12ᵛ); 1481, Sav. gr. (SM 11; ST 8); 1481-83, Amb. to Rome, stopping *en route* at Ferrara; 1483-84, Pod. of Verona; died in that office.

WORKS. *Defensio pro re publica Veneta*, to Pope Sixtus IV (1481); *In Franciscum Barocium invectiva* (1458); *[Oratio] in adventu Frederici [sic] Caesaris Tertii* (1468), not seen (Massachusetts Historical Society, cod. 22 [Z. IV. 14]); *Oratio de laudibus Bartholomaei Paierini* (other manuscript versions and selections, Tournoy, "Francesco Diedo," pp. 210-11 n. 6); *Proemium in quibusdam legibus a juristarum collegio conditum; Vita Sancti Rochi,* trans. from Greek, with prefatory letter to the city of Brescia (1478 or 1479; other manuscript and printed versions, ibid., p. 210 n. 2; prefatory letter, 225-27, and a letter praising the work by Pietro Ludovico Maldura, pp. 227-28); trans., Isocrates *De bello et pace* (1471), to Ludovico Foscarini (ibid., p. 214 n. 34; introductory letter, pp. 217-218); translated from Italian, Boccaccio's *Urbanitas* (a novella of Titus and Gisippus from the *Decameron*; ibid., p. 214 n. 31), to Marco Aurelio (1470). Also a volgare *Relazione* on the Bergamo rectorate.

CORRESPONDENCE. Exchange with Giovanni Antonio Panteo (in Tournoy, "Francesco Diedo," pp. 231-34; see also pp. 216-17 n. 83); letters to Ludovico Nogarola (see ibid., p. 217 n. 83) and from Girolamo Bologni (cf. *Iter*, I, 326), Ludovico Foscarini (*Epist.*, fol. 297ʳ⁻ᵛ), and Bartolomeo Pagello (in B. Marx, *Bartolomeo Pagello*, pp. 228-30).

DISCOURSE. Praised for his composition of the *Vita Sancti Rochi* by Pietro Ludovico Maldura (cited above). Leonello Chiericati included Diedo as an interlocutor in his *Dialogus in quo et consolatio magnifici Francisci Didii et consultatio de mittendis orationibus continetur* (see Tournoy, "Francesco Diedo," p. 210 n. 4; *Iter*, I, 14 and II, 85). Giovanni Jacopo Cane included him as an interlocutor in his dialogue *De Constantini donatione*, and dedicated to Diedo his dialogue *De arbitriis*. Giovanni Michele Alberto da Carrara dedicated to Diedo his *De pestilentia*, and poems (see Tournoy, "Francesco Diedo," p. 215 n. 50; the prefatory letter is published on pp. 218-19, and a few of the poems, pp. 219-25). Dante III Alighieri and Marco Publio Fontana addressed poems to Diedo (ibid., pp. 216 n. 82 and 215 n. 49), and Bartolomeus Centregus a letter and a poem (cf. Mazzatinti, *Inventario*, XXX, 80-81). Diedo engaged in literary circles in Bergamo (1475), Brescia (1478-79), Rome (1481-82), and Verona (1483-84). He borrowed manuscripts of classical, Christian, and philosophical works frequently from the collection of Girolamo Molin between 1452 and 1456 (see B. Cecchetti, "Una libreria circolante a Venezia nel secolo XV," pp. 162-64).

EDUCATION. Humanities with Ognibene Leoniceno, and arts and law (with Angelo Ubaldi, probably as a co-student of Bernardo Bembo) at Padua.

Dolfin, Pietro. (3) Delfino, Delphinus. Son of Vittore; nephew of the chronicler Pietro Dolfin, son of Giorgio, and cousin of Domenico and Marcantonio Morosini (for the latter relationships, see J. Schnitzer, *Peter Delfin*, pp. 36 and 51).

MONOGRAPHS AND STUDIES. J. Schnitzer, *Peter Delfin, General des Camaldulenserordens (1444-1525): ein Beitrag zur Geschichte der Kirchenreform, Alexanders VI. und Savonarolas*; G. Soranzo, "Pietro Dolfin e il suo epistolario."

CAREER. B. 1444. D. 1525. At least in the early stages of his career, Dolfin was apparently an effective administrator and earnest reformer; but see Schnitzer, *Peter Delfin*, pp. 146ff. for an account of his later struggle with the young Venetians of the circle of Paolo Giustiniani; pp. 226ff. for an assessment of his role as a reformer; and 183ff. for an overall assessment of his achievement. Soranzo's evaluation is more positive. Dolfin played an important political role, working for Venice in the troubled years following the 1492 invasion of King Charles VIII; cf. Schnitzer, *Peter Delfin*, pp. 199ff.; Soranzo, "Pietro Dolfin," pp. 158ff. He competed unsuccessfully in *probae* for the bishoprics of Padua and Treviso (cf. C. Cenci, "Senato veneto 'probae,' " pp. 410, #110; 421, #117; 419, #115) and the patriarchates of Aquileia and Venice (pp. 427, #119; 428, #120).

Titles. 1462-78, Monk of S. Michele da Murano; 1478-80, Abbot of S. Michele da Murano; 1480— General of the Camaldulensian Order.

WORKS. *Argumenta in [58] Ciceronis orationes; Dialogus in Hieronymum Ferrariensem [Savonarolam]; Epistolae CCXLII*, ed. E. Martène and U. Durand; *Epistolarum volumen libri XII* [1524]; orations to the popes Pius II and Julius II (in *Oratiunculae duae*, ed. S. Gritti) and Leo X (ed. Martène and Durand). For other works still in manuscript, see Kristeller, "Contributions of the Religious Orders" [1974], p. 136; also Mittarelli, *Bibl. codd. mss.*, cols. 316-23. For the manuscript tradition and analysis of Dolfin's *epistolario*, see Schnitzer, *Peter Delfin*, pp. 187ff.; Soranzo, "Pietro Dolfin," pp. 20ff. The printed letters are incomplete; a study of Dolfin's correspondence must be supplemented by the ms. collections: those in Berlin (West), Staatsbibliothek, Stiftung Preussischer Kulturbesitz, codd. Lat. fol. 668, 669, 670, 671; Florence, Bibl. Naz. Centrale, Fondo Conventi Soppressi, cod. Conv. Soppr. E 3, 405 (4 vols.); Venice, Marc. cod. Lat. XI, 92 (3828) (I have not seen the Berlin and Florence mss.; see *Iter*, III, 484-85 and I, 158, respectively).

CORRESPONDENCE. Among the addresses of Dolfin's letters of particular interest here are, above all, Pietro Barozzi, his friend and co-student (see the editions of letters cited, and Schnitzer, *Peter Dolfin*, pp. 342ff.), and Fra Girolamo Savonarola, his foe (ibid., pp. 328ff.); also Ermolao Barbaro G (in 1524 ed., Book II, #63), Marco Barbo (ibid., I, #46), Girolamo Donato (ibid., IX, #80), Pietro Donato (ed. of Martène and Durand, passim), Pietro Foscari (ibid., cols. 978-79), Bernardo Giustiniani (in 1524, ed. I, #39), Domenico Morosini (ibid., III, ##49, 60; IV, #42; V, #78; VII, 29; and ed. of Martène and Durand, col. 1152), Marcantonio Morosini (in 1524 ed. VII, #73), and Paolo Pisani (ibid., I, #25; III, ##64, 88; IV, #2). Also a letter from Bernardino Gadolo (in his *Epist.*, pp. 190-203). Mittarelli, *Bibl. codd. mss.*, cols. 318-23 provides an alphabetical index of persons to whom Dolfin wrote.

DISCOURSE. Dolfin's collection, transcription, and emendation of manuscripts are a frequent theme of his letters; see, for example, Schnitzer, *Peter Dolfin*, pp. 48 and nn. 21-34; 57ff.

EDUCATION. With Pietro Perleone.

de' Domenichi, Domenico. (2) Son of Pietro.

MONOGRAPHS AND STUDIES. G. degli Agostini, *Notizie*, I, 386-439; H. Jedin, *Studien über Domenico de' Domenichi (1416-1478)*.

CAREER. B. 15 July 1416. D. 17 Feb. 1478. Born in Venice of a substantial and well-established family (Agostini, *Notizie*, I, 386; the family subsequently appears among the *cittadini originari*; see da Mosto, *Archivio*, I, 75), Domenichi was possibly raised in the patrician household of Antonio Correr, nephew of Pope Gregory XII and uncle of Gregorio Correr. It is suggestive of Domenichi's wealth that he rebuilt the episcopal palace of Torcello at his own expense, and established a family tomb in Venice in the Church of S. Zaccaria shortly before his own death (see Agostini, *Notizie*, I, 401 and Cicogna, *Iscrizioni*, II, 116, respectively). He held various minor benefices during the early years of his career, and was made apostolic protonotary in 1447, *referendarius apostolicus* under Pope Calixtus III, and papal vicar in 1473; he was with the curia from 1452. During his years in Rome, he served as a consultant on theological matters, becoming an authority on papal power and sacramental issues. He performed missions for the papacy frequently in

PROFILES

the 1460s and 1470s, was at the side of Pope Pius II at Ancona in 1464, and subsequently delivered that pontiff's funeral oration. Domenichi competed unsuccessfully in *probae* for the Venetian patriarchate and the bishoprics of Vicenza and Padua (C. Cenci, "Senato veneto 'Probae,' " pp. 388, #96; 392, #99; 395, #100; 396, #101; 397, #102). He hoped for but did not obtain the cardinalate.

Titles. 1445-64, Bishop of Torcello; 1464— Bishop of Brescia.

WORKS. Many theological works (most still in manuscript) of small scale but significant interest, reflecting his humanist training and his practical experience as consultant to popes and cardinals in an age (subsequent to the era of councils) of resurgent papal authority. For these, see the chronological table in Jedin, *Studien*, pp. 51ff. The few works listed here are of special interest because related to Venetian persons or matters. *De non exigendis decimis a clericis sine licentia papae [et] sedis apostolice*, to the Doge and Senate of Venice (1468); *Oratio pro victoriis christianorum habita Rome in basilica S. Petri inter missarum solemnia in anniversario die electionis summi pontificis Pauli II* (30 Aug. 1469), in response to the recent naval victory of Niccolò Canal, not seen; *Oratio in laudem civitatis ac civilitatis Romanae ... cum in civem Romanum patricium receptus est* (1476), not seen; *Quaestio de nominibus his quidditas et essentia* (1476), to Candiano Bollani. The works not seen are in Vat. Ottob. Lat. 1035, fols. 77v-83 and 83-87v, respectively; cf. Jedin, *Studien*, p. 120.

CORRESPONDENCE. Letters to Ermolao Barbaro V (see Agostini, *Notizie*, I, 438), to and from Zaccaria Barbaro (in R. Sabbadini, "Andrea Contrario," pp. 431-33), and from Ermolao Barbaro G (*Epist.*, ed. Branca, I, 3-4), Francesco Barbaro (see *Centotrenta*, ed. Sabbadini, pp. 41, 42, 43, 55), Andrea Contrario (in Sabbadini, "Andrea Contrario," pp. 400-401) and Maffeo Vallaresso (*Epist.*, pp. 523-27).

DISCOURSE. Domenichi was widely respected for his learning: see especially the description of Ermolao Barbaro V to Flavio Biondo of Domenichi as a "universal man"; published in Agostini, *Notizie*, I, 437-38, with Domenichi's response, p. 438; also Vespasiano da' Bisticci's profile in his *Vite di uomini illustri*, p. 148. He was in contact with Poggio Bracciolini, the friend of his countryman Pietro Tommasi, and in Rome, after 1452, was in relation with Flavio Biondo and the cardinal Pietro Barbo. An early supporter of the art of printing, he also left an important collection of manuscript books; cf. P. de Nolhac, *La Bibliothèque de Fulvio Orsini*, pp. 168-69, R. Sabbadini, *Le scoperte dei codici latini e greci*, I, 187, and Cosenza, *Dict.*, II, 1243. For Domenichi's involvement in the discussion and exchange of books, see the correspondence cited and B. Cecchetti, "Una libreria circolante a Venezia nel secolo XV," p. 162. In Rome in 1460, Domenichi purchased a manuscript of Cicero's *Orationes philippicae* (Berlin [East], Deutsche Staatsbiblothek, ms. Ham. 169, not seen; see *Iter*, III, 361), noting on the flyleaf that he bought the book "quia iuvenis magna cum voluptate eas orationes audivi a preceptore meo artis oratoriae doctissimo Petro Thomasio." He was an interlocutor in Candiano Bollani's *Trialogus in rebus futuris annorum XX proximorum.*

EDUCATION. With Pietro Tommasi (see note to Berlin ms. given above). License and doctorate in arts from Padua on 6 Aug. 1435 and 22 Jan. 1436 (Zonta and Brotto, *Acta*, pp. 237, #1062, and 242, #1085; Jedin gives 1434 for the license), teaching there briefly at about that time. In 1441, he received a doctorate in theology elsewhere, perhaps from Bologna.

Donato, Antonio. (2) Donado, Donà, Donatus. Son of Andrea (also learned; see A. Zeno, ed., *Istorici*, I, x); father of Girolamo; grandson of Doge Francesco Foscari (Cicogna, *Iscrizioni*, I, 42). Miles.

CAREER. B. c. 1422 (AC-BO 163/II, c. 192^v; presented 19 Oct. 1440). M. 1450, Lucia di Bernardo Balbi (AC-BO 164/III, c. 114, presentation of Antonio's sons Girolamo and Andrea; Giomo, *Matrimoni*); thereafter, Lucia da Canal (AC-BO 163/II, c. 114^v, presentation of Antonio's son Bartolomeo). D. after 1 May 1481 (when the Senate granted him permission to leave his post in Verona to visit his severely ill brother; ST 8, c. 122), but before 1 Sept. 1481 (the date of the funeral monument erected to him in S. Maria de' Servi; Cicogna, *Iscrizioni*, I, 42). M. Foscarini (*Lett. ven.*, p. 267) suggests that the author of the *Vitae ducum venetorum* may have been Antonio di Donato, a figure of whom I find no trace; Zeno (*Istorici*, I, x) attributes the work to Antonio di Andrea, an attribution all the more likely because that family had a tradition of learning. Andrea himself was learned, as was (far more brilliantly) his grandson, Antonio's son Girolamo. Antonio's political career may have begun years earlier than the record shows. He was elected one of the *advocati proprium* 1441, and a member of the Council of Forty in 1450 (SGV 4, cc. 19, 138^v). He reappears in 1466 and 1468 on special commissions (ST 5, c. 159; 6, c. 24). During the intervening years, he may have pursued a commercial career. On 30 Jan. 1456, he was elected Capt. of the first of the galleys of the Dead Sea fleet, with nominal salary (SM 5, cc. 129-30).

Offices. 1469-70, Amb. to France (MC-Regina, c. 86^v; ST 6, cc. 78, 79^v); 1470, Pod. and Capt. of Justinopolis (MC-Regina, c. 86^v); 1471, Amb. to Ferrara (ST 6, c. 135); 1473-74, Amb. to Rome (CXM 18, cc. 9^v, 41^v; MC-Regina, c. 131^v; ST 6, cc. 191^v, 194, and 7, cc. 4^v, 48 and passim); 1474-75, Sav. tf. (ST 7); 1475, CX (CXM 18); Sav. tf. (ST 7); 1475-76, Amb. to Rome (ST 7, cc. 97 and passim); 1476-78, Avog. (CXM 18, 19; SGV 6, c. 7); 1478, Duc. el., Giovanni Mocenigo (MC-Regina, c. 177^v); Sav. tf. (ST 8); 1478-79, Amb. to Milan (ST 8, cc. 32, 44^v); 1479, Amb. to Florence and Ravenna and Prov. with the army (ST 8, cc. 60^v; *Comm.*, ed. R. Predelli, X, 231-32 [xvi, ##142, 143]; F. Pintor, "Due ambascerie," pp. 810-11); 1480, Sav. gr. (ST 8); 1480-81, Pod. of Verona (SGV 6, c. 16^v; ST 8, c. 122).

WORKS. *Vitae ducum venetorum* (c. 1473). Foscarini (*Lett. ven.*, p. 267) gives a deprecatory assessment of this work, which is repeated by Valentinelli (*Bibl. man.*, VI, 174) and A. Pertusi ("Gli inizi della storiografia umanistica," p.

305). Still, the work was used by Agostino Valier, who owned it before it descended to the collection of Apostolo Zeno.

CORRESPONDENCE. Letters from Leonardo Sanuto (*Epist.*, fols. 71^{r-v}, 75^{r-v}).

DISCOURSE. Praised by Cristoforo Persona in the dedicatory letter (to Doge Giovanni Mocenigo) of his translation of Origen (see Zeno, *Istorici*, I, x). Ludovico Cendrata dedicated to Donato his translation of Josephus' *De bello judaico* (1480; see Cicogna, *Iscrizioni*, I, 43 and Cosenza, *Dict.*, II, 1252), and Matteo Collazio dedicated to him his *De fine oratoris* (Cosenza, *Dict*, II, 1035).

EDUCATION. Studied law at Padua (Papadopoli, *Hist. gymn. pat.* II.i.22, who lists Donato among famous law students at the university).

Donato, Girolamo. (3) Donado, Donà, Donatus. Son of Antonio. Doctor.

MONOGRAPHS AND STUDIES. G. degli Agostini, *Notizie*, II, 201-39; P. Rigo, "Per il carteggio di Girolamo Donato: inventario ed epistole inedite"; Rigo, "Catalogo e tradizione degli scritti di Girolamo Donato"; P. Sambin, "Il dottorato in arti (1478) di Girolamo Donato." Rigo's "Catalogo" gives in its notes detailed information about those phases of Donato's career which pertain to the elucidation of the record of his works. Agostini is helpful in other cases. The former source, where useful, is generally used in preference to the latter; specific references are provided, to avoid confusion, in either case. See also the career summary in V. Branca, "L'umanesimo veneziano alla fine del Quattrocento, Ermolao Barbaro e il suo circolo," pp. 166-69.

CAREER. B. c. 1456 (Agostini gives c. 1457 [II, 201]; Donato was presented to the AC on 22 Nov. 1474 [BO 164/III, c. 114]). M. Maria di Ludovico Gradenigo (Agostini, *Notizie*, II, 203). D. 20 October 1511 (Rigo, "Catalogo," pp. 63-64 n. 68). He may have died poor, having attended exclusively to state business, as an archival document reports (MC-Deda, c. 74^{r-v}). During the 1470s to 1480s, the archival record is obscured by the presence of the homonym Girolamo Donato di Niccolò, who held major offices before our Donato's first diplomatic mission known to me in 1483. Several homonyms appear earlier in the century, as well, most notably a Girolamo Donato who was a peripheral figure in early Venetian humanism: cf. R. Sabbadini, *Le scoperte dei codici latini e greci*, I, 120; *Storia e critica di testi latini*, pp. 123ff.; *Vita di Guarino Veronese*, 6. Cosenza (*Dict.*, II, 1253) confounds the two figures.

Offices. 1483, Amb. to René, Duke of Lorraine (Rigo, "Catalogo," p. 52 n. 15); 1484, Amb. to Genoa (SM 12, c. 19^v); 1486, Amb. to Portugal (Rigo, "Catalogo," p. 52 n. 15); 1488, Amb. to Emperor and King Maximilian (Agostini, *Notizie*, II, 204); 1489-90, Amb. to Milan (Rigo, "Catalogo," pp. 54-55, n. 24); 1491-92, Amb. to Rome (Rigo, "Catalogo," p. 63 n. 68; Agostini, *Notizie*, II, 205); 1492, Pod. and Capt. of Ravenna (Agostini, *Notizie*, II, 207); 1494-95, Avog. (CXM 26; MC-Stella, c. 136; SGV 6, c. 132, and 7 già 12, c. 2ᵛ); 1495-97, Pod. and Vice-Capt. of Brescia (CXM 27, c. 10; also Rigo, "Catalogo," p. 55 n. 26); 1496, Amb. to Lucca (ibid.; Donato performed this mission while retaining the office of pod.); 1497-99, Amb. to Rome (Rigo, "Catalogo," pp. 63-64 n. 68); 1499-1500, Visdomino of Ferrara (MC-Stella, c. 170; Agostini, *Notizie*, II, 211; according to the latter, Donato was in Ferrara in July 1499, according to the former, in 1500; according to SGV 6, c. 15ᵛ, he entered office in Feb. 1501); 1501, Amb. to Emperor (Rigo, "Catalogo," p. 57 n. 31); Duc. el., Leonardo Loredan (MC-Stella, cc. 187, 188); 1501-2, Amb. to France (Rigo, "Catalogo," p. 58 nn. 33-45); 1503-4, Pod. of Cremona (Rigo, "Catalogo," pp. 59-60 n. 49); 1504, Sav. gr. (CXM 30, c. 107; SM 16; ST 15); 1505, Amb. in obedientia to Pope Julius II (Rigo, "Catalogo," pp. 59-61 nn. 46 and 47); 1505, Cons. (SGV 7 già 12, c. 2; SM 16); 1506-8, Duke of Crete (Rigo, "Catalogo," p. 62 n. 67); 1509, Cons. (MC-Deda; SGV 7 già 12, c. 27ᵛ); 1509-11, Amb. to Rome (Rigo, "Catalogo," p. 63 n. 68; 65-66 n. 76); died on that mission.

WORKS. Author of extensive works in Latin and Greek, of which some are no longer extant; a thorough listing in Rigo, "Catalogo." These works include translations from the Greek of Alexander of Aphrodisias (highly influential; see, for example, E. P. Mahoney, "Philosophy and Science in Nicoletto Vernia and Agostino Nifo"), John Chrysostom, John Damascene, and ps.-Dionysius the Areopagite; orations; treatises and occasional works on theological or secular topics; and verse. Most interesting or notable in the present context are: *Apologeticus ad Graecos de principatu Romanae sedis* (discussion and full listing of other manuscript versions and editions in Rigo, "Catalogo," pp. 63-64, #21); *Ad Caesarem pro re Christiana oratio* (1501; pp. 57-58, #14); *Contra Caroli Regis Francorum in Senatum Venetum calumnias apologia* (56-57, #11); *Epistola ad Oliverium Cardinalem Neapolitanum in qua Ro. Ecclesiam primatum ecclesiasticae dignitatis obtinere, et Petrum esse petram et fundamentum ecclesiae, doctissime comprobatur* (see Rigo, "Carteggio," p. 538 and n. 29); *Epistola ad Petrum Contarenum de terremotu Cretensi* (15 July 1508; ibid., p. 538 and n. 28); *Apud Iulium II Pontificem Maximum in obedientia oratio* (1505; "Catalogo," pp. 61-62, #17); *Oratio ad Ludovicum Gallorum regem* (1501; ibid., pp. 58-59, #15); *De processione Spiritus Sancti contra Graecum schisma* (ibid., pp. 64-65, #22).

CORRESPONDENCE. Inventoried by Rigo, "Carteggio," pp. 533-38, who also publishes seven letters by Donato, pp. 539-55. Among his correspondents: Ermolao Barbaro G, Pietro Bembo, Marco Dandolo, Pietro Dolfin, Marsilio Ficino, Domenico Grimani, Giovanni Lorenzi, Aldo Manuzio, Giovanni Pico della Mirandola, Angelo Poliziano, Marcantonio Sabellico.

DISCOURSE. Praised for his learning by Jacopo Boldù (see Agostini, *Notizie*, II, 213), Giovanni Battista Egnazio (*De exemplis illustrium virorum*, fols. 78-79, 295ᵛ), Erasmus (with reservations; *Ciceronianus*, p. 224), Aldo Manuzio (Agostini, *Notizie*, II, 202), Giovanni Morosini (cf. B. Nardi, "Scuola di Rialto" [UEUV ed.], p. 126), Francesco Pisani (*De universae philosophiae ornamentis*, p. 266), and Marcantonio Sabellico (*De rep. lat. ling.*, fol. 109ᵛ), among others. A humanist of very first rank (E. Garin, "Cultura filosofica toscana e veneta nel Quattrocento" [UEUV ed.], p. 28; O. Logan, *Culture and Society*, pp. 49, 51; P. Monnier, *Le Quattrocento*, I, 173), Donato enjoyed relations with many of the learned of his generation (Agostini, *Notizie*, II, 214), mirrored in part in the works dedicated to him (ibid., p. 238, except where otherwise specified) by Ermolao Barbaro G, Marino Becichemo, Girolamo Bologni, Gasparino Borro (the *Commentum super tractatum spherae mundi*, see Rigo, "Carteggio," p. 535 and n. 18), Lidio Catto, Galeazzo Pontico Facino (see J.F.C. Richards, "The Poems of Galeatius Ponticus Facinus," pp. 108-109), Niccolò Liburnio, Aldo Manuzio (the edition of Dioscorides and other works, cf. Rigo, "Carteggio," p. 537 and n. 25), Girolamo Ramusio, Raffaele Regio (his work on Quintilian, also directed to Marco Dandolo and Paolo Pisani, Rigo, "Carteggio," p. 534 and n. 13), Sabellico (*De situ venetae urbis*), Panfilo Sasso, and Pierio Valeriano (the *Lusus*, see Rigo, "Carteggio," p. 538 and n. 28). He also had cordial relations with Marsilio Ficino, Giovanni Pico della Mirandola, and Angelo Poliziano (Kristeller, "Marsilio Ficino e Venezia," p. 483 and n. 46; Rigo, "Carteggio," pp. 554-55). Donato's disputation on the subject moved Elia del Medigo to write his *Quaestio de primo motore* (B. Nardi, "Letteratura e cultura" [CVQ ed.], p. 125; Rigo, "Catalogo," p. 50 n. 8). Where opportunities arose during his various missions, Donato continued to write, to pursue antiquarian interests (ibid., pp. 59-61 and n. 49), and to engage in conversation with the learned men of foreign courts and cities. He was a patron of Marino Becichemo, whom he employed as a tutor for his sons (Agostini, *Notizie*, II, 203, 214-15; Rigo, "Catalogo," p. 55 n. 26).

EDUCATION. Greek with Theodore Gaza, and arts and law at Padua. He had received his doctorate in arts on 16 June 1478 (having studied with Nicoletto Vernia), but was still engaged in the study of law in 1489, when, with his friend Marco Dandolo, he held the post of rector (Agostini, *Notizie*, II, 202-203; Sambin, "Il dottorato"; P. Verrua, "Università di Padova circa il 1488 nell' 'Opusculum scribendi epistolas' di Francesco Negri," p. 188).

Donato, Ludovico. (3) Donado, Donà, Donatus. Son of Giovanni (Agostini, *Notizie*, I, 326) or Francesco (Zonta and Brotto, *Acta*, p. 458, #2394); cousin of Marco (see G. Zippel, "Lorenzo Valla e le origini della storiografia umanistica a Venezia," p. 96 n. 1) and nephew of Pietro Donato (ibid. and Zonta and Brotto, *Acta*, p. 233, #1039).

MONOGRAPHS AND STUDIES. G. degli Agostini, *Notizie*, I, 326-32.

CAREER. B. c. 1430. D. 20 July 1484. Before proceeding to major posts, Donato held the titles of apostolic protonotary and canon of the Cathedral of Padua (Agostini, *Notizie*, I, 327; Zonta and Brotto, *Acta*, p. 459, #2401; B. Marx, *Bartolomeo Pagello*, p. 61 and n. 24).

Titles. 1462-65, Bishop of Belluno (Eubel, *Hier. cath.*, II, 103); 1465— Bishop of Bergamo (ibid., p. 214).

WORKS. *Oratio pro summo pontifice edita* [on ascension of Doge Cristoforo Moro] (1462); *Orationes*: 1. *pro annuntiationis solenitate*; 2. *pro gloriosissimi doctoris Augustini celebritate*; 3. *pro epiphaniae festivitate; Praefatio in theologicarum textum sententiarum*, not seen (cf. *Iter*, I, 372). The three orations named are distinctly humanist in style. All were delivered in Siena in the presence of Pope Pius II, curia, and cardinals in 1460 (26 March, 28 Aug., and 6 Jan., respectively). Agostini (*Notizie*, I, 331-32) reports several other apparently similar orations that had been seen by earlier witnesses, though not by him; nor have I found them. Cosenza (*Dict.*, II, 1255) reports on oration for Guarino Veronese, not found.

CORRESPONDENCE. Letter from Bartolomeo Pagello (in Marx, *Bartolomeo Pagello*, p. 196).

DISCOURSE. Donato received the dedications of several contemporary works: Firmus de Blanconibus' dialogue *Ludovica oratio* (cf. *Iter*, I, 122); Giovanni Crastone's Greek-Latin *Psalterium* and Angelo Sabino's edition of Ammianus Marcellinus (Agostini, *Notizie*, I, 331; Cosenza, *Dict.*, II, 1255); Raffaele Zovenzoni's edition of Cicero's *De natura deorum* (Cosenza, *Dict.*, II, 1252). Donato participated in intellectual circles in Bergamo where he was bishop after 1465, and was recognized as himself learned (see G. Favre, *Vie de Jean-Marius Philelphe*, p. 112). For his reputation, see especially Pagello's letter, cited, and Giovanni Michele Alberto da Carrara's welcoming oration *in adventu novi Pontificis Ludovici Donato Senatoris eminentissimi, juris et omnium disciplinarum copia refertissimi* (1466; see Zeno, *Diss. voss.*, II, 30).

EDUCATION. With Giovanni Pietro Vitali d'Avenza (da Lucca), Lorenza Valla, and Paolo della Pergola (Agostini, *Notizie*, I, 326; for d. Pergola, also F. Lepori, "Scuola di Rialto," p. 553). Advanced studies at Padua, where he received his doctorate in arts under Gaetano da Thiene on 5 March 1450 (Zonta and Brotto, *Acta*, 458, #2394), in law 16 July 1457 (Marx, *Pagello*, p. 61 and n. 24).

Donato, Marco. (2) Donado, Donà, Donatus. Son of Natale; nephew of Pietro (G. Zippel, "Lorenzo Valla e le origini della storiografia umanistica a Venezia," pp. 96-97 n. 1), cousin of Ludovico Donato (Zonta and Brotto, *Acta*, p. 233, #1039). Doctor.

MONOGRAPHS AND STUDIES. Zippel's brief profile (cited above).

CAREER. B. c. 1415 (AC-BO 162/I, c. 175; presented 2 Dec. 1433). D. after 15 May 1465 (the last archival reference known to me of his activity: CXM 16, c. 164ᵛ).
    Offices. 1452, Amb. to Rome (*Comm.*, ed. R. Predelli, X, 69-70 [xiv, #225]); 1452, Amb. to Marquis of Montferrato; 1454, Sav. tf.; 1455-56, Sav. tf. (SGV 4, c. 147; SM 5; ST 3, c. 176, and 4); 1456, Amb. to Sigismondo

Pandolfo Malatesta, M. of Ferrara; Sav. tf. (SGV 4, c. 147; SM 5; ST 4, c. 11^v); CX (CLN 9, c. 173^v); 1457, Sav. tf. (SGV 4, c. 147^v; SM 6; ST 4, c. 35); 1458, Pod. of Vicenza; 1459, Sav. tf. (SM 6; ST 4, c. 112); 1459-60, CX (CXM 15, c. 189^v and passim, and 16); 1460, Sav. tf. (SM 6; ST 4, c. 139); Capt. of Bergamo (CLN 10, c. 8); 1463, Sav. tf. (ST 5, c. 45^v); CX (CXM 16, c. 100 and passim); 1463-64, Amb. to Duke of Burgundy; 1464, Amb. to Bartolomeo Colleoni, Capt. Gen. of the army; 1465, Cons. (CLN 10, c. 121^v; CXM 16; MC-Regina; SM 8; ST 5).

WORKS. *Oratio in laudes Zachariae Trivisani* (25 Aug. 1442); *Oratio pro principio studii Patavini.*

CORRESPONDENCE. Letters to Marco Barbo (1458), thanking the Venetian cardinal for having lent him Trebizond's invective against Gaza (in J. Monfasani, ed., *Collectanea Trapezuntiana*, pp. 419-21); from Ludovico Foscarini (*Epist.*, fols. 30-33^v; 285-86; 299^{r-v}; the second also published in G. B. Picotti, *Dieta di Mantova*, pp. 459-60).

DISCOURSE. Praised as one of Venice's learned men by Francesco Pisani (*Oratio de universae philosophiae ornamentis*, p. 266). Involved in discussion in Venice about the appointment of an official historiographer (see A. Pertusi, "Gli inizi della storiografia umanistica," p. 299; F. Gaeta, "Storiografia, coscienza nazionale," pp. 28ff.). Giorgio Bevilacqua de Lazise dedicated to Donato his *De bello gallico* (see E. Abel's preface to Isotta Nogarola's *Opera omnia*, I, cix, n. 33, and *Iter*, II, 294), and Niccolò Sagundino his translation of Plutarch's *De civili institutione.*

EDUCATION. Present at Padua from at least 26 Jan. 1434 (Zonta and Brotto, *Acta*, p. 219, #977), Donato received his license and doctorate in law on 17 and 18 Aug., respectively, 1443 (ibid., p. 350, ##1731, 1732; a student of law from 22 Jan. 1436, ibid., p. 242, #1085).

Donato, Pietro. (1) Donado, Donà, Donatus. Son of Niccolò; uncle of Ludovico and Marco. See G. Zippel, "Lorenzo Valla e le origini della storiografia umanistica a Venezia," p. 96 n. 1, and Zonta and Brotto, *Acta*, p. 233, #1039, for relationships with Marco and Ludovico, respectively.

MONOGRAPHS AND STUDIES. G. degli Agostini, *Notizie*, II, 135-56; F. Anecchini, *Cenni biografici su Pietro Donà, Vescovo di Padova*; P. Sambin, "Ricerche per la storia della cultura nel secolo XV: la biblioteca di Pietro Donato (1380-1447)." For further bibliography, see Sambin, p. 53 n. 1.

CAREER. B. c. 1380 (authorities cited; but evidence of university career suggests perhaps c. 1390). Testament, 14 Sept. 1445 (Anecchini, *Cenni biografici*, p. 14). D. 7 Oct. 1447. Donato held the title of apostolic protonotary from 1411, and served frequently in his maturity as papal legate to the Councils at Pavia and Siena (1423), Basel (1433-35), and Ferrara-Florence (1438-39). In Padua, at his own expense, he assisted the university and beautified the cathedral.

Titles. 1415-25, Archbishop of Candia (Crete). Elected in 1415 (Sambin, "Ricerche," p. 15; Eubel, *Hier. cath.*, I, 216), he appears in a university document of that year as archbishop "elect" (Zonta and Brotto, *Acta*, p. 94, #331), and early the next with the unqualified title (ibid., p. 105, #374); but Anecchini says (*Cenni biografici*, p. 7) that he acquired the title in 1417; he did not assume office until 1418 (Gams, *Ser. episc.*, p. 401). 1425-28, Bishop of Castello (Venice) (Eubel, *Hier. cath.*, I, 171, who gives the election as 1425; Gams [p. 782] says he was transferred from Crete in 1426, but never formally entered before his 1428 transfer to Padua); 1425-30, *Papal gov. of Perugia*; 1428— Bishop of Padua.

WORKS. *Oratio in exequiis Cardinalis Francisci de Zabarelis* (Padua 1418; widely diffused in manuscript versions: see, for instance, *Iter*, indices; also printed, see L. Bertalot, "Eine Sammlung Paduaner Reden des XV. Jahrhunderts," p. 256); *Oratio in laudem Pape; Oratio de laudibus philosophiae in suo principio in artibus; Oratio ... ad Reverendissimos Patres in Concilio [Basiliensi] existentes*, not seen (nor located; it was known in manuscript to Agostini, *Notizie*, see II, 155). Sansovino (*Venetia*, II, 576) and his followers also attribute a *Defensio pro Alexandro contra Averroem de augmentatione.*

CORRESPONDENCE. Exchange with Benedetto Ovetario (see Agostini, *Notizie*, II, 155; for Ovetario, see *Iter*, II, 255). Letters to Ambrogio Traversari (ibid., II, 146), and from Francesco Barbaro (see *Centotrenta*, ed. Sabbadini, pp. 17, 18, 23, 38), Poggio Bracciolini (*Epist.*, ed. Tonellis, I, 120-26 and 143-44), Antonio Carabello (see *Iter*, II, 357), Lapo da Castiglionchio (ibid., p. 432), Guarino Veronese (*Epist.*, ed. Sabbadini, I, 222), Pietro del Monte (in J. Haller, *Pier da Monte*, p. 123), Ognibene Scola (in G. Cogo, "Di Ognibene Scola, umanista padovano," pp. 156-59).

DISCOURSE. Donato was praised for his learning by Vespasiano da Bisticci (*Vite di uomini illustri*, pp. 144, 145) and Lauro Quirini (*Oratio in adventu episcopi patavini*). Several authors dedicated works to him: Guarino Veronese his translation of a dialogue of Apuleius, Michele Savonarola his *Libellus de magnificis ornamentis regie civitatis Padue*, Ambrogio Traversari his translation of some works of Athanasius, Girolamo Valle, and Mariano da Volterra, Latin religious verse (for these, see Agostini, *Notizie*, II, 151-53, with a section of Traversari's dedication published ibid., pp. 145-46); also Ciriaco d'Ancona his translation of Gregory Nazianzen's *De septem mundi spectaculis* (see Sister Way, "S. Gregorius Nazienzenus," in CTC, II, 61ff. and III, 414) and a collection of inscriptions (Berlin [East], Deutsche Staatsibliothek, cod. Ham. 254, fols. 49v-90v, with letter to Donato on fol. 81v, not seen; see *Iter*, III, 364; H. Boese, *Die lateinischen Handschriften der Sammlung Hamilton zu Berlin*, pp. 127-28); Sicco Polenton his *De confessione christiana* (see C. Trinkaus, *In Our Image and Likeness*, II, 616, and 832 n. 4); Lauro Quirini a translation from Lucian (see Sambin, "Ricerche," pp. 22, 41 and n. 211). An active participant in intellectual life at Padua, Donato restored the episcopal palace there, as he had at Perugia enlarged the cathedral; see Traversari's comment on the beautiful episcopal palace in Padua which Donato had restored in his *Hodoeporicon*, ed. L. Mehus, p. 69. He collected, copied, and engaged in the exchange of manuscripts, and left his important collection to the monastery established by his will.

EDUCATION. Present at Padua from 1410 to 1418, Donato received his license in arts on 30 Jan. 1410, and his doctorates in law and arts on 19 Oct. 1418. He was a student of Gasparino Barzizza and Francesco Zabarella; the former delivered a congratulatory oration on the occasion of his graduation (Sambin, "Ricerche," pp. 53-54).

Foscari, Jacopo. (2) Fuscarus. Son of Francesco, doge of Venice (1423-57); cousin of Pietro Foscari (for the latter's relationship to Doge Francesco and hence to Jacopo, see L. Foscarini, *Epist.*, fols. 214^v-215).

MONOGRAPHS AND STUDIES. F. Berlan, *I due Foscari, memorie storico-critiche*; M. Zannoni, "Il dramma dei Foscari nella cronica di Giorgio Dolfin." Also Romanin, *Stor. doc.*, IV, 265-85.

CAREER. B. c. 1415 (based on the dates of his first political elections and his marriage; Foscari was still young in the late 1430s when most of the letters to him from known humanists are dated). M. 1441, Lucrezia di Leonardo Contarini (Romanin, IV, 266; Cappellari, *Camp. ven.*, II, 88; the wedding was lavishly celebrated). D. 12 Jan. 1457. If the proposed date of birth is correct, Foscari would have been still too young at the time of his first condemnation in 1445 to have acquired a significant political record. This, or perhaps his close relationship to the doge, may explain the absence of an important political career. The studies cited deal centrally with Foscari's delinquency and prosecution, and are not useful for his humanist career.

Offices. (Foscari appears on election lists for the positions that follow, but in each case his name is canceled. He may never have served, or may have served only briefly.) 1438, *Senate* (SGV 4, c. 108); 1439, *Senate, zonta to the Senate* (c. 107^v, 111); 1440, *Zonta to the Senate* (c. 114); 1442, *Zonta to the Senate* (c. 119^v); 1443, *Senate* (c. 121); 1444, *Senate* (c. 124). In 1445, Foscari was condemned and exiled for prohibited acceptance of gifts and privileges. Subsequently permitted to return to Venice (1447), he was condemned again and perpetually exiled twice more (1451, 1456). For the circumstances of dereliction and punishment, see the judicious narrative in Romanin, *Stor. doc.*, IV, 265-85.

CORRESPONDENCE. Letters from Francesco Barbaro (see *Centotrenta*, ed. Sabbadini, pp. 25, 26, 27, 28); Poggio Bracciolini (*Epist.*, ed. Tonellis, II, 150-53, 153-54, 177-78); Leonardo Bruni (*Epist.*, ed. Mehus, II, 96-97, 109); Ciriaco d'Ancona (in M. Morici, *Per gli epistolari di due discepoli e di un amico di Guarino Guarini*, pp. 20-24); Guarino Veronese (*Epist.*, ed. Sabbadini, II, 292-94); Isotta and Ginevra Nogarola (in Isotta's *Opera omnia*, ed. E. Abel, I, 46-54, and II, 329-34, respectively); Lauro Quirini (Cod. Vat.

Lat. 3194, fols. 12-13; fols. 11-12 have one to Doge Francesco, also published by C. Seno in his University of Padua dissertation [1967-68], not seen).

DISCOURSE. Poggio appealed to Foscari to take part in his literary quarrel with Filelfo (see the first of his letters cited above). Bruni sent him a work for comment (see the second of his letters cited above). Ludovico Foscarini dedicated to Foscari his *Gesta martyrum Victoris et Coronae*. Foscari was probably a patron of Ciriaco's (inferred from Poggio's third letter cited above, and supported by Ciriaco's letter to Foscari) and Lauro Quirini (suggested in the latter's letter, cited above). He was known as a Hellenist and collector of manuscripts.

EDUCATION. With Bartolomeo Facio (perhaps), Francesco Barbaro, and Antonio Baratella. For Facio, see R. Sabbadini, "Bartolomeo Facio, scolaro a Verona, maestro a Venezia." Sabbadini suggests the relationship with Foscari upon the basis of letters that may not in fact be Facio's; so argues Kristeller in his "The Humanist Bartolomeo Facio and His Unknown Correspondence"; Kristeller agrees with U. Mazzini's earlier study: "Appunti e notizie per servire alla bio-bibliografia di Bartolomeo Facio." M. Foscarini (*Lett. ven.*, p. 81 n. 225) inferred that Barbaro taught Foscari from Isotta Nogarola's letter, cited above. See A. Segarizzi (*Antonio Baratella*, pp. 12-13) for the suggestion that Baratella tutored Foscari c. 1422. Foscari was present at Padua in May and July 1436 as a witness to the granting of degrees to others (Zonta and Brotto, *Acta*, 248, #1118; 249, #1119; 254, #1149).

Foscari, Pietro. (3?) Fuscarus. Son of Marco; cousin of Jacopo, nephew of Doge Francesco (see L. Foscarini, *Epist.*, fols. 214ᵛ-215).

CAREER. B. c. 1430? (based on the dates of Foscari's university attendance and degree and of his intellectual activities: the correspondence ranges from the decade of the 1450s forward). D. 11 or 22 Aug. 1485 (respectively, Eubel, *Hier. cath.*, II, 18 and M. Bolzonella, *Pietro Barozzi, Vescovo di Padova*, p. 29). During the years as *primicerius*, as we know from the same evidence, Foscari held the title of apostolic protonotary. He was in Rome on 26 June 1468 and witnessed the act by which the ambassador Paolo (not Pietro) Morosini took possession for Venice of the library of Cardinal Bessarion (*Comm.*, ed. Predelli, X, 197 [xvi, #22]).

Titles. By 1448 to at least 1477, *Primicerius Ecclesiae Sancti Marci* (Zonta and Brotto, *Acta*, 430-31, #2235; C. Cenci, "Senato veneto 'probae,' " p. 399, #103; Eubel, *Hier. cath.*, II, 18); 1477— Cardinal (Eubel, *Hier. cath.* II, 18); 1481— Bishop of Padua (ibid., p. 210).

CORRESPONDENCE. Exchange with Moro Lapi (*Opera*, fols. 1, 216ᵛ-217). Letters from Pietro Dolfin (*Epist.* CCXLII, cols. 978-79), L. Foscarini (*Epist.*, fols. cited), and Maffeo Vallaresso (*Epist.*, pp. 37-39, 106-107, 230, 254, 446-48). Several letters of Ermolao Barbaro G's, by which the younger man dedicates to Foscari successive parts of his comment on Aristotle's *Ethics*, are cited below ("Discourse"). The letter of Francesco Barbaro purportedly to

Pietro Foscari (see *Centotrenta*, ed. Sabbadini, p. 27) was surely directed to the infamous Polidoro Foscari.

DISCOURSE. Pietro Barozzi addressed to Foscari a consolatory work on the death of the latter's brother Ludovico. Ermolao Barbaro G dedicated to him his *Compendium ethicorum* (letters of dedication among Barbaro's *Epist.*, ed. V. Branca, I, 4-6), Giovanni Jacopo Cane his *Libellus de tabellionibus* (see Cosenza, *Dict.*, II, 1462), and Niccolò Perotti four monodies (see G. Mercati, *Per la cronologia della vita e degli scritti di Niccolò Perotti, arcivescovo di Siponto*, p. 70, with letter of dedication to Foscari published, pp. 151-55; also *Iter*, II, 381-82, and Kristeller, "Niccolò Perotti ed i suoi contributi alla storia dell'umanesimo," *Res Publica Litterarum*, 4 [1981], 13 and n. 33). Foscari established the cathedral library in Padua with his predecessor Jacopo Zeno's collection as nucleus, gathering dispersed works and constructing an inventory of 361 titles (see E. Govi, "La biblioteca di Jacopo Zeno," pp. 36ff.).

EDUCATION. Present at Padua c. 1448-50 (Zonta and Brotto, *Acta*, indices), Foscari received a degree in canon law there on 31 Aug. 1454. The fact and date of his law degree (identified variously in different manuscript versions as the private "license" or the "doctorate") is given by Ognibene Leoniceno's *Oratio in privato examine Petri Foscari, protonotarii apostolici et primicerii Sancti Marci Venetiarum, in iure pontificio* delivered on that occasion.

Foscarini, Ludovico (Alvise). (2) Foscareno, Fuscarenus. Son of Antonio. Doctor, miles.

MONOGRAPHS AND STUDIES. G. degli Agostini, *Notizie*, I, 45-107; G. Gardenal, "Lodovico Foscarini e la medicina"; P. Gothein, "L'amicizia fra Ludovico Foscarini e l'umanista Isotta Nogarola" and "Paolo Veneto e Prosdocimo de' Conti maestri padovani di Lodovico Foscarini"; G. B. Picotti, "Le lettere di Lodovico Foscarini"; G. dalla Santa, "Due lettere di umanisti veneziani (Lauro Querini e Lodovico Foscarini a Paolo Morosini)"; G. Zippel, "Ludovico Foscarini ambasciatore a Genova, nella crisi dell'espansione veneziana sulla terraferma (1449-50)." Also pertinent are the preface of E. Abel to his edition of Isotta Nogarola's *Opera omnia*; M. L. King, "The Religious Retreat of Isotta Nogarola"; and G. B. Picotti, *La Dieta di Mantova.*

CAREER. B. 1409. M. 1430, Lisabetta di Andrea Zane (Giomo, *Matrimoni*, II, 490). Testament 16 Dec. 1477, 17 June 1478 (AN, Testamenti G. Moysis, B. 727.119, and Cancelleria Inferiore, Miscellanea Testamenti, B. 27, n. 2596; the disposition of his books discussed in B. Cecchetti, "Libri, scuole, maestri, sussidii allo studio in Venezia nei secoli XIV e XV," p. 338). D. 17 Aug. 1480. The record of a significant property purchase on 13 Feb. 1456 in Mus. Correr, Ms. PD. C. 751/35 suggests Foscarini's wealth. Although I find no record of major offices after 1474, Foscarini continued to serve on *zonte* of the Consiglio X late in the decade.

Offices. 1437, CX (CXM 11, 12); 1438, Pod. of Ravenna (SGV 4, c. 61ᵛ); 1439, Pod. and Capt. of Feltre (SGV 4, c. 65); 1439, Lt. of Friuli; 1441-42,

Cons. (CLN 7); 1442, Castellan of Modon (SGV 4, c. 84; SM 2, c. 69ᵛ); 1444-45, Cons. (CLN 8; ST 1); 1445, CX (CXM 12, 13; SGV 4, c. 124ᵛ); Sav. tf. (SM 2; ST 1, c. 154ᵛ and passim; held in part concurrently with preceding office); 1445-46, Amb. to Bologna (ST 1, cc. 173, 174, 174ᵛ, 190ᵛ); 1446, Sav. tf. (ST 1, 2); Amb. to Milan; 1446-47, Pod. of Vicenza (SGV 4, c. 69ᵛ, 129; Barbaro, *Centotrenta*, ed. Sabbadini, p. 41; elected in 1446, Foscarini's assumption of this office may have been delayed until 1447 because of the interceding mission to Milan); 1448, Sav. tf. (SM 3; ST 2); 1448, Cons. (CLN 8; MC-Ursa; SGV 4, c. 104; SM 3; ST 2); 1449, Sav. tf. (SGV 4, c. 159; SM 3; ST 2, c. 105ᵛ and passim); 1449-50, Amb. to Genoa (Zippel, "Ludovico Foscarini ambasciatore"; Picotti, "Lettere," [1955], 208-209); 1450, Sav. tf. (SGV 4, c. 159ᵛ; SM 3, 4; ST 2); Cons. (CLN 8; CXM 13; held in part concurrently with preceding office); 1450-51, Pod. of Verona (MC-Ursa, c. 173ᵛ; SGV 4, c. 71ᵛ; Picotti, "Lettere" [1955], 209, appears to be in error giving the dates 1451-52); 1451-52, Sav. tf. (SGV 4, c. 160; ST 3); 1452, Sav. gr. (SGV 4, c. 160ᵛ; ST 3); CX (CXM 14; SGV 4, c. 142; this office held concurrently in turn with each of the two preceding); Prov. in Brescia (CXM 14, cc. 114ʳ⁻ᵛ, 115ᵛ, 116); 1452-53, Cons. (CLN 8; CXM 14; SGV 4, c. 104); 1453, Sav. gr. (ST 3); 1453-54, Pod. of Brescia; 1454, Sav. gr. (SGV 4, c. 148ᵛ; SM 5; ST 3); 1455, Cons. (CLN 9; CXM 15; SGV 4, c. 105; SM 5; ST 3); Amb. in obedientia to Pope Calixtus III; 1455, Amb. to Genoa; 1455-56, Avog. (CXM 15; SGV 4, c. 169ᵛ; SM 5); 1456-57, Capt. of Verona; 1457-58, Sav. gr. (SGV 4, c. 147ᵛ; SM 6; ST 4); 1458-59, Avog. (CXM 15; SM 6; ST 4); 1459, Amb. to Diet of Mantua (see Picotti, *Dieta di Mantova*); 1460, Avog. (CXM 16; Picotti, *Dieta di Mantova*, p. 324); 1461-62, Lt. in Friuli; 1463, Avog. (CXM 16); 1464, Amb. to Rome, then with Pope Pius II to Ancona (Picotti, "Lettere" [1955], 216-18; dalla Santa, "Due lettere," p. 93); Amb. in obedientia to Pope Paul II; 1465, Sav. gr. (SM 8); Amb. to Bartolomeo Colleoni, Capt. Gen., in Malpaga (CXM 16, cc. 154ᵛ and passim to 165ᵛ; Picotti, "Lettere" [1955], p. 218 and n. 8); 1465-66, Cons. (CLN 10; CXM 16; MC-Regina; SM 8; ST 5); 1466, Sav. gr. (ST 5, c. 153); 1466-67, Pod. of Padua; 1468, Sav. gr. (ST 6, c. 26 and passim); 1468-69, CX (CXM 17; held in part concurrently with the preceding office); 1469, Sav. gr. (SM 8, 9; ST 6, c. 49 and passim); 1470-71, Amb. to Rome (CLN 11, c. 69; MC-Regina, c. 93ᵛ; Picotti, "Lettere," [1955], p. 219; dalla Santa, "Due lettere," p. 92; originally absolved from this embassy on 24 March 1470 on the grounds of ill health—he had already received the Last Sacrament—Foscarini was reassigned and left soon after: CLN 11, c. 68; see also the comment on this mission by Pietro Marcello G in his *Oratio in funere Andreae Vendrameni*, p. 152); 1471, Proc. di San Marco (MC-Regina, c. 93ᵛ; G. Tournoy, "Francesco Diedo," p. 204; M. Vallaresso, *Epist.*, pp. 593-95); 1471, Sav. gr. (SM 9; ST 6; dalla Santa, "Due lettere," p. 93); Duc. el., Niccolò Tron (MC-Regina, cc. 101ᵛ-102ᵛ); 1472, Sav. gr. (CLN 11, c. 128ᵛ; CXM 17, c. 170; SM 9; ST 6); 1473, Duc. el., Niccolò Marcello (MC-Regina, cc. 122ᵛ, 123, 123ᵛ); 1474, Sav. gr. (CLN 11, c. 172ᵛ; ST 7).

WORKS. *Epistolae; Exempla rerum bene gestarum ac prudenter dictarum, industria studioque Ludovico Fuscareni ex doctissimorum libris collecta,* not seen (Vienna, Nationalbibliothek, cod. Lat. 3424**; cf. *Tabula codicum manuscriptorum,* ed. Academia Caesarea Vindobonensis, II [Vienna, 1868], 342, 288); *Gesta martyrum Victoris et Coronae,* to Jacopo Foscari; orations for Giovanni Marino (1435), to Pope Calixtus III (1455), against the Turkish threat (Mantua, 1459), and on the crusade (1463); these are not known to me to be extant, but there is sound evidence for them: see Agostini, *Notizie,* I, 47, 65, 69, and 83-84, respectively, and for the Mantuan orations, G. B. Picotti, *Dieta di Mantova,* p. 181. The oration to the pope cited by Kristeller (*Iter,* II, 279), however, as located in the Biblioteca Querini-Stampalia in Venice, is actually a Senate letter of 5 Oct. 1465 on which Foscarini's name appears as one of the *consiglieri* present; I am grateful to P. H. Labalme for having examined this manuscript for me. The work *De porpora* attributed to Foscarini by F. Sansovino and followers (see Agostini, *Notizie,* I, 106), like the elegy for Ludovico Gonzaga, was probably written in fact by Francesco Filelfo.

CORRESPONDENCE. Foscarini's 302 *Epistolae* (for which see Picotti's careful "Le lettere") contain notably those to Ulisse Aleotti, Guarnerio D'Artegna, Marco Aurelio, Girolamo Barbarigo, Ermolao Barbaro V, Francesco Barbaro, Paolo Barbo, Pietro Barbo, Cardinal Bessarion, Flavio Biondo, Candiano Bollani, Damiano dal Borgo, Niccolò Canal, Maffeo Contarini, Marco Donato, Francesco Filelfo, Alessandro de' Fornaci, Tito Livio Frulovisi, Bernardo Giustiniani, Lorenzo Giustiniani, Antonio Gradenigo [?], Vitale Lando, Pietro Molin, Pietro del Monte, Barbone Morosini, Paolo Morosini, Isotta Nogarola, Porcellio Pandoni (Napoletano), Filippo Paruta, Alessandro (probably Aleardo; see *Iter,* II, 65) de' Pindemonti, Girolamo da Ponte, Pantaleone Quagliano, Jacopo Ragazzoni, Pietro Tommasi, Francesco Trevisan, and Zaccaria Trevisan G. Various letters of Foscarini are also published. Several appear in Picotti's *Dieta di Mantova:* to Paolo Morosini (pp. 444-46, 457-59); to Marco Donato (pp. 459-60); to Bernardo Giustiniani (pp. 471, 480-81); to Maffeo Contarini (pp. 474-76); to Damiano dal Borgo (pp. 490-91). Abel publishes those to Nogarola in the latter's *Opera omnia* (II, 35-83, 88-126, 157-58, 183-84), two to Damiano dal Borgo (II, 84-87, 159-60), and one to Ermolao Barbaro V (II, 181-82). A. M. Quirini printed the letters of Foscarini to Barbaro in the latter's *Epistolae;* cf. *Centotrenta,* ed. Sabbadini, indices. Three letters to Baratella are printed by A. Segarizzi in *Antonio Baratella,* pp. 162-65. Mittarelli prints letters of Foscarini to Maffeo Contarini and Moro Lapi: *Bibl. codd. mss.,* cols. 413-15. A letter of Foscarini to Paolo Morosini appears in dalla Santa, "Due lettere," pp. 95-96, and one by Foscarini to Jacopo Ragazzoni appears in the introduction by F. Corner, pp. ix-x, to Lorenzo de' Monaci's *Chronicon.* Finally, a manuscript letter of Foscarini's to Maffeo Vallaresso that does not appear in the collection of the former is found in Vallaresso's *Epist.,* pp. 595-96 (Venice, 1 June 1471). Foscarini also received letters from Francesco Barbaro (see *Centotrenta,* ed. Sabbadini, indices), Giovanni Mario Filelfo (see *Iter*, II, 485), Francesco Filelfo (*Epist. fam.*, fols. 159ʳ⁻ᵛ, 166ᵛ, 167, 168ᵛ, 175, 187ʳ⁻ᵛ, 196ᵛ-197, 198ʳ⁻ᵛ, 200ᵛ, 220, 231ʳ⁻ᵛ, 237ᵛ, 238, 239ᵛ, 240ᵛ, 243ᵛ-244, 244ᵛ, 247, 250, 252, 253, 256ᵛ, 263ᵛ-264, 265ᵛ), Moro Lapi (*Opera*, fols. 221ᵛ-222ᵛ, 311ᵛ-312), Isotta Nogarola (*Opera omnia*, II, 28-34), and Maffeo Vallaresso (*Epist.*, 586, 593-95).

DISCOURSE. Praised for his learning by Benedetto Bursa (in his oration for Foscarini, the first of the *Orationes tres*); Ciriaco d'Ancona (*Itinerarium*, ed. L. Mehus, p. 18); and Francesco Pisani (*Oratio de universae philosophiae ornamentis*, p. 266), among others (Agostini, *Notizie*, I, 101). Antonio Baratella dedicated to Foscarini his *Diasodia* (Picotti, "Le lettere," [1955], p. 221 n. 3); Battista Mantovano his verse *Parthenice* (cf. *Iter*, II, 162, but perhaps doubtful; the work is dated 1481, after Foscarini's death); Bernardino Bononigena his *Epistolarum atque epigrammatum libellus*; Giovanni Jacopo Cane his verse *De ludo equestri Patavii*; Francesco Diedo his translation of Isocrates' *De bello et pace* (1471); Giorgio Merula his edition of Cicero's *De finibus* (see F. Gabotto and A. Badini Confalonieri, "La vita di Giorgio Merula," first part, p. 59); for others, see also Picotti, "Lettere" [1955], p. 221 n. 3). Foscarini participated in learned circles in Verona and Friuli while posted to those cities (Agostini, *Notizie*, I, 58, 73). He appears as an interlocutor in Nogarola's dialogue *De pari aut impari Adae atque Evae peccato*; see the discussions in Gothein, "L'amicizia," and King, "Religious Retreat," pp. 818ff. He was particularly interested in the writing of Venetian history, and was a leader in the search for a public historiographer, supporting at different times Flavio Biondo, Porcellio Pandoni (Napoletano), and Jacopo Ragazzoni (see A. Pertusi, "Gli inizi della storiografia umanistica," pp. 291ff., 298, 300ff.; F. Gilbert, "Biondo, Sabellico," pp. 277ff.; F. Gaeta, "Storiografia, coscienza nazionale," pp. 30ff.).

EDUCATION. Arts at Padua under Paolo Veneto and Prosdocimo de' Conti (cf. Gothein, "Paolo Veneto"); doctorate 27 Jan. 1429 (Zonta and Brotto, *Acta*, p. 158, #171). There he remained as a student of law, receiving his doctorate on 22 Aug. 1434 (ibid., pp. 226-227, #1010; for his frequent presence at the university in these years, see indices; for his knowledge of law, see M. Foscarini, *Lett. ven.*, p. 70).

Frulovisi, Tito Livio. (2) Forliviensis, de' Frulovisi, de Frulovisiis. Son of Domenico.

MONOGRAPHS AND STUDIES. F. Battaglia, "Il trattato 'De republica' di Tito Livio de' Frulovisi"; G. Padoan, "La commedia rinascimentale a Venezia," pp. 377-84; C. W. Previté-Orton, introduction to his edition of *Opera hactenus inedita Titi Livii de Frulovisiis de Ferrara*, pp. ix-xxxvii; R. Sabbadini, "Tito Livio Frulovisio umanista del secolo XV"; A. Stäuble, *La commedia umanistica del Quattrocento* (biographical profile, pp. 51-52, followed by synopses of the plays to p. 66, and bibliography, p. 260) and "Le sette commedie dell'umanista Tito Livio de' Frulovisi"; L. Walther, "Titus Livius de' Frulovisi—ein humanistischer Dramatiker der Renaissance"; R. Weiss, "Humphrey of Gloucester and Tito Livio Frulovisi." See these works for other studies and discussions.

CAREER. B. Ferrara, c. 1400. D. perhaps 1464. Born in Ferrara and exiled to Verona, Frulovisi was brought by his father to Venice c. 1404 when still a child, and studied there with Guarino Veronese. He completed his studies in Padua, qualifying as a notary, then taught in Venice in the parish of San Basso from 1429. In that year he was granted citizenship *de intus et extra*, along with his brothers, after fifteen years of residence, on 27 Sept.: Senato-Privilegi, R. 2, c. 10ᵛ. He continued to teach, interrupting his stay to travel to Florence, Rome, and Naples. He composed in this period the first five of his comedies and his *De republica* (addressed to the ruler of Ferrara with the aim of re-establishing himself in the city of his birth). From 1435, he resumed his wanderings, journeying first to the East, then to England, where, aided by the Venetian Pietro del Monte resident there as papal representative, he joined the household of Duke Humphrey of Gloucester and in 1437 acquired citizenship. In ensuing years, Frulovisi resided in Venice once again (1438-40, 1447), in Milan, at the University of Toulouse, where he received his doctorate in arts and medicine, and in Barcelona, where he practiced medicine. His career remains obscure for many years until his 1456 reappearance in Venice, where he probably stayed until his death in 1464.

WORKS. Frulovisi's works are amply reviewed in the studies cited; see most conveniently Stäuble, "Sette commedie," p. 25. Here it will be sufficient to note these published in *Opera hactenus inedita*: the *De republica*, to Leonello d'Este, and the seven comedies. Frulovisi denied the charge (Stäuble, *Commedia umanistica*, p. 65) that he had plagiarized a work of Jacopo Languschi's.

CORRESPONDENCE. Letters from Leonardo Bruni (reprinted with those of del Monte and those to and from Decembrio in Sabbadini, pp. 73-81), Ludovico Foscarini (*Epist.*, fols. 169ᵛ-172, 175-76, 191-92, 196ᵛ-197, 198-90) and Pietro del Monte (also in J. Haller, *Pier da Monte*, pp. 96, 63), and to and from Pier Candido Decembrio (see also V. Zaccaria, "L'epistolario di Pier Candido Decembrio," p. 106).

DISCOURSE. The relatively obscure personage of Frulovisi is actually of first importance as a social theorist (in his *De republica*), where he constitutes a link in the chain from Marsilio of Padua to Machiavelli, and as the author of the first comedies in the classical tradition to be actually performed in Italy, and thus as an author of profound significance for the history of the theater.

EDUCATION. With Guarino Veronese during the latter's 1414-19 stay in Venice.

Giorgi, Domenico. (2) Giorgio, Zorzi, Georgius. Son of Vinciguerra.

CAREER. B. c. 1407 (AC-BO 162/I, c. 147; presented 17 or 18 Oct. 1425). M. 1436, Francesca di Andrea Contarini (Giomo, *Matrimoni*, I, 266). D. after

13 May 1478 (when he was present in Venice and among the electors of Doge Giovanni Mocenigo, see below; he died not long afterwards while provveditore in Friuli). Giorgi's political career begins by at least 11 May 1438, when he was numbered among the members of the Council of Forty (SGV 4, c. 107), and he appears in the documents intermittently in the ensuing years in other lesser offices.

Offices. 1452, Sav. tf. (SGV 4, c. 147ᵛ); 1457, Sav. tf. (SM 6; ST 4, c. 35); 1458-59, Sav. tf. (SGV 4, c. 166; SM 6; ST 4); 1459, Sav. tf. (SM 6; ST 4); 1461, Sav. tf. (ST 4, c. 180ᵛ); 1462, Duc. el., Cristoforo Moro (MC-Regina, c. 39); Sav. tf. (SM 7; ST 5); 1463, Sav. tf. (SM 7; ST 5); 1464, Sav. tf. (ST 5); 1465, Sav. gr. (ST 5, c. 114); 1465-66, Cons. (CLN 10; CXM 16; MC-Regina; SM 8; ST 5); 1466, CX (CXM 17); 1467, Capt. of Verona (CLN 10, c. 161ᵛ; SGV 6, c. 16ᵛ); 1469, Avog. (CXM 17; SGV 6, c. 7; SM 9); Capt. of Padua (SGV 6, cc. 7, 50ᵛ); 1470, Cons. (SGV 6, c. 1ᵛ); 1471, Sav. gr. (ST 6); 1471-72, CX (CXM 17); 1471, Duc. el., Niccolò Tron (MC-Regina, cc. 101ᵛ, 102, 102ᵛ); 1472, Sav. gr. (ST 6, c. 153ᵛ); 1473, Cons. (CLN 11; CXM 18; MC-Regina; ST 7); 1474, Cons. (CLN 12); Sav. gr. (ST 7); 1475, CX (CXM 18); Sav. gr. (ST 7); 1476, Duc. el., Andrea Vendramin (MC-Regina, cc. 157, 157ᵛ); Sav. gr. (SM 10); 1476-77, Cons. (CLN 12; CXM 19; MC-Regina; ST 7); 1477, Sind. in Cyprus (CLN 12, cc. 58ᵛ, 61); 1477-78, Sav. gr. (CLN 12; CXM 19; SM 10; ST 8); 1478, Duc. el., Giovanni Mocenigo (MC-Regina, cc. 177ᵛ, 178); Prov. in Friuli (Malipiero, Annali, p. 112, which gives the year incorrectly as 1477; F. Gabotto and A. B. Confalonieri, "Vita di Giorgio Merula," first part, p. 284, following Sabellico, report that Giorgi died in this position).

DISCOURSE. Praised as wise by Ludovico Foscarini (Epist., fol. 174ᵛ). Antonio Broianico dedicated to Giorgi his De divina origine rei publicae venetorum; Domizio Calderini his De origine florentissimae reipublicae venetorum (see Cosenza, Dict., II, 1584); Giovanni Michele Alberto da Carrara his Liber stromathum (ibid., and Zeno, Diss. voss., II, 31); Giovanni Merula the comment on Columella in his Scriptores rei rusticae (Gabotto and Confalonieri, "Vita di Giorgio Merula," first part, p. 60).

Giuliani, Andrea. (1) Giuliano, Zulian, Julianus. Son of Francesco.

MONOGRAPHS AND STUDIES. S. Troilo, Andrea Giuliano, politico e letterato veneziano del Quattrocento; G. degli Agostini, Notizie, I, 257-68.

CAREER. B. c. 1384. M. 1401, Cristina di Niccolò Donato; 1415, Teodora Garzoni; c. 1434, Maria Dolfin. D. between 9 July and 26 Nov. 1452. Minor offices from 1408.

Offices. 1417-18, Sav. tf.; 1421, Capt. of Rovigo; 1423, Duc. el. (Francesco Foscari); 1423-25, Prov. of the citadel in Verona (with absences as noted by Troilo, Andrea Giuliano, pp. 44ff.); 1426, Amb. to the Bishop of Trent; 1426-27, Amb. to the Duke of Mantua; 1427, again Prov. of the citadel in Verona; 1428, Prov., mission to take possession of castles near Brescia and Bergamo;

1431-33, Prov. in Bergamo (interrupted by alternative assignments, as noted ibid., pp. 78ff.); 1435-36, Capt. of Brescia; 1437, Amb. to King Alfonso of Aragon; CX; 1438, Cons.; 1438-39, Amb. with Gattamelata, Capt. Gen. of the army; 1439, Sav. tf.; 1440, Vice-Capt. of Padua; 1441-42, Capt. of Bergamo; 1446-47, Cons.; 1447-48, Pod. of Bergamo; Cons.

WORKS. Four orations: 1. *Pro Manuele Chrysolora funebris oratio* (1415); 2. *Super principio orationum M. Tullii Ciceronis ad auditores* (1413); 3. *Pro civibus Veronensibus apud Thomam Mocenigo Venetorum ducem* (1414); 4. *In laudem corporis Jesu Christi* (end 1408-1409). All four orations appear in a single manuscript, not seen by me: Padua, Bibl. Antoniana, cod. Antonianus V. 90, fols. 7-10ᵛ. The first (published many times), second, and fourth I have seen in the printed editions given in the Bibliography. Giuliani is known by the testimony of Guarino to have written a fifth oration on the death of his uncle Paolo Giuliani; see Troilo, *Andrea Giuliano*, pp. 184ff. *Tabula in Eusebii Chronicon*, a lexicographical work based on Jerome's translation, not seen (Vat. Ottob. Lat. 473). Sansovino and followers attribute a translation of Dio Cassius, rejected by Troilo (pp. 190-91).

CORRESPONDENCE. Substantial correspondence with Gasparino Barzizza and Guarino Veronese (reviewed by Troilo, *Andrea Giuliano*, especially pp. x-xi for sources, 9ff. for Barzizza, and 28ff. for Guarino; see also the letters of Barzizza to Giuliani published by L. Bertalot, "Die älteste Briefsammlung des Gasparinus Barzizza," pp. 58-66). Letters from Francesco Barbaro (Troilo, pp. 195-96), Francesco Filelfo (*Epist. fam.*, fols. 3ᵛ-4), Leonardo Giustiniani (R. Sabbadini, "Sugli studi volgari di Leonardo Giustiniani," pp. 370-71), Pietro del Monte (J. Haller, *Pier da Monte*, p. 90), and Cristoforo de Scarpis (Troilo, pp. 197-98); letter to Pietro Donato (ibid., 166 n. 3).

DISCOURSE. Praised by Flavio Biondo (*It. illus.* [Venice, 1510], fol. 101ᵛ), and for the widely read oration for Chrysoloras by Barzizza (*Opera*, ed. J. A. Furiettus, p. 210), Guarino (*Epist.*, ed. Sabbadini, I, 81-83), and Poggio Bracciolini (*Epist.*, ed. Tonellis, I, 22-25; to Guarino). Expounded some of the orations of Cicero in Venice in 1413 (to which exercise the second of the orations listed above was a prelude). Niccolò Leonardi addressed to Giuliani with Francesco Barbaro his *Oratio in funere magistri Andreae phisici venetiarum*. Pietro del Monte addressed to Giuliani his *Invectiva adversus ridiculum quendam oratorem* (dedication in Troilo, *Andrea Giuliano*, pp. 198-200), and included him as one of the interlocutors in his dialogue *De vitiorum inter se differencia et comparatione*. Personally assisted del Monte and his family (see the latter's letter, cited above). Close friend and probably co-student of Daniele Vitturi. Close to Poggio and Bartolommeo da Montepulciano, whom he met in Constance in 1417 while all were attending the Council there at the time of the famous St. Gallen manuscript discoveries. Giuliani exchanged texts with Barzizza and Guarino, and was one of those who helped diffuse the manuscripts Guarino had discovered. Also transcribed from Poggio's copy a manuscript of Ascanius Pedianus (see Cosenza, *Dict.*, II, 1864) which the Florentine had discovered in Switzerland.

EDUCATION. With Barzizza (intermittently from 1407 to 1410, beginning at the advanced age of twenty-three), Lorenzo de' Monaci, and Guarino (Troilo, *Andrea Giuliano*, pp. 9ff., 163ff.).

Giustiniani, Bernardo. (2) Giustinian, Giustiniano, Zustignan, Justinianus. Son of Leonardo; grandfather of Marco Dandolo (see Ermolao Barbaro G, *Epist.*, ed. Branca, II, 48-49); also related to Lauro and Taddeo Quirini (see Labalme, *Bernardo Giustiniani*, pp. 94-95), and Carlo and Jacopo Zeno (see M. Dazzi, *Leonardo Giustiniani*, p. 35). Miles.

MONOGRAPHS AND STUDIES. P. H. Labalme, *Bernardo Giustiniani: A Venetian of the Quattrocento*. See this thorough monograph for further bibliography.

CAREER. B. 6 January 1408. M. 1433, Elisabetta di Giovanni Priuli (Giomo, *Matrimoni*, II, 264). Testament, 5 March 1489 (P. H. Labalme, "The Last Will of a Venetian Patrician"). D. 10 March 1489. Bernardo, like his father, pursued commercial and political activities at the same time; see Labalme, *Bernardo Giustiniani*, pp. 55ff., 75ff. Traces of that commercial activity also appear sporadically in archival documents; see, for instance, CLN 10, c. 68ᵛ and 78ᵛ, and ST 6, c. 160. See Labalme's full discussion of Bernardo's diplomatic career and the orations delivered on occasions associated with it on pp. 135ff. The contemporary homonym Bernardo Giustiniani di Niccolò appears from the 1480s.

Offices. 1452, Amb. to greet Emperor Frederick III; 1456, Sav. tf. (SGV 4, c. 147; SM 5; ST 4); 1457, Sav. tf. (SGV 4, c. 147ᵛ; SM 6; ST 4, c. 41ᵛ); Duc. el., Pasquale Malipiero (MC-Regina, cc. 17ᵛ, 39ᵛ); 1458, Sav. tf., two terms (SGV 4, c. 147ᵛ; SM 6; ST 4, c. 81ᵛ); 1458-59, Sav. tf. (SGV 4, c. 166); Amb. to Rome and Naples; 1459, Sav. tf.; 1459-60, CX (CXM 15, c. 189ᵛ and passim; held part of the time concurrently with the previous office); 1460, Sav. tf., two terms (SM 6; ST 4, c. 147); 1461, Sav. tf. (SM 7); 1461-62, Amb. to France (a famous embassy, performed jointly with Paolo Barbo; yet he had been reluctant to go, and was admonished, ". . . propter dictam legationem intelligatur persona publica et non privata" [CLN 10, c. 37ᵛ]); 1462, Duc. el., Cristoforo Moro (MC-Regina, c. 39ᵛ); Sav. tf. (ST 5); CX (CXM 16, c. 77 and passim); 1462-63, Amb. to Rome; 1463, Cons. (CLN 10, c. 87ᵛ); 1464, Sav. gr. (SM 7); 1464-65, Avog. (CLN 10, c. 136; CXM 16); 1466, Amb. to Rome; 1467, Sav. gr. (SM 8); Capt. of Padua; 1468, Prov. in Lombardy; 1469, Cons. (CLN 11; CXM 17; MC-Regina; SM 9; ST 6); 1469-70, Sav. gr. (SM 9; ST 6); 1470, Amb. to Naples; Sav. gr. (ST 6); 1470-71, CX (CXM 17); 1471, Sav. gr. (SM 9; ST 6, c. 115ᵛ; held part of the time concurrently with the previous office); 1471-72, Amb. to Rome; 1472, Sav. gr. (CXM 17, 18; SM 9); 1472-73, Cons. (CLN 11; CXM 17; MC-Regina; SM 9; ST 6); 1473, Duc. el., Niccolò Marcello (MC-Regina, cc. 122ᵛ, 123,

123ᵛ); Amb. to Ferrara; 1473-74, Sav. gr. (CLN 11, c. 172ᵛ; SM 9); 1474, Sav. gr. (ST 7, c. 42); Duc. el., Pietro Mocenigo (MC-Regina, cc. 143, 145ᵛ); Proc. di San Marco (for life); 1474-75, Sav. gr. (SM 10); 1475, Sav. gr. (SM 10; ST 7, c. 75ᵛ); 1476, Duc. el., Andrea Vendramin (MC-Regina, c. 157, 157ᵛ); Sav. gr. (SM 10); 1477, Prov. in Friuli; Sav. gr. (SM 10; ST 7, c. 160ᵛ); 1477-78, Sav. gr. (ST 7, c. 187); 1478, Sav. gr. (SM 10, c. 159 and passim; ST 8); Cons. (MC-Regina); Duc. el., Giovanni Mocenigo (MC-Regina, cc. 177ᵛ, 178); 1479, Sav. gr. (CXM 19; SM 11); 1479-80, Sav. gr. (ST 8); 1480, Sav. gr. (SM 11); 1481, Sav. gr. (ST 8); 1482-83, Sav. gr. (CLN 13; SM 11; ST 8, c. 180); 1483-84, Sav. gr. (SM 11, 12; ST 9); 1484, Sav. gr. (ST 9, c. 73ᵛ); 1485, Amb. to Milan (CXM 22, cc. 130, 137, 147, 148, 148ᵛ-149, 151ᵛ-152; ST 9, c. 154); Duc. el., Marco Barbarigo (MC-Stella, c. 61ᵛ); 1485-86, Sav. gr. (SM 12; ST 9, c. 154); 1486, Duc. el., Agostino Barbarigo (MC-Stella, cc. 76, 76ᵛ, 77ᵛ); Sav. gr. (SM 12); Sav. gr. (ST 10, c. 34); 1487, Sav. gr. (SM 12; ST 10); 1488, Sav. gr. (ST 10).

WORKS. *De divi Marci Evangelistae vita, translatione et sepulturae loco; De origine urbis Venetiarum rebusque gestis a Venetis libri quindecim; Vita beati Laurentii Justiniani Venetiarum protopatriarchae* (I have seen the version cited in the Bibliography, not having found the modern edition of I. Tassi [Rome: Officina Poligrafica Laziale, 1962]); *Orationes et epistolae*, including among the orations those most interesting in this context, the *Oratio funebris habita in obitu Francisci Fuscari Ducis* (1457); the *Oratio pro militia ad regem Franciae Ludovicum* (Tours, 1462); the *Oratio apud Paulum Secundum Pontificem Maximum* (1466); trans., Isocrates' *Ad Nicoclem*, to Ludovico Gonzaga. For further bibliographical information, see Labalme, *Bernardo Giustiniani*, pp. 332ff., who discusses specific works fully. For the *De origine*, see in addition to Labalme the analysis of F. Gaeta, "Storiografia, conscienza nazionale," pp. 45-65. The orations named are available in other editions than that of the *Orat. et epist*; some are cited in Bibliography. Giustiniani's other major works were also published often.

CORRESPONDENCE. Of Bernardo's epistolary relations, of special interest here are those with Sebastiano Bursa, Pietro Dolfin, Francesco Filelfo, Ludovico Foscarini, George of Trebizond, Leonardo Giustiniani, Girolamo Guarini, Pietro Perleone, Ambrogio Traversari, and Jacopo Zeno. Labalme provides a chronological list of Bernardo's letters, including some not in his *Orat. et epist.*, on pp. 321ff.

DISCOURSE. Bernardo was widely reputed for his learning and oratorical skills. He received the dedications of works by Giovanni Jacopo Cane, Justinianus Luzagus, Giorgio Merula, and Raffaele Regio (see Labalme, *Bernardo Giustiniani*, p. 326). He patronized George of Trebizond (J. Monfasani, *George of Trebizond*, pp. 46-47), Giovanni Mario Filelfo (Labalme, *Bernardo Giustiniani*, p. 102), Giorgio Merula (p. 104), Pietro Perleone (pp. 65ff.), perhaps Benedetto Brognoli (to whom Giustiniani gave principal responsibility for the posthumous edition of his *De origine urbis Venetiarum*; ibid., pp. 256-57), among others.

EDUCATION. With Cristoforo de Scarpis, Francesco Filelfo, and Guarino Veronese; perhaps studied arts and law at Padua.

Giustiniani, Leonardo. (1) Giustinian, Giustiniano, Zustignan, Justinianus. Son of Bernardo; father of Bernardo; also related to Lauro and Taddeo Quirini (P. H. Labalme, *Bernardo Giustiniani*, pp. 94-95), and to Carlo and Jacopo Zeno (M. Dazzi, *Leonardo Giustinian*, p. 35).

MONOGRAPHS AND STUDIES. G. Billanovich, "Per l'edizione critica delle canzonette di Leonardo Giustiniani" and "Alla scoperta di Leonardo Giustiniani"; M. Dazzi's three studies "Documenti su Leonardo Giustinian"; *Leonardo Giustinian, poeta populare d'amore, con una scelta di sue poesie*; "Leonardo Giustinian (1338-1446)"; B. Fenigstein, *Leonardo Giustiniani (1383?-1446), venetianischer Staatsmann, Humanist und Vulgärdichter*; M. Morici, *Per gli epistolari di due discepoli e di un amico di Guarino Guarini (Sassolo da Prato—Ciriaco d'Ancona—Leonardo Giustiniani)*; A. Oberdorfer's four studies: "Per l'edizione critica delle canzonette di Leonardo Giustiniano," "L'epistolario di Leonardo Giustiniano," "Di Leonardo Giustiniano umanista," and "Le 'Regulae artificialis memoriae' di Leonardo Giustiniano"; R. Sabbadini, "Sugli studi volgari di Leonardo Giustiniani." See also G. degli Agostini, *Notizie*, I, 135-76. See these studies for further bibliographical information.

CAREER. B. c. 1389. M. 1405, Lucrezia di Bernardo da Mula. D. 10 Nov. 1446; see Giustiniani's humble epitaph in Cicogna, *Iscrizioni*, II, 71, trans. in Labalme, *Bernardo Giustiniani*, p. 89. Fenigstein and Dazzi's studies are most fruitful for Giustiniani's career and have been used below. For the Giustiniani family's commercial activities, see Labalme, pp. 55ff., 75ff. Evidence of that commercial activity is also found in archival documents (see, for example, SM 1, cc. 23^v-24, SM 2, c. 111^v), and Leonardo's letter to King Alfonso regarding some captured ships (in B. Giustiniani, *Orat. et epist.*, sigs. L7^v-L8).

Offices. 1420, Avog.; 1421, Prov. in Friuli (MC-Ursa, c. 33); 1427, Sav. tf. (SMS 56, c. 108); 1427-28, CX (CXM 10); 1428, Sav. tf. (SMS 57, c. 46^v); 1430, Avog. (CXM 11); Sav. tf. (SMS 57, c. 224^v); 1430-31, Sav. tf. (SMS 58, c. 21); 1431, Avog. (SMS 58); Sav. tf. (SMS 58); 1432, Sav. tf. (SMS 58, c. 127); Lt. in Friuli (where he hosted Ciriaco d'Ancona [cf. Dazzi, *Leonardo Giustinian*, p. 37; Labalme, *Bernardo Giustiniani*, p. 55] and on leaving was celebrated in an oration of Giovanni da Spilimbergo [in G. B. Contarini, *Anec. ven.*, pp. 83-85]); 1433, Sav. gr., two terms (SMS 58, c. 189^v; 59, c. 7); 1434, Avog. (CLN 6; CXM 11; SMS 59); 1435, CX (CXM 11); Sav. gr. (SMS 59, c. 102^v; held concurrently with previous office); 1436, Amb. to Mantua; Sav. gr. (SMS 59, c. 150); 1436-37, Sav. gr. (SMS 59, c. 177^v); CX (CXM 11, 12; held concurrently with previous office); 1437, Sav. gr., two terms (SMS 60, cc. 5ᵛ, 38); 1438, Sav. gr. (SMS 60); 1438-39, Sav. gr. (SMS 60, c. 104ᵛ); CX (CXM 12; SGV 4, c. 108; held concurrently with previous office); 1439, Sav. gr., two terms (SMS 60, cc. 135, 171ᵛ); 1440, Sav. gr. (SM 1; SMS 60, c. 204); 1440-41, Sav. gr. (SM 1; ST 1, c. 1); 1441, Sav. gr., two terms (SM 1; ST 1, cc. 19, 44); 1442, Cons. (CLN 7; CXM 12; MC-Ursa; SGV 4, c. 103; SM 1; ST 1); 1442-43, Sav. gr. (ST 1, cc. 83ᵛ, 84ᵛ); 1443, Amb. to Naples; 1443, Sav. gr. (SM 1; ST 1, c. 91ᵛ); Proc. di San Marco; 1443-44, Sav. gr. (SM 1; ST 1, c. 108); 1445, Sav. gr. (SM 2; ST 1); 1445-46, Sav. gr. (ST 1, c. 167 and passim).

WORKS. *Funebris oratio pro Carolo Zeno* (1418; for other mss. and printed versions, cf. G. Zonta, introduction to Jacopo Zeno's *Vita Caroli Zeni*, x, n. 6); *Funebris oratio ad Georgium Lauredanum; Proemium in leges et statuta Pergami* (1420; written while Giustiniani's brother was podestà of Bergamo; see *explicit*, fol. 65ᵛ); *Regulae artificialis memoriae*; trans., Plutarch's lives of Cimon and Lucullus, to Henry Lusignan, king of Cyprus, and of Phocion, to Marco Giustiniani (see V. R. Giustiniani, "Sulle traduzioni latine delle 'vite' di Plutarco nel Quattrocento," pp. 32, 36; also A. Pertusi, "Umanesimo greco," pp. 195ff., 205ff.; Giustiniani did not translate Cato the Younger); trans., *Vita beati Nicolai Myrensis Episcopi*, to Lorenzo Giustiniani. *Epistolae*, in B. Giustiniani, *Orat. et epist.*, sigs. K-K4ᵛ, L2ʳ⁻ᵛ, L4-L8; in G. B. Contarini, *Anec. ven.*, pp. 71-91; in A. Oberdorfer, "Alcune lettere inedite," pp. 311-18. See the summary table of correspondence in Oberdorfer, "L'epistolario," and the discussion in Fenigstein, *Leonardo Giustiniani*, pp. 42ff. P. O. Kristeller has informed me that a critical edition of the *epistolario* is in progress. Giustiniani's letters, to use Oberdorfer's phrase, are "fra le più sincere e spontanee del secolo" ("Di Leonardo Giustiniano," p. 118). For Giustiniani's secular and religious verse, of great power and importance, see the studies cited above, especially Dazzi's *Leonardo Giustinian*, Fenigstein's *Leonardo Giustiniani*, and Oberdorfer's "Per l'edizione critica"; also an update in A. Tissoni-Benvenuti, "Venezia e il veneto," p. 287, #71. Not Giustiniani, as Cicogna suggested in his "Della Leandreide, poema anonimo inedito," but Gian Girolamo de' Natali was the author of the *Leandreide*.

CORRESPONDENCE. With, most notably among others, Francesco Barbaro, Gasparino Barzizza, Benedetto Bursa, Federico Corner, Francesco Filelfo, Andrea Giuliani, Bernardo Giustiniani, Guarino Veronese, Barbone Morosini, Marco Nigro, Lauro Quirini, Palla Strozzi, Pietro Tommasi, and Ambrogio Traversari.

DISCOURSE. Giustiniani was widely reputed for his learning, even more so for his involvement in the literary life of his age, engaging in discourse with humanists abroad as well as at home, and patronizing foreign professional humanists. For Giustiniani's relations with Traversari in particular, see C. Stinger, *Humanism and the Church Fathers*, index. For his patronage of Guarino Veronese, Francesco Filelfo, Cristoforo de Scarpis, and George of

Trebizond, see Labalme, *Bernardo Giustiniani,* pp. 17ff.; for relations to Filelfo see now D. Robin, "A Reassessment of the Character of Francesco Filelfo." For his patronage of Sebastiano Bursa, see Niccolò Sagundino, *Epist. et opusc.,* fol. 74. He acquired an excellent library of Greek and Latin mss. (see Dazzi, *Leonardo Giustinian,* pp. 31ff.; R. Sabbadini, *Le scoperte dei codici latini e greci,* I, 64; also Tommasi's letter to Giustiniani in Contarini, *Anec. ven.,* p. 86). The library included a valuable Petrarch ms. (P. de Nolhac, *La Bibliothèque de Fulvio Orsini,* pp. 279-80).

EDUCATION. With Guarino Veronese and Gasparino Barzizza.

Lando, Vitale. (2) Landus. Son of Marino. Doctor, miles.

MONOGRAPHS AND STUDIES. G. degli Agostini, *Notizie,* I, 542-47.

CAREER. B. c. 1421 (AC-BO 163/II, c. 294; presented 7 Oct. 1439). M. 1452, Elisabetta di Paolo Zane (Giomo, *Matrimoni,* II, 491; the sister of Lorenzo Zane). D. after 31 May 1482 when, confined in Vicenza, he was granted permission to take the baths for his health (CXM 20, c. 132); but before 21 Sept. 1485, the date of a privilege granted his son Marino (ST 9, c. 162) in which Lando is mentioned as already dead.
   Offices. 1452-54, Amb. to Siena (ST 3, cc. 37ᵛ, 95); 1456, Amb. to the Duke of Modena (ST 3, cc. 182, 188); 1456-57, Sav. tf. (SGV 4, c. 147; SM 5, 6; ST 4); 1458, Sav. tf. (SGV 4, c. 147ᵛ; SM 6; ST 4, c. 71 and passim); 1461, Amb. to the Pope (ST 4, cc. 163 and 165); 1461-62, Pod. and Capt. of Ravenna (SGV 5, c. 7; CXM 16; SM 7); 1463, Sav. tf. (SM 7; ST 5); Prov. with the army, siege of Trieste (ST 5, c. 57); 1464, Sav. tf. (SM 7; ST 5); CX (CXM 16); 1465, Sav. tf. (SM 8; ST 5); 1465-66, Sav. tf. (as above); 1466, Cons. (CLN 10; CXM 16; MC-Regina; SM 8; ST 5); 1467-68, Capt. of Brescia (SGV 6, c. 91; CXM 17; ST 5); 1468-69, Avog. (CLN 11; CXM 17; SGV 6, c. 7; SM 9; ST 6); 1468, one of 12 honorary ambs. to the Emperor (on this occasion, he delivered the oration cited below); 1469-70, Sav. tf. (CXM 17; ST 6, c. 80); 1470, Sav. gr. (CXM 17; SM 9; ST 6); 1470-71, Pod. of Verona (SGV 6, c. 16ᵛ; ST 6); 1471, Duc. el., Niccolò Tron; CX (CXM 17); 1472-73, Avog. (SGV 6, c. 7; CLN 11; CXM 17, 18); 1473, Duc. el., Niccolò Marcello (MC-Regina, cc. 122ᵛff); Amb. to Duke of Milan; 1474, Sav. gr. (CLN 11; ST 7); Duc. el., Pietro Mocenigo; 1474-75, Sav. gr. (SM 10; ST 7); 1475-76, Lt. di Friuli (SGV 6, c. 49ᵛ; ST 7); 1476, Sav. gr. (SM 10; ST 7); 1476-77, CX (CXM 18, 19); 1477, Sav. gr. (two terms) (CLN 12; SM 10; ST 7); 1478, Cons. (CLN 12; CXM 19; MC-Regina; SM 10); *Condemnation by the Council of Ten for betrayal of public secrets.* Lando's case was discussed in the CX from July through Sept. 1478 (CXM 19, cc. 79ff); he was condemned on 28 Aug. (c. 84ʳ⁻ᵛ); further consideration was given on 23 Feb. 1481 and 31 May 1482 (CXM 20, cc. 46ᵛ, 131ᵛ-132). A description of the charges and circumstances appears in Malipiero, *Annali,* pp. 668-70. Lando was implicated with his brother-in-law Lorenzo Zane.

PROFILES

WORKS. *Oratio ad Caesarem Augustum Imperatorem* (1468). Sansovino (*Venetia*, II, 577) also attributes *Quaestiones miscellaneae super potissimas philosophiae difficultates*.

CORRESPONDENCE. Letters from Giovanni Mario Filelfo (Vat. Chis. J VII 241, fols. 39ʳ⁻ᵛ; 120ᵛ-121ᵛ); Ludovico Foscarini (*Epist.*, fols. 203ʳ⁻ᵛ, 335ᵛ-339ᵛ); Pietro Perleone (with his *epistolae*, fols. 177-78ᵛ); Maffeo Vallaresso (*Epist.*, p. 233; alludes also to earlier correspondence with Lando).

DISCOURSE. Celebrated for his learning by Flavio Biondo (*It. illus.* [Venice, 1510], fol. 101). His learning is also commended by Foscarini (in the first of the letters above, fol. 203ᵛ) and alluded to by Perleone (in the letter above, fols. 177, 178ᵛ), while Niccolò Leonico Tomeo refers to Lando (alongside Bernardo Giustiniani, a humanist of first rank) as one of Venice's great orators and senators (*Dialogi*, p. 73). Also praised by Piero Carrari da Monselice, Jacopo Franco, and Michele Buono; see Agostini, *Notizie*, I, 543, 544, 547. Great confidence was placed by contemporaries in his legal knowledge and prudence. Lando was asked to arbitrate in 1456, in the controversy between Venice and Borso d'Este, duke of Modena and marquis of Ferrara; see Foscarini, *Lett. ven.*, p. 71; and in 1457, in the controversy between Vicenza and Verona; ST 4, c. 45. Bartolomeo Gerardino of Brescia addressed to Lando a poem against Ludovico Lazzarelli (see *Iter*, I, 418). Lando was among the patrician supporters of Pietro Perleone (see the *epistolae* cited) and Raffaele Zovenzoni (B. Ziliotto, *Raffaele Zonvenzoni*, pp. 26, 48). As *consigliere* on 1 Jan. 1467, Lando argued in favor of Theodore Gaza rather than Benedetto Brognoli as a replacement for Filippo Morandi da Rimini in Venice's San Marco school (CLN 10, c. 146ᵛ).

EDUCATION. Studying at Padua by 15 Dec. 1442 (when present as "utriusque iuris scolaris vicerector iuristarum"; Zonta and Brotto, *Acta*, p. 340, #1671), Lando received his doctorate in laws and arts on 6 and 7 Sept., respectively, 1445 (ibid., 388, #1969, and 389, #1970).

Languschi, Jacopo. (1) de' Languschi, de Langusco. Son of Giovanni "da Pavia."

MONOGRAPHS AND STUDIES. A. Segarizzi, "Jacopo Languschi rimatore veneziano del secolo XV"; also G. dalla Santa, review of this and other Segarizzi works, NAV, NS, 11 (1906), Parte II, 202, and A. Pertusi's sketch in "Lettera di Filippo da Rimini, cancelliere di Corfù, a Francesco Barbaro e i primi documenti occidentali sulla caduta di Costantinopoli," p. 134 n. 58.

CAREER. B. late fourteenth century (based on career record). D. after c. 1465 (Languschi was still alive, presumably, in c. 1465, the date of the composition of Candiano Bollani's *Trialogus* in which Languschi appears, an old man; see Segarizzi, "Jacopo Languschi," p. 181 and below). Born in Venice, son probably of a recent immigrant, Languschi was a practicing notary in Venice by 1409 (thus he appears on 4 Oct.: *Comm.*, ed. Predelli, VII, 334 [= x. #79]), a ducal secretary by 1410 (thus on 30 Dec.: ibid., p. 348 [= x. #116]). Subsequently he was employed by Venice in embassies to Genoa, Udine, Ferrara, and Bologna from 1416 to 1419. Probably in Constantinople in 1422, Languschi subsequently studied arts at Padua, where he taught rhetoric from as early as 1423 until 1431, and received his license in the latter year. In Padua on 15 Nov. 1429 and holding the title of "magister," Languschi was already referred to as a "secretario apostolico" (Zonta and Brotto, *Acta*, p. 164, #743). Later relocated in Rome, he served in the papal chancery under Pope Eugene IV, who granted him some property in the diocese of Padua. Languschi resided in Padua during the 1440s. He may have been in Constantinople in 1453 and witnessed the city's fall (for his report, cited below, inserted in the chronicle of Giorgio Dolfin, see Pertusi, "Lettera," expanding upon F. Babinger in *Johannes Darius*, p. 15 n. 2; see also Pertusi, "Umanesimo greco," p. 245 n. 306).

WORKS. Two sonnets; three orations, not seen (see Segarizzi, "Jacopo Languschi," pp. 180-81 and n. 1); the fragmentary *Excidio e presa di Costantinopoli nell'anno 1453*. Languschi may also have written while at Padua a comedy later plagiarized by Tito Livio Frulovisi (who denied the charge; A. Stäuble, *La commedia umanistica del Quattrocento*, p. 65, and Stäuble, "Le sette commedie dell'umanista Tito Livio de' Frulovisi," p. 44), and a work "super epistolas," sold in 1420 (S. Connell, "Books and Their Owners in Venice," p. 168).

CORRESPONDENCE. Letters to Leonardo Bruni (see Segarizzi, "Jacopo Languschi," p. 181 and n. 3) and Ambrogio Traversari (*Epist.*, ed. Mehus, II, 1005, and *Epist.*, ed. Martène and Durand, col. 726).

DISCOURSE. Praised as an orator by Antonio Baratella (Segarizzi, "Languschi," p. 180; Segarizzi, *Antonio Baratella e i suoi corrispondenti*, p. 112 n. 6) and alluded to as a well-known poet by Francesco Contarini (*Dialogus*, p. 301), Languschi appears as the main speaker in Candiano Bollani's *Trialogus*, where he is portrayed as a knowledgeable philosopher and astrologer. Languschi probably collected manuscript books, having possessed at least one ms. of Vitruvius now in Eton College Library, and having probably copied with Giovanni Aurispa in 1422 in Constantinople a ms. containing Cicero's *De finibus* and *Accademica posteriora* (Connell, "Books and Their Owners," p. 168; *Iter*, II, 415).

EDUCATION. Languschi studied arts (receiving his license on 16 May 1431; Zonta and Brotto, *Acta*, p. 186, #830) and taught rhetoric (as the successor of Gasparino Barzizza) at Padua (Facciolati, *Fasti gymn. pat.*, I.i.53, who reports Languschi's salary as eighty florins; Stäuble, "Sette commedie," p. 44).

Leonardi, Niccolò. (1) De Leonardis. Father of Girolamo.

CAREER. B. c. 1370 (based on Leonardi's university career, his son Eustachio's birth in 1401 [cf. the *Epist. di Guarino Veronese*, ed. Sabbadini, III, 35-37], and on his relations with Barbaro, Giuliani, Tommasi, and others). D. after 1452 (see Guarino's letter to him of 30 Sept.; *Epist.*, II, 577-78). A physician, born to a substantial Venetian family, Leonardi studied at Bologna and Padua, established himself in Venice, returning to Padua as a professor in the 1420s. His wealth can be inferred from his relations with prominent patricians, from his book-collecting activities, and from the status of his son Girolamo, revealed in the latter's testament (AN, Testamenti T. Tomei, B. 1240.183 [15 March 1466]). His family name subsequently appears among the list of *cittadini originari*; cf. da Mosto, *Archivio*, I, 75. He was admitted to the Venetian College of physicians, perhaps in 1392, in which year Traversari congratulates Leonardi for an unstated honor (*Epist. di Pier Paolo Vergerio*, ed. L. Smith, pp. 87-89). Leonardi was ill in his later years, having lost his sight by 1437 (Vergerio, *Epist.*, pp. 395-98; P. Perleone, *Epist. cons. ad Nicolaum Sagundinum*, p. 88).

WORK. *Oratio in funere Magistri Andreae Phisici Venetiarum*, to Francesco Barbaro and Andrea Giuliani. The *oratio* is, in the version I have seen, in the form of a letter addressed to the two patricians. The work was perhaps originally delivered in the form of an oration, then revised.

CORRESPONDENCE. Correspondence with Francesco Barbaro (in C. Griggio, "Codice berlinese," pp. 157-63), Guarino Veronese (*Epist.*, I, 110, 111, 304-306; II, 565-66, 577-78), Ambrogio Traversari (in L. Bertalot, "Zwölf Briefe des Ambrogio Traversari," pp. 253-57; cf. also the letter of Jacopo Languschi to Traversari referring to Leonardi in Traversari's *Epist.*, ed. Mehus, II, 1005, and *Epist.*, ed. Martène and Durand, col. 726), and Pier Paolo Vergerio (*Epist.*, pp. 87-89, 303-304, 307-308, 311-312, 319-21, 321-22, 360-62, 395-98; that on 360-62 is the famous one from Constance, 3 April 1417, praising Francesco Barbaro's *De re uxoria*).

DISCOURSE. Leonardi was a member of Venice's early humanist circle, having particularly close relations to Barbaro and Pietro Tommasi, to the foreigners George of Trebizond and Guarino Veronese during their early-century years of residence, and to the humanists Vergerio and Traversari outside of Venice. His learning is celebrated by Lauro Quirini (in the 1445 *Oratio in laudibus Jeronimi de Leonardi veneti, graduati Padue*, fol. 193ᵛ), who ranks him with other pioneering humanists of the elder generation. He collected Greek manuscripts, employing George of Trebizond, perhaps among others, as scribe (cf. J. Monfasani, *George of Trebizond*, p. 10; Pertusi, "Umanesimo greco," pp. 204, 230). Leonardi owned one of the manuscripts of Vergerio's letters; see Bertalot, "Zwölf Briefe," p. 252.

EDUCATION. A student at Bologna by 1390, later studying at Padua and perhaps receiving a doctorate there c. 1392 (according to Sabbadini in Guarino's *Epist.*, III, 35-37; according to Smith, he did not: Vergerio's *Epist.*, p. 87 n. 1). He was present at Padua among the *promotores* in medicine on 24 July 1424 and 15 Nov. 1429, appearing with the titles of "doctor" and "magister" on the latter date (Zonta and Brotto, *Acta*, pp. 149, #609, and

164, #743). In 1430, Traversari referred to Leonardi as a teacher of medicine—"peritissimum physicum magistrum"; Bertalot, "Zwölf Briefe," p. 255.

Lippomano, Marco. (1) Lipomano, Lipamano, Lippomanus. Son of Pietro. Doctor.

MONOGRAPHS AND STUDIES. G. degli Agostini, *Notizie* I, 487-94.

CAREER. B. c. 1390 (based on the dates of his university degrees, his marriage, his assumption of first major office). M. 1421, Marina di Fantino da Pesaro (Agostini, *Notizie*, I, 488; Giomo, *Matrimoni*, II, 219). Testament 22 and 24 Sept. 1442 (AN, Testamenti A. Gambaro, B. 558.102 and 559.55). D. after 17 Aug. 1446 (after election as *savio grande*, the last ascertained datum of his political career). Lippomano's testament sets dowries for his daughters at between 1,600 and 2,000 ducats, suggesting substantial wealth. Yet his son Francesco pleads poverty in 1466 (4 July): CLN 10, c. 149ᵛ. I do not know Marco's relationship to the fifteenth-century Lippomano bank.

Offices. 1421-22, Pod. and Capt. of Belluno (SMS 54, c. 44); 1424, Sav. tf. (SMS 55); 1426, Sav. tf. (two terms) (SMS 55, c. 133 and passim); 1426, Sav. tf. (SMS 55, c. 183ᵛ); 1427-28, Capt. of Zara (SMS 56, 57); 1429, CX (CXM 10); 1429-30, Amb. to the Pope (CXM 10; MC-Ursa, c. 80); 1430, Cons. (CLN 6; CXM 11; SMS 57); Sav. tf. (SMS 57, c. 224ᵛ); 1431, Amb. in obedientia to the Venetian Pope Eugene IV (on which occasion he delivered his oration to that pope); Sav. tf. (SMS 58); CX; 1431-32, Capt. of Verona (SMS 58, c. 91); 1433, Amb. to the Pope (SMS 58, c. 193; Senato-Secrete 12); Cons. (CLN 6; CXM 11; MC-Ursa; SMS 58, 59); 1434, Sav. tf. (SMS 59); 1434-35, Prov. with the army (Senato-Secrete 13); 1435-37, Duke of Candia (Crete) (SMS 59, c. 114ᵛ); 1438, Sav. tf. (SMS 60); 1438-40, Avog. (CXM 12; SGV 4, c. 152; SMS 60); 1440, Pod. of Padua (SGV 4, c. 57ᵛ); 1441, Cons. (CLN 7; CXM 12; MC-Ursa; SGV 4, c. 92; SM 1; ST 1); 1442-43, Sav. gr. (ST 1); 1443, Lt. di Friuli (SGV 4, c. 56ᵛ); 1444, Cons. (CLN 8; CXM 12; SGV 4, c. 92ᵛ); Amb. to Milan (MC-Ursa, c. 152ᵛ; ST 1, c. 128, 142ᵛ); 1445, Sav. gr. (SM 2, c. 87 and passim; ST 1, c. 157ᵛ and passim); 1445-46, CX (CXM 13; SGV 4, c. 114ᵛ; held in part concurrently with preceding office); 1446, Amb. to Venetian condottiere Michele Attendolo da Codignola (on this occasion he delivered the second of the two orations listed below); Sav. gr. (two terms) (SM 2; ST 1, cc. 188ᵛ, 199).

WORKS. *Oratio ad Eugenium Quartum Summum Pontificem* (1431); *Oratio ad dominum Michaelem de Codignola Capitaneum Generalem* (1446). Sansovino (*Venetia*, II, 591) also attributes *Distinctiones, in quibus continetur totum fere corpus juris civilis.*

CORRESPONDENCE. Letters from Antonio Baratella (see A. Segarizzi, *Antonio Baratella e i suoi corrispondenti*, p. 113); Francesco Barbaro (*Epist.*, ed. A. M. Quirini, p. 72); Gasparino Barzizza (*Opera*, ed. J. A. Furiettus, p. 144); Francesco Filelfo (*Epist. fam.*, fol. 1ᵛ); Ognibene Scola (see G. Cogo, "Di Ognibene Scola, umanista padovano," pp. 144-46); Giovanni Spilimbergo (see, *Iter*, I,

330); Ambrogio Traversari (see Agostini, *Notizie*, I, 492 and C. L. Stinger, *Humanism and the Church Fathers*, p. 147).

DISCOURSE. Celebrated for his learning by Antonio Baratella (*Policleome-nareis*, fol. 14ᵛ); Flavio Biondo (*It. illus.* [Basel, 1559], fol. 373ᵛ); Ciriaco d'Ancona (*Itinerarium*, ed. L. Mehus, p. 18); Giovanni Morosini (cf. B. Nardi, "La scuola di Rialto" [UEUV ed.], p. 126); Francesco Pisani (*De universae philosophiae ornamentis*, p. 266); and Giovanni da Spilimbergo (*Oratio ad Marcum Lipomanum de congratulatione sue preture*). Francesco Filelfo addressed to Lippomano a *Satira* (Paris: apud Robertum et Iohannem Gourmont, 1505; not seen) which commends his learning and reproves him for not writing. An *Antonius iuris utriusque professor* addressed to him a *Tractatus de ieiuniis* (preface, fol. 8ᵛ). Lippomano was one of several patrician supporters of Francesco Filelfo (see correspondence cited above), and one of those who welcomed Ambrogio Traversari in Venice in 1433 (*Hodoeporicon*, ed. L. Mehus, p. 62). He collected a library (M. Foscarini, *Dei veneziani raccoglitori di codici*, p. 541) which included some important Greek texts. Among these were a volume of Greek verse borrowed by Traversari (see Stinger, *Humanism and the Church Fathers*, p. 147), a Lucian, Psellus' *De operatione daemonum*, and ps. Aristotle's *Mechanics*, copied in Crete while Lippomano was duke by the *protopapas* John Simeonachos (see D. Geanakoplos, *Greek Scholars in Venice*, p. 50; J. Monfasani, *George of Trebizond*, p. 6). Lippomano shared his interest in the *Mechanics* with Francesco Filelfo, who also possessed an early copy of the work (P. Rose, "Humanist Culture and Renaissance Mathematics," p. 57). In addition to Latin and Greek, Lippomano knew Hebrew (Agostini, *Notizie*, I, xlii; Cogo, "Ognibene Scola," p. 145, both citing Filelfo's *Satira*, Decad. I, Hecatostica IV, and Spilimbergo's *Oratio*, p. 95) and perhaps also Arabic (Biondo, *It. illus.*, fol. 373ᵛ).

EDUCATION. Licensed in arts on 4 Dec. 1410 (Zonta and Brotto, *Acta*, 36, #135) and awarded doctorates in laws and arts on 14 Sept. 1417 (ibid., p. 120, ##436, 437, and p. 121, #438 respectively). He was present frequently at other degree conferrals from 1410 to 1417, and listed after 1415 as a student of law (ibid., passim).

Lorenzi, Giovanni. (3) Son of Francesco.

MONOGRAPHS AND STUDIES. A. M. Albareda, "Intorno alla fine del bibliotecario apostolico Giovanni Lorenzi"; P. de Nolhac, "Giovanni Lorenzi, bibliothécaire d'Innocent VIII"; P. Paschini, *Il carteggio fra il cardinale Marco Barbo e Giovanni Lorenzi (1481-1490)* and "Un ellenista veneziano del Quattrocento: Giovanni Lorenzi"; C. B. Schmitt, "An Unstudied Fifteenth-Century Latin Translation of Sextus Empiricus by Giovanni Lorenzi (Vat. Lat. 2990)." See also the brief profile in G. Pavanello, *Un maestro del Quattrocento (Giovanni Aurelio Augurello)*, pp. 106-108. I have been unable to consult G. dalla Santa, "Una lettera di Giovanni Lorenzi a Demetrio Calcondila," *Scintilla letteraria*, 9 (1895).

CAREER. B. c. 1440 of a humble Venetian family. D. before 23 Nov. 1501, on which date he was replaced as papal secretary. After receiving his doctorate in law at the University of Padua in 1469, Lorenzi joined (in 1472) the entourage of the Venetian Cardinal Marco Barbo, whom he accompanied on a diplomatic mission to Germany (1472-74). Having become a priest, he became Barbo's secretary (1476) and conclavist (1484), and acquired due to the powerful cardinal's influence the posts of papal scribe in 1479, papal secretary in 1484, and papal librarian in 1485. On the day Lorenzi became papal librarian, Barbo gave the library a manuscript of Jerome's letters "propter ingressum prefati domini Johannis domestici et dilecti familiaris sui"; cf. de Nolhac, "Giovanni Lorenzi," p. 4. Other honors followed, including a series of minor ecclesiastical benefices. With the accession of Pope Alexander VI, Lorenzi was replaced as librarian (1492), as was customary, but retained the position of secretary and all other accumulated honors until his death. Albareda corrects previous authors' assumption that Lorenzi fell into disgrace either in 1492 or in 1501. His brother's indiscretion in the latter year led to the confiscation of the recently dead Lorenzi's books and property in 1502. The name Lorenzi appears among those of *cittadino* families: da Mosto, *Archivio*, I, 75.

WORKS. *De passione domini oratio; Consolatoria* to Francesco Tarsio on the death of his brother, not seen (see Paschini, "Ellenista," pp. 143ff.); trans., Sextus Empiricus, *Contra grammaticos, rhetores, geometras, arithmeticos,* excerpts in Schmitt, "Unstudied Translation," pp. 250-57 (from cod. Vat. Lat. 2990, fols. 266-381ᵛ); trans. several works of Plutarch, not seen (cf. *Iter*, II, 358; Cosenza, *Dict.*, II, 1826; Foscarini, *Lett. ven.*, p. 396; Paschini, "Ellenista," p. 140; Schmitt, "Unstudied Translation," pp. 247ff.); letters to and from Barbo in Paschini, *Il carteggio*, pp. 20-214.

CORRESPONDENCE. In addition to an extensive correspondence with Barbo as noted above, of interest are letters to Girolamo Donato (see P. Rigo, "Per il carteggio di Girolamo Donato," 536 and n. 22), to and from Demetrius Chalcondylas (see especially Paschini, *Carteggio*, pp. 116-17, 121ff.; also de Nolhac, "Giovanni Lorenzi," p. 12 and Pavanello, "Un maestro," pp. 106 and 108 n. 1) and Angelo Poliziano, and from Lorenzo de' Medici (see Pavanello, p. 107; two from Poliziano published by de Nolhac, pp. 14-16 and 18; one from Lorenzo, pp. 16-17). Correspondence in cipher on political matters with Niccolò Pandolfini, Bishop of Pistoia; cf. de Nolhac, p. 9.

DISCOURSE. Widely esteemed for his learning, particularly as a Hellenist; literary relations with Niccolò Lelio Cosmico, Demetrius Chalcondylas, and Angelo Poliziano (see especially Poliziano's letters cited above, and Paschini, *Carteggio*, pp. 130ff.). He possessed a small library of his own and often borrowed Greek codices from the Vatican library (see de Nolhac, *La Bibliothèque de Fulvio Orsini*, p. 228; R. Sabbadini, *Le scoperte dei codici latini e greci*, I, 66 n. 139). His intimate relationship with his patron Barbo is documented for the years 1481-90 by the letters cited.

EDUCATION. At Padua, Lorenzi studied Greek with Chalcondylas and subsequently received his doctorate in law on 28 Aug. 1469. Later he studied with Theodore Gaza in Rome.

Marcanova, Giovanni. (2) Mercatonovo, Marchanova. Son of Tommaso (Zonta and Brotto, *Acta*, p. 299, #1406).

MONOGRAPHS AND STUDIES. L. Sighinolfi, "La biblioteca di Giovanni Marcanova," and G. M. Vitali, "L'umanista padovano Giovanni Marcanova (1410/1418-67) e la sua biblioteca." These studies supersede L. Dorez, "La Bibliothèque de Giovanni Marcanova." See also R. Weiss, *The Renaissance Discovery of Antiquity*, pp. 98, 124, 145, 148-49, 170.

CAREER. B. c. 1410/1418. Testament, 6 Dec. 1464 (in Sighinolfi, "Biblioteca," pp. 192-96). D. Bologna, 31 July 1467 (ibid., pp. 191ff., refuting earlier assumptions of last years in Padua). Born to a substantial Venetian family, after completing his studies in philosophy and medicine at Padua, Marcanova taught first there, then at Bologna (see "Education," below). Though Marcanova spent his adult years abroad and is at times signed as "Patavinus" (though other times as "Venetus"), his background was probably Venetian and he continued to be considered a Venetian citizen; for his Venetian identity, see M. Foscarini, *Lett. ven.*, p. 395, and Zeno, *Diss. voss.*, I, 140, and the discussion of Sighinolfi, "Biblioteca," p. 205, and Vitali, "Umanista padovano," pp. 127ff. On 9 Sept. 1456, long after Marcanova had established himself abroad, the Venetian Senate took significant action to aid their "citizen" to recover an unpaid loan (ST 4, c. 19).

WORKS. *Oratio pro felici ingressu D. Fantini Dandulo episcopi; Antiquitates*, a collection of inscriptions, dedicated to Novello Malatesta, Lord of Cesena, not seen. A work of first importance, it is extant in many manuscript versions: see Cosenza, *Dict.*, III, 2160; *Iter*, I, 228, 240, 373, and II, 541; S. de Ricci, *Census of Medieval and Renaissance Manuscripts in the U.S. and Canada*, with W. J. Wilson, I, 897; Weiss, *Renaissance Discovery*, pp. 148-49. Cosenza cites a published version [III, 2161], which I have been unable to locate. The preface is published by G. M. Muccioli, *Catalogus codicum manuscriptorum Malatestianae Caesenatis bibliothecae*, I, 26. For discussion of his work as an epigraphist, see Foscarini, *Lett. ven.*, pp. 395-96; Zeno, *Diss. voss.*, I, 142; Weiss, *Renaissance Discovery*, pp. 148-49, and Sighinolfi, "Biblioteca," pp. 204ff. Sighinolfi doubts the existence of a collection of orations by Marcanova mentioned by earlier writers (p. 205).

CORRESPONDENCE. Letters to Moro Lapi (*Opera*, fols. 211, 219^v), and from Matteo Bosso (see G. Soranzo, *L'umanista canonico regolare Lateranense Matteo Bosso*, p. 120 n. 33, and p. 229 and n. 20). There is also a letter of Marcanova's to an unidentified correspondent in Marc. cod. Lat. XIV, 221 (4632), fol. 45^{r-v}.

DISCOURSE. Marcanova is best known for having acquired a valuable collection of more than five hundred volumes (including classical and humanist, medical, philosophical, and legal works) of manuscript books, several transcribed in his own hand, which he left to the monastery of S. Giovanni in Verdara in Padua; see the inventory published by Sighinolfi, "Biblioteca," pp. 206-19, and the discussion on pp. 200ff. He also left a collection of coins and medals: ibid., p. 198; Weiss, *Renaissance Discovery*, p. 170. The Olivetan Antonius Bargensis dedicated to Marcanova his chronicle of his order: it exists in two copies, with dedications, and letter by the same, in a fifteenth-century ms. (without shelfmark) in Monte Oliveto Maggiore, Archivio dell'Abbazia, fols. 1-9 (dedication at 1ʳ⁻ᵛ) and 32-40 (dedication at 32ʳ⁻ᵛ), and 50-60, respectively; the chronicle was also published by P. M. Lugano (Florence, 1901), with the dedication to Marcanova on pp. 3-4; the same author, best known for his work on the dignity of man (addressed to Bartolomeo Facio), addressed to Marcanova a substantial letter on the Etruscans and on famous men of Tuscany. (I am indebted to P. O. Kristeller for this information.) Jacobus Camphora may have addressed to Marcanova his *De immortalitate animae* (see *Iter*, I, 216; the work is described as "in modum dialogi vulgariter"; the dedication to Marcanova is not certain).

EDUCATION. Having received his license and doctorate in arts at Padua on 16 March 1440 (Zonta and Brotto, *Acta*, p. 299, #1406), Marcanova had undertaken studies in medicine by 1445 (p. 388, #1968). He was teaching arts there in 1446 with the low salary of twenty ducats, and appeared among the *promotores* for degree awards from 1447 (p. 411, #2116, and several subsequent acts; cf. indices), on 29 July of which year he received a license in medicine (p. 422, #2184). On 5 March 1450, he appeared among the *promotores* in arts, his name followed with this comment: "in medicina licentiato nondum tamen doctorato sed doctissimo" (p. 458, #2394). For his Paduan teaching in the 1440s, cf. also Facciolati, *Fasti gymn. pat.*, I.ii.104, and Sighinolfi, "Biblioteca," pp. 187ff. Thereafter he taught at the University of Bologna from 1451 to 1457, and 1458 until the academic year 1466-67; in which last year he died. For Marcanova's presence on the Bolognese faculty, see U. Dallari, *I rotuli dei lettori legisti e artisti dello studio bolognese dal 1384 al 1799*, I, 31, 34, 37, 40, 43, 46, 51, 54, 56, 59, 62, 64, 67, 70, 73. He was present in Bologna c. 1460, when two manuscripts of the *Antiquitates* were signed there (see Cosenza, *Dict.*, II, 2160), in 1464, when a world chronicle was copied there at his request (see *Iter*, II, 556), and in 1466, according to a note in a manuscript of Plato's *Phaedo* (see C. Frati, "Un codice autografo di Bernardo Bembo," p. 204). See also the document described by Sighinolfi, "Biblioteca," p. 190.

Marcello, Jacopo Antonio. (1) Marcellus. Son of Francesco, brother of Pietro V. Miles.

MONOGRAPHS AND STUDIES. See R. Fabbri, "Le *Consolationes de obitu Valerii Marcelli* ed il Filelfo"; H. Martin, "Sur un portrait de Jacques-Antoine Marcelle, Sénateur vénitien (1453)"; and M. Meiss, *Andrea Mantegna as Illustrator*, chapters I and II (a discussion of his role as patron of Andrea Mantegna and correspondent of René d'Anjou); also sketches in G. Benadduci, *A Jacopo Antonio Marcello patrizio veneto parte di orazione consolatoria ed elegia di Francesco Filelfo e lettera di Giovanni Mario Filelfo*; E. A. Cicogna, *Della famiglia Marcello patrizia veneta narrazione*, pp. 18-19; J. Monfasani, *George of Trebizond*, pp. 174-76 and 413. A full study is now in preparation by M. L. King.

CAREER. B. 17 Jan. 1398 or 1399 (see Francesco Filelfo, *De obitu Valerii filii consolatio* [Glasgow ms.], at p. 55; presented to the AC 3 Dec. 1417 [BO 162/I, c. 108^v]). M. 1418, a daughter of Pietro Miani; 1442, a daughter of Cao de Vacca of Padua; 1443, Lucia di Bartolomeo dal Leone of Padua (Fabbri, p. 246; Giomo, *Matrimoni*, I, 340). D. between autumn 1464 and July 1465 (Fabbri, p. 246). Jacopo Marcello di Cristoforo, not Jacopo Antonio as often stated, fell at Gallipoli in 1484. A military figure of first rank.

Offices. 1438-39, Prov. in Val Lagarina (Fabbri, p. 247); 1440, Amb. to the condottiere Francesco Sforza (SMS 60, c. 199^v); 1440-41, Prov. in Ravenna (SM 1, c. 9^v; Fabbri, p. 247; Romanin, *Stor. doc.*, IV, 203ff.); 1442, Amb. to the condottiere Francesco Sforza (SM 1, c. 112; ST 1, c. 73); 1444, Prov. in Lombardy (ST 1, c. 122^v); 1446, Sav. tf. (ST 2, c. 4^v, 26); 1446-48, Prov. with army in Lombardy and Capt. of Verona (MC-Ursa, c. 160; SGV 4, c. 62^v; ST 2, cc. 16, 29^v, 47^v; *Comm.*, IX, 300 [xiii, 301]; X, 6 [xiv, #10], 8 [#18], 19 [#35, 38], 27 [#75]; Cicogna, *Famiglia Marcello*, p. 18); 1449, Prov. with Count Francesco Sforza (ST 2, c. 110^v; *Comm.*, X, 28 [xiv, #79]); 1449-52, Prov. of Crema (CXM 14, cc. 89, 98; ST 2, cc. 123, 128; 3, cc. 23, 25; *Comm.*, X, 45 [xiv, #126]); 1452, Cons. (SGV 4, c. 94); 1453-54, Prov. with army (ST 3, cc. 68^v, 91^v, 99^v, 101^v; *Comm.*, X, 79 [xiv, #259]; these documents do not support G. Mercati, *Ultimi contributi*, I, 73 n. 2, who suggests that Marcello parted on this mission in April 1452); 1458-59, CX (CXM 15); 1459-60, Cons. (CLN 9; CXM 15, 16; MC-Regina; SM 6; ST 4); 1462, Duc. el., Cristoforo Moro (MC-Regina, cc. 39, 39^v); Cons. (CLN 10; CXM 16; SM 7); 1462-63, Lt. di Friuli, and Prov. with army before Trieste (CXM 16, c. 100^v; ST 5, cc. 20, 51, 57; Fabbri, p. 247).

WORKS. Dedicatory *epistola* (1453) to Giovanni Cossa (minister of King René d'Anjou and prefect of the Order of the Crescent founded by that monarch) of a life of St. Maurice (the Order's patron saint) and verses, published by Martin, "Portrait," pp. 258-60 and 261-64, respectively, from Paris, Bibliothèque de l'Arsenal, ms. 940, for which see Meiss, *Andrea Mantegna*, especially chapter I and pp. 79-80. Five dedicatory letters to René d'Anjou: 1. for Lauro Quirini's translation of ps.-Suidas, *De sacerdotio Christi* (1452; in G. Mercati, *Ultimi contributi*, I, 81-82, with discussion at pp. 72-73 and n. 5); 2. for an anonymous translation of the same work (1452-53; not seen by me; ibid., pp. 72ff.); 3. for an anonymous translation of Chrysostom's *De tollerandis calamitatibus* (1453; ibid., pp. 84-85, with discussion at pp. 77 n. 2 and 82-83; the unknown translator is not to be identified with Ambrogio Traversari, who also translated the work, and with whom Marcello was in correspondence); 4. for a translation of Ptolemy's *Cosmography* (1457; Martin, pp. 264-66); 5. for Guarino Veronese's translation of all seventeen books of Strabo (1459; letter in R. Sabbadini, "La traduzione guariniana di Strabone," pp. 13-15, with accompanying discussion, as well as in many ms. and printed versions, including the original presentation ms. in Albi, Bibliothèque Rochegude, ms. 4; see Meiss, especially chapter II and p. 81; for this episode also R. Sabbadini, *Vita di Guarino Veronese*, p. 164; Sabbadini, ed., *Epist. di Guarino Veronese*, III, 483-87; A. Diller and P. O. Kristeller in CTC, II, 225-26). For other works of Marcello to René see Mercati, *Ultimi contributi*, I, 31, 70-85, and Meiss, pp. 32 and 89 n. 7. Sansovino (*Venetia*, II, 579) and others attribute to Marcello orations on "diverse subjects."

CORRESPONDENCE. Letters from Francesco Filelfo (*Epist. fam.*, fols. 116 and 116bis), Giovanni Mario Filelfo (in Benadduci, *Marcello*, pp. 25-26), and Maffeo Vallaresso (*Epist.*, pp. 427-28). Note in addition the consolatory letters cited below.

DISCOURSE. Marcello is responsible for the execution of three manuscripts of extraordinary importance. Two of the dedicatory letters cited under "Works" above (those to Cossa and to René, the fifth listed, of the Strabo text) were introductory to two of those manuscripts (in Paris and Albi, as cited), notable also for their adornment with illuminations by (probably: see Fabbri, pp. 229-30 n. 8) Andrea Mantegna. The Paris ms. contains Marcello's letter and verses, the life of Maurice, and illustrations. The Albi ms. contains the Strabo with Marcello's letter as well as two letters of Guarino (to Pope Nicholas V and Marcello, successively the commissioners of his translation; the Guarino letters in the latter's *Epist.*, ed. Sabbadini, II, 627-29 and 629-34, respectively, and in many ms. versions).

The third important ms. commissioned by Marcello was also meant as a presentation copy to King René: cod. 201 (U.1.5) of the Hunterian Museum Library of the University of Glasgow. It was prepared handsomely for illustrations that were never completed. Apparently the work was never sent to France, having migrated from Italy to Britain in the eighteenth century. A full but flawed description (in part corrected here) is found in *A Catalogue of the Manuscripts in the Library of the Hunterian Museum in the University of Glasgow*, ed. J. Young and P. H. Aitken, pp. 142-43. It contains works of consolation (and related works) to Marcello for the death of his son Valerio by these authors among others: Francesco Filelfo (with his Greek elegy and translation by Ludovico Carbone), George of Trebizond, Battista Guarini, Isotta Nogarola, Pietro Perleone, and Niccolò Sagundino.

On the death of Marcello's son Valerio on New Year's Day in 1461, just prior to his ninth birthday, these learned persons addressed works of consolation to the profoundly depressed father. (For the date of the boy's death see George of Trebizond's consolatory letter in J. Monfasani, *Collectanea Trapezuntiana*, p. 235.) The response was of such magnitude as to indicate both the great extent of Marcello's grief and his role as a patron of letters.

Filelfo's Latin prose *Consolatio* is also found in many printed and ms. versions; for these see Fabbri, pp. 233ff. and n. 31. Benadduci publishes a partial edition of the work: *Marcello*, pp. 1-15. Filelfo's Greek *elegia* (edited by Fabbri, pp. 243-45) is also found in other ms. versions, as is the Carbone translation; the latter appears with an alternate translation by Leonardo Grifo in Marc. Lat. XIV, 246 (4683), fols. 139-41 and 142-44, respectively. Not in the Hunter collection is Filelfo's Latin elegy in the name of Francesco Sforza, published by Benadduci, pp. 17-23. It is indicative of Marcello's character and wealth that he rewarded Filelfo's attempts to console him with a lavishly expensive silver vessel (Benadduci, pp. xix-xx). George's work, edited by Monfasani, Collectanea Trapezuntiana, pp. 235-48, is also in other ms. versions there cited. Nogarola's consolation also pub. by E. Abel in her Opera omnia, II, 161-78. A catalogue of other of the Glasgow works and their alternate ms. locations will appear in King's study.

In addition to these and other works of consolation, the Glasgow codex includes another version (pp. 269-94) of Michele Orsini's De origine, written in response to Filelfo's Consolatio and containing consolatory themes. I am unable to identify the authors of works to Marcello in that codex on pp. 249-68 and 295-308. I have seen only a microfilm of the manuscript, which is damaged and nearly illegible in places; yet I am able to suggest that both these works are consolatory and addressed, like most of the others, to Marcello. The final work on pp. 310-426 I can identify as the Excusatio adversus consolatores in obitu Valerii filii, written by Giorgio Bevilacqua da Lazise in the name of Marcello and at his request and addressed, as is the whole codex, to King René. A complete version of Bevilacqua's work also in a Verona ms., for which see the Bibliography; here at fols. 3-6 is a preliminary letter by Bevilacqua to Marcello revealing the circumstances of the Excusatio's authorship.

In addition to the works of the Glasgow codex, Giovanni Mario Filelfo (see Benadduci, Marcello, pp. xxi and xxvii n. 18), Janus Pannonius (see Fabbri, p. 232), and Gregorio Tifernate (an Oratio; see ibid., and Iter, II, 189, 302) wrote to Marcello in consolation. A brief consolatory letter by Perleone, probably a precursor of the major Glasgow work, appears in Marc. Lat. XIV, 266 (4502), fols. 218-21^v and several other ms. versions. An anonymous epigram appears in Marc. cod. Lat. XII, 210 (4689), fol. 16^{r-v}. Learned men wrote to Marcello also on other occasions. Janus Pannonius wrote a Panegyricus for Marcello, and a Carmen de itineribus C. Iacobi Antonii Marcelli Veneti, and other works (see Fabri, pp. 228-29 and Monfasani, George of Trebizond, p. 175 n. 198). Giovanni Michele Alberto da Carrara wrote in Marcello's honor his De bello ab Jacobo Antonio Marcello in Italia gesto. To Marcello, Giovanni Mario Filelfo dedicated his satire against Galeotto Marzio (cf. Benadduci in Marcello, pp. xxi and 25-26); George of Trebizond his translation of Ptolemy's Almagest, his commentary on the same work, and his Comparatio (see Monfasani, George of Trebizond, pp. 175-76; Monfasani publishes the prefaces to the Almagest and the Comparatio in the Collectanea Trapezuntiana, pp. 248-51 and 251, respectively); Guarino Veronese his translation of Strabo (see above). Marcello was able to tutor his young son Valerio in Greek and Latin (Orsini, De origine, [Milan cod.], fols. 15^v-20^v) and was the source of Francesco Contarini's Novella di Tedaldino e Monna Rosa (see

A. Segarizzi, "Francesco Contarini politico e letterato veneziano del secolo XV," p. 286). His role as patron to Mantegna is discussed by Meiss, *Andrea Mantegna.*

Marcello, Pietro Vecchio. (1) Marcellus. Son of Francesco, brother of Jacopo Antonio. Related by marriage to Zaccaria Trevisan V (P. Gothein, "Zaccaria Trevisan," p. 22).

MONOGRAPHS AND STUDIES. R. Sabbadini, "Antonio da Romagno e Pietro Marcello" and "Ancora Pietro Marcello."

CAREER. B. c. 1376. D. 1428. Before 1399, Marcello was named canon of Parenzo (C. Cenci, "Senato veneto 'Probae,' " p. 349, #38; Eubel, *Hier. cath.,* I, 180 n. 7); later papal vicar in Ancona (J. Monfasani, *George of Trebizond,* p. 11 n. 41).

Titles. 1399-1409, Bishop of Ceneda (Eubel, *Hier. cath.,* I, 180); 1409— Bishop of Padua (ibid.).

WORKS. *Epistola consolatoria* to Fantino Dandolo (Jan. 1405); *Principium Monasterii Montis Vendae* (24 Nov. 1427); four mock orations by "Aeschines," "Demades," "Demosthenes," and "a certain Athenian." I have seen the ms. version of the *Principium* in the Bibliography; a printed verson is cited by Sabbadini, "Antonio da Romagna," p. 218 (*Annales camaldulenses,* IV, 7-9). Sabbadini had attributed to Marcello a translation of Lucian's *Timon* in that study, printing the work on p. 238; but in "Ancora Pietro Marcello" he showed that the work was not, in fact, Marcello's.

CORRESPONDENCE. Letters from Antonio da Romagna (in Sabbadini, "Antonio da Romagno," pp. 226-33); Antonio Baratella (in A. Segarizzi, *Antonio Baratella,* p. 116), Niccolò de Cessis (published in part by P. Gothein, "Zaccaria Trevisan," p. 27), Francesco Zabarella (ibid., pp. 53-54; a consolatory on the death of Marcello's relative Zaccaria Trevisan V).

DISCOURSE. Gasparino Barzizza addressed to Marcello a consolatory work on the death of his brother Girolamo (*Oratio ad Petrum Marcellum Episcopum Patavinum in morte Hieronymi Marcelli,* in his *Opera,* ed. J. A. Furiettus, pp. 85-87). Marcello had in his household in 1403 the learned Antonio da Romagno, and in 1417, George of Trebizond, who assisted the then bishop of Padua in Greek studies (Monfasani, *George of Trebizond,* p. 11 n. 41). Also in Padua, Marcello charged Francesco Barbaro to recite an oration for the awarding of a law degree to Alberto Guidalotto (see Barbaro's *Centotrenta,* ed. Sabbadini, p. 12). While bishop of that city, Marcello himself was awarded his doctorate in law. He played a major role in the early fifteenth-century diffusion of classical texts, being one of the first to receive translations from the Greek done by Chrysoloras' Florentine pupils, and the divulgator to the Venetian humanists of Cicero's *Epistolae ad Atticum.*

EDUCATION. Marcello was perhaps a student of Giovanni Conversino da Ravenna (Sabbadini, "Antonio da Romagno," p. 216). He studied law at the

University of Bologna, c. 1392-99 (Cenci, "Senato veneto 'Probae,' " p. 349, #38), receiving his doctorate only in 1413 from Padua, on which occasion Trevisan delivered his *Oratio in doctorali et publico conventu Petri Marcelo episcopi paduani* (16 Oct. 1413).

Marcello, Pietro Giovane. (3) Marcellus. Son of Antonio.

CAREER. B. perhaps c. 1454 (AC-BO 164/III, c. 262; presented 23 Nov. 1472, by his father Antonio, son of Donato). D. after 7 June 1502 (when he was granted the privilege of printing his work on the lives of the doges: CLN 15, c. 72^v). The Balla d'oro document cited is the only one for a Pietro di Antonio in the relevant period. If our Pietro's father was the son of Jacopo, however, as is suggested by the evidence reviewed below, or of Pietro, as is given by Cappellari, *Camp. ven.*, III, 31, then the c. 1454 birthdate does not apply and I have none better to offer. Many homonyms complicate the establishment of Marcello's identity. Cappellari (III, 31^v) gives three others who had active careers in the same years. The registers of the SGV for these years contain nearly a dozen. Many of the documents record a Pietro Marcello as having held office, but provide no patronymic; one such served importantly as provveditore in Ravenna, Tuscany, and the Veneto during 1498 to 1500 (CXM 27, cc. 189^{r-v}, 198^v, 215, and 28, c. 89). Even where the patronymic Antonio appears there is no certainty, given what has been said above, that our Pietro Marcello is indicated. Having no basis for assuming that in any one of these instances our humanist was concerned, I have included none of them. Our Pietro, intriguingly, may have been the unnamed grandson of the hero Jacopo Marcello, killed at Gallipoli in 1484, to whose surviving sons and to the children of whose predeceased son Antonio were granted conspicuous privileges (see the acts of 21 Sept. 1484 and 9 April 1485: ST 9, cc. 109, 134^v). That our Pietro Marcello may have belonged to this family is suggested by the funeral oration written also by a Pietro Marcello for the captain Jacopo (see below).

No certain data regarding Marcello's career has been located. A Pietro Marcello, son of Antonio, appears in April and May of 1500 as the captain of two galleys owned by his brothers (Sanuto, *Diarii*, III, 191, 264, 315), and on 17 Aug. 1501 as one of the first of many signers of an agreement by which a company planned to discharge a large debt (ST 14, cc. 44-45^v, with Marcello's signature and the amount owed him on c. 44^v; Marcello was to be paid 170 ducats). This evidence could suggest that Marcello pursued a modest mercantile career. It is also possible that he held any number of minor government offices which, unlike the major offices in Venice and abroad, yielded a salary. Sanuto further mentions a Pietro Marcello di Antonio (surnamed "mal fine") who was condemned for usury in August, 1500 (III, 666, 754).

WORKS. *Oratio in adventu Cardinalis Grimani* (20 May 1498) (no patronymic specified; the author is probably the same as that of the oration for Vendramin, the epigram for Sanuto, and the lives of the doges, all of which are certainly the work of Pietro Marcello di Antonio); *Oratio in funere An-*

dreae Vendrameni Venetiarum Principis (9 May 1400 [sic, 1474]); *Oratio in obitu Jacobi Marcelli* (1484?), not seen (see *Iter*, II, 578; this Pietro Marcello can probably be identified with the contemporary humanist author of other works given here); *De vita, moribus et rebus gestis omnium ducum venetorum* (ed. prin. 1502); epigram *De obitu Leonardi Sanuti* (1474). The complete unoriginality of the lives of the doges, drawn from Marcantonio Sabellico's histories, is conceded even by its author; see M. Foscarini, *Lett. ven.*, pp. 267-68.

Marino, Giovanni. (2) Marinus. Son of Rosso. Doctor.

CAREER. B. c. 1410. Married, perhaps to a daughter of Andrea Giuliani. D. after 31 May 1447. The suggested birthdate is based on Marino's university career and these data: his son was presented to the AC on 29 June 1460 (BO 163/II, c. 335; by Giovanni's brother Carlo), indicating that Marino had married ("Elisabetta," without surname) before 1442; Marino's older brothers were presented in 1416, 1417, and 1419 (162/I, c. 104ᵛ). The birthdate given is also consistent with the assumption of a major political career in 1440, and a first minor office in 1438 (elected one of the *offitiales rationum novarum* on 22 June 1438; SGV 4, c. 35ᵛ). Cappellari says that Govanni Marino di Rosso, whom he confounds with another later figure (see below) was married to a daughter of Giuliani (*Camp. ven.*, III, fol. 43). That Marino married is known from the record of at least two noble sons: Antonio, presented to the AC in 1460, and Marco, to whom Paolo Ramusio dedicated his work on fasting (see below). It is not certain that he served in the title of Rector of Canea, to which he was elected on 31 May 1447. He may have died before assuming office; he had certainly died by 1460, when his son Antonio had reached eighteen. A homonym, also learned, lived in the late fifteenth to sixteenth century, and wrote a funeral oration for the Patriarch Antonio Surian (Venice: Gregorio de Gregoriis, 1508) and a poem to Marco Sanuto (Marc. cod. Lat. XIV, 266 [4502], fols. 226-29). Sansovino (*Venetia*, II, 588), like Cappellari, confounds the two figures.

Offices. 1440, Amb. to Ferrara (ST 1, c. 15); 1445, Amb. to Florence (ST 1, c. 170); Sav. tf. (ST 1); 1446, Amb. to Florence (ST 1, c. 191ᵛ); 1446-47, Sav. tf. (SM 2, 3; ST 2, c. 14ᵛ); 1447, Rector of Canea [Crete] (CLN 8, c. 59ᵛ; election only).

WORKS. *Orationes*: 1. *In licentia D. Hermolai Barbaro Romanae ecclesiae prothonotarii* (Padua, 1436); 2. *In licentia domini Montorii de Mascharelis Vicentini* (Padua, 2 April 1432); 3. *In acceptatione officii rectoratus* (Padua, 1 June 1433); 4. *Pro adventu DD. Antonii Corrario Romanae ecclesiae Cardinalis* (Padua, 1433).

CORRESPONDENCE. Letter from Francesco Barbaro (*Centotrenta*, ed. Sabbadini, pp. 40, 120-21).

DISCOURSE. Reputed for his knowledge of law, which he may have taught privately in his home to noblemen (M. Foscarini, *Lett. ven.*, pp. 70, 93).

Praised for his learning by Zaccaria Trevisan G in that fellow pupil's *Oratio pro data licentia D. Iohanni Marino in utroque iure*, and by Paolo Ramusio (*De ieiuniorum observatione*, fol. 48, and C. de' Rosmini, *L'idea dell'ottimo precettore*, pp. 162-63). Possibly it is to this Giovanni Marino that *dominus Paulus* wrote his *vocabula Servii* (cf. *Iter*, I, 414).

EDUCATION. With Vittorino da Feltre (see Trevisan's oration referred to above, fol. 44, and de' Rosmini, *L'idea*, p. 161). Marino received his license and doctorate in arts at Padua on 28 Oct. 1426 (Zonta and Brotto, *Acta*, p. 154, #670), after which he remained in attendance as a student of law (ibid., passim), receiving his doctorate 18 Dec. 1435 (ibid., p. 241, #1083). He taught law briefly, substituting for his professor Andrea Ubaldi da Perugia (Cosenza, *Dict.*, III, 2182; Ramusio, *De ieiuniorum observatione*, fol. 48).

Merula, Giorgio. (3) Son of Giovanni.

MONOGRAPHS AND STUDIES. M. E. Cosenza, *Dict.*, III, 2296-2302; F. Gabotto and A. Badini Confalonieri, "Vita di Giorgio Merula"; R. Sabbadini, "Briciole umanistiche—XLV: Giorgio Merula." See also the thorough career summaries by V. Branca in his edition of Ermolao Barbaro G's *Epistolae, orationes et carmina*, II, 152-53, and in his "L'umanesimo veneziano alla fine del Quattrocento, Ermolao Barbaro e il suo circolo," pp. 157ff.; the latter gives further bibliographical guidance.

CAREER. B. Alessandria, 1431. D. Milan, 18 March 1494. After studying and teaching in other north Italian cities, Merula came to Venice in 1465, and was appointed on 28 Nov. 1468 to the public chair of rhetoric established at San Marco alongside that for the instruction of young notaries (the document of Merula's appointment published by A. Segarizzi, "Cenni sulle scuole pubbliche a Venezia nel secolo XV e sul primo maestro d'esse," p. 651). During his years in Venice, which extended to 1484, Merula was also active as corrector and editor for the early presses of Jenson and Speyer, and developed extensive relations with learned commoners and patricians, including among the latter wealthy patrons. Merula's twenty years in Venice were those of his prime, and were decisive for the development of his intellectual method and objectives (according to Branca; "L'umanesimo veneziano," pp. 157-58). From 1484, lured by Ludovico il Moro, Merula taught at the University of Pavia and in Milan, where he stayed until his death, continuing his literary activities in Sforza employ as historian and apologist.

WORKS. See studies cited for Merula's vast production as editor of texts (some referred to below) and for the invective literature by and against him regarding literary matters; also the *De antiquitate Vicecomitum; Bellum Scodrense.*

CORRESPONDENCE. Letters to Marco Basilio (in Marc. cod. Lat. XIV, 267 [4344], fol. 60ᵛ), Antonio Calvo (in Zeno, *Diss. voss.*, II, 394-95), Marcantonio Sabellico (*Epist.*, fol. 6), Antonio Vinciguerra (in B. Beffa, *Antonio Vinciguerra*, p. 90); from Ermolao Barbaro G (*Epist.*, ed. Branca, I, 12-14,

43-44, 51-52, 54-55, 71-72, 77-79, 80-81, 98-99; II, 11-12), Francesco Filelfo (*Epist. fam.*, fols. 128ᵛ, 264, and 265), Angelo Poliziano (*Opera omnia*, I, 147-48); to and from Giovanni Pico della Mirandola (in L. Dorez, "Lettres inédites de Jean Pic de la Mirandole [1482-1492]," pp. 356-57).

DISCOURSE. Merula is one of the principal figures engaged in editing and commenting upon classical texts during the first generation of printing in Venice (see Branca, "L'umanesimo veneziano," pp. 157ff., and P. G. Ricci, "Umanesimo filologico in Toscana e nel Veneto," p. 169). He was active in literary circles in that city, notably c. 1465-66 at gatherings in the wealthy Corner household. He developed close relations with many learned patricians (see Gabotto and Confalonieri, "Vita di Giorgio Merula," first part, pp. 282ff., and the passages by Cosenza and Branca cited above under "Monographs and Studies"; also for his relations with Giustiniani, see P. H. Labalme, *Bernardo Giustiniani*, p. 104) to whom he dedicated the texts he published: among these his edition of Cicero's *De finibus bonorum et malorum* to Ludovico Foscarini (1471); his emendations of Virgil and Pliny to Antonio Vinciguerra (1471; for the Pliny, see CTC, IV, 418); his edition of *Scriptores rei rusticae*, dedicated overall to Pietro Priuli, and with specific books dedicated to Bernardo Giustiniani and Domenico Giorgi (1472); his edition of Plautus to Jacopo Zeno (1472); his comment on Ovid's *Epistola Sapphus* (1471) and his invective against Domizio Calderini (a commentary on Martial; see Gabotto and Confalonier, first part, pp. 313ff.; CTC, IV, 265-66) to Marcantonio Morosini; his comment on Cicero's *Pro Ligario* (1478) and translations of three orations of Dio Chrysostom (see V. Cian, "Per Bernardo Bembo—II," p. 53; della Torre, *Antonio Vinciguerra*, p. 153) to Bernardo Bembo; and his comment on Cicero's *epistola ad Lentulum* to Domenico Sanuto (1478). (Note also his commentary on Juvenal, 1478, and translation of Alexander of Aphrodisias, *Problemata*; see CTC, I, 22-23 and 134, respectively.) In connection with his work as editor and commentator, Merula engaged in the literary disputes that characterized the age, including notably with Domizio Calderini, Galeotto Marzio, George of Trebizond, Francesco Filelfo, and Poliziano (see Gabotto and Confalonieri, first part, pp. 311ff., and the passages by Branca and Cosenza cited). Ermolao Barbaro G dedicated to Merula—his teacher (see V. Branca, "Ermolao Barbaro e l'umanesimo veneziano," p. 196)—his paraphrase of Themistius' *De anima*. Among Merula's other students were numbered Alessandro Benedetti (see R. Massalongo, "Alessandro Benedetti e la medicina veneta del Quattrocento," p. 236), Jacopo Grasolari (cf. Gabotto and Confalonieri, first part, p. 287), and Giovanni Battista Trevisan (see *Iter*, II, 330, for the work that young patrician dedicates to "his teacher"). He was praised for his learning by Erasmus (*Ciceronianus*, p. 226), Giovio (*Elogia doctorum virorum* [1577], pp. 71-72), and Sabellico (*De rep. lat. ling.*, fol. 114). Merula collected manuscripts, and was a central figure in the Bobbio discoveries of 1493 (R. Sabbadini, *Le scoperte dei codici latini e greci*, I, 156-58 and indices).

EDUCATION. With Francesco Filelfo, Galeotto Marzio, Gabriele Paveri Fontana, Gregorio Tifernate.

Miani, Pietro. (1) Emilianus. Son of Giovanni.

CAREER. B. c. 1370. Testament 8 April 1429 (AN, Testamenti P. Zane, B. 1255, cc. 165^v-68^v). D. 1433 (see Eubel, *Hier. cath.*, I, 526; Gams, *Ser. episc.*, 807, gives 4 May). Miani belongs to the generation of Leonardo Bruni, Pier Paolo Vergerio, and Zaccaria Trevisan V. He was presumably still young in 1397-1400, when he was a student of Chrysoloras, and perhaps embarked on a political career, c. 1400, before a clerical one. When made bishop of Vicenza in 1409, he held the curial title *camerarius apostolicus*. These data suggest a birthdate no earlier than 1370, belying an earlier date suggested by L. Smith's note (*Epist. di Pier Paolo Vergerio*, p. 61 n. 2) that Miani purchased a book in 1380. Several Pietro Mianis appear in the government documents of this period, including at least one with the same patronymic but certainly not identical to ours (having held political office after the figure of concern here had been made bishop of Vicenza). But in that our Pietro Miani was clearly the author of the testament cited, which also refers to a previous marriage and to the existence of a son, he may indeed have briefly pursued a political career before turning to a clerical one. He may conceivably come to be identified with the Pietro Miani (without patronymic) who was a ducal elector in 1400 (MC-Leona, c. 111^v), a captain of the Quarantìa in 1402-1403 (CLN 3, c. 110^v; MC-Leona, c. 126), and who had by 1401-2 held the title of *auditor sententiarum* (CLN 3, passim).

Title. 1409– Bishop of Vicenza (Eubel, *Hier. cath.*, I, 526).

WORKS. Sansovino (*Venetia*, II, 580) and his followers attribute a work on the penitential psalms; modern authors repeat the attribution (e.g., by Smith, *Epist.*, p. 61 n. 2).

CORRESPONDENCE. Letters to Francesco Barbaro (in C. Griggio, "Codice berlinese," pp. 169-70) and from Leonardo Bruni (*Epist.*, ed. Mehus, I, 51-52, 67-68, 83-84, 122; II, 184-85; *Hum.-philo. Schriften*, ed. H. Baron, pp. 107-108).

DISCOURSE. Notable for his important collection of Greek and Latin manuscripts (see M. Foscarini, *Dei veneziani raccoglitori di codici*, pp. 535-39; R. Sabbadini, *Le scoperte dei codici latini e greci*, I, 52, 62, 63; Cosenza, *Dict.*, III, 2306). Miani exchanged books and book information with other bibliophiles. In his testament, he left the precious collection of "omnes libros quos habeo" to his son Faustino and nephews Marco and Filippo, prohibiting the sale of any volume for fifteen years after his death (c. 167^v). In Florence, at the papal curia, and elsewhere, he knew the principal humanists of his generation, and maintained relations with Bruni, Pietro del Monte, Ambrogio Traversari, and Pier Paolo Vergerio (see Bruni's letters, cited above; Agostini, *Notizie*, I, 351, 370; Cosenza, *Dict.*, III, 2306; Barbaro's *Centotrenta*, ed. Sabbadini, p. 15; Sabbadini, "L'ultimo ventennio della vita di Manuele Crisolora [1396-1415]," p. 326 n. 2; Smith, *Epist.*, p. 61 n. 2). He appears as the main speaker in del Monte's *De vitiorum inter se differencia et comparatione*, in which he is portrayed as a leader of informal humanist symposia (see especially fols. 3ᵛ-5 of that dialogue). Guarino Veronese addressed to Miani his translation of Isocrates' encomium of Helen (dedication to Miani, fols. 134-35, and Guarino's translation, fols. 135-46, not seen by me, in Oxford, Bodleian Library, cod. Bywater 38; P. O. Kristeller kindly permitted me to consult his typescript description of this ms.). Interested in the arts, Miani gives detailed instructions in his testament for the decoration of a chapel to be constructed for him in Vicenza (c. 166).

EDUCATION. With Manuel Chrysoloras and at Padua (Smith, *Epist.*, 61 n. 2; Sabbadini, "L'ultimo ventennio," 326 n. 2).

Molin, Pietro. (3?) De Molino, Molinus. Son of Giovanni. Doctor.

CAREER. B. c. 1430. M. 1464, daughter of Antonio di Stefano Quirini; 1480, a daughter of the knight Antonio di Bartolo Collalto. D. probably after 9 May 1482. The birthdate is hypothesized from the known data of Molin's career. A university career in the 1450s to 1460s and the letters cited below of Maffeo Vallaresso and Niccolò Sagundino, dated 1451 and 1455, respectively, suggest intellectual maturity by these mid-century years. Molin's first marriage and assumption of political responsibilities from at least 1465 are also consistent with the suggested birthdate. The death date is inferred from the career record, as well, which shows no known political role after Molin's 1482 election to the office of *provisor salis*. The determination of the boundaries of Molin's career is made more difficult by the presence of contemporary homonyms. Capellari (*Camp. ven.*, III, cc. 103ᵛ and 107) identifies our learned Pietro Molin as the son of Andrea. But archival evidence makes this identification unlikely. The son of Andrea was born c. 1441, having been presented to the AC 14 Nov. 1459 (BO 163/II, c. 346). The data given as pointing to a 1430 birthdate cannot easily be made to coincide with one so late. This figure, moreover, shows a record of minor political offices from 1467 to 1487 (SGV 6, cc. 80ᵛ, 89, 93ᵛ, 101, 106, 106ᵛ); these are inconsistent in dignity, although they partially coincide in time, with the embassies known to have been performed by our Pietro Molin. Pietro di Andrea lived until 1511, having made a testament on 1 June 1494 (AN, Testamenti C. Rizzo, B. 1228.328; 1229.245; a note at the end of the latter document gives the date of death). No document cited here nor any I have seen gives Pietro di Andrea the title of "doctor," which our figure surely held. Also appearing in SGV 4 through 8 are Pietro Molins with the patronymics Girolamo, Leone, and Marino; they may all be eliminated. A Pietro di Ludovico, born c. 1435 (AC-BO 163/II, c. 345ᵛ, presented 1 Dec. 1453), remains a weak candidate for identification with our figure.

The career table given here assumes that that figure appearing in the documents with the title "doctor" (accompanied, as it happens, by no patronymic except in a case to be noted presently) is our Pietro Molin. The Pietro Molin elected *provisor salis* in 1482 is entitled "doctor quondam Io." and can be identified with our figure. While no record of a Pietro Molin di Giovanni has been found in the AC-BO, he does appear in Barbaro's *Arbori* (V, c. 224) with the notations of marriage given above, and the description "dottore di Zuanne dottore." Pietro Molin "doctor" performed embassies to Florence and developed relations with at least two members—Naldo Naldi and Marsilio Ficino—of intellectual circles there; see Kristeller, "Marsilio Ficino e Venezia," pp. 480-81 and n. 35 (the date of Ficino's letter helps fix the date of death). B. Cecchetti, "Una libreria circolante a Venezia," pp. 166-67 presents a Pietro di Giovanni Molin who borrows books and is found in Padua in the company of Francesco Diedo in 1456. This is our man.

Offices. 1465, Pod. or Capt. of Verona (L. Foscarini, *Epist.*, fols. 305^v-306 [Malpaga, 1 May, assigned to 1465, when the author was in Malpaga]; the letter exhorts Molin to fine performance in Verona, alludes to his recent designation to one of the offices of the rectorate, and refers to Molin's previous entry to the Senate); 1465-66, Amb. to Duke Stefano of Santa Sava (MC-Regina, c. 62; SGV 8, c. 46; SM 8, c. 46); 1468, Amb. (one of four) to accompany the Emperor to Rome (ST 6, c. 42; in connection with this embassy, Molin delivered the orations cited below; of these the second, given at Chioggia on 4 Feb. of the following year, is the unique yet certain evidence of Molin's participation in an honorary delegation of twenty patricians sent to greet the Emperor as he was about to enter Venice); 1469, Pod. and Capt. of Belluno (SGV 6, c. 43); 1470, Amb. to marriage of Galeazzo Maria Sforza, duke of Milan, and Buona, daughter of duke of Savoy (Cicogna, *Iscrizioni*, III, 365); 1473, Pod. and Capt. of Justinopolis (SGV 5, c. 8, and 6, c. 61); 1477, Amb. to Florence (CLN 12, c. 64); 1482, *Provisor salis*.

WORKS. Two orations *ad Imperatorem Federicum III* (30 Nov. 1468 and 4 Feb. 1469).

CORRESPONDENCE. Letters from Marsilio Ficino (*Epist.*, 756; cf. Kristeller, "Marsilio Ficino e Venezia," pp. 481 n. 35 and 483 n. 45), Foscarini (*Epist.*, fols. 296^v-297, 305^v-306), and Maffeo Vallaresso (*Epist.*, pp. 24-26).

DISCOURSE. Molin was called "eloquens" by Vallaresso (letter cited), "doctissimus" by Niccolò Sagundino (letter to Alessandro Bono, *Epist. et opusc.*, fol. 110), "doctissimus" and "ingenio peritissimus" by Antonio Bernardo (*Oratio pro doctoratu Jacobi Molini*, fol. 50); Foscarini urged Molin in his Veronese post (c. 1465) to be the "doctorum domicilium" (second letter cited above). When Molin expressed displeasure that Sagundino had dedicated his *De origine et sectis philosophorum* to Fantino Coppo and not to himself, Sagundino wrote another work (not found) addressed to Molin; Sagundino asks Bono (*Epist. et opusc.*, fol. 110^{r-v}) to deliver the work he had composed for the complaining Molin. Paolo Marsi (cod. Marc. Lat. XII, 210 [4689], fol. 55^v) and Naldo Naldi (*Epigrammaton liber*, ed. A. Perosa, p. 15) wrote epigrams to him. Molin borrowed several theological works from the library of (his relative?) Girolamo Molin between 1450 and 1456 (Cecchetti, "Libreria," pp. 166-67).

EDUCATION. In Padua by 1456 and in relation with Francesco Diedo, and a student of arts there by 1457-58, when Antonio Bernardo mentions him (as "hic nostri ordinis Petrus bonarum artium studiis doctissimus") in an oration for Jacopo Molin's doctorate, a degree granted probably around 1457/58 (based on a reference to Barbone Morosini's death, which occurred between 12 May of the earlier and 13 Jan. of the later year). At that time, Molin was probably a student of arts, and not yet of law. That he eventually held doctorates in both fields is evident from the Brit. Mus. ms. of his orations for the Emperor Frederick; on fol. 14^v one reads "Oratio habita . . . per me petrum molinum artium et utriusque iuris doctorem," and the same title is repeated on fol. 16^v. Facciolati (*Fasti gymn. pat.*, I.ii.49) shows Molin teaching law at Padua in 1462; on 13 Nov. 1462, his salary was raised from ten to fifty ducats (ST 5, c. 23^v). See also Cecchetti, "Libreria," pp. 166-67.

del Monte, Pietro. (2) da Monte, Montanus. Son of Niccolò.

MONOGRAPHS AND STUDIES. G. degli Agostini, *Notizie*, I, 346-72; J. Haller, *Pier da Monte, ein Gelehrter und päpstlicher Beamter des 15. Jahrhunderts: seine Briefsammlung*; A. Sottili, *Studenti tedeschi e umanesimo italiano nell'Università di Padova durante il Quattrocento*, I: *Pietro del Monte nella società accademica padovana (1430-1433)*; G. Tournoy, "Un nuovo testo del periodo padovano di Pietro del Monte"; A. Zanelli, "Pietro del Monte." I have been unable to consult A. Nodari, "Pietro del Monte collettore e nunzio pontificio in Inghilterra, 1435-1440," *Memoire storiche della diocesi di Brescia*, 28 (1961), 2.

CAREER. B. 1400 or 1404 (see Haller, *Pier da Monte*, *10 n.7) to a prominent citizen family. D. 12 Jan. 1457. The name del Monte subsequently appears among the *cittadino* families: da Mosto, *Archivio*, I, 76. The family suffered reversals after 1430 (noted in del Monte's correspondence with Andrea Giuliani). Upon leaving the University of Padua after 1431, del Monte attended the Council of Basel, where he publicly favored the principle of papal authority, and thence strode forward in his career, favored by several popes. Already named apostolic protonotary, he was sent to England as papal collector from 1435 to 1440. Sent abroad again as legate to France in 1442, he returned to enter his designated see of Brescia in 1445. Retaining that see, he served as papal governor of Perugia from 1451 to 1453 and then in Rome as papal *referendarius* in the last years before his early death.

Title. 1442— Bishop of Brescia.

WORKS. In del Monte's extensive *opera* there are represented humanist genres and specialized works of theology and canon law. Only a few are cited here: *Invectiva adversus ridiculum quendam oratorem*, to Andrea Giuliani; *Monarchia in qua generalium conciliorum materia de potestate prestantia et excellentia Romani pontificis et imperatoris plenissime discutitur*, to Pope

Eugene IV; *Repertorium utriusque juris; De vitiorum inter se differencia et comparatione*, to Humphrey, Duke of Gloucester. *Epistolae*, in Haller, *Pier da Monte* (complete but often digested or excerpted), pp. *1-*185, and Zanelli, "Pietro del Monte" (selected letters from the rich Vatican cod. Lat. 2694), vol. 7, pp. 92-115; also eleven *epistolae* from the Paduan period in Sottili, *Studenti tedeschi*, pp. 66-100. For these, see Haller, pp. *108ff., and Zanelli, passim (especially vol. 7, pp. 324ff., for the orations).

CORRESPONDENCE. Among del Monte's letters published or digested in Haller are those to Jacopino Badoer, Ermolao Barbaro V, Francesco Barbaro, Pietro Barbo, Poggio Bracciolini, Pietro Donato, Tito Livio Frulovisi, Andrea Giuliani, Ambrogio Traversari, and Fantino Vallaresso. Haller indicates for each of the letters ms. sources and previous publication by Zanelli and others. Zanelli provides (vol. 8, pp. 113-15) an index of the letters in cod. Vat. Lat. 2694 used by both authors. Not included by Haller or Zanelli are letters to Pier Candido Decembrio (see V. Zaccaria, "L'epistolario di Pier Candido Decembrio," p. 108) and from Francesco Barbaro (see *Centotrenta*, ed. Sabbadini, pp. 20, 47, 60, 61), Poggio Bracciolini (*Epist.*, ed. Tonellis, II, 119-21, 281-82; III, 82-83, 101-103, 115-16, 216-17; a summary chart of the Poggio/del Monte correspondence in the former's *Opera omnia*, ed. R. Fubini, IV, 738-39), and Ludovico Foscarini (*Epist.*, fols. 281ᵛ-282).

DISCOURSE. Praised for his learning by Flavio Biondo (*It. illus.* [1510], fol. 101ᵛ), del Monte was known as both a learned humanist (especially in his early Paduan years) and canon lawyer and apologist for papal authority. Of his continuing interest in humanist studies there is the evidence of his discussion with George of Trebizond of the interpretation of John 21:22 (see J. Monfasani, *George of Trebizond*, pp. 91ff.; George's dedication to del Monte of his translation in Monfasani, *Collectanea Trapezuntiana*, pp. 311-12), and his late letters to Francesco Barbaro and from Poggio (cited above). Antonio Beccaria dedicated to del Monte his translation of Plutarch's *Pelopidas* (see *Iter*, II, 47, 193). Del Monte housed copyists in his household and collected with care his own papers, consigned by his will to the care of Pietro Barbo: cf. Haller, p. *108, and Cosenza, *Dict.*, III, 2714; also G. Zippel, ed., *Le vite di Paolo II*, p. 92 n. 2.

EDUCATION. With Guarino Veronese and Ermolao Barbaro V; subsequently at Montpellier in France, receiving a masters degree in arts, and at Padua, receiving his doctorate in law on 15 July 1433 (Zonta and Brotto, *Acta*, pp. 211-12, #944, and Zanelli, "Pietro del Monte," vol. 8, pp. 85-86).

Morandi, Filippo, called Filippo da Rimini. (2) de' Morandi; Arimineo, Arimineus, Ariminensis. Son of Federighino.

MONOGRAPHS AND STUDIES. M. L. King, "A Study in Venetian Humanism at Mid-Quattrocento: Filippo da Rimini and his *Symposium de paupertate* (Study and Text)"; A. Pertusi, "La lettera di Filippo da Rimini, cancelliere di

Corfù, a Francesco Barbaro e i primi documenti occidentali sulla caduta di Costantinopoli (1453)." See these works for further bibliographical guidance.

CAREER. B. Rimini c. 1407. D. 1497. Born to a substantial Riminese family, Filippo studied abroad and taught at Padua, Rome, and Bologna before settling in Venice in 1435, attaining Venetian citizenship in 1443 and remaining in his adopted city (except for occasional journeys abroad) until his death more than fifty years thereafter. He taught first in at least one of Venice's neighborhood schools before becoming in 1446 the first publicly appointed teacher in the famous San Marco chancery school, where he presided until 1450 and again in 1463-66. During the years between the first and second San Marco terms, Filippo held the office of chancellor of Corcyra (Corfù) and was there when Constantinople fell to the Turks in 1453, leaving an invaluable account of that event. After his second term at San Marco, he became chancellor to the newly elected patriarch of Venice, Maffeo Gerardo, whom he served for many years.

WORKS. Of Filippo's many works, including both secular and religious verse of great interest, the following should be noted here: several *epistolae*, detailed below; *Epithalamium* for Caterina Caldiera; *Excidium Constantinopolitanae urbis quae quondam Bizantium ferebatur*, to Francesco Barbaro; *Invectiva in vanissimos homines; Oratio* [in praise of Doge Francesco Foscari in the ducal court and the presence of Count Francesco Sforza] (1441); *Oratio in funere Francisci Barbari* (1454); *Symposium de paupertate*. For these works, see especially King, "A Study," Part One; also B. Marx on Filippo's political verse in "Venedig-'altera Roma,' Transformationen eines Mythos," pp. 349ff. The Paduan ms. containing the *Invectiva* was owned by Pietro Barozzi.

CORRESPONDENCE. Letters to Francesco Barbaro are printed (see *Cento-trenta*, ed. Sabbadini, pp. 56, 64). Elsewhere letters to Andrea Contrario, Vinciguerra Dandolo, Pietro Dolfin (and the monks of San Michele da Murano), Andrea and Ermolao Donato, and Cardinal Ludovico [Scarampo] Trevisan; these in Seville, Bibl. Colombina, cod. 5-6-13, respectively, on fols. 22^v (fragmentary, and with accompanying poem, both also in full elsewhere, cf. King, "A Study," Part One, p. 84 n. 15), 64^v-65, 36^{r-v}, 30^v-31, 68, 63^v-64. A long letter to Roberto Malatesta (in Bibliography).

DISCOURSE. Patronized by Francesco Barbaro, perhaps Bernardo Bembo, and others.

Morosini, Barbone. (2) Maurocenus. Son of Barbone. Doctor.

CAREER. B. c. 1414 (AC-BO 163/II, c. 302; presented 3 Dec. 1432). M. 1441, Suordamor di Giovanni Molin (Giomo, *Matrimoni*, II, 121). D. between 12 May 1457 (when the payment of a debt to Morosini was arranged: ST 4, c. 37^v) and 13 Jan. 1458 (ibid., c. 61^v).

Offices. 1446-47, Amb. to Bologna (ST 1, c. 190^v and 2, cc. 14, 20); 1448,

Amb. to Florence (ST 2, c. 85^v); 1450, Count of Trau (Dalmatia) (SGV 4, c. 80); 1451, Sav. tf. (SGV 4, c. 160; SM 4; ST 2, c. 180^v and passim); 1451-52, CX (CXM 14; SGV 4, c. 142); 1452, Sav. tf. (SGV 4, c. 148; SM 4; ST 3; this and the preceding offices held concurrently); 1452-53, Amb. to Naples (CXM 14, c. 125; SM 4; Cicogna, *Iscrizioni*, IV, 461; Barbaro, *Centotrenta*, ed. Sabbadini, pp. 58-60); 1453, Capt. of Verona (Cicogna, *Iscrizioni*, IV, 461; Francesco Barbaro, *epistola* of 2 Dec. 1453, cf. *Centotrenta*, p. 62); 1455, Sav. tf. (SGV 4, c. 147; SM 5; ST 3); 1456, Amb. to Rome (CXM 15, cc. 80^v, 93; ST 3, cc. 187^v, 188, and 4, cc. 2^v, 16; *Comm.*, ed. Predelli, X, 126 [xv, #21]); 1457-58, Pod. of Bergamo (CLN 9, cc. 93^v; ST 4, c. 61^v); died in office.

WORKS. Sansovino (*Venetia*, II, 578) and followers attribute *De immortalitate animae ad mentem Aristotelis* and a commentary on the *Somnium Scipionis*.

CORRESPONDENCE. Correspondence with Francesco Barbaro (cf. *Centotrenta*, ed. Sabbadini, pp. 58-60, 62) and Maffeo Vallaresso (*Epistolae*, pp. 1, 16-17, 22-23, 28-30, 34-35, 68, 80-82, 283-86, 346-47). Letters from Ludovico Foscarini (*Epist.*, fols. 127, 135^v-136, 152^v, 160^{r-v}) and Leonardo Giustiniani (in Bernardo Giustiniani, *Orat. et epist.*, sig. K3^v).

DISCOURSE. Celebrated for his learning by Flavio Biondo (*It. illus.* [Venice, 1510], fol. 101), and as fulfilling the combined ideal of patrician and learned man by Francesco Barozzi (*Oratio pro doctoratu Jacobi Molini*, fol. 28: "Barbonus Maurocenus integerimus atque optimus vir et in maximis ac diversissimis rei publicae nostre muneribus diutissime exercitus ac preterea omnis generis litterarum et iuris praecipue peritissimus") and Ludovico Foscarini (in his letters to Niccolò da Canal [*Epist.*, fol. 200]: "Afferebat enim magnum urbi eius iustitia emolumentum, et prudentia literario ordini decus"; and to the Patriarch Maffeo Contarini [fols. 201^v-202]: "Nullus ei defuisset in patria nostra gradus, disciplina humanitate ornatissimus, iuris consultissimus, dyaleticus acutissimus, philosophus gravissimus, in dicendi vi elloquentia nemini cedebat . . . ."). Participated in the Neapolitan literary circle while ambassador there in 1452-53, and carried back with him George of Trebizond's translation of Plato's *Laws*, dedicated to Francesco Barbaro (see letters by and to Barbaro; those of 27 Sept. and 9 Dec. 1452, 11 Feb., 27 April, 23 May, and 28 Sept. 1453, see *Centotrenta*, ed. Sabbadini, pp. 58-60; also F. Gaeta, "Giorgio da Trebisonda," p. 490 n. 3).

EDUCATION. At Padua, doctorate in arts on 26 Jan. 1434 (Zonta and Brotto, *Acta*, p. 219, #977); license and doctorate in laws on 19 Aug. 1442 (ibid., p. 335, ##1644 and 1655, respectively). While there, he served as Vice-Rector of the jurists in 1439, and perhaps substituted for a professor of law in 1442 or 1443 (Cicogna, *Iscrizioni*, IV, 460). Present at the university from at least 11 Jan. 1434 to at least 24 Nov. 1442 (*Acta*, pp. 219, #972; 340, #1666; and passim).

PROFILES

Morosini, Domenico. (2) Maurocenus. Son of Pietro; cousin of Marcantonio
Morosini and Pietro Dolfin (see J. Schnitzer, *Peter Delfin*, p. 51).

MONOGRAPHS AND STUDIES. C. Finzi, introduction (pp. 1-56) to his edition
of Morosini's *De bene istituta re publica*, with complete chronology (pp. 57-
70). G. Cozzi, "Domenico Morosini e il 'De bene istituta re publica.' "

CAREER. B. December, 1417. M. 1456, Elena di Francesco Ruzzini. Testament
10 July 1498. D. 20 March 1509. Morosini began his career in 1438, when
he was elected *capo del sestier* (Finzi, "Introduction," p. 59), to which office
he was reelected in coming years, but held no office known to me after 1441
until his political career resumed in 1471. Morosini may have pursued a
commercial career during the three decades prior to 1471. He died in possession of a fortune of more than 80,000 ducats.

Offices. 1471, Duc. el., Niccolò Tron (MC-Regina, c. 101ᵛ); 1472, CX;
1473, Duc. el., Niccolò Marcello (MC-Regina, c. 122ᵛ); CX (CXM 18, c.
24ᵛ); 1474, Duc. el., Pietro Mocenigo (MC-Regina, c. 143); 1474-75, CX;
1475-76, Cons.; 1477, Sav. tf.; 1478, Sav. tf.; Duc. el., Giovanni Mocenigo
(MC-Regina, c. 177ᵛ); 1478-79, Cons.; 1480, Sav. gr.; 1481, Sav. gr. (ST 8,
c. 124); 1482, Cons.; 1482-83, Sav. gr.; 1483, Sav. gr.; 1484, Sav. gr.; 1484-
85, Cons.; 1485, Sav. gr.; Duc. el., Marco Barbarigo (MC-Stella, cc. 61ᵛ, 62ᵛ);
1486, Sav. gr. (CXM 23; SM 12); Duc. el., Agostino Barbarigo (MC-Stella,
cc. 76, 76ᵛ, 77ᵛ); 1487, Sav. gr.; 1487-88, Cons.; 1488, Sav. gr.; 1489, Sav.
gr.; 1490-91, Sav. gr.; 1490-91, Sav. gr., three terms; 1491-92, Cons.; 1492-
93, Sav. gr., two terms; 1492, Proc. di San Marco (3 Dec.); 1493-95, Sav. gr.,
two or three terms; 1499-1500, Sav. gr.; 1501, Sav. gr.; Duc. el., Leonardo
Loredan.

WORKS. *De bene instituta re publica* [DBIRP]. Morosini is known to have
written other works, now lost: on the miracles of San Lorenzo Giustiniani,
on the prophesies of Joachim and Anselm (these two still extant in 1589),
and a translation and annotation of the Sibyl Eritrea's prophecy to the Greeks
on the way to Troy. For these works, see Finzi, "Introduction," pp. 7-8.
Morosini wrote the DBIRP between 1497 and his death, never ordering it
systematically, and leaving it unfinished. The manuscript that survives was
prepared by his loving but inexpert son.

CORRESPONDENCE. Letters from Ermolao Barbaro G (*Epist.*, ed. Branca, II,
31-32); Matteo Bosso (see Finzi, "Introduction," p. 9); Pietro Dolfin (*Epist.*
CCXLII, ed. Martène and Durand, col. 1152; *Epist. [1524]*, Book III, #49
and #60; IV, #42; V, #78 [also in Schnitzer, *Peter Delfin*, p. 361]; VII, #29);
Niccolò Sagundino (*Epist. et opusc.*, fols. 47ᵛ-49ᵛ; 58-59; 98-100ᵛ; 103ᵛ-106).

DISCOURSE. Esteemed for his learning by Pietro Dolfin, Bernardo Giustiniani,
and Francesco Negri (Finzi, "Introduction," pp. 7-9). That he possessed a
library of some value is evident from his testament (AN, Testamenti C. Rizzo

[my reading; Finzi reads Ruzini], B. 1227.122, c. 2ᵛ, and B. 1229.152, #23), where he specifically ordered that his books not be sold or distributed after his death but kept for his heirs as an encouragement to and instrument for study. Matteo Collazio dedicated to him his *De verbo civilitate* (see Bibliography), *De fine oratoris*, and a collection of *Opuscula* (cf. Cosenza, *Dict.*, II, 1036 and 1035, respectively). Paolo Orlandini dedicated to Morosini his *De notitia futurorum contra astrologos* (see *Iter*, I, 99). Niccolò Sagundino dedicated to him translations of two orations of Demosthenes, the *Pro Ctesiphonte* and *Olynthiaca prima* (ibid., II, 318, 432; also J. Monfasani, *George of Trebizond*, pp. 62-63, who cites P. Mastrodimitris, Νικόλαος ὁ Σεκουνδινός; I have been unable to utilize the sections of this work in modern Greek). From these works and the letters given above, it is evident that Morosini was Sagundino's patron.

Morosini, Marcantonio. (3) Maurocenus. Son of Roberto; cousin of Domenico Morosini and Pietro Dolfin (cf. J. Schnitzer, *Peter Delfin*, p. 51). Miles.

CAREER. B. c. 1435 (AC-BO 163/II, c. 310ᵛ, presented 13 Oct. 1453). Testament 29 March 1508 (AN, Testamenti C. Rizzo, B. 1228.248, 1229.154). D. 12 April 1509 (Sanuto, *Diarii*, VIII, 81). A contemporary, Marco Morosini (di Lorenzo), was also active in literary and political affairs. It is his poem that appears in Marc. Lat XII, 211 (4179), fol. 105; and perhaps also this figure whose biography is given by G. Pavanello, *Un maestro del Quattrocento*, pp. 141-42.

Offices. 1474-75, Amb. to Burgundy (ST 7, cc. 15ᵛ, 18, 34); 1476-77, CX (CXM 18, 19); 1477, Pod. and Capt. of Crema (SGV 6, c. 92ᵛ); 1479, Amb. to Florence (ST 8, cc. 71ᵛ, 76ᵛ); 1480, Sav. tf., two terms (CLN 12, c. 119ᵛ; SM 11; ST 8); CX (CXM 19, 20; held in part concurrently with preceding office); 1481, Pod. of Bergamo (SGV 16, c. 19); 1482, Sav. tf. (CLN 13; ST 8, c. 180); 1483, Prov. with the army (CXM 21; ST 8, c. 182ᵛ); 1484, Pod. of Brescia (SGV 6, c. 91); 1485, Avog. (CXM 22; SGV 6, c. 112); 1485-87, Amb. to Milan (Malipiero, *Annali*, pp. 681-82; B. Marx, *Bartolomeo Pagello*, p. 29 and n. 49); 1487-88, Avog. (CXM 23, 24; SGV 6, c. 112); 1488-90, Amb. to Naples (ST 10, c. 119, and 11, c. 6ᵛ); 1490-91, CX (CXM 24); 1491, Pod. of Verona (SGV 6, c. 16ᵛ); 1493-94, Avog. (CXM 26; SGV 6, c. 132, and 7, c. 2ᵛ); 1494-95, Capt. of Padua (ST 12; SGV 6, c. 50ᵛ); 1495, Prov. with the army (F. Gabotto and A. Confalonier, "Vita di Giorgio Merula," first part, p. 283 n. 2); 1496, Amb. to Emperor Maximilian at Vigevano (Malipiero, *Annali*, p. 465; Sanuto, *Diarii*, I, 277 etc.); 1497-98, CX (CXM 27; Sanuto, *Diarii*, I, 835 etc.); 1498-99, Cons. (CLN 15; CXM 27, 28; MC-Stella; SGV 7, c. 1; SM 14; ST 13; Sanuto, *Diarii*, I, 1108; II, 42 etc.); 1499, Sav. gr. (Sanuto, *Diarii*, II, 953, 1028); Prov. in the field in Brescia and Cremona, and Capt. of Cremona (Malipiero, *Annali*, pp. 557, 565; Sanuto, *Diarii*, II, 968 etc., III, 8 etc.); 1500-1, Sav. gr. (SM 15; ST 13; Sanuto, *Diarii*, III, 860 etc.); 1501-2, Cons. (CLN 15; CXM 29; SGV 7, c. 1ᵛ; SM 15; ST 14; Sanuto, *Diarii*, III, 1629 etc., IV); 1502-3, Sav. gr. (SM 15; ST 14; Sanuto,

Diarii, IV, 306 etc.); 1503, Sav. gr. (ST 14, c. 157; Sanuto, *Diarii*, V, 52 etc.);
Proc. di San Marco (Cappellari, *Camp. ven.*, III, c. 121; P. Dolfin, *Epist.*
[1524], sig. B viii^v; Sanuto, *Diarii*, V, 67, 68); 1504, Sav. gr. (SM 16; ST 15;
Sanuto, *Diarii*, VI, 5, 38, 64 etc.); 1505, Sav. gr. (MC-Deda; SM 16; Sanuto,
Diarii, VI, 189 etc.); 1506, Sav. gr. (SM 16; Sanuto, *Diarii*, VI, 323); 1507,
Sav. gr. (Sanuto, *Diarii*, VI, 518, 538; VII, 39, 41, 52).

CORRESPONDENCE. Letters from Matteo Bosso (see G. Soranzo, *L'umanista*
canonico regolare Matteo Bosso, pp. 55 and n. 36; 128 and n. 60; 274 and
n. 241; 294); Ludovico Cendrata (see *Iter*, I, 82); Pietro Dolfin (*Epist. [1524]*,
VII, #73); Matthias Drevitius (see *Iter*, II, 231); Bernardino Gadolo (*Epist.*,
162-82; also published [not seen, see *Iter*, II, 500], by A. Cacciamani in
Camaldoli, 6 [1952], 64-71, addressed to Morosini along with Sebastiano
Badoer and Girolamo Giorgi); Pietro Perleone (*Epist.*, fols. 176^v-177); and
Marcantonio Sabellico (*Opera*, fols. 10^v, 55^v-57, 60^v; see also below for ded-
icatory letters).

DISCOURSE. Praised lavishly by Panfilo Sasso in his *Epigrammata* (F. Gabotto
and A. Badini Confalonieri, "Vita di Giorgio Merula," first part, p. 283 n. 2)
and by others in dedications of works to him, listed below. Pietro Contarini
wrote a poem to him (in his *Ad Gelliam elegiae*, fol. 40), and Marino Sanuto
reported his skill at extemporaneous Latin oratory (*Diarii*, I, 304). He appeared with Domenico Morosini as an interlocutor in Sperone Speroni's dialogue *Sopra la fortuna* (Gabotto and Confalonieri, "Vita," first part, p. 283
and n. 7). Hieronymus Avantius dedicated to Morosini and Mariano Garzoni
his *De laudibus philosophiae moralis oratio* and to Morosini alone his *Emen-*
dationes (see Cosenza, *Dict.*, III, 2244); Girolamo Bologni his *Mediolanum*
sive itinerarium carmen epicum from the third book of his *Promiscuorum*
libri (Marx, *Pagello*, p. 29 and n. 49); Matteo Bosso his *De instituendo*
sapientia animo (Soranzo, *L'umanista canonico*, p. 128 and n. 60); Tristano
Calco his *De magistratibus Mediolanensibus* (1487) (*Iter*, II, 366); Coriolano
Cippico his *Petri Moceneci venetae classis imperatoris contra Ottomanum*
Turcarum principem rebus gestis, written at Morosini's suggestion (M. Palma,
"Cippico, Coriolano," in DBI, XXV [1981], 736); Aldo Manuzio his edition
of Lucan's *Pharsalia* (1502), based on a manuscript from Morosini's collection
(see Gabotto and Confalonieri, "Vita," first part, p. 283 n. 6); Giorgio Merula
his *Expositio in Sapphus epistolam* (1471) and his *Adversus Domitii [Cald-*
erini] Commentarios (1478) (ibid., pp. 283-84, and A. Zeno, *Diss. voss.*, II,
69, 71); Antonio Moretto his edition of Giasone Maino's *Commentaria in*
secundam partem Digesti Veteris (Cosenza, *Dict.*, III, 2370); Marcantonio
Sabellico his *De reparatione latinae linguae* and his *Epistolarium familiarium*
libri XII (*Opera*, fols. 108^v and 1^v); he wished to have dedicated to him, but
did not succeed in that ambition, Filippo Foresti's *Supplementa chronicarum*
(Gabotto and Confalonieri, "Vita," p. 283 n. 2). A major patron of Giorgio
Merula (ibid., pp. 283-84), he was also a supporter some years earlier of Pietro
Perleone who sent Morosini for criticism his commentary on Juvenal (see the
latter's letters to Morosini cited above). Morosini placed his rich library at

the disposal of Aldo Manuzio, and left books at his death to be distributed by his executors (Gabotto and Confalonieri, "Vita," p. 283 n. 6; Agostini, *Notizie*, I, x1). In addition to books, Morosini disposed of valuable medals and decorative objects.

Morosini, Paolo. (2) Maurocenus. Son of Egidio (Zilio).

MONOGRAPHS AND STUDIES. G. degli Agostini, *Notizie*, I, 179-88; G. dalla Santa, "Due lettere di umanisti veneziani (Lauro Quirini e Lodovico Foscarini a Paolo Morosini)."

CAREER. B. c. 1406. M. 1424, Anna di Giovanni Falier (Giomo, *Matrimoni*, I, 442 gives 1427). D. c. 1482. Morosini was certainly alive shortly prior to 9 May 1480, when Pietro Dolfin wrote in a letter to the Abbot Urbano that he "vivit adhuc, cuius vita erit nobis non inutilis" (*Epistolae CCXLII*, ed. Martène and Durand, cols. 1095-96). Morosini may have refused the honor of knighthood at Ratisbon, as he had that of the doctorate at Padua (see below). For Morosini's tomb inscription in the Church of San Gregorio, see Cicogna, *Iscrizioni*, I, 260. There are several contemporary homonyms. Paolo Morosini di Marino and di Niccolo appear in SGV 4, in substantial roles. Morosini's political career had begun by 1439 when he served as *auditor veterum sententiarum* (CLN 7, c. 20; SGV 4, c. 153).

Offices. 1449, Castellan of Coron (SGV 4, c. 84); 1451, Pod. and Capt. of Feltre (SGV 4, c. 65); Amb. to Istria; 1451-52, Sav. tf. (SGV 4, c. 160; SM 4; ST 3); 1452, one of five provveditori sent to honor Emperor Frederick III; 1453, Amb. to Rhodes (SM 4, cc. 161^v, 167, 168, 169); Amb. to Rome (ST 3, c. 66); 1454, Sav. tf. (SGV 4, c. 148; SM 5; ST 3, c. 106^v); Pod. and Capt. of Crema (SGV 4, c. 99; ST 3, c. 127^v); 1456, Pod. and Capt. of Crema (CXM 15, c. 100^v); 1458, Sav. tf. (SGV 4, c. 147^v; SM 5; ST 4); 1459, Amb. to Ferrara; Sav. tf. (SGV 4, c. 166; SM 6; ST 4); 1460, Sav. tf.; 1461, Amb. to D. Stefano of San Saba; CX (CXM 16, c. 37^v); 1461-62, Sav. tf. (ST 4, c. 180^v); 1462, Duc. el., Cristoforo Moro (MC-Regina, c. 39); Amb. to Emperor (ST 5, cc. 12^v, 13^v); 1462-63, Sav. tf. (SM 7; ST 5); 1463, Amb. to Poland and Bohemia; 1463-64, CX (CXM 16); 1464, Capt. of Vicenza (CXM 16, c. 122^v); Sav. tf. (ST 5, c. 84); Amb. to Austria (ST 5, c. 88^v); 1465-66, Pod. of Treviso; 1466, Sav. tf. (ST 5, c. 163^v); 1466-67, CX (CXM 17); 1467, Prov. to Mediterranean colonies (SM 8, cc. 110, 121; ST 6, c. 128^v); 1467-68, Avog. (CXM 17; SGV 6, c. 7); 1468, one of the ambs. charged to accompany the Emperor to Rome (CLN 11, c. 35^v; ST 6, cc. 41^v, 43; it was surely Paolo Morosini, and not Pietro, holding the title of Venetian amb. to Rome, who in the name of the Procuratori of San Marco took possession in that city on 26 June 1468 of the library of Cardinal Bessarion [*Comm.*, ed. Predelli, X, 197 (xvi, #22), and below]); 1469, CX (CXM 17); Prov. in Romagna (ST 6, c. 67^v; Ven., Bibl. del Mus. Correr, cod. PD.C 667/12); Sav. tf. (ST 6, c. 80); 1470, Sav. tf. (CXM 17, c. 97; SM 9; ST 6, c. 80 and passim); 1470-71, Prov. at Brescia (ST 6, c. 96^v); 1471, Amb. to Diet of Ratisbon; 1472, Prov. to examine terraferma fortifications; Sav. gr.; 1473, Sav. gr. (CXM

18; ST 7); Duc. el., Niccolò Marcello; 1474, Sav. gr. (CLN 11; SM 9; ST 7); Cons. (CLN 12; CXM 18; MC-Regina; SM 10; ST 7); Duc. el., Pietro Mocenigo; 1474-75, Amb. to Florence and Rome (SM 10, cc. 32ᵛ, 38ᵛ; ST 7, cc. 62, 65ᵛ, 66; F. Pintor, "Due ambascerie," p. 786); 1475, Sav. gr. (SM 10; ST 7); 1476, Duc. el., Andrea Vendramin; Sav. gr. (SM 10; ST 7); Amb. to Naples and Rome (on this occasion or soon after, Morosini addressed to Pope Sixtus IV a work on divine foreknowledge; see below); 1477, Sav. gr. (ST 7); Prov. in Friuli; 1477-78, Sav. gr. (CXM 19; ST 7); 1478, Cons. (SM 10; ST 8).

WORKS. *De aeterna temporalique Christi generatione in judaice improbationem perfidiae*, to Pope Paul II (the first book published in Padua [1473]); *Defensio venetorum ad Europae principes contra obtrectatores*, to Cardinal Marco Barbo [DVEP]; *De fato seu praescientia divina et liberi humani arbitrii libertate*, to Pope Sixtus IV; *Lettera a Cicco Simonetta*; *De rebus ac forma reipublicae venetae* [DRF], to Gregor Heimburg. I know of the *De fato* solely from *Iter*, II, 387. The ms. was copied for Pope Sixtus IV by Andreas Lazaronus on 17 July 1477, not long after Morosini had been in Rome as Venetian ambassador: the author comments that he proffered the work "pro tua in me clementia dum coram te venetus orator assiterem" (fol. 2). The work attests to Morosini's broad philosophical learning, and lends support to the suggestion that he studied at Padua and was an able but unwilling candidate for the doctorate (see below).

CORRESPONDENCE. Letters from Ludovico Foscarini (some in dalla Santa, "Due lettere," pp. 95-96, and G. B. Picotti in *Dieta di Mantova*, pp. 444-46, 457-59; others in the ms. *Epist.*, fols. 15-19ᵛ; 53ᵛ; 55-57; 346ᵛ-347; for the Foscarini-Morosini relationship, see Picotti, "Le lettere di L. Foscarini"); Lauro Quirini (in A. Pertusi, "Epistole storiche" in LQU, pp. 258-59; also in dalla Santa, "Due lettere," pp. 94-95); Antonio Vinciguerra (in B. Beffa, *Antonio Vinciguerra*, pp. 154-56).

DISCOURSE. Praised as learned by Francesco Pisani (*Oratio de universis ornamentis philosophiae*, p. 366) and Giovanni Morosini (cf. B. Nardi, "Scuola di Rialto" [UEUV ed.], p. 126). Filippo Buonaccorsi (*De his quae a Venetis tentata sunt* [1533 ed.], p. 14) and Francesco Negri (*De aristocratia*, fol. 92) reported that he was commonly called "the wise." Morosini was instrumental in persuading Cardinal Bessarion to donate his books to Venice, as he subsequently did; his collection formed the base of Venice's library (Agostini, *Notizie*, I, xxxi-xxxii, and career summary at 1468).

EDUCATION. Studied at Padua c. 1431, refusing the doctorate in arts (Agostini, *Notizie*, I, 179). Morosini knew Hebrew as well as Greek and Latin.

Negri, Francesco. (3) Son of George (Cernoëvich).

MONOGRAPHS AND STUDIES. G. degli Agostini, *Notizie*, II, 473-87; G. Mercati, "Pescennio Francesco Negro Veneto," in *Ultimi contributi*, II, 24-109; P. Verrua, "Cinque orazioni dette dall'umanista Francesco Negri nello studio di Padova" and "L'Università di Padova circa il 1488 nell' 'Opusculum scribendi epistolas' di Francesco Negri." Mercati's work is exhaustive.

CAREER. B. April, 1452, in Venice, son of a recent Dalmatian immigrant and a Venetian mother (the name Negri subsequently appears among those of *cittadino* families: da Mosto, *Archivio*, I, 76; the name is, however, exceptionally common in Venice). D. after 9 Nov. 1523. Having completed his education, Negri became a priest (c. 1478) in order to continue his literary studies, and was made *piovano* of S. Giovanni Decollato in Venice. Anticipating higher dignities, in 1483 he fell under suspicion by the Venetian government because of his close relationship to the recently deposed tyrant of Veglia, thenceforth a Venetian possession. Released the same year, he moved on to Padua and the next stages of his life which were spent abroad, perhaps in severe poverty (if Negri's own words are to be believed), and certainly in constant quest for satisfactory patronage and advancement. From 1484 to 1494, he remained for the most part in northern Italy, teaching without a stable position. From 1494 to 1505, he served the Cardinal Ippolito I d'Este in Italy and Hungary. From 1506 to 1515, he lived in Rome and the south of Italy, supporting himself as teacher and courtier.

WORKS. For Negri's many works, see Mercati's study, especially pp. 97ff. Listed here are a few representative works composed in that stage of his career when Negri was most closely linked to Venice, or those specifically related to Venice or Venetians: the *De aristocratia*, to Doge Leonardo Loredan; *Grammatica; Modus epistolandi* [= *Opusculum scribendi epistolas*]; *Orationes* for Agnesina Bondina, the mother of Pietro Roccabonella, and for Girolamo Reguardati; *Paeonicum saphicon*, for Cassandra Fedele. I have consulted the presentation copy to Loredan of the *De aristocratia*, neither the first nor the final version of the work. For its complex history, revised several times for different rulers, including two doges of Venice (Loredan, and his predecessor Agostino Barbarigo), see Mercati, "Negro," passim, but especially the Appendix, pp. 40ff. Mercati's discussion is based on the autograph cod. Vat. Lat. 4033, described on p. 24. In that version, the work is entitled *De moderanda venetorum aristocratia* and *Peri archon*. Negri also wrote a work (not seen) while a prisoner in Venice in 1483: the *De humanae conditionis miseria* to the Venetian Pat. Maffeo Gerardo; cf. Mercati, pp. 48, 50. Negri's *Grammatica* and *Modus epistolandi*, variously titled, appear in several early editions. Verrua publishes three other orations not named here.

CORRESPONDENCE. Letter to Marcantonio Sabellico (*Opera*, fol. 48). Also letters to Tebaldeo Tebaldi and Ercole and Cardinal Ippolito d'Este; see Mercati, "Negro," Appendix, pp. 59ff.

DISCOURSE. Praised for his learning by Sabellico, criticized by Erasmus (cf. Agostini, *Notizie*, II, 479; Sabellico, *De rep. lat. ling.*, fol. 114ᵛ). He taught the sons of Lorenzo Zane in Rome, 1484-85.

EDUCATION. With Pietro Bruto, Giovanni Mario Filelfo, Domizio Calderini, and Domenico Bragadin, and at Padua, where he received a doctorate in law in 1476. See Mercati's valuable discussion of Negri's education, "Negro," pp. 38ff.

Orsini, Michele. (2?) Ursinis. Son of Giovanni Orsini del Bancho.

MONOGRAPHS AND STUDIES. None, but see the brief sketch of G. Pavanello in *Un maestro del Quattrocento (Giovanni Aurelio Augurello)*, pp. 110-11, relied upon here unless otherwise noted.

CAREER. B. c. 1410/15 (based on the university career and Orsini's reputedly great age in 1497). Testament 8 Apr. 1495, codicil 17 Sept. 1497 (AN, Testamenti C. Rizzo, B. 1228.243, 1229.40). D. 1497. Orsini was still alive on the date when the codicil was signed, but had died before 16 Dec. 1497, when the bishopric of Pola, following his death, was conceded to Altobello Averoldi of Brescia (despite the previous occupant's renunciation in favor of his great-nephew; see below, and C. Cenci, "Senato veneto 'Probae,' " p. 430 n. 1; Malipiero, *Annali*, p. 707). For Orsini's family, prominent and long-established in Venice, note the comment at his doctorate of B. Pietro Donato: Orsini was "ex generosa et iam diu maximis honoribus et dignitatibus illustrata Ursinorum familia natum" (Zonta and Brotto, *Acta*, pp. 362-63, #1812). The Orsini family name subsequently appears among the *cittadini originari* of Venice (da Mosto, *Archivio*, I, 76); the Orsini family honored with Venetian nobility was foreign and held that status as an honor only, never residing in Venice (see R. Bratti, *I codici nobiliari del Museo Correr di Venezia*, p. 16). Michele was, however, related to the noble Malipiero family. In 1426, his sister Orsina married Donato di Domenico Malipiero, a nephew of the Pasquale Malipiero who became doge in 1457. It was upon Donato's grandson Giovanni that he attempted to bestow the vacated see of Pola. For these connections, see M. Barbaro, *Arbori*, IV, cc. 407, 408, 409; Giomo, *Matrimoni*, II, 192; AC-Cron. Mat., R. 107/2, c. 179; Cicogna, *Iscrizioni*, I, 362. Orsini appeared unsuccessfully in probae for the bishoprics of Torcello in 1471 and of Trau in 1483 (Cenci, "Senato veneto 'Probae,' " pp. 404, #106 and 413, #112, respectively).

Titles. 1449— Prior of San Antonio di Castello; 1475-97, Bishop of Pola (Gams [*Ser. episc.*, p. 803] inexplicably lists Jacopo Vallaresso for Pola, 1493/94); *renounced in favor of his great-nephew Giovanni Malipiero in 1497* (ST 13, c. 20ᵛ); 1483-84, *Vicar and suffragen of Pietro Foscari, Bishop of Padua* (Cenci, "Senato veneto 'Probae,' " p. 413, #112).

WORKS. *[Epistola] religiosae sorori; De summa venetorum origine*, to Francesco Filelfo (1462). The Bibliography gives Milan and Glasgow manuscripts. The Glasgow version is untitled, and appears among a series of consolations to Jacopo Antonio Marcello on the death of his son Valerio. The *De origine* contains allusions to that tragedy and a celebration of the Marcello family.

Vat. Lat. 5280 (not seen; see *Iter*, II, 332) contains a much larger work dealing with the same historiographical issue.

CORRESPONDENCE. Letters from Franceso Filelfo (*Epist. fam.*, fols. 128ᵛ, 129, 130ᵛ, 136ᵛ, 137ᵛ, 140ʳ⁻ᵛ, 142ᵛ, 149, 155ᵛ).

DISCOURSE. Giovanni Aurelio Augurello wrote a verse praising Orsini's work on Venice and celebrating his promotion to the see of Pola (Pavanello, *Maestro*). Orsini was a client of Jacopo Antonio Marcello, close to the family around the time of the child Valerio's death (1 Jan. 1461); see the *De origine*, one of the works included in the consolatory literature assembled to mark that event. While deferential to Filelfo, he was seemingly also in a position to extend favors to that humanist; *De origine*, fols. 15ᵛ-21, and Filelfo's comment in his *Epist. fam.*, fol. 137ᵛ. For Orsini's relations with Filelfo, see the letters cited.

EDUCATION. A student of law at Padua from at least 19 March 1442, Orsini received his license and doctorate in law on 26 March and 2 April, respectively, of 1444 (Zonta and Brotto, *Acta*, pp. 327, #1584; 360, #1792; 362-63, #1812, respectively).

Perleone, Pietro. (2) Perleo, Parleo, Paraleonibus, Perleonibus.

MONOGRAPHS AND STUDIES. None, but see the useful profiles in G. Pavanello, *Un maestro del Quattrocento (Giovanni Aurelio Augurello)*, pp. 83-84, and C. Tonini, *La coltura letteraria e scientifica in Rimini dal secolo XIV ai primi del XIX*, I, 179-85.

CAREER. B. Rimini, c. 1400 (based on the career record; neither Pavanello nor Tonini hazards a date). D. shortly before 22 April 1463, but after 13 June 1462. Perleone had recently died in April 1463 when he was replaced as teacher in the San Marco school (ST 5, c. 35ᵛ, published in part by B. Nardi, "Letteratura e cultura" [CVQ ed.], p. 120 n. 51; also another version of this document in CLN 10, c. 78ᵛ, published by Pavanello, *Maestro*, p. 84, who assigns the document to R. 12). He was still alive in June 1462, when he was granted permission to visit the baths for his health (CLN 10, c. 63ᵛ, published by Pavanello, *Maestro*, pp. 83-84, who assigns the document once again to R. 12). After studies in Tuscany, Perleone resided in Venice in 1436-41, then (having been granted citizenship *de intus* on 22 July 1438 [Senato-Privilegi 2, c. 21ᵛ]) journeyed to Constantinople to perfect his Greek, and subsequently taught in Milan and Genoa. Having returned to his native Rimini, he served as historiographer for Sigismondo Malatesta, then moved to Venice, where he taught from 1457 until his death in 1463 in the publicly funded San Marco school. The document of his appointment to the San Marco position is published by Pavanello, *Maestro*, p. 83 (who assigns the document to R. 11, not 9, of the series cited). At some time between 1457 and the end of 1460, Perleone also tutored privately the boy Valerio, son of the patrician patron and humanist Jacopo Antonio Marcello (see the *Laudatio in Valerium filium*, esp. pp. 242-43).

WORKS. Consolatory *epistola* to Jacopo Antonio Marcello, and full *consolatoria* (the *Laudatio in Valerium filium*) to the same; *Epistola consolatoria ad Nicolaum Sagundinum*; three *epistolae; Oratio* [on studies]; *Oratio in funere Iani Campofregosi, D. Senensium*; trans., Isocrates' *Ad Demonicum*, with preface to Brancaleo Grillus. The latter work, in addition to the version cited in the Bibliography, also appears in several other manuscripts, with and without preface, and occasionally mistitled *ad Hypponicum*; cf. *Iter*, I, 343; II, 46, 290, 475. In addition to the letters cited, a volume of letters existed in the eighteenth century but is not now known to me to be extant (Tonini, *Coltura letteraria*, I, 184). Tonini denies the attribution to Perleone of two epithalamia contained in Marc. Lat. XI, 80 (3057), along with an *Oratio de milite* also bearing Perleone's name as author (fols. 343-51^v). Tonini describes other works of Perleone's written in Rimini, which won for him recognition as court historian (I, 180).

CORRESPONDENCE. The Vatican *epistolae* cited above include two to Marcantonio Morosini (fols. 176^v-177) and one to Vitale Lando (fols. 177-78^v); also many letters from Francesco Filelfo (*Epist. fam.*, fols. 13^v-14, 30^v-31, 39, 41, 42^v, 43, 47^v-48, 50^v, 63, 66, 66^v, 70, 72, 75, 75^v, 76^v, 77, 78^v, 82^v-83, 92^v, 85bis^v, 99^v, 110, 115bis^{r-v}, and his *Cent-dix lettres grecques*, ed. E. Legrand, pp. 60-61), one from Bernardo Giustiniani (in P. H. Labalme, *Bernardo Giustiniani*, pp. 66-67 n. 89), and one to two inadequately identified Venetians, perhaps Ma[rco] Bo[no] and Leo[nardo] Lor[edan] (in Marc. Lat. XIII, 63 [4221], fols. 25^v-26).

DISCOURSE. In 1433, Bernardo Giustiniani arranged for Perleone to become tutor to the children of Fantino Michiel, whose sudden death thwarted the plan (cf. Labalme, *Bernardo Giustiniani*, pp. 65ff.). In 1460, Perleone competed along with George of Trebizond and Giovanni Mario Filelfo to win the position of public historiographer, which was in fact not created at that time; Filelfo subsequently directed an invective against his two competitors (see A. Pertusi, "Gli inizi della storiografia umanistica," pp. 302ff., and F. Gilbert, "Biondo, Sabellico," pp. 278ff.; Filelfo's *Invettiva contro Pietro Perleone e Giorgio Trapezunzio*, published by Gabotto). Perleone counted among his Venetian students (in addition to Valerio Marcello, for whom see "Career" above) the lifelong friends Pietro Barozzi and Pietro Dolfin (and with them the future doge Leonardo Loredan): see the standard sources cited; also the *Oratio funebris* for Dolfin by Eusebio Priuli, ed. E. Martène and U. Durand, III, 1218. Perleone was also one of the teachers of the Veronese Matteo Bosso; cf. G. Soranzo, *L'umanista canonico regolare Lateranense Matteo Bosso di Verona (1427-1502)*, p. 164.

EDUCATION. With Filelfo in Florence and Siena, John Argyropoulos in Constantinople.

Pisani, Paolo. (3) Pisanus. Son of Luca. Miles.

CAREER. B. c. 1454 (AC-BO 164/III, c. 283; presented 22 Oct. 1472). D. 13
Feb. 1510 (cf. P. Rigo, "Catalogo e tradizione degli scritti di Girolamo
Donato," p. 63 n. 68; Sanuto gives 3 Feb.: *Diarii,* IX, 529, 532).
Offices. 1484, Amb. to Austria (ST 9, cc. 24, 70; Malipiero, *Annali,* p.
290); 1492, Amb. to Emperor (A. Medin, "Scritti umanistici di Marco Dandolo," pp. 404-405); 1493-94, Amb. to Rome (CLN 14, c. 90ᵛ; CXM 26, cc.
82ᵛ-83, 83ʳ⁻ᵛ; ST 12, cc. 39ᵛ-40); 1495, Amb. to Rome (Malipiero, *Annali,* p.
695); 1495-96, Avog. (CXM 26, 27; SGV 6, c. 132, and 7 già 12, c. 2ᵛ; SM
14; ST 12); 1496-97, CX (CXM 27, cc. 52ᵛ and passim; SGV 9 già 13, c.
10ᵛ; Sanuto, *Diarii,* I, 382, etc.); 1497-98, Pod. of Bergamo (CXM 27, c. 52ᵛ;
SGV 6, c. 19, and 8 già 7, c. 56ᵛ; Sanuto, *Diarii,* I, 822-23, 831, II, 74); 1499,
Sav. tf. (SM 14; ST 13; Sanuto, *Diarii,* II, 285 etc.); 1499-1500, Avog. (CXM
28; SGV 6, c. 132, and 7 già 12, c. 2ᵛ; ST 13; Sanuto, *Diarii,* II, 1026 etc.,
III); 1500, Sav. tf. (ST 13; Sanuto, *Diarii,* III, 439 etc.); 1500-1, CX (CXM
28, c. 118 and passim; Sanuto, *Diarii,* III, 595 etc., IV); 1501, Duc. el.,
Leonardo Loredan (MC-Stella, cc. 187, 187ᵛ; Sanuto, *Diarii,* IV, 127, 129,
133); 1502, Vice-pod. of Cremona (SGV 6, c. 131; Sanuto, *Diarii,* IV, 246
etc.); 1503-4, Capt. of Cremona (SGV 6, c. 131; Sanuto, *Diarii,* IV, 615 etc.,
V); 1504, Sav. gr. (SM 16; ST 15; Sanuto, *Diarii,* VI, 29 etc.); 1505, Amb.
in obedientia to Pope Julius II (MC-Deda, c. 18ʳ⁻ᵛ; Sanuto, *Diarii,* VI, 139
etc.); Sav. gr. (SM 16; Sanuto, *Diarii,* VI, 143 etc.); Cons. (MC-Deda; SGV
7 già 12, c. 2; Sanuto, *Diarii,* VI, 147 etc.); 1505-7, Capt. of Padua (SGV 8
già 7, c. 29; Sanuto, *Diarii,* VI, 249 etc.); 1507, Amb. to King Louis XII in
Milan (P. Bembo, *Hist. ven.,* 237; Sanuto, *Diarii,* VII, 54 etc.); Sav. gr. (SM
16; ST 15, c. 159ᵛ; Sanuto, *Diarii,* VII, 121 etc.); 1508, Cons. (CLN 16, c.
21ᵛ; CXM 30, c. 196; MC-Deda; SGV 7 già 12, c. 27ᵛ; SM 17; ST 16; Sanuto,
Diarii, VII, 285 etc.); 1509, Sav. gr. (ST 16, c. 80; Sanuto, *Diarii,* VII, 737
etc., VIII); 1509-10, Amb. to Rome; died on mission (Rigo, "Catalogo," p.
63 n. 68).

WORKS. Pisani delivered the funeral oration (not known by me to be extant)
for Doge Marco Barbarigo (1486) according to good contemporary witnesses:
Malipiero, *Annali,* p. 680; F. Buonaccorsi, *De his quae a Venetis tentata sunt*
(1533 ed.), p. 88.

CORRESPONDENCE. Letters from Girolamo Borgia (see Rigo, "Per il carteggio
di Girolamo Donato," p. 538; Cosenza, *Dict.,* IV, 2807), Marco Dandolo (in
Medin, "Scritti umanistici di M. Dandolo," pp. 371-72, 382-83; see also 352,
353), Pietro Dolfin (*Epist. [1524],* sigs. b, 17ᵛ, m6ʳ⁻ᵛ, n3ᵛ), and Bernardino
Gadolo (among his *Epist.,* pp. 239-41).

DISCOURSE. Marino Becichemo dedicated to Pisani Chapter 91 of his
Epistolicarum quaestionum centuria (with his *Panegiricus*); Girolamo Bologni,
Book V of his *Liber promiscuorum* (see *Iter,* II, 11, among other loci); Vettore
Pisani, the preface to Giorgio Valla's edition of the *Opera* of Avienus Rufus

Sextus (see J. L. Heiberg, *Beiträge zur Geschichte Georg Vallas*, p. 23); Giorgio Valla, his edition of Rhazes' *De pestilentia* (ibid., p. 22). Raffaele Regio dedicated to Pisani, along with Girolamo Donato and Marco Dandolo, his *Dialogus* on four passages from Quintilian (see Medin, "Scritti umanistici," p. 335; Rigo, "Carteggio," p. 534 and n. 13).

EDUCATION. Perhaps with Giorgio Valla (see Heiburg, *Beiträge*, p. 24). In the dedicatory letter to Paolo of the work cited above, Vettore Pisani refers to Valla as "our teacher." Yet the phrase's meaning is vague. Vettore certainly studied with Valla (ibid., pp. 22ff.). But Paolo would have been over thirty when Valla came to Venice to teach in 1485, by which time his essential studies were probably completed.

Quirini, Lauro. (2) Querini, Quirinus. Son of Pietro; brother of Taddeo. Both Lauro and Taddeo were also related to the Giustiniani family (see P. H. Labalme, *Bernardo Giustiniani*, pp. 94-95). Doctor.

MONOGRAPHS AND STUDIES. L. Bertalot with A. Wilmanns, "Lauri Quirini 'Dialogus in gymnasiis florentinis,' ein Nachklang zum 'Certame coronario' "; V. Branca, "Lauro Quirini e il commercio librario a Venezia e Firenze"; P. O. Kristeller, "Il codice Plimpton 187 della Columbia University Library e gli scritti di Lauro Quirini sulla nobiltà"; *Lauro Quirini umanista: studi e testi a cura di Konrad Krautter, P. O. Kristeller, Agostino Pertusi, Giorgio Ravegnani, Helmut Roob e Carlo Seno*, ed. V. Branca (LQU); R. Sabbadini, "Bricciole umanistiche-XVII: Lauro Quirini"; G. dalla Santa, "Due lettere di umanisti veneziani (Lauro Querini e Lodovico Foscarini a Paolo Morosini)"; A. Segarizzi, "Lauro Quirini umanista veneziano del secolo XV." Also G. degli Agostini, *Notizie*, I, 205-28. A recent and exhaustive chronology by Seno and Ravegnani of Quirini's life and works is found in LQU, pp. 11-18, upon which this digest principally relies.

CAREER. B. c. 1420. M. 1451, Pelegrina di Marin Falier, subsequently Pentasilea Muazzo. D. c. 1475-79.

Office. 1450-51, *Auditor veterum sententiarum*. In 1452, Quirini established residence in Candia (Crete), where he remained for the rest of his life, a land proprietor and entrepreneur.

WORKS. Published in LQU: three treatises on nobility, ed. K. Krautter and H. Roob, with introductory study by P. O. Kristeller (*Epistola ad Petrum Thomasium, De nobilitate contra Poggium Florentinum, De nobilitate responsio quid iuris*); *De republica* to Doge Francesco Foscari, ed. Seno and Ravegnani; *Epistole storiche*, ed. Pertusi, on the Turkish threat in the Mediterranean, to Pope Nicholas V, Cardinal Ludovico (Scarampo) Trevisan, Pope Pius II, and Paolo Morosini. Published by Segarizzi: philosophical dialogue to Andrea Morosini, podestà of Padua (a more descriptive title in cod. Canon. Misc. 308 [Oxford, Bodleian Library]: *De philosophorum veterum dogmatibus opusculum*; discussion of themes by J. Monfasani, *George of Trebizond*, pp. 204-205); *De pace Italie*; a letter to Lorenzo Valla. Quirini's *Dialogus in*

gymnasiis florentinis published by Bertalot in "Lauri Quirini 'Dialogus.' "
Among Quirini's other works, printed or in manuscript, the following are of
particular relevance to the Venetian context: *Oratio in adventu episcopi Patavini [Petri Donati]; Oratio in laudibus Jeronimi de Leonardis veneti (graduati Padue)* (18 April 1445); *Oratio in laudem Francisci Barbari*, not seen
(known to Segarizzi ["Lauro Quirini," p. 13] who thought it no longer extant,
but found in Oxford, Bodleian Library, cod. Bywater 38 [notice courtesy of
P. O. Kristeller]); trans., from pseudo-Suidas, *Narratio de sacerdotio Jesu
Christi*, to Pope Nicholas V (Jacopo Antonio Marcello sent a version with his
own preface to King René of Anjou; cf. G. Mercati, *Ultimi contributi*, I, 72ff.,
81-82); trans., from Dio Cassius, *Oratio Caesaris ad milites*, to Leo Molin;
trans. (from a Greek version of the donation of Constantine; see W. Setz,
Lorenzo Vallas Schrift gegen die konstantinische Schenkung [Tübingen, 1975],
pp. 110ff.) *Sanctio Constantini*, to Pope Nicholas V; trans., a *fabula* of Lucian,
to Pietro Donato (cf. P. Sambin, "Ricerche per la storia della cultura nel secolo
XV: la biblioteca di Pietro Donato [1380-1447]," pp. 22, 41 and n. 211).
Refer to the studies listed above and to LQU, pp. 11-18, for other works,
printed or in ms., and other versions of the works cited.

CORRESPONDENCE. Exchanges with Michael Apostolos (cf. LQU, pp. 15ff.),
Francesco Barbaro (*Centotrenta*, ed. Sabbadini, indices), and Maffeo Valla-
resso (*Epist.*, pp. 21-22, 26-28, 283-85, 292-93, 314-15). Letters to Pietro
Dolfin (the chronicler; LQU, p. 18), Francesco and Jacopo Foscari (Vat. Lat.
3194, fols. 11-13), Isotta Nogarola (*Opera omnia*, ed. E. Abel, II, 9-22, trans.
M. L. King and A. Rabil, Jr., *Her Immaculate Hand*, pp. 111-16), and Lorenzo
Valla (ed. Segarizzi, see above). Letters from Leonardo Bruni (*Epist.*, ed.
Mehus, II, 134-44, 144-47), Francesco Filelfo (*Epist. fam.*, fols. 116ᵛ and
186), Leonardo Giustiniani (in B. Giustiniani, *Epist. et orat.*, sig. K2ᵛ), and
perhaps Bernardo Bembo (cf. V. Cian, "Per Bernardo Bembo—II," p. 77).

DISCOURSE. Widely known as learned, though often criticized as superficial,
Quirini engaged in polemics with Leonardo Bruni (1441; Quirini's letter perhaps lost [see Segarizzi, "Quirini," p. 7], but the controversy is known from
Bruni's, cited above) and Lorenzo Valla (1445; Quirini's letter to Valla cited
above; Valla's reply in L. Barozzi and R. Sabbadini, *Studi sul Panormita e sul
Valla*, pp. 112-13) on philosophical questions, and with Poggio Bracciolini
on the issue of true nobility (1449). He urged the woman humanist Isotta
Nogarola to the advanced study of philosophy (letter cited above), and his
contemporary Francesco Contarini to write a work for Ludovico Draco (Qui-
rini's influence evident from the *Epithalamium in nuptiis Ludovici Draconis
Veneti*, fol. 21). He knew Cardinal Bessarion, in whose house Quirini resided
in Florence in 1441, and whom he served as *procuratore* in Crete more than
twenty years later. With Pietro Tommasi, he visited Giannozzo Manetti (then
Florence's ambassador in Venice) on 22 Dec. 1448. Quirini taught Aristotle's
Ethics publicly in Venice during 1449, and was offered a teaching position at
Padua in 1452 (paying an inadequate annual salary of forty ducats). In Venice
and Crete, Quirini actively collected and concerned himself with the preser-

vation of ancient texts (see Branca, "Lauro Quirini e il commercio librario," and the letter from Apostolos cited in LQU, p. 16).

EDUCATION. Quirini pursued advanced studies in Venice, 1438-40, then received his doctorate in arts at Padua on 26 April 1440. Thereafter he studied canon law at Padua, where he was in residence 1443-48, receiving his doctorate 16 March 1448.

Quirini, Taddeo. (2) Querini, Quirinus. Son of Pietro; brother of Lauro. Both Lauro and Taddeo Quirini were related to the Giustiniani family; cf. P. H. Labalme, *Bernardo Giustiniani*, pp. 94-95.

MONOGRAPHS AND STUDIES. G. degli Agostini, *Notizie*, II, 314-21.

CAREER. B. Candia, c. 1428. M. 1459, Laura di Marco Piacentini. D. 1508. After beginning a secular career, Quirini left Venice for Rome in 1453, where he stayed until after the death of Pope Nicholas V in 1455. He interrupted his sacred studies to marry in 1459, then later reentered the Church, and appears in the 1460s and 1470s in the minor clerical titles noted below. He competed unsuccessfully for the bishoprics of Trau (1482), Treviso (1485), and Torcello (1485), and for the archbishopric of Nicosia (1483); cf. C. Cenci, "Senato veneto 'probae,' " pp. 413, #112; 419, #115, 420, #116; 415, #113.
    Office. 1452, honorary amb. to greet Emperor Frederick III (on this occasion he delivered the oration to that Emperor cited below).
    Titles. Before 1469, *Deacon of Cathedral of Candia* (Agostini, *Notizie*, II, 318); before 1469, *Canon of Treviso* (Rossi, "Niccolò Lelio Cosmico," p. 106); 1469-82, *Vicar Gen. to Jacopo Zeno, Bishop of Padua*; c. 1472, *Canon of Brescia*; 1482— *Archpriest of the Cathedral of Padua* (in this title, he witnessed the inventory of Zeno's library made by Pietro Foscari in 1482; cf. E. Govi, "La biblioteca di Jacopo Zeno," p. 65).

WORKS. *Ad Fridericum III romanorum imperatorem oratio gratulatoria* (18 May 1452); *Elogia Caesarum et virorum quorundam apud Romanos illustrium* (1479), not seen (in Marc. Lat. XIV, 251 [4685], cf. *Iter*, II, 249). The following works I have not found nor seen, but were known to Agostini: *Oratio in Galeatii Mussati nuptiis et Paulae de Leono* (Padua, 24 Jan. 1451); *Oratio in laudem Petri Pauli Scaziotti de Biovabutiis*; trans., St. Maximus, *De parsimonia* (*Notizie*, II, 319, 321). An *Oratio* to Pope Nicholas V is witnessed by Quirini's words to Francesco Barbaro (see the latter's *Epistolae*, ed. A. M. Quirini, p. 284).

CORRESPONDENCE. Letters from Niccolò Perotti (see R. P. Oliver's edition of his version of Epictetus' *Enchiridion*, p. 163) and to Francesco Barbaro (see *Centotrenta*, ed. Sabbadini, pp. 61, 62).

DISCOURSE. Quirini participated in the literary circle about the curia in Rome during the reign of Pope Nicholas V (see his letters to Barbaro), and collected books (see Agostini, *Notizie*, II, 317-18; A. Pertusi, "Umanesimo greco," p. 252 n. 333).

EDUCATION. A student of law at Padua on 9 March 1450, Quirini subsequently received a doctorate in that faculty (Zonta and Brotto, *Acta*, 460, #2407; Agostini, *Notizie*, II, 314).

Ragazzoni, Jacopo. (3?) Aragazonius, de Ragazonibus.

MONOGRAPHS AND STUDIES. G. degli Agostini, *Notizie*, I, 556-60.

CAREER. B. c. 1445, to a Venetian family (subsequently appearing among the list of *cittadini originari*: cf. da Mosto, *Archivio*, I, 76). D. after 1478. The birthdate is based on Ragazzoni's known activities in the early 1460s, when, still young, he was already engaged in adult intellectual discourse. In a 1461 letter to Ludovico Foscarini in the latter's *Epist.*, fol. 69^{r-v}, Ragazzoni refers to verses he had written while still a boy in praise of the patrician. In 1463, he composed a poem on the dead Bertoldo d'Este that was praised by Pietro Barozzi. By 1465, he left his position as a "youth" appointed to serve in the Great Council in order to study at Padua: "Quum Jacobus de ragazonibus, qui erat unus ex juvenibus deputatis ad servendum in maiori consilio, et habebat ducat. xx de salario in anno, recessit de venetiis, et ivit paduam ad studendum, . . . deliberatum fuit, quod loco dicti Jacobi assumantur et succedere debeant infrascripti duo . . . Inter quos duos dividatur salarium predicti Jacobi; ita quod habeant ducati decem pro quolibet in anno, sicut habeant alii, et per hunc modum habebantur duo pro uno qui serviant non augendo expensam" (CLN 10, c. 115^v, 17 Jan.); thus his "ample" veteran's salary was divided between two novices. His career after 1471 is obscure. He was apparently still in Venice in 1478 in the role of *sindaco* and procurator of the convent of S. Lucia. It is possible that our Ragazzoni may be identified with the printer Jacobus de Ragazonibus of Asolo, who published among other titles a 1494 version of Francesco Negri's *De modo epistolandi* (HC [+ Add] 11871*).

WORKS. *Oratio ad Nicolaum Tronum Venete Reipublice Principem* (1471); *Carmina*, not seen, some perhaps lost (Agostini, *Notizie*, I, 558; of these poems, one is to Pietro Barozzi in Treviso, Bibl. Comunale, cod. 566; not seen, but cf. *Iter*, II, 196).

CORRESPONDENCE. Letters to and from Foscarini (to Foscarini in the *Epist.*, fols. 44-45^v and 69^{r-v}; from Foscarini on fols. 25^{r-v}, 53^v-54, 61^v, 62^v-63^v, 69^{r-v}, 215^v, 223^v-224^v, 258^{r-v}; the famous letter to Ragazzoni about the writing of history—fols. 223^v-224^v—also published in the preface, pp. ix-x, of Lorenzo de' Monaci, *Chronicon de rebus venetis*, ed. F. Corner); from George of Trebizond (see A. Pertusi, "Gli inizi della storiografia umanistica del Quattrocento," p. 304).

DISCOURSE. Pietro Barozzi dedicated to Ragazzoni the first book of his *Versuum atque hymnorum libri III* and praised in the dedicatory letter and the following poem Ragazzoni's work on the recently slain (1463) Venetian general Bertoldo d'Este (dedicatory letter and reference to Ragazzoni's work on pp. 213ff.). Foscarini patronized Ragazzoni, bringing his Latin verse to the attention of Pope Pius II and encouraging him in the competition for the position (not yet created) of Venetian historiographer (see the correspondence cited above).

STUDIES. Ragazzoni taught arts at Padua in 1470-71 (see his oration to Tron on behalf of the artists and physicians; also Papadopoli, *Hist. gymn. pat.*, I. ii.152), where he had also studied, perhaps continually from 1465 (the date given by the document of that year cited above, establishing the inception of his studies). By 1478 (probably earlier) he possessed a doctorate in arts and medicine (in a document of that year, Ragazzoni appears with the title of doctor; see Agostini, *Notizie*, I, 558).

Ramusio, Paolo. (3). Son of Benedetto. Sire of learned family.

MONOGRAPHS AND STUDIES. See the brief profiles in E. A. Cicogna, *Iscrizioni*, II, 311-15, and V, 596; C. Tonini, *La coltura letteraria e scientifica in Rimini dal secolo XIV ai primi del XIX*, pp. 190-94; and A. del Piero, "Della vita e degli studi di Giovanni Battista Ramusio," pp. 7-12.

CAREER. B. c. 1443. Testament, Padua, 27 June 1506, and codicil Bergamo, 16 Aug. 1506. D. Bergamo 19 Aug. 1506. Born to a noble Riminese family, Ramusio moved to Venice with his younger brother Girolamo in 1458. He studied at Padua from at least 1471 until 1481, then served the Venetian government as assessor in the terraferma cities of Verona and Bergamo in 1483 and 1506, respectively, in Padua in 1480-81 in a position unknown to me (see the dedication of his *De ieiuniorum observatione*), in Udine in 1492 in an unknown position (Mazzatinti, *Inventario*, III, 196, describes a verse on the flyleaf of the Statutes of Udine by Paolo Ramusio "capitano" [an impossibility] of the city, 21 Oct. 1492), in Treviso as "judge" at a time unknown, as legate to Rimini in 1503, and in other public capacities during the twenty-five years of his maturity. Ramusio possessed substantial property in Rimini; for an indication of his wealth, see the will of Paolo's brother Girolamo (AN, Cancelleria Inferiore, Testamenti Giacomo Sappa, B. 27.2666, 2670 [13 Nov. 1483]), which disposes of considerable assets. Ramusio was close to several Venetian patricians, and established his family securely in Venice. The Ramusio family name subsequently appears among the list of *cittadini* (da Mosto, *Archivio*, I, 76). His son Giovanni Battista, grandson Paolo the Younger, and great-grandson Girolamo all figure significantly in the cultural history of the city in years to come (see Cicogna, II, 315ff.; for Giovanni Battista, see del Piero).

WORKS. *De ieiuniorum observatione* (1480), to Marco Marino and Giovanni Ludovico Dandolo; ed. and trans. Valturius' *De re militari*, not seen (see Tonini, *Coltura letteraria*, I, 191; Cicogna, *Iscrizioni*, II, 314; Cosenza, *Dict.*, IV, 3032); verses for Pietro Contarini (in the latter's *Ad Gelliam elegiae*, fol. 43) and Doge Leonardo Loredan (1501; in Cicogna, *Iscrizioni*, II, 315), and others (not seen; cf. *Iter*, II, 243; G. Biadego, *Catalogo descrittivo dei mano-scritti della Biblioteca Comunale di Verona*, p. 180; Mazzatinti, *Inventario*, III, 196). Legal works attributed to Ramusio by M. Foscarini (*Lett. ven.*, p. 62), are summarized in Tonini, *Coltura letteraria*, I, 192-93 and Cicogna, *Iscrizioni* II, 313-14.

CORRESPONDENCE. Exchange with Paolo Zanco (*Epist.*, fols. 260ᵛ-67).

DISCOURSE. A codex of Greek and Latin inscriptions owned by Marino Sanuto contains two copied in Ramusio's house (= Marc. Lat. XIV, 260 [4258]). Ramusio himself transcribed in 1486 a ms. containing works by Petrarch and Pier Paolo Vergerio (= Marc. Lat. XIV, 254 [4535] cf. *Iter*, II, 249-50), and in Padua in 1471 another containing Guarino's commentary on Persius (not seen; see Tonini, *Coltura letteraria*, I, 190, and Cicogna, *Iscrizioni*, II, 314-15). Joannes Bressanus wrote verse in Ramusio's praise; see *Iter*, I, 15.

EDUCATION. At Padua from perhaps 1471 (see the evidence cited for the Guarino ms. copied by Ramusio), for at least some period under Demetrius Chalcondylas (cf. G. Pavanello, *Un maestro del Quattrocento [Giovanni Aurelio Augurello]*, p. 7), and received his doctorate in law in 1481 (Tonini, *Coltura letteraria*, I, 190).

Renier, Daniele. (3) Rainerio, Ranieri, Raynerius. Son of Costantino.

MONOGRAPHS AND STUDIES. None, but see the brief profile in G. Pavanello, *Un maestro del Quattrocento (Giovanni Aurelio Augurello)*, pp. 145-46.

CAREER. B. c. 1458 (AC-BO 164/III, c. 304; presented 21 Nov. 1476). Testament 24 Aug. 1528 (AN, Testamenti G. M. Cavaneis, B. 217.111). D. 15? Feb. 1535. Renier was still alive on 7 Dec. 1534, when he was made Procuratore di San Marco (SGV 11 già 8, c. 22ᵛ), but died soon afterwards (Pavanello, *Maestro*, p. 145 and n. 3). His political career began as early as 3 Jan. 1484, when he was made *visdominus* of the Fondaco de' Tedeschi (SGV 6, c. 32ᵛ); he intermittently held minor offices in the following decade. These may have occupied him, or he may have pursued commercial interests during these years before his significant political career began. Renier also served repeatedly on special commissions not noted here in the early decades of the sixteenth century. I have been unable to consult for Renier the following series of ASV documents: CLN and SM for the years from 1512; CXM for the years 1513-24. The lack has been supplied by Marino Sanuto's *Diarii*, which extend through 1533, shortly before Renier's death.

Offices. 1501, Duc. el., Leonardo Loredan (MC-Stella, c. 187; Sanuto, *Diarii*, IV, 127); 1508-09, Avog. (SGV 7 già 12, c. 3; Sanuto, *Diarii*, VII, 542 etc., VIII); 1510, Avog. (CXM 33); 1517-18, Capt. of Verona (SGV 8 già 7, c. 42ᵛ; *Libro de' Reggimenti*, Marc. cod. Ital. VII, 198 [8383], c. 18; Sanuto, *Diarii*, XXIV, 252 etc., XXV, XXVI); 1519, CX (SGV 9 già 13, c. 27ᵛ; Sanuto, *Diarii*, XXVII, 87 etc.); 1520, Sav. gr. (ST 21; Sanuto, *Diarii*, XXVIII, 390 etc.); CX (SGV 9 già 13, c. 30ᵛ; Sanuto, *Diarii*, XXIX, 146 etc.); 1521, Cons. (MC-Deda; SGV 7 già 12, c. 29ᵛ; ST 22; Sanuto, *Diarii*, XXIX, 462 etc., XXX, XXXI); 1522, Sav. gr. (ST 22; Sanuto, *Diarii*, XXXIII, 365, 367); CX (SGV 9 già 13, c. 32; Sanuto, *Diarii*, XXXIII, 531); 1523, CX (CXM 46; Sanuto, *Diarii*, XXXIV, 7 etc.); 1523-24, Cons. (CXM 46; MC-Diana; SGV 7 già 12, c. 29ᵛ; ST 23; Sanuto, *Diarii*, XXXIV, 296, XXXV, XXXVI); 1525, Sav. gr. (ST 23, 24; Sanuto, *Diarii*, XXXVII, 381 etc., XXXVIII, XXXIX); 1526, Sav. gr. (ST 24; Sanuto, *Diarii*, XL, 716 etc., XLI, XLII); 1526-27, CX (CXS 1, 2; Sanuto, *Diarii*, XLIII, 17 etc., XLIV, XLV, XLVI); 1527-28, Cons. (CXS 2; MC-Diana; SGV 10 già 14, c. 1; ST 24, 25; Sanuto, *Diarii*, XLV, 586, XLVI, 120 etc., XLVII, XLVIII); 1531, Sav. gr. (ST 26; Sanuto, *Diarii*, LIV, 487 etc., LV); 1531, Amb. to marriage of Duke of Mantua (Sanuto, *Diarii*, LV, 234); 1532, Sav. gr. (ST 27; Sanuto, *Diarii*, LVI, 472 etc., LVII); 1533, Sav. gr. (ST 27; Sanuto, *Diarii*, LVIII, 382 etc.); 1534, Proc. di San Marco (SGV 11 già 8, c. 22ᵛ).

CORRESPONDENCE. Letters from Marcantonio Sabellico (*Opera*, fols. 51ᵛ-53).

DISCOURSE. Renier knew Hebrew and was especially interested in mathematics (see Agostini, *Notizie*, I, xlii, xlviii). A member of the circle that gathered around the printer Aldo Manuzio, his valuable library served as a source of manuscripts for late-Quattrocento printers (ibid., I, xl; A. Firmin-Didot, *Alde Manuce et l'hellénisme à Venise*, p. 149; Pavanello, *Maestro*; R. Sabbadini, *Le scoperte dei codici latini e greci*, I, 62 n. 119). Aldo dedicated to him his 1502 edition of Thucydides, Carteromaco (Scipione Fortiguerri of Pistoia) his Horace (1504), and Daniele Gaetani his edition of Luca Pacioli's translation of a commentary on Euclid (Molmenti, *Vita privata*, II, 214). Carteromaco also addressed to Renier his *Oratio de laudibus literarum graecarum* (1504; see A. Pertusi, "Umanesimo greco," pp. 183 n. 23 and 184ff.). Renier was close to the poet Giovanni Aurelio Augurello, who wrote at Renier's suggestion a poem on the soldier Nelfo from Treviso. Marcantonio Sabellico praised Renier as a learned patrician (*De rep. lat. ling.*, fol. 109ᵛ). Sanuto adds another glimpse of Renier on 6 Sept. 1527, when the chancery notary Alexandro Ziliol spoke at SS. Giovanni e Paolo in disputation with others learned in law: "Vi fu assà patrici invidati, tra li altri Sier Daniel di Renier Cao di X al presente, del qual è suo favorito" (XLVI, 28).

EDUCATION. With Benedetto Brognoli (cf. Sabellico, *Opera*, fol. 52).

Sabellico, Marcantonio. (3) Sabellicus. Born Coccio (Coccius). Son of Giovanni.

MONOGRAPHS AND STUDIES. R. Bersi, "Le fonti della prima decade delle 'Historiae rerum venetarum' di Marcantonio Sabellico"; C. Dionisotti, "Marcantonio Sabellico e Giovan Francesco Fortunio"; F. Gilbert, "Biondo, Sabellico, and the Beginnings of Venetian Official Historiography"; G. Mercati, "Attorno a Marco Antonio Sabellico," in *Ultimi contributi*, II, 1-23; F. Tateo,

"Marcantonio Sabellico e la svolta del classicismo quattrocentesco"; A. Zeno, ed., *Istorici delle cose veneziane, i quali hanno scritto per pubblico decreto*, I, xxix-lxxi. See also the brief account of E. Cochrane in *Historians and Historiography in the Italian Renaissance*, pp. 83-86. Mercati corrects Zeno's biography in many details.

CAREER. B. Vicovaro, c. 1436. Testament, 15 March 1506 (in Zeno, pp. lxviii-lxxi). D. 20 May 1506. Educated in Rome, Sabellico left for Udine in 1472 (witnessing the Turkish incursion of that year), where from 1473 he taught by public appointment. After staying in Udine until perhaps 1483 (cf. A. Pertusi, "Gli inizi della storiografia umanistica," p. 319), Sabellico came to Venice, fleeing again to Verona in 1484 to escape the plague. There in fifteen months (Jan. 1485 to March 1486) he composed the first thirty-two books of his famous history of Venice, which he dedicated to the doge and Senate, and for which he was rewarded with a well-paid (200 ducats annually) and honorable position. It was granted permission to be printed on 1 Sept. 1486, and was published in 1487 (Pertusi, "Inizi," p. 319). From 1485, Sabellico taught alongside Benedetto Brognoli and Giorgio Valla in the San Marco schools, from 1500 replacing the latter (who died in that year) in the superior chair of rhetoric; the relevant act of 10 Feb. is in J. L. Heiberg, *Beiträge zur Geschichte Georg Vallas*, pp. 41-42. Soon after 1486, Sabellico was also made custodian of the San Marco library founded on Cardinal Bessarion's donation of 1468 (see additionally M.J.C. Lowry, "Two Great Venetian Libraries in the Age of Aldus Manutius," p. 134). In 1505, he retired from his teaching post with a comfortable full-salary pension (the enabling act of 29 July is in Zeno, pp. lvii-lviii), and died the next year. For an alternative reconstruction of some details of Sabellico's life, see F. Gaeta, "Storiografia, coscienza nazionale," pp. 66-67 n. 193.

WORKS. See the studies cited (conveniently, Zeno, pp. xlff., as corrected by Mercati, "Sabellico," II, 14ff.) for this author's many works, which include text editions and commentaries, poems, histories and biographies, treatises and dialogues. The following are noteworthy here. Of central interest is the *Rerum venetarum ab urbe condita libri XXXIII*, to Doge Marco Barbarigo. For discussions and evaluations, see in addition to Zeno the studies cited by Bersi, Tateo, and Cochrane, above; also G. Cozzi, "Cultura politica e religione nella 'pubblica storiografia' veneziana del '500," pp. 219ff.; Pertusi, "Inizi," pp. 319ff.; and Gaeta, "Storiografia," pp. 65ff., esp. p. 68. In the *Opera* of 1502 are contained these: *Epistolarum familiarum libri XII*, to Marcantonio Morosini; *De officio scribae; De praetoris officio*, to Antonio Corner; *De reparatione latinae linguae*, to Marcantonio Morosini; *De situ Venetae urbis*, to Girolamo Donato; *De venetis magistratibus*, to Doge Agostino Barbarigo; orations *de cultu et fructu philosophiae; de origine et incrementis philosophiae; de usu philosophiae* (for these three school orations, see F. Lepori, "Scuola di Rialto," pp. 580ff.); and *Oratio in funere Zachariae Barbari*. These works also appear in the *Opera omnia* of 1560, ed. Caelius Secundus Curio, for which see G. Cozzi, "Intorno all'edizione dell'opera di Marcantonio Sabellico, curata da Celio Secondo Curione e dedicata a Sigismondo Augusto re di Polonia." Zeno lists its contents on pp. lxvff. Some works also in other earlier and later editions.

CORRESPONDENCE. The *Epistolae* include letters to Sebastiano Badoer (fols. 9^v-10), to and from Ermolao Barbaro G (fols. 3-4; also in Barbaro's *Epist.*, ed. Branca, II, 35-36), to Pietro Barozzi (fol. 11$^{r \cdot v}$), to and from Bernardo Bembo (fols. 45^v and 49$^{r \cdot v}$), to Coriolano Cippico (fols. 57-59), to Antonio Corner (fol. 60$^{r \cdot v}$), to Girolamo Donato (fols. 10^v, 35, 42^v), to Cassandra Fedele (fol. 49^v), to Girolamo Giorgi (fols. 26^v, 42^v-43), to Domenico Grimani (fols. 35^v, 41^v, 45^v), to and from Pomponio Leto (fols. 33^v-34, 46^v-47^v), from Giorgio Merula (fols. 6), to Marcantonio Morosini (fols. 10, 55^v-57 [a biography of Sabellico's teacher Pomponio Leto], 60^v), from Francesco Negri (fol. 48), to and from Angelo Poliziano (fols. 35^v, 44$^{r \cdot v}$; also in Poliziano's *Opera omnia*, I, 32), to Daniele Renier (fols. 51^v-53).

DISCOURSE. Sabellico is primarily famous for his histories, particularly his history of Venice, although he was not in fact the first of Venice's publicly appointed historiographers (Gilbert, "Biondo"). He was praised as one of Venice's teachers by Francesco Negri (*De aristocratia*, fols. 98^v-99) and Marino Sanuto (*Chronachetta*, the relevant passage translated in J. B. Ross, "Venetian Schools," p. 557), and for his learning by Paolo Giovio (*Elogia doctorum virorum* [1577], pp. 98-99, critical of his histories; note also Erasmus' slight praise in the *Ciceronianus*, p. 224). A client of Benedetto Trevisan and teacher of Gasparo Contarini (cf. Heiberg, *Beiträge*, p. 32), Giovanni Pierio Valeriano (ibid.), and Giovanni Francesco Fortunio (see C. Dionisotti, "Il Fortunio e la filologia umanistica," p. 20), Sabellico belonged to the circle of learned men who clustered around Aldo Manuzio (see A. Firmin-Didot, *Alde Manuce et l'hellénisme à Venise*, p. 149). His ample collection of books was bequeathed to his close kin (see testament).

EDUCATION. With Domizio Calderini, Pomponio Leto, Porcellio Pandoni and Gaspare Veronese.

Sagundino, Niccolò. (2) Segundino, Secundinus.

MONOGRAPHS AND STUDIES. F. Babinger, *Johannes Darius (1414-1494), Sachwalter Venedigs im Morgenland, und sein griechischer Umkreis*, pp. 9-52; P. D. Mastrodimitris, Νικόλαος ὁ Σεκουνδινὸς (1402-1464), Βίος καὶ ἔργον (Nicola Secundino, Vita e opere: Contributo allo studio dei dotti greci della diaspora). I have not been able to consult Babinger's brief "Nicolaos Sagoundinos, ein griechisch-venedischer Humanist des 15. Jahrhunderts," Χαριστήριον εἰς 'Αναστάσιον 'Ορλανδὸν, I (Athens, 1964), 198-212. The section of Babinger's *Johannes Darius* dealing with Sagundino thoroughly reconstructs his career and carefully discusses his works. Mastrodimitris' book (in modern Greek) I have been able to use only in part. Most useful have been the complete list of works (pp. 113-223), the appendix with texts (pp. 225-

42), the biographical précis in Italian (pp. 243-48), and the bibliography (pp. 249-67). See the latter and Babinger's ample notes for further information.

CAREER. B. Chalcis in Euboea (Negropont), 1402. D. 22 March 1464 (Babinger; Mastrodimitris gives 23 March; the document announcing Sagundino's death [ST 5, c. 73] is dated, as I read it, 22 March, but Babinger reports that date as 24 March). The name Sagundino subsequently appears among the list of citizen families: cf. da Mosto, *Archivio*, I, 77. At Thessalonica in 1430, Sagundino was already in Venetian service when he was seriously wounded and imprisoned with his family by Turkish conquerors. Once released, he held office from 1434 to 1437 in his native city, then under Venetian domination. Appointed official interpreter to the Council of Ferrara-Florence (1438-39), Sagundino journeyed to Italy, where he impressed the congress of learned men by his facility in both Greek and Latin and his grasp of doctrinal issues. Subsequently he was employed by Pope Eugene IV (and perhaps by his successor) as apostolic secretary and was sent on missions in Greece and Italy. By 1453, he was again in Chalcis, serving as Venetian chancellor for Euboea and as papal representative. After Constantinople's fall, he was ordered to that city by Venice to negotiate with the Sultan Mohammed II. Thence he returned to Italy in Venetian employ, and he furnished to the Venetians (and by their order to King Alfonso I of Naples and to Pope Nicholas V) his important and first-hand report of the Ottoman empire's history and ambitions, attempting to impress on these western powers the seriousness of the Turkish threat. Having returned to Venice by 1455 with the title of ducal secretary, Sagundino was sent again to Naples and Rome (1455-58), then was named to be chancellor of Crete in 1458. But he did not set out on his ill-fated journey to assume that high office until July 1460, when while still in Venetian waters shipwreck consumed his pregnant wife, two sons, a daughter, his books, and possessions. Soon after that calamity, having renounced the Cretan chancellorship, Sagundino was again named ducal secretary and dispatched on missions to Modon, Constantinople, and Trebizond. He died in Venice four years later, leaving his son Ludovico (his gifted son Giovanni having predeceased him) and grandson Niccolò a heritage of humanist learning and secretarial service (cf. Mastrodimitris, *Nicola Secundino*, p. 245, and Babinger, *Johannes Darius*, pp. 36, 44-45 for support granted them by the Venetian Senate).

WORKS. Of Sagundino's many works (a thorough catalogue is in Mastrodimitris, *Nicola Secundino*, pp. 113-223 and 261-65) especially noteworthy here are the *Epistolae*, and the following: *Consolatio in obitu Valerii filii consolatio*, to Jacopo Antonio Marcello; *De deo, de unitate essentiae eius et de trinitate personarum*, to Febo Capella; *Dialogus, opusculum de finibus*, to Girolamo Tifernate, with Sagundino, Febo Capella, and Marco Aurelio as interlocutors; *Epistola ad [Cardinalem] Bessarionem de naufragio suo; De familia otumanorum*, to Eneo Silvio Piccolomini (the title *sic* in the ms. version cited; also extant in various printed editions under diverse titles; see also A. Pertusi, "I primi studi in occidente sull'origine e la potenza dei Turchi," pp. 471ff.); *De nuptiis filiae et matrimonii commendatione*, to Pietro and Paolo Aurelio; *Opusculum* to Pietro Molin; *Oratio ad Alphonsum Regem Aragonum* (25 [elsewhere 31] Jan. 1454); *De origine et sectis philosophorum*, to Fantino Coppo; trans., Demosthenes' *For Ctesiphon (On the Crown)* and *First Olynthiac*, to Domenico Morosini, not seen (cf. *Iter*, II, 432, who cites also a third, not to Morosini, *De Chersonneso*); trans., Onosander, *De optimo imperatore eiusque officio*; trans., Plutarch, *De civili institutione*, to Marco Donato. I have seen the letters and many of the *opuscula* in the Marciana manuscript, one of the three main collections of Sagundino's works cited in the Bibliography. Many of these and others not in that manuscript appear in the valuable Vat. Ottob. Lat. 1732.

CORRESPONDENCE. Sagundino's *epistolae* (in Marc. Lat. XIII, 62 [4418]) include notably letters to Ulisse Aleotti (fols. 81ᵛ-82ᵛ, 87-88ᵛ); to Marco Aurelio (fols. 53ᵛ-57, 59-60, 62ᵛ-66, 79-81ᵛ, 83ʳ⁻ᵛ, 89ᵛ-91, 93ʳ⁻ᵛ, 101-102ᵛ, 106ʳ⁻ᵛ); to Paolo Aurelio (fols. 73-76, 91ʳ⁻ᵛ), to Ermolao Barbaro V (fols. 83ᵛ-84ᵛ), to Michele Basilio (fols. 71ʳ-72ᵛ), to Antonio Beccadelli (Panormita) (fols. 94-95), to Alessandro Bono (fols. 109ᵛ-110ᵛ), to Sebastiano Bursa (fols. 50-53ᵛ), to Francesco Contarini (fols. 57ᵛ-58), to Fantino Coppo (fols. 119ᵛ-120ᵛ), to Domenico Morosini (fols. 47ᵛ-49ᵛ, 58-59, 98-100ᵛ, 103ᵛ-106), to Bertuccio Nigro (fol. 91), to his son Giovanni Sagundino (fols. 89ʳ⁻ᵛ, 91ᵛ-92ᵛ), and to Zaccaria Trevisan G (fols. 84ᵛ-87). Published are two letters to Giovanni Sagundino (one, from the Marciana manuscript, fol. 89ʳ⁻ᵛ, in Mastrodimitris, *Nicola Secundino*, pp. 233-34; the other in R. Sabbadini, "Andrea Contrario," pp. 413-14), one to Cardinal Bessarion (ibid., p. 391), one from Andrea Contrario (ibid., pp. 414-15), and one from George of Trebizond (in J. Monfasani, *Collectanea Trapezuntiana*, pp. 305-306). Other letters still in ms. appear in the major collections of Sagundino's works not consulted by me. Mastrodimitris provides a chronological summary of all the letters, pp. 129-68.

DISCOURSE. One of the learned Greeks to find refuge in Renaissance Italy, Sagundino played a particularly important role as witness to the expansion of Ottoman power in the East; his oration to King Alfonso and description of the Ottomans are among the earliest European attempts of that kind. (See Marino Sanuto's letter to his wealthier kinsman Marco urging the latter to print Sagundino's *De familia otumanorum*, in Marc. Lat. XIV, 265 [4501], fol. 115ʳ⁻ᵛ.) He participated in learned circles at the Council of Ferrara-Florence, in Naples (1455-56), and in Rome (1462), as well as in Venice during his intermittent stays in that city between 1453 and 1464. Sagundino and George of Trebizond were the only Greeks before 1469 to write in Latin about the philosophers, and to participate usefully in the controversy on the relative merits of Plato and Aristotle; cf. J. Monfasani, *George of Trebizond*, pp. 213-14. He was praised for his learning by Vespasiano da Bisticci (*Vite di uomini illustri*, pp. 15, 26, 212, 246) and Bartolomeo Facio (*De viris illustribus*, pp. 21-22). Pietro Perleone consoled Sagundino for his calamitous 1460 losses—including his ample lifetime's collection of books—in a lengthy *epistola*.

Sanuto, Leonardo. (2) Sanudo, Sanutus. Son of Marino; uncle of Marco; father of Marino (the diarist, who refers proudly and frequently to his father Leonardo, who died nobly in his country's service). Marco Sanuto's father Francesco was Leonardo's brother and business partner. Leonardo was also nephew of the Doge Cristoforo Moro (see the letter of George of Trebizond in G. Castellani, "Giorgio da Trebisonda," pp. 141-42; now re-ed. J. Monfasani, *Collectanea Trapezuntiana*, pp. 277-78).

CAREER. B. c. 1426 (AG-BO 163/II, c. 378; presented 20 Oct. 1444). M. 1448, Celestina di Carlo Contarini; 1464, Letizia di Pellegrino Venier (Giomo, *Matrimoni*, I, 247, and II, 457). Testament 18 Sept. 1474 (AN, Testamenti T. Tomei, B. 1240.31). D. 11 Oct. 1474, in Rome (the date noted by his son Marino: Marc. Lat. XIV, 267 [4344], fol. 75^v). It is evident from Sanuto's *Ricordanza* containing notes for the years 1455-59 (ASV, Giudici di Petizion, B. 955, cc. 124-60^v) that Sanuto pursued a commercial career as well, participating in companies with his brother Francesco and Uncle Maffeo (notice of this document courtesy of Reinhold Mueller).

Offices. 1445, *Advocator mobilium* (SGV 4, c. 23); 1448, *Advocator per omnes curias* (SGV 4, c. 24); 1454-55, *Consiglo XL* (SGV 4, c. 150^v; SM 5; ST 3); 1455, *Sav. agli ordini* (SM 5, c. 83^v); 1458-59, Visdom. in Ferrara (CLN 9, c. 156; MC-Ursa, c. 26); 1462, *Treasurer to the Doge Cristoforo Moro* (see the title and Sanuto's note on fol. 7 of the collection he made of works to Moro, cited below; the note describes the orations and letters contained in the codex and adds "... quas ego Leonardus Sanutus *tunc sue excellentie suarumque fortunarum curam gerens* in unum coegi" [emphasis mine]); 1474, Amb. to Pope (ST 7, c. 48); died on that mission.

WORKS. *Oratio ad Franciscum Sanutum Brixiae Capitaneum* (1470), recited by his son Marino; *Oratio habita apud Sistum (sic) Quartum Pontificem Maximum* (1474); compiler of the *Orationes et epistolae ad Christophorum Maurum Venetiarum Principem tum Italorum tum exterorum Principum pro eius inauguratione ad Ducalem dignitatem, additis orationibus Civitatum reipublicae, quarum sequitur descriptio, uno volumine collectae, per Leonardum Sanutum eiusdem ducis fortunarum curam gerentem, anno 1462* (12 May). The first of these manuscripts is written in the hand of Leonardo's son Marino; the second was in his library. Marino also recited the oration to Francesco which his father composed, as noted on fol. 68. The codex in which the first appears also contains all but one of the letters cited below.

CORRESPONDENCE. Letter from George of Trebizond (cited above); letters to Pietro Barozzi (Marc. Lat. XIV, 267 [4344], fol. 58^{r-v}), Antonio Donato (fols. 71^{r-v} and 75^{r-v}), Francesco Sanuto (fols. 64^v-65), Jacopo Zeno (fol. 64).

DISCOURSE. Collected orations and letters addressed to Doge Cristoforo Moro, his uncle, on the occasion of Moro's election (12 May 1462) to the *dogado* (for descriptions, see *Iter*, II, 245). Epigram on his death by Pietro Marcello G: *De obitu Leonardi Sanuti Oratoris Veneti apud Pontificem Max-*

imum. Possessed a substantial library including classical, philosophical and theological, and contemporary works; on cc. 159ᵛ-60 of Sanuto's *Ricordanza* appears a list of "Libri e cose imprestade adaltri," dated 1455 and 1456, recording loans of some works to various persons and suggesting the contexts of Sanuto's library. Earlier in that document are references to Sanuto as having hired copyists and illuminators while *visdomino* of Ferrara. Copied in his own hand a codex of works by Lactantius; see Valentinelli, *Bibl. man.*, II, 9, referring to Marc. Lat. II, 75 (2198), containing the *Divinae institutiones, De ira Dei, De opificio Dei*, with a note by Sanuto at the end of the first work, fol. 120: "Ego Leonardus Sanutus q. domini Marini Venetiis, Deo adiuvante, scripsi et complevi die iunii 1457 Montesilice."

EDUCATION. Perhaps with Guarino Veronese (see Ludovico Carbone in his funeral oration for Guarino Veronese in K. Müllner, *Reden und Briefe*, p. 93).

Sanuto, Marco. (3) Sanudo, Sanutus. Son of Francesco; nephew of Leonardo; cousin of Marino; distant relation of Doge Cristoforo Moro (see profile of Leonardo Sanuto).

CAREER. B. c. 1445 (AC-BO 164/III, c. 306; presented 2 Dec. 1463). D. 22 April 1505 (cf. Sanuto, *Diarii*, VI, 154-55 for the death and splendid burial). Sanuto's career may have begun as early as 1465, when he was elected *advoc. procuratorum* (SGV 6, c. 15). The same document lists him in other minor offices sporadically for the next twenty-five years. He interrupted his career, political or commercial, to attend university in the early 1480s.

Offices. 1494, Avog. (SGV 6, c. 132 and 7, c. 2ᵛ); 1494-96, Pod. of Bergamo (SGV 6, cc. 19, 132; 7 già 12, c. 2ᵛ; Sanuto, *Diarii*, I, 143); 1496, Amb. to Savoy (ST 12, c. 142; Sanuto, *Diarii*, I, 180 etc.); Sav. tf. (Sanuto, *Diarii*, I, 322 etc.); 1497, Sav. tf. (CXM 27; SM 14; ST 13; Sanuto, *Diarii*, I, 668 etc.); CX (CXM 27, c. 121; Sanuto, *Diarii*, I, 767); 1497-99, Pod. of Brescia (SGV 6, c. 91 and 8 già 7, c. 50; ST 13, c. 72ᵛ; Sanuto, *Diarii*, I, 822 etc., II); 1499, Sav. tf. (SM 14; ST 13; Sanuto, *Diarii*, II, 558 etc.); 1499-1500, Avog. (CXM 28; MC-Stella; SGV 6, c. 132 and 7 già 12, c. 2ᵛ; ST 13; Sanuto, *Diarii*, II, 837 etc., III); 1500-1, CX (CXM 28, c. 118; Sanuto, *Diarii*, III, 673 etc.); 1501, Cons. (CLN 15; CXM 28; MC-Stella; SGV 7 già 12, c. 1ᵛ; SM 15; ST 14; Sanuto, *Diarii*, III, 1477 etc., IV); 1502-3, Sav. gr. (CXM 29; SM 15; ST 14; Sanuto, *Diarii*, IV, 235 etc., V); 1503-4, Cons. (CLN 15; CXM 30; ST 15; Sanuto, *Diarii*, V, 109 etc.); 1504, Sav. gr. (ST 15; Sanuto, *Diarii*, VI, 29 etc.); CX (CXM 30; Sanuto, *Diarii*, VI, 121 etc.); 1505, CX (CXM 30, c. 117 and passim); died in that office.

WORKS. Verse *epistola ad Benedictum Sanutum* (Bergamo, 11 June 1483), for Pylades Buccardus (Gianfrancesco Boccardi of Brescia); *Tabula stellarum fixarum* (1501).

CORRESPONDENCE. Letters from Pietro Bembo (cf. Cicogna, *Iscrizioni*, II, 111) and Marino Sanuto (Marc. Lat. XIV, 265 [4501], fol. 115ʳ⁻ᵛ).

Discourse. The funeral inscription posted by his brothers in the Church of San Zaccaria alludes to his learning: "Marco Sanuto Franc. F. Senatori in R. P. Primario, eloquentia omnique eruditione praestantiss." (Cicogna, *Iscrizioni*, II, 110). Sanuto joined in the discussions held by the group of intellectuals gathered around Filippo Buonaccorsi in 1485-86 (see the latter's *De his quae a Venetis tentata sunt* [1533 ed.], pp. 83-84). Learned especially in mathematics and astronomy (Cicogna, *Iscrizioni*, II, 110-11), he made a machine model of planetary conjunctions as well as composing the *Tabula stellarum* cited above. See also the note in Marino's diary (II, 658; 27 March 1499): "In questo zorno fu scrito per la Signoria nostra una lettera al re di Hungaria, autore sier Marco Sanudo di terra ferma, per uno astrologo qual era qui che volesse portar li soi instrumenti." Another incident on 4 Sept. 1502 (IV, 318): Bernardo Loredan, who had been *sindaco* in Cyprus appeared in the Collegio "et portò 6 pezi in astrologia, di instrumenti, grandi, antiquissimi, erano in la rocha de Famagosta, quelli fo posti en caxa dil doxe, e poi, *ex decreto Dominii*, dati a Marco Sanudo, savio dil conseio, per ducati X; ma sono ruzini e vetustissimi. E la theorica di la spera; fece il tutto di operarli, ma non poté."

Several authors dedicated works to Sanuto: Alessandro Benedetti his *Collectiones medicinae* (cf. Cosenza, *Dict.*, IV, 3190 and Zeno, *Diss. voss.*, II, 416); Giovanni Marino the Younger his poem *Sylva*; Regio his edition of Cicero's *De officiis* (cf. Cosenza, *Dict.*, IV, 3190). Giovanni Battista Egnazio addressed to Sanuto the preface of his eulogy for Benedetto Brognoli (cf. A. Firmin-Didot, *Alde Manuce*, p. 222 and Cosenza, *Dict.*, IV, 3190; I have not been able to see the work referred to, nor was that assiduous scholar J. B. Ross ["Venetian Schools," p. 537 n. 64] able to do so.). Niccolò Leonico Tomeo named two of his dialogues "Sanutus" in his honor (the *De compescendo luctu* and *De ludo talario* in his *Dialogi*, fols. 58^v-67^v and 85^v-90). Pylades Buccardus (Marc. Lat. XII, 210 [4689], fols. 28^v-29^v) and Girolamo Donato (ibid., fol. 54^v) wrote verses to him. Sanuto apparently had some weight in the circle of Aldo Manuzio; in 1503, Marino Sanuto wrote Marco regarding Niccolò Sagundino's history of the Ottomans, urging that he have it published by Aldo (letter cited above). Sanuto urged the appointment of Niccolò da Lonigo (Leoniceno) to teach in Venice in 1505 (see Marino Sanuto's *Diarii*, VI, 117).

Education. Sanuto was at Padua, c. 1482-83, and studying philosophy, when at his urging Nicoletto Vernia composed and dedicated his edition of Averroes' commentary on Aristotle to Marco's father Francesco (Cosenza, *Dict.*, IV, 3190).

Tomeo, Niccolò Leonico. (3) Leonicus Thomaeus.

Monographs and Studies. Four studies by D. de Bellis: " 'Autokineton' e 'Entelechia.' Niccolò Leonico Tomeo: l'anima nei Dialoghi intitolati al Bembo"; "Niccolò Leonico Tomeo interprete di Aristotele naturalista"; "I veicoli dell'anima nell'analisi di Niccolò Leonico Tomeo"; and "La vita e l'ambiente di Niccolò Leonico Tomeo." "La vita e l'ambiente" has been the principal source, except where otherwise noted, for the summary below. These studies replace Card. F. A. Gasquet, *Cardinal Pole and His Early Friends*, pp. 54ff.; G. Pavanello, *Un maestro del Quattrocento (Giovanni Aurelio Augurello)*, pp. 115-19; and G. Saitta, *Il pensiero italiano nell'umanesimo e nel rinascimento*, I, 443-51. I have been unable to consult A. Serena, *Appunti letterari* (Rome: Forzani e C., 1903), pp. 3-32.

CAREER. B. 1456. D. Padua, 1531, shortly before 28 March. Born in Venice, the son of a Greek immigrant (from Negropont [Euboea]), Tomeo studied at Padua, then in Florence and Milan under Demetrius Chalcondylas. Back in Padua, he received his doctorate in 1485, and there he established permanent residence by 1497, having inherited considerable family property. From 1497 (4 April) to 1507, by appointment of the Venetian Senate, Tomeo was the first to teach the Greek text of Aristotle at that university. He was absent from that post for the interval 1504 to 1506, when he taught in Venice, holding the San Marco chair previously occupied by Benedetto Brognoli. After 1507, he continued to live quietly in Padua on his personal income, studying, writing, and teaching privately.

The secondary literature reflects confusion over Tomeo's identity. He is not to be confounded with Niccolò da Lonigo (of Vicenza), also called "Leonico" or "Leoniceno," and also active in this period and in the same circles. Indeed, Pavanello, *Maestro* (p. 116), assigns the San Marco teaching position from 1504-1506 to Niccolò Leoniceno rather than Tomeo, a suggestion that de Bellis does not follow, and does not discuss; F. Lepori ("Scuola di Rialto," p. 602) follows Pavanello's lead. The seriousness of the confusion of identities will become evident in considering A. Poppi's identification of the first person to teach the Greek Aristotle at Padua as "Niccolò Tomeo da Lonigo"—who never existed (*Introduzione all'aristotelismo padovano*, p. 30).

WORKS. Famed above all for his translations of Aristotle, humanistically precise and conceptually sophisticated (see especially de Bellis, "Niccolò Leonico Tomeo interprete di Aristotele naturalista"); he intended to translate *all* of Aristotle. For Tomeo's role as a translator of scientific works—his translation of the pseudo-Aristotelian *Mechanics* became the standard one in the sixteenth century—see also P. L. Rose and S. Drake, "The Pseudo-Aristotelian *Questions of Mechanics* in Renaissance Culture," pp. 78-80. A convenient listing of Tomeo's works is in Cosenza, *Dict.*, IV, 3394ff. These are especially noteworthy here: the *Dialogi*; *De varia historia* (in many eds.); *epistolae*.

CORRESPONDENCE. With Reginald Pole and others of the English circle, Guillaume Budé (cf. de Bellis, "La vita e l'ambiente," pp. 61-62 and n. 85), Cassandra Fedele (ibid., p. 40 and n. 11), among others; for the correspondence in general, ibid., pp. 49 ff.; for the English circle, also Gasquet, *Cardinal Pole*.

DISCOURSE. In his roles as teacher and translator/commentator of Greek works pertaining mainly to natural philosophy, Tomeo is an important figure in the development of science at the University of Padua, and a participant in the continuing discussion of the relation between Plato and Aristotle, whose views were for Tomeo harmonizable. His learning was praised by Erasmus, Giovio, Pietro Bembo, Jacopo Sadoleto, and Francesco Patrizi, among others. Tomeo was in relation at Padua with leading poets (including Giovanni Aurelio Augurello and Girolamo Bologni), artists, philosophers, and politicians, including several English humanists of the circles of Thomas More and Reginald Pole and the Frenchman Christophe de Longueil, through whom he encountered in correspondence Guillaume Budé. His students included Bembo and Pole, the Englishmen Richard Pace and Thomas Lupset, Pierio Valeriano, and perhaps Nicholas Copernicus, among others. With other Venetian and Paduan litterati, Tomeo frequented the house of Filippo Buonaccorsi in 1486, when that humanist resided in Venice as ambassador from Poland. He is included as an interlocutor in Pomponio Gaurico's *De sculptura*, and amassed a considerable collection of antiquities and manuscript and printed books, some interestingly annotated.

EDUCATION. As above; received the doctorate in arts 7 May 1485.

Tommasi, Pietro. (1) Son of Tommaso.

MONOGRAPHS AND STUDIES. A. Benzoni, "Un giudizio di Pietro Tommasi"; R. Cessi, "La giovinezza di Pietro Tommasi, erudito del secolo XV"; A. Segarizzi, "La corrispondenza famigliare di un medico erudito del Quattrocento (Pietro Tommasi)"; also recent profiles by P. O. Kristeller in LQU (introduction to "Tre trattati sulla nobiltà"), pp. 32-33, and S. Connell in "Books and Their Owners in Venice, 1345-1480," pp. 175-82.

CAREER. B. c. 1375/80 (Kristeller in LQU). M. 1395, Francesca Ludovica, daughter of the Paduan giurist Giovanni Ludovico Lambertacci; a second time after 1405 to Bianca Duodo; a third time after 1436 (Segarizzi, "Corrispondenza," pp. 222, 238). Testament, 10 Nov. 1456 (Connell, "Books"). D. 1458 (ibid). A physician born of a substantial citizen family, Tommasi suffered straitened circumstances after his father's death in 1393. Immediately after receiving his doctorate at Padua, Tommasi joined Carlo Zeno's fleet, perhaps as physician, and was present at that hero's triumph off Modon in 1402 (Segarizzi, "Corrispondenza," pp. 232ff.). He taught at Padua (1407-8) and practiced in Venice after 1402, treating or advising, among others, San Bernardino, Francesco Barbaro, Poggio Bracciolini, and Ludovico Foscarini. His Venetian residence was interrupted by stays in Candia (Crete) in 1414-18, and in Vicenza, 1420-21. His testament left his property mainly to charitable causes, notably to sustain a house of pious widows; the foundation thus created survived until 1781. A Pietro Tommasi, perhaps our figure's son, was active as a Venetian secretary at mid-century; his activities greatly confuse the record, and make it doubtful that our Tommasi performed the missions. Certainly it was the younger Tommasi who performed an important mission to Hungary, where he remained after the elder had died (cf. ST 4, cc. 20, 30ᵛ, 31, 65, 70ᵛ, 97ᵛ, 133ᵛ, 168ᵛ, 175, 184; 5, c. 14ᵛ, 20ᵛ, 30ᵛ, 39).

WORKS. *Consilium medicum* (published by Benzoni, but from the same codex as the *Excerptum de astrologica inspectione*, fols. 203-208ᵛ); *Consilium de universali praeservatione contra venena*, to Pope Eugene IV; *Excerptum de astrologica inspectione; Oratio pro collegio phisicorum coram illustrissimo comite Francisco Sfortia*; also *Epistolarum familiarium liber*, not seen (Bergamo, Bibl. Civica, cod. Lambda II, 32, fols. 126-39ᵛ; published in part by E. Walser in *Poggius Florentinus*, pp. 454-84; for these letters, related to the Poggio/Filelfo quarrel, see Connell, "Books," p. 176, Kristeller, in LQU, p. 33), and autograph letters.

CORRESPONDENCE. Correspondence with Francesco Barbaro (cf. *Cento-trenta*, ed. Sabbadini, pp. 14, 31-33, 36, 46-50, 54); Poggio Bracciolini (*Epist.*, ed. Tonellis, II, 278-80, 326-33, 333-38, 339-40, 345-46, 358-60, 364-72; III, 41-43, 172-73; letters exchanged between them in Walser, *Poggius*, pp. 442-43, 455, 461-75, 479-83, 523-24, 529-33, 535-36); Francesco Filelfo (letters from Filelfo to Tommasi in the former's *Epist. fam.*, fols. 3ᵛ, 21, 21ᵛ, 29ᵛ, 33ᵛ-34, 35ᵛ, 39, 39ᵛ, 40ᵛ, 45ᵛ, 46, 47ᵛ, 48ᵛ, 50ᵛ, 51ᵛ, 61, 64, 65, 66, 66ᵛ, 68ᵛ-69, 75ᵛ, 77ᵛ-78, 81, 82, 82ᵛ, 94, 94ᵛ; letters exchanged between them in Walser, pp. 455-61, 473-79, 482, 484); Guarino Veronese (*Epist.*, ed. Sabbadini, I, 60-61, 297-99, 324-28, 664-66; II, 567-72); letters to and from Leonardo Giustiniani (in G. B. Contarini, *Anec. ven.*, pp. 74-76 and 86; another letter from Leonardo in Bernardo Giustiniani's *Orat. et epist.*, sig. K2ʳ⁻ᵛ) and Carlo Zeno (see Segarizzi, "Corrispondenza," pp. 242-43; also a letter from Zeno in G. Zonta, ed., Jacopo Zeno's *Vita Caroli Zeni*, p. 96 n. 1); letters from Gasparino Barzizza (*Opera*, ed. J. A. Furiettus, pp. 191-92, 195; in L. Bertalot, "Die älteste Briefsammlung des Gasparinus Barzizza," p. 97; in Sabbadini, "Lettere e orazioni edite ed inedite di Gasparino Barzizza," p. 574); Fantino Dandolo (cf. Segarizzi, "Corrispondenza," pp. 242-43), Ludovico Foscarini (*Epist.*, fols. 71-79ᵛ, 85ᵛ, 88, 91, 92ʳ⁻ᵛ, 99, 104ʳ⁻ᵛ), and Francesco Zabarella (cf. Segarizzi, pp. 242-43).

DISCOURSE. Widely reputed for his learning as a humanist and physician, Tommasi was close to Barbaro, Giustiniani, and other members of the first generation of Venetian humanists, as well as to the younger Domenico de' Domenichi (his student; see "Education" under the latter's profile) and Lauro Quirini and the Florentine Poggio Bracciolini. With Barbaro and Quirini, he visited Giannozzo Manetti, then Florentine ambassador, in 1448 in Venice (see Segarizzi, "Lauro Quirini," p. 3 n. 6). He was the addressee of Quirini's response (written with his friends Francesco Contarini and Niccolò Barbo) to Poggio's work on nobility. He helped settle controversies between Poggio and Filelfo and between Poggio and Lorenzo Valla (see Connell, "Books," p. 176, and Kristeller in LQU, p. 33), and assisted George of Trebizond, at Francesco Barbaro's request, in obtaining a teaching position in Vicenza (see J. Monfasani, *George of Trebizond*, p. 13, and R. Sabbadini, *Vita di Guarino Ve-*

ronese, p. 67). Tommasi collected manuscripts of medical and philosophical, humanist and classical works, including several rare Greek works that won the admiration of Ambrogio Traversari, some acquired during his stay in Crete. He accumulated a library of more than 130 volumes that were sold after his death (see Connell, "Books," pp. 163, 175ff., who provides the list of Tommasi's books sold between 23 May 1460 and 18 Sept. 1464, pp. 177-82). His concern with the exchange of books and ideas dominated his correspondence with learned men.

EDUCATION. Tommasi studied at Padua before 1392, where he was influenced by Pier Paolo Vergerio and Paolo Veneto (Nicoletti), at the University of Pavia, at Treviso, and again in Padua (from 1399), receiving his doctorate in arts and medicine on 13 Aug. 1402, and subsequently appearing among the examining professors in 1407-1408 (see Kristeller, LQU, pp. 32ff.).

Trevisan, Zaccaria Vecchio. (1) Trivisano, Trivisanus. Son of Giovanni. Miles. Father of Zaccaria G. Related by marriage to Pietro Marcello V (cf. Gothein, "Zaccaria Trevisan," p. 22).

MONOGRAPHS AND STUDIES. P. Gothein, "Zaccaria Trevisan"; *Zaccaria Trevisan il Vecchio: la vita e l'ambiente. Zacharias Trevisan: Leben und Umkreis* is a German version of the preceding work. The chronology published in the first of these works, pp. 20-23, is convenient and nearly complete. Some minor details are corrected or refined in the later monograph. The spare anatomy of the brief digest that follows cannot make clear the high significance of many of the missions entrusted to Trevisan. See also Agostini, *Notizie*, I, 310-25.

CAREER. B. c. 1370 to a popular family ennobled in 1381 for extraordinary service to Venice. M. 1395, Caterina di Giovanni Marcello. Testament 8 Jan. 1414 (published Gothein, "Zacc. Trev.," pp. 49-51). D. later that month. The Trevisan family was one of the thirty families ennobled after the Chioggian war.

Offices. 1400, Amb. to Ferrara; 1400-1401, CX (CXM 8); 1401, Sav. gr. (SMS 45, c. 68); Amb. to the Holy Roman Empire (SMS 45, c. 116); 1402, Sav. gr. (SMS 46, c. 11ᵛ); Venetian agent for purchase of Corfù from Ladislaus, king of Naples and Hungary; CX (CXM 8); 1403, Amb. to Genoa; 1403-1404, Capt. of Candia (Crete); 1405, Prov. in campo, Carrarese war; 1405-7, Vice-Capt. and Capt. of Padua (the first to hold either office); 1407, Sav. gr.; Amb. to the duke of Ferrara; 1407-8, Amb. to two rival popes; 1408-9, Pod. of Verona; 1410-11, Count of Zara (the first to hold that office); 1412, Prov. at Sebenico (for the surrender of the city); 1412-13, Capt. of Padua.

WORKS. Orations: (1) in honor of Pietro Rimondo, Trevisan's successor as Captain of Padua (March 1407); (2) to pope Gregory XII (Foiano, 31 Dec. 1407); (3) to Anti-Pope Benedict XIII (Pietrasanta, 22 Jan. 1408); (4) for the doctorate of Pietro Marcello V, B. of Padua (16 Oct. 1413).

CORRESPONDENCE. Letters from Gasparino Barzizza (Mittarelli, *Bibl. codd. mss.*, cols. 437-38), Coluccio Salutati (*Epist. di Coluccio Salutati*, ed. F. Novati, III, 349-51), Pier Paolo Vergerio (*Epist. di Pier Paolo Vergerio*, ed. L. Smith, pp. 58-61); to Ognibene Scola (Gothein, "Zacc. Trev.," pp. 55-56). Vergerio further mentioned to Niccolò Leonardi letters Trevisan had shown him; in Vergerio's *Epist.*, p. 361.

DISCOURSE. Praised by Flavio Biondo (*It. illus.* [Venice, 1510], fol. 100ᵛ), Leonardo Bruni (in a letter to Pietro Miani in the former's *Epist.*, ed. L. Mehus, II, 15), Marco Donato (in his oration for the younger Zaccaria Trevisan, published in part in Gothein, "Zacc. Trev.," pp. 57-59), and Guarino Veronese (in his *Laudatio iin praeclaros viros Zachariam [Trevisan] et Albanum [Badoer] Venetiarum cives* [1409], in R. Sabbadini, *La scuola e gli studi di Guarino Guarini Veronese*, pp. 170-72). See also the letters of Pellegrino Zambeccari on behalf of the Bolognesi, recommending Trevisan for the post of Patriarch of Aquileia: *Epist. di Pellegrino Zambeccari*, ed. L. Frati, pp. 151-56. To him Guarino dedicated his translation of Plutarch's *Themistocles*. It was Trevisan who first came into possession of Chrysoloras' Latin translation (revised by Uberto Decembrio) of Plato's *Republic*. Trevisan's service as Captain of Candia in 1403-1404 placed him opportunely for discussions of Greek learning and acquisition of texts (cf. A. Pertusi, "Le fonti greche del 'De gestis, moribus et nobilitate civitatis venetiarum' di Lorenzo de Monacis," p. 170). Mentor of Francesco Barbaro, who referred often in his *De re uxoria* to Trevisan's influence upon him (for that influence, see also Gothein, *Zaccaria Trevisan*, pp. 122ff.). Barbaro was present at his last illness, and was the scribe of Zaccaria's testament. It was perhaps Trevisan who urged Vergerio to compose his *De republica Venetorum* (see A. Pertusi, "Gli inizi della storiografia umanistica del Quattrocento," pp. 272-73).

EDUCATION. University studies at Padua, 1389-90, and Bologna, 1390-97; at Bologna, he also taught from 1394, by which year he had been granted the doctorate in canon and civil law. Present for the granting of degrees to others at Padua in 1409, 1410, and frequently in 1413.

Trevisan, Zaccaria Giovane. (2) Trivisano, Trivisanus. Son of Zaccaria. Doctor, miles.

MONOGRAPHS AND STUDIES. G. degli Agostini, *Notizie*, I, 373-85.

CAREER. B. 1414 (posthumously, after father's Jan. death). M. 1439, Dorotea di Santo Venier. D. June/July 1466. On 1 June 1466, when Trevisan held the title of *consigliere*, he was granted permission to go to the baths at Padua for his health, the privilege eventually being extended through the whole of the month (CLN 10, c. 146ᵛ). He had died before 18 July of that year when a new *consigliere* appears in his place (ibid., c. 150). For the tomb of Trevisan's wife, see Cicogna, *Iscrizioni*, II, 86ff. Trevisan had initially planned a clerical career. Francesco Barbaro wrote Ludovico (Scarampo) Trevisan on his behalf, requesting a protonotariate for his young friend; cf. *Centotrenta*, ed. Sabbadini, pp. 24, 84-85.

Offices. 1445, Amb. to Bologna; Sav. tf. (SM 2; ST 1); 1446, CX (CXM 13; SGV 4, c. 114^v); Sav. tf. (SM 2; ST 1, c. 186 and passim; 2); 1446-47, Amb. to Florence (ST 2, cc. 8, 11^v, 28); 1447, Sav. tf. (SM 3); Amb. in obedientia to P. Nicholas V; 1448, Sav. tf. (ST 2, c. 53 and passim); CX (CXM 13; SGV 4, c. 119^v; held concurrently with previous office); 1448, Cons.; Amb. to Savoy (CLN 8, c. 75^v; ST 2, cc. 72^v, 73); 1449, Sav. tf. (SGV 4, c. 145; SM 3; ST 2, c. 105^v and passim); 1449-50, Pod. of Verona (SGV 4, c. 62^v; Agostini, *Notizie*, I, 376-77; *Comm.*, ed. Predelli, X, 43 [xiv, #119]); 1450, Sav. tf. (ST 2); 1451, Cons. (CLN 8; CXM 14; MC-Ursa; SGV 4, c. 93); Amb. to Naples; CX (CXM 14; SGV 4, c. 130); Amb. to Florence; 1451-52, Sav. gr. (SGV 4, c. 146^v; SM 4; ST 3); 1452, Lt. in Friuli; 1453-54, Sav. gr. (SGV 4, c. 148^v; SM 5; ST 3); 1454, Amb. to imperial diet at Ratisbon (ST 3, cc. 103, 108); Amb. to Rome and Naples; 1455, Cons. (ST 3); Sav. gr. (SGV 4, c. 148^v; SM 5; ST 3); 1456, Cons. X (CXM 15; SGV 4, c. 142^v); Avog. (CXM 15; SGV 4, cc. 142^v, 152^v; SM 5); 1456-57, Capt. of Brescia (CLN 9, c. 90); 1458-59, Avog. (CXM 15; SM 6; ST 4); 1460, Sav. gr. (SM 6; ST 4, c. 154^v); 1461-62, Sav. gr. (ST 4, c. 180^v and passim); CX (CXM 16; held concurrently with previous office); 1462, Duc. el., Cristoforo Moro (MC-Regina, cc. 38^v, 39, 40); 1462-63, Pod. of Padua; 1464, Avog. (CXM 16); 1464-65, Amb. in obedientia to Pope Paul II (ST 5, c. 120; on this occasion Trevisan delivered an oration to the new prelate); 1465-66, Cons. (CLN 10; CXM 16; MC-Regina; SM 8, passim and c. 55; ST 5); died in this office.

WORKS. *Oratio pro data licentia D. Iohanni Marino in utroque iure* (Padua, 18 Dec. 1435); *Oratio habita ad Pontificem Barbum* (1464). Trevisan also delivered orations to Pope Nicholas V and King Alfonso of Aragon, not known to me to be extant (cf. Agostini, *Notizie*, I, 376 and 380; for the second, also Francesco Contarini, *De rebus in Hetruria gestis*, p. 42), and wrote *epistolae* to the Florentines (1451) and to the pope (San Daniele del Friuli, Bibl. Communale, in codd. 165 [cf. *Iter*, II, 568] and 104 [cf. Mazzatinti, *Inventario*, III, 126-27], respectively). Bernardo Bembo sought the text of one of Trevisan's orations (V. Cian, "Per Bernardo Bembo—II," p. 77).

CORRESPONDENCE. Substantial correspondence with Francesco Barbaro (cf. *Centotrenta*, ed. Sabbadini, indices). Letters from Ludovico Foscarini (*Epist.*, fols. 137^{r-v}, 209^{r-v}, 236^{r-v}), Niccolò Sagundino (*Epist. et opusc.*, fols. 84^v-87), and Maffeo Vallaresso (*Epist.*, pp. 67-68).

DISCOURSE. Praised for his learning by Flavio Biondo (*It. illus.* [Venice, 1510], fol. 101; cf. also Agostini, *Notizie*, I, 383) and others, and in an oration by Marco Donato (25 Aug. 1442; see Bibliography for the Marc. ms., as Gothein's edition excerpts only the section relevant to Zaccaria's father). Bartolomeo Cipolla dedicated to him his *De milite imperatore* (see Agostini, *Notizie*, I, 375). A patron of Sagundino and others (see Sagundino's letter, cited above, and Foscarini's in the *Epist.*, fol. 226).

EDUCATION. With Paolo della Pergola (see Donato's oration *in laudes Zacharie Trivisani,* fol. 163). Trevisan received his license and doctorate in arts at Padua on 8 Nov. 1434 (Zonta and Brotto, *Acta,* p. 229, #1023), after which he remained in attendance as a law student (passim), receiving his license and doctorate in laws on 25 and 26 Aug., respectively, of 1442 (p. 337, ##1648, 1649).

Valla, Giorgio. (3) Son of Andrea.

MONOGRAPHS AND STUDIES. V. Branca, ed., *Giorgio Valla tra scienza e sapienza* (especially G. Gardenal's "Cronologia della vita e delle opere" at pp. 93-97); F. Gabotto, "Giorgio Valla e il suo processo in Venezia nel 1496"; J. L. Heiberg, *Beiträge zur Geschichte Georg Vallas und seiner Bibliothek* and "Nachträgliches über Georg Valla"; P. L. Rose, "Bartolomeo Zamberti's Funeral Oration for the Humanist Encyclopaedist Giorgio Valla"; R. Sabbadini, "Briciole umanistiche—LII: Giorgio Valla" and review of Heiberg's monograph; G. dalla Santa, "Nuovi appunti sul processo di Giorgio Valla e di Placidio Amerini in Venezia nel 1496." Branca's "L'umanesimo veneziano alla fine del Quattrocento" provides a thorough career summary, pp. 162-66, the most convenient guide to further bibliography.

CAREER. B. Piacenza, 1447. D. 23 Jan. 1500. After studies in Milan and Piacenza, Valla taught in Pavia (1466-85, with interruptions), Genoa (1476-79), and Milan (1481-82). Called by the Senate to Venice late in 1485 through the efforts on his behalf of Ermolao Barbaro G (for which see also A. Ferriguto, *Almorò Barbaro,* pp. 198, 281ff.). Valla assumed the chair of rhetoric at San Marco (document of appointment in Heiberg, *Beiträge,* p. 16) which he held until his death (doc. of his replacement, ibid., pp. 41-42), his salary rising from 150 to 200 ducats. Imprisoned in Feb. 1496, suspected of having betrayed state secrets, he was released in Oct. and reinstated.

WORKS. *De expetendis et fugiendis rebus opus,* a massive humanist encyclopedia published by Aldo (1501); see Branca, p. 164 and n. 75; Heiberg, *Beiträge,* pp. 33ff.; Rose, "Oration," pp. 300ff.; Sabbadini, "Briciole umanistiche"; and A. Firmin-Didot, *Alde Manuce et l'hellénisme à Venise,* p. 176. Forty-four *epistolae* in Heiberg, *Beiträge,* pp. 44-107. For Valla's many other works, including commentaries, translations, and editions of ancient literary, scientific, philosophical, and medical texts, and grammatical and rhetorical works, see the chronological listings in Gardenal, "Cronologia," and Heiberg, *Beiträge,* pp. 36-41; for translations of Alexander of Aphrodisias, Aristarchus, Paulus Aegineta, also see CTC, I, 125-26, 130-32, 165, and IV, 151-52; commentaries on Juvenal and Pliny, ibid., I, 223-24, and IV, 350-51.

CORRESPONDENCE. Of the letters published by Heiberg (forty-seven to and from Valla), especially noteworthy here are those from and to Pietro Barozzi (pp. 83-85), to Federico Molin (93-94), and from Francesco Filelfo (97-98); also elsewhere letters from Ermolao Barbaro G (*Epist.,* ed. Branca, II, 15, 21-

PROFILES

22, 52-57), and Rutgerus Sycamber (Cologne, Historisches Archiv, cod. W 340, fol. 45ᵛ, not seen; see *Iter*, III, 594).

DISCOURSE. Translator and editor of scientific and literary works, Valla played a unique role in blending mathematical and humanist perspectives on the threshold of the sixteenth century (see Rose, "Bartolomeo Zamberti," and his "Humanist Culture and Renaissance Mathematics," pp. 98 and passim). These concerns are reflected in his magnificent library of Greek manuscripts that descended to the princely Pio family of Carpi and subsequently in part to the Biblioteca Estense in Modena (Rose, "Humanist Culture," pp. 94ff. and passim, and the inventory published by Heiberg, *Beiträge*, pp. 109-29; also R. Sabbadini, *Le scoperte dei codici latini e greci*, I, 149, indices). Promoted especially by Barbaro, Valla's relations to several Venetian noblemen (Branca, "Umanesimo," p. 162) are indicated by the dedications of many works (Heiberg, *Beiträge*, p. 21). He participated in the literary circle gathered about Filippo Buonaccorsi in 1486 (see the latter's *De his quae a Venetis tentata sunt* [1533], pp. 85-86). Among his many students (see Heiberg, *Beiträge*, pp. 22 and 25), these especially deserve mention: Gasparo Contarini, Lorenzo Loredan, Ludovico Mocenigo, and Vettore Pisani, all patricians; and Giovanni Antonio Flaminio, Giovanni Pietro Valeriano, Pontico Virunio, and Bartolomeo Zamberti (see also Rose, "Bartolomeo Zamberti," p. 301 and passim). He was praised as one of the Venetian public teachers by Francesco Negri (*De aristocratia*, fol. 99) and Marino Sanuto (*Cronachetta*, the relevant passage from which is translated in J. B. Ross, "Venetian Schools," p. 557); Paolo Giovio (*Elogia doctorum virorum* [1577], p. 199) was critical. See also the brief biography by Valla's adopted son Giovanni Pietro Valla (Cademusto; in Heiberg, *Beiträge*, pp. 3-6), and Zamberti's funeral oration (in Rose, "Bartolomeo Zamberti," pp. 303-307).

EDUCATION. With Constantine Lascaris in Milan, and at the University of Pavia, where he studied Greek with Andronico Callisto and arts and medicine under Giovanni Marliano.

Vallaresso, Fantino. (1) Valaresso, Vallaressus. Son of Vittore; uncle of Maffeo.

MONOGRAPHS AND STUDIES. G. degli Agostini, *Notizie*, I, 269-77; A. Palmieri, "Un'opera inedita di Fantini Vallaresso, Arcivescovo di Creta, sul Concilio di Firenze"; V. Peri, "Tre lettere inedite a Fantino Valaresso ed un suo catechismo attribuito a Fantino Dandolo"; B. Schultze, introduction to Vallaresso's *Libellus de ordine generalium conciliorum*, pp. xiii-xix.

CAREER. B. c. 1392 (AC-BO 162/I, c. 141, presented Dec. 1411, suggesting a birthdate of c. 1393, which confirms Agostini's date given here; Eubel [*Hier. cath.*, I, 390 n. 4] says that on 28 April 1415 Vallaresso had not yet reached twenty-three). D. 18 May 1443 (Schultze's date, following earlier sources, regardless of Palmieri's evidence of papal letters to Vallaresso as late as 1446, "Opera inedita," p. 4). Vallaresso performed several diplomatic missions for the pope, and was present as papal legate at the Councils of Basel (1434) and Ferrara-Florence (1438-39). Subsequently, he was sent as papal legate to Candia to supervise the plan of east-west church union; papal letters to him witness his stay there from 1439 to 1446. He had competed without success for Bishop of Torcello (1418), Archbishop of Zara (1419), and Bishop of Trau (1423); see C. Cenci, "Senato veneto 'Probae,' " pp. 367, #68; 370, #72; 373, #76.

Titles. 1415-25, B. of Parenzo and Pola (Eubel, *Hier. cath.*, I, 390, 216). (Vallaresso was elected to Parenzo in 1415 by Pope Gregory XII, but events prevented his assuming that position; he was confirmed by Pope Martin V in 1417. On 6 April 1418, he was still in Padua though "electo parentino" [Zonta and Brotto, *Acta*, p. 126, #462]; at the time of his 1415 election, he is identified as "clericus diocesis Castellanensis" [Eubel, *Hier. cath.*, I, 390, 216].) 1425— Archbishop of Candia (Crete) (ibid., 216).

WORKS. *Libellus de ordine generalium conciliorum et unione Florentina*, to Pope Eugene IV. This work was widely diffused in manuscript, and previously edited in Palmieri's "Opera inedita," pp. 6-26, 284-94. Extensive discussion of the tradition in Schultze's edition cited in the bibliography. Vallaresso composed the *Compendium pro instructione fidei*, which has been published from the fifteenth century under the name Fantino Dandolo; I have seen the 1490 edition entitled *Compendium catholicae fidei*. For the revised attribution, see Peri, "Tre lettere," pp. 57ff. and 66.

CORRESPONDENCE. Published by Peri ("Tre lettere," pp. 63-67) are letters from "B.AB." of Buda (for identification, see Peri, pp. 49 ff.) and Marco Zusto of Crete (two). These are published from the same codex which contains the *epistolario* of Maffeo Vallaresso, Fantino's nephew, where there are also other letters (not easily legible or identifiable) to Fantino; see Peri, p. 49. For three letters by Fantino, all related to his clerical enterprises, see ibid., p. 47. A letter from Pietro del Monte is in J. Haller, *Pier da Monte*, p. 48.

DISCOURSE. A strong supporter of papal authority, Vallaresso shows himself a humanist in method and style in his *Libellus de ordine generalium conciliorum.*

EDUCATION. With Guarino Veronese; later at Padua, where he probably attained a doctorate in canon law. That degree is reported by Agostini, *Notizie*, I, 269, but has left no record in Zonta and Brotto, *Acta*, where Vallaresso does appear as a student of arts on 15 Feb. 1412 (p. 67, #234), and is present through 1419 as a witness to degrees granted others (cf. indices). In the 1423 *proba* for Bishop of Trau to which Vallaresso was elected by the Senate (though in vain, for the pope had already chosen his candidate), he is described as "decretorum doctor" (Cenci, "Senato veneto," p. 373, #76 and n. 1).

Vallaresso, Maffeo. (2) Valaresso, Vallaressus. Son of Giorgio; nephew of Fantino.

MONOGRAPHS AND STUDIES. A. Segarizzi, "Una grammatica latina del secolo XV."

PROFILES

CAREER. B. c. 1415. D. 1496. The date of birth suggested is consistent with Vallaresso's composition in 1432 (Segarizzi, "Grammatica," p. 90), while evidently still young and engaged in elementary studies, of the grammatical *regulae* cited below, and with the dates of his university degrees, early and later dignities, and letters (mostly from the decade of the 1450s). The date of death from Cicogna, *Iscrizioni*, II, 148; Gams (*Ser. episc.*, p. 426) gives 1495. Before achieving the archbishopric with which Vallaresso would have to content himself for a lifetime, he held the titles by 1445 of canon of Crete and canon of Treviso (Zonta and Brotto, *Acta*, p. 384, #1943; Eubel, *Hier. cath.*, II, 166), and in 1449, that of apostolic protonotary (Segarizzi, "Grammatica," p. 89). He competed unsuccessfully for major sees in 1481 (Padua) and 1485 (Treviso); cf. C. Cenci, "Senato veneto 'probae,' " pp. 410, #110 and 418, #115. In the latter instance, his name appears in the *proba* with this quietly plaintive notation: "iam per triginta quinque annos archiepiscopus Iadrensis." On 26 June 1468, he witnessed in Rome the act by which the ambassador Paolo (not Pietro) Morosini took effective possession for Venice of the library of Cardinal Bessarion (*Comm.*, ed. Predelli, X, 197 [p. xvi, #22]). In 1474, he joined the reform congregation of San Giorgio in Alga (Cicogna, *Iscrizioni*, II, 147).

Title. 1450— Archbishop of Zara (Eubel, *Hier. cath.*, II, 166).

WORKS. *Epistolae* (for which see descriptions in *Iter*, II, 460-61, and *Le vite di Paolo II di Gasparo da Verona e Michele Canensi*, ed. G. Zippel, p. 179 n. 2); grammatical *Regulae* (discussed by Segarizzi). Vallaresso's unusual *epistolario* is useful for an understanding of ecclesiastical relations in this period.

CORRESPONDENCE. Vallaresso's substantial *epistolario* includes letters to, among others: Ermolao Barbaro V, Francesco Barbaro, Zaccaria Barbaro, Marco Barbo, Niccolò Barbo, Paolo Barbo, Pietro Barbo, Candiano Bollani, Fantino Dandolo, Domenico de' Domenichi, Pietro Foscari, Ludovico Foscarini, Vitale Lando, Jacopo Antonio Marcello, Pietro Molin, Barbone Morosini, Lauro Quirini, Zaccaria Trevisan the Younger, Lorenzo Zane, and Jacopo Zeno. Letters from: Francesco Barbaro, Marco Barbo, Ludovico Foscarini, Barbone Morosini, Lauro Quirini, Nicolò Sagundino, and Lorenzo Zane. Kristeller's description of the Vallaresso ms. includes names of correspondents. Some of these letters are printed: cf. Cicogna, *Iscrizioni*, II, 148. See also the letters from Simon of Ragusa to Vallaresso published by Zippel, in the *Vite*, pp. 179-81.

DISCOURSE. Although many of Vallaresso's letters are concerned primarily with ecclesiastical matters, his correspondence particularly with Pietro Barbo, Quirini, and Zane indicates an interest in the collection of antiquities and manuscripts and in the cultivation of an elegant Latin style. In Zara, Vallaresso collected and sent to Pietro Barbo, later Pope Paul II, coins and small antiquities (cf. R. Weiss, *Un umanista veneziano: Papa Paolo II*, p. 28), and completely restored the episcopal palace and cathedral (see Cicogna, *Iscrizione*,

II, 147). For further evidence of his interest in the arts, see his letter to Ermolao Barbaro V in the *Epist.*, pp. 308-10.

EDUCATION. With Guarino Veronese (see Segarizzi, "Grammatica," pp. 90ff.), and subsequently at Padua, where he received his license and doctorate in law on 26 May 1445 (Zonta and Brotto, *Acta*, pp. 384-85, #1943).

Vinciguerra, Antonio. (3) Son of Francesco.

MONOGRAPHS AND STUDIES. B. Beffa, *Antonio Vinciguerra Cronico, segretario della Serenissima*; A. Sopetto, *Le satire edite ed inedite di Antonio Vinciguerra*; A. della Torre, *Di Antonio Vinciguerra e delle sue satire*, and P. L. Rambaldi, review of the latter and other pertinent works. Della Torre's interesting but flawed study is scrupulously corrected by Rambaldi, and both by Beffa. See Beffa especially for further bibliographical direction.

CAREER. B. between 1440 and 1446. Testament, 3 Dec. 1502 (in Beffa, *Antonio Vinciguerra*, pp. 176-78, who corrects its date and the date of death as offered by his predecessors; previously printed in d. Torre, pp. 221-23). D. 9 Dec. 1502. Born in Venice to a family originating from Recanati (the family subsequently listed among the *cittadini*; see da Mosto, *Archivio*, I, 77), Vinciguerra served as a *donzello* in the Great Council before being made a ducal notary in 1459. Having accompanied Bernardo Bembo on the latter's embassy to Castille in 1468-69, in 1470-71, Vinciguerra was in Rome as secretary to the Venetian ambassadors to the pope. In the years following, he performed diplomatic missions almost continually, most notable of which perhaps are those to Florence and Ferrara in 1474-76, to Florence and Rome in 1478-79, to Veglia in 1480-81 (from which mission resulted the important *relazione*, see below) and 1488-89, to Rome in 1486-87, and to Bologna in 1495-99. In 1498 his salary, which had mounted gradually from the outset of his career, reached an ample 150 ducats per year. In 1499, he was named secretary to the Council of Ten. His 1502 will reveals that Vinciguerra had accumulated substantial possessions, including a villa outside Padua, and providing the capacity to order the construction of a funeral chapel and monument. The will also notoriously orders the burning of certain of Vinciguerra's literary work—of what number and significance we do not know.

WORKS. See the exhaustive listing of Vinciguerra's works in many ms. and printed versions in Beffa, pp. xiii-xv and 5-8. Of particular interest are the ten *satire* and the *Relazione sull'isola di Veglia*. The printed *satire* (for editions, see Beffa, *Antonia Vinciguerra*, p. xiii; for discussions and evaluations, della Torre, *Di Antonio Vinciguerra*, pp. 88-220 and Rambaldi, review, pp. 148-51) usually contain these six: *Consolatoria de morte filiae*, to Giovanni Caldiera; the *De miseria humanae conditionis* and *Contra vitia capitalia*, both to Bernardo Bembo; the *Contra falsum et imperitum vulgi iudicium*, to the unknown patrician Francesco Contarini and to Antonio Susi; the *Liber utrum deceat sapientem ducere uxorem an in coelibatu vivere* (Bologna, 31 Dec. 1494), to Marco Giorgi; the *De coelibatu, virginitate et castitate*. Four more are in Sopetto, *Satire*: the *De umbratili et vera felicitate* (pp. 64-70); *De variis hominum cupiditatibus et quod omnia non Fortunae arbitrio, sed Dei providentia reguntur* (pp. 70-76); *Contra mores huius saeculi* (pp. 77-83; also in della Torre, *Di Antonio Vinciguerra*, pp. 242-50); *Quod divinus amor in mentibus humanis diffusus aut ad ipsum Deum erigitur in beatitudine aut reflectitur ad terram in perditione* (Sopetto, *Satire*, pp. 83-89). The *Relazione* is also printed. With thanks to P. O. Kristeller for directing me to the work, and to Joyce T. Whalley of the library of the Victoria and Albert Museum, who furnished me with a xerox copy and a description, I can also report the verse *De principe libellus* (1502), to Doge Leonardo Loredan, whose accession it celebrates, now cod. Res. H. 33 of that collection. Known to have existed in the nineteenth century, this work was thought lost by scholars (della Torre, p. 87; Rambaldi, p. 151 and n. 4; Beffa, pp. 7-8).

CORRESPONDENCE. Letters to Paolo Morosini (in Beffa, *Antonio Vinciguerra*, pp. 154-56), and to Bembo (5 May 1498, New York, Pierpont Morgan Library, MA 1842 [autograph]; thanks to Dott.a Nella Giannetto for notice of this work); from Marsilio Ficino (*Epist.*, pp. 803-804, 810-11 [with Bembo], 957; all reprinted in Sopetto, *Satire*, pp. 90-92) and Giorgio Merula (in Beffa, *Antonio Vinciguerra*, p. 90).

DISCOURSE. Vinciguerra engaged in literary discussions in Rome, in Florence (with Ficino's circle, and in the company of Bembo), and in Bologna (see, in addition to the works cited, E. Raimondi, "Umanesimo bolognese e umanesimo veneziano," pp. 227-28) during his missions to those cities, and at home in Venice. There in 1491, he attempted to assist Poliziano and Giovanni Pico della Mirandola in their intention, not to be realized, to see the manuscripts Bessarion had bequeathed the city in 1468. Vinciguerra had close relations with the Venetian patricians, notably Bembo (see in addition to works cited also V. Cian, "Per Bernardo Bembo—II," p. 64, and della Torre, "La prima ambasceria di Bernardo Bembo a Firenze," pp. 283ff.; both Rambaldi [p. 135] and Beffa [pp. 30ff., 34ff.] correct their understanding of the official relations between Bembo and Vinciguerra), Ludovico Foscarini, and Paolo Morosini, and enjoyed in later years the patronage of Marco di Bertuccio Giorgi. Giovanni Caldiera dedicated to his former student Vinciguerra his *De praestantia Venetae politiae*; Giovanni Mario Filelfo his invective against Pietro Perleone and George of Trebizond; and Merula his editions of Virgil and Pliny (cf. F. Gabotto and A. Confalonieri, "Vita di Giorgio Merula," first part, p. 59). Ficino sent Vinciguerra copies of his *De religione* and *De sole*, transmitted with the first and third of the letters cited above; for relations with Ficino, see P. O. Kristeller, "Marsilio Ficino e Venezia," pp. 480 and n. 32; 482-83 and nn. 42, 43, 44.

EDUCATION. With Pietro Perleone and perhaps Filippo Morandi and Benedetto Brognoli at the San Marco chancery school, and philosophical studies with Giovanni Caldiera.

Vitturi, Daniele. (1) Vettori, Vitturius, Victurius. Son of Niccolò.

CAREER. B. late fourteenth century (presumed from his 1404 marriage and from the births of sons probably in 1406 and 1407: AC-BO 162/I, c. 140v). M. 1404, Elizabetta di Leonardo Mocenigo (Giomo, *Matrimoni*, II, 101). Testament, 10 Sept. 1440 (AN, Testamenti B. Croce, B. 1155.15). D. before 30 Jan. 1441 when, Vitturi already dead, the will was witnessed. Vitturi's political career actually began considerably earlier than the career summary below indicates. He held minor offices from 1408, when elected one of the *capi dei sestieri* (CXM 9, c. 5ᵛ).

Offices. 1423, Duc. el., Francesco Foscari (MC-Ursa, c. 50); 1424, Sav. tf. (SMS 55, c. 38); 1424-25, Cons. (CLN 6; CXM 10; SMS 55); 1425, Sav. tf., 2 terms (SMS 55, c. 133 and passim); 1425-26, CX (CXM 10); 1426, Sav. tf. (SMS 55, c. 183ᵛ); 1426-28, Avog. (CXM 10); 1428, Sav. tf. (SMS 56, c. 10); 1429, Sav. tf. (SMS 57, c. 67); Cons. (CXM 10; MC-Ursa; SMS 57); 1429-30, CX (CXM 10, 11); 1430, Sav. tf., 2 terms (SMS 57, cc. 178ᵛ, 224ᵛ); 1431, Pod. of Brescia (SMS 58, c. 26); 1432, Cons. (CXM 11; MC-Ursa; SMS 58); Sav. gr. (SMS 58, c. 146ᵛ); Prov. with the army in Brescia (SMS 58, c. 152); 1432-33, Avog. (CXM 11; SMS 58); 1435, Capt. of Verona (SMS 59, cc. 96ᵛff.); 1435-36, Cons. (CLN 6; CXM 11; MC-Ursa; SMS 59); 1436, Sav. gr., 2 terms (SMS 59, cc. 150, 177ᵛ); 1436-37, CX (CXM 11); 1437, Sav. gr., (SMS 60, c. 38); 1438, Cons. (CXM 12; MC-Ursa; SMS 60); Amb. to Pope (Ferrara) (SMS 60, cc. 102ʳ⁻ᵛ); 1439, Sav. gr. (SMS 60, cc. 135, 171ᵛ and passim); Amb. to the Pope (Flor.) (MC-Ursa, c. 122ᵛ; SMS 60, c. 166); Lt. di Friuli (MC-Ursa, c.122ᵛ; SGV 4, c. 65ᵛ); 1440, Sav. gr. (SMS 60, c. 204).

CORRESPONDENCE. Letters from Francesco Barbaro (cf. *Centotrenta*, ed. Sabbadini, indices); Gasparino Barzizza (*Opera*, ed. J. A. Furiettus, passim; L. Bertalot, "Die älteste Briefsammlung des Gasparinus Barzizza," pp. 66ff.; R. Sabbadini, "Lettere e orazioni edite ed inedite di Gasparino Barzizza," passim); Antonio Beccadelli (Panormita) (see G. Resta, *L'epist. del Panormita*, p. 243); Francesco Filelfo (*Epist. fam.*, fols. 1ᵛ, 30ᵛ); Guarino Veronese (*Epist.*, ed. Sabbadini, I, 480-82).

DISCOURSE. Member of the first-generation learned circle that also included Barbaro, Andrea Giuliani, Leonardo Giustiniani. Mentioned as one of Venice's learned men by Antonio Baratella (*Policleomenareis*, fol. 14ᵛ), Flavio Biondo (*It. illus.* [Venice, 1510], fol. 101), Pietro del Monte (*Invectiva adversus ridiculum quendam oratorem*, Quirini's *Diatriba*, p. 191); and by the author of an anonymous letter from Padua's humanist circle around Barzizza, after 1418 (see L. Bertalot, "Eine Sammlung Paduaner Reden," p. 259). In 1418, Barzizza dedicated his *De orthographia* to Daniele's young sons Domenico and Pietro (cf. R. Sabbadini, *La scuola e gli studi*, p. 50). In the 1470s, Raffaele Zovenzoni visited the library of Daniele's son Pietro, which may have contained volumes descended from his father (cf. B. Ziliotto, *Raffaele Zovenzoni*,

p. 47). A codex of ecclesiastical works transcribed at least partly in Daniele's hand is in the Bodleian Library, Oxford (see H. O. Coxe, *Catalogi codicum manuscriptorum bibliothecae Bodleianae*, III: *Codices graecos et latinos canonicianos*, p. 96).

EDUCATION. Probably a co-student of Andrea Giuliani under Gasparino Barzizza and Lorenzo de' Monaci (S. Troilo, *Andrea Giuliano*, pp. 16, 21, 165).

Zane, Lorenzo. (2) Son of Paolo. Related to Barbos; see Barbo, Pietro.

MONOGRAPHS AND STUDIES. G. degli Agostini, *Notizie*, I, 177-204; R. Weiss, "Lorenzo Zane arcivescovo di Spalato e governatore di Cesena."

CAREER. B. 1429. D. 2 October 1484 (cf. G. Mercati, *Ultimi contributi*, II, 53; Gams and Eubel [*Ser. Episc.*, p. 780; *Hier. cath.*, II, 89 n. 4, Oct. 15] give 1485). Agostini (*Notizie*, I, 177) describes Zane as the son of a citizen father and noble mother, but the records of the Avogaria di Comun show clearly that he is a nobleman. Lorenzo Zane quondam Paolo was presented to that body on 26 Nov. 1446 by Pasquale Zane, probably Paolo's brother (BO 163/II, c. 46ᵛ). Two other sons of Paolo Zane (Andrea and Alvise) were presented on 28 Nov. 1457 and 28 Nov. 1459 by Vitale Lando (Lorenzo's brother-in-law) and Paolo's widow, respectively (ibid., c. 46). Related through his mother to the popes Gregory XII and Eugene IV, Zane was early favored in his ecclesiastical career, living as a youth in Rome under the tutelage of his uncle Cardinal Francesco Condulmier. At the time of his election to Spalato—when he was twenty-three years old—Zane already held the title of apostolic protonotary. Zane was so unpopular in Spalato (which he first visited only in the fifth year of his episcopacy) that in 1463 he was recalled by Venice and forbidden for ten years to return to his see. Back in Rome, he was protected by Pope Pius II and then promoted to further honors by his relative Pope Paul II. Attached during most of his career to the curia, he was called on frequently to perform important military, administrative, and diplomatic services. From 1452 to 1457 he administered the patriarchate of Jerusalem by cession of Bessarion. In 1463, he was named papal treasurer-general. Five times between 1465 and 1484 he served as papal governor of Cesena, and served also during that period in other parts of the Romagna. For the circumstances of the 1478 case, see Malipiero, *Annali*, pp. 668-70.

Titles. 1452-73, Archbishop of Spalato (Eubel, *Hier. cath.*, II, 240); 1473, Patriarch of Antioch (ibid., II, 89); 1473-78, Bishop of Treviso (ibid., II, 249); 1478-80, Bishop of Brescia (ibid., II, 111); 1478, *exiled from Brescia and all Venetian territories after condemnation for betrayal of state secrets.*

WORKS. *De difficillimae doctrinae palma capescenda*, to Giorgio Bevilacqua (da Lazise); *epistola* in defense of Lorenzo Valla (cf. Weiss, "Lorenzo Zane," p. 165; I have been unable to consult Valla's *Antidoti*, IV, in *Opera omnia*, I, which appends it).

CORRESPONDENCE. Exchanges with Lorenzo Valla (Zane to Valla in L. Barozzi and R. Sabbadini, *Studi sul Panormita e sul Valla*, pp. 136-37; for Valla's to Zane, see A. Pertusi, "Gli inizi della storiografia umanistica del Quattrocento," p. 298) and Maffeo Vallaresso (*Epist.*, pp. 109-10, 114-18, 125-27, 129-37, 144-51, 156-57, 254-55, 344, 365-66, 376-91, 399-402, 420-21, 441-43, 475-78, 519-20, 544-45, 584-93); letter from Francesco Barbaro (see *Centotrenta*, ed. Sabbadini, p. 57). Weiss additionally notes (p. 168) correspondence with Giovanni Antonio Campano and Cardinal Ammanati, not seen.

DISCOURSE. Zane participated in the literary life of Rome centered around the curia, defending Valla, his teacher (whom he also promoted for the position of historiographer in Venice), in the latter's controversy with Poggio Bracciolini (see Agostini, *Notizie*, I, 180; Weiss, "Lorenzo Zane," p. 165; and G. Zippel, "Lorenzo Valla e le origini della storiografia umanistica a Venezia," pp. 104ff.), and assisting Pomponio Leto (see A. della Torre, *Paolo Marsi da Pescina*, p. 82). Later he encouraged Valla to undertake the task of writing a history of Venice (cf. Pertusi, "Inizi," pp. 298ff.; Zippel, "Lorenzo Valla," pp. 93ff.; and F. Gaeta, "Storiografia, coscienza nazionale," pp. 28ff.). In Spalato during his brief residence, he restored the archepiscopal palace (see Agostini, *Notizie*, I, 181). In Rome in later years, he patronized the humanists Francesco Negri, tutor to his nephews (cf. G. Mercati, *Ultimi contributi*, II, 37 n. 3, and 52), Leonardo Montagna (Weiss, "Lorenzo Zane," pp. 166-67), Gregorio (*sic*; Ludovico?) Lazzarelli (ibid.), and Girolamo Bologni, his secretary, who evidently had use of his patron's books (Agostini, *Notizie*, I, 195ff. and Weiss, "Lorenzo Zane," pp. 167-68). He was among the many learned men of his age who were interested in astrology (Agostini, *Notizie*, I, 181 and Mercati, *Ultimi contributi*, II, 52). To Zane, Giovanni Pietro Vitali d'Avenza (da Lucca) dedicated his translation of Plutarch's *Problemata* (introductory letter, fols. 1-3^v) and Leonardo Montagna two books of *Carmina, epistolae et epigrammata*, including many verses to and about his patron (cf. Weiss, "Lorenzo Zane," pp. 166, 167).

EDUCATION. In Rome with Lorenzo Valla.

Zeno, Jacopo.(2) Zen, Zenus. Son of Jacopo.

MONOGRAPHS AND STUDIES. G. degli Agostini, *Notizie*, I, 294-309; L. Bertalot, "Jacobi Zeni descriptio coniurationis patavine (das Ende des letzten Carraresen 1435)"; Bertalot with A. Campana, "Gli scritti di Jacopo Zeno e il suo elogio di Ciriaco d'Ancona"; E. Govi, "La biblioteca di Jacopo Zeno." See also G. Zonta's introduction to the *Vita Caroli Zeni*, pp. iii-xi, and the discussion in A. Zeno, *Diss. voss.*, II, 126-33.

CAREER. B. c. 1418. D. April 1481. Zeno attended the Council of Ferrara-Florence, whence he proceeded to Rome and his clerical career. By 1444, he held the title of apostolic subdeacon, and after 1447 that of papal *referendarius*. He was an unsuccessful candidate for the bishoprics of Vicenza and

Verona and the patriarchate of Venice in 1451, 1453, and 1456, respectively (C. Cenci, "Senato veneto 'Probae,' " pp. 388, #96; 389, #97; 391, #98). In Padua, he was known as a conscientious and reforming administrator.

Titles. 1447-60, Bishop of Feltre and Belluno; 1460— Bishop of Padua.

WORKS. *Consolatio pro obitu matris* (Padua, 1 August 1434) to his brother Marino (cf. Bertalot, "Jacobi Zeni Descriptio," p. 104); *Descriptio coniurationis patavine* (1435), to his brother Marino (see ibid., and A. Segarizzi, "Contributo alla storia delle congiure padovane"); laudatory letter to Ciriaco d'Ancona (see Bertalot and Campana, "Scritti"); *Epistola politica*, to Cardinal Ludovico [Scarampo] Trevisan, not seen; *Oratio . . . Collegio Paduano*, not seen (see *Iter*, I, 320); *Oratio ad Paulum Secundum Pontificem Maximum* (1464), not seen (see *Iter*, II, 322, and the fragment with discussion published by G. Zippel in his edition of *Le Vite di Paolo II di Gasparo da Verona e Michele Canensi*, p. 222); *Oratio de remeatione*, not seen (see *Iter*, II, 22); *Repetitiones et disputationes*, not seen (see ibid., II, 5); *Vita Caroli Zeni*, ed. G. Zonta; *Vita B. Nicolai Cardinalis Albergati*, to Pietro Barbo; *Vitae summorum pontificum*, to Pope Paul II, not seen (see *Iter*, II, 336, 474 and the discussion in Bertalot and Campana, "Scritti," p. 313-15). For all the works named, see the thorough indication of manuscript and printed versions in Zonta's edition of the *Vita Caroi Zeni*, pp. iiiff., notes. For lost and attributed works, see also Zonta, introduction, p. vii nn. 5, 7, 8, 14.

CORRESPONDENCE. Letters from Ludovico Foscarini (*Epist.*, fol. 62^v), Bernardo Giustiniani (*Orat. et epist.*, sigs. K4^v-K5^v), and Leonardo Sanuto (in Marc. Lat. XIV, 267 [4344], fol. 64); also letters of Zeno's (see Zonta, introduction, p. vii n. 3; V. Cian, "Per Bernardo Bembo—II," p. 77).

DISCOURSE. Praised for his learning by Vespasiano da Bisticci (*Vite di uomini illustri*, p. 146) and by Bernardo Bembo in his *Oratio in adventu Jacobi Zeni Episcopi Patavini* (for which see also Zonta, introduction, p. vi n. 1). To Zeno were dedicated several works: Zovenzoni's edition of Boccaccio's *Genealogiae deorum* (cf. Bertalot and Campana, "Scritti," p. 318 and n. 3); Guarino Veronese's translation of Plutarch's *Themistocles* (cf. *Iter*, II, 556); Giorgio Merula's edition of Plautus' comedies (see Bertalot and Campana, "Scritti," pp. 313-15, Agostini, *Notizie*, I, 305 and Cosenza, *Dict.*, III, 2300); Antonio Moretto's and Girolamo Squarciafico's edition of the letters of Leonardo Bruni (cf. Bertalot and Campana, "Scritti," pp. 313-15, Agostini, *Notizie*, I, 303-304, and Cosenza, *Dict.*, III, 2370); Giorgio Sommariva's *Enarratio sententiae laetae a Serenissimo Venetorum Imperio in infidos Hebraeos patratores atque participes martyrii beati Sebastiani novelli . . .* (cf. Agostini, *Notizie*, I, 305); Raffaele Zovenzoni's edition of Strabo's *Geographia* in the translation of Guarino and Gregorio Tifernate (ibid., I, 303, and Bertalot and Campana, "Scritti," pp. 313-15). The four 1472 editions of Boccaccio, Plautus, Bruni, and Strabo testify to Zeno's support for the new art of printing. Bernardo Giustiniani also wrote verses in praise of Zeno. Poggio Bracciolini launched against Zeno his *Invectiva*. Zeno supervised work on his episcopal palace in

Padua and the construction of the nearby Villa of Luvigliano. His extensive library of mss. and early editions was consigned to the chapter by his successor as Bishop of Padua, Pietro Foscari, who made an exact inventory of 361 volumes (see especially Govi, "Biblioteca").

EDUCATION. The *Consolatio* on his mother's death shows that Zeno's early education was greatly influenced by her. He studied with Damiano da Pola, and subsequently at Padua from about 1429, where he received a doctorate in law on 21 Aug. 1440 (see Zonta, introduction, p. i; Zeno appears in the *proba* for Bishop of Feltre as "utriusque iuris doctor ac magister theologiae": Cenci, "Senato," p. 385, #92). He also taught law at Padua, perhaps in 1439 (Facciolati, *Fasti gymn. pat.*, I.ii.38).

BIBLIOGRAPHY

Primary Sources: Documents and Chronicles

Archivio di Stato [ASV], Venice
 Avogaria di Comun [AC]
  Balla d'oro [BO]   RR. 162/I-164/III (1413-[1485])
  Cronaca matrimoni   R. 107/II (1400-1608)
  Notatorio [CLN]   RR. 5-16 (1414-1511)
 Consiglio dei Dieci [CX]—
  Deliberazioni Miste [CXM]   RR. 8-35 (1392-1513)
  Deliberazioni Secrete [CXS]   RR. 1-4 (1525-1539)
 Maggior Consiglio [MC]
  Leona (1384-1415)   Stella (1480-1502)
  Ursa (1415-1434)   Deda (1503-1521)
  Regina (1458-1479)   Dianna (1522-1536)
 Segretario alle Voci—Serie Miste [SGV]
  R. 4 (Consigli, 1438-55)   R. 8 (Miste-Reggimenti, 1492-1523)
  R. 5 (Reggimenti, 1437-90)   R. 9 (Miste-Consigli, 1492-1521)
  R. 6 (Miste, 1465-1502)   R. 10 ex 14 (Uffici, 1524-1534)
  R. 7 (Miste-Uffici, 1492-1524) R. 11 ex 8 (Uffici, 1523-1556)
 Senato
  Miste [SMS]   RR. 45-60 (1400?-1440)
  Mar [SM]   RR. 1-17 (1440-1512)
  Terra [ST]   RR. 1-28 (1440-1535)
  Privilegi   RR. 1 (1374-1495)
Archivio Notarile [AN]: Testaments
 Barbo, Paolo. AN, Cancelleria Inferiore, Miscellanea Testamenti, Notai Diversi,
  B. 31e, #3929 (c. 1460)
 Foscarini, Ludovico. AN, Testamenti Giuseppe Moysis, B. 727.119 (16 December
  1477)
 Foscarini, Ludovico. AN, Cancelleria Inferiore, Miscellanea Testamenti, Notai Di-
  versi, B. 27, n. 2596 (17 June 1478)
 Leonardi, Girolamo. AN, Testamenti T. Tomei, B. 1240.183 (15 March 1466)
 Lippomano, Marco. AN, Testamenti A. Gambaro, B. 558.102 and 559.55 (22 and
  24 September 1442)
 Miani, Pietro. AN, Testamenti P. Zane, B. 1255, cc. 165^v-68^v (8 April 1429)
 Molin, Pietro. AN, Testamenti C. Rizzo, B. 1228.328; 1229:245 (1 June 1494);
  di Andrea (d. 1511)
 Morosini, Domenico. AN, Testamenti C. Rizzo, B. 1227.122 (10 July 1498, with
  codicil of 26 April 1499) and 1229.152 (protocol, 14 April 1509)
 Morosini, Marcantonio. AN, Testamenti C. Rizzo, B. 1228.248 (29 March 1508)
  and B. 1229.154 (protocol, 8 May 1509)
 Orsini, Michele. AN, Testamenti C. Rizzo, B. 1228.243, 1229.40 (8 April 1495,
  with codicil 17 September 1497)
 Ramusio, Girolamo (di Benedetto). AN, Cancelleria Inferiore, Testamenti Giacomo
  Sappa, B. 27.2666, 2670 (13 November 1483).
 Renier, Daniele. AN, Testamenti G. M. Cavaneis, B. 217.111 (24 August 1528).
 Sanuto, Leonardo. AN, Testamenti T. Tomei, B. 1240.31 (18 September 1474)
 Vitturi, Daniele. AN, Testamenti B. Croce, B. 1155.15 (10 September 1440)

BIBLIOGRAPHY

Other documents and chronicles

Barbaro, Marco. *Arbori di patrizi veneti [Arbori].* Miscellanea codici, I: Storia Veneta, RR. 17-23

Giomo, G. *Indice per nome di donna dei matrimoni dei patrizi veneti* [Giomo, *Matrimoni*]. 2 vols. Miscellanea codici.

Sanuto, Leonardo. Cash book and *Ricordanza.* Giudici di Petizion, B. 955 (Rendimenti di conti, n. 1). *Ricordanza,* cc. 124-60ᵛ.

Toderini, Teodoro. *Genealogie delle famiglie Venete ascritte alla cittadinanza originaria* [Toderini, *Genealogie*]. 4 vols. Miscellanea codici, I.

Other Manuscript Locations

Cappellari Vivaro, Girolamo Alessandro. *Il campidoglio veneto* [Cappellari, *Camp. ven.*]. 4 vols. Marc. Ital. VII, 15-18 (8304-8307).

Cronaca di famiglie cittadini originari veneti. Venice, Biblioteca del Museo Correr, cod. Cicogna 2156.

Foscarini, Ludovico. Land purchase from Giovanni Memo, 13 February 1456. Venice, Biblioteca del Museo Correr, cod. P.D.C. 751/35.

Libro di reggimenti. Vol. I. Marc. Ital. VII, 198 (8383).

Michiel, Niccolò. Testament (17 May 1518). Venice, Biblioteca del Museo Correr, cod. P.D.C. 2166/17, vol. II, cc. 27-30.

Published

Cenci, Cesare. "Senato veneto 'probae' ai benefizi ecclesiastici." In Celestino Piana and Cenci, *Promozioni agli ordini sacri a Bologna e alle dignità ecclesiastiche nel Veneto nei secoli XIV-XV,* Spicilegium Bonaventurianum, 3 (Florence: Quaracchi, Typographia Collegii S. Bonaventurae, 1968).

Giustiniani, Bernardo. Testament (5 March 1489). In P. H. Labalme, "Last Will."

I libri commemoriali della republica di Venezia: regesti. Edited by Riccardo Predelli [*Comm.,* ed. Predelli]. 8 vols. R. Deputazione veneta di storia patria, Monumenti storici, III, Ser. I: Documenti, Vols. I, III, VII, VIII, X, XI, XIII, XVII. Venice: La Società, 1876-1914.

Marcanova, Giovanni. Testament (6 December 1464). In L. Sighinolfi, "La biblioteca di Giovanni Marcanova," pp. 192-96.

Sabellico, Marcantonio. Testament (15 March 1506). In A. Zeno, *Istorici,* I, lxviii-lxxi.

Trevisan, Zaccaria V. Testament (8 January 1414). In P. Gothein, "Zaccaria Trevisan," pp. 49-51.

Vinciguerra, Antonio. Testament (3 December 1502). In B. Beffa, *Antonio Vinciguerra,* pp. 176-78. Also A. della Torre, *Di Antonio Vinciguerra e delle sue satire,* pp. 221-25.

Zonta, Gaspare and Giovanni Brotto. *Acta graduum academicorum gymnasii patavini ab anno MCCCCVI ad annum MCCCCL* [Zonta & Brotto, *Acta*]. Istituto per la Storia dell'Università di Padova. Padua: typis Seminarii, 1922. 2nd ed. (= *Acta graduum academicorum,* Vol. I). Padua: Editrice Antenore, 1970. Vols. II-IV: *Acta graduum academicorum gymnasii patavini ab anno 1501 ad annum 1525; ab anno 1526 ad annum 1537; ab anno 1538 ad annum 1550.* Edited by E. Martellozzo Forin. Padua: Editrice Antenore, 1969, 1970, 1971.

Primary Sources: Other Manuscript and Published Works and Collections

[Anonymous]. *Oratio in laudem domini Francisci Contarini [celebrata in insignia doctoratus capescenda].* Marc. Lat. XI, 59 (4152), fols. 176-80.

452

BIBLIOGRAPHY

[Anonymous]. *Oratio* for the funeral of Fantino Vallaresso. Turin: Biblioteca Nazionale Universitaria, cod. H. III. 8, fols. 177-80ᵛ.

Aleotti, Ulisse. *Sonnets*. In A. Segarizzi, "Ulisse Aleotti," pp. 46-66.

Antonius Bargensis. Dedication to Giovanni Marcanova of *Chronicon Montis Oliveti*. Monte Oliveto Maggiore, Archivio dell'Abbazia, ms. (no shelfmark), fols. 1-9 (at 1ʳ·ᵛ), 32-40 (at 32ʳ·ᵛ). Epistola to Marcanova on the Etruscans and the Famous Men of Tuscany, ibid., fols. 50-60. The chronicle also edited by Placidius M. Lugano (Florence: ex officina typographica Cocchi & Chiti, 1901), with dedication to Marcanova, pp. 3-4.

Antonius [iuris utriusque professor]. *Tractatus de ieiuniis*, to Marco Lippomano. Vat. Lat. 1071, fols. 1-7ᵛ.

d'Avenza, Giovanni Pietro Vitali (da Lucca), trans. Plutarch, *Problemata*, to Lorenzo Zane (1453). Vat. Chis. J V 178.

Badoer, Sebastiano. *Oratio ad Alexandrum VI in prestanda Venetorum obedientia* (17 December 1492). [Rome: Andreas Freytag, after 17 December 1492]. H 2243*.

———. *Registrum litterarum magnificorum dominorum Sebastiani Baduario equitis et Benedicti Trivisano oratorum ad illustrissimum dominum ducem Mediolani . . . . (1494-95)*. Marc. Ital. VII, 547 (8529).

Baratella, Antonio. *Policleomenareis*. Marc. Lat. XII, 172 (4129), fols. 1-24. *Baratella*. Fols. 24ᵛ-61.

Barbaro, Ermolao G. *Castigationes plinianae et in Pomponium Melam*. Edited by Giovanni Pozzi. 4 vols. Thesaurus Mundi Bibliotheca Scriptorum Latinorum Mediae et Recentiores Aetatis, 11, 14, 18, 19. Padua: in aedibus Antenoreis, 1973-1979. [Ed. prin. Rome: Eucharius Silber, 1493. H2421*, GW 3340].

———. *De coelibatu*. With *De officio legati*. Edited by Vittore Branca. Nuova collezione di testi umanistici inediti o rari, 14. Florence: Leo S. Olschki, 1969, pp. 55-156.

———. *Epistolae, orationes et carmina*. Edited by Vittore Branca [*Epist.*, ed. Branca]. 2 vols. Nuova collezione di testi umanistici inediti o rari, 5, 6. Florence: "Bibliopolis," 1943.

———. *De officio legati*. With idem, *De coelibatu*, pp. 157-67.

———. *Oratio ad Federicum imperatorem et Maximilianum regem Romanorum* (1486). In *Epistolae, orationes et carmina*, II, 110-20.

———. *Oratio in funere Nicolai Marcelli Venetiarum Princeps* (1474). In *Epistolae, orationes et carmina*, II, 99-103.

Barbaro, Ermolao V. *Epistola ad D. Celsum Veronensem*. In G. B. Mittarelli, *Bibliotheca codicum manuscritorum*, cols. 103-104.

———. Ten *epistolae* in Barbaro, *Orationes contra poetas, epistolae*, pp. 145-80.

———. *Oratitones contra poetas*, with *Epistolae* [OCP]. Edited by Giorgio Ronconi. Facoltà di Magistero dell'Università di Padova, 14. Florence: G. C. Sansoni, 1972, pp. 81-142.

———. *Vita S. Athanasii Alexandrini episcopi, cum translatione eius corporis*. Marc. Lat. II, 123 (10383), fols. 23-48. *Prohemium* in Ronconi, ed., *Orationes contra poetas*, pp. 157-59.

———, trans. Aesop, fables, to Ambrogio Traversari. Brit. Mus. cod. Add. 33782. *Prohemium* in Ronconi, ed., *Orationes contra poetas*, pp. 145-47.

Barbaro, Francesco. *Centotrenta lettere inedite di Francesco Barbaro precedute dall'ordinamento critico cronologico dell'intero suo epistolario*. Edited by Remigio Sabbadini [*Centotrenta*, ed. Sabbadini]. Salerno: Tipografia Nazionale, 1884.

———. *Diatriba praeliminaris in duas partes divisa ad Francisci Barbari et aliorum ad ipsum epistolae ab anno Christi 1425 ad annum 1453*. Edited by Angelo Maria Quirini [Quirini, *Diatriba* (= I); *Epist.*, ed. Quirini (= II)]. 2 vols. Brescia: Joannes-Maria Rizzardi, 1741, 1743.

———. *Oratio funebris pro insigni viro Joannino Corradino*. In *Diatriba*, pp. 155-60.

———. *Prohemium*, to King Alfonso of Aragon, to Flavio Biondo's *Italia illustrata*. In *Diatriba*, pp. 171-73.

———. *De re uxoria liber* [DRU]. Edited by Attilio Gnesotto. *Atti e memorie della R.*

BIBLIOGRAPHY

Accademia di SLA in Padova, NS, 32 (1916), 6-105. Translated by Percy Gothein as *Das Buch von der Ehe*. Berlin: Verlag die Runde, 1933. Preface and second part translated by B. G. Kohl in Kohl and R. Witt, *The Earthly Republic*, pp. 177-228.

———, trans. Plutarch, lives of Aristides and Cato the Elder, to Zaccaria Barbaro V (di Candiano). In Plutarch, *Vitae* (Paris: venundantur ab Jodoco Badio et Joanne paruo, 1514), fols. 114-20 and 120ᵛ-126, respectively.

Barbaro, Zaccaria. *Dispacci da Napoli* (1 November 1471-7 September 1473). Marc. Ital. VII, 398 (8170).

———. Life of Francesco Barbaro. In V. Branca, "Un codice aragonese," pp. 176-77. Dedicatory letter to King Ferdinand of Naples (15 May 1472) in V. Branca, "Ermolao Barbaro poeta," pp. 409-11.

Barbo, Marco. *[Epistolae]*. In P. Paschini, *Il carteggio fra il cardinale Marco Barbo e Giovanni Lorenzi (1481-1490)*, pp. 20-214.

———. *[Epistola]* in response to Benedetto Maffei's *De moribus nostrorum temporum*. Florence, Biblioteca Nazionale Centrale, cod. Magliabecchianus VI, 191, fols. 36ᵛ-37.

Barbo, Niccolò. *Epistolae* (1438-1442) *[Epist.]*. Marc. Lat. XIV, 256 (4634), fols. 30-108.

———. *Oratio in laudem Francisci Contareni* (Padua, 27 May 1442). Marc. Lat. XIV, 257 (4050), fols. 57-84.

———. *Sermo de Sancto Romualdo*. Marc. Lat. XIV, 112 (4283), fols. 43ᵛ-44ᵛ. Attribution uncertain.

Barbo, Paolo. *Oratio in traditione insignium Bartholomeo de Colionibus* (Brescia, 1455). Florence, Biblioteca Laurenziana, cod. Ashburnham 109 (181*-112*), No. vii, fols. 26-27.

———. *Oratio ad imperatorem Federicum III* (Padua, 1452). Vat. Lat. 3194, fols. 81ᵛ-82.

———. *Oratio ad Ludovicum Francorum regem* (Tours, 8 December 1461). With Valier, *De cautione adhibenda*, pp. 183-92.

Barozzi, Francesco. *Oratio pro doctoratu Jacobi Molini in gymnasio patavino*. Marc. Lat. XI, 120 (4010), fols. 1-36.

———. *Oratio de laudibus Bonifacii Bonfilii et Iohannis Roti* (Padua, 14 May 1459). Marc. Lat. XIV, 236 (4499), fols. 77ᵛ-90ᵛ.

Barozzi, Pietro. *Consolationes* to Pietro Foscari and (two) to Giovanni Michiel. In Barozzi, *De modo bene moriendi*. The consolatory to Foscari also in G. B. Contarini, *Anecdota veneta*, I, 198-210.

———. *De factionibus extinguendis* [DFE]. In F. Gaeta, ed., *Il vescovo Pietro Barozzi e il trattato* De factionibus extinguendis, q.v.

———. *De modo bene moriendi*, to Marco Barbo. With three *consolationes* and *officia*. Venice: in aedibus Io. Antoniii et Fratrum de Sabio, 1531.

———. *Oratio ad Christophorum Maurum Ducem habita quo die Joanni Barrocio Patriarcae Venetiarum obviam cum Senatu profectus est*. With Valier, *De cautione adhibenda*, pp. 131-62. Also Orazioni, elogi e vite, I, 68-102.

———. *Oratio pro Francisco Scledo vicentino rectore juristarum Patavii*. With Valier, *De cautione adhibenda*, pp. 111-30.

———. *Oratio in funere Antoniii Roicelli aretini professoris juris civilis in Gymnasio Patavino*. With Valier, *De cautione adhibenda*, pp. 163-82.

———. *Oratio in morte Johannis patrui Patriarchae Venetiarum*. In *Orazioni, elogi e vite*, I, 103-27.

———. *Oratio Paduae habita ad Marcum Cornarium, cardinalitium galerum suscipienti*. Marc. Lat. XIV, 292 (4632), fols. 101-105.

———. *Sermo perbrevis ac simplex de moribus virtutibus et miraculis Sancti Petri Acotanti nobilis veneti*. Marc. Lat. IX, 79 (3051), fols. 82-87ᵛ.

———. *Versuum atque hymnorum libri III*. In G. B. Contarini, *Anec. ven.*, 210-68.

———, trans. (from Greek). *Basilii magni vita*. Marc. Lat. IX, 79 (3051), fols. 1-81.

———, trans., with George of Trebizond, trans. *Opera divi Joannis Chrysostomi ar-*

chiepiscopo Constantinopolitani. Basel: Ex officina Jacobi de Pfortzen; ductu ver. et impensa providi viri Uuolgangi Lachner, [4 December] 1504.

Barzizza, Gasparino, *Epistola* [to Zaccaria Trevisan V. on his orations to the Popes, 1407]. In G. M. Mittarelli, *Bibliotheca codicum manuscriptorum*, cols. 437-38.

——. *Gasparinii Barzizii Bergomatis et Guiniforti filii opera*. Ed. Joseph Alexander Furiettus [*Opera*, ed. Furiettus]. Rome: Apud Jo. Mariam Salvioni Typographum Vaticanum, 1723.

Becichemo, Marino. *Orationes duae (Gratulatio quam ad Serenissimum Venetum Principem Andream Grittum nomine Patavinae Academiae legatus in frequenti curia habuit; Funebris laudatio quam litteris publicis accitus Venetiis in Aede Divi Zachariae de meritis Joannis Petri Stellae Magni Venetiarum Cancelarii habuit)*. Venice: Sumptibus Comini Querensis, 1524.

——. *Panegiricus Principi Leonardo Lauretano dictus; Centuria epistolicarum quaestionum*; and other works. Brescia: A. & I. Brittanicus, c. 1505.

Bembo, Bernardo. *Gratulatio ad Christophorum Maurum pro clarissimi divini atque humani iuris scolasticorum ordine Patavini habita* (1462). Edited by Nella Giannetto, "Un' orazione inedita di Bernardo Bembo per Cristoforo Moro," *Atti del RIV di SLA*, 140 (1981-82), Classe di scienze morali, lettere ed arti, pp. 273-88, with dedicatory letter to Ludovico [Scarampo] Trevisan, pp. 271-73.

——, coll. [*Opera et opuscula*] to Bembo by Paolo Marsi, Marsilio Ficino, Battista Mantovano, Cristoforo Landino, Filippo Morandi da Rimini, Giorgio Merula et al. Ferrara, Biblioteca Comunale Ariostea, cod. II 162.

——. *Oratio in adventu Cardinalis Sancti Angeli Legati Apostolica habita apud Fossam Clodiam*. Marc. Lat. XIV, 2 (4590), fols. 24^v-26.

——. *Oratio [in adventu] Jacobi Zeni [Episcopi Patavini]* (1460). Marc. Lat. XIV, 236 (4499), fols. 55^v-64^v.

——. *Oratio in funere Bertholdi Marchionis Estensis* (1464). Marc. Lat. XI, 139 (4432), fols. 1^v-32. *Consolatio* to the widow Jacoba, fols. 32-40.

——. Three *Orationes ad Innocentium VIII* (1487-1488). Ferrara, Biblioteca Comunale Ariostea, cod. II 162, fols. 95-98^v, 99-100, 101^{r-v}. The first oration with Sebastiano Badoer, 24 November 1487.

——. *Zibaldone [Commonplace Book]*. Brit. Mus., cod. Add. 41068A. Cod. 41068 B contains index and notes by G. Neilson (1895).

Bembo, Pietro. *Historiae venetae libri XII*. In A. Zeno, ed., *Istorici*, II.

——. *Lettere di M. Pietro Bembo*. In *Opere del Cardinale Pietro Bembo*, vols. V-IX [Classici italiani, 59-64] (1809-1810).

——. *Opere del Cardinale Pietro Bembo*. 12 vols. Classici Italiani, 55-66. Milan: della Società Tipografica de' Classici Italiani, 1808-1810.

——. *Opere in volgare*. Edited by M. Marti. Florence: G. C. Sansoni, 1961.

Benedetti, Alessandro. *Diaria da bello carolino (Diary of the Caroline War)*. Edited and translated by Dorothy M. Schullian. Renaissance Society of America, Renaissance Text Series, 1. New York: Frederick Ungar for the RSA, 1967.

Bernardo, Antonio. *Oratio in doctoratu Albertini Baduarii*. Munich, Bayerische Staatsbibliothek, cod. Mon. Lat. 350, fols. 116-121^v.

——. *Oratio pro doctoratu Jacobi Molini in gymnasio patavino*. Marc. Lat. XI, 120 (4010), fols. 41-58.

Bevilacqua [da Lazise], Giorgio. *Epistola [in obitu Valerii filii]*, to Jacopo Antonio Marcello (Udine, 3 November 1463). Verona, Biblioteca Comunale, cod. 1472 [Biadego #224], fols. 3-6.

——. *Excusatio adversus consolatores in obitu Valerii filii*, written in name of Jacopo Antonio Marcello, to King René d'Anjou (Udine, 13 November 1463). Verona, Biblioteca Comunale, cod. 1472 [Biadego #224], fols. 7-173. Also untitled and fragmentary *ad initium* in Glasgow, Hunterian Museum Library (University of Glasgow), cod. 201 [U.1.5.], pp. 310-426.

Biondo, Flavio. *De Rome instaurata; De Italia illustrata; De gestis venetorum*. Venice: Gregorium de' Gregoriis, 1510.

BIBLIOGRAPHY

Biondo, Flavio. *De Roma triumphante libri decem; Romae instauratae libri iii; De origine et gestis Venetorum liber; Italia illustrata; Historiarum ab inclinato Romano imperio decades iii.* Basel: Froben, 1559.

da Bisticci, Vespasiano. *Vite di uomini illustri del secolo XV.* Edited by Paolo d'Ancona and Erhard Aeschilimann. Milan: Ulrico Hoepli, 1951.

Boldù, Jacopo. *Oratio de laudibus totius philosphiae.* [Venice: Manfredus de Bonellis, after 14 October 1499]. Goff B-834.

Bollani, Candiano. *Libri XVIII in tria priora capita Genesis,* to Frater Andreas Pannonius Cartusiensis (14 March 1466). Marc. Lat. I, 44 (2038). Dedication to brother Andreas in G. degli Agostini, *Notizie,* II, 160.

————. *Oratio gratulatoria de creatione Christophori Mauri.* Marc. Lat. XIV, 252 (4718), fols. 85-89.

————. *In rhetoricorum novorum Ciceronis librum primum commentum.* Olomouc [Olmütz] (Czechoslovakia), Statui Archiv [formerly Bibliotheca Cathedralis Ecclesiae Olomucensis], cod. C. O. 343, fols. 2-50ᵛ.

————. *Tractatus super canticum gloriosissimae virginis Mariae.* Brit. Mus., cod. Harl. 2508, fols. 24ᵛ-39.

————. *Trialogus in rebus futuris annorum XX proximorum.* Marc. Lat. XIV, 245 (4682), fols. 2-9ᵛ.

————, trans. (from Greek). George of Trebizond, commentary on the Magnificat to John Cuboclesios, with preface (fols. 9ᵛ-10) to Pope Eugene IV. Brit. Mus., cod. Harl. 2508, fols. 9ᵛ-24. Bollani's preface also in J. Monfasani, *Collectanea Trapezuntiana,* pp. 260-61.

Bollani, Domenico. *De conceptione beatae Virginis Mariae.* [Strasburg: the R. Printer (Adolf Rusch), not after 1475]. H. 3436*.

Bononigena, Bernardino. *Epistolarum atque epigrammatum libellus,* to Ludovico Foscarini, podestà of Padua. Venice: Biblioteca del Museo Correr, Fondo Malvezzi, cod. Malvezzi 126, fols. 1-31ᵛ.

Borro, Gasparino. *Commentum super tractatum spherae mundi* [Iohannis de Sacrobusco], to Girolamo Donato. Venice: Octaviani Scoti Civis Modoetiensis, 3 October 1490. HC 14113*.

Bracciolini, Poggio. *Epistolae.* Edited by Thomas de Tonellis [*Epist.,* ed. Tonellis]. 3 vols. Florence: Typis L. Marchini, 1832; Typis delle Murate, 1859, 1861. Reproduced in *Opera omnia,* III.

————. *Historia disceptativa de avaritia,* to Francesco Barbaro. In *Opera omnia,* I, 1-31. Translated as "On Avarice" in B. G. Kohl and Elizabeth Welles in Kohl and R. Witt, eds., *The Earthly Republic,* pp. 229-89.

————. [*Invectiva in Jacobum Zenum*]. In *Opera omnia,* IV, 649-55.

————. *In laudem rei publicae venetorum.* In *Opera omnia,* II, 925-37.

————. *De nobilitate.* In *Opera omnia,* I, 64-83. Translated as "On Nobility" by Renée Neu Watkins and David Marsh in Watkins, ed., *Humanism and Liberty,* pp. 121-48.

————. *Opera omnia.* Edited by Riccardo Fubini. 4 vols. Monumenta politica et philosophica rariora, Ser. II:6. Turin: Bottega d'Erasmo, 1964-1966. (I reproduces *Scripta in editione Basilensi anno MDXXXVIII collata;* III reproduces *Epistolae,* edited by T. de Tonellis.)

Brognoli, Benedetto. *Epistola* to Filippo Buonaccorsi [Callimaco] (15 September 1488). Marc. Lat. X, 125 (3247), fols. 137-41ᵛ. Also among Belluno *epistolae.*

————. Nine [*epistolae*]. Belluno: Bibl. Lolliniana, cod. 22, fols. 127-41ᵛ.

————, ed. Diogenes Laertius. *Vitae et sententiae eorum qui in philosophia probati fuerunt.* Translated by Ambrogio Traversari. Venice: N. Ienson, 1475. HC 6199*.

Broianico, Antonio. *De divina origine reipublicae venetorum,* to Domenico Giorgi. Venice, Biblioteca del Museo Correr, cod. Correr 172.

Bruni, Leonardo. *Epistolarum libri VIII.* Edited by Laurentius Mehus [*Epist.,* ed. Mehus]. 2 vols. Florence: ex Typographia Bernardi Paperinii, 1741.

————. *Humanistisch-philosophische Schriften, mit einer Chronologie seiner Werke und Briefe.* Edited by Hans Baron. Leipzig and Berlin: Verlag und Druck von B. G. Teubner, 1928. Rpt. Quellen zur Geistesgeschichte des Mittelalters und der Renaissance, 1. Wiesbaden: M. Sändig, [1969].

———. *Panegyric to the City of Florence.* Translated by B. G. Kohl. In Kohl and R. Witt, eds., *The Earthly Republic,* pp. 121-75.

Bruto, Pietro. *Epistola contra Judeos.* Vicenza: Leonhard Achates, [1477]. GW 5658.

———. *Victoria contra Judaeos,* to the Vicentine nobility. Vicenza: Simon Bevilaqua, 3 October 1489. HC 4027*.

Buonaccorsi, Filiippo [Callimaco]. *De bello Turcis inferendo, oratio. De his quae a venetis tentata sunt, Persis ac Tartaris contra Turcos movendis.* Haganoae: ex officina Seceriana, 1533.

———. *De his quae a Venetis tentata sunt Persis ac Tartaris contra Turcos movendis.* Edited, annotated, and translated (Polish with facing Latin text) by Andreas Kempfi, Thaddaeus Kowalewski, and Maria Cytowska. Academia scientiarum Polona, Institutum studiis classicis promovendis, 5. Warsaw: Panstwowe, Wydawnictwo Nankowe, 1962.

Bursa, Benedetto. *Orationes tres:* 1. to Ludovico Foscarini (fols. 7-10ᵛ; with Foscarini's response, fol. 11); 2. on Plautus (fols. 12-20); 3. to Alfonso, King of Aragon (fols. 21-29ᵛ). Marc. Lat. XI, 141 (3942).

Caldiera, Giovanni. *Aphorismi.* Vat. Pal. Lat. 1086, fols. 1-115ᵛ.

———. *Catonis expositio pro filia erudienda.* Modena, Biblioteca Estense, Fondo Campori, cod. 293 [Gamma T 5, 5].

———. *Centiloquium de causis et causatis.* Brussels, Bibliothèque Royale Albert I, cod. 8775-76, fols. 55-208ᵛ.

———. *De concordantia poetarum philosophorum et theologorum,* to his daughter Cataruzza. Vat. Urb. Lat. 1178. Preferred to edition of Michelangelo Biondo (Venice: apud Cominum de Tridino Montisferati, 1547).

———. *Consilia medica.* Vat. Pal. Lat. 1115.

———. *Expositio in psalmos.* Modena, Biblioteca Estense, Fondo Estense, cod. lat. 1000 [Alpha K, 3, 6].

———. *Liber canonum astrologiae ac totius orbis descriptione,* to King Alfonso of Aragon. Marc. Lat. VIII, 72 (3273).

———. *Oratio in funere Orsati Justiniani Sancti Marci Procuratoris ad senatum populumque [Veneciis] habita in eclesia sanctorum Zoanis ac Pauli.* Brit. Mus., cod. add. 15406, fols. 91-97ᵛ.

———. *Oratio habita in colegio phisicorum Venetorum pro principio prioralis.* Brit. Mus., cod. Add. 15406, fols. 98-101.

———. *Orationes.* Marc. Lat. XI, 102 (3940), fols. 44-51, 71-72, 73-83.

———. [Trilogy]. *De virtutibus moralibus et theologicis libri octo,* to Doge Cristoforo Moro [*De virtutibus*], fols. 2-77ᵛ; *De oeconomia veneta libri duo,* to Tommaso Gradenigo [*De oeconomia*], fols. 79-99ᵛ; *De praestantia venetae politiae, et artibus in eadem excultis tam mechanicis quam liberalibus [et] de virtutibus quae maxime reipublica[e] veneta[e] debentur, libri 5,* to Antonio Vinciguerra [*De politia*], fols. 101-148ᵛ (19 October 1473). Oxford, Bodleian Library, cod. Laud. Misc. 717.

Canal, Niccolò. *Epistola ad Cardinales* (9 June 1470). Marc. Lat. XIV, 9 (4267), fol. 68ʳ⁻ᵛ.

Cane, Giovanni Jacopo. *De arbitris,* to Francesco Diedo. Ferrara, Biblioteca Comunale Ariostea, cod. II, 162, fols. 78-94ᵛ.

———. *[Carmen] clarissimo iurisconsulto domino Nicolao Canali universae classis in Turchos imperatori designato.* Venice: Vindel. de Spira, [1485]. H 4333*.

———. *De Constantini donatione,* to Francesco Sanuto. Ferrara, Biblioteca Comunale Ariostea, cod. II, 162, fols. 60ᵛ-77ᵛ.

———. *De ludo equestri Patavii edito ad Ludovicum Foscarenum carmen.* [Padua: Leonardus Achates?, ca. 1475-1482]. H 4332*.

Canensi, Michele. See *Le vite di Paolo II.*

BIBLIOGRAPHY

da Carrara, Giovanni Michele Alberto. *De bello Jacobi Antonii Marcelli in Italia gesto.* In G. B. Contarini, *Anec. ven.,* pp. 309-28.

Cassirer, Ernst; Paul Oskar Kristeller; John H. Randall, Jr., eds. *The Renaissance Philosophy of Man.* Chicago: University of Chicago Press, 1948.

Cippico [Cepio], Coriolano. *Petri Mocenici venetae classis imperatoris contra Ottomannum Turcarum principem rebus gestis libri III ab anno 1470 ad 1474.* Venice: Bernhard Maler, Erhard Ratdolt, and Peter Löslein, 1477. HC 4849*.

Ciriaco D'Ancona. *Itinerarium.* Edited by Laurentius Mehus. Florence: Typ. Joannis Pauli Giovannelli, 1742.

Cirneo, Pietro. *Commentarius de bello Ferrariensi ab anno MCCCCLXXXII usque ad annum MCCCCLXXXIV.* In L. A. Muratori, ed., *Rerum italicarum scriptores,* XXI (Milan: Typographia Societatis Palatinae, 1732), cols. 1190-1218.

————. *De rebus corsicis libris quattuor a temporibus romanorum usque ad annum MDVI.* In L. A. Muratori, ed., *Rerum italicarum scriptores,* XXIV (Milan: Typographia Societatis Palatinae, 1738), cols. 410-506.

Collazio, Matteo. *De verbo civilitate,* to Domenico Morosini, with *De genere artis rhetoricae in magnos rhetores Victorinum et Quintilianum* and other works. Venice: Bernardinus Rizus Novariensis, [1486]. HC 5476*, GW 7156.

Comino, Bartolomeo. *Oratio pro funere Ioannis Dedi veneti scribae maximi.* Venice: per Gregorium de Gregoriis, 12 January 1511.

Contarini, Francesco. *Dialogus.* In A. Segarizzi, "Francesco Contarini, politico e letterato veneziano del secolo XV," pp. 288-306. Emended by L. Bertalot in "Lauri Quirini 'Dialogus,' " pp. 367-69.

————. *Dispacci* (1454-1455) from Siena. Marc. Ital. VII, 1196 (8884).

————. *Epithalamion sive oratio in nuptiis Ludovici Draconis veneti* (4 January 1440). Marc. Lat. XIV, 256 (4634), fols. 21-24ᵛ.

————. *Invectiva in ignavum poetam [Danielem de Porcilis]* (1450). *Invectiva in Marinum Baduarium obtrectatorem et vicilitigatorem* (1450). In A. Segarizzi, *Antonio Baratella,* pp. 178-80, 180-82.

————. *Oratio in conventu Iordani de Ursinis. Oratio habita in suo conventu* (3 September 1453). Milan, Biblioteca Ambrosiana, cod. C 145 inf., fols. 233ᵛ-236.

————. *Proemium in disputatione de philosophia,* addressed to Demetrius, brother of John Palaeologus, Byzantine emperor (1438). Marc. Lat. XIV, 256 (4634), fols. 143-45ᵛ.

————. *De rebus in Hetruria a Senensibus gestis cum aduersus Florentinos, tum aduersus Ildibrandinum Ursinum Petilianensem Comitem, libri tres,* [to Bernardo Bembo]. Rpt. of Lyon, 1562 edition by Giovanni Michele Bruto. Venice: apud Antonium Pinellum, 1623.

Contarini, Gasparo. *De officio episcopi, libri 2.* In Contarini, *Opera* (Paris: apud Sebastianum Niuellium, 1571).

Contarini, Giovanni Battista. *Anecdota veneta [Anec. ven.].* Vol. I (no further volumes published). Venice: Valvasensis, 1757.

Contarini, Pietro. *Ad Gelliam elegiarum libri tres. [Elegiae].* Marc. Lat. XII, 234 (4219), fols. 1-42.

————. *In funere Marci Cornelii oratio* (Venice, Church of Santi Apostoli, 27 August 1479). With Valier, *De cautione adhibenda,* pp. 202-12. Also in *Orazioni, elogi e vite,* pp. 128-40.

Contrario, Andrea. [*Epistolae* and other works]. Siena, Biblioteca Comunale degli Intronati, cod. H VI, 32.

————. [*Epistolae* and other works]. In R. Sabbadini, "Andrea Contrario," pp. 388-433.

————. *Reprehensio sive objurgatio in calumniatorem divini Platonis,* to Ferdinand, King of Sicily. Paris, Bibliothèque Nationale, Latins, cod. 12947.

Conversino, Giovanni (da Ravenna). *Dragmologia de eligibili vite genere.* Edited and translated by Helen Lanneau Eaker; introduction by Benjamin G. Kohl. Lewisburg, Pa: Bucknell University Press; London: Associated University Presses, 1980.

BIBLIOGRAPHY

Corner, Federico. [*Epistola*] to Leonardo Giustiniani. Vat. Pal. Lat. 492, fols. 188ᵛ-193.

Correr, Gregorio. *Carmina et epigrammata*. In G. B. Contarini, *Anec. ven.*, 57-58.

———. *Epistola ad novitium Cartusianum de commodis vitae regularis*. In G. B. Contarini, *Anec. ven.*, I, 24-32.

———. *Epistola ad Caeciliam virginem de fugiendo saeculo*. In G. B. Contarini, *Anec. ven.*, 33-44. Also in E. Martène and U. Durand, eds., *Veterum scriptorum collectio*, III, cols. 829-42. Translated by M. L. King and A. Rabil, Jr. as "Letter to the Virgin Cecilia Gonzaga, On Fleeing This Worldly Life," in *Her Immaculate Hand*, pp. 91-105.

———. *Hymnus ad pueros et virgines*, to Pope Martin V. Edited by Alfred von Reumont, *Beiträge zur italienischen Geschichte*, 4 (1855), 300-302.

———. *Liber satyrarum*. Edited by Joseph R. Berrigan, in "Gregorii Corrarii Veneti Liber Satyrarum," *Humanistica Lovaniensia*, 22 (1973), 10-38, at 15-38.

———. *Oratio ad Sigismundum Romanorum Imperatorem habita anno 1433 pro Concilio Basileensi*. In G. B. Contarini, *Anec. ven.*., 45-57.

———. *Quomodo educari debeant pueri*, to his brother Andrea. In C. de' Rosmini, *L'idea dell' ottimo precettore*, pp. 477-87. Also edited by E. Garin, *Il pensiero pedagogico dell'umanesimo*, I classici della pedagogia italiana, 2 (Florence: Giuntine-Sansoni, 1958), pp. 706-13.

———. *Soliloquium ad Deum de vita sua et de vita et obitu beatae memoriae Antonii Episcopi Ostiensis et Cardinalis patrui sui*. In G. B. Contarini, *Anec. ven.*, 12-24. Also in G. Musolino, A. Niero, and S. Tramontin, eds., *Santi e beati veneziani: quaranta profili* (Venice, 1963), pp. 329-41; not seen.

Dandolo, Antonio. *Pro gymnasii Patavini iuris scholasticis gratulacio* (1457), to Doge Pasquale Malipiero. Marc. Lat. XIV, 263 (4613).

Dandolo, Marco. *Catena seu expositio graecorum patrum in psalmos: In Psalterium expositionum collectio e graeco in latinum versa M. D. interpreta*. Marc. Lat. I, 33 (2133).

———. [*Epistolae* and other works]. In A. Medin, "Gli scritti umanistici di Marco Dandolo," pp. 364-98.

———. *Apud Serenissimum Ferdinandum Hispanae utriusque Siciliae, etc., regem oratio* (Naples, Castello Novo, 29 December 1507). In A. Medin, "Gli scritti umanistici di Marco Dandolo," pp. 389-98.

———. *Apud Wladislaum Boemiae atque Pannoniae regem oratio* (Budapest, 23 December 1493). In A. Medin, "Gli scritti umanistici di Marco Dandolo," pp. 384-89.

———. *Praeconium sanctissime crucis*, to King Louis XII. Pub. Lefèvre d'Etaples. Paris: in aedibus Ascensianis, 4 August 1514.

Dedo, Giovanni. [*Epistola*] ad Baptistam Fregonum (1482). Marc. Lat. XIV, 267 (4344), fols. 67ᵛ-68.

Diedo, Francesco, trans. *De bello et pace* by Isocrates. With preface to Ludovico Foscarini, Procuratore di San Marco (Vicenza, 1 August 1471). Venice, Biblioteca del Museo Correr, cod. Correr 313. Prefatory letter also in G. Tournoy, "Francesco Diedo," pp. 217-18.

———, trans. (from Italian). Giovanni Boccaccio, novella of Titus and Gisippus from the *Decameron* (1470), to Marco Aurelio. Vat. Lat. 5336, fols. 45-72ᵛ.

———. *Defensio pro re publica veneta*, to Pope Sixtus IV (Rome, 1481). In G. Tournoy, "Francesco Diedo," pp. 228-31.

———. *Epistola* to Giovanni Antonio Panteo, and response. In G. Tournoy, "Francesco Diedo," pp. 232-34.

———. *In Franciscum Barocium invectiva lacessiti iniuriis apprime* (1458). Bologna, Biblioteca Comunale dell'Archiginnasio, cod. A 172, fols. 246-52ᵛ.

———. *Oratio de laudibus Bartholomaei Paierini*. Marc. Lat. XIV, 236 (4499), fols. 64ᵛ-77.

———. *Proemium in quibusdam legibus a juristarum collegio conditum*. Bologna: Biblioteca Comunale dell'Archiginnasio, cod. A. 172, fols. 242ᵛ-245ᵛ.

BIBLIOGRAPHY

Diedo, Francesco. *Relazione di Francesco Diedo al Principe di Venezia [sul reggimento di Bergamo]*. Nozze Monzini-Borella. Milan: R. Stabillimento Ricordi, 1882.

——, trans. (from Greek). *Vita Sancti Rochi*, with prefatory letter (fols. 32-34) from Diedo as podestà to the city of Brescia (1479). Padua, Biblioteca Universitaria, cod. 239, fols. 32-56ᵛ. Preface also in G. Tournoy, "Francesco Diedo," pp. 225-27, with letter of praise from Pietro Ludovico Maldura, pp. 227-28.

Dolfin, Giorgio [Zorzi]. *[Cronaca*, excerpt]. *Belagerung und Eroberung von Constantinopel im Jahre 1453 aus der Chronik von Zorzi Dolfin*. Edited and translated by Georg M. Thomas. *Sitzungsberichte der k. bayerische Akademie der Wissenschaften*, 2 (1868). Rpt. Munich: in Verlage der k. Akademie, 1868.

Dolfin, Pietro. *Argumenta in [58] Ciceronis orationes*. Marc. Lat. XIV, 112 (4283), 94-104.

——. *Dialogus in Hieronymum Ferrariensem*. In J. Schnitzer, *Peter Delfin*, pp. 366-99.

——. *Epistolae et orationes*. Marc. Lat. XI, 92 (3828).

——. *Epistolae CCXLII* and other works [*Epist. CCXLII*, ed. Martène & Durand]. In E. Martène and U. Durand, eds., *Veterum scriptorum collectio*, III, 913-1232.

——. *Epistolarum volumen libri XII [Epist. (1524)]*. Edited by Jacobus Brixianus. Venice: Bernardinus Benalius, 1 March 1524.

——. *Oratio* to Pope Leo X. In E. Martène and U. Durand, eds., *Veterum scriptorum collectio*, III, cols. 1211-16.

——. *Oratiunculae duae habitae coram summis Pontificibus Pio Tertio et Julio Secundo*. Edited by Stefano Gritti. Venice: J. B. Merlo, 1848.

de' Domenichi, Domenico. *De non exigendis decimis a clericis sine licentia papae [et] sedis apostolice*, for Pope Paul II to the Doge and Senate of Venice (1468). Vat. Lat. 6234, fols. 23-32ᵛ.

——. *Quaestio de nominibus his quidditas et essentia*, to Candiano Bollani (1476). Vat. Lat. 6234, fols. 99-117ᵛ.

——. *De sanguine Christi tractatus. De filiatione Ioannis euangelistae ad B. Virginem pulcherrimam*. Venice: apud Petrum de Fine, 1557.

——. *Tractatus de reformationibus romane curie*. Brescia: per Baptista Farfengum, impensa Francisci Laurini, 1495. GW 8638.

Donato, Antonio. *[Vitae ducum venetorum]*, to Girolamo Giorgi. Marc. Lat. X, 145 (3533), fols. 79-93.

Donato, Girolamo. *Apologeticus ad Graecos de principatu Romanae sedis*. Edited by P. Donato. Rome: in aedibus F. M. Calvi, January 1525.

——. *Ad Caesarem pro re Christiana oratio* (1501). Venice: per Bernardinum Venetum de Vitalibus, 1501.

——. *Contra Caroli Regis Francorum in Senatum Venetum calumnias apologia*. In D. Malipiero, *Annali*, pp. 443-63.

——. *Epistola ad Oliverium Cardinalem Neapolitanum in qua Ro. Ecclesiam primatum ecclesiasticae dignitatis obtinere, et Petrum esse petram et fundamentum ecclesiae, doctissime comprobatur*. Rome: in aedibus F. M. Calvi, January 1525.

——. *Epistola ad Petrum Contarenum de terremotu Cretensi, idibus julii MDVIII*. Marc. Lat. XIV, 31 (4701), fols. 91ᵛ-96.

——. *Apud Iulium II Pont. Max. in obedientia oratio* (1505). Np, nd [Rome XVI].

——. *Oratio ad Ludovicum Gallorum regem* (1501). In *Orationes clarorum hominum*, fols. 43ᵛ-45ᵛ. Also Venice: Aldus, 1501.

——. *De processione Spiritus Sancti contra Graecum schisma*. In Mai Angelo, ed., *Scriptorum veterum nova collectio e vaticanis codicibus*, VII (Rome: Typis Vaticanae, 1833), Pars II, 1-162.

Donato, Ludovico. *Oratio pro summo pontifice edita* [on ascension of Doge Cristoforo Moro] (1462). Marc. Lat. XIII, 90 (4143), fols. 14ᵛ-16.

——. *Oratio pro S. Augustini solemnitate*. [Rome: Johann Schoenberger, after 28 August 1482?]. Goff D-356.

——. *Orationes* (1) *pro annuntiationis solenitate* (fols. 2-11ᵛ); (2) *pro gloriosissimi doctoris Augustini celebritate* (fols. 12-19); (3) *pro epiphaniae festivitate* (fols. 20-27). Pisa: Biblioteca Universitaria, cod. 537. The oration for Augustine is also printed.

Donato, Marco. Two *epistolae* to Marco Barbo, B. of Treviso (4 May, 5 March 1458). In J. Monfasani, *Collectanea Trapezuntiana*, pp. 419-21.

———. *Oratio in laudes Zacharie Trivisani* [the Elder, and his son Zaccaria the Younger] (25 August 1442). Marc. Lat. XI, 59 (4152), fols. 155-63ᵛ. Partially published by P. Gothein, "Zaccaria Trevisan," pp. 57-59.

———. *Oratio pro principio Studii Patavini.* Vat. Lat. 5197, fols. 8-9ᵛ; fragmentary.

Donato, Pietro. *Oratio in exequiis Cardinalis Francisci de Zabarelis* (Padua, 1418). Marc. Lat. XI, 101 (3939), fols. 51 (50)-55ᵛ (54ᵛ).

———. *Oratio in laudem Pape.* Marc. Lat. XI, 102 (3940), fols. 10ᵛ-11.

———. *Oratio de laudibus philosophie in suo principio in artibus.* Marc. Lat. XI, 101 (3939), fols. 55ᵛ (54ᵛ)-58ᵛ (57ᵛ).

Egnazio, Giovanni Battista. *De exemplis illustrium virorum Venetae civitatis, atque aliarum gentium.* Paris: apud Bernardum Turisanum, via Iacobea, sub Aldina Bibliotheca, 1554.

Erasmus, Desiderius. *Dialogus cui titulus Ciceronianus sive de optimo dicendi genere.* Edited and translated as *Il ciceroniano* by Angiolo Gambaro. Brescia: Editrice "La Scuola," 1965.

Facio, Bartolomeo. *De viris illustribus liber.* Edited by Laurentius Mehus. Florence: ex typis Joannis Pauli Giovanelli, 1745.

Ficino, Marsilio. *Epistolarum libri XII [Epist.].* In *Opera omnia*, I:2, 607-994.

———. *The Letters of Marsilio Ficino.* Translated and edited by members of the Language Department, School of Economic Science. 3 vols. London: Shepheard-Walwyn, 1975, 1978, 1981.

———. *Opera omnia.* 2 vols in 4. Photographic reproduction of edition of Basel: Oficina Henricpetrina, 1576. Edited by Mario Sancipriano. Introduction by Paul Oskar Kristeller. Turin: Bottega d'Erasmo, 1959.

Filelfo, Francesco. *Cent-dix lettres grecques de François Philelphe.* Edited by Emile Legrand. Publications de l'Ecole des Langues Orientales. Paris: Ernest Leroux, éditeur, 1892.

———. [Excerpt from the *Consolatio; Elegia*]. In *A Jacopo Antonio Marcello patrizio veneto parte di orazione consolatoria ed elegia*, etc., edited by G. Benadduci, pp. 1-24.

———. *Elegia in consolationem Jacobi Antonii Marcello de obitu filioli sui,* translated from Greek by Ludovico Carbone and Leonardo Grifo. Marc. Lat. XIV, 246 (4683), fols. 139-41 and fols. 142-44, respectively.

———. *Epistolarum familiarium libri XXXVII [Epist. fam.].* Venice: ex aedibus Ioannis et Gregorii de Gregoriis fratrum, 24 September 1502.

———. *De obitu Valerii filii consolatio [Consolatio].* Glasgow, Hunterian Museum Library (University of Glasgow), cod. 201 [U.1.5], pp. 38-126.

Filelfo, Giovanni Mario. *Epistolare Marii Philelfi.* [Basel: Johann Amerbach, 1495]. H 12979. Also seen: *Epistolare.* Venice: Joannes de Monteferrato de Tridino, 6 October 1492. HC 12976*.

———. *Invettiva contro Pietro Perleone e Giorgio Trapezunzio.* In F. Gabotto, "Un nuovo contributo alla storia dell'umanesimo ligure," pp. 252-55.

———. *Lettera.* In G. Benadduci, *A Jacopo Antonio Marcello patrizio veneziano parte di orazione consolatoria*, etc., pp. 25-26.

Foscarini, Ludovico. *Epistolae [Epist.].* Vienna: Österreichische Nationalbibliothek, cod. Lat. 441, fols. 11-354. Ms. copy Treviso, Biblioteca Comunale, cod. 85.

———. *Gesta martyrum Victoris et Coronae,* to Jacopo Foscari (1440). Baltimore, Walters Art Gallery, cod. W 393 (de Ricci 472), fols. 65-94ᵛ.

Frulovisi, Tito Livio. *Opera hactenus inedita Titi Livii de Frulovisis de Ferrara.* Edited by C. W. Previté-Orton. Cambridge: typis Academiae, 1932. Contains seven comedies (pp. 1-286) and *De republica* (pp. 287-389).

461

BIBLIOGRAPHY

Gadolo, Bernardino. *Epistolae.* Camaldoli, Archivio del Sacro Eremo, cod. *735.*

Garin, Eugenio, ed. *Prosatori latini del Quattrocento.* La letteratura italiana, storia e testi, 13. Milan and Naples: Riccardo Ricciardi, ed., 1952.

Gasparo da Verona. See *Le vite di Paolo II.*

Gatari, Andrea. *Diario del Concilio di Basilea, 1433-1435.* In *Concilium Basiliense: Studien und Quellen zur Geschichte des Concils von Basel,* V: *Tagebücher und Acten* (Basel: Helbing & Lichtenhahn vormals Reich-Detloff, 1904), 375-442.

George of Trebizond. *Epistola consolatoria* to Jacopo Antonio Marcello (5 April 1461). In J. Monfasani, ed., *Collectanea Trapezuntiana,* 235-48.

―――. *Oratio funebris in Fantinum Michielem* (1434). In J. Monfasani, ed., *Collectanea Trapezuntiana,* 445-58.

―――. Preface to Francesco Barbaro of his translation of Plato's *Laws.* In F. Gaeta, "Giorgio da Trebisonda," pp. 498-501; J. Monfasani, ed., *Collectanea Trapezuntiana,* 198-203.

Gianotti, Donato. *Dialogus de republica Venetorum.* In Joannes Georgius Graevius, ed., *Thesaurus antiquitatum et historiarum Italiae,* V, Part I (Leiden: Petrus Vander, 1722), cols. 1-124.

Giorgi, Francesco. *De harmonia mundi totius cantica tria,* to Pope Clement VII. Venice: in aedibus Bernardini de Vitalibus Chalcographi, September 1525.

Giovio, Paolo. *Elogia virorum literis illustrium.* Basel: P. Pernae, 1577.

Giuliani, Andrea. *Pro Manuele Chrysolora funebris oratio* (1415). In Angelo Calogerà, ed., *Raccolta d'opuscoli scientifici e filolgici,* 25 (1741), 323-38.

―――. *Oratio super principio orationum M. Tullii Ciceronis ad auditores* (1413). In K. Müllner, *Reden und Briefe,* pp. 115-18.

―――. *Oratio in laudem corporis Jesu Christi* (end 1408-1409). In S. Troilo, *Andrea Giuliani,* pp. 200-202.

Giustiniani, Antonio. *Dispacci di Antonio Giustiniani, ambasciatore veneto in Roma dal 1502 al 1505.* Edited by Pasquale Villari. 3 vols. Florence: Successori Le Monnier, 1876.

―――. *Quaestiones in secundum sententiarum.* Marc. Lat. VI, 289 (2470).

Giustiniani, Bernardo. *De divi Marci Evangelistae vita, translatione et sepulturae loco.* In Joannes Georgius Graevius, ed., *Thesaurus antiquitatum et historiarum Italiae,* V, Part I (Leiden: excudit Petrus Vander, 1722), cols. 171-96.

―――. *Oratio funebris habita in obitu Francisci Fuscari Ducis* (1457). In B. Giustiniani, *Orat. et epist.,* sigs. B2ᵛ-D2. Also *Orazioni, elogi e vite,* I, 21-59.

―――. *Oratio pro militia ad regem Franciae Ludovicum* (Tours, 6 January 1462). In B. Giustiniani, *Orat. et epist.,* sigs. E2-E4ᵛ. Also with Valier, *De cautione adhibenda,* pp. 193-201.

―――. *Oratio ad Paulum II Pont. Max.* (1466). *Oratio ad Xystum IV Pont. Max.* In B. Giustiniani, *Orat. et epist.,* fols. F5-Gᵛ, Gᵛ-G6. Also *Orationes clarorum hominum,* sigs. 1-3ᵛ, 4-9ᵛ.

―――. *Orationes et epistolae [Orat. et epist.],* with works of Leonardo Giustiniani. Venice: per Bernardinum Benalium, [1492]. HC 9638* (II)-9639.

―――. *De origine urbis venetiarum rebusque gestis a Venetis libri quindecim.* In Joannes Georgius Graevius, ed., *Thesaurus antiquitatum et historiarum Italiae,* V, Part I (Leiden: excudit Petrus Vander, 1722), cols. 1-172.

―――. *Vita beati Laurentii Justiniani venetiarum protopatriarchae* [1475]. In Lorenzo Giustiniani, *Opera omnia,* I, i-xxiv. Also edited with Italian translation by Idelfonso Tassi (Rome: Officina Poligrafica Laziale, 1962), not seen.

―――, trans. Isocrates, *Ad Nicoclem de regno,* to Ludovico Gonzaga. In B. Giustiniani, *Orationes et epistolae,* sigs. H6ᵛ-I6ᵛ.

Giustiniani, Leonardo. *[Epistolae].* With B. Giustiniani, *Orat. et epist.,* sigs. K-K4ᵛ, L2ʳ⁻ᵛ, L4-L8.

―――. *[Epistolae].* In A. Oberdorfer, "Alcune lettere inedite di Leonardo Giustiniani," 311-18.

———. *Epistolae aliquot necnon aliorum ad ipsum*. In G. B. Contarini, *Anec. Ven.*, I, 71-91.

———. *Funebris oratio pro Carolo Zeno* (1418). In *Rerum italicarum scriptores*, New Ed., XIX, Parte VI, fasc. 2 (Bologna: Nicola Zanichelli, 1941), 141-46. Also in *Orazioni, elogi e vite*, I, 1-11.

———. *Funebris oratio ad Georgium Lauredanum*. In *Orazioni, elogi e vite*, I, 12-20.

———. *Proemium in leges et statuta Pergami* (1420). Marc. Lat. XIV, 256 (4634), fols. 61v-65v.

———. *Regulae artificialis memoriae*. In A. Oberdorfer, "Le 'Regulae artificialis memoriae' di Leonardo Giustiniani," pp. 117-27.

———, trans. Plutarch, lives of Cimon and Lucullus, to Henry Lusignan, King of Cyprus, and life of Phocion (to his brother Marco Giustiniani). In Plutarch, *Vitae*, ed. G. A. Campano (Rome: Udalricus Gallus, [1470]), II, fols. 1-22 and 123-34v. H 13125.

———, trans. (from Greek). *Vita beati Nicolai Myrensis Episcopi*, with preface to his brother Lorenzo Giustiniani, Patriarch of Venice. In Ludovico Lippomano, ed., *Sanctorum priscorum patrum vitae* (Venice: ad signum spei, 1551), fols. 138v-149v (preface, 138v-139v). Preface in Lorenzo Giustiniani, *Opera omnia* (2 vols. Venice: excudebat Jo. Baptista Albritius et Joseph Rosa, 1751), I, liii.

Grasolari, Jacopo. *Oratio ad illustrissimum venetorum dominium in assumptione Reverendissimi Domini Ludovico Contareni ad Patriarchatum*. Venice: per Bernardinum de Vitalibus, 1508.

Grassello, Antonio. *De gratia recuperanda ad instantiam Angele sororis sue*. Venice: per Peregrinum de Pasqualibus Bononiensem, 1487. H 7871*.

———. *De eucharistia et de extrema untione*. Venice: per Peregrinum de Pasqualibus Bononiensem, 1487. H 7872*.

Guarino Veronese. *Dedica della Geografia di Strabone a Iacopo Antonio Marcello*. Edited by Guglielmo Berchet. Nozze Marcello-del Mayno. Venice: Stabilimento tipografico Ferrari, 26 July 1893. The Strabo dedication also in Guarino's *Epist.*, II, 629-34.

———. *Epistolario di Guarino Veronese*. Edited by R. Sabbadini [*Epist.*, ed. Sabbadini]. R. Deputazione Veneta di Storia Patria. Ser. III: Miscellanea di Storia Veneta. Vols. VIII [= I], XI [= II], XIV [= III]. Venice: la Società, 1915-19. Photographic reproduction, Turin: Bottega d'Erasmo, 1967.

———. *Oratio funebris in Georgium Lauretanum venetum*. Marc. Lat. XIV, 256 (4634), fols. 38-46.

———. *Laudatio in praeclaros viros Zachariam [Trevisan] et Albanum [Badoer] Venetiarum cives*. In R. Sabbadini, *La scuola e gli studi di Guarino Veronese*, pp. 170-72.

King, Margaret L. and Albert Rabil, Jr., eds. *Her Immaculate Hand: Selected Works by and about the Women Humanists of Quattrocento Italy*. Medieval and Renaissance Texts and Studies, 20. Binghamton, N.Y.: State University of New York, 1983.

Kohl, Benjamin G. and Ronald Witt, eds. *The Earthly Republic: Italian Humanists on Government and Society*. Philadelphia: University of Pennsylvania Press, 1978.

Lando, Vitale. *Oratio ad Caesarem Augustum Imperatorem* (1468). Venice, Biblioteca del Museo Correr, cod. Cicogna 2855 (2757), fol. 187r-v.

Languschi, Jacopo. *Excidio e presa di Costantinopoli nell'anno 1453*. Incorporated in Giorgio Dolfin's chronicle, fragment edited by G. M. Thomas, *Die Eroberung*, pp. 9ff.; uncertain boundaries.

———. Two Sonnets. In A. Segarizzi, "Jacopo Languschi," pp. 181-82.

Lapi, Moro. [*Opera*]. Marc. Lat. XIV, 295 (4348).

de Lauris, Lauro. *Oratio coram Jacobo Zeno in ipsius felici ingressu* (1 May 1460). Milan: Biblioteca Ambrosiana, cod. C 145 inf., fols. 170v-176.

da Legge, Donato. *Historia turchesca (1300-1514)*. Edited by I. Ursu. Editinnea Aca-

BIBLIOGRAPHY

demiei romane. Bucharest: Inst. de arte grafiche "Carol Göbl," s-r I. S. Rasidescu, 1909.

Leonardi, Niccolò. *Oratio in funere magistri Andreae phisici venetiarum,* in form of letter to Francesco Barbaro and Andrea Giuliano. Marc. Lat. XIV, 12 (4002), fols. 119ᵛ-120ᵛ.

Leoniceno, Ognibene. *Oratio in privato examine Petri Foscari, protonotarii apostolici et primicerii Sancti Marci Venetiarum, in iure pontificio* (Padua, 31 August 1454). Marc. Lat. XI, 52 (4355).

Lippomano, Marco. *Oratio ad Eugenium Quartum Summum Pontificem* (1431). *Oratio ad dominum Michaelem de Codignola Capitaneum Generalem illustrissimi dominii venetiarum* (1446). Vat. Lat. 5220, fols. 79-83, 83-84ᵛ, respectively.

Lorenzi, Giovanni. *De passione domini oratio.* Vat. Capponianus 235, fols. 47ᵛ-60ᵛ.

———. *[Epistolae].* In P. Paschini, *Il carteggio fra il Cardinale Marco Barbo e Giovanni Lorenzi (1481-90),* pp. 20-214.

———, trans. Sextus Empiricus, *Contra grammaticos, rhetores, geometras, arithmeticos,* excerpts (from Vat. Lat. 2990, fols. 266-381ᵛ) in C. B. Schmitt, "An Unstudied Fifteenth-Century Latin Translation," pp. 250-57.

Maffei, Benedetto. *De moribus nostrorum temporum,* to Marco Barbo. Florence: Biblioteca Nazionale Centrale, cod. Magliabecchianus VI, 191, fols. 3-36.

Malipiero, Domenico. *Annali veneti dall'anno 1457 al 1500* [Malipiero, *Annali*]. Edited by F. Longo and Agostino Sagredo. ASI, 7, Parts I and II (1843-1844), 1-720.

Marcanova, Giovanni. *Oratio pro felici ingressu D. Fantini Dandulo Episcopi.* Milan, Biblioteca Ambrosiana, cod. C. 145 inf, fols. 166ᵛ-171ᵛ.

Marcello, Cristoforo. *In reverendissimi episcopi Petri Barocii funus oratio.* With A. Valier, *De cautione adhibenda in edendis libris,* pp. 102-107.

Marcello, Francesco. *Libellus ad Leonardum Lauredanum Venetiarum Principem, in quo excursus describit turcarum, epistola dedicatoria* (1508). Marc. Lat. XIV, 225 (4497).

Marcello, Jacopo Antonio. *Epistola* to Giovanni Cossa, prefatory to anonymous translation of a Life of St. Maurice. In H. Martin, "Portrait," pp. 258-60. Also verse at pp. 261-64.

———. *Epistola* to King René d'Anjou, prefatory to a translation of Ptolemy's *Cosmography.* In H. Martin, "Portrait," pp. 264-66.

———. *Epistola* to King René d'Anjou, prefatory to anonymous translation of Chrysostom, *De tollerandis calamitatibus.* In G. Mercati, *Ultimi contributi,* I, 84-85. The work with preface in Padua, Biblioteca del Museo Civico, cod. C M 525, no. 5, fols. [1-5].

———. *Epistola* to King René d'Anjou, prefatory to Guarino Veronese's translation of Strabo. In R. Sabbadini, "La traduzione guariniana di Strabone," pp. 13-15.

———. *Epistola* to King René d'Anjou, prefatory to Lauro Quirini's translation of ps.-Suidas, *De sacerdotio Christi.* In G. Mercati, *Ultimi contributi,* I, 81-82.

Marcello, Pietro G. *De obitu Leonardi Sanuti oratoris veneti apud Pontificem Maximum,* epigram (1474). Marc. Lat. XII, 211 (4179), fol. 167.

———. *Oratio in adventu Cardinalis Grimani* (20 May 1498). Marc. Lat. XIV, 246 (4683), fols. 110-14.

———. *Oratio in funere Andreae Vendrameni Venetiarum Principis* (9 May 1400 [sic; 1478]). In *Orazioni, elogi e vite,* I, 144-60.

———. *De vita, moribus et rebus gestis omnium ducum venetorum.* Frankfurt am M.: apud Paulum Reffeloi, impensis Sig. Feierabent, 1574.

Marcello, Pietro V. *Epistola consolatoria* to Fantino Dandolo (January 1405). In R. Sabbadini, "Antonio da Romagno e Pietro Marcello," pp. 236-37.

———. *Principium Monasterii Montis Vendae* (24 November 1427). Padua, Biblioteca del Seminario, cod. 135.

———. Mock orations: "Aeschines," "Demades," "Demosthenes," "a certain Athenian." In R. Sabbadini, "Antonio da Romagno e Pietro Marcello," pp. 241-44.

Marino, Giovanni. *Orationes:* 1. *in licentia Hermolai Barbaro Romanae ecclesiae pro-*

464

thonotarii (Padua, 1436; fols. 20-29); 2. *in licentia domini Montorii de Mascharelis Vicentini* (Padua, 2 April 1432; fols. 30-32ᵛ); 3. *in acceptatione officii rectoratus* (Padua, 1 June 1433; fols. 32ᵛ-34); 4. *pro adventu Antonii Corrario Romane ecclesie Cardinalis* (Padua, 1433; fols. 34-36ᵛ). Vat. Lat. 5119, fols. 20-36ᵛ.

Marino, Giovanni (G). *Oratio funebris pro Antonio Suriano Venetiarum Patriarcha,* with prefatory letter to Marino by Paolo Pisani. Venice: Gregorius de Gregoriis, 28 May 1508.

———. *Sylva.* Marc. Lat. XIV, 266 (4502), fols. 226-29.

Marsi, Paolo. *De crudeli Europeontinae urbis excidio, sacrosanctae religionis Christiane lamentatio,* to Pope Paul II. In A. della Torre, *Paolo Marsi,* Appendix, 287-95.

———. *Elegia ad Joannem Canalem Nicolai doctoris filium* ("Ex peloponneso," 30 July 1469). In A. della Torre, *Paolo Marsi da Pescina,* pp. 177-78.

Martène, Edmond, and Ursin Durand. *Veterum scriptorum et monumentorum historicorum, dogmaticorum moralium amplissima collectio.* 9 vols. Paris: apud Montalant, 1724-1733.

Merula, Giorgio. *De antiquitate Vicecomitum.* Edited by Alexander Minutianus. Milan: Guillermus Le Signerre, 1500? H C *11095.

———. *Bellum scodrense.* Venice: Gabriele di Pietro, [not before 10 September 1474]. HC (+ Add) 11093.

Miscellaneous Marciani Latini manuscripts containing various and scattered humanist *opuscula:* XI, 101 (3939); XI, 102 (3940); XII, 210 (4689), hand of Marino Sanuto; XII, 211 (4179), hand of Marino Sanuto; XIV, 221 (4632), copied by Jacopo Morelli; XIV, 230 (4736); XIV, 254 (4535); XIV, 260 (4258); XIV, 265 (4501); XIV, 266 (4502), partly by the hand of Marino Sanuto; XIV, 267 (4344), Sanuto miscellany.

Molin, Pietro. Two *Orationes ad imperatorem Federicum III* (30 November 1468 and 4 February 1468 mv = 1469). Brit. Mus., Cod. Add. 15906, fols. 14ᵛ-16, 16ᵛ-20.

de' Monaci, Lorenzo. *Chronicon de rebus venetis ab urbe condita ad annum MCCCLIV.* Edited by Flaminio Corner. Venice: ex typographia Remondini, 1758.

———. *Oratio ad serenissimum principem et ducem Venetorum in laude et edificatione alme civitatis Venetiarum.* In M. Poppi, "Un orazione del cronista Lorenzo de Monacis," 483-97.

del Monte, Pietro. [*Epistolae*], whole and excerpted. In J. Haller, *Pier da Monte* [Appendix], pp. 1-185.

———. [*Epistolae*]. In A. Zanelli, "Pietro del Monte," 8, 92-115.

———. *Invectiva adversus ridiculum quendam oratorem,* to Andrea Giuliani. Vat. Lat. 3194, fols. 13-28. Preface to Giuliani in S. Troilo, *Andrea Giuliani,* pp. 198-200. Preface and excerpts in Barbaro, *Diatriba,* edited by A. M. Quirini, pp. 186-92.

———. *Monarchia in qua generalium conciliorum materia de potestate prestantia et excellentia Romani pontificis et imperatoris plenissime discutitur,* to Pope Eugene IV. Rome: apud Antonium Bladum, 1537.

———. *Repertorium utriusque juris.* Rome: apud Sanctum Marcum (Vitus Paecher), 5 February 1476. H 11587*.

———. *De vitiorum inter se differencia et comparatione,* with prefatory letter to Humphrey, Duke of Gloucester (fols. 1-3ᵛ). Vat. Lat. 1048. The prefatory letter also published (from Oxford, Bodleian Library, cod. Auct. F. 5. 26) in the *English Historical Review,* 10 (1895), 101-103.

Morandi, Filippo, da Rimini. [*Epistolae et alia opera*]. Seville: Biblioteca Columbina, cod. 5-6-13.

———. *Epistola* to Roberto Malatesta. Florence: Biblioteca Marucelliana, cod. B I 26, fols. 1-23ᵛ [recent numeration].

———. *Epithalamium* for Caterina Caldiera. San Daniele, Biblioteca Guarneriana, cod. 57, fol. 76. Partially published R. Sabbadini, "Briciole umanistiche-XIII: Caterina Caldiera," p. 245.

———. *Excidium Constantinopolitanae urbis quae quondam Bizantium ferebatur,* to Francesco Barbaro. In A. Pertusi, "La lettera di Filippo da Rimini," pp. 152-57.

465

BIBLIOGRAPHY

Morandi, Filippo, da Rimini. *Invectiva in vanissimos homines.* Seville, Biblioteca Columbina, cod. 5-6-13, fols. 40ᵛ-48ᵛ. Padua, Biblioteca Capitolare, cod. B. 62, fols. 65ᵛ-77.

———. *Oratio* [in praise of Doge Francesco Foscari, given in the ducal palace and in the presence of Count Francesco Sforza] (1441). Seville, Biblioteca Columbina, cod. 5-6-13, fols. 18-19.

———. *Oratio in funere Francisci Barbari* (1454). Marc. Lat. XIV, 250 (4717), fols. 8-12.

———. *Symposium de paupertate,* to Francesco Barbaro. In M. L. King, "A Study in Venetian Humanism at Mid-Quattrocento: Filippo da Rimini and his *Symposium de paupertate* (Study and Text)," second part (SV, NS 3), pp. 168-86.

Morosini, Albano. *Oratio habita in suo conventu legum et in assumptione offitii rectoratus.* Marc. Lat. XI, 102 (3940), fols. 72ᵛ-73ᵛ.

Morosini, Domenico. *De bene instituta re publica* [DBIRP]. Edited by Claudio Finzi. Collectanea Caralitana, testi e documenti inediti o rari pubblicati a cura dei seminari di scienze politiche, 2. Milan: Giuffré editore, 1969.

Morosini, Michele. *Oratio in suo conventu iuris civilis.* Marc. Lat. XI, 102 (3940), fol. 72ʳ⁻ᵛ.

Morosini, Paolo. *De aeterna temporalique Christi generatione in judaice improbationem perfidiae,* to Pope Paul II. Padua: Bartholomeus de Valdezoccho with Martinus de Septem Arboribus (also with variant colophon: Bartholomaeus Campanus Ponticuruanus), 28 April 1473. HC 10924.

———. *Defensio venetorum ad Europae principes contra obtrectatores* [DVEP], to Cardinal Marco Barbo. In Valentinelli, *Bibl. manu.,* III, 189-229.

———. *De fato seu praescientia divina et liberi humani arbitrii libertate,* to Pope Sixtus IV. Vat. Lat. 13157 (copied 1477).

———. *Lettera a Cicco Simonetta [Lettera].* Marc. Ital. VII, 762 (7668). Translated (Italian to Latin) by Giovanni Corner (Marc. Ital. VII, 2296 [7385]); retranslated (Latin to Italian) and published by A. Bonicelli, *Memoria storica intorno alla repubblica di Venezia scritta da Paolo Morosini e da Giovanni Cornaro* (Venice: stamperia di Carlo Palese, 1796), i-liii.

———. *De rebus ac forma reipublicae venetae* [DRF], to Gregory Heimburg. In Valentinelli, *Bibl. manu.,* III, 231-264.

Müllner, Karl. *Reden und Briefe italienischer Humanisten: Ein Beitrag zur Geschichte der Pädagogik des Humanismus.* Vienna: Alfred Hölder, 1899.

Naldi, Naldo. *Epigrammaton liber.* Edited by Alexander Perosa. Bibliotheca scriptorum medii recentisque aevorum, saecula XV-XVI. Budapest: Nyomda, 1943.

Navagero, Andrea. *Historia veneta ab origine urbis usque ad annum 1498.* In L. A. Muratori, ed., *Rerum italicarum scriptores,* XXIII (Milan: Societas Palatinae, 1733), cols. 919-1218.

Negri, Francesco. *De aristocratia,* to Doge Leonardo Loredan. Marc. Lat. VI, 6 (2753).

———. *Grammatica.* Edited by J. L. Santritter. Venice: Theodorus Herbipolensis, 21 March 1480. HC 11858*.

———. *Modus epistolandi.* Venice: arte quoque impensis Hermanni Lichtenstein, 5 February 1488. HC 11963*.

———. *Orationes:* 1. for Agnesina Bondina, mother of Pietro Roccabonella, pp. 204-209; 2. for Girolamo Reguardati, pp. 209-13; 3. for I. I. Putei, pp. 213-17; 4. for Andrea Planchnerii, pp. 218-22; 5. for Francesco Maltraversi, pp. 222-27. In P. Verrua, "Cinque orazioni."

———. *Paeonicum Saphicon* for Cassandra Fedele. In Fedele, *Epistolae et orationes,* edited by J. F. Tomasini (Padua: apud Franciscum Bolzettam, 1636), pp. 151-55.

Nogarola, Isotta. *De pari aut impari Adae attque Evae peccato.* In *Opera omnia,* edited by E. Abel, II, 187-216. Translated by M. L. King & A. Rabil, Jr., in *Her Immaculate Hand,* 59-69.

———. *Opera quae supersunt omnia,* with works of Angela and Ginevra Nogarola. Edited by Eugenius Abel. 2 vols. Vienna: apud Gerold & Socios, 1886.

De obitu Valerii Marcelli, [consolationes] Nicolae Secundini et aliorum, to Jacopo

BIBLIOGRAPHY

Antonio Marcello (1463). Glasgow: Hunterian Museum Library (University of Glasgow), cod. 201 [U.1.5].

Orationes clarorum hominum, vel honoris officiique causa ad principes vel in funere de virtutibus eorum habitae. Venice: In Academiae Venetae, 1559.

Orazioni, elogi e vite scritte da letterati veneti patrizi in lode di dogi, ed altri illustri soggetti. Edited by Girolamo Ascanio Molin. 2nd ed. rev. 2 vols. Venice: A. Curti, 1798.

Orsini, Michele. *[Epistola] religiosae sorori*. Milan, Biblioteca Ambrosiana, cod. E 66 sup., fols. 1-13.

———. *De summa venetorum origine*, to Francesco Filelfo (26 August 1462). Milan: Bibl. Ambrosiana, cod. H 122 inf. Autograph. Also Glasgow, Hunterian Museum Library (University of Glasgow), cod. 201 [U.1.5], pp. 269-94.

Paruta, Paolo. *Orazione funebre in lode dei morti nella vittoriosa battaglia contra i Turchi*. In *Orazioni, elogi e vite*, II.

Pasqualigo, Pietro. *Ad Hemanuelem Lusitaniae regem oratio* (20 August 1501). Venice: per Bernardinum Venetum de Vitalibus, 22 December 1501. Facsimile in D. Weinstein, *Ambassador from Venice*, pp. 35-42, with translation, 43-51.

Perleone, Pietro. *Consolatoria epistola* to Jacopo Antonio Marcello. Marc. Lat. XIV, 266 (4502), fols. 218-21ᵛ.

———. *Epistola [consolatoria] ad Nicolaum Sagundinum [Epist. cons.]*. In Giovanni Maria Lazzaroni, ed., *Miscellanea di varie operette*, II (Venice; appresso Lazzaroni, 1740), 43-98.

———. *Three [epistolae]*. Vat. Chis. J VI 215, fols. 176ᵛ-178ᵛ.

———. *Epithalamia duo* et *Oratio pro milite* (honoring Sismondo Pandolfo Malatesta). Marc. Lat. XI, 80 (3057), fols. 343-46ᵛ, 347-51ᵛ. Attribution uncertain.

———. *Laudatio in Valerium filium*, to Jacopo Antonio Marcello (copied 1 November 1463). Glasgow, Hunterian Museum Library (University of Glasgow), cod. 201 [U.1.5], pp. 189-248.

———. *Oratio* [on studies]. In K. Müllner, ed., *Reden und Briefe*, pp. 144-46.

———. *Oratio in funere Iani Campofregosi, D. Senensium*. Vat. Lat. 5336, fols. 35-43ᵛ.

———, trans. Isocrates, oration to Demonicus, with preface to Brancaleo Grillus. Vat. Lat. 5336, fols. 25-34ᵛ.

Perotti, Niccolò. *Niccolò Perotti's Version of the Enchiridion of Epictetus*. Edited by Revilo Pendleton Oliver. Urbana: University of Illinois Press, 1954.

Petrarch, Francesco. *Letters*. Selected and translated by Morris Bishop. Bloomington: Indiana University Press, 1966.

———. *On His Own Ignorance and That of Many Others* (translation of *De sui ipsius et multorum aliorum ignorantia* by Hans Nachod). In E. Cassirer, P. O. Kristeller, and J. H. Randall, Jr., eds., *The Renaissance Philosophy of Man*, 47-133.

Piccolomini, Eneo Silvio. *Opera inedita*. Edited by Josephus Cugnoni. *Atti della R. Accademia dei Lincei, Memorie della classe di scienze morali, storiche e filologiche*, Ser. 3, 8 (1883), 319-686.

Pico della Mirandola, Giovanni. *De hominis dignitate, Heptaplus, De ente et uno, e scritti vari*. Edited by Eugenio Garin. Florence: Vallecchi, 1942. The *De hominis dignitate* also translated by Elizabeth Livermore Forbes ("Oration on the Dignity of Man") in E. Cassirer, P. O. Kristeller, and J. H. Randall, Jr., eds., *The Renaissance Philosophy of Man*, 223-54.

Pisani, Francesco (di Silvestro). *Oratio de universae philosophiae ornamentis*. With A. Valier, *De cautione adhibenda in edendis libris*, pp. 245-67.

Polenton, Sicco. *La Catinia, le orazioni, e le epistole di Sicco Polenton, umanista trentino del secolo XV*. Edited by Arnaldo Segarizzi. Bergamo: Istituto italiano d'arte grafiche, 1899.

Poliziano, Angelo. *Opera omnia*. Edited by Ida Maïer. 3 vols. Monumenta politica philosophica humanistica rariora, Ser. I, ## 16, 17, 18. Turin: Bottega d'Erasmo,

BIBLIOGRAPHY

1971, 1970, 1971. Vol. I reproduces *Scripta in editione Basilensi anno MDLIII collecta* and includes the *epistolae*.

Pontano, Giovanni. *I dialoghi*. Edited by Carmelo Previtera. Florence: Sansoni, 1943.

Porcia, Jacopo, Count of Porsigli [Purliliarum, Jacobus Comes]. *De reipublicae venetae administratione domi et foris liber*, to Sebastiano Priuli. Treviso: [Gerardo da Fiandra?], 1492. H 13604.

Priuli, Eusebio. *Oratio funebris* for Pietro Dolfin. In E. Martène and U. Durand, *Veterum scriptorum collectio*, III, 1215-32.

Quirini, Giovanni. *Consolatoria oratio pro obitu eximii ac integerrimi viri Benedicti Brugnoli utriusque preceptoris*, to Girolamo Raimundo. Np, [c. 1503].

Quirini, Lauro. [*Dialogus in gymnasiis florentinis*]. In L. Bertalot and A. Wilmanns, eds. "Lauri Quirini 'Dialogus in gymnasiis florentinis,' " *Studien*, I, 349-54.

——. [*Dialogus* on philosophy] *Andree Mauroceno clarissimo pretori patavino*. In A. Segarizzi, "Lauro Quirini umanista veneziano del secolo XV," pp. 17-22.

——. [*Epistola*] to Doge Francesco and Jacopo Foscari (9 January 1448). Vat. Lat. 3194, fols. 11-13.

—— *Epistola Laurentio Vallensi*. In A. Segarizzi, "Lauro Quirini umanista veneziano del secolo XV," pp. 23-24.

——. *Epistola ad Petrum Thomasium*. In K. Krautter, P. O. Kristeller, and H. Roob, eds., "Tre trattati sulla nobiltà," LQU, pp. 67-73.

——. [*Epistolae*]: 1. to Pope Nicholas V, pp. 223-33; 2. to Ludovico [Scarampo] Trevisan, pp. 234-40; 3. to Pope Pius II, pp. 241-57; 4. to Paolo Morosini, pp. 258-59. In A. Pertusi, ed., "Epistole storiche sulla caduta di Costantinopoli e la potenza dei Turchi," in LQU, pp. 163-259. The letter to Morosini was previously published by G. dalla Santa, "Due lettere di umanisti veneziani," 94-95.

——. *De nobilitate contra Poggium Florentinum* [DN]. In K. Krautter, P. O. Kristeller, and H. Roob, eds., "Tre trattati sulla nobiltà," LQU, pp. 74-98.

——. *De nobilitate responsio quid iuris*. In K. Krautter, P. O. Kristeller, and H. Roob, eds., "Tre trattati sulla nobiltà," LQU, pp. 99-102.

——. *Oratio in adventu episcopi Patavini [Petri Donati]*. Marc. Lat. XI, 59 (4152), fols. 164-65ᵛ.

——. *Oratio in laudibus Jeronimi de Leonardis veneti [graduati padue]* (18 April 1445). Milan, Biblioteca Ambrosiana, cod. Ambros. O 124 sup, fols. 93-94ᵛ.

——. *De pace italie*. In A. Segarizzi, "Lauro Quirini umanista veneziano del secolo XV," pp. 24-28.

——. *De republica*, to Francesco Foscari [DR]. Edited by C. Seno and G. Ravegnani in LQU, pp. 121-61.

——, trans. (from Greek). Ps.-Suidas, *Narratio de sacerdotio Jesu Christi*, to Pope Nicolaus V. Rome, Biblioteca dell'Accademia Nazionale dei Lincei e Corsiniana, cod. 839 (43 D 8), fols. 78-80; preface of J. A. Marcello to King René d'Anjou published by G. Mercati, *Ultimi contributi*, I, 81-82.

——, trans. Cassius Dio, Caesar's oration to his soldiers, with preface to Leo Molin. In J. M. Mucciolus, *Catalogus codicum manuscriptorum Malatestianae Caesenatis Bibliothecae*, II, 233-36.

——, trans. (from Greek version of the donation of Constantine), *Sanctio Constantini*, to Pope Nicholas V. In W. Setz, *Lorenzo Vallas Schrift gegen die konstantinische Schenkung*, pp. 118-20.

Quirini, Taddeo. *Ad Fridericum III Romanorum Impertorem oratio gratulatoria* (18 May 1452). In Marquardus Freherus, ed., *Rerum germanicorum scriptores* (3rd ed., Burcardus Gotthelffius Struvius; 3 vols.; Argentorati: Sumptibus Johannis Reinhold Dulsseckeri, 1717), II, 972.

Ragazzoni, Jacopo. *Oratio ad Nicolaum Tronum Venete Reipublice Principem* (1471). [Northern Italy]: tip. del Mesue, 1471. H 1544, GW 2308.

Ramusio, Paolo. *De ieiuniorum observatione* (1480), to the Venetian patricians Marco Marino and Giovanni Ludovico Dandolo. Venice, Biblioteca del Museo Correr, cod. Cicogna 948 (852).

BIBLIOGRAPHY

Regio, Raffaele. *Ducenta problemata in totidem institutionis oratoriae Quintiliani deprauationes; Quaestio utrum ars rhetorica ad Herenium falso Ciceroni inscribatur; De laudibus eloquentiae panegyricus*. [Venice: Octavianus Scotus], 1492. Goff R-115.

Roselli, Antonio. *Monarchia seu tractatus de potestate imperatoris et papae*. Edited by Giacomo Perticone. Bologna: N. Zanichelli, 1944.

Sabellico, Marcantonio. *De cultu et fructu philosophiae [oratio] Venetiis recitata in Rivoaltino gymnasio frequentissimo philosophorum consessu. Opera*, fols. 75ᵛ-77ᵛ.

———. *Enneades sive rhapsodia historiarum*. In *Opera omnia* (1560), II.

———. *Epistolarum familiarium libri XII*, to Marcantonio Morosini [*Epist*.]. *Opera*, fols. 1ᵛ-61bis.

———. *De officio scribae liber unus, dialogus. Opera*, fols. 115-117ᵛ.

———. *Opera*. Venice: per Albertinum de Lisona Vercellensem, 24 December 1502.

———. *Opera omnia*. Edited by Caelius Secundus Curio. 4 vols. in 3. Basel: per Ioannem Heruagium, 1560.

———. *Oratio in funere Benedicti Rugii, Alfonsi Neapolitanorum Regis apud Venetam Rempublicam oratoris. Opera*, fol. 71. Also in *Orationes clarorum hominum*, fols. 173ᵛ-76.

———. *Oratio in funere Zachariae Barbari. Opera*, fols. 70-71. Also in *Orationes clarorum hominum*, fols. 135ᵛ-137ᵛ.

———. *De origine et incrementis philosophiae [oratio] Venetiis recitata frequenti philosophorum conventu in gimnasio rivoaltino. Opera*, fols. 72ᵛ-75ᵛ.

———. *De praetoris officio*, to Antonio Corner. *Opera*, fols. 104ᵛ-108ᵛ.

———. *De reparatione latinae linguae libri 2*, to Marcantonio Morosini [*De rep. lat. lingu*.]. *Opera*, fols. 109-115ᵛ.

———. *Rerum venetarum ab urbe condita libri XXXIII*, to Doge Marco Barbarigo. A. Zeno, ed., *Degl'istorici delle cose veneziane*, I.

———. *De situ Venetiae urbis libri tres*, to Girolamo Donato. *Opera*, fols. 82ᵛ-94.

———. *De usu philosophiae [oratio]. Opera*, fols. 77ᵛ-79.

———. *De venetis magistratibus liber unus*, to Doge Agostino Barbarigo. *Opera*, fols. 94ᵛ-104ᵛ.

———. *De vetustate Aquileiensis patriae*. In *Opera omnia* (1560), II.

Sagundino, Niccolò. *Consolatio in obitu Valerii filii*, to Jacopo Antonio Marcello. Glasgow, Hunterian Museum Library (University of Glasgow), cod. 201 [U.1.5], pp. 1-25. Also Vat. Ottob. Lat. 1732, fols. 1-13.

———. *De deo, de unitate essentiae eius et de trinitate personarum*, to Febo Capella. Marc. Lat. XIII, 62 (4418), fols. 121-30ᵛ.

———. *Dialogus, opusculum de finibus*, to Girolamo Tifernate (fols. 157ᵛ-158ᵛ). Vat. Ottob. Lat. 1732, fols. 157ᵛ-69ᵛ.

———. *Epistola ad Bessarionem de naufragio suo [De naufragio suo]*. In Giovanni Maria Lazzaroni, ed., *Miscellanea di varie operette*, II (Venice: appresso Lazzaroni, 1740), 5-42.

———. *Epistola ad Joannem Gallinetam de oratoris subjecto*. Marc. Lat. XI, 47 (4151), fols. 43-46.

———. *Epistolae et alia opuscula [Epist. et opusc.]*. Marc. Lat. XIII, 62 (4418) (entire) and 63 (4221), fols. 1-26. NB: first codex intended unless otherwise indicated.

———. *De epistolari dicendi genere ad Joannem filium*. Marc. Lat. XIII, 62 (4418), fols. 37-46.

———. *De familia otumanorum* (sic), to Eneo Silvio Piccolomini. Marc. Lat. XIII, 62 (4418), fols. 1-10ᵛ.

———. *De nuptiis filiae et matrimonii commendatione*, to the brothers Pietro and Paolo Aurelio (Venice, 19 March 1462). Vat. Ottob. Lat. 1732, fols. 31-55ᵛ.

———. *Opusculum*, to Pietro Molin, Marc. Lat. XIII, 62 (4418), fols. 111-19.

———. *Oratio ad Alphonsum Regem Aragonum* (25 [elsewhere 31] January 1454). Marc. Lat. XIV, 228 (4498), fols. 102ᵛ-119.

Sagundino, Niccolò. *De origine et sectis philosophorum*, to Fantino Coppo. Marc. Lat. XIII, 62 (4418), fols. 25-36.

———, trans. Onosander, *De optimo imperatore eiusque officio*. Basel: n.p., 1541, pp. 1-115.

———, trans. Plutarch, *De civili instructione*, to Marco Donato. Brescia: Jacobus Brittanicus, 1485. H 11776.

Salutati, Coluccio. *Epistolario di Coluccio Salutati*. Edited by F. Novati. 4 vols. Fonti per la storia d'Italia, Epistolari: Secolo XIV, Vols. XV-XVIII. Rome: nella sede dell'Istituto, 1891-1911.

Sanuto, Leonardo. Five [*Epistolae*]. Marc. Lat. XIV, 267 (4344), fols. 64-65, 71ʳ⁻ᵛ, 75ʳ⁻ᵛ.

———. *Oratio ad Franciscum Sanutum Brixiae Capitaneum* (1470), recited by his son Marino (1470). Marc. Lat. XIV, 267 (4344), fol. 68.

———. *Oratio habita apud Sistum* (sic) *Quartum pontificem Maximum* (1474). Marc. Lat. XIV, 252 (4718), fols. 162-65ᵛ.

———, comp. *Orationes et epistolae ad Christophorum Maurum Venetiarum Principem tum Italorum tum exterorum Principum pro eius inauguratione ad Ducalem dignitatem, additis orationibus Civitatum reipublice, quarum sequitur descriptio, uno volumine collectae, per Leonardum Sanutum eiusdem ducis fortunarum curam gerentem, anno 1462* [12 May]. Marc. Lat. XIII, 90 (4143).

Sanuto, Marco. [Verse] *epistola ad Benedictum Sanutum* (Bergamo, 11 June 1483). Marc. Lat. XII, 210 (4689), fol. 15.

———. *Tabula stellarum fixarum* (1501). Marc. Lat. VIII, 86 (3580), fols. 55-60.

Sanuto, Marino. *I diarii di Marino Sanuto, 1496-1533* [Sanuto, *Diarii*]. 58 vols. in 59. Edited by Rinaldo Fulin et al. R. Deputazione Veneta di Storia Patria. Venice: Visentini, 1879-1903.

———. *Vitae ducorum venetorum*. In L. A. Muratori, ed., *Rerum italicarum scriptores*, XXII (Milan: Typographia Societatis Palatinae, 1733), cols. 399-1252. Also *Le vite dei dogi*, edited by Giovanni Monticolo. In *Rerum italicarum scriptores*, New Ed., XXII, Part IV (Città di Castello: coi tipi dell'editore S. Lapi, 1900), 337-432.

da Spilimbergo, Giovanni. *Oratio in Leonardum Justinianum*. In G. B. Contarini, ed., *Anec. ven.*, 83-85.

———. *Oratio ad Marcum Lipomanum de congratulatione sue preture*. Padua, Biblioteca del Museo Civico, cod. B. P. 1223, pp. 94-97.

Tomeo, Niccolò Leonico. *Dialogi*. Venice: in aedibus Gregorii de Gregoriis, September 1524.

———. [*Epistolae*]. Vat. Ross. 997.

———. *De varia historia libri tres*. Venice: in aedibus Lucae Ant. Juntae, 1531.

Tommasi, Pietro. *Consilium medicum* (1434). In A. Benzoni, "Un giudizio di Pietro Tommasi," pp. 33-40.

———. *Consilium de universali praeservatione contra venena*, to Pope Eugene IV (Venice, 18 February 1437). Vat. Urb. Lat. 1425.

———. *Epistolarum familiarium liber*. Published in part (from Bergamo: cod. Lambda II, 32, fols. 126-39ᵛ) by E. Walser, *Poggius Florentinus* (Leipzig and Berlin, 1914), pp. 454-84.

———. *Excerptum de astrologica inspectione*. Marc. Lat. XIV, 265 (4501), fols. 201-202ᵛ.

———. *Lettere autografe*. ASV. Procuratori di San Marco de Citra, Atti depositati della Congregazione di Carità, Buste 120-22. Excerpts published by R. Cessi, "La giovinezza di Pietro Tommasi," and A. Segarizzi, "La corrispondenza famigliare di un medico erudito del Quattrocento."

———. *Oratio pro collegio phisicorum coram illustrissimo comite Francisco Sfortia*. Vat. Lat. 5385, fols. 78-84ᵛ.

Traversari, Ambrogio. *Aliorumque ad ipsum, ed ad alios de eodem Ambrosio latinae epistolae*. Ordered by Petrus Cannetus; edited by Laurentius Mehus [*Epist.*, ed.

Mehus (= Vol. II)]. 2 vols. Florence: ex typographia Caesareo, 1759. Rpt. of vol. I (with title *Historia litteraria florentina*), Munich, 1968.

———. *Epistolarum libri XX* [*Epist.*, ed. Martène & Durand]. In E. Martène and U. Durand, eds., *Veterum scriptorum collectio*, III, 1-752.

———. *Hodoeporicon*. Edited by Laurentius Mehus, with notes by Alessandro Dini-Traversari. In Dini-Traversari, *Ambrogio Traversari e i suoi tempi* (Florence: Succ. B. Seeber, 1912).

Trebanius, Aurelius. *De felicitate libellus*, to Marco Barbo. Vat. Lat. 2924.

Trevisan, Zaccaria G. *Oratio pro data licentia Iohanni Marino in utroque iure* (Padua, 18 December 1435). Vat. Lat. 5119, fols. 40-45ᵛ.

———. *Oratio habita ad Pontificem Barbum* (1464). In Mittarelli, *Bibl. codd. mss.*, cols. 1158-63.

Trevisan, Zaccaria V. [*Epistola*] to Ognibene Scola. In P. Gothein, "Zaccaria Trevisan," pp. 55-56.

———. Four *Orationes*: 1. for his successor as captain of Padua Pietro Rimondo (Petrus Arimundus; March 1407), pp. 28-30; 2. to Pope Gregory XII (Foiano, 31 December 1407), pp. 34-42; 3. to the Antipope Benedict XIII (Pietrasanta, 22 January 1408), 43-46; 4. for the public conferral of the doctorate on Pietro Marcello V, B. of Padua (16 October 1413), pp. 47-49. In P. Gothein, "Zaccaria Trevisan."

Valier, Agostino. *De cautione adhibenda in edendis libris*, with other works. Padua: Excudebat Josephus Cominus, 1719.

———. Three [*Epistolae*] *ad Philippum Mocenicum Cypri archiepiscopum*, pp. 280-81; *ad Aloisium Contarenum*, pp. 281-96; *ad Laurentium Priulum*, pp. 296-302. In K. Müllner, *Reden und Briefe*.

Valla, Giorgio. Forty-four *epistolae*. In J. L. Heiberg, *Beiträge*, pp. 44-107.

———. *De expetendis et fugiendis rebus opus*. 2 vols. Venice: in aedibus Aldi Romani, impensa ac studio Ioannis Petri Vallae filiee pientiss., December 1501.

———. *Rhetorica*. Venice: S. de Luere, sumptibus L. Orii de Portesio, 1514.

Valla, Lorenzo. [Invective *epistola* to Lauro Quirini]. In L. Barozzi and R. Sabbadini, *Studi sul Panormita e sul Valla*, pp. 112-13.

———. *De vero falsoque bono*. Edited by Maristella de Panizza Lorch. Bari: Adriatica Ed., 1970.

Vallaresso, Fantino. *Compendium Catholicae fidei*. [Venice: Rainald von Nimewegen, ca. 1490]. H 5920, GW 7903. (In this and other editions, the author's name is given erroneously as Fantino Dandolo.)

———. *Libellus de ordine generalium conciliorum et unione Florentina*, to Pope Eugene IV. Edited by Bernard Schultze. Concilium Florentinum, documenta et scriptores, Ser. B, v. 2, fasc. 2. Rome: Pontificium Institutum Orientalium Studiorum, 1944.

Vallaresso, Maffeo. [*Epistolae*]. Vat. Barb. Lat. 1809 (XXIX 153).

———. *Regule*. Venice, Biblioteca del Museo Correr, cod. Cicogna 59.

Vergerio, Pier Paolo. *Epistolario di Pier Paolo Vergerio*. Edited by Leonardo Smith [*Epist.*, ed. Smith]. Fonti per la storia di'Italia, 74. Rome: Tipografia del Senato, 1934.

———. *De republica venetorum*. In Robey and Law, "Venetian Myth," pp. 38-50. Previously published by E. A. Cicogna (Venice: tip. Picottiana, 1830).

Vinciguerra, Antonio. Lettera to Bernardo Bembo (5 May 1498). New York, Pierpont Morgan Library, MA 1842.

———. *De principe libellus* (2 October 1502?). London, Victoria and Albert Museum, cod. Res. H. 33.

———. *Relazione sull'isola di Veglia*. Marc. Ital. VI, 220 (5915).

———. *Satire di Antonio Vinciguerra, Lodovico Ariosto, Ercole Bentivoglio, Luigi Alamanni, Lodovico Dolce*. Londra [sic], 1786; "Si vende in Livorno presso Tommaso Masi e Compagni."

———. Four *satire*. In A. Sopetto, *Le satire edite ed inedite di Antonio Vinciguerra*, pp. 64-89.

Le vite di Paolo II di Gasparo da Verona e Michele Canensi. Edited by Giuseppe Zippel.

BIBLIOGRAPHY

In *Rerum italicarum scriptores*, New Ed., III, Part XVI (Città di Castello: S. Lapi, 1904-1911).

Watkins, Renée Neu, ed. *Humanism and Liberty: Writings on Freedom from Fifteenth-Century Florence*. Columbia: University of South Carolina Press, 1978.

Zambeccari, Pellegrino. *Epistolario di Pellegrino Zambeccari*. Edited by Ludovico Frati. Fonti per la storia d'Italia. Rome: Tipografia del Senato, 1929.

Zamberti, Bartolomeo. *In funere Georgii Vallae Placentini philosophi praestantissimi oratio*. In P. Rose, "Bartolomeo Zamberti's Funeral Oration," pp. 303-307.

Zanco, Paolo. *Epistolae*. Rome, Biblioteca Alessandrina, cod. 103.

Zane, Lorenzo. *De difficillimae doctrinae palma capescenda*, to Giorgio Bevilacqua da Lazise. In G. degli Agostini, *Notizie*, I, 198-204.

Zeno, Apostolo, ed. *Istorici delle cose veneziane, i quali hanno scritto per pubblico decreto*. 10 vols. in 11 parts. Venice: appresso il Lovisa, 1718-1722.

Zeno, Jacopo. *Consolatio pro obitu matris*, to his brother Marino (Padua, 1 August 1434). British Museum, cod. Arundel 70, fols. 169-74.

―――. *Descriptio coniurationis patavine*, to his brother Marino (1435). In L. Bertalot, "Iacobi Zeni descriptio coniurationis patavine (das Ende des Letzten Carraresen 1435)," *Studien*, II, 109-28.

―――. [Laudatory letter to Ciriaco d'Ancona.] In L. Bertalot and A. Campana, "Gli scritti di Jacopo Zeno e il suo elogio di Ciriaco d'Ancona," pp. 323-32.

―――. *Vita Caroli Zeni*, to Pope Pius II (1458). Edited by Gasparo Zonta. In *Rerum italicarum scriptores*, New Ed., XIX, Part vi, fasc. 1-2 (Bologna: Nicola Zanichelli, 1940).

―――. *Vita B. Nicolai Cardinalis Albergati*, to Pietro Baro. In *Acta sanctorum*. Edited by G. Henschenius and D. Papebrochius, T. Maii 2 (3rd ed.; Paris and Rome: apud Victorem Palmé Biblipolam, 1866), 467-74.

Secondary Sources

Abbondanza, Roberto. [Review]. "Franco Gaeta, 'Il vescovo Pietro Barozzi' e il trattato 'De factionibus extinguendis.' " BIS, 1 (1959), 241-56.

Agostinelli, Lavinio, and Giovanni Benadduci. *Biografia e bibliografia di Giovan Mario Filelfo*. Tolentino: Stabilimento tipografico Francesco Filelfo, 1899.

degli Agostini, Giovanni. *Notizie istorico-critiche intorno la vita e le opere degli scrittori viniziani* [Agostini, *Notizie*]. 2 vols. Venice: S. Occhi, 1752, 1754.

Albareda, A. M. "Intorno alla fine del bibliotecario apostolico Giovanni Lorenzi." In *Miscellanea Pio Paschini: studi di storia ecclesiastica, Lateranum*, NS, 14-15 (Rome: Facultas Theologica Pontificii Athenaei Lateranensis, 1948-1949), II, 191-204.

Alberici, Giacomo. *Catalogo breve degl'illustri et famosi scrittori venetiani*. Bologna: presso gli heredi di G. Rossi, 1605.

Alcaro, Arturo. *Lodovico Scarampo*. I grandi cardinali italiani nella vita e nella storia, 5. Bologna: I. Cappelli, 1931.

d'Amico, John F. *Renaissance Humanism in Papal Rome: Humanists and Churchmen on the Eve of the Reformation*. Johns Hopkins University Studies in Historical and Political Science, 101st Series, 1. Baltimore and London: Johns Hopkins University Press, 1983.

Anecchini, Ferdinando. *Cenni biografici su Pietro Donà, Vescovo di Padova*. Nozze Albani-Donà dalle Rose/dalle Rose-Danioni. Padua: Tipografia del Seminario, 1900.

Antal, Frederick. *Florentine Painting and Its Social Background: The Bourgeois Republic before Cosimo de' Medici's Advent to Power, XIV and Early XV Centuries*. London: Kegan Paul, 1948.

Arnaldi, Girolamo. "Andrea Dandolo doge-cronista." In Pertusi, ed., *Storiografia veneziana*, pp. 127-268.

472

Avesani, Rino. "Una 'lectura' di Domenico da S. Gemignano erroneamente attribuita a Ermolao Barbaro il Vecchio." In *Misc. Branca*, III/1, 221-25.

Babinger, Franz. *Johannes Darius (1414-1494), Sachwalter Venedigs im Morgenland, und sein griechischer Umkreis.* Bayerische Akademie der Wissenschaften, philosophisch-historische Klasse, Sitzungsberichte, 1961, Heft 5. Munich: Verlag der Bayerischen Akademie, 1961.

――――. "Le vicende veneziane nella lotta contro i Turchi durante il secolo XV." In CVQ, pp. 49-73.

Banfi, Luigi. "Ermolao Barbaro, Venezia, ed il patriarcato di Aquileia." *Nuova antologia*, 91 (1956), 421-28.

Barbaro, Marco. *Arbori di patrizi veneti.* See "Primary Sources: Other Documents and Chronicles."

Baron, Hans. *The Crisis of the Early Italian Renaissance: Civic Humanism and Republican Liberty in an Age of Classicism and Tyranny.* 2nd ed. Princeton: Princeton University Press, 1966.

――――. "Franciscan Poverty and Civic Wealth in Humanist Thought." *Speculum*, 13 (1938), 1-37.

Barozzi, Luciano, and Remigio Sabbadini. *Studi sul Panormita e sul Valla.* Pubblicazioni del R. Istituto di Studi Superiori Practici e di Perfezionamento. Sezione di filosofia e filologia, 25. Florence: coi tipi dei successori di Monnier, 1891.

Baruffaldi, Girolamo. "Relazione, o sia esame d'un codice manoscritto del secolo XV, nel quale si contengono diversi opuscoli appartenenti, per qualche titolo, a Bernardo Bembo Cavalliere, e Senatore Veneziano." *Raccolta d'opuscoli scientifici e filologici* (edited by Angelo Calogerà), 26 (1742), 155-82.

Battaglia, Felice. "Il trattato 'De republica' di Tito Livio de' Frulovisi." *Rivista internazionale di filosofia del diritto*, 15 (1935), 487-505.

Bec, Christian. *Les Marchands écrivains à Florence, 1375-1434.* Paris: Ecole Pratique des Hautes Etudes (Mouton), 1967.

Beffa, Bruno. *Antonio Vinciguerra Cronico, segretario della Serenissima e letterato.* Publicazioni Universitarie Europee. Bern: Herbert Lang; Frankfurt: Peter Lang, 1975.

de Bellis, Daniela. " 'Autokineton' e 'Entelechia.' Niccolò Leonico Tomeo: l'anima nei Dialoghi intitolati al Bembo." *Annali dell'Istituto di Filosofia*, 1 (1979), 47-68.

――――. "Niccolò Leonico Tomeo interprete di Aristotele naturalista." *Physis*, 17 (1975), 71-93.

――――. "I veicoli dell'anima nell'analisi di Niccolò Leonico Tomeo." *Annali dell'Istituto di Filosofia*, 3 (1981), 1-21.

――――. "La vita e l'ambiente di Niccolò Leonico Tomeo." *Quaderni per la storia dell'Università di Padova*, 13 (1980), 37-75.

Benadduci, Giovanni. *A Jacopo Antonio Marcello patrizio veneto parte di orazione consolatoria ed elegia di Francesco Filelfo e lettera di Giovanni Mario Filelfo.* Nozze Marcello-Giustiniani (31 January 1891). Tolentino: Stabilimento Tipografico Francesco Filelfo, 1894.

Benzoni, A. "Un giudizio di Pietro Tommasi." *Ateneo veneto*, 30:2 (1907), 24-40.

Berlan, Francesco. *I due Foscari, memorie storico-critiche.* Turin: Tipografia G. Favale e Comp., 1852.

Berrigan, Joseph R. "The Latin Aesop of Ermolao Barbaro." *Manuscripta*, 22:3 (1978), 141-48.

――――. "The Latin Tragedy of the Quattrocento." *Humanistica lovaniensia*, 22 (1973), 1-9.

――――. "The *Libellus Fabellarum* of Gregorio Correr." *Manuscripta*, 19:3 (1975), 135-38.

Bersi, Ruggiero. "Le fonti della prima decade delle *Historiae rerum venetarum* di Marcantonio Sabellico." NAV, NS, 19, Parte II (1910), 422-60; 20, Parte I (1910), 115-62.

Bertalot, Ludwig. "Die älteste Briefsammlung des Gasparinus Barzizza." *Beiträge zur*

Forschung, Studien aus dem Antiquariat Jacques Rosenthal, N.F. 2 (Munich, 1929), 39-84. Rpt. Bertalot, *Studien zum italienischen und deutschen Humanismus*, II, 31-102.

———. "Jacobi Zeni descriptio coniurationis patavine (das Ende des letzten Carraresen 1435)." *Quellen und Forschungen aus italienischen Archiven und Bibliotheken*, 20 (1928-1929), 333-58. Rpt. Bertalot, *Studien zum italienischen und deutschen Humanismus*, II, 103-30.

———. "Eine Sammlung Paduaner Reden des XV. Jahrhunderts." *Quellen und Forschungen aus italienischen Archiven und Bibliotheken*, 26 (1935-1936), 245-67. Rpt. Bertalot, *Studien zum italienischen und deutschen Humanismus*, II, 209-36.

———. *Studien zum italienischen und deutschen Humanismus*. Edited by Paul Oskar Kristeller. 2 vols. Storia e Letteratura: Raccolta di Studi e testi, 129-30. Rome: Edizioni di storia e letteratura, 1975.

———. "Zwölf Briefe des Ambrogio Traversari." *Römische Quartalschrift*, 29 (1915), 91*-106*. Rpt. Bertalot, *Studien zum italienischen und deutschen Humanismus*, I, 251-67.

———, with A. Campana. "Gli scritti di Jacopo Zeno e il suo elogio di Ciriaco d'Ancona." *La bibliofilia*, 41 (1939-1940), 356-76. Rpt. Bertalot, *Studien zum italienischen und deutschen Humanismus*, II, 311-32.

———, with A. Wilmanns. "Lauri Quirini 'Dialogus in gymnasiis florentinis,' ein Nachklang zum 'Certame coronario.' " *Archivum Romanicum*, 7 (1923), 478-509. Rpt. Bertalot, *Studien zum italienischen und deutschen Humanismus*, I, 339-72.

Besta, E. *Il Senato veneziano (origine, costituzione, attribuzioni e riti)*. R. Deputazione di Storia Patria per le Venezia, Ser. IV: Miscellanea, Ser. II, 5 (Venice: la Deputazione, 1899).

Biadego, Giuseppe. *Catalogo descrittivo dei manoscritti della Biblioteca Comunale di Verona*. Verona: Stabilimento tipografico G. Civelli, 1892.

Bigi, Emilio. "Barbaro, Ermolao" [Vecchio]. DBI, VI (1964), 95-96.

———. "Barbaro, Ermolao" [Giovane]. DBI, VI (1964), 96-99.

Billanovich, G. "Alla scoperta di Leonardo Giustiniani." *Annali della R. Scuola Normale Superiore di Pisa*, Ser. 2, 8 (1939), 99-130, 333-57.

———. "Per l'edizione critica delle canzonette di Leonardo Giustiniani." GSLI, 110 (1937), 197-252.

Boèse, Helmut. *Die lateinischen Handschriften der Sammlung Hamilton zu Berlin*. Wiesbaden: Otto Harrassowitz, 1966.

"Bollani, Domenico." (Author unstated). DBI, XI (1969), 289-90.

Bolzonella, Mario. *Pietro Barozzi, Vescovo di Padova (1487-1507)*. Padua: Tipografia del "Messaggero," 1941.

Borsari, Silvano. "Barbaro, Zaccaria." DBI, VI (1964), 118-19.

———. "Barbo, Paolo." DBI, VI (1964), 254-55.

Bottin, Francesco. "Logica e filosofia naturale nelle opere di Paolo Veneto." In A. Poppi, ed., *Scienza e filosofia*, pp. 85-124.

Bouwsma, William J. *Venice and the Defense of Republican Liberty: Renaissance Values in the Age of the Counter-Reformation*. Berkeley and Los Angeles: University of California Press, 1968.

———. "Venice and the Political Education of Europe." In Hale, ed., *Renaissance Venice*, pp. 45-66.

Branca, Vittore. "Un codice aragonese scritto dal Cinico. La silloge di epistole di Francesco Barbaro offerta dal figlio Zaccaria a Re Ferrante." In *Studi di bibliografia e di storia in onore di Tammaro de Marinis*, 4 vols. Verona: stamperia Valdonega, 1964, I, 163-215.

———. "Ermolao Barbaro in Francia." In *Studi in onore di Carlo Pellegrini*, Biblioteca di studi francesi, 2. Turin: Società Editrice Internazionale di Torino, 1963, pp. 97-106.

———. "Ermolao Barbaro and Late Quattrocento Venetian Humanism." In Hale, ed., *Renaissance Venice*, pp. 218-43.

BIBLIOGRAPHY

————. "Ermolao Barbaro 'poeta' e la sua 'presentazione' alla corte degli Aragonesi." In *Classical, Medieval and Renaissance Studies in Honor of Berthold Louis Ullman*, edited by Charles Henderson, 2 vols. Rome: Edizioni di storia e letteratura, 1964, II, 385-411.

————. "Ermolao Barbaro e l'umanesimo veneziano." In UEUV, pp. 193-212.

————. "Lauro Quirini e il commercio librario a Venezia e Firenze." In *Venezia centro di mediazione tra Oriente e Occidente, secoli XV-XVI: Aspetti e problemi*, edited by H. G. Beck, M. Manoussacas, Agostino Pertusi. 2 vols. Florence, 1977, I, 369-77.

————. *Poliziano e l'umanesimo della parola*. Turin: Einaudi, 1983.

————. "Un trattato inedito di Ermolao Barbaro: il 'De coelibatu libri.' " BHR, 14 (1952), 83-98.

————. "L'umanesimo veneziano alla fine del Quattrocento, Ermolao Barbaro e il suo circolo." In *Storia della cultura veneta*, III/1, 123-75.

————, and Giorgio Padoan, eds. *Dante e la cultura veneta*. Fondazione Giorgio Cini, Civiltà Veneziana, Studi, 21. Florence: Leo S. Olschki, 1966.

Bratti, Ricciotti. *I codici nobiliari del Museo Correr di Venezia*. Rome: Collegio Araldico, 1908.

Braudel, Fernand. "La vita economica di Venezia nel secolo XVI." In CVR, pp. 81-102.

Breen, Quirinus. "Giovanni Pico della Mirandola on the Conflict of Philosophy and Rhetoric." *Journal of the History of Ideas*, 13 (1952), 384-426; rpt. in idem, *Christianity and Humanism*, edited by Nelson Peter Ross. Grand Rapids: William B. Eerdmans, 1968, pp. 1-68.

Brown, Alison. *Bartolomeo Scala, 1430-97, Chancellor of Florence: The Humanist as Bureaucrat*. Princeton: Princeton University Press, 1979.

Brown, Horatio F. *The Venetian Printing Press*. London: John C. Nimmo, 1891.

Brucker, Gene A. *The Civic World of Early Renaissance Florence*. Princeton: Princeton University Press, 1977.

————. "Humanism, Politics and the Social Order in Early Renaissance Florence." In *Florence and Venice*, I, 3-11.

Buck, August. " 'Laus Venetiae' und Politik im 16. Jahrhundert." *Archiv für Kulturgeschichte*, 57 (1975), 186-94.

Bughetti, Benvenuto. "Alcune lettere di Francesco Barbaro riguardanti l'Ordine Francescano." *Archivum Franciscanum historicum*, 11 (1918), 287-304.

Burke, Peter. "Back to Burckhardt." *New York Review of Books*. 26:15 (1979), 35-37.

————. *Culture and Society in Italy, 1420-1540*. London: B. T. Batsford; New York: Charles Scribner's Sons, 1972.

Bustico, Guido. "Due umanisti veneti: Urbano Bolzanio e Pierio Valeriano." *Civiltà moderna*, 4 (1932), 86-103; 344-79.

Caccamo, Domenico. "Buonaccorsi, Filippo." DBI, XV (1972), 78-83.

Campana, Augusto. "The Origin of the Word 'Humanist.' " JWCI, 9 (1946), 60-73.

Cappellari Vivaro, Girolamo Alessandro. *Il campidoglio veneto*. See "Primary Sources: Other Manuscript Locations."

Caravale, M. "Bernardo, Antonio." DBI, IX (1967), 304-305.

Carile, Antonio. "Aspetti della cronachista veneziana nei secoli XIII e XIV." In A. Pertusi, ed., *Storiografia veneziana*, pp. 75-126.

Carotti, Natale. "Un politico umanista del Quattrocento: Francesco Barbaro." RSI, Ser. 5, 2 (1937), 18-37.

Casarsa, Laura. "Contributi per la biografia di Gregorio Correr." *Quaderni della Facoltà di Magistero di Trieste, Miscellanea I (1979)*. Udine: Del Bianco Editore, 1979. I, 29-88.

Casella, Maria T., and Giovanni Pozzi. *Francesco Colonna, biografia e opere*. 2 vols. Medioevo e umanesimo, 1-2. Padua: Editrice Antenore, 1959.

Castellani, Carlo. "Il prestito dei codici manoscritti dalla Biblioteca di San Marco in

475

BIBLIOGRAPHY

Venezia ne' suoi primi tempi e le conseguenti perdite de' codici stessi." *Atti del RIV di SLA*, 55 (1896-1897), 311-77.

Castellani, Giorgio. "Documenti veneziani inediti relativi a Francesco e Mario Filelfo." *ASI*, Ser. 5, 17 (1896), 364-70.

————. "Giorgio da Trebisonda, maestro d'eloquenza a Vicenza ed a Venezia." *NAV*, 11 (1896), 123-42.

A Catalogue of the Manuscripts in the Library of the Hunterian Museum in the University of Glasgow. Edited by John Young, continued by P. Henderson Aitken. Glasgow: James Maclehose & Sons, 1908.

Catalogus translationum et commentariorum: Medieval and Renaissance Latin Translations and Commentaries [CTC]. Edited by P. O. Kristeller and F. Edward Cranz. Washington, D.C.: Catholic University of America Press. Vol. I, 1960; Vol. II, 1971; Vol. III, 1976; Vol. IV, 1980.

Cecchetti, Bartolomeo. "Una libreria circolante a Venezia nel secolo XV." *AV*, 32, Parte I (1886), 161-68.

————. "Libri, scuole, maestri, sussidii allo studio in Venezia nei secoli XIV e XV." *AV*, 32, Parte II (1886), 329-63.

Cenci, Cesare. "Senato veneto 'probae' ai benefizi ecclesiastici." See "Primary Sources: Published."

Cervelli, Innocenzo. "Storiografia e problemi intorno alla vita religiosa e spirituale a Venezia nella prima metà del '500." *SV*, 8 (1966), 447-76.

Cesarini, Remo. "Bologni, Girolamo." *DBI*, XI (1969), 327-31.

Cessi, Roberto. "La caduta di Costantinopoli nel 1453." *Atti del RIV di SLA*, 97 (1937-1938), Classe di scienze morali e letterarie, Parte II, 551-75.

————. "La giovinezza di Pietro Tommasi, erudito del secolo XV." *Athenaeum*, 1:2 (1913), 129-62.

————. "La 'Lega italica' e la sua funzione storica nella seconda metà del secolo XV." *Atti del RIV di SLA*, 102 (1942-1943), Classe di scienze morali e letterarie, Parte II, 99-176.

————. "Paolinismo preluterano." *Rendiconti delle sedute dell'Accademia Nazionale dei Lincei*, Classe di scienze morali, storiche e filologiche, Ser. 8, 12 (1957), 3-30.

————. *Storia della repubblica di Venezia*. 2 vols. Biblioteca Storica Principato, 23-24. Milan-Messina: Casa editrice Giuseppe Principato, 1944.

Chabod, Federico. "Venezia nella politica italiana ed europea del Cinquecento." In *CVR*, pp. 27-55.

Chambers, David S. *The Imperial Age of Venice, 1380-1580*. History of European Civilization Library. London: Thames and Hudson; New York: Harcourt Brace Jovanovich, 1970.

Chastel, André. "Art et humanisme au Quattrocento." In *UEUV*, pp. 395-405.

Chojnacki, Stanley. "Crime, Punishment, and the Trecento Venetian State." In Lauro Martines, ed., *Violence and Civil Disorder in Italian Cities, 1200-1500*, UCLA Center for Medieval and Renaissance Studies, Contributions, 5. Berkeley and Los Angeles: University of California Press, 1972, pp. 184-228.

————. "In Search of the Venetian Patriciate: Families and Factions in the Fourteenth Century." In Hale, ed., *Renaissance Venice*, pp. 47-90.

————. "Kinship Ties and Young Patricians in Fifteenth-Century Venice," *RQ*, 38 (1985), 240-70.

Cian, Vittorio. "Per Bernardo Bembo—I: Le sue relazioni coi Medici." *GSLI*, 28 (1896), 348-61.

————. "Per Bernardo Bembo—II: Le relazioni letterarie, i codici e gli scritti." *GSLI*, 31 (1898), 49-81.

————. *Un decennio della vita di M. Pietro Bembo (1521-1531)*. Turin: Ermanno Loescher, 1885.

————. "Pietro Bembo e Isabella d'Este Gonzaga." *GSLI*, 9 (1882), 81-136.

Cicogna, Emmanuele Antonio. *Della famiglia Marcello patrizia veneta narrazione*. Venice: dalla tipografia di G. B. Merlo, 1841.

BIBLIOGRAPHY

———. *Delle iscrizioni veneziane. [Iscrizioni].* 6 vols. Venice: G. Orlandelli, 1824-1853.

———. "Della Leandreide, poema anonimo inedito." *Memorie dell'IV di SLA,* 6 (1857), Parte II, 415-72.

La civiltà veneziana del Quattrocento [CVQ]. Fondazione Giorgio Cini, Centro di Cultura e Civiltà. Florence: Sansoni, 1957.

La civiltà veneziana del Rinascimento [CVR]. Fondazione Giorgio Cini, Centro di Cultura e Civiltà. Florence: Sansoni, 1958.

La civiltà veneziana del Trecento [CVT]. Fondazione Giorgio Cini, Centro di Cultura e Civiltà. Florence: Sansoni, 1956.

Cloetta, Wilhelm. "Gregorio Correr." In Cloetta, *Beiträge zur Literaturgeschichte des Mittelalters und der Renaissance,* I: *Die Anfänge der Renaissancetragödie* (Halle am S.: Max Niemeyer, 1892), Zweites Buch, C, 147-221.

Clough, Cecil H. "Becichemo, Marino." DBI, VII (1965), 511-15.

———. *Pietro Bembo's Library as Represented Particularly in the British Museum.* Rev. ed. London: British Museum, 1971.

———, ed. *Cultural Aspects of the Italian Renaissance: Essays in Honor of Paul Oskar Kristeller.* Manchester: Manchester University Press; New York: Alfred F. Zambelli, 1976.

Cochrane, Eric. *Historians and Historiography in the Italian Renaissance.* Chicago and London: University of Chicago Press, 1981.

Cogo, Gaetano. "Di Ognibene Scola, umanista padovano." NAV, 8 (1894), 115-71.

Coletti, L. "Le arti figurative." In CVT, pp. 111-45.

Collodo, Silvano. "Temi e caratteri della cronachista veneziana in volgare del Tre-Quattrocento (Enrico Dandolo)." SV, 9 (1967), 127-51.

Colombo, Cesare. "Gasparino Barzizza a Padova: nuovi ragguagli di lettere inedite." *Quaderni per la storia dell'Università di Padova,* 2 (1969), 1-28.

———, and Kristeller, P. O. "Some New Additions to the Correspondence of Guarino of Verona." IMU, 8 (1965), 213-48.

Connell, Susan. "Books and Their Owners in Venice, 1345-1480." JWCI, 35 (1972), 163-86.

Contarini, Giovanni Battista. *Anecdota veneta [Anec. ven.].* See Primary Sources: Other Manuscript and Published Works and Collections.

Cortesi, Mariarosa. "Alla scuola di Gian Pietro d'Avenza in Lucca." *Quellen und Forschungen aus italienischen Archiven und Bibliotheken,* 61 (1981), 109-67.

Cosenza, Mario Emilio. *Biographical and Bibliographical Dictionary of the Italian Humanists and of the World of Classical Scholarship in Italy, 1300-1800* [Cosenza, *Dict.*]. 2nd ed. 5 vols. Boston: G. K. Hall, 1962.

Coser, Lewis A. *Men of Ideas: A Sociologist's View.* New York: Free Press; London: Collier-Macmillan, 1965.

Coxe, H. O. *Catalogi codicum manuscriptorum Bibliothecae Bodleianae.* Pars III: *Codices graecos et latinos canonicianos complectens.* Oxford: e Typographeo academico, 1854.

Cozzi, Gaetano. "Authority and Law in Renaissance Venice." In Hale, ed., *Renaissance Venice,* pp. 293-345.

———. "Cultura politica e religione nella 'pubblica storiografia' veneziana del '500." BIS, 5-6 (1963-64), 215-94.

———. *Il doge Nicolò Contarini: ricerche sul patriziato veneziano agli inizi del Seicento.* Venice: Istituto per la Collaborazione Culturale, 1958.

———. "Domenico Morosini e il 'De bene instituta re pubblica.' " SV, 12 (1970), 405-58.

———. "Federico Contarini, un antiquario veneziano tra rinascimento e controriforma." BIS, 3 (1961), 190-221.

———. "Intorno all'edizione dell'opera di Marcantonio Sabellico, curata da Celio Secondo Curione e dedicata a Sigismondo Augusto re di Polonia." In *Venezia e la Polonia nei secoli dal XVII al XIX,* edited by Luigi Cini, Civiltà veneziana, Studi, 19. Venice: Istituto per la Collaborazione Culturale [1965], pp. 165-77.

BIBLIOGRAPHY

Cozzi, Gaetano. "Marino Sanuto il Giovane: dalla cronaca alla storia." RSI, 80 (1968), 297-314. Rpt. Pertusi, ed., *Storiografia veneziana*, pp. 333-58.

Cracco, Giorgio. "Badoer, Sebastiano." DBI, V (1963), 124-26.

————. "Barbarigo, Girolamo." DBI, VI (1964), 66-67.

————. "La cultura giuridico-politica nella Venezia della 'serrata.' " In SCV, II: Il Trecento, pp. 238-71.

————. "Patriziato e oligarchia a Venezia nel Tre-Quattrocento." In *Florence and Venice*, I, 71-98.

————. "Il pensiero storico di fronte ai problemi del comune veneziano." In Pertusi, ed., *Storiografia veneziana*, pp. 45-74.

————. *Società e stato nel medioevo veneziano, secoli XII-XIV*. Fondazione Giorgio Cini, Civiltà Veneziana, Studi, 22. Florence: Leo S. Olschki, 1967.

Dahrendorf, Rolf. "The Intellectual and Society: The Social Function of the 'Fool' in the Twentieth Century." In P. Rieff, ed., *On Intellectuals*. Garden City, N.Y.: Doubleday, 1969, pp. 49-52.

Dallari, Umberto. *I rotuli dei lettori legisti e artisti dello studio bolognese dal 1384 al 1799*. 4 vols. Bologna: Regia tipografia dei Fratelli Merlani, etc., 1888-1919.

Darnton, Robert. "Intellectual and Cultural History." In Michael Kammen, ed., *The Past Before Us: Contemporary Historical Writing in the United States*. Ithaca and London: Cornell University Press, 1980, pp. 327-55.

Davis, James C. *The Decline of the Venetian Nobility as a Ruling Class*. Johns Hopkins University, Studies in Historical and Political Science, Ser. 80 (1962), 2. Baltimore: Johns Hopkins University Press, 1962.

Dazzi, Manlio. "Documenti su Leonardo Giustinian." AV, Ser. 5, 15 (1934), 312-19.

————. "Leonardo Giustinian (1388-1446)." In UEUV, pp. 173-92.

————. *Leonardo Giustinian, poeta populare d'amore, con una scelta di sue poesie*. Bari: Giuseppe Laterza e Figli, 1934.

Diller, Aubrey. "The Library of Francesco and Ermolao Barbaro." IMU, 6 (1963), 253-62.

Dionisotti, Carlo. "Aldo Manuzio umanista." In UEUV, pp. 213-43.

————. "Bembo, Pietro." DBI, VIII (1966), 133-51.

————. "Chierici e laici nella letteratura italiana del primo Cinquecento." In *Problemi di vita religiosa in Italia nel Cinquecento. Atti del Convegno di Storia della Chiesa in Italia (Bologna, 2-6 settembre 1958)*. Padua: Editrice Antenore, 1960, pp. 167-85.

————. "Ermolao Barbaro e la fortuna di Suiseth." *Medioevo e rinascimento, studi in onore di Bruno Nardi*. Florence: G. C. Sansoni, 1955, pp. 217-54.

————. "Il Fortunio e la filologia umanistica." In RERV, pp. 11-23.

————. "Marcantonio Sabellico e Giovan Francesco Fortunio." In Dionisotti, *Gli umanisti e il volgare fra Quattro e Cinquecento* (Florence: Felice le Monnier, 1968), pp. 15-26.

————. "Niccolò Liburnio e la letteratura cortigiana." In RERV, pp. 26-37.

————. "Pietro Bembo e la nuova letteratura." In RERV, pp. 47-60.

Dizionario biografico degli italiani [DBI]. Rome: Istituto della Enciclopedia Italiana, 1960—.

Doglio, Maria Luisa. "Ambasciatore e principe: l'*Institutio legati* di Ermolao Barbaro." In *Misc. Branca*, III/1, 297-310.

Dorez, Leon. "La bibliothèque de Giovanni Marcanova (—— 1467)." *Mélanges G. B. de Rossi: Recueil de travaux publiés per l'Ecole Française de Rome en l'honneur de M. le Commandeur Giovanni Batista de Rossi*. Paris: E. Thorin, 1892 (= Mélanges d'archéologie et d'histoire, Supp. XII), pp. 113-26.

————. "Lettres inédites de Jean Pic de la Mirandole (1482-1492)." GSLI, 25 (1895), 352-61.

Dunston, A. J. "Pope Paul II and the Humanists." *Journal of Religious History*, 7 (1973), 287-306.

BIBLIOGRAPHY

Dupuigrenet Desroussilles, François. "L'università di Padova: dal 1405 al Concilio di Trento." In SCV, III/2, 607-47.

Edwards, William F. "Niccolò Leoniceno and the Origins of Humanist Discussion of Method." In Mahoney, ed., *Philosophy and Humanism*, pp. 283-305.

Eisenstadt, Samuel N., and Stephen R. Graubard, eds. *Intellectuals and Tradition. Daedalus*, 1972. Rpt. New York: Humanities Press, 1973.

Elwert, W. Theodor. "Pietro Bembo e la vita letteraria del suo tempo." In CVR, pp. 125-76.

———. *Studi di letteratura veneziana*. Fondazione Giorgio Cini, Centro di Cultura e Civiltà, Studi, 5. Venice: Istituto per la Collaborazione Culturale, 1958.

Eubel, Conrad. *Hierarchia catholica medii aevi* [Eubel, *Hier. cath.*]. 2nd ed. Vols. II, III. Monasterii: Sumptibus et Typis Librariae Regensbergianae, 1913, 1914.

Fabbri, Renata. "Le *Consolationes de obitu Valerii Marcelli* ed il Filelfo." In *Misc. Branca*, III/1, 227-50.

Facciolati, Jacopo. *Fasti gymnasii patavini* [Facciolati, *Fasti gymn. pat.*]. Padua: Typis Seminarii, apud Joannem Manfrè, 1757.

Fasoli, Gina. "I fondamenti della storiografia veneziana." In Pertusi, ed., *Storiografia veneziana*, pp. 11-44.

———. "Nascita di un mito." In *Studi storici in onore di Gioacchino Volpe per il suo 80 compleanno*. 2 vols. Florence: G. C. Sansoni, 1958, I, 445-79.

———. "Veneti e veneziani fra Dante e i primi commentatori." In Branca and Padoan, eds., *Dante e la cultura veneta*, pp. 71-85.

Favre, Guillaume. *Vie de Jean-Marius Philelphe*. In *Mélanges d'histoire litteraire par Guillaume Favre*, I. Geneva: Imprimerie Ramboz et Schuchardt, 1856, 2-221.

Fedalto, Giorgio. "Stranieri a Venezia e a Padova." In SCV, III/1, 499-535.

Fenigstein, Berthold. *Leonardo Giustiniani (1383?-1446), venetianischer Staatsmann, Humanist und Vulgärdichter*. Halle am Sein: Verlag von Max Niemeyer, 1909.

Ferriguto, Arnaldo. *Almorò Barbaro: l'alta cultura nel settentrione d'Italia nel '400, i "sacri canones" di Roma e le "santissime leze" di Venezia*. Deputazione Veneta di Storia Patria, Monumenti Storici, Ser. IV, Miscellanea di Storia Veneta, Ser. III, T. XV. Venice: la Società, 1922.

Finlay, Robert. "The Foundation of the Ghetto: Venice, the Jews, and the War of the League of Cambrai." *Proceedings of the American Philosophical Society*, 126 (1982), 140-54.

———. *Politics in Renaissance Venice*. New Brunswick, N.J.: Rutgers University Press, 1980.

———. "The Venetian Republic as a Gerontocracy: Age and Politics in the Renaissance." *Journal of Medieval and Renaissance Studies*, 8 (1978), 157-78.

———. "Venice, the Po Expedition, and the End of the League of Cambrai, 1509-1510." *Studies in Modern European History and Culture*, 2 (1976), 37-72.

Fiocco, Giuseppe. "Palla Strozzi e l'umanesimo veneto." In UEUV, pp. 349-58.

Firmin-Didot, Ambroise. *Alde Manuce et l'hellénisme à Venise*. Paris: Typographie d'Ambroise Firmin-Didot, 1875.

Flamini, Francesco. "Girolamo Ramusio (1450-86) e i suoi versi latini e volgari." *Atti e Memoire della R. Accademia di SLA in Padova*, NS, 16 (1899-1900), 11-41.

Florence and Venice: Comparisons and Relations. Acts of Two Conferences at Villa I Tatti in 1976-1977. 2 vols. I: *Quattrocento*. II: *Cinquecento*. Florence: La Nuova Italia Editrice, 1979, 1980.

Foffano, Francesco. "Marco Musuro, professore di greco a Padova ed a Venezia." NAV, 3 (1892), 453-72.

Folena, Gianfranco. "Il primo imitatore veneto di Dante, Giovanni Quirini." In Branca and Padoan, eds., *Dante e la cultura veneta*, pp. 395-421.

Foligno, Cesare. "Codici di materia veneta nelle biblioteche inglesi." NAV, 10 (1905), Parte I, 89-128; 11 (1906), Parte I, 171-86; Parte II, 162-93; 12 (1906), Parte I, 193-207; Parte II, 332-47; 13 (1907), Parte I, 185-200; Parte II, 352-63; 15 (1908), Parte I, 210-224.

BIBLIOGRAPHY

Foscarini, Marco. *Della letteratura veneziana ed altri scritti intorno essa [Letteratura veneziana]*. 2nd ed. by Francesco Berlan. Venice: co' tipi di Teresa Gattei, 1854 [orig. 1752].

———. *Dei veneziani raccoglitori di codici*. ASI, 5 (1843). Rpt. in *Letteratura veneziana*, 2nd ed. (1854), pp. 529-52.

Fossati, F. "Sulla partenza degli oratori Leonardo Botta da Venezia e Francesco Diedo da Milano." NAV, 14 (1907), Part II, 229-57.

Fragnito, Gigliola. "Cultura umanistica e riforma religiosa: il 'De officio boni viri ac probi episcopi' di Gasparo Contarini." SV, 11 (1969), 75-189.

Frati, Carlo. "Un codice autografo di Bernardo Bembo." In *Raccolta di studi critici dedicati ad Alessandro d'Ancona*. Florence: Tipografia di G. Barbèra, 1901, pp. 193-208.

Freudenberger, Theobald. "Die Bibliothek des Kardinals Domenico Grimani." *Historische Jahrbuch*, 56 (1936), 15-45.

Fubini, Riccardo. "Biondo, Flavio." DBI, X (1968), 536-39.

Fulin, Rinaldo. "Documenti per servire alla storia della tipografia veneziana." AV, 23 (1882), 84-212; 390-405.

———. "Primi privilegi di stampa a Venezia." AV, 1 (1871).

Gabotto, Ferdinando. "Giorgio Valla e il suo processo in Venezia nel 1496." NAV, NS, 1 (1891), 201-20.

———. "Un nuovo contributo alla storia dell' umanesimo ligure." *Atti della Società Ligura di Storia Patria*, 24 (1892), 5-323.

———, and A. Badini Confalonieri. "Vita di Giorgio Merula." *Rivista di storia, arte, archeologia della Provincia di Alessandria*, 2 (1893), 7-66, 281-356; 3 (1894), 3-70, 151-75, 227-350.

Gaeta, Franco. "Alcune considerazioni sul mito di Venezia." BHR, 23 (1961), 58-75.

———. "Barbo, Niccolò." DBI, VI (1964), 252-53.

———. "Barozzi, Pietro." DBI, VI (1964), 510-12.

———. "Giorgio da Trebisonda, le 'Leggi' di Platone e la costituzione di Venezia." *Bullettino dell'Istituto Storico Italiano per il Medio Evo e Archivio Muratoriano*, 82 (1970), 479-501.

———. "Storiografia, coscienza nazionale e politica culturale nella Venezia del rinascimento." In SCV, III/1, 1-91.

———. "Sul 'de potestate pontificis' di Gasparo Contarini." *Rivista della storia della chiesa in Italia*, 13 (1959), 391-96.

———. *Il vescovo Pietro Barozzi e il trattato De factionibus extinguendis [DFE]*. Fondazione Giorgio Cini, Civiltà Veneziana, Saggi, 3. Venice-Rome: Istituto per la Collaborazione Culturale, 1958.

Gams, Pius Bonifacius. *Series episcoporum ecclesiae catholicae*, with *supplementa* [Gams, *Ser. episc.*]. Regensburg: Josef Manz, 1873-86; München: Ernst Stahl, 1879 (Supp. I); Regensburg: Josef Manz, 1886 (Supp. II). Rpt. Graz: Akademische Druck-u. Verlaganstalt, 1957.

Gardenal, Gianna. "Cronologia della vita e delle opere di Giorgio Valla." In *Giorgio Valla tra scienza e sapienza*, Appendix, pp. 93-97.

———. "Lodovico Foscarini e la medicina." In *Misc. Branca*, III/1, 251-63.

Gargan, Luciano. *Cultura e arte nel Veneto al tempo del Petrarca*. Ente Nazionale Francesco Petrarca, Studi sul Petrarca, 5. Padua: Editrice Antenore, 1978.

———. "Il preumanesimo a Vicenza, Treviso e Venezia." In SCV/II: *Il Trecento*, pp. 142-70.

———. *Lo studio teologico e la biblioteca dei Domenicani a Padova nel Tre e Quattrocento*. Contributi alla storia dell'Università di Padova, 6. Padua: Editrice Antenore, 1971.

Garin, Eugenio. "I cancellieri umanisti della repubblica fiorentina da Coluccio Salutati a Bartolomeo Scala." RSI, 81 (1959), 185-208. Rpt. Garin, *Scienza e vita civile nel rinascimento italiano* (Bari: Laterza, 1972), pp. 1-32.

——. "Cultura filosofica toscana e veneta nel Quattrocento." *Rinascimento*, Ser. 2, 2 (1962), 57-75. Rpt. in UEUV, pp. 11-30.

——. "La cultura milanese nella prima metà del XV secolo." In *Storia di Milano*, V. Milan: Fondazione Treccani degli Alfieri per la Storia di Milano, 1955, 547-608.

——. "La cultura milanese nella seconda metà del XV secolo." In *Storia di Milano*, VI. Milan: Fondazione Treccani degli Alfieri per la Storia di Milano, 1956, 539-97.

——. *Italian Humanism, Philosophy and Civic Life in the Renaissance*. Translated by Peter Munz. Oxford: Basil Blackwell, 1965 [orig. *Der italienische Humanismus*. Bern, 1947].

——. *La letteratura degli umanisti*. In *Storia della letteratura italiana*, edited by Emilio Cecchi and Natalino Sapegno, III: *Il Quattrocento e l'Ariosto* (Milan: Garzanti, 1965 [1966]), pp. 7-353.

——. *Prosatori latini del Quattrocento*. See Primary Sources: Other Manuscript and Published Works and Collections.

——. "Le traduzioni umanistiche di Aristotele nel secolo XV." *Atti e memorie dell'Accademia Fiorentina di Scienze Morali "La Columbaria,"* 16 (1947-1950), 55-104.

Gasquet, Francis A., Cardinal. *Cardinal Pole and His Early Friends*. London: G. Bell & Sons, 1927.

Geanakoplos, Deno J. *Greek Scholars in Venice: Studies in the Dissemination of Greek Learning from Byzantium to the West*. Cambridge: Harvard University Press, 1962.

Gerulaitis, Leonardas V. *Printing and Publishing in Fifteenth-Century Venice*. Chicago: American Library Association; London: Mansell Information Publishing, 1976.

Giannetto, Nella. "Un messaggio autografo di Bernardo Bembo a Baldassar Castiglione." Lettere italiane, 32 (1980), 235-43.

——. "Un'orazione inedita di Bernardo Bembo per Cristoforo Moro." *Atti dell' IV di SLA*, 140 (1981-82), Classe di scienze morali, lettere ed arti, 257-88.

Gianturco, Elio. "Bodin's Conception of the Venetian Constitution." *Revue de littérature comparée*, 18 (1938), 684-95.

Gilbert, Felix. "Biondo, Sabellico, and the Beginnings of Venetian Official Historiography." In J. G. Rowe and W. H. Stockdale, eds., *Florilegium Historiale: Essays Presented to Wallace K. Ferguson* (Toronto: University of Toronto Press, 1971), pp. 275-93.

——. "Contarini on Savonarola: An Unknown Document of 1516." *Archiv für Reformationsgeschichte*, 59 (1968), 145-50.

——. "Cristianesimo, umanesimo e la bolla 'Apostolici Regiminis' del 1513." RSI, 79 (1967), 976-90.

——. "The Date of the Composition of Contarini's and Giannotti's Books on Venice." *Studies in the Renaissance*, 14 (1967), 172-84.

——. *History: Choice and Commitment*. Cambridge, Mass. and London: Belknap Press of Harvard University Press, 1977.

——. "Humanism in Venice." In *Florence and Venice*, I, 13-26.

——. "The Last Will of a Venetian Grand Chancellor." In Mahoney, ed., *Philosophy and Humanism*, pp. 502-17.

——. "Religion and Politics in the Thought of Gasparo Contarini." In Theodore K. Rabb and Jerrold E. Seigel, eds., *Action and Conviction in Early Modern Europe: Essays in Memory of E. H. Harbison*. Princeton: Princeton University Press, 1969, pp. 90-116. Rpt. Gilbert, *History: Choice and Commitment*, pp. 247-67.

——. "The Venetian Constitution in Florentine Political Thought." In Nicolai Rubinstein, ed., *Florentine Studies: Politics and Society in Renaissance Florence* (Evanston, Ill.: Northwestern University Press, 1968), pp. 463-500. Rpt. Gilbert, *History: Choice and Commitment*, pp. 179-214.

——. "Venetian Diplomacy before Pavia: from Myth to Reality." In J. H. Elliott and H. G. Koenigsberger, eds., *The Diversity of History: Essays in Honor of Sir Herbert*

BIBLIOGRAPHY

Butterfield. London: Routledge and Kegan Paul, 1971, pp. 79-116. Rpt. Gilbert, *History: Choice and Commitment*. pp. 295-321.

——. "Venice in the Crisis of the League of Cambrai." In Hale, ed., *Renaissance Venice*, pp. 274-92. Rpt. Gilbert, *History: Choice and Commitment*, pp. 269-91.

Gilmore, Myron. "Myth and Reality in Venetian Political Theory." In Hale, ed., *Renaissance Venice*, pp. 431-44.

Giomo, G. *Indice per nome di donna dei matrimoni dei patrizi veneti*. See "Primary Sources: Published."

Giorgio Valla tra scienza e sapienza: studi di Gianna Gardenal, Patrizia Landucci Ruffo, Cesare Vasoli. Edited by Vittore Branca. Florence: Leo S. Olschki, 1981.

Giustiniani, Vito R. "Sulle traduzioni latine delle 'Vite' di Plutarco nel Quattrocento." *Rinascimento*, Ser. 2, 1 (1961), 3-62.

Gloria, Andrea. *Monumenti della Università di Padova, 1318-1405*. 2 vols. Padua: Tipografia del Seminario, 1888.

Le Goff, Jacques. "Dépenses universitaires à Padoue au XVe siècle." *Mélanges d'archéologie et d'histoire de l'Ecole Française de Rome*, 68 (1956), 376-95.

Gothein, Percy. "L'amicizia fra Ludovico Foscarini e l'umanista Isotta Nogarola." *Rinascita*, 6 (1943), 394-413.

——. *Francesco Barbaro (1390-1454): Frühhumanismus und Staatskunst in Venedig*. Berlin: Verlag die Runde, 1932.

——. "Paolo Veneto e Prosdocimo de' Conti maestri padovani di Lodovico Foscarini." *Rinascita*, 5 (1942), 236-43.

——. "Zaccaria Trevisan." AV, Ser. 5, 21 (1937), 1-59.

——. *Zaccaria Trevisan il Vecchio: La vita e l'ambiente*. R. Deputazione di Storia Patria per le Venezia, Miscellanea di Studi e Memorie, IV. Venice: la Deputazione, 1942. German version: *Zacharias Trevisan, Leben und Umkreis*. Amsterdam-Antwerp: Pantheon Verlag, 1944.

Gouldner, Alvin W. *The Future of Intellectuals and the Rise of the New Class*. New York: Seabury Press, 1979.

Govi, Eugenia. "La biblioteca di Jacopo Zeno." *Bollettino dell'Istituto di Patalogia del Libro*, 10 (1951), 34-118.

——. "Petri Barocii bibliothecae inventarium." Appendix of *Patavinae cathedralis ecclesiae capitularis bibliotheca librorum XV saec. impressorum index*. Padua: Typographia Antoniana, 1958, pp. 143-70.

Grayson, Cecil. "Alberti, Poliziano, e Bernardo Bembo." In *Poliziano e il suo tempo. Atti del IV Convegno Internazionale di Studi sul Rinascimento*. Florence: G. C. Sansoni, 1957, pp. 111-17.

——. "Un codice del 'De re aedificatoria' posseduto da Bernardo Bembo." In *Studi letterari: Miscellanea in onore di Emilio Santini*. Palermo: Palermo Università, Lettere e Filosofia, 1956, pp. 181-88. Reprinted with alterations as "Alberti, Poliziano, e Bernardo Bembo."

Grendler, Paul F. *Critics of the Italian World, 1530-1560: Anton Francesco Doni, Nicolò Franco, and Ortensio Lando*. Madison: University of Wisconsin Press, 1969.

——. "Five Italian Occurrences of Umanista, 1540-1574." RQ, 20 (1967), 317-24.

——. "Francesco Sansovino and Italian Popular History, 1560-1600." *Studies in the Renaissance*, 16 (1969), 139-80.

——. *The Roman Inquisition and the Venetian Press, 1540-1605*. Princeton: Princeton University Press, 1977.

Griggio, Claudio. "Il codice berlinese lat. fol. 667: nuove lettere di Francesco Barbaro." In *Misc. Branca*, III/1, 133-75.

Gualdo, Germano. "Barbaro, Francesco." DBI, VI (1964), 101-103.

——. "Barbo, Marco." DBI, VI (1964), 249-52.

Hale, John R., ed. *Renaissance Venice*. London: Faber & Faber; Totowa, N.J.: Rowman & Littlefield, 1973.

Haller, Johannes. *Pier da Monte, ein Gelehrter und päpstlicher Beamter des 15. Jahr-*

hunderts: Seine Briefsammlung. Bibliothek des Deutschen Historischen Instituts in Rom, 19. Rome: W. Regenberg, 1941.

Hazlitt, William C. *The Venetian Republic, Its Rise, Its Growth, and Its Fall, A.D. 409-1797.* 4th ed. 2 vols. London: Adam and Charles Black, 1915.

Heiberg, Johan L. *Beiträge zur Geschichte Georg Vallas und seiner Bibliothek. Centralblatt für Bibliothekswesen,* Beiheft XVI. Leipzig: Otto Harassowitz, 1896, pp. 353-481 (= 1-129).

————. "Nachträgliches über Georg Valla." *Centralblatt für Bibliothekswesen,* 15 (1898), 189-97.

Herde, Peter. "Politik und Rhetorik in Florenz am Vorabend der Renaissance." *Archiv für Kulturgeschichte,* 47 (1965), 141-220.

Hill, Juliana Cotton. "Caldiera, Giovanni." DBI, XVI (1973), 626-28.

de Huszar, George B., ed. *The Intellectuals: A Controversial Portrait.* Glencoe, Ill.: Free Press, 1960.

Hyde, J. K. *Padua in the Age of Dante: A Social History of an Italian City-State.* Manchester: Manchester University Press; New York: Barnes & Noble, 1966.

————. [Review], L. Gargan, *Cultura e arte.* RQ, 33 (1980), 95-96.

Jedin, Hubert. "Contarini und Camaldoli." *Archivio italiano per la storia della pietà,* 2 (1959), 51-117.

————. "Gasparo Contarini e il contributo veneziano alla riforma cattolica." In CVR, pp. 103-24.

————. *Studien über Domenico de' Domenichi (1416-1478).* Akademie der Wissenschaften und der Literatur, Abhandlungen der Geistes- und Socialwissenschaftlichen Klasse, 5. Wiesbaden: F. Steiner, 1957, pp. 175-300.

————. "Ein 'Turmerlebnis' des jungen Contarini." *Historisches Jahrbuch,* 70 (1950), 115-30.

Kibre, Pearl. "Cardinal Domenico Grimani, *Quaestio de Intensione et Remissione Qualitatis*: A Commentary on the Tractate of that Title by Richard Suiseth (Calculator)." In *Didascaliae: Studies in Honor of Anselm M. Albareda,* edited by Sesto Prete (New York: Bernard M. Rosenthal, 1961), 147-203.

King, Margaret L. "Caldiera and the Barbaros on Marriage and the Family: Humanist Reflections of Venetian Realities." *Journal of Medieval and Renaissance Studies,* 6 (1976), 19-50.

————. "The Patriciate and the Intellectuals: Power and Ideas in Quattrocento Venice." *Soundings,* 5 (1975), 295-312.

————. "Personal, Domestic and Republican Values in the Moral Philosophy of Giovanni Caldiera." RQ, 28 (1975), 535-74.

————. "The Religious Retreat of Isotta Nogarola." *Signs,* 3 (1978), 807-22.

————. "A Study in Venetian Humanism at Mid-Quattrocento: Filippo da Rimini and His *Symposium de paupertate* (Study and Text)." SV, NS, Part One: 2 (1978), 75-96; Part Two: 3 (1979), 141-86; Part Three: 4 (1980), 27-44.

————. "Venetian Ideology and the Reconstruction of Knowledge: Giovanni Caldiera (c.1400-c.1474)." Ph.D. dissertation, Stanford University, 1972.

————, and Albert Rabil, Jr., eds. *Her Immaculate Hand.* See Primary Sources: Other Manuscript and Published Works and Collections.

Kohl, Benjamin G. "Conversino, Giovanni, da Ravenna." In DBI, XXVIII (1983), 574-78.

————. "The Manuscript Tradition of Some Works of Giovanni da Ravenna." In *Acta Conventus Neo-Latini Amstelodamensis, Proceedings of the Second International Congress of Neo-Latin Studies (Amsterdam, 19-24 August 1973),* edited by P. Tuynman et al. Munich: Wilhelm Fink Verlag, 1979, pp. 610-19.

————. "The Works of Giovanni di Conversino da Ravenna: A Catalogue of Manuscripts and Editions." *Traditio,* 31 (1975), 351-67.

————, and Ronald Witt, eds. *The Earthly Republic.* See Primary Sources: Other Manuscript and Published Works and Collections.

BIBLIOGRAPHY

Krautter, Konrad; Paul Oskar Kristeller, and Helmut Roob, eds. "Tre trattati di Lauro Quirini sulla nobiltà." In LQU, pp. 19-102.

Kretschmayr, Heinrich. *Geschichte von Venedig.* 3 vols. II: *Die Blüte.* Gotha: Friedrich Andreas Perthes A.-G., 1920. Rpt. Darmstadt: Sonderausgabe für die Mitglieder der Wissenschaftlichen Buchgesellschaft, 1964.

Kristeller, Paul Oskar. "Un codice padovano di Aristotele postillato da Francesco ed Ermolao Barbaro: il manoscritto Plimpton 17 della Columbia University Library." *La bibliofilia,* 50 (1948), 162-78. Rpt. in Kristeller, *Studies in Renaissance Thought and Letters,* pp. 337-353.

——. "Il codice Plimpton 187 della Columbia University Library e gli scritti di Lauro Quirini sulla nobiltà." In *Miscellanea Marciana di Studi Bessarionei,* Medioevo e umanesimo, 24. Padua: Editrice Antenore, 1976, pp. 201-22.

——. "The Contribution of Religious Orders to Renaissance Thought and Learning." *American Benedictine Review,* 21 (1970), 1-55. Rpt. in Kristeller, *Medieval Aspects of Renaissance Learning,* edited and translated by Edward P. Mahoney, Duke Monographs in Medieval and Renaissance Studies, 1. Durham, N.C.: Duke University Press, 1974, pp. 95-158.

——. *Eight Philosophers of the Italian Renaissance.* Stanford: Stanford University Press, 1964.

——. "Giovanni Pico della Mirandola and His Sources." In *L'opera e il pensiero di Giovanni Pico della Mirandola nella storia dell' umanesimo, convegno internazionale (Mirandola: 15-18 settembre 1963).* 2 vols. Florence: Istituto Nazionale di Studi sul Rinascimento, 1965, pp. 35-42.

——. "The Humanist Bartolomeo Facio and His Unknown Correspondence." In *From the Renaissance to the Counter-Reformation: Essays in Honor of Garrett Mattingly,* edited by Charles H. Carter. New York: Random House, 1965, pp. 56-74.

——. "The Humanist Movement." In Kristeller, *Renaissance Thought and Its Sources,* edited by M. Mooney, pp. 21-32.

——. *Iter Italicum: A Finding List of Uncatalogued or Incompletely Catalogued Humanistic Manuscripts of the Renaissance in Italian and Other Libraries* [Kristeller, *Iter*]. 3 vols. and continuing. London: Warburg Institute; Leiden: E. J. Brill, 1963, 1967, 1983.

——. *Latin Manuscript Books before 1600.* 3rd ed. New York: Fordham University Press, 1965.

——. "Marsilio Ficino e Venezia." In *Misc. Branca,* III/2, 475-92.

——. "Niccolò Perotti ed i suoi contributi alla storia dell'umanesimo." *Res Publica Litterarum,* 4 (1981), 7-25.

——. "Il Petrarca, l'umanesimo e la scolastica a Venezia." In CVT, pp. 149-78.

——. "Petrarch's 'Averroists.' A Note on the History of Aristotelianism in Venice, Padua and Bologna." *Mélanges Augustin Renaudet,* BHR, 14 (1952), 59-65.

——. *The Philosophy of Marsilio Ficino.* Translated by Virginia Conant. New York: Columbia University Press, 1943.

——. *Renaissance Concepts of Man and Other Essays.* New York: Harper & Row, 1972.

——. *Renaissance Thought: The Classic, Scholastic and Humanistic Strains.* New York: Harper & Row, 1961.

——. *Renaissance Thought II: Papers on Humanism and the Arts.* New York: Harper & Row, 1965.

——. *Renaissance Thought and Its Sources.* Edited by Michael Mooney. New York: Columbia University Press, 1979.

——. *Studies in Renaissance Thought and Letters.* Rome: Edizioni di storia e letteratura, 1956.

——. *Supplementum Ficinianum: Marsilii Ficini Florentini opuscula inedita et dispersa.* Florence: Leo S. Olschki, 1937.

―――. *La tradizione aristotelica nel rinascimento*. Saggi e Testi, 2. Padua: Editrice Antenore, 1962.

―――. "An Unknown Letter of Giovanni Barbo To Guarino." In Colombo and Kristeller, "Some New Additions to the Correspondence of Guarino da Verona," pp. 243-48.

Labalme, Patricia H. *Bernardo Giustiniani: A Venetian of the Quattrocento*. Uomini e Dottrine, 13. Rome: Edizioni di Storia e Letteratura, 1969.

―――. "The Last Will of a Venetian Patrician (1489)." In Mahoney, ed., *Philosophy and Humanism*, pp. 483-501.

Labowsky, Lotte. "Bessarione." DBI, IX (1967), 686-96.

―――. *Bessarion's Library and the Biblioteca Marciana: Six Early Inventories*. Sussidi eruditi, 31. Rome: Edizioni di storia e letteratura, 1979.

Lane, Frederic C. "The Enlargement of the Great Council of Venice." In J. G. Rowe and W. H. Stockdale, eds., *Florilegium Historiale: Essays Presented to Wallace K. Ferguson* (Toronto: University of Toronto Press, 1971), pp. 236-74.

―――. "Naval Actions and Fleet Organization, 1499-1502." In Hale, ed., *Renaissance Venice*, pp. 146-73.

―――. "Recent Studies on the Economic History of Venice." *Journal of Economic History*, 23 (1963), 312-34.

―――. *Venice: A Maritime Republic*. Baltimore: Johns Hopkins University Press, 1973.

Lauro Quirini umanista: studi e testi a cura di Konrad Krautter, P. O. Kristeller, Agostino Pertusi, Giorgio Ravegnani, Helmut Roob e Carlo Seno. [LQU]. Edited by Vittore Branca. Fondazione Giorgio Cini, Civiltà Veneziana, Saggi, 23. Florence: Leo S. Olschki, 1977.

Lazzarini, Lino. "Amici del Petrarca a Venezia e Treviso." AV, Ser. 5, 14 (1933), 1-14.

―――. " 'Dux ille Danduleus,' Andrea Dandolo e la cultura veneziana a metà del Trecento." In Padoan, ed., *Petrarca, Venezia e il Veneto*, pp. 123-56.

―――. "Francesco Petrarca e il primo umanesimo a Venezia." In UEUV, pp. 63-92.

―――. "Un libro su Francesco Barbaro." ASI, Ser. 7, 20 (1933), 97-104.

―――. "Nuovi documenti su Giovanni Gerolamo Nadal e la *Leandreide*." In *Misc. Branca*, II, 377-404.

―――. *Paolo de Bernardo e i primordi dell'umanesimo in Venezia*. Biblioteca dell' "Archivum Romanicum," 13. Geneva: Leo S. Olschki, 1930.

Lazzarini, Vittorio. "Beni carraresi e proprietari veneziani." In *Studi in onore di Gino Luzzatto*. 4 vols. Milan: A. Giuffrè, 1949-1950, I, 274-88.

―――. "I più antichi codici di Dante." NAV, 41 (1921), Parte I, 171-74.

―――. "Il preteso documento della fondazione di Venezia e la cronaca del medico Jacopo Dondi." *Atti del RIV di SLA*, 75 (1915-1916), Parte II, 1263-81.

―――. *Rimatori veneziani del secolo XIV*. Padua: Stabilimento Tipografico Veneto, 1887.

Ledos, Eugène-Gabriel. "Lettre inédite de Cristoforo Landino à Bernardo Bembo." *Bibliothèque de l'Ecole des Chartes*, 54 (1893), 721-24.

Lee, Egmont. *Sixtus IV and Men of Letters*. Temi e testi, 26. Rome: Edizioni di storia e letteratura, 1978.

Leicht, Pier S. "Ideali di vita dei veneziani del Cinquecento." AV, Ser. 5, 14 (1933), 217-31.

di Lennas, Niccolò. "Giosafat Barbaro (1413-94) e i suoi viaggi nella regione russa (1436-51) e nella Persia (1474-78)." NAV, 28 (1914), 5-105.

Lepori, Fernando. "Bruto, Pietro." DBI, XIV (1972), 735-37.

―――. "La scuola di Rialto dalla fondazione alla metà del Cinquecento." In SCV, III/2, 539-605.

Levi, Eugenia. "Lo zibaldone di Bernardo Bembo." *Rassegna della letteratura italiana*, 4 (1896), 46-50.

Libby, Lester J. "Venetian History and Political Thought after 1509." *Studies in the Renaissance*, 20 (1973), 7-45.

I libri commemoriali della republica di Venezia: regesti. Edited by Riccardo Predelli. See "Primary Sources: Published."

Linz, Juan J. "Intellectual Roles in Sixteenth- and Seventeenth-Century Spain." In Eisenstadt and Graubard, eds., *Intellectuals and Tradition,* pp. 59-108.

Logan, Oliver. *Culture and Society in Venice, 1470-1790: The Renaissance and Its Heritage.* London: B. T. Batsford; New York: Charles Scribner's Sons, 1972.

————. "The Ideal of the Bishop and the Venetian Patriciate: c. 1430-c. 1630." *Journal of Ecclesiastical History,* 29 (1978), 415-50.

Lopez, Robert S. "Il principio della guerra veneto-turca nel 1463." AV, Ser. 5, 15 (1934), Parte I, 45-131.

Lowry, M.J.C. "The 'New Academy' of Aldus Manutius: A Renaissance Dream." *Bulletin of the John Rylands Library,* 58 (1976), 378-420.

————. "Two Great Venetian Libraries in the Age of Aldus Manutius." *Bulletin of the John Rylands Library,* 57 (1974), 128-66.

————. *The World of Aldus Manutius: Business and Scholarship in Renaissance Venice.* Ithaca, N.Y.: Cornell University Press; Oxford: Basil Blackwell, 1979.

de Luca, Giuseppe. "Letteratura de pietà." In CVT, pp. 207-30.

————. *Letteratura di pietà a Venezia dal '300 al '600.* Edited by Vittore Branca. Lettere italiane, 3. Florence: Leo S. Olschki, 1963.

Ludwig, Walther. "Titus Livius de' Frulovisi—ein humanistischer Dramatiker der Renaissance." *Humanistica Lovaniensia,* 22 (1973), 39-76.

Luzzatto, Gino. "L'economia veneziana nei secoli '400 e '500." *Bergomum,* 58 (1964), 57-71.

————. "Navigazione di linea e navigazione libera nelle grandi città marinare del Medio Evo." [1941]. In Luzzatto, *Studi di storia economica veneziana,* pp. 53-79.

————. "Les noblesses: les activités économiques du patriciat vénitien (X^e-XIVe siècles)." *Annales: ESC,* 9 (1937), 25-57. Rpt. in Luzzatto, *Studi di storia economica veneziana,* pp. 125-65.

————. "Per la storia delle costruzioni navali a Venezia nei secoli XV e XVI." [1931]. In Luzzatto, *Studi di storia economica veneziana,* pp. 37-51.

————. *Storia economica di Venezia dall'XI al XVI secolo.* Venice: Centro Internazionale delle Arti e del Costume, 1961.

————. *Studi di storia economica veneziana.* Istituto Universitario di Economia e Commercio Veneziano. Padua: Cedam, 1954.

Magni, Domenico. "Gasparino Barzizza—una figura del primo umanesimo." *Bergomum,* 11:2-4 (1937), 104-18, 143-70, 205-22.

Mahoney, Edward P., ed. *Philosophy and Humanism: Renaissance Essays in Honor of Paul Oskar Kristeller.* Leiden: E. J. Brill, 1976.

————. "Philosophy and Science in Nicoletto Vernia and Agostino Nifo." In Poppi, ed., *Scienza e filosofia,* pp. 135-202.

Mallett, Michael. "Preparations for War in Florence and Venice in the Second Half of the Fifteenth Century." In *Florence and Venice,* I, 149-64.

————. "Venice and Its Condottieri, 1404-54." In Hale, ed., *Renaissance Venice,* pp. 121-45.

Manfroni, C. "La battaglia di Gallipoli e la politica veneto-turca (1381-1420)." *Ateneo veneto,* 25 (1902), Parte II, 3-34, 129-69.

Mann, Nicholas. "Benintendi Ravagnani, il Petrarca, l'umanesimo veneziano." In Padoan, ed., *Petrarca, Venezia e il Veneto,* pp. 109-22.

————. "Petrarca e la cancelleria veneziana." In SCV/II: *Il Trecento,* pp. 517-35.

Mannheim, Karl. *Ideology and Utopia: An Introduction to the Sociology of Knowledge.* Translated by Louis Wirth and Edward Shils. London: K. Paul, Trench, Trubner; New York: Harcourt Brace, 1936.

————. "The Problem of Generations." In Mannheim, *Essays on the Sociology of Knowledge.* New York: Oxford University Press, 1952, pp. 276-320.

————. "The Sociological Problem of the 'Intelligentsia.' " In de Huszar, ed., *The Intellectutals. A Controversial Portrait,* pp. 62-68.

Maranini, G. *La costituzione di Venezia dopo la serrata del Maggior Consiglio.* Venice, Perugia, Florence: 'La Nuova Italia' Editrice, 1931.

Martellotti, Guido. "Barzizza, Gasparino." DBI, VII (1965), 34-39.

Martene, Edmond, and Ursin Durand. *Veterum scriptorum et monumentorum historicorum, dogmataticorum, moralium amplissima collectio.* See Primary Sources: Other Manuscript and Published Works and Collections.

von Martin, Alfred. *Sociology of the Renaissance.* Translated by W. L. Luetkens. London: Kegan Paul, Trench, Trübner & Co., 1944. Rpt. New York: Harper & Row, 1963.

Martin, Henri. "Sur un portrait de Jacques-Antoine Marcelle, sénateur vénitien (1453)." *Mémoires de la société nationale des antiquaires de France, 59* [= Ser. 6, vol. 9] (1898), 229-67.

Martines, Lauro. *Lawyers and Statecraft in Renaissance Florence.* Princeton: Princeton University Press, 1968.

———. *Power and Imagination: City-States in Renaissance Italy.* New York: Alfred A. Knopf, 1979.

———. *The Social World of the Florentine Humanists.* Princeton: Princeton University Press, 1963.

Marx, Barbara. *Bartolomeo Pagello: Epistolae familiares (1464-1525), Materialien zur Vicentiner Kulturgeschichte des 15. Jahrhunderts und kritische Edition des Briefwechsels.* Padua: Editrice Antenore, 1978.

———. "Venedig—'Altera Roma,' Transformationen eines Mythos." *Quellen und Forschungen aus italienischen Archiven und Bibliotheken, 60* (1980), 325-73.

———. [Review], LQU. *Paideia, 33* (1978), 43-50.

Massalongo, Roberto. "Alessandro Benedetti e la medicina veneta del Quattrocento." *Atti del RIV di SLA, 76* (1916-1917), Parte II, 197-259.

Mastrodimitris, Panagiotis D. Νικόλαος ὁ Σεκουνδινός *(1402-1464), βίος καὶ ἔργον (Nicola Secundino (1402-64). Vita e opere. Contributo allo studio dei dotti greci della diaspora.)* Athens: Ethnikon kai Kapodistriakon Panepistemion Athenon, Philosophike Schole, 1970.

Mazzatinti, Giuseppe and continuators. *Inventario dei manoscritti delle biblioteche d'Italia* [Mazzatinti, *Inventario*]. 97 vols. Forli: Luigi Bordandini tipografo editore, 1891-1911; Florence: Leo S. Olschki, 1912-1980.

Mazzini, Ubaldo. "Appunti e notizie per servire alla bio-bibliografia di Bartolomeo Facio." *Giornale storico e letterario della Liguria, 4* (1903), 400-54.

Mazzuchelli, Giovanni Maria. *Gli scrittori d'Italia.* 2 vols. in 6. Incomplete. Brescia: presso Giambattista Bossini, 1753-1763.

Medin, Antonio. "Il culto del Petrarca nel Veneto fino alla dittatura del Bembo." NAV, NS, 8 (1904), Parte II, 421-65.

———. "Raffaele Regio a Venezia, epigrammi per la sua morte." AVT, Ser. 4, 1 (1922), 237-44.

———. "Gli scritti umanistici di Marco Dandolo." *Atti del RIV di SLA, 76* (1916-1917), Parte II, 335-414.

———. "Per la storia della fortuna del Boccaccio nel Veneto." *Atti del RIV di SLA,* Ser. 8, 72 (1912-1913), Parte II, 853-63.

———. *Per la storia della Repubblica di Venezia nella poesia.* Milan: Ulrico Hoepli, 1904.

Meiss, Millard. *Andrea Mantegna as Illuminator: An Episode in Renaissance Art, Humanism and Diplomacy.* New York: Columbia University Press, 1957.

Meneghel, R. "La 'Leandride' di Giovanni Girolamo Nadal." IMU, 16 (1973), 163-78.

Mercati, Giovanni. *Per la cronologia della vita e degli scritti di Niccolò Perotti, arcivescovo di Siponto.* Studi e testi, 44. Rome: Biblioteca Apostolica Vaticana, 1955.

———. *Ultimi contributi alla storia degli umanisti.* 2 vols. Studi e testi, 90-91. Città del Vaticano: Biblioteca Apostolica Vaticana, 1939.

Merores, Margarete. "Der venezianische Adel." *Vierteljahrschrift für Sozial- und Wirtschaftsgeschichte*, 19 (1926), 193-237.

Minio-Paluello, Lorenzo. "Attività filosofico-editoriale aristotelica dell'umanesimo." In UEUV, pp. 245-62.

Mioni, Elpidio. "Brugnoli, Benedetto." DBI, XIV (1972), 501-503.

Miscellanea di studi in onore di Vittore Branca [Misc. Branca]. Biblioteca dell'"Archivum Romanicum," Ser. 1, vols. 178-81 (= 4 vols. in 6; I, II, III/1, III/2, IV/1, IV/2). Florence: Leo S. Olschki, 1983. II: *Boccaccio e dintorni.* III: *Umanesimo e Rinascimento a Firenze e a Venezia.*

Mittarelli, Giovanni Benedetto. *Bibliotheca codicum manuscriptorum monasterii S. Michaelis Venetiarum prope Murianum* [Mittarelli, *Bibl. codd. mss.*]. Venice: ex typographia Fentiana, 1779.

Molmenti, Pompeo G. *La storia di Venezia nella vita privata dalle origini alla caduta della Repubblica* [Molmenti, *Vita privata*]. 3 vols. 5th ed., rev. Bergamo: Istituto italiano d'arte grafiche, 1910-1912.

Momigliano, Felice. *Paolo Veneto e le correnti del pensiero religioso e filosofico nel suo tempo: Contributo alla storia della filosofia del secolo XV.* Udine: Tip. G. B. Doretti, 1907.

Monfasani, John, ed. *Collectanea Trapezuntiana: Texts, Documents and Bibliographies of George of Trebizond.* Medieval and Renaissance Texts and Studies, 25; Renaissance Society of America: Renaissance Texts Series, 8. Binghamton, N.Y.: MRTS, 1984.

———. *George of Trebizond: A Biography and a Study of His Rhetoric and Logic.* Columbia Studies in the Classical Tradition, 1. Leiden: E. J. Brill, 1976.

Monnier, Philippe. *Le Quattrocento.* 2nd ed. 2 vols. Paris: Librairie Académique, Perrin et Cie. Libraires-Editeurs, 1912.

Monzani, C. "Di Guglielmo Favre e della vita di Gianmario Filelfo scritta da lui." ASI, Ser. 2, 9 (1859), 87-127.

Moore, Barrington, Jr. *Injustice: The Social Bases of Obedience and Revolt.* White Plains, N.Y.: M. E. Sharpe, [1978].

Mor, Carlo Guido. "Problemi organizzativi e politica veneziana nei riguardi dei nuovi acquisti di terraferma." In UEUV, pp. 1-10.

Morici, Medardo. *Per gli epistolari di due discepoli e di un amico di Guarino Guarini (Sassolo da Prato—Ciriaco d'Ancona—Leonardo Giustiniani).* Nozze Tommasini-Guarini. Pistoia: con tipi di G. Flori, 1897.

da Mosto, Andrea. *L'Archivio di Stato di Venezia, indice generale storico, descrittivo ed annalitico* [da Mosto, *Archivio*]. 2 vols. Bibliothèque des "Annales Institutorum," 5. Rome: Biblioteca d'arte editore, 1937-1940.

Muccioli, Giuseppe Maria. *Catalogus codicum manuscriptorum Malatestianae Caesenatis Bibliothecae.* 2 vols. in 1. Cesena: typis G. Blasinii, 1780-1784.

Mueller, Reinhold C. "Charitable Institutions, the Jewish Community, and Venetian Society: A Discussion of the Recent Volume by Brian Pullan." SV, 14 (1972), 37-82.

———. "Effetti della guerra di Chiogga sulla vita economica e sociale di Venezia," *Ateneo veneto*, NS, 19 (1981), 27-41.

———. "The Procurators of San Marco in the Thirteenth and Fourteenth Centuries: A Study of the Office as a Financial and Trust Institution." SV, 13 (1971), 105-220.

Muir, Edward. *Civic Ritual in Renaissance Venice.* Princeton: Princeton University Press, 1981.

———. "Images of Power: Art and Pageantry in Renaissance Venice." *American Historical Review*, 84 (1979), 16-52.

Müllner, Karl. *Reden und Briefe italienischer Humanisten.* See Primary Sources: Other Manuscript and Published Works and Collections.

Musatti, Eugenio. *Storia di Venezia.* 2nd ed. 2 vols. Milan: Fratelli Treves, Editori, 1919.

Nardi, Bruno, "Ancora qualche notizia e aneddoto su Nicoletto Vernia." In Nardi, *Saggi sull'aristotelismo padovano*, pp. 115-26.

———. "Contributo alla biografia di Vittorino da Feltre." *Bollettino del Museo Civico di Padova*, 45 (1956), 111-42.

———. "Letteratura e cultura veneziana del Quattrocento." In CVQ, pp. 99-145. Rpt. in Nardi, *Saggi sulla cultura veneta*, pp. 3-43.

———. *Saggi sull'aristotelismo padovano dal secolo XIV al XVI*. Florence: G. C. Sansoni, 1958.

———. *Saggi sulla cultura veneta del Quattro e Cinquecento*. Edited by Paolo Mazzatinti. Medioevo e umanesimo, 12. Padua: Editrice Antenore, 1971.

———. "La scuola di Rialto e l'umanesimo veneziano." In UEUV, pp. 93-139. Rpt. in Nardi, *Saggi sulla cultura veneta*, pp. 45-98.

Narducci, Enrico. "Intorno all'autenticità d'un codice Vaticano contenente il trattato di Boezio 'De consolatione philosophiae' scritto di mano di Giovanni Boccaccio, seguita da un'appendice di documenti riguardanti le ambascerie di Bernardo Bembo." *Atti dell'Accademia Nazionale dei Lincei*, Classe di scienze morali, storiche e filologiche, Ser. 3, 8 (1882-83), 243-64.

Nielson, George. "A Venetian's Commonplaces [Bernardo Bembo]." *Athenaeum* (21 December 1895), 871-72.

Nigro, Salvatore S., Francesco Tateo, and Antonia Tissoni-Benvenuti, eds. *Il Quattrocento: L'età dell'umanesimo*, II (= *La letteratura italiana: storia e testi*, edited by C. Muscetta, III/2). Bari: Editori Laterza, 1972.

de Nolhac, Pierre. *La Bibliothèque de Fulvio Orsini: Contribution à l'histoire des collections d'Italie et à l'étude de la Renaissance*. Bibliothèque de l'Ecole des Hautes Etudes, 74. Paris: F. Vieweg, Libraire Editeur, 1887.

———. "Giovanni Lorenzi, bibliothécaire d'Innocent VIII." *Mélanges d'archéologie et d'histoire*, 8 (1888), 3-18.

Oberdorfer, Aldo. "Alcune lettere inedite di Leonardo Giustiniano." GSLI, 53 (1909), 309-18.

———. "Per l'edizione critica delle canzonette di Leonardo Giustiniano." GSLI, 57 (1911), 193-217.

———. "L'epistolario di Leonardo Giustiniano." *Ateneo veneto*, 34, Parte I (1911), 5-19.

———. "Di Leonardo Giustiniano umanista." GSLI, 56 (1910), 107-20.

———. "Le 'Regulae Artificialis Memoriae' di Leonardo Giustiniani." GSLI, 60 (1912), 117-27.

Olivieri, Achille. "Calbo, Antonio." DBI, XVI (1973), 476-77.

O'Malley, John W. *Praise and Blame in Renaissance Rome: Rhetoric, Doctrine, and Reform in the Sacred Orators of the Papal Court, c. 1450-1521*. Duke Monographs in Medieval and Renaissance Studies, 3. Durham, N.C.: Duke University Press, 1979.

Padoan, Giorgio, ed. *Petrarca, Venezia e il Veneto*. Fondazione Giorgio Cini, Civiltà veneziana, Saggi, 21. Florence: Leo S. Olschki, 1976.

Pallucchini, Rodolfo. "L'arte a Venezia nel Quattrocento." In CVQ, pp. 147-77.

Palma, Marco. "Cippico (Cepione), Coriolano." DBI, XXV (1981), 735-36.

Palmieri, Aurelio. "Un'opera inedita di Fantino Vallaresso, Arcivescovo di Creta, sul Concilio di Firenze." *Bessarione*, 29 (1913), 1-26, 284-94.

Panofsky, Erwin. *Renaissance and Renascences in Western Art*. Gottesman Lectures, Uppsala University, 7. Stockholm: Olmquist & Wiksell, 1960.

Papadopoli, Niccolò C. *Historia gymnasii patavini* [Papadopoli, *Hist. gymn. pat.*]. 2 vols. Venice: apud Sebastianum Coleti, 1726.

Parsons, Talcott. " 'The Intellectual': A Social Role Category." In Rieff, ed., *On Intellectuals*, pp. 3-24.

Paschini, Pio. "I benefici ecclesiastici del cardinale Marco Barbo." *Rivista di storia della chiesa in Italia*, 13 (1959), 335-54.

BIBLIOGRAPHY

Paschini, Pio. *Domenico Grimani, Cardinale di S. Maria (+ 1523)*. Storia e letteratura, 4. Rome: Edizioni di storia e letteratura, 1943.

———. *Il carteggio fra il cardinale Marco Barbo e Giovanni Lorenzi (1481-1490)*. Studi e testi, 137. Città del Vaticano: Biblioteca Vaticana, 1948.

———. "Daniele Barbaro, letterato e prelato veneziano nel Cinquecento." *Rivista di storia della chiesa in Italia*, 16 (1962), 73-107.

———. "Un ellenista veneziano del Quattrocento: Giovanni Lorenzi." AV, Ser. 5, 32-33 (1943), 114-46.

———. "Gli scritti religiosi di Daniele Barbaro." *Rivista di storia della chiesa in Italia*, 5 (1951), 340-49.

———. *Tre illustri prelati del rinascimento: Ermolao Barbaro, Adriano Castellesi, Giovanni Grimani*. Lateranum, NS, 23:1-4. Rome: Facultas Theologica Pontificii Athenaei Lateranensis, 1957.

———. "Umanisti intorno a un cardinale." *Rinascita*, 1 (1938), 52-73.

von Pastor, Ludwig. "Life of Paul II." In *The History of the Popes from the Close of the Middle Ages*, IV. 5th ed. London: Routledge and Kegan Paul; St. Louis, Mo.: B. Herder Book Co., 1949, pp. 3-194.

Pastore Stocchi, Manlio. "Scuola e cultura umanistica fra due secoli." In SCV, III/1, 93-121.

Pastorello, Esther. *Bibliografia storico-analitica dell'arte della stampa a Venezia*. R. Deputazione di storia patria per le Venezie, Miscellanea di studi e memorie, I. Venice: la Deputazione, 1933.

———. *L'epistolario manuziano: inventario cronologico-analitico (1483-1597)*. Fondazione Giorgio Cini, Civiltà veneziana, Studi, 3. Florence: Leo S. Olschki, 1957.

Pavanello, Giuseppe. *Un maestro del Quattrocento (Giovanni Aurelio Augurello)*. Venice: Tipografia Emiliana, 1905.

Pecchioli, Renzo. "Il 'mito' di Venezia e la crisi fiorentina intorno al 1500." *Studi storici*, 3 (1962), 451-92.

Peri, Vittorio. "Tre lettere inedite a Fantino Vallaresso e un suo catechismo attribuito a Fantino Dandolo." In *Misc. Branca*, III/1, 41-68.

Perry, Marilyn. "Cardinal Domenico Grimani's Legacy of Ancient Art to Venice." JWCI, 41 (1978), 215-44.

Pertusi, Agostino. "Le fonti greche del 'De gestis, moribus et nobilitate civitatis venetiarum' di Lorenzo de Monacis, cancelliere di Creta (1388-1428)." IMU, 8 (1965), 162-211.

———. "Gli inizi della storiografia umanistica del Quattrocento." In Pertusi, ed., *Storiografia veneziana*, pp. 269-332.

———. "La lettera di Filippo da Rimini, cancelliere di Corfù, a Francesco Barbaro e i primi documenti occidentali sulla caduta di Costantinopoli (1453)." In Μνημό-συνον Σοφίας Ἀντωνίαδη. Biblioteca dell'Istituto Ellenico di Studi Bizantini e Postbizantini di Venezia. Venice, 1974, pp. 120-57.

———. "I primi studi in occidente sull'origine e la potenza dei Turchi." SV, 12 (1970), 465-552.

———. "L'umanesimo greco dalla fine del secolo XIV agli inizi del secolo XVI." In SCV, III/1, 177-264.

———, ed. "Epistole storiche" [of Lauro Quirini]. In LQU, pp. 163-259.

———, ed. *La storiografia veneziana fino al secolo XVI: Aspetti e problemi*. Fondazione Giorgio Cini, Civiltà veneziana, Saggi, 18. Florence: Leo S. Olschki, 1970.

Pesce, Luigi. *Ludovico Barbo vescovo di Treviso (1437-43): cura pastorale, riforma della chiesa, spiritualità*. 2 vols. Italia sacra, studi e documenti di storia ecclesiastica, 9-10. Padua: Editrice Antenore, 1969.

Picotti, Giovanni Battista. *La Dieta di Mantova e la politica dei veneziani*. R. Deputazione Veneta di Storia Patria, Miscellanea di storia veneta, Ser. III, Vol. IV. Venice: La Società, 1912.

———. "Le lettere di Lodovico Foscarino." *Ateneo Veneto*, 32 (1909), 21-49. Rpt. in

Picotti, *Ricerche umanistiche*, Studi di lettere, storia e filosofia, 24. Florence: La Nuova Italia, 1955, pp. 205-26.

del Piero, Antonio. "Della vita e degli studi di Giovanni Battista Ramusio." NAV, NS, 4 (1902), 5-112.

Pillinini, Giovanni. "Bollani, Candiano." DBI, XI (1969), 287-89.

——. "Marino Falier e la crisi economica e politica della metà del '300 a Venezia." AV, Ser. 5, 84 (1968), 45-71.

——. "L'umanista veneziano Francesco Barbaro e l'origine della politica di equilibrio." AV, Ser. 5, 72 (1963), 23-28.

Pintor, Fortunato. "Le due ambascerie di Bernardo Bembo a Firenze e le sue relazioni coi Medici." In *Studi letterari e linguistici dedicati a Pio Rajna* (Milan: Ulrico Hoepli, 1911), pp. 785-813.

Piovene, Guido. "L'anacronismo della Venezia quattrocentesca." In CVQ, pp. 1-21.

Pommier, Edouard. "La société vénitienne et la réforme protestante au XVIᵉ siècle." BIS, 1 (1959), 3-27.

Pontieri, Ernesto. "L'atteggiamento di Venezia nel conflitto tra Papa Innocenzo VIII e Ferrante I d'Aragona (1485-1492)." *Archivio storico per le provincie napoletane*, 81 (1963), 197-324.

Poppi, Antonino. *Introduzione all'aristotelismo padovano*. Saggi e testi, 10. Padua: Editrice Antenore, 1970.

——, ed. *Scienza e filosofia all 'Università di Padova nel Quattrocento*. Contributi alla storia dell'Università di Padova, 15. Padua: Editrice Antenore, 1983.

Poppi, Mario. "Un'orazione del cronista Lorenzo de Monacis per il millenario di Venezia (1421)." *Atti dell'IV di SLA*, 131 (1972-1973), Classe di scienze morali, lettere ed arti, 463-97.

——. "Ricerche sulla vita e cultura del notaio e cronista veneziano Lorenzo de Monacis, cancelliere cretese (ca. 1351-1428)." SV, 9 (1967), 153-86.

Pozza, Neri. "L'editoria veneziana da Vindelino ad Aldo Manuzio." In SCV, III/2.

Pratesi, Alessandro. "Barbo, Ludovico." DBI, VI (1964), 244-49.

Predelli, Riccardo, ed. *I libri commemoriali della republica di Venezia: regesti*. See "Primary Sources Published."

Prete, Sesto. "Capella, Febo." DBI, XVIII (1975), 470-71.

Prodi, Paolo. "The Structure and Organization of the Church in Renaissance Venice: Suggestions for Research." In Hale, ed., *Renaissance Venice*, pp. 409-30.

Pullan, Brian. "The Occupations and Investments of the Venetian Nobility in the Middle and Late Sixteenth Century." In Hale, ed., *Renaissance Venice*, pp. 379-408.

——. "Poverty, Charity and the Reason of State: Some Venetian Examples." BIS, 2 (1960), 17-60.

——. *Rich and Poor in Renaissance Venice: The Social Institutions of a Catholic State, to 1620*. Oxford: Basil Blackwell; Cambridge: Harvard University Press, 1971.

Queller, Donald E. "The Civic Irresponsibility of the Venetian Nobility." *Economy, Society, and Government in Medieval Italy, Essays in Memory of Robert L. Reynolds*. Edited by David Herlihy, Roberto S. Lopez, and Vsevolod Slessarev. Kent, Ohio: Kent State University Press, 1969, pp. 223-35.

——. *Early Venetian Legislation on Ambassadors*. Travaux d'humanisme et renaissance, 88. Geneva: Librairie Droz, 1966.

——. "The Myth of the Venetian Patriciate: Electoral Corruption in Medieval Venice." In Queller, *Two Studies on Venetian Government*, with Francis R. Swietek, Etudes de philosophie et d'histoire, 33 (Geneva: Librairie Droz, 1977), pp. 99-166.

Quirini, Angelo Maria, Cardinal. *Diatriba praeliminaris in duas partes divisa ad Francisci Barbari et aliorum ad ipsum epistolae ab anno Christi 1425 ad annum 1453*. See "Primary Sources: Other Manuscript and Published Works" Francesco Barbaro.

Raimondi, Ezio. "Umanesimo bolognese e umanesimo veneziano." In UEUV, pp. 263-94.

Rajna, Pio. "Il codice Vaticano 3357 del trattato 'De vita solitaria' di Francesco Petrarca." In *Miscellanea Ceriani*. Milan: Ulrico Hoepli, 1910, pp. 641-86.

Rambaldi, Pier L. [Review of Arnaldo della Torre, *Di Antonio Vinciguerra e delle sua satire*]. NAV, NS, 10 (1905), Parte I, 129-63.

Randall, John H., Jr. "Paduan Aristotelianism Reconsidered." In Mahoney, ed., *Philosophy and Humanism*, pp. 275-82.

————. *The School of Padua and the Emergence of Modern Science*. Padua: Editrice Antenore, 1961.

Recchilongo, Benito. "Borro, Gasparino." DBI, XIII (1971), 22-23.

Resta, Gianvito. *L'epistolario del Panormita. Studi per una edizione critica*. Università degli Studi di Messina, Studi e testi diretti da Michele Catalano, 3. Messina: Università degli Studi, 1954.

Ricci, Pier Giorgio. "Umanesimo filologico in Toscana e nel Veneto." In UEUV, pp. 159-72.

de Ricci, Seymour. *Census of Medieval and Renaissance Manuscripts in the U.S. and Canada*. With W. J. Wilson. 3 vols. New York: H. W. Wilson Co., 1935-40. Supplement by W. H. Bond. New York: Bibliographical Society of America, 1962.

Riccoboni, Antonio. *De gymnasio patavino commentariorum libri sex*. Padua: apud Franciscum Bolzetam, 1598.

Richards, J.F.C. "The Poems of Galeatius Ponticus Facinus." *Studies in the Renaissance*, 6 (1959), 94-128.

Rieff, Philip, ed. *On Intellectuals: Theoretical Studies, Case Studies*. Garden City, N.Y.: Doubleday, 1969.

Rigo, Paola. "Per il carteggio di Girolamo Donato: Inventario ed epistole inedite." *Rendiconti dell'Accademia Nazionale dei Lincei*, Classe di scienze morali, storiche e filologiche, Ser. 8, 29 (1974), 531-55.

————. "Catalogo e tradizione degli scritti di Girolamo Donato." *Rendiconti dell'Accademia Nazionale dei Lincei*, Classe di scienze morali, storiche e filologiche, Ser. 8, 31 (1976), 49-80.

Rinascimento europeo e rinascimento veneziano [RERV]. Edited by Vittore Branca. Civiltà europea e civiltà veneziana, Aspetti e problemi, 3. Florence: G. C. Sansoni, 1967.

Rizzi, P. "Aleotti, Ulisse." DBI, II (1960), 155.

Robey, David, and John Law. "The Venetian Myth and the 'De Republica Veneta' of Pier Paolo Vergerio." *Rinascimento*, Ser. 2, 15 (1975), 3-59.

Robin, Diana. "A Reassessment of the Character of Francesco Filelfo (1398-1481)." RQ, 36 (1983), 202-24.

della Rocca, Raimondo Morozzo, and Maria Francesca Tiepolo. "Cronologia veneziana del Quattrocento." In CVQ, pp. 179-241.

Romanin, Samuele. *Storia documentata di Venezia* [Romanin, *Stor. doc.*]. 10 vols. Venice: Pietro Naratovich Editore, 1853-1861.

Ronconi, Giorgio. "Lettere di Ermolao Barbaro il Vecchio ai Gonzaga di Mantova." *Atti e Memorie dell'Accademia Patavina di SLA*, 83 (1970-1971), Parte III, 381-412.

Rosand, Ellen. "Music and the Myth of Venice." RQ, 30 (1977), 511-37.

Rose, Charles. "Marcantonio Venier, Renier Zeno, and the 'Myth of Venice.' " *The Historian*, 26 (1974), 479-97.

Rose, Paul L. "The Accademia Venetiana, Science and Culture in Renaissance Venice." SV, 11 (1969), 191-242.

————. "Bartolomeo Zamberti's Funeral Oration for the Humanist Encyclopaedist Giorgio Valla." In Clough, ed., *Cultural Aspects of the Italian Renaissance*, pp. 299-310.

————. "Humanist Culture and Renaissance Mathematics: The Italian Libraries of the Quattrocento." *Studies in the Renaissance*, 20 (1973), 46-105.

————, and Stillman Drake. "The Pseudo-Aristotelian *Questions of Mechanics* in Renaissance Culture." *Studies in the Renaissance*, 18 (1971), 65-104.

de' Rosmini, Carlo. *L'idea dell'ottimo precettore, della vita e disciplina di Vittorino da Feltre e de' suoi discepoli.* Bassano: Tipografia Remondiniana, 1801.

————. *Vita e disciplina di Guarino Veronese e de' suoi discepoli.* 3 vols. Brescia: Nicolò Bettoni tipografia dipartimentale, 1805-1806.

————. *Vita di Francesco Filelfo da Tolentino.* 3 vols. Milan: Presso Luigi Mussi, 1808.

Ross, James Bruce. "The Emergence of Gasparo Contarini: A Bibliographical Essay." *Church History*, 41 (1972), 22-45.

————. "Gasparo Contarini and His Friends." *Studies in the Renaissance*, 17 (1970), 192-232.

————. "Venetian Schools and Teachers, Fourteenth to Early Sixteenth Century: A Survey and a Study of Giovanni Battista Egnazio." *RQ*, 39 (1976), 521-66.

Rossi, Vittorio. "Niccolò Lelio Cosmico, poeta padovano del secolo XV." *GSLI*, 13 (1889), 101-58.

————. *Il Quattrocento.* 7th ed., revised by Aldo Vallone. Milan: F. Villardi, 1960.

Rubinstein, Nicolai. "Italian Reactions to Terraferma Expansion in the Fifteenth Century." In Hale, ed., *Renaissance Venice*, pp. 197-217.

Ruggiero, Guido. *Violence in Early Renaissance Venice.* New Brunswick, N.J.: Rutgers University Press, 1980.

Sabbadini, Remigio. "Andrea Contario." *NAV*, NS, 31 (1916), Parte II, 378-433.

————. "Antonio da Romagno e Pietro Marcello." *NAV*, NS, 30 (1915), Parte I, 207-46.

————. "Ancora Pietro Marcello." *NAV*, NS, 31 (1916), Parte II, 260-62.

————. "Bartolomeo Facio, scolaro a Verona, maestro a Venezia." In *Scritti storici in memoria di Giovanni Monticolo*, edited by C. Cipolla et al. Venice: Carlo Ferrari, [1922], pp. 29-36.

————. "Briciole umanistiche—XIII: Caterina Caldiera." *GSLI*, 43 (1904), p. 245.

————. "Briciole umanistiche—XVII: Lauro Quirini." *GSLI*, 43 (1904), 248-50.

————. "Briciole umanistiche—XXX: Gregorio Correr." *GSLI*, 46 (1905), 65-69.

————. "Briciole umanistiche—XLV: Giorgio Merula." *GSLI*, 47 (1906), 39-40.

————. "Briciole umanistiche—LII: Giorgio Valla." *GSLI*, 50 (1907), 50-52.

————. *Centotrenta lettere inedite di Francesco Barbaro precedute dall'ordinamento critico cronologico dell'intero suo epistolario.* See "Primary Sources: Other Manuscript and Published Works," Francesco Barbaro.

————. "Codici latini posseduti, scoperti, illustrati da Guarino Veronese." *Museo italiano di antichità classica*, 2:2 (1887), cols. 373-456.

————. "La gita di Francesco Barbaro a Firenze nel 1415." In *Miscellanea di studi in onore di Attilio Hortis*. 2 vols. Trieste: Stabilimento artistico tipografico G. Caprin, 1910, II, 615-27.

————. *Guariniana* [photostatic reproduction of Sabbadini's *Vita di Guarino Veronese* and *La scuola e gli studi di Guarino Guarini Veronese*]. Edited by Mario Sancipriano. Turin: Bottega d'Erasmo, 1964.

————. "Lettere e orazioni edite ed inedite di Gasparino Barzizza." *Archivio storico lombardo*, Ser. 2, 3 (1886), 363-78, 563-83, 825-36.

————. "Delle nuove lettere di Gasparino Barzizza." *Rendiconti dell'Istituto Lombardo di Scienze e Lettere*, 62, fasc. 16-20 (1929), 881-90.

————. *Le scoperte dei codici latini e greci ne' secoli XIV e XV.* 2 vols. Florence: G. C. Sansoni, 1905, 1914. Photostatic reproduction, revised and edited by Eugenio Garin. 2 vols. Florence: G. C. Sansoni, 1967.

————. *La scuola e gli studi di Guarino Guarini Veronese.* Catania: Tipografia Francesco Galati, 1896. Reproduced in *Guariniana*.

————. *Storia e critica di testi latini* [1914]. 2nd ed. Medioevo e umanesimo, 11. Padua: Editrice Antenore, 1971.

————. "Sugli studi volgari di Leonardo Giustiniani." *GSLI*, 10 (1887), 363-71.

————. "Tito Livio Frulovisio umanista del secolo XV." *GSLI*, 103 (1934), 55-81.

————. "La traduzione guariniana di Strabone." *Il libro e la stampa*, 3 (1909), 5-16.

BIBLIOGRAPHY

Sabbadini, Remigio. "L'ultimo ventennio della vita di Manuele Crisolora (1395-1415)." *Giornale ligustico di archeologia, storia e letteratura*, 17 (1890), 321-36.

———. *Vita di Guarino Veronese. Giornale ligustico di archeologia, storia e letteratura*, 18 (1891), 3-40, 109-35, 185-206, 261-82, 321-48, 401-32. Extract in monograph form, Genoa: Tipografia dele R. Istituto Sordo-Muti, 1891. Reproduced in *Guariniana*.

———. [Review of J. L. Heiberg, *Beiträge zur Geschichte Georg Vallas*]. GSLI, 29 (1897), 525-27.

Saitta, Giuseppe. *Il pensiero italiano nell'umanesimo e nel rinascimento*. 3 vols. 2nd ed. Florence: Sansoni, 1961.

Sambin, Paolo. "Il dottorato in arti (1478) di Girolamo Donato." *Quaderni per la storia dell'Università di Padova*, 6 (1973), 215-16.

———. "Ricerche per la storia della cultura nel secolo XV: la biblioteca di Pietro Donato (1380-1447)." *Bollettino del Museo Civico di Padova*, 48 (1959), 53-98.

San Lorenzo Giustiniani, protopatriarca di Venezia nel V centenario di morte: 1456-1956. Venice: F. Ongania, 1959.

de Sandre Gasparini, Giuseppina. "Uno studio sull'episcopato padovano di Pietro Barozzi (1478-1507) e altri contributi sui vescovi veneti nel Quattrocento: Problemi e linee di ricerca." *Rivista di storia della chiesa in Italia*, 34 (1980), 81-122.

Sansovino, Francesco. *Della Venetia città nobilissima et singolare* [Sansovino, *Venetia*]. (Orig. 1581.) Additions by Giustiniano Martinioni [orig. 1663]; index by Lino Moretti. 2 vols. Venice: Filippi (Tipolitografia Armena), 1968.

dalla Santa, Giuseppe. "Due lettere di umanisti veneziani (Lauro Querini e Lodovico Foscarini a Paolo Morosini)." NAV, 19 (1900), Parte I, 92-96.

———. "Nuovi appunti sul processo di Giorgio Valla e di Placido Amerini in Venezia nel 1496." NAV, 10 (1895), Parte I, 13-23.

———. "Di un patrizio mercante veneziano [Guglielmo Quirini] del Quattrocento e di Francesco Filelfo suo debitore." NAV, NS, 11 (1906), Parte II, 63-90.

———. "Un testamento ed alcune note biografiche di Pietro Cirneo, prete, storico, umanista." *La scintilla*, a. 9 (1895), 40: 159-60; 41: 164.

———. "Uomini e fatti dell'ultimo Trecento e del primo Quattrocento, da lettere a Giovanni Contarini, patrizio veneziano, studente ad Oxford e a Parigi, poi Patriarca di Costantinopoli." NAV, NS, 32 (1916), Parte I, 5-105.

———. "Una vicenda della dimora di Ermolao Barbaro a Roma nel 1492." In *Scritti storici in memoria di Giovanni Monticolo*, edited by C. Cipolla et al. Venice: Carlo Ferrari, [1922], pp. 221-28.

———. [Review of Arnaldo Segarizzi, "Jaopo Languschi rimatore veneziano del secolo XV," etc.]. NAV, NS, 11 (1906), Parte II, 200-205.

Schmitt, Charles B. *A Critical Survey and Bibliography of Studies on Renaissance Aristotelianism, 1958-1969*. Università di Padova, Centro per la storia della tradizione aristotelica nel Veneto; Columbia University, University Seminar on the Renaissance, Saggi e testi, 11. Padua: Editrice Antenore, 1971.

———. "An Unstudied Fifteenth-Century Latin Translation of Sextus Empiricus by Giovanni Lorenzi (Vat. Lat. 2990)." In Clough, ed., *Cultural Aspects of the Italian Renaissance*, pp. 244-61.

Schnitzer, Joseph. *Peter Delfin General des Camaldulenserordens (1444-1525): Ein Beitrag zur Geschichte der Kirchenreform, Alexanders VI und Savonarolas*. [1902] 2nd ed. Munich: Verlag von Ernst Reinhardt, 1926.

Schumpeter, Joseph A. "The Sociology of the Intellectuals." In de Huszar, ed., *The Intellectuals, A Controversial Portrait*, pp. 69-79.

Segarizzi, Arnaldo. *Antonio Baratella e i suoi corrispondenti*. R. Deputazione Veneta di Storia Patria, Miscellanea di storia patria, Ser. III, X. Venice: la Deputazione, 1916.

———. "Cenni sulle scuole pubbliche a Venezia nel secolo XV e sul primo maestro d'esse." *Atti del RIV di SLA*, 75 (1915-16), Parte II, 637-67.

494

————. "Contributo alla storia delle congiure padovane." NAV, NS, 31 (1916), Parte I, 48-78.

————. "La corrispondenza famigliare di un medico erudito del Quattrocento (Pietro Tommasi)." *Atti dell'Accademia di SLA degli Agiati in Rovereto*, Ser. 3, 13:3-4 (1907), 219-48.

————. "Cristoforo de Scarpis." NAV, NS, 29 (1915), Parte I, 209-20.

————. "Francesco Contarini, politico e letterato veneziano del secolo XV." NAV, NS, 12 (1906), Parte II, 272-306.

————. "Una grammatica latina del secolo XV." *Atti del RIV di SLA*, 75 (1915-1916), Parte II, 89-96.

————. *Jacopino Badoer rimatore veneziano del secolo XV*. Nozze Onestinghel-Alberti (Trento, 19 novembre 1904). Venice: Tipografia Visentini, 1904.

————. "Jacopo Languschi rimatore veneziano del secolo XV." *Atti della R. Accademia di SLA degli Agiati in Rovereto*, Ser. 3, 10 (1904), 179-82.

————. "Lauro Quirini umanista veneziano del secolo XV." *Memorie della R. Accademia delle Scienze di Torino*, Ser. 2, 54 (1904), Classe di scienze morali, storiche e filologiche, 1-28.

————. "Niccolò Barbo patrizio veneziano del secolo XV e le accuse contro Isotta Nogarola." GSLI, 43 (1904), 39-54.

————. "Ulisse Aleotti, rimatore veneziano del secolo XV." GSLI, 47 (1906), 41-66.

Seneca, Federico. *Venezia e Papa Giulio II*. Padua-Liviana Editrice, 1962.

Seno, Carlo, and Giorgio Ravegnani, eds. 'Il 'De republica' di Lauro Quirini." In LQU, pp. 103-61.

Setz, Wolfram. *Lorenzo Vallas Schrift gegen die konstantinische Schenkung*, De falso credita et ementita Constantini donatione: *Zur Interpretation und Wirkungsgeschichte*. Bibliothek des Deutschen Historischen Instituts in Rom, 44. Tübingen: Max Niemayer Verlag, 1975.

Seznec, Jean. *The Survival of the Pagan Gods*. Translated by Barbara F. Sessions. New York: Harper & Row, 1961.

Sforza, G. "Della vita e delle opere di Giovanni Pietro d'Avenza, grammatico del secolo XV." *Atti e memorie delle RR. Deputazioni di Storia Patria per le provincie modenesi e parmensi*, 5 (1868), 393-411.

Shils, Edward. "Intellectuals." In *International Encyclopedia of the Social Sciences*, edited by David L. Sills. New York: Macmillan Co. and the Free Press, 1968, VII, 399-415.

————. "The Intellectuals and the Powers: Some Perspectives for Comparative Analysis." In P. Rieff, ed., *On Intellectuals*, pp. 25-48.

————. "The Traditions of Intellectuals." In de Huszar, ed., *The Intellectuals, A Controversial Portrait*, pp. 55-61.

Sighinolfi, Lino. "La biblioteca di Giovanni Marcanova." In *Collectanea variae doctrinae Leoni S. Olschki*, edited by Ludwig Bertalot et al. Munich: Jacques Rosenthal, 1921, pp. 187-222.

Siraisi, Nancy G. *Arts and Sciences at Padua: The Studium of Padua before 1350*. Pontifical Institute of Medieval Studies, Studies and Texts, 25. Toronto: Pontifical Institute, 1973.

Sopetto, Adelaide. *Le satire edite ed inedite di Antonio Vinciguerra*. Ciriè: Tipografia Giovanni Capella, 1904.

Soranzo, Giovanni. "Pietro Dolfin e il suo epistolario." *Rivista di storia della chiesa in Italia*, 13 (1959), 1-31; 157-95.

————. *L'umanista canonico regolare Lateranense Matteo Bosso di Verona (1427-1502): I suoi scritti e il suo epistolario*. Padua: Libreria Gregoriana Editrice, 1965.

Sottili, Agostino. *Studenti tedeschi e umanesimo italiano nell'Università di Padova durante il Quattrocento. I: Pietro del Monte nella società accademica padovana (1430-1433)*. Contributi alla storia dell' Università di Padova, 7. Padua: Editrice Antenore, 1971.

Stabile, Giorgio. "Bragadin, Domenico." DBI, XIII (1971), 668-69.

BIBLIOGRAPHY

Stäuble, A. *La commedia umanistica del Quattrocento*. Florence: Istituto Nazionale di Studi sul Rinascimento, 1968.

———. "Le sette commedie dell'umanista Tito Livio de' Frulovisi." *Rinascimento*, Ser. 2, 3 (1963), 23-51.

Stickney, Joseph T. *De Hermolai Barbari vita atque ingenio*. Lutetiae Parisiorum: Société Nouvelle de Librairie et d'Edition, 1903.

Stinger, Charles L. *Humanism and the Church Fathers: Ambrogio Traversari (1386-1439) and Christian Antiquity in the Italian Renaissance*. Albany: State University of New York Press, 1977.

Storia della cultura veneta [SCV]. II: *Il Trecento*. Vicenza: Neri Pozza, Editore, 1976. III: *Dal primo Quattrocento al Concilio di Trento*. Vols. 1-3. 1980.

Struever, Nancy. *The Language of History in the Renaissance: Rhetoric and Historical Consciousness in Florentine Humanism*. Princeton: Princeton University Press, 1970.

Superbi, Agostino. *Trionfo glorioso d'heroi illustri, et eminenti dell'inclita, et maravigliosa città di Venetia*. Venice: per Evangelista Deuchino, 1629.

Suttles, G. "Friendship as a Social Institution." In Suttles, *Social Relationships* (Chicago: University of Chicago Press, 1970), chap. iv.

Tabulae codicum manuscriptorum praeter graecos et orientales in Bibliotheca palatina vindobonensi asservatorum (Vienna, Nationalbibliothek). Edited by Academia Caesarea Vindobonensis. 10 vols. Vienna: Venumdat Caroli Geroldi Filius, 1864-1899.

Tartaro, Achille, and Francesco Tateo, eds. *Il Quattrocento: l'età dell'umanesimo*, I (= *La letteratura italiana: storia e testi*, edited by C. Muscetta, III/1). Bari: Editori Laterza, 1971.

Tassi, Ildefonso. *Ludovico Barbo (1381-1443)*. Uomini e dottrine, 1. Rome: Edizioni di storia e letteratura, 1952.

Tateo, Francesco. *La cultura umanistica e i suoi centri*, in Tartaro and Tateo, *Il Quattrocento*, pp. 39-146.

———. "Marcantonio Sabellico e la svolta del classicismo quattrocentesco." In *Florence and Venice*, I, 41-63.

Tenenti, Alberto. "Il 'De perfectione rerum' di Nicolò Contarini." BIS, 1 (1959), 155-66.

———. "The Sense of Space and Time in the Venetian World of the Fifteenth and Sixteenth Centuries." In Hale, ed., *Renaissance Venice*, pp. 17-46.

Tiara et purpura veneta ab anno MCCCCLXXIX ad annum MXCCLIX. Brescia: Excudebat Joannes-Maria Rizzardi, 1761.

Tiraboschi, Girolamo. *Storia della letteratura italiana* [Tiraboschi, *Stor. lett. ital.*]. (1772—). Rpt. 4 vols. Milan: Niccolò Bettoni, 1833.

Tissoni-Benvenuti, Antonia. *Venezia e il veneto*. In Nigro, Tateo, and Tissoni-Benvenuti, eds., *Il Quattrocento*, pp. 249-89.

Toderini, Teodoro. *Genealogie della famiglie Venete ascritte alla cittadinanza originaria*. See "Primary Sources: Other Documents and Chronicles."

Toffanin, Giuseppe. *History of Humanism*. Edited and translated by Elio Gianturco, from the 2nd ed.: *L'Umanesimo italiano (dal XIV al XVI secolo)*, Bologna: Zanichelli, 1950. New York: Las Americas Publishing Co., 1954.

Tomasini, Jacopo Filippo. *Gymnasium patavinum*. Udine: ex typographia Nicolae Schiratti, 1654.

Tonini, Carlo. *La coltura letteraria e scientifica in Rimini dal secolo XIV ai primi del XIX*. 2 vols. Rimini: Tipografia Danesi già Albertini, 1884.

della Torre, Arnaldo. *Di Antonio Vinciguerra e delle sue satire*. Rocca S. Casciano: Stabilimento titpografico Capelli, 1902.

———. *Paolo Marsi da Pescina. Contributo alla storia dell'Accademia Pomponiana*. Indagini di storia letteraria, 1. Rocca S. Casciano: Licinio Cappelli, 1903.

———. "La prima ambasceria di Bernardo Bembo a Firenze." GSLI, 35 (1900), 258-333.

496

BIBLIOGRAPHY

Torrioli, Ascanio. *Publio Gregorio Tifernate*. Urbino: Tipografia Melchiorre Arduini, 1927.

Tournoy, Gilbert. "Francesco Diedo, Venetian Humanist and Politician of the Quattrocento." *Humanistica lovaniensia*, 19 (1970), 201-34.

———. "Un nuovo testo del periodo padovano di Pietro del Monte." *Quaderni per la storia dell'Università di Padova*, 8 (1975), 67-72.

Tramontin, Silvio. "La cultura monastica del Quattrocento dal primo patriarca Lorenzo Giustiniani ai Camaldolesi Paolo Giustiniani e Pietro Quirini." In SCV, III/1, pp. 431-57.

Trebbi, Giuseppe. "La cancelleria veneta nei secoli XVI e XVII." *Annali della Fondazione Luigi Einaudi*, 14 (1980), 65-125.

Trinkaus, Charles. *In Our Image and Likeness: Humanity and Divinity in Italian Humanist Thought*. 2 vols. Chicago: University of Chicago Press; London: Constable, 1970.

Trithemius, Johannes. *De scriptoribus ecclesiasticis*. Cologne: ex officina Petri Quentel, March 1546.

Troilo, Sigfrido. *Andrea Giuliano, politico e letterato veneziano del Quattrocento*. Biblioteca dell' "Archivum Romanicum," Ser. I, 18. Geneva-Florence: Leo S. Olschki, 1932.

Tucci, Ugo. "The Psychology of the Venetian Merchant in the Sixteenth Century." In Hale, ed., *Renaissance Venice*, pp. 346-78.

Ughelli, Ferdinandus. *Italia sacra, sive de episcopis Italiae*. 10 vols. in 9. Venice: apud Sebastianum Coleti, 1717-22.

Umanesimo europeo ed umanesimo veneziano [UEUV]. Edited by Vittore Branca. Civiltà europea e civiltà veneziana, Aspetti e problemi, 2. Florence: G. C. Sansoni, 1963.

Valentinelli, Giuseppe. *Bibliotheca manuscripta ad S. Marci Venetiarum* [Valentinelli, *Bibl. manu.*]. 6 vols. Venice: ex typographia Commercii, 1868-1873.

Valeri, Nino. "Venezia nella crisi italiana del rinascimento." In CVQ, pp. 23-48.

Vecchi, Alberto. *Correnti religiose nel Sei-Settecento veneto*. Fondazione Giorgio Cini, Civiltà veneziana, Studi, 15. Venice: Istituto per la Collaborazione Culturale, 1962.

Ventura, Angelo. "Canal, Niccolò." DBI, XVII (1974), 662-68.

———. "Il dominio di Venezia nel Quattrocento." In *Florence and Venice*, I, 167-90.

———. *Nobiltà e popolo nella società veneta del '400 e '500*. Bari: Ed. Laterza, 1964.

———, and M. Pecoraro. "Bembo, Bernardo." DBI, VIII (1966), 103-109.

Verrua, Pietro. "Cinque orazioni dette dall'umanista Francesco Negri nello studio di Padova." AVT, Ser. 4, 1 (1922), 194-236.

———. "L'Università di Padova circa il 1488 nell' 'Opusculum scribendi epistolas' di Francesco Negri." *Atti e Memorie della R. Accademia di SLA di Padova*, NS, 36 (1920), 183-214.

Viscardi, Antonio. "Lingua e letteratura." In CVT, pp. 179-205.

Vitali, Maria Cristina. "L'umanista padovano Giovanni Marcanova (1410/1418-67) e la sua biblioteca." *Ateneo veneto*, 21 (1983), 127-61.

Voigt, Georg. *Il risorgimento dell'antichità classica, ovvero il primo secolo dell'umanesimo*. Translated by D. Valbusa. Additions and corrections by Giuseppe Zippel. 3 vols. Florence: G. C. Sansoni, 1888, 1890, 1897. Rpt., edited by Eugenio Garin. Biblioteca storica del rinascimento, 5. Florence: G. C. Sansoni, 1968. [Based on 3rd German edition of *Die Wiederbelebung des classischen Althertums*, edited by M. Lehnerdt, Berlin, 1888-1897].

Volpe, Gioacchino. "L'Italia e Venezia." In CVT, pp. 23-83.

Walser, Ernst. *Poggius Florentinus, Leben und Werke*. Beiträge zur Kulturgeschichte des Mittelalters und der Renaissance, 14. Leipzig-Berlin: Druck u. Verlag von B. G. Teubner, 1914.

Watanabe, Morimichi. "Gregor Heimburg and Early Humanism in Germany." In Mahoney, ed., *Philosophy and Humanism*, pp. 406-22.

BIBLIOGRAPHY

Watkins, Renée Neu, ed. *Humanism and Liberty*. See Primary Sources: Other Manuscript and Published Works and Collections.

Weinstein, Donald. *Ambassador from Venice: Pietro Pasqualigo in Lisbon, 1507*. Minneapolis: University of Minnesota Press, 1960.

Weiss, Roberto. "Augurelli, Giovanni Aurelio." DBI, IV (1962), 578-81.

――――. "Humphrey of Gloucester and Tito Livio Frulovisi." In D. J. Gordon, ed., *Fritz Saxl, 1890-1948: A Volume of Memorial Essays from His Friends in England* (London: Thomas Nelson & Sons, 1957), pp. 218-27.

――――. "Lorenzo Zane arcivescovo di Spalato e governatore di Cesena." *Studi romagnoli*, 16 (1965), 163-69.

――――. *The Renaissance Discovery of Classical Antiquity*. Oxford: Basil Blackwell, 1969.

――――. *Un umanista veneziano: Papa Paolo II*. Fondazione Giorgio Cini, Civiltà veneziana, Saggi, 4. Venice-Rome: Istituto per la Collaborazione Culturale, 1958.

Witt, Ronald. "The De tyranno and Coluccio Salutati's View of Politics and Roman History." NRS, 53 (1969), 434-74.

――――. *Hercules at the Crossroads: Life, Works and Thought of Coluccio Salutati*. Durham, N.C.: Duke University Press, 1983.

――――. "Medieval 'Ars Dictaminis' and the Beginnings of Humanism: A New Construction of the Problem." RQ, 35 (1982), 1-35.

Wohl, Robert. *The Generation of 1914*. Cambridge: Harvard University Press, 1979.

Wolf, Eric R. "Kinship, Friendship and Patron-Client Relations in Complex Societies." In Michael Banton, ed., *The Social Anthropology of Complex Societies* (New York and Washington, D.C.: Frederick A. Praeger, 1966), pp. 1-22.

Woodward, W. H. *Vittorino da Feltre and Other Humanist Educators*. Cambridge: Cambridge University Press, 1897. Rpt. Introductiton by Eugene F. Rice, Jr. Classics in Education, 18. New York: Bureau of Publications, Teachers College, Columbia University, 1963.

Woolf, S. J. "Venice and the Terraferma: Problems of the Change from Commercial to Landed Activities." BIS, 4 (1962), 415-41. Rpt. in B. Pullan, ed., *Crisis and Change in the Venetian Economy in the Sixteenth and Seventeenth Centuries* (London: Methuen, 1968), pp. 175-203.

Wyrobisz, Andrze. "L'attività edilizia a Venezia nel XIV e XV secolo." SV, 7 (1966), 307-43.

Zaccaria, Vittorio. "L'epistolario di Pier Candido Decembrio." *Rinascimento*, 3 (1952), 85-118.

Zanelli, Agostino. "Pietro del Monte." *Archivio storico lombardo*, 34 (1907), 7, 317-78; 8, 46-115.

Zannoni, Maria. "Il dramma dei Foscari nella cronica di Giorgio Dolfin." NRS, 26 (1942), 201-15.

――――. "Le fonti della cronaca veneziana di Giorgio Dolfin." *Atti del RIV di SLA*, 101 (1941-42), Parte II, 515-46. Extract: Venice: Ferrari, 1942.

――――. "Giorgio Dolfin, cronista veneziano del secolo XV." *Atti e Memorie della R. Academia di SLA in Padova*, 58 (1941-42), Parte II, 37-55.

Zanocco, Rinieri. "La biblioteca di un grande nostro vescovo umanista (Pietro Barozzi, 1441-1507)." *Bollettino diocesano di Padova*, 12 (1927), 442-52.

Zeno, Apostolo. *Dissertazioni vossiane [Diss. voss.]*. 2 vols. Venice: Giambatista Albrizzi Q. Gir., 1752-1753.

――――, ed. *Istorici delle cose veneziane*. See Primary Sources: Other Manuscript and Published Works and Collections.

Zeno, Pietro Angelo. *Memoria de' scrittori veneti patritii ecclesiastici et secolari*. Venice: Paolo Baglioni, 1662.

Ziliotto, Baccio. "Baratella, Antonio." DBI, V (1963), 778-80.

――――. *Raffaele Zovenzoni: la vita, i carmi*. Comune di Trieste, Celebrazioni degli istriani illustri, 3. Trieste: "Smolars," 1950.

Zippel, Gianni. "Lorenzo Valla e le origini della storiografia umanistica a Venezia." *Rinascimento*, 7 (1956), 93-133.

——. "Ludovico Foscarini ambasciatore a Genova, nella crisi dell'espansione veneziana sulla terraferma (1449-50)." *Bullettino dell'Istituto Storico Italiano per il Medio Evo e Archivo Muratoriano*, 71 (1959), 181-255.

Zippel, Giuseppe. "La morte di Marco Barbo cardinale." In *Scritti storici in memoria di Giovanni Monticolo*, edited by C. Cipolla et al. Venice: Carlo Ferrari, [1922], pp. 193-203.

——. *Le vite di Paolo II di Gasparo da Verona e Michele Canensi*. See Primary Sources: Other Manuscript and Published Works, *Le vite*.

Znaniecki, Florian. *The Social Role of the Man of Knowledge*. New York: Columbia University Press, 1940.

Zonta, Gasparo. "Un conflitto tra la repubblica veneta e la curia romana per l'episcopato di Padova (1459-60)." *Atti e Memorie della R. Accademia di SLA in Padova*, NS, 40 (1923-1924), 221-38.

——, ed. Jacopo Zeno, *Vita Caroli Zeni*, to Pope Pius II (1458). See "Primary Sources: Other Manuscript and Published Works," Zeno.

——, and Giovanni Brotto. *Acta graduum academicorum gymnasii patavini ab anno MCCCCVI ad annum MCCCCL*. See "Primary Sources: Published," Zonta and Brotto.

INDEX

In this index, a distinction is made between entries from Part I or the Preface to Part II on the one hand, and from the Part II Profiles on the other. Entries in **boldface** following the *Profiles* heading refer to the full bio-bibliographical profiles of the concerned figure.

Acotantus, Petrus (Saint), *Profiles*, 334
Active vs. contemplative life, 129, 189, 198ff., 241
Aesop, 168, 229; *Profiles*, 320, 321
degli Agli, Lotto, *Profiles*, 332
Albergati, Niccolò (Cardinal), 167; *Profiles*, 448
Alberti, Leon Battista, 9
Alberto, Giovanni Michele, da Carrara, 273; *Profiles*, 318, 341, 362, 369, 379, 396
Aleotti, Ulisse, 78n371, 266, 294-95, 289, 296; *Profiles*, 315, 376, 429
Alexander of Aphrodisias, 168; *Profiles*, 367, 401, 439
Alexander VI (Pope), 205n329; *Profiles*, 318, 391
Alfonso I of Aragon, King of Naples, *Profiles*, 352, 353, 383, 428, 429, 438
Alighieri, Dante III, 273; *Profiles*, 337, 362
Aliotti, Girolamo, *Profiles*, 356
Amaseo, Gregorio, 271
Amateurism, 258, 288, 298, 303
Ambassador, E. Barbaro G's view of role, 202ff.
Ammianus Marcellinus, *Profiles*, 369
Andrea (physician), 62; *Profiles*, 388
Anselm, *Profiles*, 409
Anti-Semitism, 37, 230
Antiquario, Jacopo, 204n328; *Profiles*, 322
Antonio da Romagna, *Profiles*, 397
Antonius (professor of laws), 390
Apostolos, Michael, *Profiles*, 420
Appian, 7; *Profiles*, 354
Apuleius, *Profiles*, 371

Archivio di Stato (ASV), Venice, 257; *Profiles*, 308ff.
Argyropoulos, John, 20; *Profiles*, 417
Aristarchus, *Profiles*, 439
Aristocracy, best form of rule, for L. Quirini, 126-28
Aristotle, Aristotelianism: and E. Barbaro G, 5, 15, 202; and P. Barozzi, 149n184, 152n192, 154ff.; and Caldiera, 98ff.; and Lippomano, 8; and D. Morosini, 141n145, 148-49; and L. Quirini, 12, 15, 120ff.; and N. L. Tomeo, 234; and Venetian humanism, 168, 175, 182, 184, 189-90, 212, 224-25, 230, 234, 241; *Profiles*, 318, 322, 343, 373, 390 (ps.-Aristotle), 420, 429, 432, 433, 434
Arnold of Bost, 197n306; *Profiles*, 323
d'Artegna, Guarnerio: xviii, 7, 12; *Profiles*, 376
d'Arzignano, Oliviero, *Profiles*, 344
Ascanius Pedianus, *see* Pedianus, Ascanius
Astrology, Venetian humanist works of, 165-66
Athanasius, 158; *Profiles*, 320, 371
Attendolo, Michele, da Codignola, *Profiles*, 389
Augurello, Giovanni Aurelio: 232n67, 267; *Profiles*, 338, 416, 425, 434
Augustine, 6, 93, 158
Aurelio, Marco: 11, 19, 76-79, 85, 265, 266, 274n17, 290, 294-96; *Profiles*, 315-16, 349, 361, 376, 428, 429
Aurelio, Niccolò (father of Marco), 290; *Profiles*, 315-16
Aurelio, Niccolò (son of Marco):

501

INDEX

Calixtus III (Pope), *Profiles*, 376
Callimaco Esperiente, *see* Buonaccorsi,
 Filippo
Callisto, Andronico, *Profiles*, 440
Calvo, Antonio, 5, 9n6, 16, 73, 202,
 204n328, 266; *Profiles*, 322, **345-47**
 (**homonyms, 345-46**)
Calvo, Girolamo, 271
Campano, Giovanni Antonio, *Profiles*,
 447
Camphora, Jacobus, *Profiles*, 393
Campofregosus, Janus, *Profiles*, 417
Canal, Giovanni (son of Niccolò), *Pro-
files*, 348
Canal, Niccolò, 10, 17, 163, 193, 266,
 267, 274n17, 282; *Profiles*, 324, **347-
48**, 364, 376, 408
Cane, Giovanni Jacopo, 57, 273; *Pro-
files*, 338, 348, 362, 376, 377, 382
Canon law, works of by second-genera-
tion humanists, 230
Capella, Febo, 8, 11, 48n238, 77, 78,
 266, 274n17, 289, 294-96, 303; *Pro-
files*, 316, 324, **348-49**, 428
Capello, Andrea, *Profiles*, 349
Capistrano, Giovanni, 33
Capodilista, Francesco, 10
Carabello, Antonio, *Profiles*, 371
Caravello, Marino, 206-207
Carbone, Ludovico, *Profiles*, 395, 431
Careers: of commoner humanist clerics,
 291ff.; of physicians, 296; of secre-
taries, 294ff.; of teachers, 293-94; of
lay patrician humanists, 279ff.; of pa-
trician humanist clerics, 283ff.; of
Venetian humanists, commercial, 303;
presentation in profiles, 304, 307-308,
309ff.
de' Caresini, Raffaino, 215, 270
Carrari, Piero, da Monselice, *Profiles*,
 386
Carteromaco (Scipione Fortiguerri), *Pro-
files*, 425
Cassarino, Antonio, *Profiles*, 355
Cassius, Dio, 168; *Profiles*, 420
da Castiglionchio, Lapo, *Profiles*, 356,
 357, 371
Castiglione, Baldassar, *Profiles*, 338
Catto, Lidio, *Profiles*, 368
Catullus, 8
Cavalcanti, Ginevra, 93

Celibacy, as condition permitting pursuit
 of studies, 197ff.
Celsano, Barnaba, *Profiles*, 344
Celso, Ermolao, *Profiles*, 353
Cendrata, Ludovico, *Profiles*, 366, 411
Censorship, 111, 124n92, 176n239
Centregus, Bartolomeus, *Profiles*, 362
Cesano, Lorenzo, 25; *Profiles*, 327
de Cessis, Niccolò, *Profiles*, 397
Chalcondylas, Demetrius, 20; *Profiles*,
 391, 392, 424, 433
Chancery humanism, 227n59; in Tre-
cento Venice, 214-15
Charles VIII, King of France, 237; *Pro-
files*, 367
Chiericati, Leonello, *Profiles*, 361
Children, as viewed by E. Barbaro G,
 198; by F. Barbaro, 97; by G. Caldi-
era, 102, 104
Chioggia, battle of (1381), 209
Christian tradition: and moral thought
 of P. Barozzi, 152n190, 155ff.; and
 moral thought of G. Caldiera, 98ff.;
 and third-generation humanism, 234;
 fundamental to Venetian humanism,
 175, 183-84nn267-68, 185-86
Chronicle tradition, 210ff.
Chrysoloras, Manuel, 3, 6, 10, 20, 44,
 170, 222n44, 270; *Profiles*, 380, 397,
 402, 403, 437
Chrysostom, Dio, *Profiles*, 401
Chrysostom, John, 168; *Profiles*, 334,
 338, 367, 394
Cicero, 4, 6, 8, 43, 93, 130n113, 158,
 168; *Profiles*, 341, 343, 355, 362,
 364, 369, 377, 380, 387, 397, 401,
 432
Cipolla, Bartolomeo, *Profiles*, 321, 438
Cippico, Coriolano, 47n234, 232n67,
 268; *Profiles*, 411, 427
Ciriaco (Pizzicoli) d'Ancona, 10, 164,
 269; *Profiles*, 355, 371-73, 448
Cirneo, Pietro, 7, 19, 72, 166, 292-94;
 Profiles, 338, 343, **349-50**
Citizenship, 289-91, 293; and physician
 humanists, 296; and secretariat, 290,
 294; consideration of in profiles, 308
Cittadini, Antonio, *Profiles*, 318
City, ideal of for P. Barozzi, 155n196;
 for L. Quirini, 127-29, 131
Civic duty, *see* Virtue, civic

INDEX

Filelfo, Francesco: and N Canal (*cont.*) 193; and L. Giustiniani, 195n297; and J. A. Marcello, 283; and P. Perleone, 70, 72; and formation of Venetian humanism, 220, 227; comments on condition of learning in Venice, 20; criticizes Venice, 133n120; letters as source for core group definition, 257; literary quarrels mediated by Venetian humanists, 11; seeks patronage among Venetian patricians, 52; teacher in Venice, 18-20, 267; urges sons to seek advancement in Venice, 71; *Profiles*, 316, 320, 321, 323-26, 328, 331, 332, 337, 347-49, 354, 355, 373, 376, 377, 380, 382-84, 389, 390, 395, 401, 402, 415-17, 420, 435, 439, 445
Filelfo, Giovanni Mario, 18, 47, 52, 54, 71-72, 226, 232n67, 233, 236n78, 267, 269; *Profiles*, 306, 320, 321, 377, 382, 386, 395, 415, 417, 444
Filelfo, Senofonte, 71, 78n371
Filippo da Rimini, *see* Morandi, Filippo
Filippo (teacher), 21
Fiocchi, Andrea, 11; *Profiles*, 330
Flaminio, Giovanni Antonio, *Profiles*, 440
Fontana, Gabriele Paveri, *Profiles*, 402
Fontana, Marco Publio, *Profiles*, 362
Foreigners, 260ff., 267ff.; and formation of Venetian humanism, 220-21; resident, 293, 308; role of in second-generation humanism, 226-27; role of in third-generation humanism, 232; role of in Venetian humanism, 299; role of for G. Caldiera, 108; status of, 70ff., 82n392, 85 and n409, 90; transient, 258, 260ff., 267ff., 275; transient in first generation, 220-21; transient in second generation, 226; transient in third generation, 232
Foresti, Filippo, da Bergamo, *Profiles*, 411
de' Fornaci, Alessandro, 78n371, 265, 295; *Profiles*, 376
Fortiguerri, Scipione, *see* Carteromaco
Fortunio, Giovanni Francesco, 271; *Profiles*, 427
Foscari, Francesco (Doge), 11, 31, 124,

179n252, 193, 219, 267, 272, 288; *Profiles*, 372, 373, 382, 407, 419, 420
Foscari, Jacopo, 9 and n36, 11, 20, 31, 35, 193, 266, 267, 274n17, 282, 288; *Profiles*, 324, 372-73, 376, 420
Foscari, Ludovico (brother of Pietro), *Profiles*, 374
Foscari, Pietro, 33n160, 178n247, 283, 288; *Profiles*, 322, 324, 334, 363, 373-74, 415, 421, 442, 449
Foscari, Polidoro, *Profiles*, 374
Foscarini, Ludovico: alleges Jewish atrocities, 37; and U. Aleotti, 78n371, 266; and G. d'Artegna, 7; and M. Aurelio, 78; and P. Barbo, 12; and L. Barozzi, 288; and Bessarion, 269n14; and G. J. Cane, 273-74n17; and F. Filelfo, 193n290; and A. d. Fornaci, 78n371; and J. Foscari, 35; and G. Merula, 72; and P. d. Monte, 64; and P. Morosini, 133n120; and I. Nogarola, 12; and G. Reguardati, 78; and P. Tommasi, 60; and F. Trevisan, 273-74n17; and second-generation humanism, 229; as patron, 50, 56, 57, 58, 297; comments on Council of Ten, 176n239; criticizes public policy, 194; disobeys Senate instructions, 193-94; exhorts son's teacher, 21; friendships with Venetian humanists, 17; intellectual conversation in Paduan podestariate, 13; intellectual conversation in Veronese podestariate, 12; knowledge of law approved by B. Bursa, 41; land purchase, 283; letters as source for core group definition, 257; letters to secretaries, 295; letters to various Venetians, 265; piety, 33, 55n269; political concerns in letters, 48; praises B. Morosini's learning, 39-40; prominent member of Venetian humanist circle, 303; seeks for a historian of Venice, 46ff.; seeks works of D. d. Borgo, 9; sees learning as proper preparation for office, 40; sees study of history as reverence for past, 182n263; works noted in overview, 167, 170-71; *Profiles*, 315, 316, 319-21, 324, 330, 331, 333, 341, 347, 348, 361, 370, 373, 374-77,

510

INDEX

sistance of Doge Agostino Barbarigo, 69; career, 67ff., 261n7, 293; clerical status of, 70n337; immigrant origin of, 290; magnitude of major works, 117n66; praises P. Morosini, 41; recommends city care for poor, 191n282; patrician houses as centers for humanist discourse, 15; student of D. Bragadin, 19; urges restraint of adolescent passions, 176n236; works noted in overview, 163, 169; *Profiles*, 318, 343, 344, 409, 413-15, 422, 427, 440, 447

Niccoli, Niccolò, 11

Niccolò da Lonigo, *see* Leoniceno, Niccolò

Nicholas V (Pope), *Profiles*, 353, 356, 395, 420, 421, 428, 429, 438

Nicholas, Bishop of Myra (Saint), *Profiles*, 384

Noletti, Paolo (Veneto), 264; *Profiles*, 377, 436

Nifo, Agostino, *Profiles*, 317, 318

Nigro, Bertuccio, *Profiles*, 429

Nigro, Marco, *Profiles*, 384

Nobility: conception of in Venetian humanism, 61, 68, 94, 95, 176, 180, 181; G. Caldiera's, 108-109; D. Morosini's, 149; P. Morosini's, 134ff.; L. Quirini's, 118ff.

Nogarola, Isotta, 12, 186n275; *Profiles*, 321, 329, 353, 355, 372, 373, 376, 377, 395, 396, 420

Nogarola, Ginevra, *Profiles*, 372

Nogarola, Ludovico, *Profiles*, 361

Ognibene da Lonigo, *see* Leoniceno, Ognibene

Old age, evaluation of, 32, 143, 149

Oligarchy, L. Quirini's view, 127

Oliverius (Cardinal), *Profiles*, 367

Onosander, 168; *Profiles*, 429

Opportunity for social advancement: assessed by F. Filelfo, 71; by T. L. Frulovisi, 88n423; by D. Morosini, 144-45; by L. Quirini, 122n83; by P. Perleone, 88; case of P. Cirneo, 72; of A. Contrario, 70; of G. Merula, 73; of P. d. Monte, 65-66; of F. Negri, 67; of L. Quirini, 124n92; of C. de

Scarpis, G. B. Egnazio, 76n361; of two physicians, 62-63; for commoners, 76n362, 77, 90; for foreigners, 70ff.; lack of in Venice, 73

Orationes contra poetas, see Barbaro, Ermolao V

Orations, 43-44, 222n44, 228; as genre of Venetian humanism, 29, 169-70, 258; funeral, 3, 10, 19, 22, 44, 170, 177n241, 228; school or university, 26, 170, 228; Z. Trevisan V's to P. Gregory XII opens Venetian humanist era, 206-207

Orlandini, Paolo, *Profiles*, 410

Orsini, Michele, 134n122, 164, 165, 229, 289, 292, 297; *Profiles*, 396, 415-16

Orsini, Orsina (sister of Michele), 415

Ovetario, Benedetto, *Profiles*, 371

Ovid, 169n224; *Profiles*, 401

Pace, Richard, *Profiles*, 434

Pacioli, Luca, 267; *Profiles*, 425

Pagello, Bartolomeo, *Profiles*, 339, 360, 361, 369

Pagliarino, Bartolomeo, *Profiles*, 332, 361

Paierinus, Bartholomaeus, *see* Pagliarino, Bartolomeo

Paleologus, Demetrius (brother of Emperor John), *Profiles*, 350

Paleologus, John (Emperor), *Profiles*, 350

Palmieri, Matteo, *Profiles*, 328

Pandolfini, Niccolò, *Profiles*, 391

Pandoni, Porcellio, 47, 56, 228; *Profiles*, 331, 376, 377, 427

Pannonius, Janus, *see* Janus Pannonius

Panormita, *see* Beccadelli, Antonio

Panteo, Giovanni Antonio, *Profiles*, 361

Paolo Veneto, *see* Nicoletti, Paolo (Veneto)

Paruta, Filippo, *Profiles*, 376

Paruta, Paolo, xviii, 241

Pasqualigo, Pietro, 270

Patrician humanism, 216, 220-51 passim, 275, 277, 288, 300ff.

Patrician values, 23ff., 25ff., 37ff., 93ff., 100, 102, 107-109, 121-23, 192-93, 216, 222, 223, 244; expressed in

INDEX

Patrician values (*cont.*)
Venetian humanism, 177, 190-91
Patricians: role of in Venetian humanism, 300, 301; status of, 58ff., 91. *See also* Patrician humanism
Patriciate, formation, nature, structure of in Venice, xix, 208-209, 231, 237, 244, 276-77, 287n25, 309; described by L. Quirini, 126-27
Patrizi, Francesco, *Profiles*, 321
Patron-client relations: 49ff., 54ff., 71, 74, 75, 79, 239, 258, 297; case of N. Sagundino, 82ff. *See also* Patronage
Patronage, 90, 259. *See also* Patron-client relations
Paul (Apostle), 158
Paulus Aegineta, *Profiles*, 439
Pedianus, Ascanius, *Profiles*, 381
della Pergola, Paolo, 19, 28, 183n267, 264; *Profiles*, 317, 318, 329, 351, 369, 439
Perleone, Pietro: and G. M. Filelfo, 71-72; and J. A. Marcello, 297; and F. Michiel, 273n17; candidate for Venetian historiographer, 47, 236n78; career, 227n60, 269, 293, 294; commoners' need for patrician patronage assumed, 90; congratulated by F. Filelfo on teaching appointment, 70; consoles N. Sagundino for misfortune of shipwreck, 87ff.; friendship relations, 296; student of F. Filelfo, 19; of G. Argyropoulos, 20; support of patricians M. A. Morosini and V. Lando, 71; teacher of Venetians, 19, 22; works noted in overview, 164, 168, 170-71; *Profiles*, 316, 335, 349, 355, 363, 382, 386, 395, 411, 415-17, 429, 444
Perotti, Niccolò, *Profiles*, 343, 374, 421
Persius, *Profiles*, 424
Persona, Cristoforo, *Profiles*, 366
Petrarca, Francesco, *see* Petrarch
Petrarch, xviii-xix, 8, 9, 157n201, 168, 175, 212, 213, 270; *Profiles*, 342, 357, 385, 424
Philology, as pursuit of Venetian humanists, 72, 73, 183n267, 189-90, 233-

34, 236, 238-39, 242. *See also* Textual criticism
Philosophy: and Venetian humanism and culture, 19, 29, 164-65, 167, 183-84 and nn267-68, 186, 213, 230, 234, 239, 264; F. Contarini's mastery of, 28; N. Contarini's, 27; Z. Trevisan V's and G's, 30; viewed by E. Barbaro V, 159; by E. Barbaro G, 199; by P. Barozzi, 151; by G. Caldiera, 112, 115; by L. Quirini, 124n90; by N. Sagundino, 81. *See also* Moral philosophy
Physicians: role of in Venetian humanism, 214n25, 226, 298; status of, 59ff., 90, 119, 297; Jewish, contemporary views of, 37
Piccolomini, Enea Silvio, 133n120; *Profiles*, 428
Piccolomini, Jacopo Ammannati (Cardinal), *Profiles*, 328, 447
Pico, Giovanni, della Mirandola, 10, 172, 175, 186n275, 192, 273; *Profiles*, 322, 323, 367, 368, 401, 444
Piety: and the Venetian humanists, 31ff., 185-86, 216n33, 224, 235, 240; and Venice, 29, 35ff.; of F. Barbaro, 33-34; of C. Bollani, 32; of C. Correr, 35; of F. Diedo, 13; of P. Dolfin, 9, 35; of L. Foscarini, 35; of L. Giustiniani, 34; of C. Moro, 31; of Z. Trevisan G, 30. *See also* Repudiation of secular learning
de' Pindemonti, Aleardo, *Profiles*, 321, 376
de' Pindemonti, Alessandro [Aleardo?], *Profiles*, 376
Pio, family, *Profiles*, 440
Pisani, Francesco, 24, 184n268
Pisani, Paolo, 19, 234n72, 266; *Profiles*, 360, 363, 368, **418-19**
Pisani, Vettore, *Profiles*, 418, 419, 440
Pius II (Pope), 70n337; *Profiles*, 353, 362, 369, 419, 422, 446
Pizzamano, Antonio, 270
Pizzicoli, *see* Ciriaco d'Ancona
Platina, *see* de' Sacchi, Bartolomeo
Plato, Platonism, 9, 110n52, 124, 130n113, 158, 183n267, 185n269,

Library of Congress Cataloging-in-Publication Data

King, Margaret L., 1947-
Venetian humanism in an age of patrician dominance.

Bibliography: p.
Includes index.
1. Venice (Italy)—Intellectual life.   2. Humanism—History.
3. Venice (Italy)—697-1508.   4. Humanists—Italy—Venice—Biography.
5. Venice (Italy)—Biography.   I. Title.

DG677.85.K56 1986   945'.31   85-43294
ISBN 0-691-05465-7

Made in the USA
Lexington, KY
12 August 2015